STRANGERS TO THESE SHORES: Race and Ethnic Relations in the United States

STRANGERS TO THESE SHORES: Race and Ethnic Relations in the United States

SECOND EDITION

Vincent N. Parrillo
The William Paterson
College of New Jersey

JOHN WILEY & SONS
NEW YORK   CHICHESTER   BRISBANE   TORONTO   SINGAPORE

COVER PHOTO: A. Choisnet *(Image Bank)*

Library of Congress Cataloging in Publication Data

Parrillo, Vincent N.
  Strangers to these shores.

  Includes bibliographies and index.
  1. United States—Race relations. 2. United States—Ethnic relations. 3. Minorities—United States—History.
I. Title.
E184.A1P33 1985   305.8'00973   84-17435
ISBN 0-471-80742-7

Printed in the United States of America

10 9 8 7 6 5 4 3 2

To my Italian-American father
And my Irish-American mother

FOREWORD

Race and minority relations have been major issues in the development of American society and social thought. From its beginnings to the present day, the question of how this country would accommodate its racially, ethnically and religiously diverse groups has preoccupied religious and secular thinkers, political scientists and economists, sociologists and psychologists. Solutions have been sought in both an idealized version of an American religious utopia and in a state-regulated secular social order. Recognizing that race, ethnicity and religious diversity are intrinsic to the American scene, some have sought a way out of the racial problem through what they imagined was the inexorable operation of the social process; others in the reorganization of public ideologies and personal beliefs; and still others in public policies of affirmative action and racial justice. From both religious and secular points of view the key issue has seemed to be that of determining the criteria for inclusion within or exclusion from the American commonweal. Addressing this issue, secular sociologists have differed from their religious counterparts in their usage of mundane language and expectancies but not in their commitment to the establishment of a nationally-inclusive moral community.

In much of American sociology, America has been conceived as a society comprising a secularized confessional community. While the originating model for this image of society was distinctively Puritan, its religious and ethical ideals have had a far longer afterlife, surviving into the secular age, and profoundly influencing the development of social scientific thought in the United States. American sociology is unique (and distinctly different from the sociologies that developed in Europe during the same period) in that it was founded upon and took as its major intellectual resource Protestant ideals of the covenanted community. In the Puritan variant, the central question was: Who is eligible for inclusion within the covenant of visible saints? For the Puritans, proofs of qualifications would have to be demonstrated; an applicant's moral conduct and admission could only be granted by consensus among the ever-watchful magistrates. American sociologists, governed by this ideal even as they sought to emancipate themselves from the chains of ecclesiolatry, sought to establish a mundane science of American society founded upon its tenets and creeds, and thus they too faced the question of determining criteria for inclusion and exclusion. For the sociologists, however, their secular science of society would transvalue the old moral terminologies by which to judge the acceptability of persons of different racial strain, exotic ethnic origin, and non-Protestant religious affiliation.

Nowhere was this question of inclusion greater than in the sociological debates over the several racial, ethnic and religious groups that had recently come to or were already residing in less than equal circumstances in the United States. American sociology itself was born in the position, put forward by the Southern Comteans—Henry Hughes, George Fitzhugh, George Frederick Holmes, and Joseph Le Conte—that slave labor could be recognized as a morally *warranted* but legally *subordinated calling* for a select body of people—Negroes—who might thereby be included within a permanently stratified American racial caste order. Their conception of America was that of a social system that would oversee a subservient caste of "warranteed" black workers and that might extend the warranted status to other peoples of inferior color or degraded culture. These Southern sociologists provided the first thoroughgoing descriptive and prescriptive theory of race relations. As support for their idea, these sociologists offered an impressive scholarly *tour de force:* a major critique of free market capitalism, a comparative and historical sociology of ancient and modern slavery, a critical discussion of race and gender-oriented literature, and a functional analysis that justified the hierarchical place of races, minorities, and women in the American social order. However, their proposal for a slave oriented confessional community of permanently segregated Americans did not survive the Civil War. Except for the transplantation of seigneurial statism to the quasi–regulated market of Chinese, Japanese, East Indian, Korean, and Mexican laborers in the agribusiness of the West, Southern sociological ideals on race did not become a part of sociology.

Another and more durable sociology of race and ethnic relations developed in the Northeast, the Middlewest and parts of the Far West in the decades after the Civil War. Central to this newly developing sociology were those theoretical orientations that resonated with America as an industrializing, urbanizing, and immigrant receiving nation–in–the–making. Northeastern and Middlewestern sociologists, most of whom had received a part of their education in Germany, combined the German idea of *Kultur* with the inner-worldly activity and millenial promise of the Social Gospel. One result of this synthesis was the concept and theory of *assimilation*. The German *Kultur* concept had been an instrument of national policy under Bismarck, designated through a *Kulturkampf* to establish the intellectual basis for Prussian hegemony over the various Germanic communities within the Kaiserian realm. American sociologists adapted this concept to American conditions, democratized it, and applied it as a processual description of how, ultimately, the diverse American population would be forged into a single national community. That the moral basis of this proposed national community would be the Protestant ideal is best illustrated in Nathaniel Shaler's influential work, *The Neighbor,* which openly avowed a Christian basis for the theory of American neighborliness and social inclusion.

Shaler's analysis of the neighbor, focussing on the challenge posed by the presence of Blacks and Jews in the United States, laid a religious basis for later theories of racial and ethnic incorporation. Sociologists who followed in this tradition, the most important of whom were Robert E. Park and his disciples at the University of Chicago, muted or transvalued the Christian aspects of Shaler's thesis. Assimilation was presented as an evolutionary and linear process that would eventually absorb all of the peoples in America without undermining the basic American value system. However, just as the Puritan magistrates had required proofs of the right to membership in the Christian community, so the sociologists also established grounds, qualifications or evidence of assimilability for the different peoples coming to a living in the United States. In some cases this meant acknowledging that certain peoples were beyond the pale of inclusion; others were includable because, over time, their excludable characteristics would erode; still others were includable almost immediately because of the similarity or coordination of their ethno–cultural characteristics with those of established Americans. However, assimilation–oriented sociologists faced two recalcitrant challenges: ineradicable racial characteristics, and resistant cultural differences. The seemingly inherent physical basis of race posed a special problem—how or whether to incorporate Blacks, Asians, and Amerinds in the American covenant. The resistances of certain religions and cultures to the fires of the American melting pot posed another kind of challenge to the inclusion of Catholics, Jews, Moslems, and Buddhists. The entire body of assimilationist theory grappled unsuccessfully with the dilemmas imposed by racial and cultural differences.

Other social scientists had become impressed by the biosocial basis for community cohesion. The most important of the first of these was William Z. Ripley of Harvard University. Others included Vacher de la Pouge and Carlos Closson. Building their theories upon the physical basis of culture and the anatomical underpinnings of social attitudes, these theorists proposed natural, irreducible limits to the establishment of an American community. The patterned differences in human physiognomy, especially as they found form and expression in racial differences, were barriers to inclusion. For these "anthropo-sociologists" the American covenant could only be established among those who shared a common natural history—the same skin color, the same hair texture, and the same range on the cephalic index. To these scientists, nature had provided the grounds and circumference for both community organization and nation building. But, the biosocial challenge to the assimilation of everyone might be met by physical amalgamation. Both biosocial and assimilation oriented sociologists were divided then, and are uncertain now, about the ethical implications and scientific value of marriage across racial, ethnic and religious lines.

The very idea of a culturally uniform American covenant was challenged by other bodies of thinkers who either celebrated the positive value of human variety, upheld theories of class conflict, or believed in a grounded public philosophy of basic civic rights guaranteed to all within a *plural* society. These challenges to the consensus orthodoxy have arisen from disparate quarters of the sociological community. Frank Hankins made the first major assault on the Nordic version of the racial basis of American civilization. Horace Kallen and Randolph Bourne proposed that the true test of democracy was the public assurance that a plurality of cultures could thrive side by side. Marxist theorists admitted the deterrent effect that racial and cultural distinctiveness had on the development of class consciousness but looked forward to the proletarianization of minorities and to their eventual liberation through a racially congregative class revolution. A public philosophy based on United States Constitutional doctrines, and especially on the principle enunciated in the Equal Protections clause of the 14th Amendment, opposed the central claim of the assimilationists' thesis: viz., that cultural distinctiveness would have to be given up in exchange for civil rights and economic opportunities.

The sociological discussions of race relations theory today are encumbered by the legacies of and the contradictions between assimilationist, pluralist, biological, and civil rights perspectives. The present book provides an excellent survey and analysis of the issues contained in these discussions. None of the overarching theories of inclusion inspired by the Protestant ideal, such as Park's theory of the race relations cycle, or Talcott Parson's theory of inclusion by queuing, or Thomas Sowell's reassertion of the Protestant Ethic, enjoy unambiguous acceptance in either the discipline or among the peoples they seek to prescribe for. The variety of pluralist and Marxist theories thrive or founder upon the political, cultural and economic bases for separate maintenance, or for liberation through cataclysm. For the modern sociobiologist, the claims of anatomy, inheritance, and kinesics provide a limitation on racially inclusive destiny, but the limits are far from unequivocal recognition or social approval. For some theorists the failure of the American covenanted communities to solidify in either theory or practice has led to a despair over the possibility of any sociological contribution to race relations. For others the dream of community and consensus is postponed to a later date on the evolutionary timetable. And for still others, hopes of revolutions, liberation, or of ethnic renaissance inspire continued analysis and hope. Race relations theory ought now to recognize its separation from religion but its need for a normative base line. It might better be served by a reconsideration of those concepts of public philosophy and theories derived from the Enlightenment that ground rights in law, and by a closer attention to the historical and phenomenological dimensions of racial, ethnic, and religious group life in America. Professor Parrillo's text asks each reader to reconsider the racial, ethnic, and religious situation in America and to wrestle once again with this age-old problem. The book is thence an invitation to the quest for how the good society in America might be established.

Stanford M. Lyman
New School for Social Research

PREFACE

This revised and expanded edition, like the original one, is a basic text for courses on minority groups in the United States. Changes in the format of the first and fifth parts of the book, the addition of new chapters on religious minorities and on women, and sociological analyses at the end-of-the-chapters reflect the helpful suggestions of instructors and reviewers. Where appropriate, sections have been updated and a few groups have been added (Haitians, Jamaicans, Samoans, several Native American tribes). Otherwise, this edition retains the content, approach, and special features about which readers have spoken so favorably.

Strangers to These Shores attempts to provide comprehensive coverage of the enormous variety of minority peoples in the United States, placing their experiences within both a sociological framework and a sociohistorical perspective. The intent has been to offer a highly readable and thematically organized text, giving students both a solid foundation in this subject and insight into the complex social fabric which constitutes American society.

The first four chapters present a conceptual and theoretical overview of the subject area, providing students with a basis from which they can examine the experiences of the different minority groups discussed in subsequent chapters. Major sociological perspectives—functionalist, conflict, interactionist—as well as some middle–range theories are applied throughout the book, though overall it remains eclectic in treatment of topics. Instructors can similarly follow this approach or emphasize their own theoretical viewpoint, since the book's structure allows for varying applications.

After some introductory concepts in the first chapter, particularly that of the stranger as a social phenomenon, we examine differences in culture, reality perceptions, social class, and power as reasons for intergroup conflict. In addition, we look at the dominant group's varying expectations about how minorities should "fit" into its society. Chapters 1 and 2 include some middle–range interactionist theories also. Chapter 3 explores the dimensions and interrelationships of prejudice and discrimination, while Chapter 4 covers the dominant–minority response patterns regardless of a specific group or time period. Included in this chapter are middle–range conflict theories about economic exploitation.

Chapters 5 through 13 offer the reader some insights into the experiences of a wide array of minority groups. In–depth studies of the cultural orientations and assimilation/non–assimilation of each group are not possible, since the intent is to provide a broad scope rather than extensive coverage of only a few groups. Not every racial and ethnic group is discussed, though almost fifty have been included to illustrate the diversity among North Americans. For a more comprehensive examination of any subject or group discussed in this book, the reader should consult the sources listed in the chapter notes or suggested readings.

Chapter 14 provides insights into the mosaic of American society through demographic analysis and intergroup comparisons from various field investigations. Specifically, we look at ethnic consciousness, differing forms of ethnic behavior, and ethnic stratification. Present concerns about legal and illegal immigration and bilingual education follow. A discussion of the future of ethnicity completes our study of minorities.

Many people helped in the writing of this book. Yvonne Chilik provided excellent research assistance. The following students completed exceptional immigrant tape projects, whose excerpts appear in Chapters 5 through 12: Bruce Bisciotti, Doris Brown, Hermione Cox, Milly Gottlieb, Daniel Kazan, David Lenox, Sarah Martinez, Chairath Phaladiganon, Terrence Royful, Michelle Schwartz, Geri Squire, Luba Tkatchov, Leo Uebelein, and Yu-Jie Zeng. Their contributions bring a very human touch to the study of minority peoples.

The following reviewers provided many helpful comments for this edition: Margaret Brooks-Terry, Baldwin-Wallace College; Anthony J. Cortese, Colorado State University; Juan L. Gonzalez, Jr., California State University at Hayward; Kathleen M. Handy, Louisiana State University at Shreveport; Maurice Jackson, University of California at Riverside; Christopher Jay Johnson, Northeast Louisiana University; Terry Jones, California State University at Hayward; Michael C. LeMay, Frostburg State College; R. Paul Maiden, University of Maryland; Cynthia Rolling, Edgewood College; Earl Smith, Washington State University; Marios Stephanides, Spalding University; W. Austin Van Pelt, Arapahoe Community College; Bruce B. Williams, Vanderbilt University.

I am especially grateful to Stanford M. Lyman of the New School for Social Research for writing the foreward to this edition. His gudiance in the development of the first edition was of immense value.

At John Wiley and Sons, the editorial and production staffs have been outstanding in their efforts to make this book a reality. My special thanks go to Carol Luitjens and Butch Cooper, whose consistent encouragement and support have made this association both pleasant and positive.

Finally, I want to thank my wife, Beth, for her patience and understanding during the researching and writing of this book.

V.N.P.

CONTENTS

STRANGERS TO THESE SHORES: Race and Ethnic Relations in the United States

PART ONE

SOCIOLOGICAL FRAMEWORK

CHAPTER 1

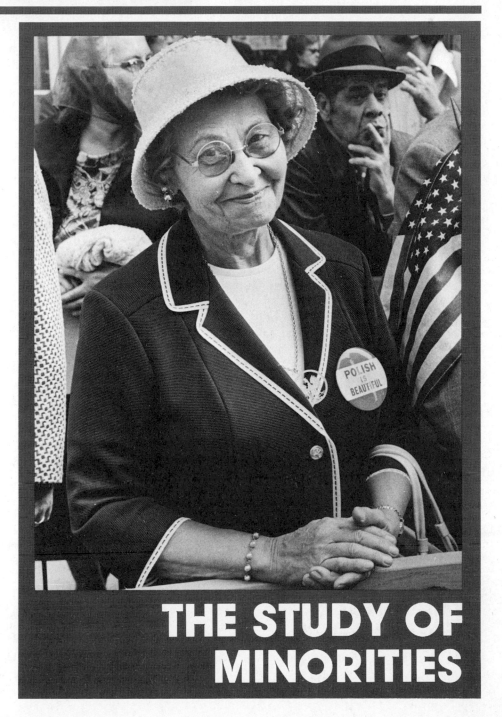

THE STUDY OF MINORITIES

We pride ourselves on being a nation of immigrants, many calling the United States a great "melting pot" where people of all races, religions, and nationalities come to be free and improve their lives. Certainly, a great number of immigrants offer living testimony to that ideal, their enthusiasm for their adopted country evident in countless interviews, some of which you will read in this book. Most of you, as college students, regardless of how long ago your family emigrated to the United States, also give evidence to the American Dream of freedom of choice, economic opportunity, and upward mobility.

Yet, beneath the Fourth of July speeches, the nation's absorption of diverse peoples over the years, and the numerous success stories, lies a disquieting truth. Native-born Americans have not always welcomed the newcomers with open arms; indeed they have often responded with overt acts of discrimination ranging from avoidance to violence and murder. Our treatment of native-born Blacks and American Indians (Native Americans) is a disturbing illustration of subjugation and entrenched inequality. Today we still face serious problems in attitudes and treatment of reservation Indians, poor Blacks in urban ghettos, and large concentrations of recent Asian and Hispanic immigrants. For some, the American Dream becomes a reality; for others, blocked opportunities create an American nightmare.

Problems in intergroup relations are worldwide, regardless of culture or form of government. Religious factions in Lebanon and Northern Ireland continue to kill each other. Animosity remains among the Hausa, Ibo, and Yoruba tribes in Nigeria where a bloody war raged among them a few years ago. Kampucheans (Cambodians), Chinese, Laotians, and Vietnamese have been mired for years in hostilities and appalling bloodletting. Elsewhere, occasional violence or continuing problems of prejudice and discrimination occur: West Indians in Britain, Turks, Yugoslavs, and Greeks in West Germany, Kurds in Iran, Blacks in South Africa, to name but a few. In fact, every country encounters such problems within its borders to some degree because all have various groupings of people by race, religion, tribe, culture, or life-style.

Many sociologists take a strong interest in the field of race and ethnic relations. Although individuals personally involved tend to see specific reasons for a particular group's situation (for example, their slowness in learning the main language of the country or supposed lack of the work ethic), sociologists note distinct patterns of interaction among different groups that transcend national boundaries, specific time periods, or idiosyncrasies of particular groups. Opinions may vary as to the causes for these patterns of behavior, but a consensus does exist about their presence.

THE STRANGER AS A SOCIAL PHENOMENON

To understand intergroup relations, we must recognize that differences among various peoples cause each group to look upon other groups as strangers. Among isolated peoples, the arrival of a stranger has always been a momentous occasion, often eliciting strong emotional responses. Reactions might range from warm hospitality to conciliatory or protective ceremonies to hostile acts. In an urbanized and mobile society, the stranger often still evokes similar responses. From the Tiwi of northern Australia, who consistently killed intruders, to the nativists of any country or time, who continually strive to keep out "undesirable elements," the underlying premise is the same: the outsiders are not good enough to share the land and resources with the "chosen people" already there.

Similarity and Attraction

Since Aristotle observed, "We like those who resemble us, and are engaged in the same pursuits," social observers have been aware of the similarity-attraction relationship.[1] Numerous studies have examined the extent to which a person likes another having similar attitudes, values, beliefs, social status, or physical appearance. Examining the development of attraction among people initially strangers to one another, an impressive number of these studies have found a positive relationship between the similarity of one person and that person's liking for the other. Most significantly, the findings show that people's perception of the similarity between themselves is a more powerful determinant than actual similarity.[2] Cross-cultural studies also support this conclusion.[3] Considerable evidence exists showing greater human receptivity to strangers perceived as similar than to those who are perceived as different.

Social Distance

One excellent technique for evaluating how perceptions of similarity attract closer interaction patterns is the use of *social distance* ranking. First devised by Emory Bogardus in 1926, this measurement device has been used repeatedly since then, with social scientists finding a consistent pattern regardless of respondents' ethnicity, income, education, or occupation.[4] In four studies spanning five decades, Bogardus obtained responses from fairly evenly divided undergraduate and graduate students aged 18 to 35, about 10 percent of them Black. He asked the students to select the degree of social closeness or distance personally acceptable with members of a particular group. Specifically, the choices were:

To close kinship by marriage (1 point)
To my club as personal chums (2 points)
To my street as neighbors (3 points)
To employment in my occupation (4 points)
To citizenship in my country (5 points)
As visitors only to my country (6 points)
Would exclude from my country (7 points)

Researchers then total, average, and rank the responses, creating social-distance indices. The scale ranges from a 1.00 to 7.00, the higher the number the

TABLE 1.1
Four Studies of Social Distance in the United States

I — Social Distance Indices Given Groups in 1926 by 1,725 Selected Persons throughout the U.S.	II — Social Distance Indices Given Groups in 1946 by 1,950 Selected Persons throughout the U.S.	III — Social Distance Indices Given Groups in 1956 by 2,053 Selected Persons throughout the U.S.	IV — Social Distance Indices Given Groups in 1966 by 2,605 Selected Persons throughout the U.S.
1. English — 1.06	1. Americans (U.S. white) — 1.04	1. Americans (U.S. white) — 1.08	1. Americans (U.S. white) — 1.07
2. Americans (U.S. white) — 1.10	2. Canadians — 1.11	2. Canadians — 1.16	2. English — 1.14
3. Canadians — 1.13	3. English — 1.13	3. English — 1.23	3. Canadians — 1.15
4. Scots — 1.13	4. Irish — 1.24	4. French — 1.47	4. French — 1.36
5. Irish — 1.30	5. Scots — 1.26	5. Irish — 1.56	5. Irish — 1.40
6. French — 1.32	6. French — 1.31	6. Swedish — 1.57	6. Swedish — 1.42
7. Germans — 1.46	7. Norwegians — 1.35	7. Scots — 1.60	7. Norwegians — 1.50
8. Swedish — 1.54	8. Hollanders — 1.37	8. Germans — 1.61	8. Italians — 1.51
9. Hollanders — 1.56	9. Swedish — 1.40	9. Hollanders — 1.63	9. Scots — 1.53
10. Norwegians — 1.59	10. Germans — 1.59	10. Norwegians — 1.66	10. Germans — 1.54
11. Spanish — 1.72	11. Finns — 1.63	11. Finns — 1.80	11. Hollanders — 1.54
12. Finns — 1.83	12. Czechs — 1.76	12. Italians — 1.89	12. Finns — 1.67
13. Russians — 1.88	13. Russians — 1.83	13. Poles — 2.07	13. Greeks — 1.82
14. Italians — 1.94	14. Poles — 1.84	14. Spanish — 2.08	14. Spanish — 1.93
15. Poles — 2.01	15. Spanish — 1.94	15. Greeks — 2.09	15. Jews — 1.97
16. Armenians — 2.06	16. Italians — 2.28	16. Jews — 2.15	16. Poles — 1.98
17. Czechs — 2.08	17. Armenians — 2.29	17. Czechs — 2.22	17. Czechs — 2.02
18. Indians (Americans) — 2.38	18. Greeks — 2.29	18. Armenians — 2.33	18. Indians (American) — 2.12
19. Jews — 2.39	19. Jews — 2.32	19. Japanese Americans — 2.34	19. Japanese Americans — 2.14
20. Greeks — 2.47	20. Indians (American) — 2.45	20. Indians (American) — 2.35	20. Armenians — 2.18
21. Mexicans — 2.69	21. Chinese — 2.50	21. Filipinos — 2.46	21. Filipinos — 2.31
22. Mexican Americans — —	22. Mexican Americans — 2.52	22. Mexican Americans — 2.51	22. Chinese — 2.34
23. Japanese — 2.80	23. Filipinos — 2.76	23. Turks — 2.52	23. Mexican Americans — 2.37
24. Japanese Americans — —	24. Mexicans — 2.89	24. Russians — 2.56	24. Russians — 2.38
25. Filipinos — 3.00	25. Turks — 2.89	25. Chinese — 2.68	25. Japanese — 2.41
26. Negroes — 3.28	26. Japanese Americans — 2.90	26. Japanese — 2.70	26. Turks — 2.48
27. Turks — 3.30	27. Koreans — 3.05	27. Negroes — 2.74	27. Koreans — 2.51
28. Chinese — 3.36	28. Indians (from India) — 3.43	28. Mexicans — 2.79	28. Mexicans — 2.56
29. Koreans — 3.60	29. Negroes — 3.60	29. Indians (from India) — 2.80	29. Negroes — 2.56
30. Indians (from India) — 3.91	30. Japanese — 3.61	30. Koreans — 2.83	30. Indians (from India) — 2.62
Arithmetic Mean of 48,300 Racial Reactions 2.14	Arithmetic Mean of 58,500 Racial Reactions 2.12	Arithmetic Mean of 61,590 Racial Reactions 2.08	Arithmetic Mean of 78,150 Racial Reactions 1.92
Spread in Distance 2.85	Spread in Distance 2.57	Spread in Distance 1.75	Spread in Distance 1.56

Source: Emory S. Bogardus, "Comparing Racial Distance in Ethiopia, South Africa, and the United States," Sociology and Social Research 52 (1968): 152.

greater the social distance (*see* Table 1.1). Responses of minority-group members remain very similar to those of dominant-group members, except that their own group moves to the top of the scale. While social distance indices have declined over the years, their relative consistency in pattern illustrate the similarity-attraction relationship.

Perceptions

By definition, the stranger is not only an outsider but also someone different and personally unknown. People perceive strangers primarily through **categoric knowing,** the classification of others based on limited information obtained visually and perhaps verbally.[5] People make judgments and generalizations on the basis of scanty information, confusing an individual's characteristics with typical group-member characteristics. For instance, if a visiting Swede asks for tea rather than coffee, the host might incorrectly conclude that all Swedes dislike coffee.

Immigrants, first-generation Americans of different racial and ethnic groups, have been perceived as a particular kind of stranger: one who intends to stay. As the presence of immigrants became less of a novelty, fear, suspicion, and distrust often replaced the natives' initial curiosity. The strangers often remained strangers as each group sought its own kind for personal interaction.

The role of a stranger can be analyzed regardless of the particular period in history. Georg Simmel (1858–1918) theorized that strangers represent both *nearness,* because they are physically close, and *remoteness,* because they react differently to the immediate situation and have different values and ways of doing things.[6] The stranger is both inside and outside: physically present and participating, but also outside the situation, being from another place.

The native perceives the stranger in an abstract, typified way. That is, the individual becomes the *totality,* or stereotype, of the group. The stranger, however, perceives the natives in concrete, individual terms. Simmel suggests that strangers have a higher degree of objectivity about the natives because the strangers' geographical mobility reflects mobility in their minds as well. The stranger is free from indigenous habit, piety, and precedent. Furthermore, because strangers do not participate fully in society, they have a certain mental detachment, causing them to see things more objectively.

Interactions

Simmel approaches the role of the stranger through an analysis of the formal structures of life. In contrast, Alfred Schutz—himself an immigrant to the United States—analyzes the stranger as lacking "intersubjective understanding."[7] By this he means the reciprocity of perspectives among those from the same social world. Because this is a shared world, it is an intersubjective one. For the native, then, every social situation is a coming together not only of roles and identities, but also of shared realities—the intersubjective structure of consciousness. What is taken for granted by the native is problematic to the stranger. In a familiar world, people live through the day by responding to daily routine without questioning or reflection. To strangers, however, every situation is new and is therefore experienced as a crisis.

Strangers experience a "lack of historicity"—a lack of the shared memory of those with whom they live. Human beings who interact together over a period of time "grow old together"; strangers, however, are "young," being newcomers, and they experience at least an approximation of the freshness of childhood. They are aware of things that go unnoticed by the natives, such as their customs, social institutions, appearance, and life-style.

Sometimes the stranger may be the comical butt of jokes because of unfamiliarity with the everyday routine of life in this new setting. In time, however, strangers take on the natives' perspective; the strangers' consciousness is lowered because the freshness of their perceptions is lost. Also, the natives' **abstract typifications** about the strangers become more concrete through social interaction. As Schutz says, "The vacant frames become occupied by vivid experiences." As acculturation takes place, the native begins to view the stranger more concretely and the stranger becomes less questioning about daily activities. Use of the term *naturalized* citizen takes on a curious connotation when examined from this perspective, as it implies that people are in some way odd or unnatural until they have taken on the characteristics of the natives.

As its title suggests, this book is about the many strangers who came to the United States in search of a better life. Through an examination of sociological theory and the experiences of many racial and ethnic groups, the story of how the stranger perceives the society and is received by it will be continually retold. The adjustment from stranger to neighbor may be viewed as movement along a continuum, but this continuum is not cyclical nor is assimilation inevitable. Rather, it is the process of social interaction among different groups of people.

ETHNOCENTRISM

An understanding of the concept of the stranger is important in order to understand **ethnocentrism,** a term meaning the "view of things in which one's own group is the center of everything, and all others are scaled and rated with reference to it."[8] Ethnocentrism thus refers to people's tendency to identify with their own ethnic or national group as a means of fulfilling their needs for group belongingness and security. (The word is derived from two Greek words: *ethnos,* meaning nation, and *kentron,* meaning center.) As a result of ethnocentrism, people usually view their own cultural values as somehow more real and thus superior to those of other groups, and they prefer their own way of doing things. Unfortunately for human relations, such ethnocentric thought is often extended until it negatively affects attitudes and emotions toward those who are perceived as different.

Sociologists define an **ingroup** as one to which individuals belong and feel loyalty; thus everyone—whether a member of a majority group or a minority group—is part of an ingroup. **Outgroups** are defined, in relation to ingroups, as groups consisting of all people who are not members of one's ingroup. Studying majority groups as ingroups helps to understand their reactions to strangers of another race or culture entering their society. Similarly, considering minority groups as ingroups enables us to understand their efforts to maintain their ethnic identity and solidarity in the midst of the dominant culture.

There is ample evidence about people from past civilizations who have regarded other cultures as inferior, incorrect, or immoral. This assumption that *we* are better than *they* are generally results in outgroups becoming objects of ridicule, contempt, or hatred. Such attitudes may lead to stereotyping, prejudice, discrimination, and even violence. What actually does occur depends upon many factors, including structural and economic conditions, which will be discussed in subsequent chapters.

Despite its ethnocentric beliefs, the ingroup does not always view the outgroup as inferior. There are numerous documented cases of groups who have retained their values and standards while recognizing the superiority of another group in some specific areas.[9] Also, countless people reject their own ingroup by being "voluntary exiles, expatriates, outgroup emulators, social climbers, renegades, and traitors."[10] An outgroup may become a positive **reference group**—that is, it may serve as an exemplary model—if members of the ingroup perceive it as having a

"Free Trade Lunch"

The immigrant laborer was often seen as an economic threat. Here English, Italian, Mexican, Russian, and German immigrants are shown devouring meat—symbolizing American workingmen's wages—and bread—symbolizing prosperity. In the background, immigrants are shown preventing the American laborer from entering the restaurant to get his share of the free lunch. Cartoon appeared in *Judge*, July 28, 1888.

conspicuous advantage over them in terms of survival or adaptation to the environment, success in warfare, a stronger political structure, greater wealth, or a higher occupational status.[11]

Ethnocentrism is an important factor in determining minority-group status in society, but because of many variations in intergroup relations, it alone cannot explain the causes of prejudice. For example, majority-group members may view minority groups with suspicion, but not all minority groups become the targets of extreme prejudice and discrimination.

Some social-conflict theorists argue that when the ingroup perceives the outgroup as a real threat competing for scarce resources, the ingroup reacts with increased solidarity, ethnocentrism, and hostility toward the outgroup.[12] According to this view, ethnocentrism can lead to prejudice, discrimination, and hostility, the degree of which depends upon several economic and geographic considerations. It would thus appear that ethnocentrism leads to negative consequences when the ingroup feels threatened. One counterargument to this view would be that ethnocentric attitudes—thinking that because others are different, they are thus a threat—initially caused the problem. However, the major difficulty with this approach is that it does not explain variations in the frequency, type, or intensity of intergroup conflict from one society to the next or between different immigrant groups and the ingroup.

In the United States

An ethnocentric attitude is often not deliberate, but instead an outgrowth of growing up and living within a familiar environment. Consider, for example, that Americans have labeled their major-league baseball championship games a *World Series,* although until recently, not even Canadian teams were included in an otherwise exclusively United States professional sports program. *American* is another word we use—even in this book—to identify ourselves to the exclusion of people in other parts of North and South America. The Organization of American States (OAS), which consists of countries in both North and South America, should remind us that others are equally entitled to call themselves Americans.

At one point in this country's history, many state and national leaders identified their expansionist goals as a "manifest destiny," as if Divine Providence had ordained specific boundaries for the United States. Indeed, many a member of the clergy has preached a fiery sermon over the years regarding God's special plans for this country, and all presidents have invoked the Deity in their inaugural addresses for special assistance to this country.

In Other Times and Lands

Throughout history, people of many cultures have demonstrated an ethnocentric view of the world. For example, the British once believed they were obliged to carry the "white man's burden" in "civilizing" the nonwestern world. Yet two thousand years earlier, the Romans thought natives of Britain to be an inferior people, as indicated in this excerpt from a letter written by the orator Cicero to his friend Atticus:

Do not obtain your slaves from Britain because they are so stupid and so utterly incapable of being taught that they are not fit to form a part of the household of Athens.

The Greeks, whose civilization predated the Roman Empire, considered all those around them—Persians, Egyptians, Macedonians, and others—distinctly inferior and called them barbarians *(barbarikos)*, a Greek word describing those who did not speak Greek as making noises that sounded like *bar-bar.*

Religious chauvinism blended with ethnocentrism in the Middle Ages when the Crusaders, spurred on by their beliefs, considered it their duty to free the Holy Land from the control of the "infidels." They traveled a great distance, by land and sea, taking with them horses, armor, and armaments, to wrest control from the native inhabitants because the "infidels" had the audacity to follow the teachings of Mohammed rather than Jesus. On their journey across Europe, the Crusaders slaughtered Jews (whom they incorrectly labeled "Christ-killers"), regardless of whether they were men, women, or children, all in the name of the Prince of Peace. The Crusaders looked upon both Moslems and Jews as inferior peoples as well as enemies.

In the following passage, Brewton Berry offers several other examples of ethnocentric thinking in past times:

Some writers have attributed the superiority of their people to favorable geographical influences, but others incline to a biological explanation. The Roman, Vitruvius, maintained that those who live in southern climates have the keener intelligence, due to the rarity of the atmosphere, whereas "northern nations, being enveloped in a dense atmosphere, and chilled by moisture from the obstructing air, have a sluggish intelligence." A certain Ibn Khaldun argued that the Arabians were the superior people, because their country, although in a warm zone, was surrounded by water, which exerted a cooling effect. Bodin, in the sixteenth century, found an astrological explanation for ethnic group differences. The planets, he thought, exerted their combined and best influence upon that section of the globe occupied by France, and the French, accordingly, were destined by nature to be the masters of the world. Needless to say, Ibn Khaldun was an Arab, and Bodin a Frenchman. The Italian, Sergi, regarded the Mediterranean peoples as the true bearers of civilization and insisted that Germans and Asiatics only destroy what the Mediterraneans create. In like manner, the superiority of Nordics, Alpines, Teutons, Aryans, and others has been asserted by those who were members of each of these groups, or thought they were.[13]

Anthropologists, in examining the cultures of other peoples, have identified countless instances of ethnocentric attitudes. One frequent practice has been in geographic reference and map making. There have, for example, been commercially prepared Australian world maps that depicted that continent in the center in relation to the rest of the world.

There is nothing unusual about this type of thinking: the Chinese, who called their country the Middle Kingdom, were convinced that China was the center of the world, and similar beliefs were held by other nations—and are still held. The British drew the Prime Meridian of longitude to run through Greenwich, near London. Europeans drew maps of the world with Europe at the center, Americans with the New World at the center.[14]

Ethnocentrism is more than just a group-centered approach to living. It is also of utmost significance in understanding motivation, attitudes, and behavior when members of racially or ethnically distinct groups interact.

OBJECTIVITY

When discussing people, usually those who are different from ourselves, it is not unusual for us to offer our own assumptions and opinions more readily than in some other area such as statistics or biology. But if we are to undertake a socio-logical study of ethnicity, we must question our assumptions and opinions—everything we have always believed without question. How can we scientifically investigate a problem if we have already reached a conclusion?

Sociologists attempt to examine group relationships objectively, but it is impos-sible to exclude their own subjectivity altogether. All human beings have **values,** socially shared conceptions of what is good, desirable, and proper or bad, unde-sirable, and improper. Because we are human, we cannot be completely objec-tive, as these values influence our orientations, actions, reactions, and interpreta-tions. For example, selecting intergroup relations as an area of interest and concern, emphasizing the sociological perspective of this subject, and the thematic organi-zation of the material in this book all represent value judgments regarding priori-ties.

Although **value neutrality** may be impossible to attain (and many would even argue that it is undesirable), it is nevertheless most important that the reader ex-ercise a conscientious effort to maintain an open mind in order to examine this subject as objectively as is humanly possible. You must be aware of your own strong feelings about these matters and be willing to examine new concepts, even if they challenge previously held beliefs. To study this subject properly, you should try to be a stranger in your familiar world. Look at everything as if you were seeing it for the first time, trying to understand how and why it is, rather than just taking it for granted.

Trying to be *objective* about race and ethnic relations presents a strong chal-lenge. People tend to use selective perception, accepting only information that agrees with their values or interpreting information so that it remains consistent with their attitudes about other groups. Many variables in life influence people's subjectivity about minority relations. Some views may be based upon personal or emotional considerations, or even upon false premises. However, sometimes quite reasonable and responsible people disagree on the matter in an unemotional way. Whatever the situation, the study of minority-group relations poses a challenge for objective examination.

The subject of race and ethnic relations is a very complex one, and it touches our lives in many ways. All who are reading this book must face the realization that they are in fact coming to this subject with preconceived notions. Because many individuals have a strong tendency to "tune out" disagreeable information, the reader must make a continual, conscientious effort to remain open-minded and receptive to new data.

BEHAVIOR

Contrary to popular belief, most forms of social behavior are not "natural." We learn how to do things through the socialization process, which propagates cultural values, attitudes, customs, and beliefs. We even satisfy our hunger and sexual needs in culturally determined ways.

Certain Native American tribes consider dog stew a fine delicacy to serve honored guests, although someone from a different culture may not find the prospect of such a meal very appetizing. Many Americans eat beef and pork, much to the chagrin of Hindus, Moslems, and Orthodox Jews, respectively. Westerners may find distasteful the Chinese fondness for aged, foul-smelling eggs, but the Chinese may find equally repugnant the Westerners' fondness for aged, foul-smelling milk, better known as cheese. Others enjoy eating raw fish, cooked squid, eel, snake, or insects, to the clear disgust of still others.

Incest has not been an acceptable practice in most societies, but certain cultures have considered it critically important, as, for example, did the pharaohs of ancient Egypt. During the Eighteenth Dynasty, the daughter inherited the throne, and the son acquired title to the throne by marrying his sister.[15] Many Americans do not condone extramarital affairs, although they occur in our society, and many resent women being treated as sex objects. However, among the central Eskimo peoples of Alaska and the Bahimas of East Africa, a man would be branded a poor host if he did not share his wife (or wives) with his overnight guest.

Therefore, what we consider "proper" behavior, or "pleasurable," or "right," or "wrong," does not necessarily correspond to what others believe. What we consider to be "natural" is more likely to be culturally prescribed. Yet our ethnocentric judgment of behavior different from our own, including such basic areas as eating and sex, often results in our branding the behavior with such labels as "strange," "inferior," "disgusting," or "immoral." Although some of the behavior one would regard as most exotic is practiced by peoples who are rather isolated from the rest of the world, the United States itself, as the greatest receiving nation of immigrants, has always comprised many diverse types of people who have had varying orientations to living.

The diversity of culturally learned behavior patterns is interesting in itself, but what happens when different groups interact? Sociologists are interested in why prejudicial attitudes and discriminatory actions may or may not arise when groups whose actions or appearances differ come into contact with one another. What factors influence attitudes, expectations, and behavior toward the other group? Numerous theories and findings about such matters exist, and these will be examined in this book.

A SOCIOLOGICAL PERSPECTIVE

Sociology is the study of human relationships and patterns of behavior. Through scientific investigation, sociologists seek to determine the social forces that influence behavior, as well as the recurring patterns through which they can better understand that behavior.

When two different groups of people come into contact with one another, many possible forms of interaction can occur, ranging from open conflict to close cooperation. The initial relationship, whatever it is, may later change or become even more solidly entrenched. For instance, the two groups may adopt some of each other's culture and intermarry. In contrast, they may live separately in the same area, with one group dominant over the other and with continuing prejudice and hostility toward one another. These examples do not exhaust the possibilities, of course, but they do illustrate various behavior patterns and indicate that behavior might change over a period of time.

Using historical documents, reports, surveys, ethnographies, journalistic materials, and direct observation, the sociologist systematically gathers empirical evidence about such intergroup relations. The sociologist then analyzes these data in an effort to discover and describe the causes, functions, relationships, meanings, and consequences of intergroup harmony or tension. Ascertaining reasons for the beginning, continuance, intensification, or alleviation of readily observable patterns of behavior among different peoples is a complex and difficult matter, and not all sociologists concur in interpreting the data. Different theories, ideas, concepts, and even ideologies and prejudices may also influence a sociologist's conclusions.

Disagreement among sociologists is no more unusual than in other areas of scientific investigation where such matters as the way in which the universe was created, what constitutes a mental disorder, or whether heredity or environment is more important in shaping behavior are discussed. In sociological investigation, three major perspectives shape analysis of the study of minorities. Each has a contribution to make, and should be considered as a different lens providing a separate focus on the subject.

Functional Theory

Proponents of *functional theory* perspective believe that a stable, cooperative social system is the basis of society. All the elements of a society function together to maintain order and stability. Under ideal conditions, a society would be in a state of balance, with all its parts working in harmony with each other. When problems arise, it is because some parts of the system have become dysfunctional, upsetting the social equilibrium. This system disorganization can occur for many reasons, but the most frequent cause is rapid social change. Changes in any one part of the system require compensating adjustments elsewhere, but these usually do not occur fast enough, thereby creating tensions and conflict.

Functionalists view dysfunctions as temporary maladjustments to an otherwise interdependent, relatively harmonious society. Since this perspective focuses upon societal stability, the key factor in this analysis of social disorganization is whether to restore the equilibrium as it was or to seek a new and different equilibrium. For example, how do we overcome the problem of illegal aliens? Do we expel them to eliminate their exploitation, depression of regional wage scales, and high costs to taxpayers for health, education, and welfare benefits? Or, do we grant them amnesty, help them enter the economic mainstream, and seal our borders against further illegal entries? Whatever the solution, and the above two do not exhaust the possibilities, functionalists emphasize that all problems regarding minorities can be resolved through adjustments to the social system, returning it to a state of equilibrium. Instead of major changes in the society, they prefer smaller corrections in the already functioning society.

Conflict Theory

Conflict theorists see society as being continually involved in a series of disagreements, tensions, and clashes, as different groups compete for limited resources. Rejecting the concept of societal parts usually working harmoniously, they see disequilibrium and change as the norm. Their focus is upon the inequalities generating racial and ethnic antagonisms between groups. To understand why discrimination persists, conflict theorists ask the question, "Who benefits?" Those already in power, the employers and holders of wealth and property, exploit the powerless, seeking even greater profits at the expense of unassimilated minorities. Since lower wages allow higher profits, ethnic discrimination serves investors and owners by weakening workers' bargaining power.

According to this view, one major technique of maintaining power and control of resources is *false consciousness,* getting workers to adopt attitudes not accurately reflecting the objective facts of the situation. If workers believe the economic gains of other groups would adversely affect their own living standards, they will not be supportive of actions to end discriminatory practices. If workers struggling to improve their situation believe other groups entrenched in better job positions are holding them back, they will view their own gains as possible only at the expense of the other ethnic groups. In both cases the wealthy and powerful benefit by pitting racial and ethnic groups against each other, causing each to have strong negative feelings about the other. This distorted view foments conflict and occasional outbursts of violence between groups, preventing workers' realization of their common bond of joint oppression.[16]

Interactionist Theory

A third theoretical approach, ***interactionist theory,*** examines the microsocial world of personal interaction patterns in everyday life rather than the macrosocial aspects of social institutions and their harmony or conflict. ***Symbolic interaction,*** the shared symbols and definitions people use in communicating with one another, provides the focus for understanding how individuals create and interpret the life situations they experience. Symbols are what constitute our social worlds: our spoken language, expressions, body language, tone of voice, appearance, and images of television and other mass media.[17] By means of these symbols we communicate, create impressions, and develop understandings of the world about us.

Essential to this perspective, suggest Peter L. Berger and Thomas Luckmann, is how people define their reality through a process they called the ***social construction of reality.***[18] Individuals create a background against which to understand their separate actions and interactions with others. When a social situation is a continuing one, the participants' interactions create a shared history resulting in ***reciprocal typifications*** or mutual categorizations of each other. Taken-for-granted routines emerge, based upon shared expectations. Participants see this socially constructed world as legitimate, by virtue of its "objective" existence. When problems arise, specific "universe-maintenance" procedures become necessary to preserve stability; such conceptual machineries as mythology, theology, philosophy, or science may be used. In short, people create cultural products: material artifacts, social institutions, ideologies, and so on (externalization); they lose awareness of having created their own social and cultural environment (objectification); and then they learn these supposedly objective facts of reality through the socialization process (internalization).

MINORITY GROUPS

Although the term *group* is commonly used to refer collectively to a racial or ethnic people, it is a very problematic word. ***Group,*** in its sociological usage, usually connotes a small, closely interacting set of persons. The term *minorities* sometimes refers to aggregates of millions of persons, clearly a size even larger than a ***secondary group,*** people who interact on an impersonal or limited emotional basis for some practical or specific purpose. Nonetheless, *group* is a familiar term to most readers, and with the above caveat in mind, I shall use that term throughout this book in referring to racial and ethnic groupings.

Development of a Definition

Sociologists use the term ***minority*** to designate not a group's numerical representation, but rather its relative power and status in a society. The term was first used in the World War I peace treaties to protect approximately 22 million out of 110 million people in East Central Europe, but it was most frequently used as a description of biological features or national traits. Donald Young in 1932 thus observed that Americans make distinctions among people according to race and national origin.[19]

Louis Wirth expanded Young's original conception of minority groups to include the consequences of those distinctions: group consciousness and differential treatment.[20] The significance of Wirth's contribution was that it marked two important turning points in sociological inquiry. First, by broadening the definition to include any physical or cultural trait instead of just race or national origin, he enlarged the range of variables to include also the aged, handicapped, members of various religions or sects, and groups with unconventional life-styles. Second, his emphasis upon the social consequences of minority status leads to a focus on prejudice, discrimination, and oppression. Not everyone agrees with this approach. Richard Schermerhorn, for example, notes that this "victimological" approach does not adequately explain the similarities and differences among groups or analyze relationships between majority and minority groups.[21]

A third attempt to define minority groups rests upon examining relationships between groups in terms of each group's position in the social hierarchy.[22] This approach stresses a group's social power, which may vary from one country to another, as, for example, does that of the Jews in the Soviet Union and in Israel. The emphasis upon stratification instead of population size explains situations in which a small-sized group subjugates a larger number of people (for example, the European colonization of African and Asian populations). A variation on this viewpoint is represented by Schermerhorn. He also viewed social power as an important variable in the determination of a group's position in the hierarchy, but he believed that other factors were equally important. Size (a minority group must be less than one-half the population), ethnicity (as defined by Wirth's physical and cultural traits), and group consciousness also help to define a minority group.[23]

Minority Group Characteristics

As an acceptable definition of minority groups evolved, anthropologists Charles Wagley and Marvin Harris identified five characteristics shared by minorities worldwide:

1. The group receives unequal treatment compared to other groups.

2. The group is easily identifiable because of distinguishing physical or cultural characteristics which are held in low esteem.

3. The group feels a sense of peoplehood, that each of them shares something in common with others like themselves.

4. Membership in the minority group is *ascribed;* one is born into it.

5. Group members practice *endogamy;* they tend to marry within their group, either by choice or necessity because of their social isolation.[24]

In our discussion of racial and ethnic minorities, the above five features will serve as helpful guidelines. However, we should also understand that the last two characteristics do not apply to certain other types of minority groups: women obviously do not fit the last category, nor necessarily do the aged or handicapped. One is not born old, nor are handicapped people always born that way.

Because our discussion of various minority groups rests upon their subordination by a more powerful, though not necessarily larger group, we shall use the term *dominant group* in referring to a minority group's relationships with the rest of society. Another consideration is that dominant and minority group memberships are not mutually exclusive categories. For example, an American Roman Catholic belongs to a prominent religious minority group but, if white, is also a member of the racially dominant group.

RACIAL AND ETHNIC GROUPS

Race may seem at first glance an easy way to group people, but it is not. Among the more than 4 billion humans inhabiting this planet, we find a wide range of physical differences in body build, hair texture, facial features, and skin color. Centuries of migration, conquest, intermarriage, and evolutionary physical adaptation to the environment have caused these varieties. Anthropologists have attempted racial categorizations, ranging from three to more than a hundred. Some, like Ashley Montagu, even argue that only one race exists, the human race.[25] Just as anthropologists apply different interpretations to biological groupings, so do most people. It is in these social interpretations that sociologists attempt to analyze and explain racial prejudice.

Racism may be defined as linking the biological conditions of a human organism with its sociocultural capabilities and behavior. When people believe one race is superior over another due to economic advantages or specific achievements, racist thinking prevails. The subordinate group will experience prejudice and discrimination, which the dominant group justifies by means of such perceptions. In this book, we shall discuss how not only Blacks, but American Indians, Asians, Hispanics, and even white southern Europeans have encountered hostility because of social categorizations of their abilities based simply on their physical appearances.

Members of an ethnic group (which may or may not be racially different from the dominant group in a society) have a common cultural heritage. As Max Weber observed, they share a sense of belonging, based upon national origin, language, religion, and/or other cultural attributes.

The word *race* is often incorrectly used as a social rather than a biological concept. Thus, the British and Japanese are often classified as races, as are Hindus, Latins, Aryans, Gypsies, Arabs, American Indians, Basques, and Jews.[26] Many people, even sociologists, anthropologists, and psychologists, use *race* as the general rubric to include both racial and ethnic groups, thereby giving the term both a biological and a social meaning. Recently, *ethnic group* has been used more frequently as the general rubric to include the three elements of race, religion, and national origin.[27] Needless to say, the misuse and reuse of these terms result in endless confusion.

In this book, the word *race* will refer to biological distinctions such as skin color, hair texture, *eye* shape, and so on. If a sociologist has used this term but actually means both racial and ethnic groups, I will bring that point to the reader's attention. Similarly, the term *ethnic group* will refer only to social groupings that the superordinate group considers unique because of religious, linguistic, or cultural characteristics. If a sociologist has used this word but means to include racial groups also, I will make this clear. Both terms will be used when discussing groups with an overlapping of racial and ethnic characteristics.

THE DYNAMICS OF INTERGROUP RELATIONS

The study of intergroup relations is both fascinating and challenging because they are continually changing. The patterns of relating may change for many reasons: industrialization, urbanization, shifts in migration patterns, social movements, upward or downward economic trends, and so on. However, sometimes the changing relationships also reflect changing attitudes, as, for example, the interaction between the Whites and the American Indians. There was a continually changing emphasis: exploitation, extermination, isolation, segregation, paternalism, forced assimilation, and, more recently, tolerance for pluralism and restoration of certain, but not all, Indian ways. Similarly, Blacks, Asians, Jews, Catholics, and other minority groups have all had varying relations with the host society.

Some recent world events also illustrate changing orientations toward minority groups. In 1982 economic difficulties prompted Nigerian leaders to expel once-welcomed immigrants from other African countries. A few years earlier, Ugandan leader Idi Amin had expelled all Asians who had formerly enjoyed harmonious relations in that country. After experiencing economic problems and numerous racial incidents, Britain severely curtailed its liberal immigration policy for the people of all its former colonies. When Iranians seized American hostages at the U.S. Embassy in November 1979, hostile attitudes and actions against Iranian Americans in this country suddenly manifested themselves. Similarly, Blacks and Whites in South Africa, Hindus and Moslems in India, Moslems and Christians in Lebanon, Arabs and Jews in the Middle East, Catholics and Protestants in Northern Ireland, and many other groups too numerous to mention all go through varying periods of stability and instability in their dealings with one another.

The field of race and ethnic relations is alive with theoreticians and investigators. Each year a vast outpouring of information from papers presented at meetings and from articles, books, and other sources adds to our knowledge. New insights, new concepts, and new interpretations of old knowledge inundate the interested observer. What both the sociologist and the student must attempt to understand, therefore, is not a fixed and static phenomenon, but rather a dynamic, ever changing one, about which more is still being learned.

RETROSPECT

Human beings follow certain patterns in responding to strangers. Their perceptions of newcomers are a result of categoric knowing; if the perception is that the newcomers are similar, people are more receptive to their presence. What makes interaction with strangers difficult is the varying perceptions of each to the other, occasioned by a lack of shared understandings and perceptions of reality.

Ethnocentrism, the tendency to identify with one's own group, is a universal human condition contributing to potential problems in relating to outgroups. Examples of ethnocentric thinking and actions can be found in all countries throughout history.

The study of minorities presents a difficult challenge because our value orientations and life experiences can impair our objectivity. Sociologists, being human, also encounter difficulty in maintaining value neutrality. Some argue that sociologists should take sides and not attempt a sterile approach to the subject.

Functional theory stresses the orderly interdependence of a society and adjustments needed to restore equilibrium when dysfunctions occur. Conflict theorists emphasize the tensions and conflicts from exploitation and competition for limited resources. Interactionists concentrate on everyday interaction patterns operating within a socially constructed reality perception.

Minority groups, regardless of size, receive unequal treatment, possess identifying physical or cultural characteristics held in low esteem, have a self-consciousness about their shared, ascribed status, and tend to practice endogamy. Racial groups are biologically similar groups while ethnic groups are ones sharing a learned cultural heritage.

KEY TERMS

Ascribed status
Abstract typifications
Categoric knowing
Conflict theory
Dominant group
Endogamy
False consciousness
Functional theory
Ingroup
Interactionist theory

Minority group
Outgroup
Parallel social institutions
Racial group
Reciprocal typifications
Reference group
Social construction of reality
Social distance
Symbolic interaction
Values

REVIEW QUESTIONS

1. What is the difference between a race and an ethnic group? between a minority group and an ethnic group?

2. What is ethnocentrism and why is it important in relations between dominant and minority groups?

3. Why is the objective study of racial and ethnic minorities a difficult matter?

4. What are the focal points of the functional, conflict, and interactionist theories?

SUGGESTED READINGS

Berger, Peter L. and Thomas Luckmann. *The Social Construction of Reality.* Garden City, NY: Doubleday, 1963.

   A highly influential work discussing how people define their reality and interact based upon shared expectations.

Levine, Robert A. and Donald T. Campbell. *Ethnocentrism: Theories of Conflict, Ethnic Attitudes, and Group Behavior.* New York: John Wiley & Sons, 1972.

   A detailed, analytical, and quantitative study of the interplay of ethnic attitudes and outgroup interactions.

Simmel, Georg. "The Stranger," in *The Sociology of Georg Simmel,* Kurt H. Wolff (ed.). New York: Free Press, 1950.

   A classic analysis of the role of the stranger through an analysis of the formal structures of life.

Schutz, Alfred. "The Stranger," *American Sociological Review, 69* (May 1944), 449–507.

   An early, influential essay, still highly pertinent today, explaining the interaction problems of a stranger.

CHAPTER 2

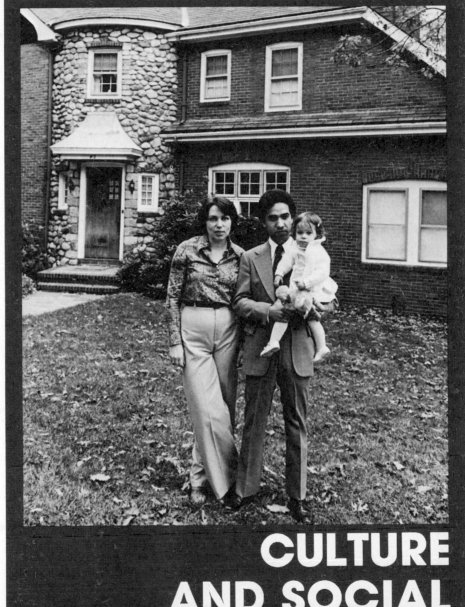

CULTURE AND SOCIAL STRUCTURE

Understanding what makes people receptive to certain strangers and not others requires knowledge about the role of culture and social structure in affecting perceptions and response patterns. Culture provides the guidelines for people's interpretations of situations they encounter and the actions they should take. **Social structure,** the organized patterns of behavior among the basic components of a social system, establishes the nature of the interrelationships among the different peoples in a society. The distinctions and interplay between culture and social structure are important to the assimilation process as well. For example, cultural orientations shape expectations about how a minority group should fit into the society.

In this chapter we shall first examine the various aspects of culture impacting upon dominant–minority relations. Following that will be a discussion of the significance of social class within the social structure. Both cultural and structural differentiation as a basis for conflict then come under study, followed by varying cultural expectations about minority integration.

THE CONCEPT OF CULTURE

Most sociologists emphasize the impact of culture in shaping behavior.[1] Through language and other forms of symbolic interaction, the members of a society learn the thought and behavior patterns that constitute their commonality as a people.[2] In this sense culture is the social cement that binds a society together. **Culture,** then, consists of the values, attitudes, customs, beliefs, and habits that are shared by members of a society; anything contrary to this "normal" state is seen as negative or deviant. Minority groups often change their distinctive cultural traits to those of the host society, and this process is called **acculturation.**

Shared cultural norms encourage solidarity and orient the behavior of members of the ingroup. **Norms** are a culture's rules of conduct—internalized by the members—embodying the fundamental expectations of society. Through norms, ingroup members (majority or minority) know how to react toward the acts of outgroup members that surprise, shock, or annoy them, or in any way go against their shared expectations. When minority-group members "act uppity" or "don't know their place," majority-group members often get upset, and sometimes act out their anger. Violations of norms usually result in strong reactions because they appear to threaten the social fabric of a community or society.

The Reality Construct

Our perception of reality is related to our culture; that is to say, through our culture we learn how to perceive the world about us. Cultural definitions help us to interpret the sensory stimuli from our environment and tell us how to respond to them. Thus, "culture is something that intervenes between the human organism and its environment to produce actions."[3] It is the screen through which we "see" (Figure 2.1).

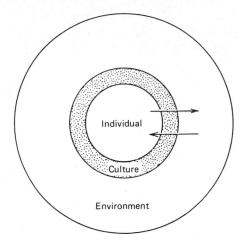

FIGURE 2.1
Cultural Reality

INDIVIDUAL observes the world through SENSE PERCEPTIONS; which are evaluated in terms of CULTURE: values, attitudes, customs, and beliefs.

Language and Other Symbols

Culture is learned behavior, acquired chiefly through verbal communication or language. A word is nothing more than a symbol—something that stands for something else. Whether it be tangible *(chair)* or intangible *(honesty),* the word represents a mental concept that is based on empirical reality. However, words reflect the culture, and one word may have different meanings in different cultures. If you have a *flat* in England, you have an apartment, not a deflated tire; if you could use a *lift,* you want an elevator, not a ride or a boost to your spirits. Because words symbolically interpret the world to us, the **linguistic relativity** of language may connote both intended and unintended prejudicial meanings. For example, the word *black* sometimes suggests dirty, or evil, and white sometimes suggests clean, or good, and these meanings may be subtly transferred to black and white people.

Walter Lippmann, a prominent political columnist, once remarked, "First we look, then we name, and only then do we see." What he meant was that until we learn the symbols of our world, we cannot understand the world. A popular pastime in the early 1950s called "Droodles" illustrates Lippmann's point. The object was to interpret drawings such as those in Figure 2.2. Many people were unable to see the meaning of the drawings until it was explained. They looked but did not see until they knew the "names."[4] (See "Notes" for answers.)

FIGURE 2.2
"Droodles"

Interpreting symbols is not just an amusing game; it is extremely significant in real life. Human beings do not respond to stimuli, but to their definitions of those stimuli, as mediated by their culture.[5] The definition of beauty is one example. Beyond the realm of personal taste, definitions of beauty have cultural variations. For instance, in different times and places a woman's beauty has been based upon her having distended lips, scar markings, tattoos, or beauty marks, or upon how plump or thin she was.

Nonverbal communication, or body language, is highly important too. Body movements, gestures, physical proximity, facial expressions (there are between 100 and 136 facial expressions, each of which conveys a distinct meaning![6]), and *paralinguistic signals* (sounds but not words) all convey information to the observer-listener. Body language is important in intergroup relations, whether in conversation, interaction, or perception. Body language may support or belie one's words; it may suggest friendliness, or aloofness, or deference.

Although some body language is fairly universal (for example, most facial expressions), many cultural variations exist in body language itself and in the interpretion of its meanings. Body movements such as posture, bearing, or gait vary from culture to culture. The degree of formality in a person's environment (both past and present) and other cultural factors have an influence on such forms of nonverbal communication. Consider the different meanings one could attach to a student's being unwilling to look directly into the eyes of a teacher. The teacher may consider this to reflect embarrassment, guilt, shyness, inattention, or even disrespect. Yet if the student were Hispanic, such an action would be a mark of respect. The symbol's definition, in this case the teacher's interpretation of what the student's action meant, determines the response.

A person who is foreign to a culture must learn both its language and the rest of its symbol system. Certain gestures may be signs of friendliness in one culture but obscene or vengeful symbols in another. For example, in America, placing thumb and forefinger in a circle with the other fingers upraised indicates that everything is fine, but in Japan this sign refers to money, and in Greece it is an insulting anal expression.[7] Kisses, tears, dances, emblems, silence, open display of emotions, and thousands of other symbols can, and often do, have very different meanings in different cultures. Symbols, including language, help construct a reality for an ingroup that may be unknown to or altogether different for an outgroup. Members of one group may then select, reject, ignore, or distort their sensory input regarding the other group because of cultural definitions.

The Thomas Theorem

Many years ago, William I. Thomas made an oft-repeated observation that if people define situations as real, those situations become real in their consequences.[8] His statement is further testimony to the truth of reality constructs: human beings respond to their definitions of stimuli rather than to the stimuli themselves. People behave according to the meaning they assign to the situation, and the consequences of their behavior serve to reaffirm the meaning; the definition becomes a self-fulfilling prophecy. For example, when Whites define Blacks as inferior and then offer them fewer opportunities because of that alleged inferiority, the result is that Blacks are disadvantaged, which in turn supports the initial definition.

Several variables determine the initial definition, but culture is a very important one. Culture establishes the framework through which an individual perceives others, classifies them into groups, and assigns them certain general characteristics. Because ethnocentrism leads people to consider their way of life as the best and most natural, their culturally defined perceptions of others often lead to suspicion and differential treatment of other groups. In effect, each group constructs myths about other groups and supports those myths through ingroup solidarity and outgroup hostility. As each group's attitudes and actions toward other groups continue, the *vicious-circle phenomenon* is at work.[9] In such instances, people create a culturally determined world of reality, and their actions reinforce their beliefs. Social interaction or social change may counteract such situations, leading to their redefinition.

Gregory Razran conducted a study illustrating how cultural definitions can influence perception.[10] Twice within a two-month interval, he showed the same set of thirty pictures of unknown young women to the same group of one hundred male college students and fifty noncollege men. Using a five-point scale, the subjects rated each woman's beauty, character, intelligence, ambition, and general likableness. At the first presentation, the pictures had no ethnic identification, but at the second presentation, they had Irish, Italian, Jewish, and old American (English) surnames. All women were rated equally on the first presentation, but when the names were given, the ratings changed. The "Jewish" women received higher ratings in ambition and intelligence. Both "Jewish" and "Italian" women suffered a large decline in general likableness and a slight decline in beauty and character evaluations. This study illustrates how cultural definitions affect judgments about others.

Through *cultural transmission,* each generation passes on its culture to the next generation, which learns those cultural definitions at an early age. This fact is dramatically expressed in the Rodgers and Hammerstein musical *South Pacific.* The tragic subplot is the touching romance between Lieutenant Cable and Liat. Although he and the Tonkinese girl are sincerely in love, his friends remind him that the couple's life would not be the same in America. Their differences in race and culture would work against a happy marriage for them, as would his own acceptance in Philadelphia high society. Miserable because of the choice his cultural values force him to make, he sings "Carefully Taught," a poignant song about how prejudice is taught to children.

> *You've got to be taught to hate and fear,*
> *You've got to be taught from year to year.*
> *It's got to be drummed in your dear little ear,*
> *You've got to be carefully taught.*
>
> *You've got to be taught to be afraid,*
> *Of people whose eyes are oddly made,*
> *Of people whose skin is a different shade.*
> *You've got to be carefully taught.*

You've got to be taught before it's too late,
Before you are six or seven or eight,
To hate all the people your relatives hate.
You've got to be carefully taught.
You've got to be carefully taught.[11]

These lyrics help reinforce the reality construct discussed earlier and illustrated in Figure 2.1. From family, friends, school, mass media, and all other sources of informational input, we learn our values, attitudes, and beliefs. Some of our learning reflects the prejudices of others which we may incorporate in our own attitudes and actions.

CULTURAL CHANGE

Culture is continually changing. Discoveries, inventions, technological advances, innovations, or natural disasters can all alter the customs, values, attitudes, and beliefs of a society.

Cultural Diffusion

A striking paradox is that although the members of a dominant culture wish to keep their society untainted by the influence of foreign elements, all cultures are inevitably influenced by other cultures. Ideas, inventions, and practices spread from one culture to another, though the rate of diffusion varies considerably. Negative attitudes and a large distance between groups can be effective barriers, and sometimes cultural diffusion occurs only under the right conditions. Also, sometimes ideas are modified or reinterpreted before being accepted, such as the Latin American Indians' fondness for automobile tires: they use them to make sandals, for they neither own nor drive cars.[12]

American anthropologist Ralph Linton calculated that any given culture contains about 90 percent borrowed elements. To demonstrate both the enormity and the subtlety of cultural diffusion, he offered a classic portrait of the "100 per cent American."

Our solid American citizen awakens in a bed built on a pattern which originated in the Near East but which was modified in Northern Europe before it was transmitted to America. He throws back covers made from cotton, domesticated in India, or linen, domesticated in the Near East, or wool, from sheep, also domesticated in the Near East, or silk, the use of which was discovered in China. All of these materials have been spun or woven by processes invented in the Near East. He slips into his moccasins, invented by the Indians of the Eastern woodlands, and goes to the bathroom, whose fixtures are a mixture of European and American inventions, both of recent date. He takes off his pajamas, a garment invented in India, and washes with soap invented by the ancient Gauls. He then shaves, a masochistic rite which seems to have been derived from either Sumer or ancient Egypt.

Returning to the bedroom, he removes his clothes from a chair of southern European type and proceeds to dress. He puts on garments whose form originally derived from the skin clothing of the nomads of the Asiatic steppes, puts on shoes made from skins tanned by a process invented in ancient Egypt and cut to a pattern derived from the classical civilizations of the Mediterranean, and ties around his neck a strip of bright-colored cloth which is a vestigial survival of the shoulder shawls worn by the seventeenth-century Croatians. Before going out for breakfast he glances through the window, made of glass invented in Egypt, and if it is raining puts on overshoes made of rubber discovered by the Central American Indians and takes an umbrella, invented in southeastern Asia. Upon his head he puts a hat made of felt, a material invented in the Asiatic steppes.

On his way to breakfast he stops to buy a paper, paying for it with coins, an ancient Lydian invention. At the restaurant a whole new series of borrowed elements confronts him. His plate is made of a form of pottery invented in China. His knife is of steel, an alloy first made in southern India, his fork a medieval Italian invention, and his spoon a derivative of a Roman original. He begins breakfast with an orange, from the eastern Mediterranean, a cantaloupe from Persia, or perhaps a piece of African watermelon. With this he has coffee, an Abyssinian plant, with cream and sugar. Both the domestication of cows and the idea of milking them originated in the Near East, while sugar was first made in India. After his fruit and first coffee, he goes on to waffles, cakes made by a Scandinavian technique from wheat domesticated in Asia Minor. Over these he pours maple syrup, invented by the Indians of the Eastern woodlands. As a side dish he may have the egg of a species of bird domesticated in Indo-China, or thin strips of the flesh of an animal domesticated in Eastern Asia which have been salted and smoked by a process developed in northern Europe.

When our friend has finished eating he settles back to smoke, an American Indian habit, consuming a plant domesticated in Brazil in either a pipe, derived from the Indians of Virginia, or a cigarette, derived from Mexico. If he is hardy enough he may even attempt a cigar, transmitted to us from the Antilles by way of Spain. While smoking he reads the news of the day, imprinted in characters invented by the ancient Semites upon a material invented in China by a process invented in Germany. As he absorbs the accounts of foreign troubles he will, if he is a good conservative citizen, thank a Hebrew deity in an Indo-European language that he is 100 per cent American.*

Culture Contact

Another way in which culture can undergo change is through people of different cultures coming into contact with one another. Because people tend to take their own culture for granted, it operates at a subconscious level in forming their expectations. When people's assumptions are jolted through contact with another culture with different expectations, they often experience *culture shock,* which is characterized by feelings of disorientation and anxiety and a sense of being threatened.

*Ralph Linton. *The Study of Man,* 1936, pp. 326–327. Reprinted by permission of Prentice-Hall, Inc., Englewood Cliffs, New Jersey.

BOX 2.1 | **Basic American Values**

Within this diverse American society of many different racial, ethnic, and religious groups with their distinctive set of values exists a common core of mainstream values. Sociologist Robin Williams, after decades of study, has identified fifteen value orientations, the foundation of our beliefs, behaviors, definitions of social goals and life expectations. Some are contradictory—freedom, individualism, and external conformity; equality and group-superiority; nationalism and freedom—and thus spark divisions among people. Still widely held by powerful groups, these values continue to have enormous impact in shaping our society.

1. **Achievement and Success.** Competition oriented, our society places much value on gaining power, prestige, and wealth.
2. **Activity and Work.** We firmly believe in everyone working and we condemn as lazy those who do not work.
3. **Moral Orientation.** We tend to moralize, seeing the world in absolutes of right and wrong.
4. **Humanitarian Mores.** Through charitable and crisis aid we lean toward helping the less fortunate and the underdog.
5. **Efficiency and Practicality.** We seek problem solutions through the quickest and least costly means.
6. **Progress.** We think technology can solve all problems and hold an optimistic future outlook.
7. **Material Comfort.** We share the American Dream of a high standard of living and owning many material goods.
8. **Equality.** We believe in this abstract ideal, relating to each other informally, as equals.
9. **Freedom.** Individual freedom from domination of others is a highly cherished value.
10. **External Conformity.** Despite our professed belief in individualism, we join, conform, or go along, suspicious of those who do not.
11. **Science and Rationality.** We believe through science we can gain mastery over our environment and secure a better life-style.
12. **Nationalism.** We think the American way of life is the best, and distrust ''un-American'' behavior.
13. **Democracy.** We believe everyone has the right of political participation, that our government is highly democratic.
14. **Individualism.** We emphasize personal rights and responsibilities, giving the individual priority over the group.
15. **Racism and Group-Superiority Themes.** We place higher value on some racial, religious, or ethnic groups than others through our attitudes and actions.

Source: Robin M. Williams, Jr., *American Society: A Sociological Interpretation* 3rd ed. (New York: Knopf, 1970).

Culture shock does not always occur. When people of two different cultures interact, many possible patterns can emerge. The two groups may live in peaceful coexistence with a gradual cultural diffusion occurring. History offers some excellent examples of connections between migrations and innovations, wherein geographical conditions and native attitudes have determined the extent to which a group has resisted cultural innovations, despite invasions, settlements, or missionary work. The persistent pastoralism of Bedouin tribes and the long-sustained resistance to industrialization of the American Indians are but two examples.[13] Stanley Lieberson, however, suggests that power alone determines the outcome, causing one group to become dominant and the other subservient.[14] If the subordinate group was not the migratory group, the changes to their social organization can be particularly devastating. No longer possessing the flexibility and autonomy they once enjoyed, they may suffer material deprivation and find their institutions undermined. If the migratory group finds itself in the subordinate position, it must adapt to its new environment to survive. Most commonly, the minority group draws from its familiar world as it attempts to cope with the different conditions. Group members form a subculture in which their behavior and interests are unique to themselves, not shared with others in the larger society. In doing so, they create a modified version of the culture of the old country that also reflects the influence of the new country. For example, both Catholicism and Judaism have undergone changes in form and expression since taking root in America. Each of the ethnic subcultures has represented a blend of native and American cultures, as group members have acclimated to their new environment.

Subcultures

Most large societies—especially complex, industrial ones—contain various subgroupings of people. Quite commonly, people share some characteristics of the society at large, but they have other characteristics unique to their own group. Such groups are called subcultures, which can be regional, age-related, occupational, racial, ethnic, and so on.

Usually, immigrants follow a *chain migration* pattern, settling in an area already containing family, friends, or compatriots who had located there earlier. An ethnic community evolves, providing an emotional support system to these strangers in a strange land striving to forge a better life for themselves. Part of this process of cultural insulation among others like themselves is the re-creation in miniature of the world they left behind. Appearing are *parallel social institutions*—their own clubs, organizations, newspapers, stores, churches, and schools duplicating those of the host society—which create cohesiveness within the minority subculture.

As ethnic subcultures among immigrants in the United States evolved in response to conditions within the host society, the immigrants sometimes developed a group consciousness unknown in their old countries. Many first-generation Americans possessed a village orientation toward their homeland rather than a national identity. They spoke different dialects, feuded with other regions, and had different values. However, their common experience in the United States caused them to coalesce into a national grouping. One example is the Italian-Americans, who at first identified with their cities of origin: Calabria, Palermo, Naples, Genoa, Salerno, and so on. Within a generation, many came to view themselves as Italians, partly because the host society classified them as such.

Convergent Subcultures

Most ethnic subcultures are *convergent;* that is, they tend toward assimilation with the dominant society. Although recognizable by residential clustering and adherence to the language, dress, and cultural norms of their native land, these ethnic groups are nonetheless becoming assimilated. As the years pass—possibly several generations—the distinctions between the dominant culture and the convergent subculture gradually lessen. Eventually this form of subculture becomes completely integrated into the dominant culture.

Because this subculture is undergoing change, its members may experience the problems of **marginality,** living under stress in two cultures simultaneously. The older generation may seek to preserve its traditions and heritage, but the younger generation may be impatient to be fully accepted within the dominant society. Because the impetus is to assimilate, time obviously favors the younger generation. Some examples of once prevalent ethnic subcultures are the Irish, Germans, and Dutch, in order of decreasing visibility today. These nationality groups still exhibit ethnic pride in many ways, but, for the most part, they are no longer set apart by place of residence or subcultural behavior. Based upon their multigenerational length of residence, these nationality groups are less likely to live in clustered housing arrangements or to display particular behavior patterns such as conflict, deviance, or endogamy, to any greater degree than the rest of the majority group.

Persistent Subcultures

Not all subcultures assimilate, and some do not even desire to do so. Some steadfastly adhere to their own way of life as much as possible, resisting absorption into the dominant culture. Two relatively isolated religious groups, the Amish and the Hutterites, have long insisted upon maintaining a way of life different from that of the "ungodly" majority and may represent the purest form of a persistent subculture in American society. Other ethnic groups adopt a few aspects of the dominant culture but remain adamant about preserving their own way of life; examples are most Indians who live on reservations and many Spanish-Americans in the Southwest. Chinatowns also manifest in many ways the preservation of the Chinese way of life.

A minority group's insistence upon the right to be different has not usually been very well received among dominant-group members. This clash of wills has the potential for conflict; at the very least, it is the breeding ground for stereotyping and prejudice on both sides.

Just as convergent subcultures illustrate assimilation, persistent subcultures illustrate pluralism. We shall discuss these two forms of minority integration shortly.

STRUCTURAL CONDITIONS

Relationships between majority and minority groups are influenced as much by structural conditions as by differences in culture. The nature of those conditions influences not only the distribution of power resources (economic, political, social) but also the accessibility of those resources to groups who are seeking upward mobility. An expanding economy and an open social system allow for increased opportunities for minority-group members, thereby reducing the possibility of frustrations and tensions arising. A stagnant or contracting economy thwarts many efforts to improve status and antagonizes those who feel most threatened by another group's competition for scarce resources. Such a situation may breed conflicts among minority groups even more than between majority and minority groups, because the group next highest on the socioeconomic ladder may perceive a threat more quickly and react negatively.

The state of the economy is just one of the important structural factors influencing the opportunities for upward mobility. Another factor is the degree of change between a minority group's old society and the new one. A traditional or agrarian society will have a much more stable social structure than a society undergoing a

Three street urchins asleep in New York's Lower East Side, circa 1890. Homeless children, usually orphaned though occasionally runaways, were not uncommon in the immigrant communities. Fending for themselves through hawking newspapers, doing odd jobs, or stealing, they would usually band together in small groups and sleep wherever they could.

transformation through industrialization. The latter society will offer dramatic changes in opportunities and life styles, not all of them for the better. For a minority group migrating to another country, its compatibility with the social structure of the new land will be contingent upon the degree of similarity with structural conditions in its homeland. A person who leaves an agrarian society for an industrial one is poorly prepared to do anything but enter the lowest stratum in a low-paying position. Opportunities for upward mobility, however, may exist if the economy is growing rapidly. In this sense, the structural conditions of 1880 to 1920 were better for the unskilled immigrant than are conditions today. Low-skill jobs are not as plentiful today as they once were, and an unskilled worker's desire to support a family through hard work and sweat may not be matched by the opportunity to do so.

Another change in structural conditions has been the advancement in technology, which has made for a smaller world. Rapid transportation and communications (radio, television, telephone, telegraph, satellites, air mail) make it possible for ties to other parts of the world to remain stronger than in the past.[15] Accessibility to one's homeland, friends, or relatives may make one less interested in becoming fully assimilated in a new land. Befriending strangers in the new country becomes less necessary. Additionally, people's greater knowledge of the world, the rising social consciousness of a society, and structural opportunities for mobility all help to create a more hospitable environment for minority-group members.

STRATIFICATION

Social stratification is the hierarchical classification of the members of society based upon the unequal distribution of resources, power, and prestige. *Resources* refer to such factors as income, property, and borrowing capacity. *Power*, usually reflected by the stratified layers, concerns the ability to influence or control others. *Prestige* relates to status, either *ascribed*—based on age, sex, race, or family background—or *achieved*—based on individual accomplishments.

The process of stratification may serve to moderate or exacerbate any strains or conflicts between groups, depending upon the form that the stratification takes. The form can range from rigid to flexible and subtle, from slavery, caste, and forced labor to class distinctions and discrimination based on race or ethnic group. Whether racial and ethnic groups face insurmountable barriers or minor obstacles in achieving upward mobility is determined by the form of stratification. The more rigid the stratification, the more likely racial, religious, or other ideologies justifying the existing arrangements are to arise.

The form of stratification affects how groups within the various strata of society view one another. Some people confuse structural differentiation with cultural differentiation. For example, they may believe a group's low socioeconomic status is the result of its values and attitudes rather than the result of such structural conditions as racism, economic stagnation, or high urban unemployment. The form of stratification is an important determinant of the potential for intergroup conflict. In the United States, both the possibility of upward mobility and structural obstacles to that possibility have existed. When the disparity between the perception of the American Dream and the reality of the difficulty of achieving it grows too great, the possibility of conflict increases.

Culture of Poverty

Beginning in 1932 with E. Franklin Frazier's conception of a disorganized and pathological lower-class culture,[16] a controversial school of thought has existed that has become known as the *culture-of-poverty* theory. The culmination of this idea came in 1965 with the release of a U.S. Department of Labor document known as the "Moynihan Report."[17] The report actually contained nothing new, relying heavily on Frazier's observations. However, this time it came from a federal government agency, at a time when the civil rights movement was at its height. The report angered a great many people, including Blacks, civil rights workers, and social workers.

Family Disintegration

In examining the problems of high unemployment, welfare dependency, illegitimacy, low achievement, juvenile delinquency, and adult crime, Moynihan argued that family deterioration was a major factor.

At the heart of the deterioration of the fabric of Negro society is the deterioration of the Negro family. It is the fundamental source of weakness of the Negro community at the present time. . . . The white family has achieved a high degree of stability and is maintaining that stability. By contrast, the family structure of the lower class Negroes is highly unstable, and in many urban centers is approaching complete breakdown.[18]

Moynihan described black males as occupying an unstable place in the economy, which prevents their being strong fathers and husbands. This environment serves as a breeding ground for a continuing vicious cycle: the women often not only raise the children, but also earn the family income. Consequently, the children grow up in a poorly supervised, unstable environment; they often do not do well or stay in school; they can secure only low-paying jobs—and so the cycle begins anew.[19]

At the center of the tangle of pathology is the weakness of the family structure. Once or twice removed, it will be found to be the principal source of most of the aberrant, inadequate, or anti-social behavior that did not establish but now serves to perpetuate the cycle of poverty and deprivation. . . .

What then is the problem? We feel that the answer is clear enough. Three centuries of injustice have brought about deep-seated structural distortions in the life of the Negro American. At this point, the present tangle of pathology is capable of perpetuating itself without assistance from the white world. The cycle can be broken only if these distortions are set right.[20]

Perpetuation of Poverty

The crux of the culture-of-poverty thesis, and its most controversial point, was the contention that distinctive lower-class values were transmitted from one generation to the next. Oscar Lewis gave perhaps the most persuasive commentary for the culture-of-poverty school in his introduction to his classic case study of a Puerto Rican family.[21]

The culture of poverty, however, is not only an adaptation to a set of objective conditions of the larger society. Once it comes into existence it tends to perpetuate itself from generation to generation because of its effect on the children. By the time slum children are age six or seven they have usually absorbed the basic values and attitudes of their subculture and are not psychologically geared to take full advantage of changing conditions or increased opportunities which may occur in their lifetime.[22]

This proposition—that poverty continues because of subcultural patterns—has had important implications. Those who hold this view often believe that federal efforts to eliminate poverty would be more successful if they turned to a more direct, sociopsychological approach. Edward Banfield, for example, felt that this was the best solution to the poverty problem. He argued that good jobs, good housing, tripled welfare payments, new schools, quality education, and armies of police officers would not stop the problem. He continued:

If, however, the lower classes were to disappear—if, say, its members were over-night to acquire the attitudes, motivations, and habits of the working class—the most serious and intractable problems of the city would all disappear with it. . . . The lower-class forms of all problems are at bottom a single problem: the existence of an outlook and style of life which is radically present-oriented and which therefore attaches no value to work, sacrifice, self-improvement, or service to family, friends, or community.[23]

Public opinion appears to support the culture of poverty hypothesis. Although many social scientists decry the view, numerous survey polls have indicated the majority of Americans think the poor are responsible for their own poverty. For example, in one national cross section of adults, 53 percent said that the poor were at fault for their dilemma and 22 percent felt that the social structure was at fault.[24]

Other Explanations

Critics of the culture-of-poverty school have argued that fatalism, apathy, low aspiration, and other similar orientations are situational responses within each generation and are not passed down. In 1963, Michael Harrington's *The Other America* helped spark the federal government's "War on Poverty" program. He maintained that society was to blame for poverty.

The real explanation of why the poor are where they are is that they made the mistake of being born to the wrong parents, in the wrong section of the country, in the wrong industry, or in the wrong racial or ethnic group.[25]

Charles Valentine stated that the distinctive patterns of life among the poor result from structural conditions in the larger society that are beyond the control of low-income people, not from socialization to different cultural values.[26] Others argued that all people would desire the same things and cherish the same values if they were in an economic position to do so. Because they are not, they adopt an alternative set of values in order to survive.[27] Eliot Liebow, in a participant-observer study of lower-class black males, concluded that they try to achieve many of the goals of the larger society, but fail for many of the same reasons as their fathers did: discrimination, unpreparedness, lack of job skills, and self-doubt.[28] The similarities between generations are due not to cultural transmission, but to the sons' independent experience of the same failures. What appears to be a self-

This impoverished woman and her son live in this small, one—room apartment. Lacking job skills or access to child care facilities and thus unable to secure a decent—paying job, she typifies the growing segment of female—headed households living in poverty with little hope of extricating themselves from their situation.

sustaining cultural process is in reality a secondary adaptation to an adult inability to overcome structural constraints.

The debate between those who argue that ghetto culture is the product of *economic determinism* (structural differentiation) and those who believe it is caused by *cultural determinism* (a culture of poverty) continues. A person's attitudes toward welfare, toward the urban poor, who are mostly racial and ethnic minorities, and toward different orientations to life all reflect the individual's beliefs about this issue. About the only common ground shared by the two schools of thought is their mutual support of increased employment and educational opportunities.

Scientific studies have failed to document an actual culture of poverty among ghetto residents.[29] Furthermore, the presence of confused sexual identifications, delinquency, or other pathological conditions directly resulting from absence of a father still has not been proved.[30] Moreover, investigators often found evidence of great strength in poor black families, with an extended family structure of several generations headed by competent and emotionally strong women maintaining family stability within a positive home environment.[31]

Yet some sociologists believe the economic determinist and cultural determinist positions can be reconciled. Hyman Rodman suggested all social classes share the general values of a society but that the lower class, while not rejecting those values, adopts additional values representing realistic levels of attainment.

Lower-class persons . . . do not maintain a strong commitment to middle-class values that they cannot attain, and they do not continue to respond to others in a rewarding or punishing way simply on the basis of whether these others are living up to the middle-class values. A change takes place. They come to tolerate and eventually to evaluate favorably certain deviations from the middle-class values. In this way they need not be continually frustrated by their failure to live up to unattainable values. The resultant is a stretched value system.[32]

L. Richard Della Fave adds that this *value-stretch* approach of the poor occurs when the gap between ideal value preference and achievement expectations becomes too great.[33] In other words, the poor do not have different values but different behaviors resulting from coping mechanisms. Since they expect less, they become satisfied with less.

SOCIAL CLASS

Social class is one categorization by which sociologists designate people's place in the stratification hierarchy; people in a particular social class have similar income, amount of property, degree of power, status, and life style. Many factors help to determine a person's social class, including that individual's membership in particular racial, religious, and status groups. Although no clearly defined boundaries exist between class groupings in the United States, people have a tendency to cluster together according to certain socioeconomic similarities. Classes result from sociopsychological distinctions people make about one another based, for example, on where they live and what they own, as well as on the types of interactions that occur because of those distinctions.

Social class becomes important in intergroup relations because it serves as a basis for expectations. As Alan Kerckhoff states, social class provides a particular setting for the interplay between the formative experiences of a child, others' expectations of the child, and what kind of adult the child becomes.[34] First as a significant determiner and later as a point of reference in others' responses and in a person's self-view, social class helps to shape an individual's world of reality and influences group interactions. This view is in some ways similar to the culture-of-poverty hypothesis, but it does not negate a person's receptivity to change given increased opportunities. Social class is an important determiner of attitudes and behavior, but that does not necessarily mean they are immutable.

In the 1930s, W. Lloyd Warner headed a classic study of social-class differentiation.[35] Using the **reputational method**—asking people how others compared to them—Warner found a well-formulated class system existing. In Newburyport, Massachusetts, a small town of about seventeen thousand which he called "Yankee City," Warner identified six classes: upper-upper, lower-upper, upper-middle, lower-middle, upper-lower, and lower-lower. When he and his associates examined the distribution of ethnic groups among the various classes, certain factors emerged. First, a significant relationship existed between an ethnic group's length of residence and class status; the more recent arrivals tended to be in the lower classes. Other factors were also found to have an important influence on class status. An ethnic group tended to be less assimilated and less upwardly mobile if its population in the community was relatively large, if its homeland was close (such as in the case of the French-Canadians), if its members had a sojourner rather than a permanent-settler orientation, and if limited opportunities for advancement existed in the community.[36]

Class Consciousness

Just how important are the ethnic factors that Warner and others have reported in shaping an awareness of social class? The answer is that the significance of ethnic factors depends on a great many variables; some of these variables are economic conditions, mobility patterns, and prevailing attitudes. John Leggett found that class consciousness depends on the ethnic factor: the lower a group's ethnic status in the society, the higher the level of class consciousness.[37] Other studies have shown that working-class ethnic groups tend to view their class as hostile to, and under the political control of, the higher classes.[38]

Because ethnic minorities are disproportionately represented among the lower classes, and because middle-class values dominate in the United States, a reasonable assumption is that at least some of the attitudes of each group result from people's value judgments about social class. That is to say, the dominant group's criticism and stereotyping of the minority group probably rests in part on class distinctions.

Ethnicity and Social Class

Social-class status plays an important role in determining a minority group's adjustment to and acceptance by society. For example, because the Cuban and Vietnamese refugees arrived possessing the education and occupational experience of the middle class, they succeeded in overcoming early native concerns and did not encounter the same degree of negativism as had earlier groups. On the other hand, when unskilled and often illiterate peasants have entered the lower-class positions in American society, many Americans have belittled, avoided, and discriminated against them because of their supposedly inferior ways. Frequently, these attitudes and actions have represented an awareness of class differences as well as cultural differences. Since the dominant group usually represents a higher stratum in the social-class hierarchy, the differing social-class values and life styles provide a source of friction in addition to the ethnic cultural differences.

Social class and ethnic group membership are closely intertwined, but, according to Colin Greer, many social observers have placed too much emphasis on ethnic-centered analyses and ignored the larger question of class.

This kind of ethnic reductionism forces us to accept as predetermined what society defines as truth. Only through ethnicity can identity be securely achieved. The result is that ethnic questions which could, in fact, further our understanding of the relationship of individuals to social structures are always raised in a way that serves to reconcile us to a common heritage of miserable inequities. Instead of realizing that the lack of a well-defined stratification structure, linked to a legitimated aristocratic tradition, led Americans to employ the language of ethnic pluralism in exchange for direct divisions by social class, we continue to ignore the real factors of class in our society. . . . What we must ultimately talk about is class. The cues of felt ethnicity turn out to be the recognizable characteristics of class position in this society: to feel black, Irish, Italian, Jewish has meant to learn to live in accommodation with that part of your heritage that is compatible with the needs and opportunities in America upon arrival and soon thereafter.[39]

In 1964, ten years before Greer's observations, Milton Gordon had suggested that dominant-minority relations be examined within the larger context of the social structure.[40] This proposition marked an important turning point in racial and ethnic studies.[41] Although he believed that all groups would eventually become assimilated, Gordon offered an explanation of the present pluralistic society. His central thesis was that four factors or social categories play a part in forming subsocieties within the nation: ethnicity (by which Gordon also meant race), social class, rural or urban residence, and regionalism.[42] These factors unite in various combinations to create a number of *ethclasses.* These subsocieties result from the intersection of the stratifications of race and ethnic group with the stratifications of social class. Additional determinants are the rural or urban setting and the particular region of the country in which a group lives. Examples of ethclasses are lower-middle-class white Catholics in a northeastern city, lower-class black Baptists in the rural South, and upper-class white Jews in a western urban area.

Numerous studies have supported the concept that race and ethnicity, together with social class, are important in social structures and intergroup conflicts.[43] Not only do ethclass groupings exist, but people tend to interact mostly within them for their intimate primary relationships. To the extent that this is true, multiple allegiances and conflicts will occur. According to this view, both cultural and structural pluralism currently exist. Even those whose families have been here for several generations are affiliated with, and participate in, subsocieties. Gordon does, however, view assimilation as a linear process in which eventual assimilation, including structural, will occur.

INTERGROUP CONFLICT

Is conflict inevitable when culturally distinct groups interact? Do structural conditions encourage or reduce the probability of conflict? Robert E. Park, respected head of the highly influential Chicago school of sociology, concluded that a universal cycle of events repeatedly occurs in all countries, making conflict always a reality. In Park's day, the term *race* referred to both racial and ethnic groups, and his comments should thus be given the broader application.

Park saw an inevitable process that was irreversible and could take a long period of time. The stages of this cycle were contact between the groups, then competition, followed by some kind of adjustment or accommodation. The final stage was assimilation and amalgamation.

The race relations cycle which takes the form, to state it abstractly, of contact, competition, accommodation, and eventual assimilation, is apparently progressive and irreversible. Customs regulations, immigration restrictions, and racial barriers may slacken the tempo of the movement; may perhaps halt it altogether for a time; but cannot change its direction, cannot, at any rate, reverse it. . . . It does not follow that because the tendencies to the assimilation and eventual amalgamation of races exist, they should not be resisted and, if possible, altogether inhibited. . . . Rising tides of color and oriental exclusion laws are merely incidental evidences of this diminishing distance   . In the Hawaiian Islands, where all the races of the Pacific meet and mingle . . . the native races are disappearing and new peoples are coming into existence. Races and cultures die—it has always been so—but civilization lives on.[44]

There are several problems with Park's race relations cycle. By its very nature, this hypothesis of an inevitable cycle is not testable.[45] Park could not cite any racial group that had passed through all four stages. Instead of seeing these negative data as refuting the theory, Park and other cyclical theorists explained the lack of assimilation as the result of obstacles or interference. As a result of such tautological reasoning, this theory lacks an essential element of empirical science: it cannot be proved or disproved.[46] Moreover, the universality of the cyclical theory falters because there are cases in which conflict and competition did not occur when different groups came into contact.

Conflict does not necessarily occur when different peoples make contact. Brazil and Hawaii are just two examples of places where peaceful and harmonious interactions have existed among different peoples. In many other instances of intergroup relations, however, some form of stress, tension, or conflict does occur. In this chapter we have presented the major factors that may set the stage for such conflict: cultural and structural differentiation. Those factors may be applied to an understanding of conflict between dominant and minority groups.

Cultural Differentiation

When similarities between the minority group and the indigenous group exist, the probability is greater that the relationship will be relatively harmonious and that assimilation will eventually occur.[47] The greater and more visible the cultural differences, the greater the likelihood that conflict will occur. When large numbers of German and Irish Catholics came to this country in the midnineteenth century, Protestant America grew uneasy. As priest and nuns also arrived, and as the Catholics built churches, convents, and schools, Protestant America became alarmed at what it considered a papal conspiracy to gain control of the country. Emotions ran high, and the result was unrest and violence.

Religion is often a basis for cultural conflict, as demonstrated by the examples of the Mormons, Jews, and Quakers, who have all suffered discrimination in this country. Yet many other aspects of cultural visibility can also serve as sources of contention. Cultural differences might range from clothing (for example, Sikh turbans and saris) to leisure activities (for example, Hispanic cockfights). Americans once condemned the Chinese as opium smokers, even though the British had introduced opium smoking into China and promoted it among the lower-class Chinese population.

Cultural differences do not necessarily cause intergroup conflict. Part of the explanation about variance in relations between culturally distinct groups comes from interactionist theory. As you will recall, this perspective holds that the extent of shared symbols and definitions between groups in mutual intercommunication determines the nature of interaction patterns. While it is true that actual differences may provide a basis for conflict, interactionists say the key to harmonious or disharmonious relations lies in the definitions or interpretations of those differences. Tolerance or intolerance, acceptance or rejection of others thus depends upon perceptions of others as threatening or nonthreatening, assimilable or nonassimilable, worthy or unworthy.

Structural Differentiation

Because they offer macrosocial analyses of a society, both functional theory and conflict theory provide a basis for understanding how structural conditions affect intergroup relations. Functionalists seek explanations in the adjustments needed in the social system to compensate for other changes. Conflict theorists emphasize the conscious, purposeful actions of dominant groups to maintain systems of inequality.

Functional Analysis

Sometimes economic and technological conditions facilitate minority integration. When the economy is healthy and jobs are plentiful, newcomers find it easier to get established and work their way up the socioeconomic ladder. In present-day America, however, technological progress has reduced the number of low-status blue-collar jobs and increased the number of high-status white-collar jobs, which require more highly skilled and educated workers. The result is that fewer jobs are available for unskilled, foreign, marginal, and unassimilated people.

Perhaps because of the importance of one's job as a source of economic security and status, **occupational mobility**—the ability to improve one's job position—seems to be an important factor in determining whether prejudice will increase or decrease. A number of studies have shown that downward social mobility increases ethnic hostility.[48] Bruno Bettelheim and Morris Janowitz report from seven studies that persons moving downward in status are not only more prejudiced than the group they left but also more prejudiced than the lower-status group they enter. Additionally upwardly mobile people are generally more tolerant than nonmobile individuals.[49] It would appear that loss of status and prestige increases hostility toward outgroups, whereas upward gains enable people to be more magnanimous toward others.

Conflict Analysis

If one group becomes dominant and another subservient, obviously one group has more power than the other. Social-class status partly reflects this unequal distribution of power, which may also fall along racial or ethnic lines. For ethnicity to become a basis for stratification, it appears that several factors must be present.

Ethnic stratification will emerge when distinct ethnic groups are brought into sustained contact only if the groups are characterized by a high degree of ethnocentrism, competition, *and* differential power. Competition provides the motivation for stratification; ethnocentrism channels the competition along ethnic lines; and the power differential determines whether either group will be able to subordinate the other.[50]

This **power differential** is of enormous importance in race and ethnic relations. If the stratification system is rigid, as in a slave or caste system, with no hope or means of improving status, then intergroup relations may be stable though perhaps far from mutually satisfactory. Dominant power, whether expressed in legalized ways or through structural discrimination, intimidation, or coercion, maintains the social system. Even if the stratification system allows for upward mobility, some members of the dominant group may believe that the lower-class racial and ethnic groups are challenging the social order as they strive for their share of the "good life." If the dominant group does not feel threatened, the change will be peaceful. If the minority group meets resistance but retains hope and a sense of belonging to the larger society, the struggle for more power will be within the system (for example, by means of demonstrations, boycotts, voter-registration drives, or lobbying) rather than through violence.[51]

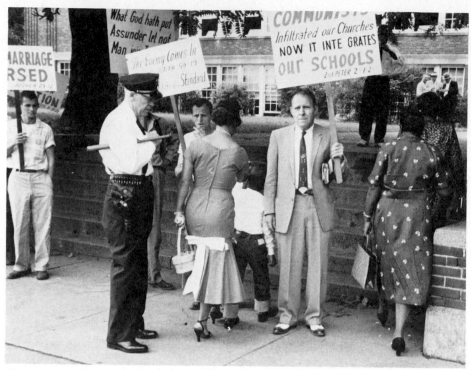

Court—ordered integration ran counter to a lifetime's value orientations and beliefs in the early 1960s, prompting numerous incidents of picketing, such as that pictured above. Threatened by these mandates, some Whites sincerely believed communist agitators or sympathizers were responsible, and found Biblical passages to support their position.

As a minority group struggles for a larger share of economic and political power, another group—either a majority group or another minority group—may resist, especially if it views the situation as threatening to its own power resources. Inter-group competition for scarce resources is a breeding ground for racial and ethnic hostilities. Most regional antiforeign flare-ups—such as the late-nineteenth-century race-baiting riots on the West Coast against Chinese and Japanese workers or the 1919 Chicago race riots against Blacks entering the meat-packing industry—have occurred as a reaction to minority-group strivings for greater power resources.

Social Class Antagonisms

Conflict theorists such as Ralf Dahrendorf suggest that social class is an important variable affecting conflict. Dahrendorf maintains that a correlation exists between a group's economic position and the intensity of its conflict with the dominant society. The greater the deprivation in economic resources, social status, and social power, the more probable it is that the weaker group will resort to intense and violent conflict to achieve gains in any of these three areas. As the social-class position of a group increases, intergroup conflict will be less intense and less violent.[52]

Years earlier, Max Weber argued that when economic resources become more evenly distributed among classes, relative status will become the issue of conflict, if conflict occurs at all.[53] Conflict occurs not only because a lower-class group seeks an end to deprivation, but also because the group next higher on the socioeconomic ladder feels most threatened. Quite often the working-class group displays the most prejudice and most frequently engages in violence against the upward-striving minority group. Other factors may also be at work, but status competition is significant in causing conflict.

Social-class antagonisms also influence people's perceptions of racial and ethnic groups.[54] Some social scientists maintain that the problem of Black–White relations is more a problem of social class than of racism. Illustrative of this view is James M. O'Kane:

The gap exists between the classes, not the races; it is between the white and black middle classes on the one hand, and the white and black lower classes on the other. Skin color and the history of servitude do little to explain the present polarization of the classes. . . . Class differentials, not racial differentials, explain the presence and persistence of poverty in the ranks of the urban Negro.[55]

O'Kane suggests several parallels between Irish, Italian, and Polish immigrants and Southern Blacks who migrated to Northern cities (the Chinese, some of the Japanese, and others could also be included). All came from agrarian poverty to industrial slums. Encountering prejudice and discrimination, some sought alternative routes of upward mobility: crime, ethnic politics, stable but unskilled employment.[56] Other social scientists argue that the black experience does not equate with that of European immigrants. They hold, as did the Kerner Commission investigating the urban riots of the late 1960s, that the dominant society's colonization of Blacks deprived them of the strong social organizations that other groups had. Moreover, today's labor market offers fewer unskilled jobs for Blacks than it once offered for other immigrant groups, thereby depriving Blacks of a means to begin moving upward.[57]

This debate about race versus social class as the primary factor in assessing full integration of Blacks in America continues to rage, particularly among black social scientists. We shall devote more attention to this topic in a subsequent chapter on American Blacks.

THEORIES OF MINORITY INTEGRATION

Over 51 million immigrants have come to the United States since its founding as a nation. During this vast ethnic experience, three different theories have emerged concerning how these ethnically different peoples either should or did fit into American society. These schools of thought have been (1) **assimilation,** or the majority-conformity theory; (2) **amalgamation,** or the "melting pot" theory; and (3) **accommodation,** or the pluralistic theory.

The type of interaction between minority peoples and those of the dominant culture has been partly dependent upon which of these ideologies was then accepted by those already established in the community. People formulate attitudes and expectations based upon the values they hold. If those values include a clear image of how an "American" should look, talk, and act, then people who are different from that model will find their adjustment and acceptance by others a more difficult matter. Conversely, if those values allow for diversity, then a greater possibility exists that harmonious relationships will evolve.

Assimilation

Generally speaking, **assimilation** means the functioning of racial or ethnic minority-group members within a society without any marked cultural, social, or personal differences from the people of the majority group. Physical or racial differences may persist, but they do not serve as the basis for group prejudice or discrimination. In effect, the minority groups no longer appear to be strangers because they have forsaken their own cultural traditions and successfully imitated the dominant group. Assimilation may be thus described as $A + B + C = A$.[58]

Anglo-Conformity

Because the majority of the people living in the United States during the eighteenth century were of English descent, English influence upon the new nation's culture was enormous—in language, institutional forms, values, and attitudes. By the first quarter of the nineteenth century, a distinct national consciousness had emerged, and many wanted to de-emphasize their English origins and influences. However, when migration patterns changed the composition of the American population in the 1880s, the Yankees re-established the Anglo-Saxon as the superior archetype.[59] Anglo-Saxonism remained dominant well into the twentieth century as the mold into which any newcomers must fit.

In order to preserve their Anglo-Saxon heritage, Americans often attempted, sometimes with success, to curtail the large numbers of non-Anglo-Saxon immigrants. For those who did come, social pressures demanded that they shed their native culture and attachments as quickly as possible and be remade into Americans along cherished Anglo-Saxon lines. The schools served as an important socialization agent in promoting the shedding of cultural differences.

Sometimes insistence upon assimilation reached feverish heights, as evidenced by the **Americanization** movement during World War I. United States participation in a European conflict caused questions to be raised about those who were not "100 percent American." Governmental agencies at all levels, together with many private organizations, acted to implement more immediately foreigners' adoption of American practices: citizenship, reverence for American institutions, and use of the English language.[60] Because this policy required that all minority groups divest themselves of their distinctive ethnic characteristics and adopt those of the dominant group, George R. Stewart suggested that it be called the "transmuting pot" theory.[61]

Saluting the flag in the Mott Street Industrial School, circa 1890. These children of immigrants, often wearing mended, hand–me–down clothing, were the promise for both their parents and the dominant society. A better life for their children motivated many immigrants to migrate, while native–born Americans looked to the schools as a major means of acculturation.

Other assimilation efforts have not been very successful—for example, with people whose ancestral history in an area predates the nation's expansion into that territory. Most Indian tribes throughout the country as well as the Mexican-Americans of the Southwest have resisted this cultural hegemony. In fact, some critics argue that assimilation has not yet occurred for most racial and ethnic groups.

Types of Assimilation

Milton Gordon has suggested assimilation has several aspects or subprocesses.[62] One early phase is **cultural assimilation** or **acculturation,** the internalization of the norms, values, and behavior patterns of a society. **Marital assimilation,** intermarriage with members of the dominant society, is another aspect. Most importantly, cultural assimilation (acculturation) and **structural assimilation** (large-scale entrance into the cliques, clubs, and institutions of the host society on a primary-group level) best reveal the extent of acceptance of minority groups in the larger society. Gordon states that "Once structural assimilation has occurred, either simultaneously with or subsequent to acculturation, all other types of assimilation will naturally follow."[63] Other sociologists disagree with Gordon, claiming that cultural assimilation does not necessarily result from structural assimilation. Some studies have shown that structural assimilation has not yet occurred to any significant degree.[64]

Louis Wirth maintained that situational variables are important in the assimilation of minority groups.[65] Wirth distinguished among pluralism, assimilation, secession, and militancy as successive minority responses to majority-group prejudice and discrimination. As groups begin to gain some power, they generally attempt to gain social tolerance of the group's differences *(pluralism),* then go beyond this and become absorbed by the dominant society *(assimilation).* Those groups who are prevented from assimilating withdraw *(secession),* but if conflict then ensues, they seek more extreme remedies *(militancy).*

Assimilation may be both a majority-group and a minority-group goal, but it is also possible that one or both may view assimilation as undesirable. Accordingly, the preceding typologies are not always helpful in examining dominant-minority relationships. Gordon shows the complexity of the assimilation process; Wirth suggests that the dynamics of the situation shape the evolvement of dominant-minority relations throughout the assimilation process. The larger question, whether the assimilation process is linear, remains in all cases. Not all groups seek assimilation, nor do all groups who seek assimilation attain it. Varying goals, social arrangements, and historical conditions may also affect majority-minority patterns.

Assimilation—as a belief, goal, or pattern—helps explain many aspects of dominant-minority relations, particularly acceptance and adjustment. For many members of the dominant society, assimilation of minorities has meant their absorption into the mold, reflecting what Barbara Solomon calls "the Anglo Saxon complex."[66] For physically or culturally distinct groups (for example, Blacks, Indians, Asians, or Moslems), such a concept has raised an often insurmountable barrier. Even without the Anglo-Saxon role model, assimilation has been preceded by a transitional period in which the newcomer has gradually blended in with majority-group members. In doing so, the individual has acquired a new behavioral identity, perhaps at some personal cost.

The Melting-Pot Theory

The democratic experiment in the new land of America fired many an imagination. Here a new society was being shaped, peopled by immigrants from different European nations and not slavishly dependent upon the customs and traditions of the past. This set of circumstances generated a romantic notion of America as a melting pot. The **melting-pot theory,** or the theory of amalgamation, states that all the diverse peoples blend their biological and cultural differences into an altogether new breed—the American. This concept may be expressed as $A + B + C = D$.[67]

Advocates

J. Hector St. John de Crèvecoeur, a French settler in New York, first popularized the idea of a melting pot. Envisioning the United States as more than just a land of opportunity, de Crèvecoeur in 1782 spoke of a new breed of humanity coming forth from the new society. That Crèvecoeur included only white Europeans partly explains the weakness of this approach to minority integration.

What is an American? He is either a European, or the descendant of a European; hence that strange mixture of blood which you will find in no other country. I could point out to you a man whose grandfather was an Englishman, whose wife was Dutch, whose son married a French woman, and whose present four sons have now four wives of different nations. He is an American, who, leaving behind him all his ancient prejudices and manners, receives new ones from the new mode of life he has embraced, the new government he obeys and the new rank he holds. . . . Here individuals of all nations are melted into a new race of men, whose labors and posterity will one day cause great changes in the world.[68]

This idealistic concept found many advocates over the years. In 1893, Frederick Jackson Turner updated it with his frontier thesis, a notion that greatly influenced historical scholarship for more than forty years. Turner believed that the challenge of frontier life was the catalyst that fused the immigrants into a composite new national stock within an evolving social order.

Thus the Middle West was teaching the lesson of national cross-fertilization instead of national enmities, the possibility of a newer and richer civilization, not by preserving unmodified or isolated the old component elements, but by breaking down the line-fences, by merging the individual life in the common product—a new product, which held the promise of world brotherhood.[69]

In 1908 English author Israel Zangwill's play *The Melting-Pot* began an extraordinarily popular run, enthusiastically etching a permanent symbol on the assimilationist ideal:

There she lies, the great melting pot. Listen! Can't you hear the roaring and the bubbling? There gapes her mouth—the harbor where a thousand mammoth feeders come from the ends of the world to pour in their human freight. Ah, what a stirring and a seething—Celt and Latin, Slav and Teuton, Greek and Syrian. America is God's Crucible, the great Melting Pot where all the races of Europe are melting and reforming!—Here you stand good folk, think I, when I see you at Ellis Island, here you stand, in your fifty groups, with your fifty languages and histories, and your fifty hatreds and rivalries. But you won't be long like that, brothers, for these are the fires of God you come to—these are the fires of God! . . . Germans and Frenchmen, Irishmen and English, Jews and Russians, into the Crucible with you all! God is making the American! . . . the real American has not yet arrived . . . He will be the fusion of all races, perhaps the coming superman. . . . Ah, Vera, what is the glory of Rome and Jerusalem, where all races and nations come to worship and look back, compared with the glory of America, where all races and nations come to labor and look forward.[70]

Both the frontier thesis and the melting-pot concept have since come under heavy criticism. Although many people still pay homage to the melting-pot concept, few social scientists still accept this explanation of minority integration into society.

Did We Melt?

Over several generations, intermarriages frequently have occurred between people of different nationalities and, to a lesser degree, of different religions and, to a still lesser degree, of different races. One could thus argue that a biological merging of previously distinct ethnic stocks, although not so much of different races, has taken place.[71] However, the melting-pot theory spoke not only of intermarriages among the different groups but also of a distinct new national culture evolving from elements of all other cultures. Here the theory has proven unrealistic. This country, from its founding, has been dominated by an Anglo-Saxon population and thus by the English language and Anglo-Saxon institutional forms. Rather than a melting of various cultural patterns into a new American culture, what actually has occurred is a metamorphosis of elements of minority cultures into the Anglo-Saxon mold.

Milton Gordon suggests that only in the institution of religion have minority groups altered the national culture; the United States is now a land of three major faiths: Protestant, Catholic, and Jewish.[72] Some social observers have viewed the emergence of three major faiths as evidence that America was actually a **"triple melting pot."** Based on her studies in New Haven in 1944 and 1952, Ruby Jo Reeves Kennedy concluded that intermarriage was occurring between various nationalities, but only within the three major religious groupings.[73] A few years later, Will Herberg echoed this analysis, arguing that ethnic differences were disappearing as religious groupings became the primary foci of identity and interaction.[74] Subsequent studies have offered conflicting evidence of assimilation versus pluralism based on religion, national origin, social class, and residence. We shall examine some of these findings shortly.

In other areas, the entry of many diverse minority groups into American society has not resulted in new social structures or institutional forms in the larger society. Instead, subcultural social structures and institutions have evolved to meet group needs, and the dominant culture has benefited from the labors and certain cultural aspects of minority groups within the already existing dominant culture. For example, minority influences are found in word usage, names of places, cuisine, architecture, art, and recreational activities.

Sociologist Henry Pratt Fairchild offered a physiological analogy for comprehending how the absorption of various cultural components or peoples explains assimilation and dismisses amalgamation.[75] An organism consumes food and is somewhat affected (nourished) by it; the food, though, is assimilated in the sense that it becomes an integral part of the organism, retaining none of its original characteristics. This is a one-way process. In a similar manner, American culture has remained basically unchanged, though strengthened, despite the influx of many minority groups.

"Uncle Sam's Troublesome Bedfellows"

This cartoon pictures Uncle Sam annoyed by groups who were seen as unassimilable. Both racial differences (Blacks, Chinese, and Indians) and religious differences (Irish Catholics and Mormons) were cause for being kicked out of the symbolic bed. Cartoon appeared in San Francisco illustrated weekly, *The Wasp,* February 8, 1879.

Most social scientists now believe that the melting-pot theory is a myth and always has been. Its idealistic rhetoric has attracted many followers and still does. In reality, the melting meant Anglo-conformity, being remade according to the idealized Anglo-Saxon mold. Herberg offered some observations on the theory of Anglo-conformity as opposed to the idea of the melting pot.

But it would be a mistake to infer from this that the American's image of himself— and that means the ethnic group member's image of himself as he becomes American—is a composite or synthesis of the ethnic elements that have gone into the making of the American. It is nothing of the kind; the American's image of himself is still the Anglo-American ideal it was at the beginning of our independent existence. The "national type" as ideal has always been, and remains, pretty well fixed. It is the *Mayflower,* John Smith, Davy Crockett, George Washington, and Abraham Lincoln that define the American's self-image, and this is true whether the American in question is a descendent of the Pilgrims or the grandson of an immigrant from southeastern Europe.[76]

The rejection of the melting-pot theory by many people, coupled with an ethnic consciousness, spawned the third ideology, cultural pluralism.

Pluralism

Pluralism recognizes the persistence of racial and ethnic diversity. Pluralist theorists argue that minorities can maintain their distinctive subcultures and simultaneously interact with relative equality in the larger society. In countries such as Switzerland and the United States, this combination of diversity and togetherness is possible in varying degrees because the people agree on certain basic values (for example, the American Creed in the United States). At the same time, minorities may interact mostly among themselves, live within well-defined communities, have their own forms of organizations, work in similar occupations, and marry within their own group. Applying our descriptive equation, pluralism would be $A + B + C = A + B + C$.[77]

Early Analysis

Horace Kallen is generally recognized as the first exponent of cultural pluralism. In 1915, he published "Democracy Versus the Melting Pot," in which he rejected the assimilation and amalgamation theories.[78] Not only did each group tend to preserve its own language, institutions, and cultural heritage, he maintained, but the very nature of democracy gave them the right to do so. To be sure, minority groups learned the English language and participated in American institutions, but what the United States really had become was a "cooperation of cultural diversities." Seeing Americanization movements as a threat to minority groups and the melting-pot notion as unrealistic, Kallen believed that cultural pluralism could be the basis for a great democratic commonwealth. A philosopher, not a sociologist, Kallen nonetheless directed scholarly attention to a practice that many Americans had long followed.

Pluralistic Reality

From its colonial beginnings, the United States has been a pluralistic country. Early settlements were small ethnic enclaves, each peopled by different nationalities or religious groups. New Amsterdam and Philadelphia were exceptions, both heavily pluralistic within their boundaries. Chain migration patterns resulted in immigrants settling in clusters. Germans and Scandinavians in the Midwest, Poles in Chicago, Irish in New York and Boston, French in Louisiana, Asians in California, Cubans in Miami, and many others all illustrate how groups ease adjustment in a new country by re-creating in miniature the world they left behind. Current immigrant groups and remnants of past immigrant groups are testimony to the pluralism in American society.

As Gordon observes, "Cultural pluralism was a fact in American society before it became a theory—at least a theory with explicit relevance for the nation as a whole and articulated and discussed in the general English-speaking circles of American intellectual life."[79] **Cultural pluralism,** two or more culturally distinct groups living in the same society in relative harmony, has been the more noticeable form of pluralism. **Structural pluralism,** the coexistence of racial and ethnic groups in subsocieties also divided by social class and regional boundaries, is less noticeable but also existent. Many minority groups lose their visibility because they have acculturated, but may retain identification with and pride in their heritage, having primary relationships mostly with members of their ethclass.

RETROSPECT

Culture provides the definitions by which members of a society perceive the world about them. Language and other forms of symbolic interaction provide the means through which this knowledge is perceived and transmitted. Becoming acculturated requires learning both the language and the symbol system of the society. Unless it is isolated from the rest of the world, a society undergoes change through culture contact and the diffusion of ideas, inventions, and practices. Within large societies, subcultures usually exist. They may be gradually assimilated (convergent subcultures) or they may remain distinct (persistent subcultures).

Structural conditions also influence people's perceptions of the world, whether they live in an industrialized or agrarian society, a closed or open social system, a growing or contracting economy, a friendly or unfriendly environment, or whether or not their homeland, friends, and relatives are accessible. Distribution of power resources and compatibility with the existing social structure will greatly determine majority-minority relations as well. Interactionists concentrate upon the perceptions of cultural differences as they affect intergroup relations. Functionalists and conflict theorists emphasize the structural conditions.

The interplay between the variables of race, ethnic group, and social class are important for understanding how some problems and conflicts arise. What often gets mistaken for an attribute of race or ethnic group may be a broader aspect of social class. Because many attitudes and values are situational responses to socioeconomic status, a change in status or opportunities will also bring about a change in those attitudes and values. Investigative studies have not supported the culture-of-poverty hypothesis of family disintegration and a self-perpetuating poverty value system.

Three theories of minority integration have evolved since the nation's beginning. The romantic notion of a melting pot, in which a new breed of people with a distinct culture would emerge, proved unrealistic. Assimilation, or majority-conformity, became a goal of many, both native-born and foreign-born; yet not all sought this goal or were able to achieve it. Finally, pluralism emerged as a school of thought in recognition of the persistence of ethnic diversity in a society with a commonly shared core culture.

KEY TERMS

Accommodation

Acculturation

Amalgamation

Anglo-conformity

Assimilation

Chain migration

Convergent subculture

Culture

Culture of poverty

Cultural assimilation

Cultural determinism

Cultural differentiation

Cultural diffusion

Cultural pluralism

Cultural transmission

Economic determinism

Ethclass

Marginality

Marital assimilation

Melting-pot theory

Norms

Persistent subculture

Pluralism

Power differential

Race

Reputational method

Social class

Social structure

Structural assimilation

Structural conditions

Structural differentiation

Structural pluralism

Thomas Theorem

Triple melting-pot theory

Value stretch

Vicious circle

REVIEW QUESTIONS

1. What is the relationship between culture, reality, and intergroup relations?

2. What are subcultures? What forms do they take? What significance do these forms have for intergroup relations?

3. What is the relationship between a society's structural conditions and intergroup relations?

4. What is meant by the culture of poverty? What criticisms exist about this thinking?

5. How do the functional, conflict, and interactionist perspectives approach factors likely to contribute to intergroup conflict?

6. Discuss the major theories of minority integration.

SUGGESTED READINGS

Gordon, Milton M. *Assimilation in American Life.* New York: Oxford University Press, 1964.

A highly influential and still pertinent book offering an analysis of the role of race and ethnicity in American life.

Hall, Edward T. *The Silent Language.* Garden City, N.Y.: Doubleday, 1959.

Excellent introduction to how nonverbal communication conveys cultural values and behavior characteristics, often leading to misunderstandings.

Morris, Desmond. *Manwatching: A Field Guide to Human Behavior.* New York: Abrams, 1977.

Helpful book, with extensive color photo illustrations, about importance of expressions, gestures, signals, and actions in human behavior.

Newman, William M. *American Pluralism.* New York: Harper & Row, 1973.

A comprehensive analysis of pluralism in American society, synthesizing the contributions of other social scientists.

Williams, Robin M., Jr. *American Society: A Sociological Interpretation.* New York: Random House, 1970.

Useful examination of American culture, with influential analysis of impact of norms and values on social life.

Yankelovich, Daniel. *New Rules.* New York: Random House, 1981.

Summary evaluation of changed American norms and attitudes about cultural pluralism and self-fulfillment, based on national surveys.

CHAPTER 3

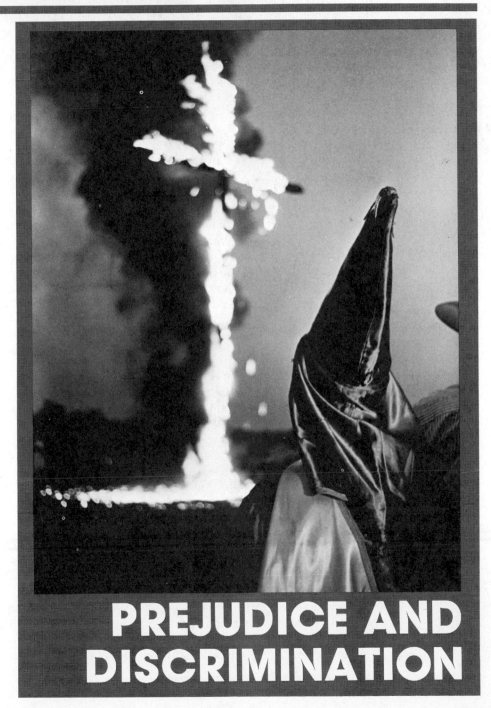

PREJUDICE AND DISCRIMINATION

When strangers from different groups come into contact with one another, their interrelationships may take several forms. The nature of their social interaction depends upon many variables. This book stresses particularly (1) the values and attitudes prevailing among members of both the majority and minority groups; (2) the degree of physical, cultural, and social-class differences between the groups; and (3) the structural conditions within the society, particularly the distribution of resources and power. This chapter examines the various patterns of behavior that may emerge when prejudice and discrimination become the basis of interaction.

PREJUDICE

The word **prejudice** is derived from the Latin word *praejudicium* and originally meant prejudgment. Thus some scholars defined a prejudiced person as one who hastily reached a conclusion before examining the facts.[1] However, this definition proved inadequate because social scientists discovered that prejudice often arose *after* groups came into contact and had at least some knowledge of one another. For that reason, Louis Wirth described prejudice as "an attitude with an emotional bias."[2]

Because feelings shape our attitudes, they reduce our receptivity to additional information that may alter those attitudes. Ralph Rosnow had this fact in mind when he broadened the definition of prejudice to encompass "any unreasonable attitude that is unusually resistant to rational influence."[3] In fact, a deeply prejudiced person is one who is almost totally immune to information. Gordon Allport offers a classic example of such an individual in the following dialogue:

Mr. X: The trouble with the Jews is that they only take care of their own group.

Mr. Y: But the record of the Community Chest campaign shows that they gave more generously, in proportion to their numbers, to the general charities of the community, than did non-Jews.

Mr. X: That shows they are always trying to buy favor and intrude into Christian affairs. They think of nothing but money; that is why there are so many Jewish bankers.

Mr. Y: But a recent study shows that the percentage of Jews in the banking business is negligible, far smaller than the percentage of non-Jews.

Mr. X: That's just it; they don't go in for respectable business; they are only in the movie business or run night clubs.*

It is almost as if Mr. X is saying, "My mind is made up; don't confuse me with the facts." He does not refute the argument; rather, he ignores the new and contradictory information, and moves on to a new area in which he distorts other facts to support his prejudice against Jews.

Prejudicial attitudes may be either positive or negative; however, negative prejudice is of primary concern to the sociologist studying minorities because only negative attitudes can lead to turbulent social relations between dominant and minority groups. Numerous writers, therefore, have defined prejudice as an attitu-

*Gordon W. Allport, *The Nature of Prejudice*, 1954, Addison-Wesley, Reading, Mass., pp. 13–14.

dinal "system of negative beliefs, feelings, and action-orientations regarding a certain group or groups of people."[4] The status of the strangers is an important factor in the development of a negative attitude. Prejudicial attitudes exist among members of both the dominant and minority groups. In seeking to understand the nature of relations between dominant and minority groups, it is important to realize that the antipathy felt between groups is quite often prevalent on both sides.

Levels of Prejudice

Bernard Kramer suggests that prejudice exists on three levels: cognitive, emotional, and action orientation.[5]

Cognitive Level

The **cognitive level** refers to a person's beliefs and perceptions of a group as threatening or nonthreatening, inferior or equal (for example, in terms of intellect, status, or biological composition), seclusive or intrusive, impulse-gratifying, acquisitive, or possessing other positive or negative characteristics. Mr. X's cognitive beliefs are that Jews are intrusive and acquisitive. Other illustrations of cognitive beliefs are that the Irish are heavy drinkers and fighters, Blacks are musical and lazy, and the Polish are thick-headed and unintelligent. Generalizations shape both ethnocentric and prejudicial attitudes, but there is a difference. *Ethnocentrism* is a generalized rejection of all outgroups based on an ingroup focus, whereas **prejudice** is a rejection of certain people based solely upon their membership in a particular group or groups.

In many societies, majority-group members often believe that a particular low-status minority group is "dirty," "immoral," "violent," or "law-breaking." In the United States, the Irish, Italians, Blacks, Mexicans, Chinese, Puerto Ricans, and others have at one time or another been labeled with most, if not all, of the above adjectives. In most European countries and the United States, the group that was lowest on the socioeconomic ladder has often been depicted in caricature as also lowest on the evolutionary ladder. The Irish and Blacks in the United States, peasants and ethnic groups in Europe, have each been pictured at one time as apelike in cruel jokes and cartoons.

> The Victorian images of the Irish as "white Negro" and simian Celt, or a combination of the two, derived much of its force and inspiration from physiognomical beliefs . . . [but] every country in Europe had its equivalent of "white Negroes" and simianized men, whether or not they happened to be stereotypes of criminals, assassins, political radicals, revolutionaries, Slavs, gypsies, Jews or peasants.[6]

Emotional Level

The **emotional level** refers to the feelings that a minority group arouses in an individual. Although these feelings may be based upon stereotypes from the cognitive level, they represent a more intense stage of personal involvement. The emotional attitudes may be negative or positive, such as fear, distrust, trust, disgust, sympathy, nonsympathy, contempt, admiration, envy, or anger. These feelings, based upon beliefs about the group or groups, may come about through social interaction or the possibility of interaction. For example, Whites might react with fear or anger to the integration of their schools or neighborhoods, or Protestants might be jealous of the life-style of a highly successful Catholic business executive.

Action-orientation Level

An **action orientation** is the positive or negative predisposition to engage in discriminatory behavior. If someone harbors strong feelings about members of a certain racial or ethnic group, that individual may have a tendency to act for or against them—being aggressive or nonaggressive, offering assistance or withholding it. Such individuals would also be likely to want to exclude or include members of that group both in their close, personal social relations and in their peripheral social relations. For example, some people would want to exclude members of the disliked group from doing business with them or living in their neighborhood. Another manifestation of the action-orientation level of prejudice is the desire to change or maintain the status differential or inequality between the two groups, whether the area be economic, political, educational, social, or a combination. Note that an action orientation refers to a predisposition to act, not the action itself.

Stereotyping

One of the most common reactions to strangers is broad categorization of them. Prejudice at the cognitive level is often the result of false perceptions of others, which are enhanced by stereotypes, either cultural or racial. A **stereotype** is an oversimplified generalization by which we attribute certain traits or characteristics to any person in a group without regard to individual differences. Most cultural stereotypes emphasize variance from societal norms. Racial stereotypes suggest that there are peculiarities about certain traits or characteristics that are hereditary and will thus continue, regardless of what society does. Both forms of stereotypes are doubly abusive. Not only do they deny an individual the right to be judged and treated on the basis of merit, but by being applied to the image of the entire group, they become a justification for discriminatory behavior.

Negative stereotypes also serve as important reference points in people's evaluations of what they observe in everyday life. Following is an excellent illustration of how we attribute motives and causes that are consistent with our stereotypes to other people's behavior:

Prejudiced people see the world in ways that are consistent with their prejudice. If Mr. Bigot sees a well-dressed, white, Anglo-Saxon Protestant sitting on a park bench sunning himself at three o'clock on a Wednesday afternoon, he thinks nothing of it. If he sees a well-dressed black man doing the same thing, he is liable to leap to the conclusion that the person is unemployed—and he becomes infuriated,

"Mutual: Both are glad there are bars between 'em!"

This visual stereotype of an apelike Irishman reinforced prevailing beliefs that the Irish were emotionally unstable and morally primitive. Cartoon appeared in *Judge*, November 7, 1891.

because he assumes that his hard-earned taxes are paying that shiftless good-for-nothing enough in welfare subsidies to keep him in good clothes. If Mr. Bigot passes Mr. Anglo's house and notices that a trash can is overturned and some garbage is strewn about, he is apt to conclude that a stray dog has been searching for food. If he passes Mr. Garcia's house and notices the same thing, he is inclined to become annoyed, and to assert that "those people live like pigs." Not only does prejudice influence his conclusions, his erroneous conclusions justify and intensify his negative feelings.[7]

Once established, stereotypes are difficult to eradicate, even among succeeding generations. Evidence of the pervasiveness and persistence of stereotypes came from replicated studies of three generations of Princeton undergraduates in 1932, 1951, and 1967.[8] (See Table 3.1.) The psychologists conducting each study asked students to select five characteristics, from a list of eighty-four, they considered most representative of different racial and ethnic groups. Although each group became increasingly reluctant to make such generalizations, a high level of uniformity nonetheless marked their responses.

TABLE 3.1
Stereotypes in Three Generations of Princeton Undergraduates

Trait	% Checking Trait			Trait	% Checking Trait		
	1933	1951	1967		1933	1951	1967
Americans				*English*			
Industrious	48	30	23	Sportsmanlike	53	21	22
Intelligent	47	32	20	Intelligent	46	29	23
Materialistic	33	37	67	Conventional	34	25	19
Ambitious	33	21	42	Tradition loving	31	42	21
Progressive	27	5	17	Conservative	30	22	53
Pleasure loving	26	27	28	Reserved	29	39	40
Alert	23	7	7	Sophisticated	27	37	47
Efficient	21	9	15	Courteous	21	17	17
Aggressive	20	8	15	Honest	20	11	17
Straightforward	19	—	9	Industrious	18	—	17
Practical	19	—	12	Extremely			
Sportsmanlike	19	—	9	nationalistic	18	—	7
Individualistic[a]	—	26	15	Humorless	17	—	11
Conventional[b]	—	—	17	Practical[b]	—	8	25
Scientifically							
minded[b]	—	—	15	*Germans*			
Ostentatious[b]	—	—	15				
				Scientifically			
				minded	78	62	47
Chinese				Industrious	65	50	59
				Stolid	44	10	9
Superstitious	34	18	8	Intelligent	32	32	19
Sly	29	4	6	Methodical	31	20	21
Conservative	29	14	15	Extremely			
Tradition loving	26	26	32	nationalistic	24	50	43
Loyal to				Progressive	16	3	13
family ties	22	35	50	Efficient	16	—	46
Industrious	18	18	23	Jovial	15	—	5
Meditative	19	—	21	Musical	13	—	4
Reserved	17	18	15	Persistent	11	—	4
Very religious	15	—	6	Practical	11	—	9
Ignorant	15	—	7	Aggressive[a]	—	27	30
Deceitful	14	—	5	Arrogant[a]	—	23	18
Quiet	13	19	23	Ambitious[b]	—	—	15
Courteous[b]	—	—	20				
Extremely				*Irish*			
nationalistic[b]	—	—	19				
Humorless[b]	—	—	17	Pugnacious	45	24	13
Artistic[b]	—	—	15	Quick tempered	39	35	43

TABLE 3.1 (continued)

Trait	% Checking Trait			Trait	% Checking Trait		
	1933	1951	1967		1933	1951	1967
Irish				*Japanese*			
Witty	38	16	7	Shrewd	22	13	7
Honest	32	11	17	Sly	20	21	3
Very religious	29	30	27	Quiet	19	—	14
Industrious	21	8	8	Imitative	17	24	22
Extremely				Alert	16	—	11
nationalistic	21	20	41	Suave	16	—	0
Superstitious	18	—	11	Neat	16	—	7
Quarrelsome	14	—	5	Treacherous	13	17	1
Imaginative	13	—	3	Aggressive	13	—	19
Aggressive	13	—	5	Extremely			
Stubborn	13	—	23	nationalistic[a]	—	18	21
Tradition loving[b]	—	—	25	Ambitious[b]	—	—	33
Loyal to				Efficient[b]	—	—	27
family ties[b]	—	—	23	Loyal to			
Argumentative[b]	—	—	20	family ties[b]	—	—	23
Boastful[b]	—	—	17	Courteous[b]	—	—	22
Italians				*Jews*			
Artistic	53	28	30	Shrewd	79	47	30
Impulsive	44	19	28	Mercenary	49	28	15
Passionate	37	25	44	Industrious	48	29	33
Quick tempered	35	15	28	Grasping	34	17	17
Musical	32	22	9	Intelligent	29	37	37
Imaginative	30	20	7	Ambitious	21	28	48
Very religious	21	33	25	Sly	20	14	7
Talkative	21	23	23	Loyal to			
Revengeful	17	—	0	family ties	15	19	19
Physically dirty	13	—	4	Persistent	13	—	9
Lazy	12	—	0	Talkative	13	—	3
Unreliable	11	—	3	Aggressive	12	—	23
Pleasure loving[a]	—	28	33	Very religious	12	—	7
Loyal to				Materialistic[b]	—	—	46
family ties[b]	—	—	26	Practical	—	—	19
Sensual[b]	—	—	23	*Negroes[c]*			
Argumentative[b]	—	—	19				
Japanese				Superstitious	84	41	13
				Lazy	75	31	26
Intelligent	45	11	20	Happy-go-lucky	38	17	27
Industrious	43	12	57	Ignorant	38	24	11
Progressive	24	2	17	Musical	26	33	47

TABLE 3.1 (continued)

Trait	% Checking Trait			Trait	% Checking Trait		
	1933	1951	1967		1933	1951	1967
Negroes[c]				*Turks*			
Ostentatious	26	11	25	Treacherous	21	3	13
Very religious	24	17	8	Sensual	20	4	9
Stupid	22	10	4	Ignorant	15	7	13
Physically dirty	17	—	3	Physically dirty	15	7	14
Naive	14	—	4	Deceitful	13	—	7
Slovenly	13	—	5	Sly	12	7	7
Unreliable	12	—	6	Quarrelsome	12	—	9
Pleasure loving[a]	—	19	26	Revengeful	12	—	6
Sensitive[b]	—	—	17	Conservative	12	—	11
Gregarious[b]	—	—	17	Superstitious	11	—	5
Talkative[b]	—	—	14	Aggressive[b]	—	—	17
Imitative[b]	—	—	13	Quick tempered[b]	—	—	13
				Impulsive[b]	—	—	12
Turks				Conventional[b]	—	—	10
Cruel	47	12	9	Pleasure loving[b]	—	—	11
Very religious	26	6	7	Slovenly[b]	—	—	10

[a] Indicates the additional traits reported by Gilbert (1951).

[b] Indicates the new traits needed in 1967 to account for the 10 most frequently selected traits today.

[c] The title "Negroes" is the word employed in the study.

Source: Marvin Karlins, Thomas L. Coffman, and Gary Walters, "On the Fading of Social Stereotypes: Studies in Three Generations of College Students," *Journal of Personality and Social Psychology* 13 (1969): Table 1, pp. 4–5. By permission.

Notably, students either showed a tendency to agree on the same attributes others had chosen in earlier studies, or picked a similar new adjective. Positive stereotypes regarding work achievement continued for Americans, Germans, Japanese, and Jews. Emotional stereotypes for Irish and Italians, a carefree image for "Negroes" (the acceptable word in those years), a negative stereotype for Turks, a positive and conservative image for English, and commitment to family and tradition for Chinese, all remained constant generalizations over the 35-year span.

Ethnophaulisms

An **ethnophaulism** is a derogatory word or expression used to describe a racial or ethnic group. This is the language of prejudice, the verbal picture of a negative stereotype. Howard J. Ehrlich believes that ethnophaulisms can be of three types: (1) disparaging nicknames (chink, dago, polack, jungle bunny, honky); (2) explicit group devaluations ("jew him down" for trying to get something for a lower price, "luck of the Irish" suggesting undeserved good fortune, "to be in Dutch" meaning to be in trouble); (3) irrelevant ethnic names used as a mild disparagement ("jewbird" for black cuckoos having prominent beaks, "Irish confetti" for bricks thrown in a fight).[9]

Although ethnophaulisms are good indications of intergroup relations and of the relationship between attitudes and actions, they have not received much scientific study. Erdman Palmore, however, did such a study and concluded that all racial and ethnic groups use ethnophaulisms. He also observed that a correlation exists between the number of them used and the degree of group prejudice, and that they express and support negative stereotypes about the most visible racial or cultural differences.[10]

Sometimes members of a racial or ethnic minority group will use an ethnophaulism directed against themselves in their conversations with one another. On occasion they may use the term as a reprimand to one of their own kind for acting out the stereotype, but more often they mean it as a humorous expression of friendship and endearment. However, when an outsider uses that same term, they resent it because of its prejudicial derision.

Ethnic Humor

Why do some people find ethnic jokes so funny, while others find them distasteful? Studies show the response often reflects the listener's attitude toward the group being ridiculed. If you hold favorable or positive attitudes toward the group which is the butt of the joke, then you are less likely to find it funny than if you hold unfavorable or negative views. If you dislike a group about which a joke implies something negative, you will tend to appreciate the joke much more than others.[11]

Sometimes people tell or laugh at derogatory jokes about their own group. Jeffrey Goldstein suggests several reasons for such action. One is to strengthen ingroup cohesiveness by reminding members of the perceptions and threats of outgroups. Another is to dissociate oneself from stereotypes of one's group through self-disparaging group humor. A third possibility is that we use ethnic humor to affirm ourselves, point out the absurdity of our predicaments, and objectify our faults and make them laughable. The key to ethnic humor then, lies in both the joker's and audience's attitudes.[12]

Television Influence

Virtually every American household owns at least one television set, with families averaging over seven hours of TV viewing daily. Does all this viewing make us think or act differently? Does it change our attitudes or shape our feelings and reactions about minority groups? Or is it only entertainment with no appreciable effect on perceptions and behavior? Abundant research evidence indicates television programming distorts reality, promotes stereotypical role models, and significantly shapes and reinforces our attitudes about men, women, and minority groups.

In a 1977 report, updated in 1979, the U.S. Commission on Civil Rights charged the television industry with perpetuating racial and sexual stereotypes in programming and news.[13] Aside from the almost exclusively negative racial portrayals on police shows over the preceding six years, the report attacked the television industry for portraying "a social structure in which males are very much in control of their lives . . . older, more serious, more independent, and more likely to hold prestigious jobs. Women, on the other hand, were younger, often unemployed, more 'family bound,' and often found in comic roles. Those women who were employed were in stereotyped and sometimes subservient occupations."

George Gerbner, generally acknowledged as the nation's foremost television authority, has analyzed television programming and viewer attitudes and perceptions for more than 17 years. In 1982 he reported that little had changed since the Commission's reports.[14] A tiny percentage of black characters, for example, were "unrealistically romanticized" but the overwhelming majority of them were in subservient, supporting roles—such as the white hero's comic sidekick. Gerbner commented:

When a black child looks at prime time, most of the people he sees doing interesting things are white. That imbalance tends to teach young Blacks to accept minority status as naturally inevitable and even deserved.[15]

Measuring the impact of such portrayals on the general audience, one of Gerbner's surveys asked questions like "Should white people have the right to keep Blacks out of their neighborhoods?" and "Should there be laws against marriages between Blacks and Whites?" The more people watched television, the more they answered "Yes" to such questions.

Television influences attitudes toward racial or ethnic groups by the status of the parts assigned to their members, the kind of behavior they display within these parts, or even the type of products they promote.[16] Television greatly influences children's attitudes in this area. Sheryl Graves, for example, found how positive and negative portrayals of black characters in cartoons affected black and white children's attitudes toward Blacks. She found a positive attitude change among black children seeing either portrayal and among white children seeing a positive portrayal. The most dramatic change, however, was in a negative direction for white children exposed to even a single program showing Blacks portrayed negatively. Conversely, the more a child watches "Sesame Street," the less likely that child will have negative attitudes toward Blacks.[17]

"All in the Family," a popular comedy series in the 1970s now in syndicated reruns, received an NAACP award for its contribution to race relations but divided critics as to its reducing or reinforcing racial bigotry.[18] Finding an explanation for both views, Neil Vidmar and Milton Rokeach reported findings that selective perception, prior attitudes determining reactions, governed viewers' affective responses.[19] Liberal viewers saw the program as satire, with son-in-law Mike effectively rebutting Archie's ignorance and bigotry, or minority members besting Archie by the end of the program. In contrast, prejudiced viewers—particularly adolescents—were significantly more likely to admire Archie over Mike and to perceive Archie as winning in the end. While most respondents indicated they thought Mike made better sense than Archie, high prejudiced adolescents were significantly more likely to perceive Archie as making better sense. (See Table 3.2.) It appears the program is more likely reinforcing prejudice and discrimination than combating it.

TABLE 3.2
Differences Between High and Low Prejudiced Viewers
in Their Reactions to *All in the Family*

Variable	U.S. Adolescents			Canadian Adults		
	High Prejudice	Low Prejudice	p	High Prejudice	Low Prejudice	p
3 How enjoyable is it?						
very enjoyable	27%	26%		18%	20%	
enjoyable	19	15	n.s.	29	26	n.s.
not enjoyable	5	3		1	4	
very unenjoyable	4	1		2	0	
4 How funny is it?						
extremely funny	12%	12%		8%	7%	
very funny	17	22		22	22	
somewhat funny	12	12	n.s.	14	14	n.s.
mildly funny	2	5		4	5	
not funny	2	4		2	2	
5 Who do you like or admire?						
Archie	38%	24%		40%	26%	
Mike	18	20	.05	13	21	.05
6 Who makes better sense?						
Archie	10%	3%		8%	3%	
Mike	44	43	.01	43	46	.10
7 Does Archie win?						
Wins	29%	13%		26%	14%	
Loses	25	33	.01	26	34	.05
8 Who is made fun of?						
Archie	4%	6%		11%	21%	
Others	50	40	n.s.	40	28	n.s.
9 Ethnic slurs?						
not wrong	22%	13%		29%	14%	
wrong	18	15	.10	14	19	.01
very wrong	15	17		7	17	
10 Whose values will be similar?						
Archie	16%	7%		—	—	
Others	39	38	.05	—	—	—

Source: Neil Vidmar and Milton Rokeach, "Archie Bunker's Bigotry," *Journal of Communication,* 24 (1974), 36–47.

Causes of Prejudice

There appears to be no single cause of prejudice, but rather, many causes that are frequently interrelated. Because fear and suspicion of outgroups are so widespread, scholars and scientists once believed that prejudice was a natural or biological human attribute. Today, because of increased knowledge about the growth of prejudices in children and about the varying patterns of interaction throughout world history, behavioral scientists realize that prejudices are socially determined. A great many theories exist concerning exactly how we become prejudiced.

Socialization

In the **socialization** process, individuals acquire the values, attitudes, beliefs, and perceptions of their culture or subculture, including religion, nationality, and social class. Generally, the child conforms to the parents' expectations in acquiring an understanding of the world and its people. Being young and therefore impressionable, and knowing of no alternative conceptions of the world, the child usually accepts these concepts without questioning. We thus learn the prejudices of our parents and others, and they subtly become a part of our values and beliefs. Even if they are based on false stereotypes, prejudices shape our perceptions of various peoples and influence our attitudes and actions toward particular groups. For example, if we develop negative attitudes about Jews because we are taught that they are shrewd, acquisitive, and clannish—all-too-familiar stereotypes—as adults we may refrain from business or social relationships with them. We may not even realize the reason for such avoidance, so subtle has been the prejudice instilled within us.

People may learn certain prejudices because of their pervasiveness. The cultural screen that we develop and through which we view the world around us is not always accurate, but it does reflect shared values and attitudes, which are reinforced by others. Prejudice, like cultural values, is taught and learned through the socialization process. The prevailing prejudicial attitudes and actions are often deeply embedded in custom or law (for example, Jim Crow laws), and the new generation may accept them as proper, maintaining them in their adult lives.

Although socialization explains how prejudicial attitudes may be transmitted from one generation to the next, it does not explain their origin nor why they intensify or diminish over the years. These aspects of prejudice must be explained in another way.

Herbert Blumer suggests that prejudice always involves the notion of group position in society.[20] Prejudiced people believe that one group is inferior to another, and they place each group in a hierarchical position in society. This perception of group position is an outgrowth of the individual's experiences and understanding of them. The group stereotypes are socially approved images held by members of one group about another.[21]

Self-Justification

Through **self-justification,** we denigrate a person or group to justify our maltreatment of them. In this situation, self-justification leads to prejudice and discrimination against another's group.

Some philosophers argue that we are not so much rational creatures as we are rationalizing creatures. We require reassurance that the things we do and the lives we live are proper, that good reasons for our actions exist. If we are able to convince ourselves that another group is inferior, immoral, or dangerous, then we can feel justified in discriminating against them, enslaving them, or even killing them.

History is replete with examples of people who thought their maltreatment of others was just and necessary: As defenders of the true faith, the Crusaders killed "Christ-killers" (Jews) and "infidels" (Moslems). Participants in the Spanish Inquisition imprisoned, tortured, and executed "heretics," "the disciples of the Devil." The Puritans burned witches, whose refusal to confess "proved" they were evil. Indians were "heathen savages," Blacks were "an inferior species," and thus both could be mistreated, enslaved, or killed. The civilians in the Vietnamese village of My Lai were "probably" aiding the Vietcong, so the soldiers felt justified in slaughtering the old men, women, and children they found there.

Some sociologists believe that self-justification works the other way around.[22] That is, instead of self-justification serving as a basis for subjugation of a people, the subjugation occurs first and the self-justification follows, resulting in prejudice and continued discrimination. The evolvement of racism as a concept after the establishment of the African slave trade would seem to support this idea. Philip Mason offers an insight into this view:

> A specialized society is likely to defeat a simpler society and provide a lower tier still of enslaved and conquered peoples. The rulers and organizers sought security for themselves and their children; to perpetuate the power, the esteem, and the comfort they had achieved, it was necessary not only that the artisans and labourers should work contentedly but that the rulers should sleep without bad dreams. No one can say with certainty how the myths originated, but it is surely relevant that when one of the founders of Western thought set himself to frame an ideal state that would embody social justice, he—like the earliest city dwellers—not only devised a society stratified in tiers but believed it would be necessary to persuade the traders and work-people that, by divine decree, they were made from brass and iron, while the warriors were made of silver and the rulers of gold.[23]

Another example of self-justification serving as a cause of prejudice is the dominant group's assumption of an attitude of superiority over other groups. In this respect, establishing a prestige hierarchy—ranking the status of various ethnic groups—results in differential association. To enhance or maintain one's own self-esteem, one may avoid social contact with groups deemed inferior and associate only with those identified as being of high status. Through such behavior, self-justification may come to intensify the social distance between groups. *Social distance* refers to the degree to which ingroup members do not engage in social or primary relationships with members of various outgroups.

Personality

In 1950, T. W. Adorno and his colleagues reported a correlation between individuals' early childhood experiences of harsh parental discipline and their development of authoritarian personalities as adults.[24] If parents assume an excessively domineering posture in their relations with a child, exercising stern measures and threatening the withdrawal of love if the child does not respond with weakness and submission, then the child tends to be very insecure, nurturing much latent hostility against the parents. When such children become adults, they may demonstrate **displaced aggression,** directing their hostility against a powerless group as compensation for feelings of insecurity and fear. Highly prejudiced individuals tend to come from families that emphasize obedience.

The authors identified authoritarianism by the use of a measuring instrument called an F scale (the F standing for potential fascism). Other tests included the A-S (anti-Semitism) and E (ethnocentrism) scales, the latter measuring attitudes toward various minorities. One of their major findings was that people who scored high on authoritarianism also consistently showed a high degree of prejudice against all minority groups. These highly prejudiced persons were characterized by rigidity of viewpoint, dislike for ambiguity, strict obedience to leaders, and intolerance of weakness in themselves or others.

No sooner did *The Authoritarian Personality* appear than controversy began. H. H. Hyman and P. B. Sheatsley challenged the methodology and analysis.[25] Solomon Asch questioned the assumptions that the F-scale responses represented a belief system and that structural variables, such as ideologies, stratification, mobility, and other social factors, do not play a role in shaping personality.[26] E. A. Shils argued that the authors were only interested in measuring authoritarianism of the political right while ignoring such tendencies in those at the other end of the political spectrum.[27] Other investigators sought alternative explanations for the authoritarian personality. D. Stewart and T. Hoult extended the framework beyond family childhood experiences to include other social factors.[28] H. C. Kelman and Janet Barclay demonstrated that substantial evidence exists showing that lower intelligence and less education also correlate with high authoritarianism scores on the F scale.[29]

Despite the critical attacks, the underlying conceptions of *The Authoritarian Personality* were important, and research on personality as a factor in prejudice has continued. Subsequent investigators have refined and modified the original study. Correcting scores for response bias, they have conducted cross-cultural studies. Respondents in Germany and Near East countries, where a more authoritarian social structure exists, scored higher on authoritarianism. In Japan, Germany, and the United States, authoritarianism and social distance were moderately related. Others frequently have shown that an inverse relationship exists between social class and F-scale scores.[30]

Although the authoritarian-personality studies have been helpful in the understanding of some aspects of prejudice, they have not provided a causal explanation. Most of the findings in this area show a correlation, but the findings do not prove, for example, that harsh discipline of children *causes* them to become prejudiced adults. Perhaps the strict parents were themselves prejudiced, and the child learned those attitudes from them. Or, as George Simpson and J. Milton Yinger say,

---

One must be careful not to assume too quickly that a certain tendency—rigidity of mind, for example—that is correlated with prejudice necessarily causes that prejudice. . . . The sequence may be the other way around. . . . It is more likely that both are related to more basic factors.[31]

For some people, prejudice may indeed be rooted in subconscious childhood tensions, but we simply do not know whether these tensions directly cause a high degree of prejudice in the adult or whether other powerful social forces are the determinants. Whatever the explanation, authoritarianism is a significant phenomenon and worthy of continued investigation. Recent research, however, has stressed social and situational factors, rather than personality, as important causes of prejudice and discrimination.[32]

Frustration

Frustration is the result of relative deprivation in which expectations remain unsatisfied. **Relative deprivation** refers to a lack of resources, or rewards, in one's standard of living in comparison with others in the society. A number of investigators have suggested that frustrations tend to increase aggression toward oth-

Bandits' roost, 39½ Mulberry Street in New York's Little Italy section, circa 1888. Street crime was a serious problem in the immigrant slum communities, creating problems for the residents and tarnishing the image of the entire community in the minds of native–born Americans.

ers.[33] Frustrated people may easily strike out against the perceived cause of their frustration. However, this reaction is not always possible because the true source of the frustration is often too nebulous to be identified or too powerful to act against. In such instances, the result may be a displaced or free-floating aggression; in this situation, the frustrated individual or group usually redirects the aggressiveness against a more visible, vulnerable, and socially sanctioned target, one unable to strike back. Minorities meet these criteria and are thus frequently the recipients of displaced aggression by the dominant group.

Placing blame on others for something that is not their fault is known as **scapegoating.** The term comes from the ancient Hebrew custom of using a goat during the Day of Atonement as a symbol of the sins of the people. In an annual ceremony, a priest placed his hands upon the head of a goat and listed the people's sins in a symbolic transference of guilt; he then chased the goat out of the community, thereby freeing the people of sin.[34] Since those times, the powerful group has usually punished the scapegoat group rather than allowing it to escape.

There have been many instances throughout world history of minority groups serving as scapegoats, including the Christians in ancient Rome, the French Huguenots, the Jews, the Chinese, the Irish, the Japanese, the Quakers, and many more. Gordon Allport suggests that certain characteristics are necessary for a group to become a suitable scapegoat.[35] The group must be (1) highly visible in physical appearance or observable customs and actions; (2) not strong enough to strike back; (3) situated within easy access of the dominant group or, ideally, concentrated in one area; (4) a past target of hostility, for whom latent hostility still exists; and (5) the symbol of an unpopular concept.

Some groups fit this typology better than others, but racial and ethnic groups have continually been a favorite choice. Irish, Italians, Catholics, Jews, Quakers, Mormons, Chinese, Japanese, Blacks, Puerto Ricans, and Chicanos have all been, at one time or another, the scapegoat in the United States. Especially in times of economic hardship, there seems to be a tendency to blame some group for the general conditions, often leading to aggressive action against the group as an expression of frustration. For example, a study by Carl Hovland and Robert Sears found that between 1882 and 1930, a definite correlation existed between a decline in the price of cotton and an increase in the number of lynchings of Blacks.[36]

In several controlled experiments, sociologists have attempted to measure the validity of the scapegoat theory. Neal Miller and Richard Bugelski tested a group of young men 18 to 20 working in a government camp about their feelings toward various minority groups.[37] They were re-examined about these feelings after experiencing frustration by being obliged to take a long, difficult test and denied an opportunity to see a film at a local theater. This group showed some evidence of increased prejudicial feelings, whereas a control group, which did not experience any frustration, showed no change in prejudicial attitudes.

Donald Weatherley conducted an experiment with a group of college students to measure the relationship between frustration and aggression against a specific disliked group.[38] After identifying students who were or were not highly anti-Semitic and subjecting them to a strong frustrating experience, he asked the students to write stories about pictures shown to them. Some of the students were shown pictures of people who had been given Jewish names; other students were presented with pictures of unnamed people. When the pictures were unidentified, no difference appeared between the stories of the anti-Semitic students and those of other students. However, when the pictures were identified, the anti-Semitic students wrote stories reflecting much more aggression against the Jews in the pictures than did the other students. Frustration had led to aggression against an identifiable group, predetermined to have been disliked beforehand, but frustration did not increase aggression against any specific group when it had not been identified.

Talcott Parsons suggests that the family and the occupational system are both likely to produce anxieties and insecurities that create frustration.[39] According to this view, the growing-up process (gaining parental affection and approval, identifying with and imitating sexual role models, competing with others in adulthood) may involve severe emotional strain. The result is an adult personality with a large reservoir of repressed aggression that becomes **free-floating**—susceptible to redirection against convenient scapegoats. Similarly, the occupational system is a source of frustration: its emphasis on competitiveness and individual achievement, its function of conferring status, its requirement that people inhibit their natural impulses at work, and its relationship to the state of the economy are but a few of the factors that generate emotional anxieties. Parsons pessimistically concludes that minorities fulfill a functional ''need'' as targets for displaced aggression and will therefore remain targets.[40]

The scapegoat is not always the weakest target. Sometimes the scapegoat is similar to the actual source of frustration and is thus perceived as an acceptable substitute. In other situations, a more powerful person or group is falsely identified as the root cause of the problem. Some presumed flaw of that scapegoat (a negative stereotype) is then used as solace by those who are frustrated: ''Things may be bad, but at least I'm not deceitful like them,'' or ''I'm not greedy,'' and so on.

For over 20 years Leonard Berkowitz and his associates have studied and experimented with aggressive behavior. Their conclusions are that, confronted with equally frustrating situations, highly prejudiced individuals are more likely to seek scapegoats than nonprejudiced individuals.[41] Another intervening variable is that certain kinds of frustrations—personal (marital failure, injury, mental illness) rather than shared (dangers of flood or hurricane)—make people more likely to seek scapegoats.[42]

Frustration–aggression theory, while helpful, is not completely satisfactory. It ignores the role of culture and the reality of actual social conflict, while failing to show a causal relationship. Most of the responses measured in these studies were of people already biased. Why did one group rather than another become the object of the aggression? Moreover, frustration does not necessarily precede aggression, nor aggression necessarily flow from frustration.

Competition

People tend to be more hostile toward others when they feel their security is threatened; thus, many social scientists conclude that economic competition and conflict breed prejudice. Certainly a great amount of evidence shows that negative stereotyping, prejudice, and discrimination increase strongly whenever competition for a limited number of jobs increases.

An excellent illustration concerns the Chinese sojourners in the nineteenth century. Prior to the 1870s, the transcontinental railroad was being built, and the Chinese filled many of the jobs made available by this project in the sparsely populated West. Although they were expelled from the gold mines and schools, having no redress of grievances in the courts, they managed to convey to some Whites an image of a clean, hard-working, law-abiding people. The completion of the railroad, the flood of former Civil War soldiers into the job market, and the economic depression of 1873 worsened their situation. The Chinese were even more frequently the victims of open discrimination and hostility. Their positive stereotype among some Whites became more commonly a negative one: they were now "conniving," "crafty," "criminal," "the yellow menace." Only after they retreated into Chinatowns and entered specialty occupations not in competition with Whites did the intense hostility abate.

One of the early pioneers in the scientific study of prejudice, John Dollard, demonstrated how prejudice against the Germans, which had been virtually nonexistent, came about in a small American industrial town when times got bad.

> Local whites largely drawn from the surrounding farms manifested considerable direct aggression toward the newcomers. Scornful and derogatory opinions were expressed about the Germans, and the native whites had a satisfying sense of superiority toward them. . . . The chief element in the permission to be aggressive against the Germans was rivalry for jobs and status in the local woodenware plants. The native whites felt definitely crowded for their jobs by the entering German groups and in case of bad times had a chance to blame the Germans who by their presence provided more competitors for the scarcer jobs. There seemed to be no traditional pattern of prejudice against Germans unless the skeletal suspicion of all out-groupers (always present) be invoked in this place.[43]

Both experimental studies and historical analyses have added credence to the economic-competition theory. Muzafer Sherif has directed several experiments showing how intergroup competition at a boys' camp leads to conflict and escalating hostility.[44] Donald Young has shown that, throughout American history, in times with high unemployment and thus intense job competition, strong nativist movements against minorities have existed.[45] This pattern has held true regionally—with the Asians on the West Coast, the Italians in Louisiana, and the French Canadians in New England—and nationally, with the antiforeign movements always peaking during periods of depression. So it was with the Native American Party in the 1830s, the Know-Nothing Party in the 1850s, the American Protective Association in the 1890s, and the Ku Klux Klan after World War I. More recently, Andrew Greeley and Paul Sheatsley have reported that most antiblack prejudice occurs in groups that are just slightly above the Blacks socioeconomically.[46] The group that applies the pressure of job competition most directly upon another group will be the target of the strongest prejudicial attitudes.

Once again, a theory offers some excellent insights into prejudice—there is a correlation between economic conditions and hostility toward minorities—but also has some serious shortcomings. Not all groups who have been objects of hostility have been economic competitors (for example, Quakers and Mormons). Moreover, why is there greater hostility against some groups than against others? Why do the negative feelings in some communities run against groups whose numbers are so small that they cannot possibly be an economic threat? It would appear that other values, besides economic ones, cause people to be antagonistic to a group perceived as an actual or potential threat.

Social Norms

Some sociologists have suggested that a relationship exists between prejudice and a person's tendency to conform to societal expectations.[47] **Social norms**—the norms of one's culture—provide the generally shared rules of what is and is not proper behavior; by learning and automatically accepting the prevailing prejudices, the individual is simply conforming to those norms. This theory says that there is a direct relationship between degree of conformity and degree of prejudice. If this is true, then people's prejudices would decrease or increase significantly when they move into areas where the prejudicial norm is either lesser or greater. Evidence supports this view. Thomas Pettigrew found that Southerners became less prejudiced against Blacks when they interacted with them in the army, where the social norms were less prejudicial.[48] In another study, Jeanne Watson found that people moving into an anti-Semitic neighborhood in New York City became more anti-Semitic.[49]

In 1937, John Dollard published his major study, *Caste and Class in a Southern Town,* providing an in-depth look into the emotional adjustment of Whites and Blacks to rigid social norms.[50] In his study of the processes, functions, and maintenance of accommodation, Dollard shows how the "carrot-and-stick" method is employed. Intimidation, or sometimes even severe reprisals for going against social norms, ensures compliance. However, such actions are usually unnecessary. The advantages Whites and Blacks gain in psychological, economic, or behavioral terms serve to perpetuate the caste order. These gains in personal security and stability set in motion a vicious circle. They encourage a way of life that reinforces the rationale of the social system in this community.

The problem with the social-norms theory is that although it explains prevailing attitudes, it explains neither their origins nor the reasons for the development of new prejudices when other groups move into an area. In addition, the theory does not explain why prejudicial attitudes against a particular group continue to rise and fall in cyclical fashion over the years.

Although many social scientists have attempted to identify the causes of prejudice, no single factor has proven to be an adequate explanation. Prejudice is a complex phenomenon, and it is most likely to be the product of more than one causal agent. Sociologists now tend either to emphasize multiple-causation explanations or else to stress social forces at work in specific and similar situations, such as economic conditions, stratification, or hostility toward an outgroup.

Can Prejudice Be Reduced?

A great many organizations and movements whose prime objective was to reduce prejudice have existed over the years. Though they have varied in their orientation and focal point of activity, their techniques have basically been two: (1) to promote greater interaction between dominant and minority groups in all aspects of living, by either voluntary or compulsory means; and (2) to dispense information that will destroy stereotypes and expose rationalizations (self-justifications). Neither approach has been successful in all instances, probably because the inequalities that encourage such attitudes still exist.

Contact

Contact between people of different racial and ethnic backgrounds does not necessarily lead to friendlier attitudes. In fact, the situation may worsen, as has happened frequently when schools and neighborhoods experienced the influx of a different group of people. However, many instances show that interaction reduces prejudice.[51] It would appear that a great many other variables determine the effect of contact, including the frequency and duration of contacts, the relative status of the two parties and their backgrounds, whether their meeting is voluntary or compulsory, competitive or cooperative, and whether they meet in a political, religious, occupational, residential, or recreational situation.[52]

A good example of the significance of the type of contact lies in the "**jigsaw method**" experiments of Elliot Aronson and his associates.[53] This research team observed that classroom competition for teacher recognition and approval often wreaked special hardships on minority children less fluent in English or less self-assured about participating in class. Creating interdependent learning groups of five or six children, each member charged with learning one portion of the day's lesson in a particular subject, the researchers then learned the complete lesson from one another, thereafter taking a test on all the material. This cooperative technique, highly structured and teacher facilitated, has successfully taught content and cooperative skills while enhancing self-esteem and peer liking (see Box 3.1).

Information

Many people have long cherished the hope that education would reduce prejudice. Some studies, such as that by Gertrude Selznick and Stephen Steinberg, have found a definite correlation between level of education and degree of tolerance;[54] but other studies have not.[55] Charles Stember's research led him to conclude that more highly educated persons were not more tolerant—they were simply more sophisticated in recognizing measures of bias and more subtle in expressing their prejudices.[56] In sum, it appears that formal education is far from a perfect means of reducing prejudice. One reason for this failure is that people tend to use **selective perception;** that is, they learn information that accords with their own beliefs and rationalize away that which does not. Another reason is the almost quantum leap from the classroom to real-life situations. Dealing with prejudice from

BOX 3.1

The Jigsaw Method

The experience of a Mexican-American child in one of our groups serves as a useful illustration. We will call him Carlos. Carlos was not very articulate in English, his second language. Because he was often ridiculed when he had spoken up in the past, over the years he learned to keep quiet in class. He was one of those students . . . who had entered into an implicit contract of silence with his teacher, he opting for anonymity and she calling on him only rarely.

While Carlos hated school and was learning very little in the traditional classroom, at least he was left alone. Accordingly, he was quite uncomfortable with the jigsaw system, which required him to talk to his groupmates. He had a great deal of trouble communicating his paragraph, stammering and hesitating. The other children reacted out of old habits, resorting to insults and teasing. "Aw, you don't know it," Susan accused. "You're dumb, you're stupid. You don't know what you are doing."

One of the researchers, assigned to observe the group process, intervened with a bit of advice when she overheard such comments: "Okay, you can tease him if you want to. It might be fun for you, but it's not going to help you learn about Eleanor Roosevelt's young adulthood. And let me remind you, the exam will take place in less than an hour." Note how this statement brings home the fact that the reinforcement contingencies have shifted considerably. Now Susan does not gain much from putting Carlos down. And she stands to lose a great deal, not just from the teacher singling her out for criticism but because she needs to know Carlos's information.

Gradually, but inexorably, it began to dawn on the students that the only chance they had to learn about Carlos's segment was by paying attention to what he had to say. If they ignored Carlos or continued to ridicule him, his segment would be unavailable to them and the most they could hope for would be an 80 percent score on the exam—an unattractive prospect to most of the children. And with that realization, the kids began to develop into pretty good interviewers, learning to pay attention to Carlos, to draw him out, and to ask probing questions. Carlos, in turn, began to relax more and found it easier to explain out loud what was in his head. What the children came to learn about Carlos is even more important than the information about the lesson that they got from him. After a couple of days, they began to appreciate that Carlos was not nearly as dumb as they had thought he was. After a few weeks they noticed talents in him they had not seen before. They began to like Carlos, and he began to enjoy school more and to think of his Anglo classmates as helpful friends and interested colleagues rather than as tormentors.

Source: Elliot Aronson and Neal Osherow, "Cooperation, Prosocial Behavior, and Academic Performance: Experiments in the Desegregated Classroom," *Applied Social Psychology Annual* 1 (1980), 174–175.

a detached perspective is one thing, but dealing with it in actuality quite another, as emotions, social pressures, and many other factors are all involved.

Despite these criticisms, courses in race and ethnic relations certainly have value in that they raise the students' level of consciousness about intergroup dynamics. However, a significant reduction or elimination of prejudice is more likely to occur by changing the structural conditions of inequality, which promote and maintain prejudicial attitudes. As Herbert Blumer suggests, the sense of group position dissolves and racial prejudice declines when major shifts in the social order overtake the current definition of a group's characteristics.[57] So long as the dominant group does not react with fear, instituting a countermovement, the improvement of a minority's social position changes the power relations and reduces the negative stereotypes. Therefore, continued efforts at public enlightenment and extension of constitutional rights and equal opportunities to all Americans, regardless of race, religion, or national origin, appear to be the most hopeful means of attaining a prejudice-free society.

DISCRIMINATION

Discrimination is actual behavior, the practice of differential and unequal treatment of other groups of people, usually along racial, religious, or ethnic lines. The Latin word *discriminatus* from which the English word is derived, means to divide or distinguish, and so its negative interpretation has remained relatively unchanged down through the centuries.

Levels of Discrimination

Actions, like attitudes, may have different levels of intensity. Discrimination may thus be analyzed at five levels.[58] The first level is *verbal expression,* a statement of dislike or use of a derogatory term. The next level is *avoidance,* in which the prejudiced person takes steps to avoid any social interaction with that group. At the third level, *exclusion* from certain jobs, housing, education, or social organizations would occur. In the United States, the practices of **de jure segregation** (established through law) and **de facto segregation** (established in social customs and institutions) illustrate this form of behavior. The fourth level of discrimination is *physical abuse,* the beatings and attacks upon members of the disliked group, as was frequently done against Blacks and Chinese in the late nineteenth century. The final level is *extermination,* when massacres, genocide, or pogroms are conducted against a people.

Prejudice can lead to discrimination and, conversely, discrimination can lead to prejudice. Depending upon the situation, either discrimination or prejudice may cause the other, but no certainty exists that one will follow the other. Although our attitudes and our overt behavior are closely interrelated, they are not identical. We may harbor hostile feelings toward certain groups without ever making them known through word or deed. Similarly, through our overt behavior we may effectively conceal our real attitudes.

It is true that prejudiced people are more likely than others to practice discrimination; discrimination is thus quite often the overt expression of prejudice. However, it is wrong to assume that discrimination is always the acting out of prejudice. It may be instead the result of a policy decision protecting the interests of the majority group, such as the curtailment of immigration for economic reasons. It may be due to social conformity, such as when people submit to outside pressures despite their personal views.[59] Discriminators may explain their actions with reasons other than prejudice toward a particular group, and those reasons may be valid to the discriminators. Sometimes the discriminatory behavior may precede prejudicial attitudes as, for example, when organizations insist that all job applicants take aptitude or IQ tests based on middle-class experiences and then judge negatively the lower-income people who do not score well.

Relationship Between Prejudice and Discrimination

Robert Merton formulated a model (see figure 3.1) showing the possible relationships between prejudice and discrimination. Merton demonstrates that, quite conceivably, a nonprejudiced person will discriminate and a prejudiced person will not. In his paradigm, Merton classifies four types of people according to how they accept or reject the American Creed, "the right of equitable access to justice, freedom and opportunity, irrespective of race or religion, or ethnic origin."[60]

The Nonprejudiced Nondiscriminator or All-weather Liberal

All-weather liberals are consistent. They are neither prejudiced nor practicers of discrimination. Accordingly, they are properly motivated to illuminate others and to fight against all forms of discrimination. However, says Merton, they have their shortcomings in that they confuse discussion with action. They talk chiefly to others sharing their viewpoint, and so they deceive themselves into thinking that they represent the consensus of the community. Further, because their "own spiritual house is in order," they feel no pangs of conscience pressing them to work collectively on the problem. A counterargument would be that some all-weather lib-

	Discriminates	
Prejudiced:	No	Yes
No	All—weather liberal	Fair—weather liberal
Yes	Timid bigot	Active bigot

FIGURE 3.1

Interrelationship Between Prejudice and Discrimination

erals are activists and do speak to others with different viewpoints, thereby transforming discussion into action.

The Nonprejudiced Discriminator or Fair-weather Liberal

Expediency is the byword for those in this category, for their actions often conflict with their personal beliefs. They may, for example, be free of racial prejudice, but they will keep silent when bigots speak out, they will not condemn acts of discrimination, and they will join in efforts to keep Blacks out of their neighborhood for fear of its deterioration. These people frequently feel guilt and shame because they are acting against their beliefs.

The Prejudiced Nondiscriminator or Fair-weather Illiberal

Merton's term "timid bigots" best describes fair-weather illiberals. They believe in many of the stereotypes about minorities and definitely feel hostility toward these groups. However, they keep silent in the presence of those who are more tolerant; they conform because they must. If there were no law or pressure to be unbiased in certain actions, they would discriminate.

The Prejudiced Discriminator or All-weather Illiberal

Without doubt, such folks as the all-weather illiberals are active bigots. They have no conflict between attitudes and behavior. Not only do they openly express their beliefs, practice discrimination, and defy the law, if necessary, but they also believe that it is their duty to do so.

The second and third categories, the nonprejudiced discriminator and the prejudiced nondiscriminator, are the most helpful classifications, showing us that social-situational variables often determine whether or not discriminatory behavior occurs. Individuals may act in a manner inconsistent with their beliefs because of the pressure of group norms.

Other Aspects of Discrimination

Discriminatory practices are frequent in the areas of employment and residence, although such actions are often covert and denied. Another dimension of discrimination, often unrealized, is **social discrimination,** or the creation of a "social distance" between groups. Simply stated, in their intimate primary relationships, people tend to associate with those of a similar ethnic background and socioeconomic level; the dominant-group members thus usually exclude minority-group members from close relations with them.

Hubert Blalock, offering conflict perspective reasoning, suggests extreme discrimination will usually result when the dominant group feels that its self-interests—such as primacy and the preservation of cherished values—are threatened.[61] Blalock believes that the dominant group will not hesitate to employ discriminatory action if it thinks that this will be an effective means of undercutting the minority group as a social competitor. Also, the dominant group will aggressively discriminate if it interprets minority variation from cultural norms as a form of social deviance threatening society's sacred traditions (for example, the large influx of Catholic immigrants in nineteenth-century America, or the appearance of "dishonest" Gypsies among "decent, hard-working" people). Discrimination, in this view, is "a technique designed to neutralize minority group efforts."[62]

Reverse Discrimination

At what point do efforts to secure justice and equal opportunities in life for one group infringe upon the rights of other groups? Is justice a utilitarian concept—the greatest happiness for the greatest number—or is it a moral concept—a sense of good that all people share? Is the proper role of government to provide a climate in which there is equal opportunity to participate in a competitive system, or is it government's responsibility to ensure equal results in any competition? These issues have engaged moral and political philosophers for centuries, and they go to the core of the affirmative-action controversy.

Over 2,300 years ago, Plato wrote in the *Republic* that justice must be relative to the needs of the people who are served, not to the desires of those who serve them. For example, physicians are obliged to make the patients' health their primary concern if they are to be just. In *A Theory of Justice,* John Rawls interprets justice as fairness, which maximizes equal liberty for all.[63] Society must eliminate social and economic inequalities in order to provide the greatest benefit to the least advantaged, placing disadvantaged persons in offices and positions that are open to all under conditions of fair equality of opportunity. Both men see the ideal society as well ordered and strongly pluralistic: each of the component elements performs functionally differentiated roles in working harmony; society must arrange its practices to make this so.

Shift in Government Policy

Anticipating the emergence of the equal-protection-under-the-law clause of the Fourteenth Amendment as a major force for social change, Joseph Tussman and Jacobus tenBroek examined the problems of the doctrine of equality five years before the 1954 Supreme Court desegregation ruling.[64] Americans, they argued, have always been more concerned with liberty than with equality, identifying liberty with the absence of governmental interference.

> What happens, then, when government becomes more ubiquitous? Whenever an area of activity is brought within the control or regulation of government to that extent equality supplants liberty as the dominant ideal and constitutional demand.[65]

Tussman and tenBroek note that those who insist upon constitutional rights for all are not so much demanding the removal of governmental restraints as they are asking for positive governmental action to provide equal treatment for "minority groups, parties, or organizations whose rights are too easily sacrificed or ignored in periods of popular hysteria."[66] Responsibility for promoting individual rights is increasingly being placed upon public authority.

In the past thirty years, the three branches of the federal government have acted to promote minority rights in judicial decisions, legislative programs, and executive actions. As their impact was felt at state and local levels; in college and graduate school admissions; in hiring, training, and promotion policies; and in other facets of life, many Whites reacted with anger, feeling that their own rights were now being denied. They argued that they were being penalized for past societal wrongs and were thus victims of reverse discrimination.

Supreme Court Rulings

The issue was partially resolved with the *Bakke* decision in July 1978. In what one observer termed a "Solomonic" compromise, the Supreme Court ruled 5-4 that it is illegal for a university to use racial or ethnic quotas in its admissions program, but also that race may be considered as one factor in the admissions policy. The principle of affirmative action, designed to improve educational and job opportunities for racial minorities and women, was thus upheld, though in refined form. The ruling was not a definitive one, however. Other cases pending before the Supreme Court will further clarify the matter in areas other than university admissions. In the same week as the *Bakke* decision, for example, the Court ruled that the use of racial quotas at AT&T (American Telephone and Telegraph) was justified because of long-standing discriminatory practices in this corporation that required corrective action.

Two of the majority opinions from the *Bakke* decision seem to best summarize the Court's assessment of this extremely complex matter. Justice Lewis F. Powell stated: "The guarantee of equal protection cannot mean one thing when applied to one individual and something else when applied to a person of another color. If both are not accorded the same protection, then it is not equal." Justice Harry A. Blackmun pointed out the other part of the problem: "In order to get beyond racism, we must first take account of race. There is no other way. And in order to treat some persons equally, we must treat them differently. We cannot—we dare not—let the Equal Protection Clause perpetuate racial superiority."

Another important case involved the United Steelworkers of America and Kaiser Aluminum & Chemical Corporation, which reserved half of the positions in its skilled-craft training programs for minorities and women. Brian Weber, a white Louisiana factory worker, filed a class action suit when two Blacks with less seniority were picked ahead of him for this program. When the U.S. Supreme Court handled the case of *Weber v. Kaiser* in July 1979, it further upheld affirmative action in ruling that private employers may voluntarily adopt quotas to remedy past discrimination, even if blameless themselves. Considered by some analysts a potentially more significant decision than the *Bakke* case, the Court considered the spirit and intent of the law, the serious racial imbalance among craft employees, and the fact that the temporary plan did not deny promotions to, or cause firings of, Whites.

The 1980–1982 recession generated other charges of **reverse discrimination,** prompting court challenges and decisions about compliance. In June 1984, a 6–3 U.S. Supreme Court ruling put a new limit on Affirmative Action, upholding the last-hired, first-fired principle. As long as seniority systems are unbiased, the Court declared, they may not be disrupted to save jobs of newly hired minority workers. This decision appears to signal a new era of aid to direct victims of past discrimination, not whole groups. The entire issue promises to remain with us for some time to come.

RETROSPECT

Prejudice may exist at three levels: cognitive, emotional, and action orientation. Stereotyping, difficult to erase once established, is found in use of ethnophaulisms and ethnic humor. Television has a profound impact in shaping and reinforcing attitudes; unfortunately it continues to perpetuate racial and sexual stereotypes instead of combating them.

No single cause can account for all instances of prejudice. Among the explanations social scientists offer are socialization, self-justification, personality factors, frustration, competition, and social norms. Each of these factors explains some cases of prejudice, and sometimes various combinations of them explain other cases. Social-situational variables, such as economic conditions, stratification, and hostility toward the outgroup, also are important in understanding the existence of prejudice.

Increased contact between groups and improved information as in courses about minorities do not necessarily reduce prejudice. The nature of the contact, particularly if it is competitive or cooperative, is a key determinant. Information can develop heightened awareness as a means of improved relations, but external factors (economic conditions, social pressures) may override rational considerations.

Discriminatory behavior operates at five levels of intensity: verbal expression, avoidance, exclusion, physical abuse, extermination. Discrimination is not necessarily an acting out of prejudice. Social pressures may oblige nonprejudiced individuals to discriminate or prevent prejudiced people from discriminating.

Reverse discrimination remains an emotionally charged issue. Is it a democratic government's responsibility to provide a climate for equal opportunity or to ensure equal results? If the latter, at what point do efforts to secure equality for one group infringe upon the rights of other groups?

KEY TERMS

Action-orientation level of prejudice
Authoritarian personality
Cognitive level of prejudice
Displaced aggression
Emotional level of prejudice
Ethnophaulism

Frustration
Institutionalized discrimination
Jigsaw method
Prejudice
Relative deprivation
Reverse discrimination
Scapegoating

Selective perception	**Socialization**
Self-justification	**Stereotype**
Social norms	**Value judgment**

REVIEW QUESTIONS

1. What is prejudice? What are some of its manifestations?
2. What are some of the possible causes of prejudice?
3. What role does television play in combating or reinforcing stereotypes?
4. What is discrimination? What are some of its manifestations?
5. What is the relationship between prejudice and discrimination?
6. What is reverse discrimination? Why is it so difficult an issue?

SUGGESTED READINGS

Blalock, Hubert M., Jr. *Race and Ethnic Relations.* Englewood Cliffs, NJ: Prentice-Hall, 1982.

A theoretical "roadmap" of race and ethnic relations offering a macrosocial view of prejudice and discrimination.

Clark, Kenneth B. *Prejudice and Your Child,* 2nd ed. Boston: Beacon Press, 1963.

A thorough examination of the effects of race prejudice on children, both majority and minority group members, with specific suggestions to overcome prejudicial feelings in children.

Feagin, Joe R. and Clairece B. Feagin. *Discrimination American Style.* Englewood Cliffs, NJ: Prentice-Hall, 1978.

An excellent overview of the forms and dimensions of discriminatory actions practiced in American society against various minority groups.

Jones, James M. *Prejudice and Racism.* Reading, Mass.: Addison-Wesley, 1972.

A comprehensive and helpful summary about racial prejudice determined by years of social scientific investigation.

CHAPTER 4

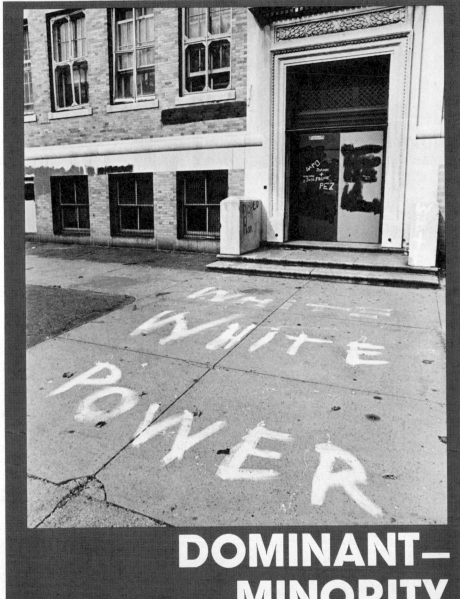

DOMINANT—MINORITY RELATIONS

So far we have looked at behavioral patterns in relating to strangers, the role of culture and social structure in shaping perceptions and interactions, and the complexity of prejudice and discrimination. In this chapter we shall discuss response patterns that dominant and minority groups follow in their dealings with each other.

What we are suggesting in the following pages is that these patterns occur in varying degrees for most groups regardless of race, ethnicity, or time period. They are not mutually exclusive categories, nor do groups necessarily follow all these patterns at one time. While each group has its own unique characteristics and many factors determine actual responses, the experiences of each minority and dominant group of a given society share these pattern commonalities in some fashion.

MINORITY-GROUP RESPONSES TO PREJUDICE AND DISCRIMINATION

Although personality characteristics play a large role in determining how individuals respond to unfavorable situations, behavioral patterns for the group in general will be similar to that of other groups in comparable circumstances. External factors play an important part, but social interpretation is also a critical determinant. The minority group's perception of its power resources—its power to change established relationships with the dominant group in a significant way—will, to a large extent, determine which response it will be more likely to make.[1]

Avoidance

One way of dealing with discriminatory practices is to avoid encountering them, if possible. Throughout history, minority groups—from the ancient Hebrews to the Pilgrims to the Soviet Jews today—have attempted to solve their problems by leaving them behind. One motivation for migration, then, is avoidance of discrimination. If leaving is not possible, minorities may turn inward to their own group for their social and economic activities. This approach serves to insulate minority groups against the antagonistic actions of the dominant group, but it also promotes charges of "clannishness" and "nonassimilation." However, lacking adequate economic, legal, or political power, avoidance may be the only choice open to the minority group.

By clustering together in small subcommunities, minority peoples not only recreated a miniature version of their familiar world in the strange land, they also established a safe place in which they could live, relax, and interact with others like themselves who could understand their needs and interests. For some minority groups, seeking such shelter from the prejudices of others was probably a secondary motivation, following a primary choice to live amongst their own kind.

Asian immigrants, for example, followed this pattern. When the Chinese first came to this country, they worked in many occupations in which workers were needed, frequently clustering together in neighborhoods close to their jobs. Prejudicial attitudes had always existed against the Chinese, but in the post-Civil War period, they became even more the targets of bitter hatred and discrimination, for economic and other reasons. Evicted from their jobs by race-baiting union strikes and limited in residential choice by restrictive housing covenants, many had no choice but to live in Chinatowns within the larger cities. They entered occupations not competitive with Whites [curio shops, laundries, restaurants, and so on], and followed their tradition of settling their disputes among themselves, rather than subjecting themselves to public law adjudication.

Deviance

When a group is continually rejected and discriminated against, some of the members find it difficult to identify with the dominant society and to accept its norms. People at the bottom of the socioeconomic ladder, particularly members of victimized racial and ethnic groups, may respond to the pressures of everyday life in ways they consider reasonable but others view as deviant. In particular, this situation occurs when laws represent an attempt to impose the moral standards of the dominant group on the behavior of other groups. Many minority groups in the United States—Irish, Germans, Chinese, Italians, Blacks, Native Americans, Hispanics—have been, at one time or another, arrested and punished in disproportionate numbers for so-called crimes of personal disorganization. Included among the outrages to the morality of the dominant group have been public drunkenness, drug abuse, gambling, and sexual "misconduct." It is a matter of dispute whether this is a function of the frequency of misconduct or of selective arrests.

Part of the problem regarding law enforcement is its subjective nature and the discretionary handling of violations. Many people have criticized the American criminal justice system for its disparities in according fair and equal treatment to the poor and minority group members as compared with the middle and upper classes.[2] The complaints have included (1) the tendency of police to arrest suspects from minority groups more than those from the majority group when discretionary judgment is possible; (2) the overrepresentation of certain dominant social, ethnic, and racial groups on juries; (3) the difficulty for the poor in affording bail; (4) the poor quality of free legal defense; and (5) the disparities in sentences for dominant and minority groups. Because social background constitutes one of the factors that the police and courts consider, those who belong to a racial or ethnic group with a negative stereotype are at a severe disadvantage.

Often when a particular racial or ethnic group commits a noticeable number of deviant offenses, such as delinquency, crime, drunkenness, or some public-nuisance problem, the public may extend a negative image to all members of that group. Some common associations, for example, are Italians and gangsters, Irish and heavy drinking and fighting, Chinese and opium, Blacks and street crimes such as mugging and purse snatching, and Puerto Ricans and knife fighting. Even though a very small percentage of a group actually engages in such behavior, sometimes the entire group becomes negatively stereotyped. A number of factors—including values, behavior patterns, and structural conditions in both the native and adopted lands—help explain the various kinds of deviance among different minority groups. The best means of stopping the deviance is a debatable issue between proponents of corrective versus preventative measures.

Deviant behavior among minority groups occurs not because of race or ethnicity, as prejudiced people would claim, but partly because of poverty and lack of opportunity. Clifford Shaw and Henry McKay, in a classic study of juvenile delinquency in Chicago, suggested that structural conditions, not membership in a particular minority group, determine crime and delinquency rates.[3] They found that the highest juvenile-delinquency rates occured in areas with poor housing, few job opportunities, and the widespread incidence of prostitution, gambling, and drug use. The delinquency rate was consistently high over a thirty-year period, even though five different ethnic groups had moved in and out of those areas during that period of time. Nationality was unimportant; the unchanged conditions brought unchanged results. Other studies have also demonstrated a correlation between higher rates of either juvenile or adult crime and income level and place of residence.[4]

Because many minority groups are heavily represented among low-income populations, studies emphasizing social-class variables provide insight into the minority experience. For example, Albert Cohen found that a lack of opportunities encourages delinquency by lower-class males.[5] Social aspirations may be similar in all levels of society, but opportunities are not. Belonging to a gang may give a youth a sense of power and help overcome feelings of inadequacy; hoodlumism becomes an expression of resentment against a society whose norms seem impossible to follow.[6] The large majority of racial and ethnic-group members do not join gangs or engage in criminally deviant behavior. Nevertheless, because some minority groups are represented disproportionately in such activities, despite the small percentage of the total group involved, the public image of the group as a whole suffers. Some social factors, particularly parental attitudes about education and social ascent, appear to be related to delinquency rates. For example, parental emphasis on academic achievement may partially explain the low juvenile-delinquency rate among second-generation Jews compared with the high juvenile-delinquency rate among second-generation Italians, whose parents often viewed formal education as a frill.[7]

Defiance

If a minority group is sufficiently cohesive and conscious of its growing economic or political power, its members may act openly to challenge and eliminate discriminatory practices. In defying discrimination, the minority group is taking a strong stance regarding its position in the society. Prior to this time, certain individuals of that group may have been in the vanguard (for example, by challenging laws in court).

Sometimes the defiance is violent and appears to be spontaneous, although it is usually the outgrowth of long-standing conditions. One example is the Irish draft riot in New York in 1863 during the Civil War. When its volunteer armies proved insufficient, the Union utilized a military draft to secure the needed troops. In those days, if a male were well-to-do, he could legally buy the military services of a substitute. Because the Irish were mostly poor and concentrated in urban areas,

A police officer stands amidst the bombed wreckage from Fraunces Tavern in New York City, an important historical site from the days of George Washington. This violent act of defiance in 1975 by FALN members seeking independence for Puerto Rico, shocked even the Puerto Rican community where either nonsympathizers or those fearful of dominant hostility expressed concern over the incident.

many of them were drafted. Their defiance of what they considered an unfair practice became a riot, in which the Blacks became the scapegoats, with lives lost and property destroyed or damaged.

A militant action, such as the takeover of a symbolic site, is a moderately aggressive act of defiance. The late 1960s witnessed many building takeovers by Blacks and other disaffected, angry, alienated students on college campuses. In many instances the purpose of the action was to call public attention to what the group considered indifference or discrimination accorded their people. Similar actions occurred in this period to protest the war in Vietnam. A small group of American Indians took this approach in the 1970s to protest their living conditions; they seized Alcatraz Island in California, the Bureau of Indian Affairs in Washington, D.C., and the village of Wounded Knee in South Dakota. The influence of the media helped to validate and spread the idea of using militant actions to obtain one's ends.

Any peaceful action that challenges the status quo is less aggressive but is defiant, nonetheless; parades, marches, picket lines, mass meetings, boycotts, and demonstrations are examples. Another form of peaceful protest is to deliberately break discriminatory laws to challenge their constitutionality or to break a discriminatory tradition. The civil rights actions of the 1960s—sit-ins, lie-ins, and freedom rides—challenged Jim Crow laws that restricted access by Blacks to public establishments in the South. Shop-ins at stores that had previously catered to an exclusively white clientele illustrated deliberate efforts to break traditional store practices.

Acceptance

Many minority people, to the frequent consternation of their leaders and sympathizers, accept the situation in which they find themselves. Some do so stoically, even justifying it by subtle rationalizations. Others are resentful but accept the situation for reasons of personal security or economic necessity. Although this approach maintains the superior position in society of the dominant group and the subordinate position of minority groups, it does ease the open tensions and conflicts between the two groups.

Conforming to prevailing patterns of interaction between dominant and minority groups can also be a subconscious action, the end result of social conditioning. Just as socialization can serve as a cause of prejudice, so too it can cause minority-group members to disregard or be unaware of alternative status possibilities. How much acceptance of lower status is of this nature and how much is characterized by resentful submission is a question that has not been completely answered. However, some sociologists believe that instances of conscious but disliked role-playing by minority peoples in order to survive are quite common.[8] Brewton Berry and Henry Tischler state: "It is not uncommon for one to conform externally while rejecting the system mentally and emotionally."[9]

Blacks, Chicanos, and American Indians have experienced a multigenerational subordinate position in the United States. Until the 1960s, a combination of structural discrimination, racial stratification, and a sense of powerlessness and the futility of trying to change things caused many to accommodate to the situation imposed upon them. Similarly, Japanese-Americans had little choice when, following the bombing of Pearl Harbor and the subsequent rise in anti-Japanese sentiment in the United States, the government in 1942 uprooted and imprisoned 110,000 of them in "temporary relocation centers."

Acceptance as a minority response is not as common in the United States as it once was. More aware of the alternative ways of living that are presented on television and in the movies, minorities are hopeful of sharing in them. No longer are they receptive to the status quo, which denies them the comfortable living and leisure pursuits others have. Society—as evidenced by court decisions, legislation, new social services, and other efforts—has created a more favorable climate for improvement of the status of minority groups. Perhaps televised news features and behavioral science courses have helped to heighten the public's social awareness.

Negative Self-image

The apathy that militant leaders find among their own people often results from a negative self-image, a rather common consequence of prejudice and discrimination. Continual treatment as an inferior encourages a loss of self-confidence. If everything about a person's position and experiences—jobs with low pay, substandard housing, the hostility of others, the need for assistance from governmental agencies—works to destroy pride and hope, that person may become apathetic. To remain optimistic and determined in the face of constant negative experiences from all directions is almost impossible.

Over thirty-five years ago Kurt Lewin observed that among minority-group members, development of a negative self-image was a fairly general tendency.[10] According to this view, the pervasiveness of dominant-group values and attitudes, which include negative stereotypes of the minority group, may cause the minority-group member to accept them. A person's self-image includes race, religion, and nationality; thus, individuals may feel embarrassed and inferior if they are aware that any of these attributes are held in low esteem within the society. In effect, minority-group members begin to perceive themselves as negatively as the dominant group originally perceived them.

This negative self-image, or self-hatred, manifests itself in many ways. People may try to ''pass'' as members of the dominant group and deny membership in a disparaged group. They may fully agree with the dominant group's prejudices and accept their state. They may also engage in ego defense by blaming others within the group for their low status.

Some Jews refer to other Jews as ''kikes''—blaming them exclusively for the anti-Semitism from which all alike suffer. Class distinctions within groups is often a result of trying to free oneself from responsibility for the handicap from which the group as a whole suffers. ''Lace curtain'' Irish look down on ''shanty'' Irish. Wealthy Spanish and Portuguese Jews have long regarded themselves as the top of the pyramid of Hebraic peoples. But Jews of German origin, having a rich culture, view themselves as the aristocrats, often looking down on Austrian, Hungarian, and Balkan Jews, and regarding Polish and Russian Jews at the very bottom.[11]

Negative self-image, then, can cause people to accept their fate passively. It can also cause a sense of personal shame for possessing undesired qualities or can create antipathy toward other members of the group for possessing them. Minority-group members frequently attempt to overcome their negative self-image by changing their name or religion, having cosmetic surgery, or moving into a locale where the stereotype is not as prevalent.

Portraying negative self-image as a fairly general tendency among minority-group members, as Lewin does, may be too broad a generalization. For example, members of tightly cohesive religious groups could draw emotional support from their faith and from one another. The insulation of living in an ethnic community, strong ingroup loyalty, or the determination to maintain their cultural heritage may also prevent minority-group members from developing a negative self-image.

The Vicious Circle

Sometimes the relationship between prejudice and discrimination is circular. Gunnar Myrdal refers to this pattern as **cumulative causation,** a vicious circle wherein prejudice and discrimination each cause the other.[12] The dynamics of the relations between dominant and minority groups set in motion an almost perpetual sequence of reciprocal stimuli and responses. For example, a discriminatory action in jobs leads to a minority reaction, poverty, which in turn reinforces the dominant-group attitude that the minority group is inferior, which leads to still more discrimination, and so on.

Myrdal points out that this pattern may be desirable or undesirable. The expectations held about the newcomers are the key to the nature of the pattern that develops.[13] If the dominant group makes the newcomers welcome, they in turn are likely to react in a positive manner, which reinforces their friendly reception. If the new group is ignored and made to feel unwelcome, the members may react negatively, which also reaffirms original attitudes and actions. As Allport says, "If we foresee evil in our fellow man, we tend to provoke it; if good, we elicit it."[14] In other words, negative expectations engender negative reactions. The reactions encourage greater prejudicial opinions, broaden the social distance between the groups, and cause the vicious circle to continue.

When the Jews were denied access to many vacation resorts in the nineteenth century, their reaction served to reinforce their negative stereotype in the minds of some, thus reinforcing the discrimination. Some Jews demanded the right of equal access, showing the resort operators that Jews were "pushy." As the Jews, because of this discriminatory policy, began going to their own resorts in the Catskill Mountains, they were then labeled "clannish." Similarly, the Irish encountered severe job discrimination in the midnineteenth century, and because of the poverty that resulted, many of them lived in urban slums and had trouble with the law. With this evidence of their "inferiority" and "undesirability," their job opportunities became even more limited. In the same way, white discrimination against Blacks, based partly on their low standard of living, furthers the problems of poverty, thus fueling even more any white antipathy for Blacks.

Marginality

Minority-group members sometimes find themselves caught in a conflict between their own identity and values and the necessity to behave in a certain way in order to be accepted by the dominant group. This situation is usually found when a member of a minority group is undergoing a transitional period. In an attempt to enter the mainstream of society, the *marginal* person internalizes the dominant group's cultural patterns but has not yet gained full acceptance. Such individuals are in an ill-defined role, no longer at ease within their own group but not yet fully a part of the *reference group*, the one to which they refer when evaluating themselves and their behavior.[15]

Over the years, sociologists have differed in their interpretation of the effects of marginality. Robert E. Park, who gave this social phenomenon its name, believed it caused the individual a great deal of strain and difficulty. Such a person, he observed, is one "whom fate has condemned to live in two societies and in two not merely different but antagonistic cultures."[16]

According to Park's thesis, this situation can cause the marginal person to suffer anxiety over a conflict of values and loyalties. This inner conflict can occur among both adults and children. The adults leave the security of their cultural group, thereby risking being labeled renegades by their own people. They seek sustained social contacts with the dominant group, which may view them as outsiders. No longer comfortable with the old ways, but influenced by them and identified with them nonetheless, the adults often experience feelings of frustration, hypersensitivity, and self-consciousness.

The children of immigrants also find themselves caught between two worlds. At home their parents attempt to raise them in their social heritage, according to the established ways of the old country. The children, through school and other outside experiences, become exposed to the American culture, and want to be like the other children. Moreover, they quickly learn that the dominant group views the ways of their parents as inferior and that they too are socially rejected because of their background. Consequently, many young people may develop emotional problems and be embarrassed to bring classmates home.

Marginality, according to this view, is an example of cultural conflict, primarily due to the clash of values within the individual. However, many sociologists now believe that the reaction to marginal status depends in large measure upon whether or not the individual receives reassurances of self-worth from the community. Thus, defining the situation and adjusting to it are contingent upon the individual's sense of security within the community.[17] In addition, ethnic subcommunities and institutions and a sense of solidarity among members of the ethnic group contribute to that sense of well-being. These observations have led some sociologists to emphasize stable individuals in a marginal culture rather than marginal persons in a dominant culture.[18] In other words, individuals in a marginal culture share their cultural duality with many others in primary-group relationships, institutional activities, and interaction with members of the dominant society, without encountering any dichotomy between their desires and actuality.

Whether this phase of the assimilation process represents an emotionally stressful experience or an insulated one, minority-group members nonetheless pass through a transitional period during which they are not fully a part of either world. An immigrant group may move into the mainstream of American society within the lifetimes of the first-generation members, or they may choose not to do so or simply be unable to. Usually, marginality is a one- or two-generational phenomenon. After that, members of the minority group have either assimilated or formed a distinctive subculture. No matter which route they take, they are no longer caught between two cultural worlds.

"Middleman" Minorities

Building upon theories of marginality, Hubert Blalock suggested the concept of "middleman" minorities.[19] This model, based on a dominant-subordinate stratification system, places middleman minorities in an intermediate rather than low-status position.[20] Feudal or colonial societies, with their ruling elite and large peasant masses often have middleman minorities performing mediating commerce links between the two. Consequently, such minorities are commonly trading peoples whose history of persecution (Jews, Greeks, and Armenians) or whose sojourner orientation (Chinese, Japanese, and Koreans) obliged them to perform risky or marginal tasks that permitted easy liquidation.[21]

Middleman groups often serve as buffers, the target of hostility and conflict from both the top and bottom strata. Jews in Nazi Germany and Asians in Uganda in the early 1970s, for instance, became scapegoats for economic stresses in those societies. Their susceptibility to such antagonism, or their sojourner self-definition of not remaining long in the host society, promote among them high ingroup solidarity.

Systematic discrimination can make middleman minority status a rather permanent one, as in the case of European Jews in the medieval period. Sometimes the entrepreneural skills developed in trade and commerce provide middleman minorities with highly adaptive capabilities and competitive advantages, enabling them to achieve upward mobility and assimilate more easily; this occurred for Jewish immigrants to the United States and may also occur for the Korean-Americans. In other cases, a group may emerge as a middleman minority because of changing residential patterns. One example is Jewish store owners in cities who once serviced their own people who have now moved away; unable to follow them, these urban merchants now serve the new urban minority groups situated lower on the socioeconomic ladder.

DOMINANT-GROUP RESPONSES TO MINORITY GROUPS

Members of a dominant group frequently react to minority peoples with tolerance and compassion, although they may sometimes be condescending in their attitudes. This type of favorable response usually occurs when the minority is small in number, not perceived as a threat, or both. As the minority group increases in population, threatening the natives' monopoly on jobs and other claims to privileged cultural resources, the dominant group's attitude is likely to become suspicious or fearful. If the fear becomes great enough, the dominant group may take some form of action against the minority group.

Legislative Controls

If the influx of racial and ethnic groups appears too great for a country to absorb, or if prejudicial fears prevail, that nation may act to regulate and restrict their entry. Australia, Canada, and the United States—the three greatest receiving countries in international migration—once had discriminatory immigration laws that either excluded or curtailed the number of immigrants from countries other than those in northern and western Europe. Following similar patterns of policy change, Canada (in 1962), the United States (in 1965), and Australia (in 1973) began to permit entry from all parts of the world.

To maintain a paternalistic social system, the dominant group frequently restricts the educational opportunities and voting of the subordinate group. This denial assures the dominant group of maintaining its system of control, whether over internal minorities such as the Blacks in the Old South and the various ethnic minorities in the Soviet Union, or over colonized peoples such as those ruled by the Belgians, British, Dutch, French, Japanese, and Portuguese. Colonial powers have usually committed themselves to stability, trade, and tapping the natural resources of a country rather than to its development and self-governance. Token local leadership without real power in important matters, limited educational opportunities, and restricted political participation have been the usual experience of native populations under colonial rule. Other means of denying political power have been disenfranchising voters through high property qualifications (British West Indies), high income qualifications (Trinidad), and poll taxes (United States), although none of these practices exist today in those areas. The most conspicuous recent example of rigid social control is in South Africa, where a legislated apartheid society denies not only equal education and the ballot to Blacks, but almost every other privilege as well.

Segregation

Through a policy of containment, by avoiding social interaction with members of a minority group as much as possible and keeping them "in their place," the dominant group can effectively create both spatial and social segregation.

Spatial segregation refers to the physical separation of a minority people from the rest of society. This most commonly occurs in residential patterns but also takes place in education, in the use of public facilities, and in the occupational area. The majority group may institutionalize this form of segregation by law (**de jure** segregation) or establish it as an ongoing practice through norms (**de facto** segregation).

Spatial segregation of minorities has been quite common for a long time. Since the days of the preindustrial city with its heterogeneous populations, the dominant group has relegated racial and ethnic minorities to special sections of the city, often the least desirable areas.[22] In Europe, this medieval ecological pattern resulted in minority groups being situated on the city outskirts nearest the encircling wall. Because this pattern remains in much of Europe today, Europeans, unlike Americans, consider it a sign of high prestige to live near the center of the city.[23]

The dominant group may use covert or overt means to achieve spatial segregation of a minority group. Some examples of covert actions are restrictive covenants, "gentlemen's" agreements, and collusion between the community and real estate agents to steer "undesirable" minorities only into certain neighborhoods.[24] Overt actions may include restrictive zoning, segregation laws, or intimidation. Both covert and overt segregation actions have been targets of U.S. court rulings over the past twenty-five years.

An important dimension of spatial segregation is that the dominant group can also achieve it through avoidance, or residential mobility. Usually referred to as the **invasion-succession** ecological pattern, this process has been a common one, involving different religions and nationalities as well as different races. The most recognized example in the United States is previously all-white neighborhoods becoming black, but any study of most urban neighborhoods would reveal the same pattern as successive waves of immigrants came here over the years. Residents of a neighborhood may attempt to resist the influx of a minority group, eventually abandoning the area when their efforts are not successful. This pattern results in neighborhoods with a concentration of a new racial or ethnic group, a new segregated area.

Social segregation involves confining participation in social, service, political, and other types of activities to members of the ingroup. The dominant group excludes the outgroup from any involvement both in meaningful primary-group activities and in secondary-group activities. Organizations have screening procedures to keep out unwanted types, and informal groups also act to preserve their composition.

Segregation, whether spatial or social, can be either involuntary or voluntary. Minority-group members may choose not to live among the dominant group but by themselves instead; such a course of action is an avoidance response, discussed previously. On the other hand, minority-group members may have no choice at all about where they live because of economic or residential discrimination.

Whether by choice or against their will, minority groups form ethnic subcommunities, whose existence in turn promotes and maintains the social distance between the minority groups and the rest of society. Not only are minority-group members physically congregated in one area and thus spatially segregated, but they are also not engaging in any social interaction with others outside of their own group.

Frequent interaction usually lessens prejudice, but when interaction is severely limited, the acculturation process is slowed considerably. Instead, a reinforcement of values occurs concerning what is regarded as normal or different, paving the way for stereotyping, social comparisons, and prestige ranking.

Expulsion

When other methods of dealing with a minority group fail, an intolerant dominant group may persecute or expel the minority group from the territory in which it resides. Henry VIII banished the Gypsies from England in the sixteenth century, Spanish rulers drove out the Moors in the early seventeenth century, and the British expelled the Acadians from Nova Scotia in the mideighteenth century. A more recent example is Idi Amin, the former authoritarian ruler of Uganda, who decreed in 1972 that all Asians must leave his country.

The United States also has its examples of mass expulsion. In colonial times, the Puritans forced Roger Williams and his followers out of Massachusetts for their nonconformity, and they settled in what became Rhode Island. The forcible removal of the Cherokee from rich Georgia land and the subsequent "Trail of Tears," in which four thousand perished along the thousand-mile forced march, is another illustration.

Mass expulsion reflects an effort to remove a group that is seen as a social problem rather than attempting to resolve the problem. This policy often takes

"The Trail of Tears"

Forcibly removed from their land in the East in 1838 by federal troops, despite their peaceful assimilation efforts, the Cherokee trekked westward to Oklahoma under heavy guard. Over 4,000 died during the winter journey. This dominant act of expulsion occurred despite a U.S. Supreme Court ruling in favor of the Cherokee.

form after other methods, such as assimilation or extermination, have failed. Whether a dominant group chooses to remove a minority group by extermination or by the somewhat more humane method of expulsion depends in part on how sensitive the country is to world opinion. Sensitivity to world opinion is often related to the country's economic dependency on other nations.

Xenophobia

If the dominant group's suspicions and fears of the minority group become greatly heightened, they sometimes result in volatile, irrational feelings and actions. This overreaction is known as **xenophobia,** the undue fear of or contempt for strangers or foreigners. This almost hysterical response—reflected in print, in speeches and sermons, in legislation, and in violent actions—begins with ethnocentric views. Ethnocentrism encourages the creation of negative stereotypes, which in turn can lead to prejudice and discrimination, and which can escalate through some catalyst into a highly emotional reaction.

The Federalists, fearful of "wild Irishmen" and French radicals" and anxious to eliminate what they saw as a foreign threat to the country's stability, succeeded in passing the Alien and Sedition Acts in 1798. When a bomb exploded at an anarchist gathering at Chicago's Haymarket Square in 1886, many Americans thereafter linked foreigners with radicals. The Bolshevik Revolution in 1917 led to the Palmer raids, in which Russian-Americans were illegally rounded up and incarcerated, and some even deported, Similarly, in 1942 the placement in concentration camps of 110,000 Japanese-Americans, many of them second- and third-generation Americans; was an irrational overreaction. All of these are examples of a xenophobic reaction to people and events.

Annihilation

The Nazi extermination of over 6 million Jews brought the term *genocide* into the English language, but the practice of killing all the men, women, and children of a particular group goes back to ancient times. In warfare among the ancient Hebrews, Assyrians, Babylonians, Egyptians, and others, the usual practice was for the victor in battle to slay all the enemy, partly to prevent their children from seeking revenge. For example, preserved in Deuteronomy are these words of Moses:

---

when Sehon offered battle at Jasa, coming out to meet us with all his forces. . . . We made an end of him and of his sons and of all his people, took all his cities there and then, putting all that dwelt there, men, women, and children, to the sword, and spared nothing except the beasts we drove off for our use, and such plunder as captured cities yield.

. . . Og, that was king of Basan, came out to meet us with all his forces, and offered battle at Edrai. . . . So the Lord our God gave us a fresh victory over Og, king of Basan, and all his people, and we exterminated them, there and then laying waste all his cities. . . . We made an end of them as we had made an end of Sehon, that reigned in Hesebon, destroying all the inhabitants of their cities, men, women, and children, plundering their cattle and all the plunder their cities yielded.[25]

In modern times various countries have used extermination as a means of solving a so-called race problem. Arnold Toynbee once said that the "English method of settlement" followed this pattern.[26] The British, through extermination and close confinement of survivors, succeeded in annihilating the entire Tasmanian race between 1803 and 1876.[27] The Dutch considered South African Bushmen less than human and attempted to obliterate them.[28] When the Indians of Brazil resisted the settlement of Portuguese in their land, the Whites solved the problem by systematically killing them. One of their favored means of doing so was to place the clothing of recent smallpox victims in their villages and allow the contagion to decimate the native population.[29] In the 1890s and again in 1915, the Turks massacred hundreds of thousands of Armenians, events still solemnly remembered each year by Armenian-Americans. One classic example in the United States was the massacre at Wounded Knee in 1890, when the Seventh Cavalry killed about two hundred Indian men, women, and children.

Lynchings are not a form of annihilation, for the intent is not to exterminate an entire group but to set an example through selective and drastic punishment.

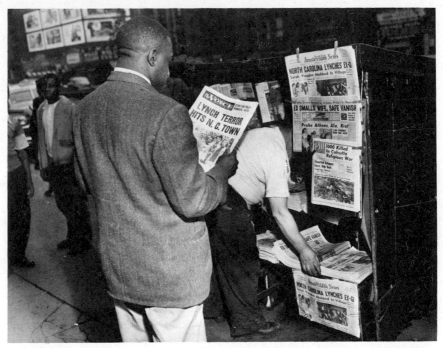

This mid–twentieth century lynching was one of over 5,000 occurring since 1882. Dominant groups have often lynched minority group members not only as a drastic punishment but as an intimidating form of social control to keep others "in line."

Nonetheless, the victims are usually minority-group members, and often that fact is the reason they were hanged instead of receiving some other punishment. Although lynchings have occurred in the United States throughout its history, only since 1882 have reasonably reliable statistics been kept (Figure 4.1). Sources such as the *Chicago Tribune* and Tuskegee Institute, which have kept data on this subject, reveal that five thousand lynchings have occurred since 1882. They have happened in every state except the New England states, with the Deep South (including Texas) claiming the most victims. In fact, 90 percent of the lynchings in this period have occurred in the Southern states; Blacks have accounted for 80 percent of the victims and other minority-group members the remainder. The statistics do not, however, include lynchings during the nation's first hundred years, including those in the western frontier, which would increase the total number of victims, many of them white majority-group members.

Annihilation is sometimes unintended, as when Whites inadvertently spread their sickness to the American and Canadian Indians, Eskimos, and Polynesians. With such ailments as measles, mumps, chicken pox, and smallpox unknown to them, the native populations had little resistance and thus often succumbed to these contagious diseases. Other forms of annihilation, usually intentional, occur during times of mob violence, overzealous police actions, and quiet, calculated small-group actions.[30]

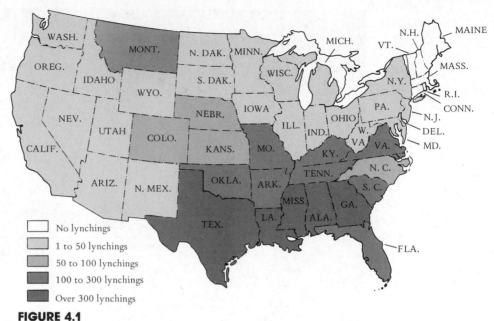

FIGURE 4.1
Lynchings in the United States Since 1882.

EXPLOITATION

Countless writings have enumerated instances of minority group exploitation in all countries. Sometimes the perpetrators of this abuse are members of the same group as, for instance, the crew chiefs of migrant workers and the *padroni* of old Italian immigrant communities, both of whom often benefited at the expense of their own people. Most often, however, dominant-group members exploit minority groups, a practice emphasized by conflict theorists.

Although we shall be utilizing functionalist, conflict, and interactionist theories throughout this book, three conflict analyses will sometimes prove helpful in understanding ethnic antagonism: the power differential, internal colonialism, and the split labor market.

The Power Differential

Stanley Lieberson suggested a **power theory** in which intergroup relations depend on the relative power of the migrant group and the indigenous group.[31] Since the two groups usually do not share the same culture, each will strive to maintain its own institutions. Which group becomes superordinate and which becomes subordinate governs what will follow.

If the newcomers are superior in terms of technology (particularly weapons) and social organization, then conflict may occur at an early stage, and there is likely to be a numerical decline as a result of warfare, disease, or disruption of sustenance activities. The local inhabitants find their institutions undermined or co-opted, and may eventually participate in the institutions of the dominant group. In time a group consciousness may arise, and sometimes the indigenous group will even succeed in ousting the superordinate migrant group. In many former African colonies and in Southeast Asia, when this happened, interethnic fights among the many indigenous groups often led to new forms of superordination and subordination within countries (as was the case in Nigeria and Uganda).

Lieberson maintains that neither conflict nor assimilation is an inevitable outcome of racial and ethnic contact. Instead, the particular relationship between two groups determines which alternative will occur. Conflict between a superordinate migrant group and a subordinate indigenous group can be immediate and violent. If the relationship is the reverse, and the indigenous group is superordinate, conflict will be limited and sporadic, and the host society will exert a great deal of pressure upon the subordinate migrant group to assimilate, acquiesce, or leave. Additionally, the superordinate indigenous group can limit the numbers and groups entering, to reduce any threats of demographic and institutional imbalance. Restrictive immigration laws against the Chinese in 1882 and against all but northern and western Europeans in 1921 and 1924 illustrate this process. Violent union attempts to remove Asian workers, labor union hostility to Blacks, efforts to expel foreigners (such as Indians, Japanese, or Pilipinos) or to revolutionize the social order (Indian boarding schools, the Americanization movement) all illustrate the use of power against minority groups.

Another sociologist, William Wilson, has suggested that power relations between **superordinate** and **subordinate** groups are different in paternalistic and competitive systems.[32] With **paternalism,** (such as South Africa and the Old South), the dominant group has almost absolute control over the subordinate group and can exert almost unlimited coercion to maintain societal order. In a competitive system, such as the United States today, there is some degree of power reciprocity, and so society is somewhat vulnerable to political pressures and economic boycotts.

Rapid social change—industrialization, unionization, urbanization, migration, political changes—usually loosens the social structure, leading to new tensions as both groups seek new power resources. If the minority group increases its power resources through protective laws and improved economic opportunities, it may foresee even greater improvement in its condition. This heightened awareness is likely to lead to conflict unless additional gains are forthcoming. For example, the civil rights movement of the mid-1960s brought about legislation ensuring minority rights and opportunities in jobs, housing, education, and other aspects of life, but this led to new tensions. In the late 1960s there were urban riots and burnings, protest demonstrations and human barricades to stop construction at low-income housing sites, school busing controversies, and challenges against labor discrimination.

The Internal Colonialism Theory

In dealing with the issue of black militancy in the late 1960s, Robert Blauner attempted to integrate the factors of caste and racism, ethnicity, culture, and economic exploitation.[33] Though he focused on American Black–White relations, he did suggest that the Mexican-Americans might also fit his internal colonialism model, and the Native Americans could be added as another suitable example.

Although in this text we shall discuss some similarities between the experiences of Blacks and those of other ethnic groups, Blauner rejects any such comparison.

Of course many ethnic groups in America have lived in ghettoes. What makes the Black ghettoes an expression of colonized status are three special features. First, the ethnic ghettoes arose more from voluntary choice, both in the sense of the choice to immigrate to America and the decision to live among one's fellow ethnics. Second, the immigrant ghettoes tended to be a one and two generation phenomenon; they were actually way-stations in the process of acculturation and assimilation. When they continue to persist as in the case of San Francisco's Chinatown, it is because they are big business for the ethnics themselves and there is a new stream of immigrants. The Black ghetto on the other hand has been a more permanent phenomenon, although some individuals do escape it. But most relevant is the third point. European ethnic groups like the Poles, Italians and Jews generally only experienced a brief period, often less than a generation, during which their residential buildings, commercial stores, and other enterprises were owned by outsiders. The Chinese and Japanese faced handicaps of color prejudice that were almost as strong as the Blacks faced, but very soon gained control of their internal communities, because their traditional ethnic culture and social organization had not been destroyed by slavery and internal colonization. But Afro-Americans are distinct in the extent to which their segregated communities have remained controlled economically, politically, and administratively from the outside.[34]

Several of the above statements need to be modified. Chinatowns have persisted not because of any business advantage, but because of racial discrimination. In proportion to the Chinatown population, only a few Chinese actually benefit from the tourist trade. Second, the Chinese and Japanese *always* had "control of their internal communities," although they differ greatly from one another with respect to their structure and cohesiveness.

The exploitation that was limited for other groups, Blauner sees as more permanent for Blacks and possibly Chicanos. He believes that conflict and confrontation, as well as real or apparent chaos and disorder, will continue, since this may well be the only way in which an internally colonized group can deal with the dominant society. This conflict orientation suggests that the multigenerational exploitation of certain groups creates both a unique situation in comparison with the situation of other groups, and a basis for the conflict—often violent—that marked the late 1960s.

The Split Labor Market Theory

Edna Bonacich theorizes that ethnic antagonism is the result of a combination of economic exploitation by employers and economic competition between two or more groups of laborers that produces a wage differential for labor.[35] She contends that much of the ethnic antagonism is based not on ethnicity and race but on the conflict between higher-paid and lower-paid labor.

> Ethnic antagonism is specifically produced by the competition that arises from a price differential. An oversupply of equal-priced labor does not produce such antagonism, though it too threatens people with the loss of their job. However, hiring practices will not necessarily fall along ethnic lines. . . . All workingmen are on the same footing, competing for scarce jobs. When one ethnic group is decidedly cheaper than another (i.e., when the labor market is split), the higher paid worker faces more than the loss of his job; he faces the possibility that the wage standard in all jobs will be undermined by cheaper labor.[36]

If the higher-paid labor group is racist and is strong enough, it may be able to stop the real or potential cheaper competition through an exclusion movement or caste system. To some degree, America's restriction of Chinese and Japanese immigrant labor, and Australia's restriction of Asian and Polynesian immigrants, are victories for organized labor against lower-paid competition. In a caste system, higher-paid labor controls certain high-paying jobs exclusively and limits the minority group to other, lower-paying jobs. This creates an aristocracy of labor and submerges the labor-market split by stratifying the differentially priced workers. This phenomenon can be seen in the job differentials between Blacks and Whites in certain trade unions.

Some factors lowering the price of one group's labor might be their exploitation by management, their unfamiliarity with wage standards, their language and customs, their lack of economic resources, all of which force them to take even low-paying jobs to survive, contractual commitments before emigrating, or political support from a labor organization or government.

> Governments vary in the degree to which they protect their emigrants. Japan kept close watch over the fate of her nationals who migrated to Hawaii and the Pacific coast. . . . In contrast Mexican migrant workers to the United States have received little protection from their government, and African states were unable to intervene on behalf of slaves brought to America.[37]

When a labor market splits along ethnic lines, racial and ethnic stereotyping becomes a key factor in the labor conflict, and prejudice, ethnic antagonism, and racism become overt. The conflict is not the result of religious differences, nor is it a matter of which group was first to move into the area, since there are examples of ethnic antagonism in which these variables have been controlled. Bonacich argues that the one characteristic shared by all societies high in ethnic antagonism is that they have an indigenous working class that earns higher wages than immigrant workers. Not everyone agrees with this theory. In the case of the anti-Chinese movement led by labor unions, racism was the motivating factor, and white workers offered to work for lower wages if this meant that the Chinese would be removed from their jobs.[38]

In applying the split labor market theory to the history of the Chinese in America between 1848 and 1882, Hilton suggested several modifications.[39] If the economy is expanding and labor shortages occur, ethnic antagonisms are disarmed. Most importantly, an ethnic bourgeoisie necessarily evolves because of the existence of an ethnic labor force.

Native capitalists are seldom equipped to locate and reproduce that ethnic labor force by themselves. Unfamiliarity with the language and customs of Chinese workers made it necessary that white capital rely on an intermediary class of Chinese businessmen for two purposes. First, locating and hiring an adequate number of Chinese workers required that capital act through an intermediate class of Chinese compradors. Second, once obtained, the Chinese labor force had to be provisioned according to their accustomed tastes. This requirement fostered the development of a class of Chinese merchants.[40]

Hilton also indicates that ethnic bourgeoisie is both exploitative, in that it benefits from the ethnic worker, and benevolent, in that it solidifies the ethnic community and provides for its social needs. The ethnic bourgeoisie can affect a split labor market because its stronger economic and political base, and often higher educational level, enable it to act on behalf of the ethnic group. Although it does not always do so, the ethnic bourgeoisie can articulate the injustices of a caste system and challenge restrictive institutions.

A bourgeoisie arises from within the ranks of any ethnic group at some stage in their readjustment to life in America. Most notable are the *padroni* among the Italian and Greek immigrants and the *padrinos* among Puerto Rican and Mexican laborers.

Limitations of These Theories

The power theory offers one variable to explain conflict or acceptance patterns; this does not provide insight into all conflicts, however, such as those between a superordinate indigenous group and a subordinate migrant group. Blauner's internal colonialism theory applies only to three groups—Blacks, Chicanos, and Native Americans. Bonacich's emphasis on the labor market is helpful, but her theory does not deal with other sources of prejudice, such as racial or religious antipathy or culture clash. In short, none of these theories can satisfactorily explain most dominant-minority interaction. Many situations are quite complex and defy a single causative explanation. Other instances do show recurring patterns; in these cases, given an understanding of their limitations, theories such as those proposed by Lieberson, Blauner, and Bonacich can provide some insights into the minority experience.

RETROSPECT

Minority-group responses to prejudice and discrimination may be acceptance, avoidance, deviance, or defiance, depending in large measure upon the group's perception of its power to change the status quo. After continual treatment as an inferior, a negative self-image may result. Another consequence of continued inequality is its intensification through a vicious circle or cumulative causation process.

Marginality is a social phenomenon occurring during the transitional period of assimilation; it can be either a stressful or sheltered experience, depending upon the support system of the ethnic community. Some groups become middleman minorities because of their historical background or sojourner orientation; they can remain indefinitely in that intermediate place in the social hierarchy, the potential scapegoat target of those above and below them, or achieve upward mobility and assimilation.

Dominant-group actions toward the minority group may also take various forms, including favorable or indifferent responses. When the reaction is a negative one, the group in power may place restraints upon the minority group (for example, legislative controls, segregation, or suppression). If the reaction becomes more emotional or even xenophobic, expulsion or annihilation may occur. Sensitivity to world opinion and economic dependency on other nations in the modern world may curtail such actions. When the dominant group reacts more favorably to the minority group, intergroup tensions may be resolved through genuine or token reform.

Whether the indigenous or migrant group possesses superior power determines the nature of intergroup relations. Another influence is whether the social system is paternalistic or competitive. Consideration of black and Hispanic ghettoes or Indian reservations as examples of internal colonialism offers a second conflict perspective. A third is a split-labor market view of differential wage levels sparking ethnic antagonism. A final consideration is the rise of an ethnic bourgeoisie which is both exploitative and benevolent.

KEY TERMS

Acceptance	**Cumulative causation**
Annihilation	**Defiance**
Avoidance	**Deviance**

Exploitation

Expulsion

Internal colonialism

Marginality

Middleman minority

Negative self-image

Paternalism

Power differential

Power theory

Social segregation

Spatial segregation

Split labor market

Subordinate

Superordinate

Vicious circle

Xenophobia

REVIEW QUESTIONS

1. What are some common minority-group responses to prejudice and discrimination?

2. What are some common majority-group responses to minorities?

3. Explain marginality and why it may or may not be a stressful experience.

4. What are middleman minorities and how do they affect acceptance?

5. Discuss three conflict viewpoints about exploitation of minorities.

SUGGESTED READINGS

Blalock, Hubert M., Jr. *Toward a Theory of Minority Group Relations.* New York: John Wiley & Sons, 1967.

Still an influential work, describing conceptual frameworks for understanding dominant-minority relations, including self-serving discrimination and middleman minorities.

Bonacich, Edna and John Modell. *The Economic Basis of Ethnic Solidarity.* Berkeley, Calif.: University of California Press, 1980.

Building upon middleman minority theory, an examination of Japanese cohesiveness leading to socioeconomic advancement.

Curran, Thomas J. *Xenophobia and Immigration, 1820–1930,* Boston: Twayne, 1975.

A detailed historial account of the persistence of the xenophobic spirit in America, the fear the stranger threatened American culture.

Mason, Philip. *Patterns of Dominance.* New York: Oxford University Press, 1970.

Readable and comprehensive analysis of dominant-group actions to maintain their privileged position in society.

PART TWO

WHITE ETHNIC MINORITIES

CHAPTER 5

THE "OLD" IMMIGRANTS: NORTHERN AND WESTERN EUROPEANS

A trickle of immigrants from almost all parts of the world arrived during the early history of the United States. The story of the colonial period and the first one hundred years as an independent nation, however, is predominantly the experience of immigrants from the British Isles, France, Holland, Scandinavia, and Germany, and their descendants.

SOCIOHISTORICAL PERSPECTIVE

At first, all Europeans were strangers to these shores, and they responded with wonder and excitement in their journals and reports about the vastness, resources, and promise of the New World. In those early years, all shared in the adventure of creating a new society. First the necessity to survive, then pro- or anti-British sentiments dominated relations among diverse peoples. As life stabilized and a common culture evolved, many newcomers not only found themselves in strange surroundings, but were more quickly perceived as strangers in a society in which homogeneity had come to be taken for granted. Thus, many Irish and Germans, with their cultural, religious, and social-class differences from the natives, often experienced open hostility upon their arrival.

Before examining the connection between theory and the actual experience of any group, note that a pitfall is inherent in considering ethnic groups only within a limited historical framework. A tendency to do so results from the fact that immigration patterns have varied among countries and have peaked at different times. The word *peak* provides a clue to how the experiences of each racial or ethnic group should be viewed. Although each minority group usually has had a significant period of migration, thus providing a focal point for examination, each country has sent a continual flow of immigrants over the years. It follows, then, that the immigrants' experiences have varied with changing conditions and that each nationality has usually had a first-generation American grouping at any given time.

The Colonial Period

Members of each ethnic group came to the New World for economic, political, or religious reasons, or sometimes for the adventure of beginning a new life in a new land. As strangers, most encountered yet another ethnic group—the American Indians—who at a much earlier time may have been immigrants to this land as well. Although limited social interaction between the European settlers and the natives occurred, their cultural differences frequently resulted in a xenophobic reaction from both sides. The story of Indian–White relations is usually one of misunderstanding, fear, suspicion, exploitation, hostility, and violence. Coming from vastly different cultural worlds, they quickly came into conflict with one another.

Cultural Diversity

From the moment the first Europeans settled in America, cultural differences existed throughout the land. The settlements were culturally distinct from one another in nationality or religion, like, for example, the Puritans in Massachusetts and the Congregationalists in Connecticut. Some settlements, even in their very early stages, were composed of a mixture of ethnic groups. To strengthen his Pennsylvania colony, the English Quaker William Penn recruited several hundred Dutch and many more German settlers. In fact, the "Pennsylvania Dutch" are actually Germans, the word *Dutch* being a corruption of *Deutsch,* which means German. The settlement of New Amsterdam in the colony of New Netherland was also a pluralistic community, reflecting the home country's positive attitude toward minorities and refugees within its border.

In 1660, William Kieft, the Dutch governor of New Netherland, remarked to the French Jesuit Issac Jogues that there were eighteen languages spoken at or near Fort Amsterdam at the tip of Manhattan Island. . . . The first shipload of settlers sent out by the Dutch was made up largely of French-speaking Protestants. British, Germans, Finns, Jews, Swedes, Africans, Italians, Irish [quickly] followed, beginning a stream that has never yet stopped.[1]

Religious differences caused social problems more frequently than did nationality during this period. Many people who first crossed the Atlantic as immigrants had been religious dissenters in their native land and were seeking a utopia in the new land—a place with religious harmony. Unfortunately, they brought with them their own religious prejudices. Although they themselves came seeking religious freedom, they were intolerant of others with different religious beliefs. When the Colonies were mostly Protestant, there was antagonism among the various denominations and sects. Later, when Catholic immigrants arrived, the old hostilities that had existed in Europe generations earlier manifested themselves once again in the United States.

Expulsion and Avoidance

The most frequently cited example of expulsion during the colonial period is that of the Puritans driving out the "heretic" Roger Williams and his followers, who settled in Rhode Island. Of course, the settlers also displaced the Indians, often forcibly. Many of the early settlers—for example, the Pilgrims, the French Huguenots, and the Sephardic Jews—had themselves been driven from their native lands in Europe.

With ample land available in the seventeenth and eighteenth centuries, religious, national, or racial groups experiencing prejudice and discrimination could move elsewhere if they wished. As long as there was open land, many did so, forming new societies or living in isolation in small family groups. Driven from New York State at gunpoint in the early nineteenth century, the Mormons exemplify both expulsion and avoidance. As they journeyed westward, they frequently encountered intense hostility and violence because of their religious beliefs and their practice of polygamy. They crossed the country seeking a place of refuge until they were able to make their home in the still unsettled regions of Utah, Nevada, and California.

Spatial Segregation

The early settlements of the seventeenth century—Jamestown (Virginia), Plymouth (Massachusetts), New Sweden (Delaware and New Jersey). New Amsterdam (New York), Philadelphia (Pennsylvania)—were actually small ethnic enclaves. Immigrants from different countries and with differing religious beliefs settled among their own kind. Even in the pluralistic settlements in Philadelphia and New Amsterdam, members of the various ethnic groups sought to live near their own people. Each of these instances of residential clustering in a recognizable ethnic community was a voluntary act of spatial segregation. In the years to follow, other minority groups would also congregate within well-defined communities, either by choice or because of societal demands.

During the colonial period these Americans welcomed the newer immigrants as buffers along the frontier, but it was a "welcome tinged with misgivings."[2] The immigrants' good character and ability to support themselves were considered more important than their nationality; nevertheless, the Germans, French, and Scotch-Irish did encounter hostility from time to time.

The immigrants originally lived in scattered ethnic settlements. As the English came to dominate, they inhabited primarily the Eastern Seaboard. Some minority peoples settled in ethnic pockets in this region, while others settled on the edge of the frontier. Most of this spatial segregation was voluntary, as virgin land was available to all who wished to strike out on their own. The immigrants had come to the new land to start a new life, and found their own land to do so.

The Early National Period

Many new immigrants arrived during the immediate post-Revolution period, and an antiforeign attitude, sporadic and localized until then, asserted itself. Both political factions feared that their opponents would benefit from the newcomers. The Jeffersonians were alarmed at the arrival of so many refugees, particularly the French, from the collapsing European aristocracies. The Federalists, the conservatives of their day, feared that the ranks of the anti-Federalists would grow, since poor immigrants, particularly the Irish, had no commitment to preserving a strong central government.

Whatever their motives, the dominant English-Americans' beliefs about and actions toward the newly arriving northern and western European immigrants followed a familiar pattern in dominant-minority relations. Suspicious of those different from themselves, the members of the dominant culture felt threatened.

In a letter to John Adams in 1798, George Washington indicated his reservations about newcomers, especially when they settled in their own little communities. His words are similar to others to be uttered in the nineteenth and twentieth centuries.

My opinion, with respect to immigration, is that except of useful mechanics and some particular descriptions of men or professions, there is no need of encouragement, while the policy or advantage of its taking place in a body (I mean the settling of them in a body) may be much questioned; for, by so doing, they retain the language, habits and principles (good or bad) which they bring with them.[3]

Xenophobia

Many Federalists, in fact, believed that the large foreign-born population was the root of all the evil in the United States. In letters, speeches, and newspapers they expressed the fear that

coming from "a quarter of the world so full of disorder and corruption" as Europe, it was to be feared that immigrants would "contaminate the purity and simplicity of the American character"; warned "their principles spread like the leaven of unright-eousness; the weak, the ignorant and the needy are thrown into a ferment, and corruption threatens the whole mass." True some immigrants were industrious, peaceable, and voted the Federalist ticket—but for one such "good" European, la-mented Noah Webster, "we receive three or four discontented, factious men—the convicts, fugitives of justice, hirelings of France, and disaffected offscourings of other nations." "Generally speaking," said a Federalist, "none but the most vile and worthless, none but the idle and discontented, the disorderly and the wicked, have inundated upon us from Europe." Clearly, the property and the virtue of the United States would not be secure until foreign immigration had been reduced to a mere trickle of hand-picked newcomers of approved political sympathies.[4]

William Smith Shaw, the young nephew of President John Adams, wrote to the First Lady in 1798, "The grand cause of our present difficulties may be traced . . . to so many hordes of Foreigners imigrating [sic] to America. . . . Let us no longer pray that America may become an asylum to all nations."[5]

Legislative Action

The Federalists attempted to limit all office holding to the native-born and to ex-tend the period for naturalization from five to fourteen years. Although they suc-ceeded in having the longer periods enacted, the states—faced with the problems of establishing a new nation—successfully evaded this legislation.

In 1798, with a volatile situation in Europe and a distinct possibility of war with France, the Federalists succeeded in passing a series of laws known collectively as the Alien and Sedition Acts. Many factors contributed to the successful passage of this notorious legislation. One factor was the presence of a large foreign-born population, perceived as a threat to the stability of the country. Significantly, the legislation passed because of sectional block voting, with New England almost unanimously in favor of the bills. Few foreigners resided in New England, and hence little contact had occurred; nonetheless, widespread negative stereotyping existed in that region. Jefferson's election to the presidency in 1800 ended this xenophobia, and the acts were abrogated.

Population Composition

At this stage in history, the young nation possessed several distinct ethnic groups, differing in heritage, language, customs, and religion. Within the several states ad-mitted to the Union lived the northern and western Europeans, dominated by the

English Protestants. The French lived in the New Orleans region and gave the country its only ethnic flavor truly distinct from the English and the various Indian tribes. In the territories awaiting conquest and statehood were other Indian tribes and the Spanish. Of course, many other ethnic groups were present—though relatively small in numbers—and contributed to the growth and development of the young nation.

The Pre-Civil War Period

Not until 1820 did the national census include a person's country of origin as part of its data, and new regulations required shipmasters to submit passenger lists to customs officials. This census (which excluded the Indians) listed approximately 9.6 million Americans, of whom 20 percent were Blacks and most of the remainder white Protestants from northern and western Europe. Between 1820 and 1860, over 5 million immigrants—more than half the U.S. population in 1820 and more than the entire population in 1790—would cross the Atlantic and Pacific oceans to disembark on American shores.

In these forty years preceding the Civil War, the first great wave of immigrants produced still more arrivals from England and Scandinavia. Ireland and Germany, however, supplied the greatest numbers. In fact, so great was the Irish immigration that they accounted for 44 percent of all immigration in the 1830s and 49 percent of all immigration in the 1840s. Consequently, they accounted for 7 percent of the total population by the end of the Civil War. Not only was the arrival of so many foreigners overwhelming, but many of the newcomers were Catholic—a religion to which many Protestant groups were openly hostile.

The Battery, New York City, 1855, where European immigrants disembarked. Castle Garden, the Predecessor of Ellis Island as the government's immigrant processing center, is on the left.

Structural Conditions

The land the immigrants came to in the first half of the nineteenth century was quite different from that of past centuries. From rudimentary beginnings a nation had evolved, bursting with exuberance and confidence. A common culture now prevailed, marked by strong beliefs in Protestantism, individual enterprise, and political democracy. The institutions of society were strongly linked to an Anglo-Saxon heritage. Americans admired and emulated English writers. In a new country filled with nationalistic fervor, England was still the model for a civilization.

Along the East Coast and in the large cities west of the Appalachian Mountains, life was stable and established. Although regional variations as well as differences in religion and social status existed, the prevailing cultural norms were relatively homogenous.

Urban living conditions, particularly for the poor Irish immigrants, were very substandard, even for those days. The poverty-stricken newcomers, forced to live in a squalid environment, suffered high disease and mortality rates, as well as the condemnation of the dominant society for living the way they did. Like so many others in the generations that followed, such critics did not realize that their own attitudes and actions might well have helped to create the situation in the first place.

Typical of overcrowded cellars was a house in Pike Street which contained a cellar ten feet square and seven feet high, with one small window and an old-fashioned

This immigrant poses upon his bed for the previous four years, circa 1890. Many poverty-stricken immigrants lived in such damp, unlit, unventilated, dirt-floor cellars, often contracting tuberculosis and other debilitating diseases.

inclined cellar door; here lived two families consisting of ten persons of all ages. The occupants of these basements led miserable lives as troglodytes amid darkness, dampness, and poor ventilation. Rain water leaked through cracks in the walls and floors and frequently flooded the cellars; refuse filtered down from the upper stories and mingled with the seepage from outdoor privies. From such an abode emerged the "whitened and cadaverous countenance" of the cellar dweller.[6]

Xenophobia

Americans perceived the large influx of immigrants between 1820 and 1860 as a threat to their institutions and their social order. Not only were many of the newcomers Catholic, but they were also from countries embroiled in political turmoil. Anxiety mounted over the imagined radical threat as well as the Catholic threat.

In the 1830s, antiforeign organizations, calling themselves "Native" Americans, originated in many cities. They frequently raised up "mobs" to burn Catholic convents, churches and homes, assault nuns, and murder Irishmen, Germans, and Negroes."[7] These sporadic outbursts gradually coalesced into the powerful Know-Nothing movement of the 1850s. They unleashed a vicious hate campaign, frequently accompanied by brutal violence, particularly in the large cities where many immigrants lived. Surprisingly successful, the Know-Nothings "became the magnet for all dazed elements in the political whirlpool; they fed on pathological fears and fanned to white heat all the petty animosities that had bored into the public mind."[8]

A Whig presidential candidate, General Winfield Scott, waged an anti-Catholic, antiforeign campaign with Know-Nothing support, but lost badly to Democrat Franklin Pierce in 1852. By 1854 the Know-Nothing Party was strong enough to elect seventy-five congressmen and many city, county, and state officials.[9] In 1855 the party elected six governors, and many contemporaries believed that this reactionary movement would capture the White House in the 1856 election.[10] A strong candidate, former President Millard Fillmore, sought to return to office on the Know-Nothing ticket. The conservative Whig party endorsed Fillmore, but a serious split within its ranks, with defections to Republican candidate John C. Fremont, enabled Democrat James Buchanan to win the three-way race. The bitter sectional rivalry of the Civil War period effectively ended this ethnocentric-turned-xenophobic movement.

Not all voices were raised against the European expatriates. In defense of the newcomers, Harriet Martineau (*Society in America,* 1837) answered some of the criticisms:

It would certainly be better that the immigrants should be well-clothed, educated, respectable people (except that, in that case, they would probably never arrive). But the blame of their bad condition rests elsewhere, while their arrival is, generally speaking, a pure benefit. . . . Every American can acknowledge that few or no canals or railroads would be in existence now in the United States, but for the Irish labor by which they have been completed; and the best cultivation that is to be seen in the land is owing to the Dutch and Germans it contains.[11]

Ralph Waldo Emerson, an articulate literary figure of the times, was also a popular speaker on the lyceum lecture circuit. In those days many communities had a *lyceum,* or association, for discussion and popular instruction by lectures or other means. In his lectures, Emerson tried to convince his listeners through an eloquent expression of deeply felt ideas. One of his journal entries in 1845 shows how he tried to combat the nativism movement by stressing the "smelting-pot" concept.

I hate the narrowness of the Native American Party. It is the dog in the manger. It is precisely opposite to true wisdom. . . . Well, as in the old burning of the Temple at Corinth, by the melting and intermixture of silver and gold and other metals, a new compound more precious than any, called Corinthian brass, was formed; so in this continent—asylum of all nations,—the energy of Irish, Swedes, Poles, and Cossacks, and all the European tribes,—of the Africans, and of the Polynesians, will construct a new race, a new religion, a new state, a new literature, which will be as vigorous as the new Europe which came out of the smelting-pot of the Dark Ages, or that which earlier emerged from the Pelasgic and Etruscan barbarism.[12]

Currents and countercurrents occurred then, as now. Not all members of the same ethnic group encountered problems, nor did all native-born Americans react so negatively to the newcomers. Yet patterns of harmony or conflict did exist, and they very often depended upon the degree of cultural and structural differentiation that existed in each region.

THE ENGLISH

Despite earlier explorations by other countries, the English were the first white ethnic group to establish permanent settlements in the New World. The first two successful ones were Jamestown and Plimmoth (Plymouth) Plantation (the word *plantation* was first used in the North).

These two settlements were culturally quite different from one another; they offer an excellent example of cultural diversity among the same nationality as opposed to a stereotyped concept of a people. Jamestown served as the seed from which the Southern aristocracy and slavery would grow. Plymouth was the forerunner of town meetings (participatory democracy), the abolition movement, and "Yankee ingenuity" (capitalistic enterprise). Many factors, such as the different purposes of the settlements, and different religions, climates, and terrains, played a role in determining the unfolding of events and life styles.

The writings of William Bradford, the first governor of the Plymouth colony, provide evidence that the English were an ethnically conscious people. More than 360 years have passed since the time of the Pilgrims, but Bradford's words regarding their experiences could apply to many other immigrant groups—past, present, and future.

The Departure

Leaving one's native land for another country known only by reputation can be an awesome experience. For many it is a time of joy and sorrow, anticipation and trepidation. People know what they are leaving behind, but they are not certain what they will find. The Pilgrims first fled England for Holland, which opened its doors to all refugees, and later journeyed to the United States. In the following passages, Bradford is speaking about the Pilgrims' journey to Holland, but the locale is only incidental to the expression of the immigrant's typical sensations.

Being thus constrained to leave their native soil and country, their lands and livings, and all their friends and familiar acquaintances, it was much, and thought marvelous by many. But to go into a country they knew not but by hearsay, where they must learn a new language and get their livings they knew not how, it being a dear place and subject to the miseries of war, it was by many thought an adventure almost desperate; a case intolerable and a misery worse than death.[13]

Culture Shock

Arrival at one's destination brings with it culture contact. One's world of reality, that familiar way of life one accepts subconsciously, is jolted to some degree as the group encounters a different civilization. Bradford continues:

Being now come into the Low Countries, they saw many goodly and fortified cities, strongly walled and guarded with troops of armed men. Also, they heard a strange and uncouth language, and beheld the different manners and customs of the people, with their strange fashions and attires, all so far differing from that of their plain country villages (where they were bred and had so long lived) as it seemed they were come into a new world.[14]

Resisting Assimilation

Not all immigrants desire to be full, participating citizens in the country to which they move. Many, in fact, do not become naturalized citizens. Although they are starting a new life, they do not necessarily intend to forsake their cultural heritage. More often, they seek to preserve that heritage as a familiar world in a strange land, and to pass it on to their children. Often the children become assimilated into the new ways despite their parents' efforts. The Pilgrims feared that their children would be assimilated into the Dutch culture, and viewed such an outcome as an evil to be avoided.

But that which was more lamentable, and of all sorrows most heavy to be borne, was that many of their children, by these occasions and the great licentiousness of youth in that country, and the manifold temptations of the place, were drawn away by evil examples into extravagant and dangerous courses, getting the reins off their necks and departing from their parents. . . . So that they saw their posterity would be in danger to degenerate and be corrupted.[15]

English Influence

The English immigrants' major impact on American culture occurred during the colonial period. Settling in the thirteen original Colonies, they so established themselves that succeeding generations were culturally and numerically dominant by the time of the American Revolution. In 1790, about 78 percent of the population could claim nationality or descent from the British Isles (see Table 5-1). This large majority of English-speaking citizens made an indelible imprint upon American culture in language, law, customs, and values. The wars of 1776 and 1812 notwithstanding, the descendants of English immigrants still prided themselves on their heritage, as indicated in their writings at that time. For example, in his *Sketchbook,* Washington Irving encouraged Americans to pattern themselves after the English nation rather than any other.

After 1825, when the British Parliament repealed the ban on the emigration of artisans, many English, Scottish, and Irish mill hands came to southern Massachusetts and Philadelphia. There they found work in the textile factories, often at twice or more the salary they had been earning at home. As experienced mill operatives, the English continued to come throughout the nineteenth century, especially to the Massachusetts towns of Fall River and New Bedford. When the American silk industry clustered in Paterson, New Jersey, in the 1840s, many British immigrants moved there, several of them starting their own factories. British immigrants formed a solid base for the rising American textile industry, and many became managers and proprietors.[16]

TABLE 5.1
U.S. White Ethnic Population in 1790

	%
English	60.1
Scottish, Scotch-Irish	14.0
German	8.6
Irish	3.6
Dutch	3.1
French, Swedish	3.0
Other	7.6
Total	100.0%

These estimates from the American Historical Association come from a surname analysis of the 3.9 million people listed in the 1790 census. Slaves accounted for approximately 20% of the total population.

Many British coal miners also came, but by the latter part of the nineteenth century they were being replaced by Slavic and Italian workers. Those who remained in the coal industry were usually supervisors and foremen. Some British farmers also emigrated to the United States, scattering throughout the Midwest. British immigrants of all occupations seldom concentrated in any one area, going instead wherever the job market led them.

As foreigners with the same language and cultural heritage as the dominant society, British immigrants seldom experienced prejudice or discrimination in the United States. Rowland Berthoff cites numerous studies and reports indicating that the English were rarely ridiculed on the vaudeville stage except as titled fops (an inaccurate representation). Ethnophaulisms did not exist, except for such inoffensive nicknames as "John Bull" or "limey," and even these were not widely used.[17]

Yet the British were not always comfortable in the new land. Ilja M. Dijour found similar results among immigrants to other countries and reported, "The return of British from Australia, South Africa, and Canada or of Portuguese from Brazil, or Spaniards and Italians from the rest of Latin America is incomparably higher than the re-emigration of say Japanese from Brazil, Slavic people from Australia or Canada, or others." Dijour explained that a major cause of these findings was that the first group had the exaggerated expectation of finding no differences in the new country, whereas the second group was psychologically prepared to find everything different in the new country.[18] Those not expecting to be strangers were unprepared when they realized that they actually were strangers.

During the first hundred years after American independence, many British immigrants found the new country less inviting than England. Comparing the criticisms of seventy-five returnees prior to 1865, Wilbur Shepperson found some common themes reflecting a failure of the new land to live up to their expectations.

The Republic was peopled by men of action who cared little for the deeper meaning of life, who were blind to the beauties of their natural environment, and who were hostile to refinement and sensitivity.

. . . Rather than vigorous, they found America boring; rather than questioning and vital, republican communities were suspicious and moribund. Although they were often unemployed, Americans boasted of their economic opportunities; although they condemned politicians, they defended the political system; although they advocated freedom, they enforced conformity. . . .

Knowledge of the language allowed for rapid assimilation of English immigrants, but at the same time it permitted them to compare critically American authors, newspapers, and theaters with those at home. Acquaintance with English government and legal traditions provided easy understanding of American law, but it sometimes provoked censure of political methods and frontier justice. Nearness to markets, cheap labor, and advanced technological methods in Britain often led immigrants of the entrepreneur class to despair of the New World's inefficient agricultural methods and unorthodox business practices. British workers once associated with the trade union or Chartist movements found American labor groups lacking in organization, leadership, and purpose.[19]

In the post-Civil War period, some degree of Anglophobia still prevailed, and British immigrants discovered that they had to exercise self-restraint to be accepted as Americans. An ethnic consciousness led many British to resent this necessity and to dislike the ways of the new country. Between 1881 and 1889, a total of 370,697 British and Irish aliens left the United States for their native land.[20]

In fact, in all things but money and quick promotion, British-Americans thought the United States a debased copy of their homeland. Many seemingly familiar customs and institutions had lost their British essence. "The Land of Slipshod," one immigrant in 1885 called the country, its language not English but a "silly idiotic jargon—a mere jumble of German idioms and popular solecisms, savored by a few Irish blunders," the enforcement of its basically English legal code "totally farcical," and its children half-educated, spoiled, and unruly. . . . Many returned home discontented with "the manners and habits of the people."
. . . Although as the years passed the immigrants' personal ties came to be in America rather than in Britian, their fondness for and pride in the old country waxed. British travelers found them everywhere, "British in heart and memory,
. . . always with a touch of the exile, eager to see an English face and to hear an English voice!"[21]

Despite certain similarities, enough differences and ethnic consciousness remained to restrain British immigrants from merging in a totally smooth fashion. Second-generation British-Americans, however, had no such problem and identified with the United States as their country.

England was the source of great many immigrants over the years; between 1820 and 1980, a total of 3.2 million people came to the United States from England.[22] It ranks seventh in the list of nations that have supplied immigrants to the United States since 1820. Even though England has been one of the four largest European suppliers of immigrants throughout much of the 1970s, these immigrants are not a very visible ethnic group because they are not readily detected as strangers.

THE DUTCH

In recent years Dutch immigration has been low, around 1,000 per year in the 1970s; however, the total immigration from the Netherlands in the 1820–1980 period was 361,994, placing it among the twenty-five nations supplying the largest number of immigrants.[23] Curiously, almost 50 percent of the Dutch immigration occurred from 1880 to 1920, when immigrants from southern, central, and eastern Europe dominated among the incoming nationalities. Despite these statistics, the major impact of Dutch influence upon American society, which is quite significant, comes from a much earlier period.

During the Age of Exploration, sea captains for the Dutch East India Company sailed into the uncharted waters of the New World. From their explorations, they provided important information that encouraged the organization of a trading center, Fort Nassau, on an island in the Hudson just south of Albany. Some of these sea captains became famous—for example, Henrik Hudson and Adriaen Block, for whom, respectively, a river and an island are named.

In 1624 thirty Dutch families settled in Beverwyck, later called Albany, and in 1625 the Dutch built a moat and fort on Manhattan Island and called it New Amsterdam. A year later Governor Peter Minuit concluded his famous deal and bought the whole island from the Indians for sixty guilders—twenty-four dollars—worth of merchandise.

Pearl Street in present-day New York City marks the limit of dry land in the days of New Amsterdam, where palisades had been erected against Indian raiders. In Dutch, these were called *de wal,* and thus the northern boundary gave its name to the Wall Street of today. Breukelen (later Brooklyn) became a town in 1646. Peter Stuyvesant's farm or *bouwerij* in Manhattan, where he lived after the English takeover in 1664 until his death in 1672, gave its name to the Bowery, a well-known street in New York.

Other Dutch settlements sprang up in the Bronx, on Staten Island, in New Jersey at Bergen (named after a town in Holland, and later known as Jersey City), at Ridgewood, at Hackensack, in the Raritan and Ramapo valleys, and in South Carolina at St. James Island. So widespread were the Dutch settlements and so strong was the Dutch imprint that Dutch remained a major language in American society for quite some time.

Structural Conditions

During the colonial period, few Dutch were willing to exchange the security at home for the hardships of the New World. With their stable economy and a harmonious society, the Dutch had little inducement to venture forth in great numbers as other ethnic groups had. Urban areas in Holland had heterogeneous populations because the Dutch had offered shelter to many refugees from other countries. In seeking to establish trading settlements in the New World, the Dutch therefore sought other minority-group members willing to journey to the New World. As a result, immigrant Dutch settlements became as heterogeneous as their counterparts in Holland.

The spirit of seventeenth-century Holland resulted in a cosmopolitan and tolerant atmosphere in New Amsterdam that outlasted Holland's rule. The somewhat more relaxed atmosphere of New Amsterdam contrasted with that of the English colonies to the north, restricted by their rigid blue laws. New York City, with its large number of places to eat, drink, and dance, seems to have inherited this New Amsterdam characteristic. Sports were popular too. The colonists loved boat and carriage races, and from Holland they imported the game of *kolf,* which later became golf.

The English takeover of New Amsterdam in 1664 caused no hardship for the Dutch settlers. They enjoyed a basically favorable social environment during the time of the American Colonies, in the post-Revolutionary War period, and thereafter. A relatively tolerant people in an intolerant age, similar in physical appearance and religious beliefs to other Americans, the Dutch were generally accepted, though sometimes they were the butt of gentle humor as illustrated in the writings of Washington Irving.

Holland's early support of the American Revolution and its status as the second country to give formal recognition to the United States further strengthened positive American attitudes toward the Dutch. In 1782, John Adams succeeded in securing the first loan for Congress from three Amsterdam banking houses; the loan was for five million guilders, or 2 million dollars—a very substantial amount in those days. By 1794 the total amount loaned by Holland had risen to thirty million guilders, or twelve million dollars. This amount comprised most of the foreign debt incurred by the United States.

In 1846 a group of religious separatists settled in what became Holland, Michigan. Spurred by religious and economic motives, a new wave of Dutch immigrants followed suit, settling mostly in Michigan, Iowa, Wisconsin, and Illinois because of their favorable soil and climate conditions. The social bond proved to be religion rather than nationality, and schisms ensued, resulting in the Dutch Reformed Church, the Christian Reformed Church, and the Netherland Reformed Church. The success of the first group's efforts to propagate the faith and achieve higher social standing rested partly upon Hope College in Holland, Michigan. Their success encouraged the Christian Reformed Church, a more conservative group, to establish Calvin College in Grand Rapids to achieve the same objectives for their people.

Pluralism

The Dutch immigrants who came here, whether during the colonial period or the nineteenth century, found their liberal attitude toward other groups was usually reciprocated. They were a distinct ethnic group in language as well as in other ways—but they generally found a friendly atmosphere wherever they went. Nonetheless, like many other nationalities yet to come, some of whom would not find such openness, they formed their own enclaves and tried to preserve their language and traditions through their own churches, schools, and associations.

Dutch culture and influence persisted for many generations despite the Anglo-Saxon cultural dominance, for several reasons. The Dutch were self-sufficient and enjoyed high social standing in the society. Their church, rather than American ways, formed the basis of their social life; the more orthodox they were, the more they resisted assimilation. A steady migration into concentrated residential communities reinforced the old ways. Finally, a friendly atmosphere enabled the Dutch to coexist in a pluralistic society.

The following passage gives some insight into the extensive use of the Dutch

"Departure From Home"

Sweethearts, wives, and children leave the ship before it sails, carrying to America the men seeking a better life. Some returned after earning money, while others eventually could afford to send for the rest of their family. Engraving from *Harper's Weekly,* June 26, 1858.

language and the resistance to the English language. Note, for example, that not until 1774 were the children taught English, more than one hundred years after New York became an English colony.

In 1764 Dr. Archibald Laidlie preached the first English sermon to the Dutch Reformed congregation in New York City. Ten years later English was introduced in the schools. In Kingston, Dutch was used in church as late as 1808. A few years before, a traveler had reported that "on Long Island, in New York, along the North River, at Albany, how Dutch was in general still the common language of most of the old people." Francis Adrian van der Kemp, who had come to this country as a refugee in 1788, wrote that his wife was able to converse in Dutch with the wives of Alexander Hamilton and General George Clinton. Much later, in 1847, immigrants from Holland were upon their arrival welcomed in Dutch by the Reverend Isaac Wyckoff of New York, a descendant of one of the first settlers in Rensselaerwyck, who only in school had learned to speak English; and until very recently many communities in New Jersey adhered to the tradition of a monthly church service in Dutch. As late as 1905 Dutch was still heard among the old people in the Ramapo Valley of that state.[24]

Although most of the Dutch immigrants have come to the United States during the same period as the southern, central, and eastern Europeans, they have not encountered ethnic antagonism and they have assimilated more easily. Their physical features, their religion, their comparatively small numbers, and their more urbanized background have enabled them to both adapt to and gain approval from the dominant society more easily than other groups.

THE FRENCH

French-Americans fall into three population segments: migrants from France, migrants from French Canada (who have settled primarily in New England), and French Louisianans brought under U.S. jurisdiction. (The French Louisianans, also known as "Cajuns," were expelled from Acadia, French Canada, by the British in 1755, and by 1790 about 4,000 of them had resettled in Louisiana.) Each group's experiences have been somewhat different, illustrating different patterns in dominant-minority relations.

Marginality and Assimilation

In the seventeenth century, the Huguenots fled either to Holland or to the United States to escape religious persecution. It is often thought that because of their Protestantism, their willingness to work hard, their conversion to the Anglican Church, and their rapid adoption of the English language, the Huguenots assimilated easily into colonial society. However, the transition was not altogether a smooth one, and the second generation apparently agonized over their marginal status in the same way as other groups did.

> By 1706, sufficient time had elapsed since the Revocation[in 1685 Louis XIV formally eliminated religious liberty, causing the renewal of persecution and extermination of the Huguenots] to give rise to a younger generation unsatisfied with the adherence to old French forms, a generation adverse to a language not in general use in the province, clamoring for the new and the popular. . . . The children of many of the refugees were even ashamed to bear French names. The idea of remaining foreigners in a land in which they were born and reared was alien to their thought.[25]

Encountering distrust and some violence from the dominant society, partly explained by the frequent hostilities between England and France, the Huguenots tried to Anglicize themselves as quickly as possible to avoid further unpleasantness. They changed their names and their customs, learned to speak English, and soon succeeded in assimilating completely into American society. For them, assimilation and loss of ethnic identity was the desired goal. Not all Americans or ethnic groups agree with such a goal; many prefer instead a pluralistic society.

With time, attitudes changed. The Revolutionary War period made England an enemy and France an ally. The Marquis de Lafayette was a war hero, and such popular figures as Benjamin Franklin and Thomas Jefferson openly admired the French and their culture.

Francophobia

When the French Revolution was still in its moderately liberal stage, the Jeffersonians were French sympathizers and the Federalists vehemently anti-French. Then came the celebrated XYZ Affair, in which French officials demanded bribes before permitting U.S. diplomats to secure desired conferences or agreements. This inflamed public opinion against the French and their sympathizers. The lives of French immigrants during those passionate times were at best uncomfortable, and at worst filled with trouble and turmoil.

The fear and detestation in which American "Jacobins" were held were no less powerful than the abhorrence felt for the French revolutionists themselves. "Medusa's Snakes are not more venomous," declared a Federalist, "than the wretches who are seeking to bend us to the views of France." "The open enemies of our country," declared the *Albany Centinel,* "have never taken half the pains to render our Government and our rulers infamous and contemptible in the eyes of the world, than those wretches who call themselves Americans, Patriots and Republicans." This "Gallic faction" was believed to be in close communication with Paris, "the immense reservoir, and native spring of all immorality, corruption, wickedness and methodized duplicity."

. . . In the eyes of the Federalists, however, every Frenchman was a potential enemy: whether royalists or revolutionists, they were eager to extend French influence over the United States, and actuated by national pride, they might join a French army of invasion. Moreover, their notoriously loose morals and irreligion threatened to infect Americans.[26]

By 1801 the Republicans effectively ended the Federalists' political dominance. President Thomas Jefferson purchased the Louisiana Territory from France in 1803, and with it the French city of New Orleans, which retains much of its ethnic flavor to this day, including the famed Mardi Gras celebration.

Pluralism

The persistence of a French subculture in southern Louisiana is interesting in that not only has it remained strong over the years, but it has succeeded in absorbing other ethnic groups in that area.

The French assimilated the Germans while both were under Spanish rule and both subject to strenuous programs designed to stamp them with a Spanish cultural heritage. But the virile French culture was not content with this, even made a beginning at swallowing the politically dominant Spaniards themselves, a beginning which has been practically consummated during the American period while both were enveloped in the so-called melting pot which was heralded as bringing about Americanization. Under American rule the Louisiana French have, to the present time, perpetuated their language and culture and, at the same time, have absorbed most of the diverse Anglo-Saxon elements which have settled among them.[27]

T. Lynn Smith and Vernon Parenton attribute this social phenomenon to the intermarriage of Louisiana-French women with outgroup men, high fertility rates, and the dominance of the French mother in the socialization process. The strong influence and control of the French Catholic priest and the appeal of the French way of life to outgroup members are other factors.[28]

For many, French is still the principal language spoken in the home. In 1940, the Census Bureau estimated that 1,412,060 persons spoke French primarily, of whom 300,000 lived in Louisiana. In 1980, 1.5 million French-speaking people were in the United States, with about one-fifth of them in Louisiana. As native language usage continues, so is a distinctive ethnic subculture still in evidence.

Today, urbanizing influences are permeating the entire section. These include improved communication, mechanization of agriculture (with its concomitant social implications) and, particularly, mass media of education (radio, movies, and newspapers) as well as increased contacts outside French-speaking Louisiana. Nevertheless, the system of common values which was generated by language, national origin, settlement pattern, as well as familial, kinship, and religious ties, has thus far retained its societal integrative forces in this period of rapid and far-reaching technological changes now operative among these people.[29]

In addition to the nineteenth-century French aristocrats and the present-day Louisiana French, the French-Canadians living in New England offer a third example of a persistent subculture. The Industrial Revolution brought rapid expansion to the New England factories, and the owners actively recruited labor in French Canada. Many French-Canadians flocked from Quebec to the mill towns, competing with the Irish and others for jobs. The heaviest migration occurred in the forty years followed in Civil War. By 1873, approximately 400,000 French-Canadians were living in the United States, half of them in New England and most of the remainder in the Midwest, primarily Illinois and Michigan.[30]

As in Louisiana, the family and the church have served as strong cohesive units in retaining language and culture. French parochial schools have also had a unifying effect upon the community. The French-Canadians still remain a distinct ethnic group, and their loyalties to their institutions and to their original home, Quebec, suggest that they will continue to remain a strong subculture in the foreseeable future.

TABLE 5.2
U.S. Population Ancestry in 1980

	Million	%
English	50	22
German	49	21
Irish	40	17
African	21	9
French	13	6
Italian	12	5
Scottish, Scotch-Irish	10	4
Scandinavian	10	4
Polish	8	3
Mexican	8	3
American Indian	7	3

Source: U.S. Bureau of the Census, "Ancestry of the Population by State: 1980" (Washington, D.C.: U.S. Government Printing Office, April 1983), p. 2.

The Census Bureau also reported that California had the most people with ancestors from England, Germany, Ireland, and Scandinavia. Massachusetts had the largest concentration of Irish-Americans, 27.3% of its residents. Maine had the largest concentration of residents with French roots, 25% of its population.

Americans claiming English ancestry are slightly greater than the current population of England. Irish-Americans are twice that of Ireland today. Note also that almost 75% of the total U.S. population trace their bloodlines to northern and western Europe.

GERMANS

Germany has supplied the greatest number of immigrants, about 7 million since 1820. Today 49 million people, about one of five Americans, trace their bloodlines to Germany (see Table 5.2). In several earlier periods the large concentrations of German Americans raised nativist fears, but today's average citizen no longer thinks of them as a distinct ethnic group even though around 6,000 new German immigrants arrive annually.

Early Reactions

William Penn was so successful in recruiting German immigrants to his Pennsylvania colony that by the outbreak of the Revolutionary War, they numbered over 100,000—one third of the colony's total population. England's deployment of Hessian (German) mercenary troops in this area may have been done in part to secure sympathetic German colonial assistance in such areas as supplies, intelligence reports, and so on.

The Germans' situation provides a good example of a dominant culture reacting to a perceived threat from a distinct minority group. They were different in language, customs, and religion (being primarily Lutherans), as were other groups, but their high visibility due to their numbers and settlement patterns brought them to public attention.

Many Germans also had the additional disadvantage of having been placed in a subservient position at the outset. A very popular system, particularly in Pennsylvania, was the use of indentured servants or "redemptioners." Through this plan, persons unable to pay their passage would serve from three to seven years as laborers, artisans, domestics, or tutors. Upon their arrival in the harbor, such persons were advertised for sale in the newspapers, and the ship became a market as the ship captain or entrepreneur was paid for advancing the passage money. Occasionally families were separated. Such a situation could not help but encourage ethnocentric feelings of superiority among native-born Americans over such "poor foreigners."[31] Some English immigrants also came to the New England colonies as indentured servants, but in Pennsylvania the Germans represented a different ethnic group as well.

By 1750 the influx of German immigrants had become so great that Benjamin Franklin became quite disturbed and asked:

Why [should] the Pennsylvanians . . . allow the Palatine Germans to swarm into our settlements, and by herding together to establish their Language and Manners to the exclusion of ours? Why should Pennsylvania, founded by the English, become a colony of Aliens, who will shortly be so numerous as to Germanize us instead of our Anglifying them?[32]

These expressed fears were to be repeated by others at a later time, with respect to different immigrant groups. Franklin's worries about the duality of language display a marked similarity to some twentieth-century concerns regarding the Spanish-speaking populace and bilingual education. Franklin particularly opposed the Mennonites, fearing that members of this religious sect were pacifists. Maurice Davie reports that Franklin had misgivings about the Germans also because of their clannishness, their meager knowledge of English, their separate German press, and their increasing need for interpreters. Speaking of the latter, Franklin said, "I suppose in a few years they will also be necessary in the Assembly, to tell one-half of our legislators what the other half say."[33] Franklin was not arguing for restriction on immigration, but rather for rapid assimilation (Anglo-conformity).

The Second Wave: Segregation and Pluralism

The German immigrants of the eighteenth century settled first in Pennsylvania and then in other mid-Atlantic states, but the nineteenth-century immigrants went to the Midwest. So many migrated to the Ohio, Mississippi, and Missouri river valleys

In Hamburg, circa 1885, these prospective German emigrants await processing for clearance to travel to the United States. The promise of "Golden America," often conveyed by letters of friends or relatives or by steamship advertisements, lured millions of people to the "land of opportunity."

that by the middle of the nineteenth century they were looked upon as a factor to be reckoned with. They became homesteaders, preserving their heritage through their schools, churches, newspapers, language, multi-aid societies, and recreational activities.

The failure of the liberal German revolution brought many political refugees to the United States in 1848. Known as "Forty-eighters," these Germans settled in the large cities of the East and Midwest. Most settled in Baltimore, New York, St. Louis, Milwaukee, and Minneapolis. Having been political activists in their homeland, the Forty-Eighters quickly became active in American politics. Many Germans even gave serious thought to an all-German state within the union with German as the official language; some considered creating a separate German nation, believing that the slavery issue would cause the dissolution of the Union.

An often overlooked ethnic footnote to American history is Abraham Lincoln's astute realization of the value of German-American political activism. With a sizeable German population in Illinois before the Civil War, Lincoln tried to master the German tongue and became owner of a German-language newspaper.[34] His efforts earned rich dividends as the Forty-Eighters, who had adopted the Republican Party, persuaded thousands of their compatriots to do the same. They also exerted considerable influence in 1860 to secure the nomination for Lincoln and to elect him to the Presidency.

The subcommunities of Germans in the cities were similar to the separate German communities in the agrarian regions. In both situations, the Germans were physically and socially segregated, mostly by their own choice. In a city like Milwaukee, Germans at one time were in the absolute majority; the 1850 census showed six thousand Germans and four thousand native-born Americans. Today the Germantown sections of most of these cities still retain some vestige of their ethnic identity.

Societal Responses

Tensions were increased by the large numbers of Germans, most of them Catholics and Jews, and by the mid-nineteenth century, many violent confrontations occurred with native-born Americans. During the height of the Know-Nothing movement in the 1850s, the Germans were often victims of verbal abuse, open discrimination, and even mob violence. On August 5, 1855, a day long remembered in Louisville, Kentucky, as Bloody Monday, a mob of Know-Nothings—incited by fiery articles in the Louisville *Journal*—stormed into the German section of the city. When the riot was over, twenty-two men had been killed, several hundred were wounded, and sixteen houses had been burned.[35]

German immigrants assimilated fairly rapidly, but because of the large, continual flow of newcomers, a significant ethnic subculture was always in evidence. Some 230 years after the arrival of the first German settlers, this continuing subculture came under xenophobic attack. Becoming embroiled for the first time in 1917 in a European war so traumatized Americans that a strong wave of anti-German feeling prevailed for several years. Patriotic hysteria brought intense pressure upon the

Box 5.1

"When I—I tell the news 'You are free.' I choke up."

"When I got to Ellis Island, we all had to line up and they would examine us. Some people could pass and they marked their coat. Some they marked on the left and some they marked on the right lapels. Those that were marked on one side could go through right away. Maybe they had been here before, I don't know. But I got a mark—'This is back.' So they let us through a big hall and we had to strip naked. And we met two fellas, they were doctors with stethoscopes. I didn't know what a stethoscope was—I learned that after. They tapped us on the chest and on the back and then I had to run around. I was the only one they examined.

"All of a sudden one raised his fist. He was gonna knock the other fella down, the other doctor. I didn't know what it meant, I was told afterward. One said I had consumption and the other doctor said there was nothing wrong with me—all I needed was a bellyful of food for a couple of months, I was undernourished. Well, finally, I got passed. And when I got out, I had to go before an examiner. "My brother had arranged for relatives that lived in Brooklyn. The examiner said to my cousin, 'You will have to put up $50,000 bail so this young man will not become a burden of the United States.'

". . . Then the examiner said, 'You are free to go.' And [voice breaking] when I—I tell the news 'you are free,' I choke up. The judge says, 'The boy [pause, tears streaming] may be undernourished [Pause, then very emotionally] but he has a wonderful mind.' And he said again, 'You are free to go,' and we went out."

German immigrant who came to the United States in 1910 at age 16.

Germans to eliminate their cultural manifestations. This Americanization movement, which was sometimes brutal, did succeed in eliminating distinct "Little Germany" subsocieties. This was one instance where forced assimilation succeeded, because the Germans wanted to identify with the land of their children, not the land of their forebears.

Cultural Impact

American speech, eating, and drinking reflect German influence. Frankfurters, sauerkraut, sauerbraten, hamburgers, wiener schnitzel, pumpernickel bread, liverwurst, pretzels, zwieback, and lager beer were introduced by German immigrants. The words *stein* and *rathskeller* are also of German origin, as are the concepts of the kindergarten and the university. Germans almost exclusively dominated the brewing industry, founding Anheuser-Busch, Schaefer, Schlitz, Schmidt's, Pabst, Ruppert, and many others.

Some leading German industrialists were George Westinghouse, electrical engineering; Frederick Weyerhaeuser, lumber; John Jacob Astor, fur trade; Bausch and Lomb, optical instruments; Chrysler, Studebaker, and Kaiser, car manufacturers; Steinway and Wurlitzer, piano makers; and Heinz, food canning. A German immigrant, Thomas Nast, was America's first great caricaturist and political cartoonist, and he created the Democratic donkey, the Republican elephant, and the "I want you" Uncle Sam recruiting poster of World War I vintage.

The Germans no longer predominate as a distinct ethnic minority, even though some remain unassimilated. Their earlier experiences, particularly those of mid-nineteenth-century German Catholics and of German-Americans during World War I, were a forerunner of the types of conflict certain other minority groups also would encounter.

THE IRISH

Their religion, their peasant culture, and their rebelliousness against England not only marked the Irish as strangers to the Americans, but also set the stage for the most overt discrimination and hostility any ethnic group had thus far encountered. Almost all theoretical considerations discussed in the earlier chapters can be applied to the history of the Irish in the United States.

Originally made unwelcome in the New England settlements, most of the early Irish immigrants settled in Pennsylvania or in Maryland, which had been founded as an English Catholic colony in 1634 but which had become Protestant-controlled by the mid-eighteenth century. By 1790 the Irish accounted for almost 2 percent of the total population of 3,172,444. Their numbers became a source of increasing concern to the Federalists, especially during the presidency of John Adams. Fearing that the "wild Irish" rebels would attempt to turn the United States against England, and also that they would join the Republican party, the Federalists were strongly against the incoming "hordes of wild Irishmen." Rufus King, American minister in London, was one of the foremost opponents of Irish emigration to the United States. He expressed to Secretary of State Timothy Pickering his fear that the disaffected Irish would "disfigure our true national character," which was purest in untainted New England. Massachusetts-born John Quincy Adams agreed that the United States had "too many of these people already."[36]

After 1830, emigration to America became increasingly essential to the Irish, whose oppression under British rule prevented their becoming successful in their native land. The successive failures of the potato crop and the resulting famine in the late 1840s accelerated the exodus. Approximately 1.2 million people emigrated between 1847 and 1854, the peak year being 1851, when almost a quarter of a million Irish came to the United States.

Cultural Differentiation

The Irish attracted attention because of their sheer numbers, and also because they were Catholic and had strong anti-British feelings. Both factors weighed heavily against them in Anglo-Saxon Protestant America. In addition, they were a poverty-stricken rural people who settled in groups mainly in the slum areas of cities on the East Coast. Because they could find only unskilled jobs, they began life in America with a lower-class status, bearing that stigma at a time when America was becoming increasingly class conscious.

The Irish were the first ethnic group to come to the United States in large numbers as a minority very different from the dominant culture of the country. They were to be the harbingers of the "new" immigrants yet to come. As Charles Marden and Gladys Meyer point out:

This was America's first confrontation with a peasant culture. The English, Scandinavians, or Germans who came to America in the nineteenth century came from towns or from freehold farming patterns. The Irish had been long exploited by the English landholding system. The unchallenged position of the Catholic church cemented bonds of identity. A history of famine, a family and inheritance system that led to late marriage and many unmarried men and women, the ambivalent situation of being English-speaking but not part of English-derived institutions, and migration in large numbers put the Irish in a peculiar relationship to dominants. Some welcomed them as a necessary working-class contingent; others engaged in flagrant discrimination.[37]

Even when they were welcomed as people who would fill the working-class jobs, it was with an ethnocentric attitude of superiority over a lowly breed of people, typified by these comments of a Massachusetts senator in 1852:

That inefficiency of the pure Celtic race furnishes the answer to the question: How much use are the Irish to us in America? The Native American answer is, "none at all." And the Native American policy is to keep them away.

A profound mistake, I believe. . . . We are here, well organized and well trained, masters of the soil, the very race before which they have yielded everywhere besides. It must be, that when they come in among us, they come to lift us up. As sure as water and oil each finds its level they will find theirs. So far as they are mere hand-workers, they must sustain the head-workers, or those who have any element of intellectual ability. Their inferiority as a race compels them to go to the bottom; and the consequence is that we are, all of us, the higher lifted because they are here.[38]

Societal Reaction

The Native American movement, which had briefly been evident in the immediate post-Revolutionary War period, now swept across the land in a shameful display of bigotry and intolerance. The growth of anti-Irish feeling was strongly linked to anti-Catholic feeling. Fears of ''Popery'' arose, strengthened by the influx of priests to minister to the needs of the Irish Catholics. The Irish were brutalized by this movement far more than the Germans were by Know-Nothing violence; destruction of property, beatings, and loss of life occurred in the Irish sections of many cities. In addition to frequent street brawls, the mob violence sometimes resulted in the burning of churches and convents. In an ironic twist of fate, the

"The American River Ganges"

Many consider this the most vicious anti–Catholic, anti–Irish cartoon ever printed in a mass–circulation magazine. It illustrates the belief that the Irish Catholics were endangering public education (symbolized by the upside–down American flag). Notice the Irish harp and papal tiara flying above Tammany Hall, the teachers being led to the gallows, and children being thrown to the river bank by Democratic politicians. One Protestant teacher (Bible under his jacket) is protecting children from the crocodiles, which represent Catholic bishops. Their jaws are mitres, their scales are vestments, and their faces are Irish stereotypes. Cartoon by German immigrant Thomas Nast, *Harper's Weekly,* September 30, 1871.

Irish later tended to dominate some urban police forces, and they would be the ones to either control or arrest unruly Know-Nothing mobs, thus maintaining the American way of life that the Irish had once been accused of destroying.

Antagonism toward the Irish was manifested most strongly in social and job discrimination. For a long time, job advertisements in Boston and elsewhere included the line "No Irish need apply."

Indeed, they suffered severe discrimination in the new land and most often found employment only in the lowest-paying and hardest-working jobs: as ditchdiggers, or dockers, or "terriers" working on the railroads and in the canal beds. In some respects (clearly not in all), the urban experience for Blacks in the twentieth century—in terms of the attitudes of others and in terms of occupations—has its parallel in the Irish experience in the middle of the previous century.[39]

Cultural Impact

Irish labor played a key role in the industrial expansion of the United States, particularly in building the great systems of canals, waterways, and railroads. As Roman Catholicism evolved into a major faith in a Protestant country, through increased membership and the power of the church hierarchy, Irish-Americans exerted a great moral force upon the nation. As the Irish began to assimilate, they often served as a "middleman minority," aiding new European immigrant groups in work, church, school, and city life.[40] The Irish were not so hospitable to the Chinese, however, often clashing with them in the cities and in railway labor disputes.

Minority Response

The Irish experience was the prototype for the experiences of later immigrants, not only in their hostile reception by the dominant culture, but also in their reaction to the prejudice and discrimination that they frequently encountered. One should not underestimate the hardship involved in leaving one's native land—alone or with family—journeying far to another country, feeling both anxieties and hopes, and then finding oneself an unwanted stranger in a strange land.

Actions and Reactions

Irish responses were both retreatist and aggressive, as demonstrated through their social behavior and their involvement in the labor movement and in the urban political machine. Because these activities frequently offended American norms of behavior, they reaffirmed the suspicions of native-born Americans, thereby reinforcing the stereotypes of the Irish and prolonging the vicious circle.

Unable to participate in the normal associational affairs of the community, the Irish felt obliged to erect a society within a society, to act together in their own way. In every contact therefore the group, acting apart from other sections of the community, became intensely aware of its peculiar and exclusive identity.[41]

The small degree of intermarriage both reflected and buttressed the distinction between the Irish and other Americans. Among the Irish, religious and social considerations encouraged a tendency to mate with their own kind. As Catholics, they were repeatedly warned that union with Protestants was tantamount to loss of faith, and the great majority of non-Irish in the city considered marriage with them degrading. As a result, the percentage of Irish intermarriage was extremely low.

As the colonial forces had once usurped "Yankee Doodle," the British satirical song about them, the Irish now seized upon their group identity as a rallying point for pride and camaraderie. That ebullience still manifests itself across the country each Saint Patrick's Day. In the nineteenth century, the Irish community was united through family, church, and school, as well as through their social and recreational activities. Such "clannishness" only added fuel to the fires of resentment among the American assimilationists, even though the Anglo-Saxon community had helped to cause the situation. Jewish immigrants would later experience similar problems when their community was subject to charges of clannishness.

Box 5.2

> *"The nicest thing I ever experienced was seeing the Statue of Liberty. It meant we were here and we were all right."*

"Like many more immigrants like myself, I came to this country to seek a living because living over there was very, very poor. Work was scarce and hard. I decided that I ought to try the United States to make a living.

"I left home in Ireland on a Friday morning. I went to a place then called Queenstown in County Cork. I was there for the greater part of Friday and Saturday because you had to go through quite a number of tests and screening to be allowed to board ship. On Sunday morning around eight o'clock I boarded the ship.

"We arrived in the United States a week from that Monday, around two o'clock in the afternoon in the harbor of New York. The nicest thing I saw after being so seasick—and I might say I was very, very seasick—the nicest thing I ever experienced was seeing the Statue of Liberty. It meant we were here and we were all right. We had landed and we were safe. Then, of course, I had to go through customs and things like that.

"I had heard a great deal about the United States, that it was a good country, and I might very well say that it was a good country, although at that time I was disappointed because I wasn't the one to find the gold in the streets. I really had to go out and look for a job. I worked for awhile in a doctor's office and from there I went to work for a chemical company. There was disappointment. There were loans from my family and my friends. It's something you wonder if you can make it. Thank God I did."

Irish immigrant who came to the United States in 1920 at age 18.

Quite often, some members of a low-status minority group are arrested more frequently than members of other groups for certain crimes, particularly those of personal disorganization. The Irish, for example, were disproportionately represented in arrests and convictions for brawling, drunkenness, disturbing the peace, and more serious crimes during the nineteenth century. These occurrences reinforced the dominant society's stereotyped attitudes toward them.

Labor Conflict

Irish labor was diversified, but it was concentrated in low-status unskilled or semi-skilled occupations. The Irish worked at the hard, physical jobs in the cities, in the mines of Appalachia, or in railroad construction from the Alleghenies to the Rockies. With their knowledge of the English language, the Irish provided strong, articulate membership and leadership in such early labor movements as the Knights of Labor. The greatest notoriety surrounded the violence and murders committed by the Molly Maguires, a secret terrorist group that aided the Irish miners in their struggle with the mine owners. Following infiltration of their group by a secret agent for the Pinkerton Detective Agency and a highly questionable court proceeding, the Molly Maguire movement ended in the hanging of twenty men, the largest mass execution in the nation's history.

Bonacich's split labor market theory helps explain much of the conflicts involving the Irish. Irish–German conflict, particularly in Pennsylvania, was intense in the late eighteenth and early nineteenth centuries, because of economic competition and use of Germans as strikebreakers.[42] On the West Coast, Irish workers held meetings and demonstrations, demanding curtailment of further Chinese immigration, viewing those lower-paid ethnics as a serious economic threat.[43] The Irish also fiercely resisted abolition, fearing labor competition from released slaves. Antiblack riots in Chicago, Cincinnati, and Detroit followed.[44] Most notorious was the so-called "Draft Riot" of 1863 in New York City, in which about 400 rioters were killed, as well as dozens of Blacks, police, and soldiers. This riot, the worst in American history, was led by Irish longshoremen, angry over the recent use of black strikebreakers to undermine efforts to secure better wages.[45]

Upward Mobility

Grassroots politics speeded along Irish upward mobility, triggering a nativist concern over Catholic priests controlling American politics. Through political machine organization, the Irish controlled Tammany Hall in New York by the 1860s, and the Brooklyn Democratic party by the 1870s.[46] By the 1890s they also controlled Boston, Buffalo, Chicago, Philadelphia, St. Louis, and San Francisco. Through a paternalistic patronage system, the boss-controlled urban political machine offered economic and political opportunities, as well as social welfare provisions for the Irish community.[47]

Irish Catholics made slow but steady progress in entering the societal mainstream. Antipathy against them gradually lessened as their command of English,

"The balance of trade with Great Britain seems to be still against us" was the caption to this 1883 newspaper editorial cartoon. The arrival of 650 paupers in Boston from Galway, Ireland, sent by the British government on the steamship *Nestoria* on April 15, 1883, was the basis for this anti-Irish attack, designed to stir fears about large numbers of Irish poor coming here. The dynamite shipment identifies those Irish in the United States as active supporters of rebellion overseas.

improved economic position, and physical appearance made them less objectionable to Anglo-American Protestants than the "new" immigrants arriving from other parts of Europe.

THE SCANDINAVIANS

Some Swedes and Finns came to what is now the United States as early as 1638, making their landfall at the mouth of the Delaware River. They established a colony, New Sweden, a land of promise encompassing parts of modern-day Delaware, Pennsylvania, and New Jersey. Combating the Dutch and the English as well as the heat and the mosquitoes, these settlers constructed the first log cabin in the New World.

Although small numbers of Norwegians, Swedes, and Danes continued to emigrate to the United States, they did not come here in substantial numbers until after 1865. Thereafter, motivated by religious dissension, voting disenfranchisement, crop failures, and other economic factors, the Scandinavians emigrated in large numbers.

A great many of these immigrants settled in the northern region of the Midwest, in rural communities where the soil was highly fertile and where they could enjoy social and political equality and yet retain their ethnicity. Their settlements in the farmlands of the northern Middle West became strongholds of church-centered Norwegian and Swedish traditions. Isolation from the dominant drift of American social patterns permitted their widespread and long-lived retention of indigenous lifeways, which continue, in some measure, to this day.[48] Ole Rolvaag presented an eloquent and poignant saga of late-nineteenth-century Norwegian pioneers in the Dakota Territory in *Giants in the Earth,* a vivid social-psychological portrait of pioneer life. Capturing the exuberant hopes, fears, despair, struggles, and interactions of the immigrants in the heartland of America, this monumental work offers vivid testimony to the human quest of a dream.

And it was as if nothing affected people in those days. They threw themselves blindly into the Impossible, and accomplished the Unbelievable. If anyone succumbed in the struggle—and that happened often—another would come and take his place. Youth was in the race; the unknown, the untried, the unheard-of, was in the air; people caught it, were intoxicated by it, threw themselves away, and laughed at the cost. Of course it was possible—everything was possible out here. There was no such thing as the Impossible any more. The human race had not known such faith and such self-confidence since history began. . . . And so had been the Spirit since the day the first settlers landed on the eastern shores; it would rise and fall at intervals, would swell and surge on again with every new wave of settlers that rolled westward into the unbroken solitude.[49]

Ingroup Solidarity

Like other immigrant groups, the Scandinavians attempted to resist Americanization and cling to their Old World traditions. Intermarriage was frowned upon, often far into the twentieth century. An ethnic newspaper's 1897 lament about exogamy illustrated the concern "that the national spirit is not particularly strong among the Danes of this region" and that intermarriage would "strike out our mother tongue and all we received as a heritage from our fathers."[50]

As greater numbers of Norwegians settled in Minnesota and Wisconsin, they eventually outnumbered the native-born population, creating social tensions and political competition. A typical example occurred in 1878 in Trempealeau County, Wisconsin, a beautiful region of wooded hills and valleys. When the Norwegians practiced their custom of picnicking and drinking on Sunday afternoons—the Continental Sabbath—their American neighbors increasingly censured them. When a Norwegian running as an independent was elected sheriff on a vote split along party lines, the Sunday custom continued without further interference; political party leaders also realized they could no longer ignore or antagonize this ethnic majority.[51]

Ethnic Identity

Norwegians, Swedes, and Danes have come to the United States from lands with different governments, different traditions, and different languages. Because of the physical similarities among the three groups and because they frequently settled together in the new land, use of the term *Scandinavian* to designate all three groups became common throughout American society.

The common use of the term *Scandinavian* to describe Swedes, Norwegians, and Danes in a broad and general way is one of the products of the commingling of these three peoples on the American side of the Atlantic. The word really fits even more loosely than does the word *British* to indicate the English, Welsh, and Scotch. It was applied early in the history of the settlements in Wisconsin and Illinois, to groups which comprised both Norwegians and Danes on the one hand, or Norwegians and Swedes on the other hand, when no one of the three nationalities were strong enough to maintain itself separately, and when the members of one were inclined . . . to resent being called by one of the other names; for example, when a Norwegian objected to being taken for a Swede. The Scandinavian Synod of the Evangelical Lutheran Church, organized in 1860, included both Norwegians and Danes.

. . . The use and acceptability of the word steadily grew; the great daily paper in Chicago took the name *Skandinaven;* in 1889, the editor of *The North* declared: "the term has become a household word . . . universally understood in the sense in which we here use it to designate the three nationalities . . .[52]

In addition to farming, the Scandinavians primarily worked as lumberjacks, sailors, dock workers, and craftsmen in the building and machine trades. Since they came from countries with compulsory education, their literacy rate was very high, and a large percentage of them acquired U.S. citizenship. Danes tended to spread out more and to downplay the role of the church and fraternal organizations, in comparison to Norwegians and Swedes. For that reason, the Danes assimilated more quickly, although all groups succeeded in blending into the American social fabric fairly easily. The Swedes hit their peak year of immigration in 1913, and the Norwegians in 1924. The total number of Scandinavians who have emigrated to the United States is now approximately 2.5 million.

THE SCOTS

The first wave of Scottish migration occurred during the colonial period; by 1790 they were second in number only to the English, totaling 221,562, or 7 percent of the population, compared with the 2,605,699 English, who made up 82 percent. Consequently, Scottish-Americans played a prominent role during the formative years of the new nation. As an illustration, eleven of the fifty-six signers of the Declaration of Independence were Scottish-Americans. Almost 80 percent of all Scottish emigrants came to America later, however; between 1871 and 1930, more than 640,000 Scots arrived. This group was primarily from the working class, and they entered various semiskilled occupations.

The Scots should not be confused with the Scotch-Irish, who were mostly Lowland Scots who came from the Irish city of Ulster. Before the Revolution, 50,000 of them had settled on the southern frontier and in the central Appalachians. They were concentrated primarily in North Carolina and Pennsylvania. Living on the American frontier, the Scotch-Irish did not mingle with outgroup members, interacting and marrying within their group boundaries.[53] They often took the law into their own hands when they felt their interests were threatened, rebelling violently against taxation, massacring Indians, and forming lynch mobs. Numerous recorded incidents attest to their involvement in ethnic conflict and community violence.[54]

Although the Scotch-Irish activity supported the rebel cause, the Scots from the Highlands of Scotland were loyalists throughout the Revolutionary War. They settled in established areas rather than along the frontier and insisted upon maintaining their ethnic identity even though they were easily assimilated almost from the outset.

The rigid discipline of Scottish church life—either Presbyterian or Episcopalian—was reflected in their life-style. Deeply religious, they adhered to a strict moral code; the Protestant Ethic of hard work, frugality, and honesty was as evident among them as among Calvinist New Englanders. Like many other communities, they also sought to preserve their culture and to duplicate the way of life from the old country.

Scottish emigration did not maintain its magnitude after 1936. Lack of new Scottish immigrants in sizable numbers reduced their proportional representation in the total population, and the assimilation process mostly removed their visibility. Maintaining their ethnic identity was a losing battle. The Scots did continue, however, to wear disguises on Halloween (a practice now followed by many children in the United States on this holiday) and to regularly celebrate the January 25 birthday of Robert Burns, the Scottish poet.

THE WELSH

Though frequently lumped together with the English, the Welsh were a distinct ethnic minority in the United States; there were sufficient numbers during the pre–Civil War period to warrant the printing of newspapers and some books in Welsh.

Welsh immigrants came here with the early colonists, settling together to a much greater degree than the English. They were very active during the Revolution, and five Welsh-Americans—William Floyd, Button Gwinnett, Thomas Jefferson, Francis Lewis, and Lewis Morris—were signers of the Declaration of Independence.

As with other immigrants, economic and religious motives lured the Welsh to the United States. They were of different Protestant denominations; Baptists and Quakers came first, followed later by Anglicans and Presbyterians. Primarily farmers and miners, many settled in Cambria County, Pennsylvania, where they exerted a strong social and political influence; others settled in Oneida County, New York, a region in which "Welsh butter" became famous. By the late nineteenth century, many Welsh miners—like their English counterparts—had become superintendents and foremen of coal mines in many states, including Ohio, Illinois, and Washington.

SOCIOLOGICAL ANALYSIS

In our study of the northern and western European immigrants, we have discussed their experiences within a sociohistorical context, as well as the specific patterns of dominant-minority interaction. To understand better the meaning of those patterns, we shall now place them within conceptual frameworks of the three major sociological perspectives.

The Functionalist View

With their emphasis upon a societal network of interrelated parts working together for survival or stability, functionalists see the arrival of large groups of people to forge a civilization out of a vast, undeveloped country rich in natural resources as highly desirable. The New World offered the newcomers economic opportunity and freedom from religious and political oppression, while benefiting from their presence. The unskilled newcomers helped build the cities, canals, and railroads; clear the land for farming; and create demand for goods and services. Others used their entrepreneural skills or craftsmanship to supply the growing nation with needed commerce. The evolution of an independent American society and of poor immigrants Crevecoeur had called "useless and withered plants" that "have taken root and flourished" was the outgrowth of a smoothly functioning social system.[55]

Sometimes the large numbers of Irish and Germans entering the country created dysfunctions; the society could not absorb them that quickly. They clustered together, culturally distinct from the dominant Anglo-American model, a situation that generated prejudice and discrimination against them. The ensuing conflict, like that involving French-Americans in earlier years, disrupted the social system, preventing cooperative efforts toward common goals and denying attainment of personal goals to many newcomers. In time the necessary adjustments occurred; education and upward mobility through economic growth and the Civil Service (in the case of the Irish) allowed both acceptance and assimilation.

The Conflict View

The beginning point of this theoretical perspective is the dominance of Anglo-Americans in the new nation. Not only did they influence the adoption of language, customs, and social institutions derived from Great Britain, they also held economic and political power. In this context, the Federalist hostility toward the French and Irish becomes more than ethnic antagonism; the propertied elite saw the influx of so many "common" people and the possible spread of Jacobin revolutionary ideas as threats to their power, thereby taking various actions to safeguard their interests (Alien and Sedition Acts, Native American party, and so on). Political considerations also weighed heavily in dealings with the Irish and Germans. The rise of power of Irish city politicians and the political activism of the Forty-Eighters caused nativist reactions through mob violence, political movements, and state legislative countermeasures.

Economic exploitation, particularly in the case of the Irish, brought prosperity to the owners of mines, factories, and railroads. Often working under brutal conditions in physically demanding jobs, many Irish struggled to survive in the slums where their low wages obliged them to reside. The captains of industry, when confronted with strikes or labor organization efforts, used their power to thwart such efforts through the courts, law enforcement personnel, or vigilante groups to break up demonstrations, or by hiring other workers. Much of the industrial expansion in the nineteenth century, conflict theorists maintain, was at the expense of the immigrant workers who made it possible. The resultant conflict did eventually bring about change, as Irish and Germans organized and gained a greater share of the nation's wealth.

Lieberson's power theory seems quite appropriate for the Irish in particular. As unskilled, peasant migrants, the Irish were the subordinate group to the indigenous Anglo-Americans. The conflict was sporadic and limited, with the Irish kept in their subordinate role until they too gained their share of power.

The Interactionist View

Understanding how people perceive and define the strangers in their midst is the basis of interactionist analysis. The Dutch in New Amsterdam and the Quakers in Philadelphia, for example, were receptive to cultural pluralism, and so harmonious relations ensued between them and the diverse peoples in their respective colonies. In contrast, the Puritans were intolerant of anyone different, resulting in the expulsion of such religious dissidents as Roger Williams and Anne Hutchinson and their followers. Long-standing violent conflict in Europe between the English and Irish and between the English and French partially explains negative Anglo-American perceptions of French and Irish-Americans; cultural prejudices, transmitted from generation to generation, helped foster ethnic antagonism in the United States, often on a reciprocal basis.

In a country predominantly Protestant throughout its colonial and early national periods, the arrival of large numbers of Irish Catholics and German Jews disturbed the native population. They interpreted the presence of these groups as a threat to the "American" way of life, labeling them as inferiors and worse. Note the use of "hordes" (William Shaw), "swarm" and "herding" (Benjamin Franklin)—words used frequently by others as well. Words are symbols, and here they connote both animalistic qualities and massive numbers, the latter often perceived as a contaminating menace to society. With this social interpretation of reality, confrontations and conflict were inevitable.

RETROSPECT

Structural and cultural differentiation played important roles in determining the nature of intergroup relations among northern and western Europeans in the United States. Generally, as long as the social structure was in its formative period and thus very fluid, the ethnic groups did not experience discrimination or low status for long. Relative isolation from European influences and sharing the commonality of forging a new life in the wilderness helped reduce any nationalistic biases. Although sporadic flare-ups occurred due to nationalistic rivalries, the different ethnic groups were usually hospitable to one another, welcoming strangers coming to settle because they themselves would benefit from the community's growth.

As life became more settled, residential patterns more densely clustered, and the social structure more solidified, recently arrived strangers became more conspicuous. Their cultural differences were often accentuated by their less fortunate economic circumstances. German and Irish immigrants of the nineteenth century, for example, encountered hostility not only because of their religion and culture but also because of their lack of power. Many settled in already established areas and thus started a new life in a region already dominated by others who looked upon them with scorn. Those who kept to themselves by settling in rural areas—the Scandinavians, the French, and some of the German immigrants—fared better than those who tried to settle in already urbanized areas.

Prevailing attitudes were of critical importance to a minority group's experience. The Dutch and Quakers, tolerant of those who were different, encouraged religious and cultural diversity within their settlements. Cultural diffusion and assimilation were least likely among the religiously orthodox. This was true not only for a dominant group such as the New Englanders, who expelled or denied welcome to dissenters, Quakers, Catholics, and Jews. It was also true for minority groups who resisted intermarriage and assimilation, such as the nineteenth-century Dutch, Scandinavians, and Irish.

Cultural diversity was a reality from the outset. Each settlement was an ethnic enclave, in which people of similar beliefs and values clustered together and helped one another to adjust in a new land. As the settlements became more populated, growing into towns and cities, the ethnic enclaves formed by the newer immigrants were actually sub-communities within a larger society. Although they were not as physically isolated as earlier ethnic groups, they were, nonetheless, socially and spatially segregated, often voluntarily, from those unlike themselves.

All immigrants, in varying degrees, faced hardships in adjusting to the strangeness of a new land and people. To ease that adjustment, they tried to re-create the familiar old world here in the new, through their churches, schools, newspapers, and fraternal and mutual-aid societies. Their efforts to preserve their language and culture helped to bring them a measure of security, but the attempts also often led to suspicion, dissension, and hostility between the dominant and minority cultures.

Discrimination and xenophobia occur especially when the superordinate group views the size and influence of the subordinate group as a threat to the stability of the job market, the community, or the nation itself. The nativist movements against the French and the Irish during John Adams' presidency, and against the Germans and the Irish in the midnineteenth century, testify to that pattern. Through legislative efforts and violent actions, the dominant-group members sought to justify their discriminatory behavior as appropriate to preserve the American character.

For the ''old'' immigrants, the Civil War brought to an end the difficulties they had encountered because of their background, for they were now comrades-in-arms for a common cause. Then too, a new threat loomed on the horizon as ''new'' immigrants—shorter, swarthier, with unfamiliar dress, foods, and customs—began the second great wave of migration to the United States. These new immigrants seemed to be totally unlike all that Americans were or should be. People found a new target for their fears, distrust, prejudices, and discrimination in these ''undesirable'' aliens.

The functionalist perspective stresses the young nation's need for newcomers and problems arising from large numbers of Irish and Germans hampering more rapid absorption. Conflict theorists emphasize Anglo-American dominance and the economic exploitation of other nationalities. Interactionists discuss how differing social interpretations of strangers—Dutch versus Puritan, Federalists toward foreigners, Protestants toward Catholics—set the stage for ethnic conflict.

REVIEW QUESTIONS

1. What are some examples of cultural pluralism among the Dutch, French, German, Irish, Scandinavian, and Scottish peoples in the United States?

2. What significance attaches to the fact that English-Americans comprised 82 percent of the population at the nation's beginning?

3. What similarities of dominant-minority patterns were shared by most northern and western European immigrants?

4. Apply the sociological concepts about strangers to those immigrant groups suffering from the xenophobic reactions of dominant groups toward them.

5. Apply the three major theoretical perspectives to the experiences of the immigrant groups discussed in this chapter.

SUGGESTED READINGS

Anderson, Charles H. *White Protestant Americans.* Englewood Cliffs, N.J.: Prentice-Hall, 1970.

A readable, comprehensive account of the cultural dominance of Anglo-Americans and their role in interethnic relations.

Beals, Carleton. *Brass Knuckle Crusade,* rev. ed. New York: Hastings House, 1960.

   Enlivened with graphic anecdotes, a fine portrait of mob violence and political activism during the days of the Know-Nothings.

Billigmeier, Robert H. *Americans from Germany: A Study in Cultural Diversity.* Belmont, Calif.: Wadsworth, 1974.

   A thorough coverage of German immigrants, its title referring to both the differences among those immigrating and their subcommunities.

Dolan, Jay P. *The Immigrant Church: New York and German Catholics, 1815–1865.* Baltimore, Md.: Johns Hopkins Press, 1975.

   A penetrating insight into the immigrant Catholic Church as it encountered many forms of Anglo-Saxon Protestant attack.

Higham, John. *Strangers in the Land.* New York: Atheneum, 1973.

   An excellent historical narrative of the patterns of American nativism from 1860 to 1925.

Fallows, Marjorie R. *Irish Americans: Identity and Assimilation.* Englewood Cliffs, N.J.: Prentice-Hall, 1979.

   Overview of the Irish-American experience, from rejection to acceptance, with analysis of subcultural values and behavior.

Kleppner, Paul. *The Cross of Culture: A Social Analysis of Midwestern Politics, 1850–1900.* New York: Free Press, 1970.

   Solid analysis of the German and Scandinavian role in local and state politics, showing ethnic solidarity as a means to political power.

Leyburn, James G. *The Scotch-Irish: A Social History.* Chapel Hill, N.C.: University of North Carolina Press, 1962.

   One of the better books about this ethnic group, from the pre-Revolutionary years to modern times, providing subcultural analysis and history.

CHAPTER 6

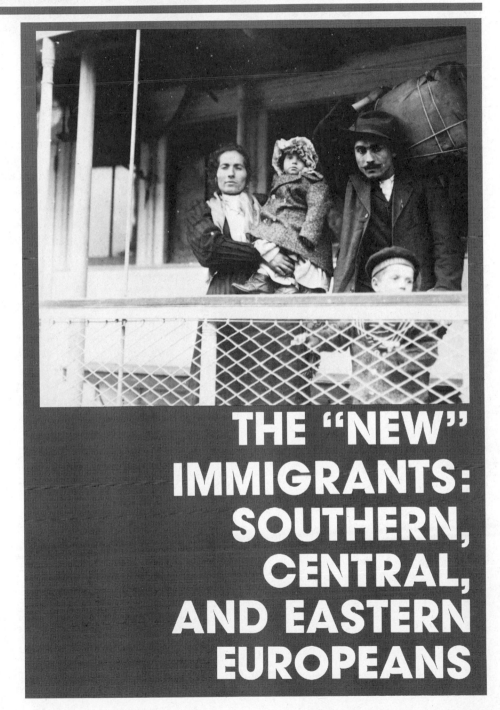

THE "NEW" IMMIGRANTS: SOUTHERN, CENTRAL, AND EASTERN EUROPEANS

During its colonial period, immigrants came to the United States from southern, central, and eastern Europe. Many, in fact, played important roles in the Revolutionary War and during the early years of the new nation. Not until the late nineteenth century, however, would immigrants come from this part of the world in any significant numbers.

SOCIOHISTORICAL PERSPECTIVE

In the late nineteenth century, a noticeable shift occurred in the kind of immigrant coming to America. By 1896 the turning point was reached: the number of immigrants from northern and western Europe was surpassed by the number of immigrants from the rest of Europe. Their physical and cultural differences made the newcomers easier to identify as strangers, and they were often broadly categorized as being alike, despite their many intrinsic differences as individuals and as separate ethnic groups. They arrived in large enough numbers to be able to preserve their culture and social boundaries within an urban subcultural setting, but this also increased the probability of prejudice and discrimination against them.

The Push–Pull Factors

A number of reasons accounted for the great wave of immigration from 1880 to 1920 (Figure 6.1). During that time American industry was growing rapidly, requiring ever larger numbers of workers. Improved transportation—quicker, sturdier steamships with their highly competitive rates for steerage dropping to ten dollars or less—encouraged an ocean crossing.

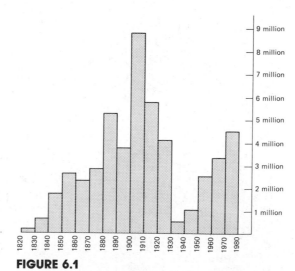

FIGURE 6.1

Total Immigration to the United States 1820–1980, by Decades

Peasant life was especially harsh in Europe. The ruling classes and local landed estate farmers exploited the common people. They crushed most peasant revolts and protests instead of reforming the basic agricultural economy. Peasants saw their sons drafted into the army for periods of twelve to thirty-one years. Trying to eke out an existence amid poverty, unemployment, sickness, and tyranny, some of Europe's poor looked elsewhere for a better life.

Letters from friends or relatives already in America were eagerly read and circulated among villagers. Newspapers, books, pamphlets, and transportation and labor recruiting agents all stimulated what contemporaries came to call "America fever." Following a familiar minority pattern of avoidance, Europe's poor and persecuted peoples fled their homelands for the promise of "Golden America."

Political and economic unrest in Europe also encouraged the exodus. Governments faced the pressures of overpopulation, chronic poverty, the decline of feudalism, dissident factions, and a changing agrarian economy. For them, large-scale emigration to America was an expedient solution to many problems, so they sponsored emigration drives that served as an additional impetus.

And so they came—Italians, Portuguese, Greeks, and Armenians from the southern part of the continent; Hungarians, Poles, Czechs, Slovaks, and others from the plains of central Europe; Byelorussians, Ukrainians, Ruthenians, and others

On—deck scenes such as these were quite common during the steamship journeys of immigrants in the early twentieth century. Whether getting fresh air by day or retiring by night to their dormitory-style steerage quarters, the immigrants interacted with one another, sharing their hopes and concerns.

from the western regions of Czarist Russia; Jewish emigrants, whose religion and Yiddish culture had frequently made them targets of discrimination and persecution, from all parts of eastern and central Europe, particularly Russia. All of these different peoples came, leaving behind their familiar world and seeking a new destiny.

Structural Conditions

The America the immigrants came to was far different from what earlier immigrants had found. The frontier was rapidly disappearing; industrialization and urbanization were changing the life style of the nation. The immigrants, mostly illiterate, unskilled, rural peasants, were plunged into a new cultural and social environment.

Since they had virtually no resources, many of these immigrants settled in the cities that had been their ports of entry or in the inland cities along railroad lines, such as Chicago. At the turn of the century, living conditions in the cities were far worse than they are today. Overcrowding, disease, high mortality rates, crime, filth, and congestion were commonplace. Crowded into poorly ventilated tenements and cellars, the immigrants often lived in squalor.

Box 6.1

> *"It was so hot in the shop, the sweat was running from the body and from the hand. . . . Big people used to faint."*

"Working conditions were terrible, terrible. If you have to sit two-three hours overtime for ten cents, what can I explain you? It don't get worse. But these ten cents I need. Whenever it was overtime, I was the first one to raise my hand.

"The boss watches you. You shouldn't talk to one another. He watches you between lunch and supper, you know. So you want something, you have something in your drawer like candy. He watches. No, no, no, nothing. You can't eat while you're working. So, you watch, you put the candy in your mouth.

"It was so hot in the shop, the sweat was running from the body and from the hand and the material got stained. The boss didn't care, the foreman didn't care. Once two policemen came in. They stopped the power. They said we couldn't work in such a heat. You haven't even got a fan here to have a little coolness. Nothing! People used to faint. Big people used to faint.

"In winter—it was such a hard winter. When I opened the door in the morning to go to work, I couldn't take away my hand from the knob—the frost. Terrible, terrible. At work in the big shop in the middle was a stove. It kept us a little warm. But, you know, young people, young blood—we put on a sweater. Yeah, the conditions was terrible. Can't be worse. Can't be worse. It was terrible. And the boss had a fresh mouth always for the workers."

Austrian Jewish immigrant who came to the United States in 1914 at age 17

Settling in the oldest city sections, the immigrants formed ethnic sub-communities, re-creating the nationality quilt of Europe. Although these groups were neighbors because of necessity, intermarriage or joint organizational activities were rare. In an effort to find security in a strange land, they repeated the adjustment patterns of the "old" immigrants. They sought and interacted with their own people, establishing their own churches, schools, and organizations to preserve their traditions and culture.

As unskilled workers, most found employment in the low-status, manual labor jobs in the factories, mines, needle trades, and construction. At that time the worker had no voice in working conditions, for labor unions had not yet become effective. The fourteen-hour day, six-day week for low wages was common. There were no vacations, sick pay, or pension plans. Child labor was the norm, and entire families often worked to provide family income. Lighting, ventilation, and heating were poor; in the factories, moving pieces of machinery were dangerously exposed. There was no worker's compensation if, as was likely, someone was injured on the job. A worker who objected was likely to be fired and blacklisted. Exploited by the captains of industry, the immigrants became deeply involved with the labor union movement, so much so that to tell the story of one without the other is virtually impossible.

It is true that many immigrants embraced the industrial ethos and found fulfillment in it. But many could not adjust to the new work discipline required of them and drifted from job to job; a good percentage returned to the Old Country, defeated and disillusioned. Some tried and failed to find work for which their skills and previous experience equipped them. Others turned to collective action—temperance societies, workers' educational associations, fraternal benefit societies, cooperatives, and unions—either to protect themselves from a system that was often pitiless, or to try in a small way to change the social and economic environment in which they found themselves. Still others resorted to radical and "direct" action to forcibly change a system which did not yield what they had crossed the Atlantic to find.[1]

Despite the adverse conditions, many immigrants worked hard and made sacrifices. Things were still better than what they had left behind. More importantly, America gave them hope and a promise of better things—if not for themselves, then surely for their children.

Societal Reactions

Although the immigrant groups kept themselves socially segregated from one another, outsiders mostly saw them as un-American strangers and tended to lump them all together. Italians and Jews stood out from the others because of their large numbers, clustering, religion, language, appearance, and cultural practices. Although many people viewed all "new" immigrants as both undesirable and nonassimilable, American society directed the greatest antagonism against the more visible Italians and Jews.

As an Ellis Island inspector checks for eye disease, other immigrants anxiously await their turn. Earlier, doctors had watched at the top of steps to stop anyone limping or showing shortness of breath. Because any form of disability resulted in deportation, many immigrants believed only healthy people lived in the United States.

Racism

A negative reaction to incoming minority groups had occurred many times before. This time, however, it developed a new dimension—actions based on physical features.

The arrival on American shores of these darker swarms of migrants—the so-called "new immigration"—was countered by the development of a new note in American nativism: the racist claim of ineluctable biological superiority for those with lighter skins, fairer hair, and earlier debarkation dates. Together with the older nativist themes of anti-Catholicism, fear of "foreign radicalism," and general xenophobia, this newer development in collective hatred, along with an awakening anti-Semitism, combined to produce the onslaught on the immigrant's culture, social organization, and self-regard known as the Americanization movement—a development which as we have seen before, was brought to its highest pitch by the events of World War I and the immediate post-war period.[2]

Probably the most significant blending of the nativist and racist thinking of this period came from Madison Grant's influential book, *The Passing of the Great Race*, which appeared in 1916. Relying upon what he considered scientific truth, Grant used race as the key factor determining culture and behavior. He argued that racial hybridism can only lead to a reversion to the "lower type." As his pessimistic title suggests, Grant saw the vastly superior Old American stock as disappearing ("racial suicide") as a result of lower birth rates because they chose not to contaminate their racial purity.

[Native Americans of colonial stock] will not bring children into the world to compete in the labor market with the Slovak, the Italian, the Syrian and the Jew. The native American is too proud to mix socially with them and is gradually withdrawing from the scene, abandoning to these aliens the land which he conquered and developed. The man of the old stock is being crowded out of many country districts by these foreigners just as he is today being literally driven off the streets of New York City by the swarms of Polish Jews. These immigrants adopt the language of the native American, they wear his clothes, they steal his name and they are beginning to take his women, but they seldom adopt his religion or understand his ideals; and while he is being elbowed out of his own home, the American looks calmly abroad and urges on others the suicidal ethics which are exterminating his own race.[3]

Grant's book was highly influential with other writers and congressional leaders. Popular magazines, such as the *Saturday Evening Post,* quoted and praised Grant. Scholars offered eugenic explanations to show a correlation between racial physique and culture.

Previously vague and romantic notions of Anglo-Saxon peoplehood were combined with general ethnocentrism, rudimentary wisps of genetics, selected tidbits of evolutionary theory, and naive assumptions from an early and a crude imported anthropology (later, other social sciences, at a similar stage of scientific development added their contributions) to produce the doctrine that the English, Germans, and others of the "old immigration" constituted a superior race of tall, blonde, blue-eyed "Nordics" or "Aryans." Whereas the peoples of Eastern and Southern Europe made up the darker Alpines or Mediterraneans—both inferior breeds whose presence in America threatened, either by intermixture or supplementation, the traditional American stock and culture.[4]

Ronald M. Pavalko maintains that racism was the fundamental basis for the negative response to the "new" immigrants, and that any economic argument for immigration restrictions was a smokescreen.[5] He cites economist Isaac A. Hourwich, who reported that in reality unemployment rates tended to be lowest in years of *high* immigration and highest during years of *low* immigration.[6] However, "specific economic and political events—industrial conflict, World War I, and the Russian Revolution—contributed to [a] redefinition" of these groups in nonracial terms.[7] As the emphasis shifted to national loyalty and stability, the Americanization movement marked a "crucial turning point."

"An Interesting Question"

"How long will it be before the rats own the garden and the man gets out?" This cartoon shows Uncle Sam relaxing in his garden, while foreign rats invade it. The rat faces are stereotyped depictions of Jews, Russians, Italians, Greeks, and other immigrants from southern and eastern Europe. Cartoon by E. M. Ashe appeared in Life, June 22, 1893.

> The transformation of the new immigrants from a stigmatized racial entity to a threat to economic and political order represents a shift in the definition of them as *unassimilable* to one emphasizing the point that they *must be assimilated*. We can only speculate on whether the new immigrants would have continued to be the focus of a racist ideology if this redefinition had not occurred. It does seem clear that the conscious and explicit emphasis on "Americanization" did not represent a rejection of racist assumptions about them as much as the substitution of economic and political concerns as more pressing.[8]

Americanization

Without any assistance from governmental agencies, and with little or no knowledge of the language or customs, the immigrants were expected to "fit" into the society quickly. Moreover, Americans expected them to speak only English, strip away their old culture, and avoid any ethnic institutions or organizations. These demands often led to ethnic self-hatred or a negative self-image because of the newcomers' ambivalence, or their inability or slowness to assimilate.[9]

To preserve the stability of the country, many people attempted to hasten the assimilation of the new immigrants already here. They looked upon the schools as agents of socialization, one of the key forces in effecting Anglo-conformity. The following quotation, by an educator of the early twentieth century, is representative of the prevailing dominant-group attitudes of that period.

These southern and eastern Europeans are of a very different type from the north Europeans who preceded them. Illiterate, docile, lacking in self-reliance and initiative, and not possessing the Anglo-Teutonic conceptions of law, order, and government, their coming has served to dilute tremendously our national stock, and to corrupt our civic life. The great bulk of these people have settled in the cities of the North Atlantic and North Central states and living, moral and sanitary conditions, honest and decent government, and proper education have everywhere been made more difficult by their presence. Everywhere these people tend to settle in groups or settlements, and to set up here their national manners, customs, and observances. our task is to break up these groups or settlements, to assimilate and amalgamate these people as a part of our American race, and to implant in their children, so far as can be done, the Anglo-Saxon conception of righteousness, law and order, and popular government, and to awaken in them a reverence for our democratic institutions and for those things in our national life which we as a people hold to be of abiding worth.[10]

The children of the immigrants felt the conflicts between majority-group expectations and their minority perspective more keenly than did their parents. They were truly marginal people, caught between two worlds. The schools were promoting the shedding of cultural differences, and the children were growing up in a society contemptuous of foreigners. Because the land they knew was America and because they wanted to be accepted, the children began to be self-conscious about themselves. Many, for example, were embarrassed to bring friends to their homes, where a foreign language, foreign cooking, and a different atmosphere prevailed.

Xenophobia

Historians often cite the Haymarket Affair as the single most important factor in causing a xenophobic reaction against all immigrants. In Chicago, in May 1886, at the height of a general strike for an eight-hour workday, the anarchist organizers—almost all of them immigrants—held a rally in Haymarket Square. As nervous police approached the peaceful gathering, someone threw a bomb at the police. It exploded in their midst, killing one officer and wounding seventy. The bomb thrower's identity was never discovered, but the courts sentenced six immigrants and one native-born American to death; another immigrant received a long prison term. Newspapers fostered a negative stereotype of the immigrant and attacked immigrants on this basis. National hysteria and fear of anarchy built up, particularly in the large cities of the Northeast and Midwest.

The current social scene presented a troubling contrast to the image of America that Anglo-Saxon intellectuals cherished. The tradition of racial nationalism had always proclaimed orderly self-government as the chief glory of the Anglo-Saxons—an inherited capacity so unique that the future of the mid-eighties cast doubt on the survival of a free society. The more anxious of the Anglo-Saxon apostles knew that the fault must lie with all the other races swarming to America. Did they not, one and all, lack the Anglo-Saxon's self-control, almost by definition? So, behind the popular image of unruly foreigners, a few caught sight of unruly races; and Anglo-Saxon nativism emerged as a corollary to anti-radical nativism—as a way of explaining why incendiary immigrants threatened the stability of the republic.[11]

Reflecting public hostility about these other "different" groups, one editorial writer said:

These people are not Americans, but the very scum and offal of Europe . . . long-haired, wild-eyed, bad-smelling, atheistic—reckless foreign wretches, who never did an honest hour's work in their lives . . . crush such snakes . . . before they have time to bite.[12]

A magazine writer warned Americans that anarchy was a "blood disease" unknown to the Anglo-Saxons but common to the "darker swarms" from Europe:

I am no race worshipper but . . . if the master race of this continent is subordinated to or overrun with the communistic and revolutionary races, it will be in grave danger of social disaster.[13]

For a long time after the Haymarket Affair, *foreign* and *radical* were linked together in American culture. Negative stereotyping and nativistic movements increased. Calls for restrictions on immigration mounted and continued until the Immigration Law of 1921 was passed.

Legislative Action

In 1907, in response to public pressure, Congress established a joint Senate-House commission to investigate the entire immigration situation. Chaired by Senator William P. Dillingham of Vermont, the commission issued a voluminous report in 1911. This report was the first to use the concept of "old" versus "new" immigration. The Dillingham Commission reported that the "new" immigrants tended to congregate, slowing the assimilation process, unlike the "old" immigrants, who had dispersed. Also, "new" immigrants were less skilled and less educated, had greater criminal tendencies, and were more willing to accept lower wages and a lower standard of living. As a solution, the commission suggested that either a literacy test be required of immigrants or immigration be restricted based upon a percentage of the immigrants from a given country already here.

Although it supposedly used social science statistics, the commission made several major errors. First, by using two simplistic categories, it failed to take into consideration vast differences in ability, opportunity, and social organization among the various ethnic groups. Second, it overlooked the longer period of time the "old" immigrants had had to achieve economic stability. Released during a time of economic recession, the report further encouraged calls for restrictions on immigration.

Congress' first response, in 1913, was to pass a literacy bill requiring all immigrants over 16 to be able to read some language. President Taft vetoed the bill, however, just as President Cleveland had vetoed a similar proposal in 1896. Finally, in 1917, Congress overrode President Wilson's veto of a new literacy bill similar in content to the earlier bills that had been vetoed. This law did little to stem the tide of immigrants, however, for it exempted those fleeing religious persecution, of whom there were a great many. Also, the literacy rate in Europe had risen, and so the literacy test was not a serious obstacle for many people. Because of the continual flow of immigrants from war-ravaged Europe, the fear that such political upheavals as the Bolshevik revolution would spread to the United States, and the general mood of isolationism that swept over postwar America, pressures for immigration restrictions mounted.

Although outgoing President Wilson vetoed the congressional bill dealing with immigration, it became law after it was reintroduced in a special session of Congress and signed by President Harding. The National Origins Quota Act of 1921, adopting a proposal that the Dillingham Commission had made ten years earlier, limited the numbers of immigrants. It imposed, for three years, a quota system under which the number of new immigrants allowed was only 3 percent of the number of people of that nationality already in the United States in 1910. The effect of this legislation was to reduce the number of southern, central, and eastern European immigrants from the 780,000 annual average in 1910–1914 to about 155,000 annually.

When the act expired, it was replaced by the even tougher Johnson-Reed Act of 1924, which reduced each country's annual quota to 2 percent of its emigrants already in the United States in 1890. This legislation discriminated even more strongly against the "newer" immigrant countries.

Henry Pratt Fairchild, a sociologist, summed up the ethnocentric attitudes of his time when he said:

The highest service of America to mankind is to point the way, to demonstrate the possibilities, to lead onward to the goal of human happiness. Any force that tends to impair our capacity for leadership is a menace to mankind and a flagrant violation to the spirit of liberalism.

Unrestricted immigration was such a force. It was slowly, insidiously, irresistibly eating away at the very heart of the United States. What was being melted in the great Melting Pot, losing all form and symmetry, all beauty and character, all nobility and usefulness, was the American nationality itself.[14]

Although an exception was made to receive approximately 400,000 Displaced Persons following World War II, the 1924 legislation remained in effect until the McCarran-Walter Act of 1952 was passed. This new law, passed over President Truman's veto, still reflected nativist biases. It simplified the quota formula to one-

"Spoiling the broth!" ran the caption to this February 1921 cartoon first appearing in the Los Angeles Times and reprinted elsewhere. This sentiment of inundation and nonassimilation of immigrants led to passage of a restrictive immigration law later that year.

sixth of one percent of the foreign-born population from each country in the 1920 census.

The Immigration and Nationality Act of 1965 ended the quota system, coming into effect in 1968. A numerical limit of 120,000 from the Western Hemisphere and 170,000 from the Eastern Hemisphere was set, based on a complicated preference system stressing job skills and close family kinship. In 1977, a 20,000 per-country annual limit was established, followed in 1978 with replacement of hemisphere quotas with a single worldwide ceiling of 290,000, later changed to 270,000, excluding refugees. Immediate relatives of U.S. citizens are admitted above the 270,000 limit, however, bringing annual legal immigration totals to about 400,000 on the average.

THE SLAVIC PEOPLES

Often included under the general classification "Slavic peoples" are the Poles, Russians, Ukrainians, Ruthenians, Bulgarians, Rumanians, Czechs, Serbs, Croatians, Slovaks, and Slovenians. The first four groups came to the United States in much greater numbers during the 1880–1920 mass migration period. Since these were more visible minorities, more information is available about their experiences, allowing separate discussions. However, American public opinion during the 1880–1920 period usually made no distinctions among these groups, and as a result their experiences in this country were frequently similar.

Slavic people had been in the New World since colonial times. New Amsterdam and New Sweden, for example, received Protestant refugees from this region in the seventeenth century, and Moravians fled to the Quaker colony of Pennsylvania in the eighteenth century. In the mid-nineteenth century many political refugees came to America, and almost all of them remained. In the post–Civil War period, however, Slavic people began to come in steadily increasing numbers, and this influx continued until the Immigration Act of 1921 sharply curtailed it.

These "new" immigrants scattered throughout the country, although a good many tended to concentrate in the mining and industrial areas in Pennsylvania and the Midwest. Beginning as unskilled workers, they formed the large majority of the workers in the coal fields, the iron and steel factories, and the slaughterhouses of Chicago. By 1917 they outnumbered all other ethnic groups in those places of occupation. The normal pattern was for the males to come first and their families later, if at all. Like many Greeks and Italians, many Slavic males merely came as sojourners to earn money for land, dowries, or just a better life, returning to their native land after a year or two. These various nationalities were the majority of the more than 2 million aliens who returned to Europe between 1908 and 1914.

In his book *The Slavic Community on Strike,* Victor R. Greene offers many vivid pictures of the immigrant experience in the mining industry. In the following excerpt he portrays the anxiety and arrival of a newcomer to the Pennsylvania coal region:

The typical greenhorn would have alighted from the immigrant train in the Pennsylvania hard-coal region undoubtedly apprehensive if he had not yet met his correspondent. With luck, one or both had a photograph to aid in recognizing the other. Otherwise, the weary traveler at the depot asked or shouted the name of his sponsor. One can imagine the tears of joy on both sides when to the immigrant's call his countryman responded, and their relief was expressed in a demonstrative embrace. . . .

The sponsor then led his charge to a group of shacks usually at the edge of town. This ghetto was separated from the rest of the populace, just as in other places in America where the East Europeans lived. Here in the coal country inhabitants term the foreign nest the Slavic mining "patch." If he arrived at night, the bundle-laden traveler would have to grope through the darkness, as no street illumination, paved roads or signs (even if he could have read them) facilitated this last, short trip.[15]

Here we can visualize the social segregation and the resulting ethnic enclave so common to all the immigrant groups. Although their languages and customs varied, the Slavic peoples commonly experienced economic hardship. Children were often put to work to help the family survive, instead of being sent to school. This not only deprived these immigrant children of a "normal" childhood but also delayed upward mobility by at least a generation.

The sight of so many children employed in mining along with their fathers appalled many Americans. The Slav would give a ready answer when accused of practising child labor—economic necessity. Popular American abhorrence of the evil forced through minimum age laws, but to little avail, as parents and employers violated them with rare penalty. Some child labor reformers announced that they had found boys as young as six working at the mines; nine or ten was probably the actual minimum. A leading reformer sympathized with the East European youngster as the "helpless victim of the frugality, ignorance, and industrial instincts of his parents." The value placed by Americans on educating the young little interested the Slav, for the valuable child was the working one. Above a minimum education was useless, and the pressing need for income forced sons into the pits at or before their teens. . . . All of the workers here, men and boys, labored the normal ten-hour, six-day week, when at full time.[16]

In the case of the Slavic immigrants, a combination of factors—their peasant background, economic deprivation, child labor and little education—slowed their rise up the socioeconomic ladder. A high proportion of second- and third-generation Slavic-Americans, for example, have lower income and educational levels than the Greek- and Jewish-Americans.[17] Among the reasons for these differences was the fact that the latter groups often came from more urbanized areas and were able to establish effective community organizations in the United States more quickly. Many Slavic-Americans today are blue collar workers whose income and standard of living have been improving as a result of the bargaining power of their unions.

THE POLES

Included among other Slavic groups until 1899, when they began to be counted separately, the Poles constituted the third largest ethnic group of the "new" immigration. With their homeland under the divided control of Germany, Russia, and Austria-Hungary, 1 million Poles came here between 1899 and 1914, fleeing poverty and seeking economic opportunity. In fact, the desire for economic improvement was so common to almost all the new immigrants that the expression to be "after bread" is found in the vocabularies of most central and eastern Europeans.

A 30-year-old Polish, Nobel Prize-winning writer, Henryk Sienkiewicz, visiting the United States from 1876 to 1878, illustrates this last point in his classic observation of the difficulties his people first encountered here. Note also the traces of ethnocentrism in his observation of Americans.

Their lot is a severe and terrifying one and whoever would depict it accurately would create an epic of human misery. . . . Is there anyone whose hand is not against them? Their early history is a tale of misery, loneliness, painful despair and humiliation. . . . They are primarily peasants and workers who have come in quest of bread. Thus you will easily understand that in a country inhabited by a people who are not at all sentimental, but rather energetic, industrious, and whose competition it is difficult to survive, the fate of these newcomers, poorly educated, unfamiliar with American conditions, ignorant of the language, uncertain how to proceed, must be truly lamentable.[18]

Although Sienkiewicz recorded his observations before the large influx of Polish immigrants, which peaked in 1907, he found a great many Polish immigrants in the United States. At that time there were Polish communities at Radom, Illinois; Krakow, Missouri; Polonia, Wisconsin; and Panna Maris, Texas.[19] Buffalo, Detroit, Milwaukee, and Chicago—the chief Polish center—all had a very sizable Polish population also.

Culture Shock

The effects of culture shock—bewilderment and disorganization, particularly in family life—can be seen in many immigrants' writings and in the records of courts and social service agencies. This initial immigrant reaction has received considerable attention from sociologists. One of the early sociological classics, *The Polish Peasant in Europe and America*, by William I. Thomas and Florian Znaniecki, explored this theme, and the framework they used has dominated other studies of Polish-American life.[20]

Leaving behind a **Gemeinschaft** society, where behavior was regulated by custom and habit, the Polish immigrants found themselves isolated, surrounded by unsympathetic and even hostile people whose language and customs they did not comprehend. Thomas and Znaniecki maintained that even if active demoralization and antisocial behavior did not occur, those who made the transition suffered a "partial or general weakening of social interests, a growing narrowness or shallowness of the individual's social life." The authors showed how many immigrant families found the adjustment too difficult, and how crime, delinquency, divorce, desertion, prostitution, and economic dependency were often the by-product of family disorganization. Such tendencies could often be found in immigrant communities caught in a web of economic and social instability.

Community Organization

The values and forms of village life in rural Poland were reintegrated, though not completely, in the parish structure of the urban American Roman Catholic Church.[21] For example, St. Stanislaus Kostka Church in Chicago in 1899 became the world's largest parish. The church blended staunch Roman Catholicism, Polish culture, and a full range of social services to help the immigrants become Americanized.

Not all Poles wanted to become Americanized, however, and many wanted the church to reflect Polish culture. Many were also frustrated by vain attempts to have Polish priests elevated in a church hierarchy dominated by the Irish and Germans. Consequently, representatives from various "independent" parishes formed the Polish National Catholic Church; Lithuanians formed a similar movement. Both church groups used their native languages in the Mass rather than Latin. They also added other elements of their culture (patriotic songs, patron saint feast days) to their church activities.

The peasants of pre-World War I Poland had negative attitudes toward edu-

"Looking Backward"

"They desire to ban the newest arrivals at the bridge over which they and theirs arrived." Five wealthy men—from left to right, an Englishman, an German Jew, an Irishman, a German, and a Scandinavian—prevent the new immigrant from coming ashore and enjoying the same privileges that they now enjoy. The shadows of the five wealthy men are representations of their social status before immigration: the Englishman's shadow is a stableman, the German Jew's is a notions peddler, and the Irishman's is a farm worker. Cartoon by Joseph Keppler, Puck, January 11, 1893.

cation. Summarizing the numerous scholarly references to this point, Helena Znaniecki Lopata reported:

> The attitudes of the Polish peasants toward education—which defined it as a waste of time at best, and as a dangerous thing undermining the traditional way of life at worst—were transplanted to the American soil. Ideally, the children of Polonia began working at an early age to help the family in its endless struggle for money. The United States Immigration Commission, which undertook an intensive study of immigrants in 17 American cities in 1911, found the children of Poles following this typical educational career: parochial school from the ages of 8 to 12, first communion, public school for two years, and then work.[22]

At that time all the Polish immigrant wanted education to do was to provide children with a strict moral upbringing in a well-disciplined atmosphere. Lopata reports that there has been a dramatic change in educational achievement among newer generations of Polish-Americans, but the median is still low because of first- and second-generation immigrants.[23]

Polonia Today

The Polish community did not fall into complete family disorganization and demoralization, as reported by Thomas and Znaniecki. Lopata reports that today these ethnic communities are stable and integrated, sources of prestige and status competition. The reason for this appears to be that the peasant culture was not a rigid set of norms subject to collapse from constant attack.

> The history of Polonia over the years, locally or as a superterritorial community, indicates that its cultural fabric was much more flexible and viable, based on the social structure and gradually changing, bending, and modifying as new norms were introduced purposely or through unconscious diffusion by its members.[24]

Several studies have shown the rate of Polish upward mobility to have been below that of other ethnic groups.[25] While this was true of the first two generations, recent studies show a change. The older Polish-Americans are at the top of the blue collar world, and most of their offspring are entering the professions and the white collar world.[26]

Examining the Polish-American community in Los Angeles, Neil C. Sandberg found a lessening in cultural ethnicity among the third- and fourth-generation members.[27] Since successive generations had experienced upward mobility, he found an inverse correlation between social class and ethnicity.[28] In other words, greater individualism and less group cohesiveness accompanied social mobility. Lopata also suggests that the Polish communities could dissolve through continued assimilation, but that a Polish national cultural base could conceivably replace the organizational and institutional base of the immigrants.[29]

THE HUNGARIANS

In the nineteenth century the Hungarians, or Magyars, were a minority in control of the Kingdom of Hungary. They began a campaign of "Magyarization"—imposing the Magyar language and culture—on all peoples living within their boundaries. As emigration to the United States increased, the Hungarian government financed both Catholic and Protestant churches and various immigrant societies in an effort to maintain its influence over Hungarians living in America. The government was not successful, as many of the immigrants sought their own identity and attempted to preserve their own languages and culture.

Like others before and after them, the Hungarians congregated in their own ethnic clusters. Most settled in New Jersey, New York, Ohio, Pennsylvania, Illinois, Indiana, and West Virginia. Cleveland and New York City attracted the greatest concentration of immigrants. With over 76,000 Hungarians living in New York City in 1920, it was the "third largest Hungarian city in the world."[30]

In each such ethnic community the Hungarians established their own institutions and organizations, embodying the same religious division among Catholics, Protestants, and Jews as in their homeland. They established their own social and fraternal organizations to provide sick benefits and to pay for funerals. They also founded their own newspapers and nationalistic cultural groups.

Labor Conditions

America was seeking industrial workers, and so the Hungarians forsook farming and worked instead in the mines, steel factories, and other heavy industries. The labor agitation of the late nineteenth century often included Hungarian as well as Lithuanian and Slavic workers. These confrontations were frequently violent and bloody.

The most violent episode occurred outside of Hazelton, Pennsylvania in 1897. A posse, headed by a sheriff who was a former mine foreman, fired several vollies into an unarmed group of 150 strikers, mostly Hungarian, who were marching to a nearby town to urge other miners to join the strike. Twenty-one immigrants were killed and another forty wounded. There was general agreement among other mine foremen that there would have been no bloodshed if the strikers had not been foreign-born.[31]

It may have been because of the prominence of Hungarians in the labor unrest that the ethnophaulisms "hunky" (for Hungarian) and "bohunk" (For Bohemian) were applied to all Central Europeans except the Jews, for whom there were special epithets. Some believe that the former term evolved into "honky" as a black reference to a White.[32]

The number of Hungarians in America at this time is somewhat difficult to determine exactly, since the U.S. government did not distinguish Hungarians from Austrians until 1905, and even the Poles living in that country were included with the Hungarians until 1919. However, based upon immigration records and the research of Emil Lengyel, it is estimated more than 2 million Hungarians came to the United States between 1871 and 1920, many from the middle Danube region. As many as half may have returned to their homeland once they had saved enough money to buy their own farms or for some other purpose.

Political Refugees

More recently, an entirely different group of Hungarians has come to America for political rather than economic reasons. When the Soviet Union crushed the Hungarian rebellion in 1956, Congress passed special legislation to circumvent the restrictive national quotas of the McCarran-Walter Bill of 1952. The United States airlifted the refugees—families, minors unaccompanied by parents, and students—and gave them temporary shelter at Camp Kilmer, New Jersey. Many voluntary agencies and Hungarian-Americans assisted the 30,000 newcomers, who, after the initial shock of displacement, quickly adjusted to America and began to rebuild their lives.

THE GYPSIES

Gypsies are perhaps America's most elusive minority. Although more than 5,000 books have been written about them, many of these are fictional and few are based on close observation. Although Gypsies number somewhere around 500,000 or more in the United States,[33] they have been studied less than some American Indian tribes just one-hundredth their size. Several reasons account for this: census and immigration authorities have never kept official statistics on them; Gypsies actively discourage any form of "snooping"; and they are frequently on the move.

Who are the Gypsies? Because they are nomads and without territorial confinement, their major distinguishing characteristics are language and culture. They speak Romany, a form of Sanskrit, which has enabled researchers to trace their origins to northern India.[34] There are the *Rom* (Gypsies) and the *gadje* (others). Words that distinguish between the ingroup and the outgroup in this way are quite common in tribal societies. When individual Gypsies assimilate into the dominant culture, they are no longer considered to be Gypsies. Thus we must view the Gypsies as a persistent subculture, maintaining a unique cultural system.

Throughout the second half of the seventeenth century, Gypsies from Scotland came to work the Virginia plantations. Records indicate that Gypsies also settled among the French in New Amsterdam.[35] In the 1840s, because of repressive actions against them in England, Gypsies began migrating to the United States in substantial numbers.[36] What with the Nazis having exterminated somewhere between 300,000 and 500,000 Gypsies, and their being generally unwelcome throughout Europe, many legal and illegal Gypsy immigrants undoubtedly came to the United States during the postwar period. Our only evidence for this, however, is their increased visibility at that time.

At the core of Gypsy culture is the family (the *familia*), which is actually a functional extended family. Parents, siblings, aunts, uncles, cousins, assorted relatives, and adopted children all live and work together, caring for one another in times of joy and sorrow.[37] The *familia* is an effective support institution for all problems, offering also a safe refuge from the gadje. The second unit of identity for the Rom is the *vitsi,* a clan or band of a few to over a hundred *familiyi,* forming a cognitive kinship group of affiliation through which Gypsies classify one another.[38]

The *familia* is strongly patriarchal, with the males working for short spans of time in a variety of trades: roofing, driveway blacktopping, auto body repair, scrap metal, and carnival work.[39] Women also provide a valuable source of income, usually fortune-telling which the Rom practice only with the *gadje,* not among themselves.[40] Although parents do not force matches, they are the principals in the mate-selection process, encouraging marriages within the *vitsa* beyond first cousin relationships. A bride-price, or *daro,* ranging from under $1,000 to $10,000, goes toward the bride's trousseau, the wedding festivities, and household articles for the new couple.[41] Most marry between the ages of 12 and 16, their age no doubt contributing to the high rate of failed Gypsy marriages. The wife traditionally lives with her husband's family, is known as a *bori,* subject to the supervision of her in-laws.[42]

Rom culture has as its linchpin the concept of *marimé,* which extends to all areas of life. The term means *defilement* or *pollution,* referring to rigid lines between good and bad, clean and unclean, health and disease, Rom and *gadje.*[43] Most notable is its application to the upper and lower halves of the human body. The pure and clean upper portion cannot come into contact in any way with the lower portion, which is *marimé,* or with objects that have been in contact with it. For example, each person uses soaps and towels of different colors for the two body portions.[44] A woman brings shame on herself for exposing too much leg, but breasts are unashamedly squeezed by both men and women.[45] A *marimé* woman—one who has given birth or is having her monthly period—cannot cook or serve food to men, step over anything belonging to a man, or allow her skirts to touch his things.[46]

The *gadje* are conceived as a different race whose main value is economic, and whose raison d'être is to trouble the Rom. The major offense of the *gadje,* the one offense the Rom can never forgive, is their propensity to defilement. *Gadje* confuse the critical distinction between the pure and the impure. They are observed in situations which the Rom regard as compromising: forgetting to wash in public bathrooms; eating with the fork that they rescued from the floor of the restaurant; washing face towels and tablecloths with underwear at the laundromat; relaxing with their feet on the top of the table.

> Because they do not protect the upper half of the body, the *gadje* are construed as marimé all over, head to foot.[47]

Both honest and dishonest Gypsies exist, but their negative attitudes toward the *gadje* make them "fair game" as targets of prejudice. Depending on chance and opportunity, some Gypsies do make individuals or companies targets for *bujo*, a flimflam or swindle. Other Rom disapprove of the bujo because it brings down community wrath on them all.

Most Gypsies cannot read or write. They have little faith in formal education, believing it will "de-Gypsy" them. Gypsies have always been remarkably adaptable to their cultural environment, however, and today they effectively use banks, credit cards, and charge accounts. They distrust the bureaucracy yet use it to their advantage.

> No gypsy likes to be pinned down on anything. Real birth certificates, for example, are anathema to him. If he needs a passport or otherwise requires proof of date and place of birth, he will obtain an affidavit for this purpose supplied and sworn to by other gypsies, or he will get a "delayed" certificate of birth one way or another from a cooperative doctor or midwife. The main thing is to be flexible about such matters, since he never knows what kind of potential bureaucratic booby trap lies in wait for him, and he always operates on the theory that it is best to expect the worst. . . .
>
> In thwarting the great computer numbers game that pigeonholes the rest of us, any self-respecting gypsy carries at least three social security cards, a handful of driver's licenses and a revolving collection of credit cards in a variety of names.[48]

Gypsy sexual mores concerning intimacy are very strict; this is an outgrowth of their normally confined living arrangements and their social structure. Premarital chastity remains highly regarded and Gypsy women rarely resort to prostitution. Birth control and abortions are rare, and as a result the birth rate is very high. Since Gypsies do not officially record these births, our only information on the birth rate comes from case studies. Peter Maas, for example, reports on one couple that has 14 children and 76 grandchildren, most under 30 years of age; these have already produced 183 children, with more likely to come.[49]

The safety valve within the social organization is the *kris*, or Gypsy court. Through an effective grapevine, Gypsies send word to the different tribes of the time and place of the kris. Much like Indian chieftains at a powwow, the tribal leaders confer, settle disputes, and place restraints upon more powerful members. The most potent social sanction is shunning, no longer acknowledging someone as a Rom. Since Gypsies spend virtually all their waking moments in group activities with other Rom, shunning is a feared social death keeping the Rom effectively in line.[50] The kris operates with ceremonial dignity; it forms the social cement that binds Gypsy society together. Once it is over, the convention becomes an occasion for general feasting, renewal of friendships, bartering, and bridebuying, since such large gatherings are not very frequent.

The Gypsies have kept their tribal codes and morals virtually unchanged in an urbanized and industrialized society by remaining outside the educational institutions and being passively antagonistic to the larger society. Although they are highly conscious of ritual, Gypsies survive through adaptation to their environment. Despite enormous pressure from every society in which Gypsies have lived, they have retained their identity and resisted assimilation. Gypsies live mostly in cities, about 10,000 in Chicago and 15,000 in Los Angeles. Residing in all states, their largest concentrations are in New York, Virginia, Illinois, Texas, Massachusetts, and the Pacific Coast.[51]

THE UKRAINIANS AND RUTHENIANS

Ukrainians and Ruthenians speak a common language and are quite alike culturally, except for their religious beliefs. The Ukrainians, who sometimes call themselves Carpatho-Russians or Little Russians, are mostly Greek Orthodox; the Ruthenians, on the other hand, are usually Roman Catholic. For both peoples religion is a very important part of life, and it serves as the strongest cultural bond in a new land.

From the Middle Ages to the close of the First World War, both peoples were at various times part of the Russian, Polish, or Austro-Hungarian Empires. Though they tried to distinguish themselves from the Russians through their language and culture, other Americans usually thought of them as Russians. Immigration authorities did not treat them as separate groups until 1896; because of this, their actual number in this country is only an estimate. Based on census data, church records, and immigration reports, historians believe that about 700,000 Ukrainians and several hundred thousand Ruthenians had emigrated to the United States by 1914.

Contact and Conflict

Although a few Ukrainians settled in the western United States and Canada and became farmers, most settled in the urban industrial centers of the Northeast and Midwest, working in the factories and coal mines. Wasyl Halich offers a good example of one Ukrainian group's early contacts with Americans and their fights with Irish miners who saw them as a serious economic threat.

The experience of the first Ukrainian group in America contains some of the basic elements of that of other pioneers on this continent. When they landed in New York, they did not understand a word of English; their colorful attire attracted much attention, and they were regarded as a curiosity. Being unable to get lodgings, they had to leave the city. They walked to Philadelphia, being forced to sleep outdoors because people were afraid to give shelter to such curious strangers. . . .

This group of immigrants arrived in the mining communities during a labor strike. Not understanding the conditions, or probably because of necessity, they went to work as strike-breakers; consequently they brought upon themselves the hatred of old miners, mostly Irishmen. There were frequent assaults on the strikebreakers which ended in riots. The influx of fresh immigrants tended to keep the wages low, and this prolonged the racial and labor antagonism between the Ukrainian and Irish groups. In connection with this racial animosity not infrequently the newcomer became a victim of "accidental" injury in the mine, or even death.[52]

Like the Ukrainians and other nationality groups, the Ruthenians settled mostly in large industrial cities, taking whatever industrial jobs they could find. Their experiences paralleled those of other immigrant groups, as shown by this excerpt from Jerome Davis' *Russians and Ruthenians in America* concerning their spatial and social segregation and their first taste of America at Ellis Island.

The majority of Russians and Ruthenians are almost as completely isolated from the American people as if they were in the heart of giant Russia. They have no points of contact with the sound elements of American life. The dream of the Russian as he leaves his native shore is that everything is beautiful in America. It is the land of liberty and equality but he begins to feel that perhaps he has been hoodwinked almost as soon as he reaches Ellis Island. The Russians claim that the coarse and brutal treatment they received at the immigrant stations is far worse than that in the Russia of the Tsars. Certainly, the wholesale tagging of the immigrant, the physical inspection, the turning back of the eyelids, rushed through with machine-like regularity resembles more the inspection of cattle than of thousands of human souls.[53]

Later Immigrants

After World War II, there were thousands of Ukrainian Displaced Persons in Europe. In 1948 Congress passed the Displaced Persons Act, allowing homeless people from war-ravaged Europe to enter, in addition to the annual quota under existing immigration laws. Under this special legislation and with the assistance of many Ukrainian-Americans, about 85,000 Ukrainian refugees came to America. The new arrivals were better educated, more politically oriented, and better able to adapt to American life than the older immigrants; they were refugees, not "economic" immigrants, and, significantly, structural conditions in their homeland had changed.

BOX 6.2

"During our first six months stay in Maryland, our home must have been the first case of integration in the South and we were not even aware of it."

"Finally in 1949 we were given permission to come to the United States as Displaced Persons, to be taken by sponsors who were to provide for us in America, where food and clothing were plentiful and freedom was everyone's right. The D.P. families boarded a huge ship where the men stayed in one part and the women and children remained in another. There were no separate compartments, but one large barrack filled with beds. Because the passengers were not used to the ocean, most of them spent their trip in sick bay or on deck trying to survive the voyage.

"On July 7, 1949, our ship landed in Baltimore, Maryland, where we were greeted by the Red Cross. We were taken to a depot and given blankets which were to be placed on the cement floor for the purpose of sleeping. At that time food and old clothes were distributed while we waited for the arrival of our sponsors. An American man bought me a Coca Cola from a vending machine. I had never tasted anything so delicious before and to this day I can still recall the incident so vividly that I can actually taste that first Coke although all others lack that particular flavor.

". . . My sister and I were sent to a public school in the local town. This experience was devastating to me since I did not know one word of English. The teacher, who seemed like a friendly person, must have tried with much frustration to communicate with me, but I was frustrated too, and so did what most children do under those circumstances—I turned her off and did what my imagination led me to do. I colored, cut, played imaginary games and had an all-around good time till I finally started to put some of the sounds together and began to realize the meaning of a few English words.

". . . Because we lived in Maryland, race prejudice was the first unpleasant and embarrassing situation which my family had to encounter. My father was the only white man to work in the fields. During the lunch break he was allowed to come into the farmhouse to eat while the others ate their lunch outside. Soon my father learned that dark-skinned men were not allowed to eat with fair-skinned men. I heard my parents discussing this problem. Since they did not know American history and did not speak English, they had to figure that for some reason the dark people were not liked in this country. We did not even know what they were called except that the farmer sometimes called them 'niggas', which later I learned was niggers.

"One day the farmer became very angry because he learned that we were entertaining the other farm hands in our home. My mother, being a good neighbor, invited the other workers to our house for supper. We had pirogis and the men drank corn liquor. The Negro families reciprocated and we were invited to their homes. It seemed a very natural thing to do and we could not understand why the farmer became so excited. During our first six months stay in Maryland, our home must have been the first case of integration in the South and we were not even aware of it.

"Although I was only seven years old at the time, my observations of the treatment which the Whites inflicted on the Blacks had a lasting effect on me. While riding in the all-white school bus, I was shown the shabby school for the 'niggas.' I could not understand why two schools were needed in the first place. While shopping for food in the town, I saw only Whites were served in most stores. No matter where I went, the Blacks were excluded. . . . Looking back, I guess that my education in Maryland did not take place in the segregated public school but on the farm, where I learned more about human behavior than any college course could ever offer."

Ukrainian refugee who came to the United States in 1949 at age 7

THE RUSSIANS

Of the more than 3 million Russian immigrants who came to the United States between 1881 and 1920, approximately 43 percent were Jewish.[54] Because many Jewish immigrants also came from other countries and all Jewish immigrants are often grouped together, and because the majority of Russian immigrants were not Jewish, we shall discuss the two groups separately.

Included among the peoples of Russia who came to the United States were the Ukrainians and Ruthenians previously mentioned, the Jews, the "Great Russians" from the medieval Duchy of Muscovy, the Byelorussians or White Russians from the western region, and to a lesser extent the Finns, Estonians, Latvians, and Lithuanians. In its efforts to "Russianize" its empire and to solve its problems with political dissidents and poverty, the Czarist government openly encouraged its ethnic minorities to leave.

Cultural Differentiation

The great majority of Russian-Americans are members of the Russian Orthodox Church, but in other respects they differ from one another. In addition to ethnic distinctions based on regional residence in eastern Europe, the emigrants also came from all levels of society.

The first wave of Russian immigrants were Mennonites, who were actually of German origin and had maintained the German language and German customs within the Russian borders for a century. As they became targets of forced assimilation, military conscription, and persecution in the 1870s, they began to emigrate to the Great Plains of the United States. Though there were never a substantial number—only thirty to forty thousand in total by 1900—they made a significant contribution to American agriculture by introducing Turkish wheat, a hard winter wheat that had become the leading first-class wheat product by the turn of the century.

The peak Russian migration occurred between 1881 and 1914, with poor, illiterate peasants emigrating for economic reasons and others seeking political or religious freedom. In America they had to make the transformation from a rural to an industrial environment. They settled in the industrialized regions, joining other immigrants in the grueling labor in the mines and factories of America. They were heavily exploited and often complained about the harshness of their work situation. Not at all passive, they were active in the labor movement and sought to improve their working conditions.

Following the Bolshevik revolution, a new type of Russian immigrant sought asylum in the United States. Czarist army officers, landowners, professional people, and political activists all fled from the new regime. Thereafter Soviet restrictions sharply curtailed Russian emigration, except for those Russians who succeeded in coming to the United States as Displaced Persons.

Life in America

During the boom immigration period, the Russian peasants were at the bottom of the socioeconomic ladder in their newly adopted country. Two excerpts, although they refer to Russian immigrants, are excellent illustrations of the recurring pattern of the minority experience. They could just as easily be applied to other groups who live or have lived in the urban slums. In the first, a religious-newspaper editor tells of the toll exacted by the long working hours under wretched conditions in 1916:

> Each working day shortens the worker's life for a few months, saps the living juice out of him, dries out the heart, dampens the noblest aspirations of the soul; transforms a living man into a sort of machine, embitters the whole life. The ragged soul and body of the worker bring forth to the world half-sick children, paralytic, idiotic—therefore the factory's poison kills not merely the unfortunate workers, but also whole generations.[55]

Orchard Street in New York City's Lower East Side, 1896. On the streets outside the crowded tenements, immigrant children talked, played, and watched the bustle of daily activity. Peddlers and sidewalk vendors were commonplace throughout this densely populated community.

Closely related to working conditions are poor living conditions because of low wages. This timeless commentary by a social worker of that period analyzes the effects of the squalor and apathy in the urban ghettoes upon the Russian immigrants:

> Parental neglect, congestion of population, dirty milk, indigestible food, uncleaned streets, with the resulting contaminated atmosphere, the prevalence of infectious diseases, multiplied temptations to break the law. . . . Add a twelve-hour day, and a seven-day week, irregular, casual employment, sub-standard wages, speeding processes which have no regard to human capacities or nervous strains for which the system is unprepared, indecent housing, unsanitary conditions both in home and factory, and we have an explanation amply adequate to account for sub-normal wage earners.[56]

Xenophobia

Many Russian-Americans who had worked hard to achieve some economic security in America found themselves jobless and unable to find work after the Bolshevik Revolution in 1917. Employers, fearful of any threat to capitalism in the United States, removed all Russian workers from their labor force lest they be Bolsheviks. Most Russian peasant immigrants were probably ignorant of the ideology of Bolshevism or, in the case of second-generation Americans, more attuned to American values and attitudes, but they were identified as "Bolsheviks" because of their nationality alone. Some may have been sympathetic to the Bolshevik regime, but only because it had overthrown the hated Czarist government. The thought of spreading that revolution to the United States, where the political, labor, and social conditions were very different, appears to have been in the minds of only a very small percentage.[57]

BOX 6.3

"I thought we came into a palace and I used to correspond with my girl-friends overseas and I told them what beautiful things we have."

"The closer we came to the United States the better we felt after being so dizzy and nauseous. The trip took us ten days and we landed in Ellis Island in 1924. We saw a big, big building. It was like an armory and, yes, we went through inspection. Before we went on the boat we went through inspection and the physical, and when we came to Ellis Island it was the same thing. They inspected all the clothing of ours and the physical too. Everything was all right with us. Some people didn't pass the inspection and they had to go back, with their health and all.

"All the immigrants were holding their bundles, the baggage, by them. Also we ate by huge tables and most of the food they served was herring. There were some young immigrant boys and they played the mandolin and I was dancing and I didn't think about anything. We were laughing and dancing. I didn't understand what they were saying but we had a lot of fun. We stayed in Ellis Island three days because we came in on a Friday and on the weekend they didn't let anyone out. So we stayed there three days.

"When my father came in—they told me it's my father, of course, but I didn't know him because I hadn't seen him in ten years—I was thrilled to see him. And, of course, as a young girl, I was very happy and I was giggling a lot and that worried my father because he heard a lot of girls came here in this country and they got in trouble. He asked me, 'My dear daughter, why are you giggling so much?' I didn't have an answer for him then. I never saw my father and yet I saw him worry for me and giving me orders what to do, what not to do. It was very strange to me, but we were all very happy to see him and finally he took us on a subway. The subway was very new to me. This I didn't see in Europe.

"When we came to America I was not of age yet to go to work, so from the Board of Education they came and they told me I must go to day school, and so my brother and I did. When I went into the school all the children spoke English and the teacher—whatever she said to me—I didn't understand. When it came to arithmetic I was tops but as far as language, she couldn't teach me much because she was busy with all the children.

"But I saw my father was struggling very much and he didn't make too good of a living here, so I went on my own and I took out working papers and I found a job. I was working in a silk mill and I went to night school.

"All the immigrants who came here were there and the teacher was teaching us, 'Open the door,' 'Close the door,' and so everyone had these advantages to learn how to speak.

"Now I see it wasn't such a big palace my father took us in. It was four rooms but everything looked so nice. It was a piece of carpet on the floor with a victrola with the letters, chairs, and a little sofa, and I thought we came into a palace and I used to correspond with my girlfriends overseas and I told them what beautiful things we have. But now when I look back it wasn't really so beautiful.

"It was a nice experience but I wouldn't like to go through with it again. I like this country. I'm very happy that we came to this country. After I got married, we had two children and we brought them up in a free country and that makes me very happy by this day that we are here."

Russian immigrant who came to the United States in 1923 at age 15

Nevertheless, labor unrest and radical agitation during that period caused a strong xenophobic reaction against many foreigners. A. Mitchell Palmer, a new attorney general, stepped into the federal power vacuum caused by the incapacity of President Wilson. His first target was the Union of Russian Workers, and his men raided eleven of their meeting places in various cities. About a month later 249 immigrants were deported, many forced to leave their wives and children behind in most dire circumstances. The Palmer raids continued with a vast dragnet of East Europeans, primarily Russians.

Officers burst into homes, meeting places, and pool rooms, as often as not seizing everyone in sight. The victims were loaded into trucks, or sometimes marched through the streets handcuffed and chained to one another, and massed by the hundreds at concentration points, usually police stations. . . . Many remained in federal custody for a few hours only; some lay in crowded cells for several weeks without a preliminary hearing. For several days in Detroit eight hundred men were held incommunicado in a windowless corridor, sleeping on the bare stone floor, subsisting on food which their families brought in, and limited to the use of a single drinking fountain and single toilet. Altogether, about three thousand aliens were held for deportation, almost all of them eastern Europeans.[58]

Opposition to these brazen and illegal actions arose, and many of the immigrants were freed. Yet more than five hundred of them actually were deported. Expulsion was still an effective weapon of the government in America. Eventually the growing strength of the CIO (Congress of Industrial Organizations) within the labor movement would bring these people a measure of economic security and domestic tranquility.

THE ITALIANS

Though few in number, the first Italians to come to the New World were significant among the early explorers. Cristoforo Colombo (Columbus), Giovanni Cabotto (John Cabot), Amerigo Vespucci, and Giovanni da Verrazano all explored and charted the new land. Father Marcos da Nizza explored Arizona in 1539, and other Italians were among the settlers throughout the Colonies. Filippo Mazzei was an influence upon the writings and the farming of his neighbor Thomas Jefferson. Many Italians fought in the Revolution, the Civil War, and the other wars that followed. Antonio Meucci invented the first primitive version of the telephone 26 years before Alexander Graham Bell, and Constantino Brumidi painted the frescoes in the rotunda of the United States Capitol building.

Throughout the nineteenth century the parallels and relationship between Italians and Blacks were somewhat unusual. In some pre–Civil War Southern localities futile efforts were made to replace black slaves with Italian workers. In other areas Southerners barred Italian children from the white schools because of their dark complexions. General Edward Ferraro commanded an all-black combat division during the Civil War. In 1899 five Sicilian storekeepers were hanged in Tallulah, Louisiana, for the unforgivable crime of treating black customers the same as Whites.

The Great Migration

The major story of the Italian immigrants began after great numbers of them arrived between 1880 and 1920. Of the more than 5 million Italians who have come to the United States throughout its history, 80 percent came during this 40-year period. Many Italian males engaged in "shuttle migration," going back and forth between America and Italy. Fleeing abject poverty and economic disaster in the harsh "Mezzogiorno" east and south of Rome, they quickly became so visible to American society that they were subject to vicious anti-Italian bigotry.

Most Italian immigrants were peasants from rural areas who were ill prepared for the occupations of an industrial nation. They therefore labored in low-status, low-paying manual jobs as railroad laborers, as miners, on the waterfront; in construction they dug ditches, laid sewer pipes, and built roads, subways, and other basic structures in urban areas.

Societal Hostility

Strong negative attitudes against the Italians sometimes resulted in violence and even killings. Several Italians were lynched in West Virginia in 1891. In the same year, when ten Sicilians were tried and acquitted of killing the New Orleans police chief, an angry mob that included many of the city's leading citizens stormed the prison and executed them, adding an eleventh victim who had been serving a minor sentence for a petty crime. Four years later coal miners and other residents of a southern Colorado town murdered six Italians. The following year three Italians were torn from a jail in Hahnsville, Louisiana, and hanged. After a street brawl in 1914, in a southern Illinois mining town, that left one Italian and two native-born Americans dead, a lynch mob hanged the only survivor, an Italian, with the apparent approval of the town's mayor. A few months later another Italian was lynched in a nearby town because he had been arrested on suspicion of conspiracy to murder a mining supervisor. Actually there was no evidence to substantiate the charge other than his nationality.

In Massachusetts, Nicola Sacco and Bartolomeo Vanzetti—an immigrant shoe factory worker and a poor fish peddler—were charged with and convicted of robbery and murder in 1920. The prosecutor insulted Italian defense witnesses and appealed to the prejudices of a bigoted judge and jury. Despite someone else's later confession and other potentially exonerating evidence, their seven-year appeals fight was futile, and they were executed in 1927. The point here is not their guilt or innocence, but that racism should never have figured in the case. At his sentencing in 1927, Vanzetti gave his famous address to presiding Judge Webster Thayer. At one point in his moving speech, he said:

> I would not wish to a dog or a snake, to the most low and misfortunate creature of the earth—I would not wish to any of them what I have had to suffer for the things that I am not guilty of. . . . I have suffered because I was an Italian, and indeed I am an Italian.[59]

These incidents are extreme examples of society's reaction to the Italian immigrants. Because they came in sizable numbers, the public became increasingly aware of their presence, and they quickly became the stereotype of all that was objectionable in the "swarm" of immigrants coming here. When an Italian got into trouble, newspaper headlines often magnified the event and stressed the of-

Nicola Sacco and Bartolomeo Vanzetti (second and third from right) walk under heavy guard to the courthouse in 1920. Their conviction of robbery and murder triggered worldwide protests and demonstrations. Despite exonerating evidence, after a seven–year appeals fight, they were executed. Their case remains an illustration of justice gone awry through bigotry.

fender's nationality.[60] Italians, like Jews, found certain occupations, fraternities, clubs, and organizations closed to them; and they were excluded from certain areas of the city and suburbs by restrictive covenants.

Social Patterns

The Italians mainly settled in the eastern cities in "Little Italies," the North End of Boston and Mulberry Street on the Lower East Side of New York City being two of the better known areas. In the west, San Francisco's North Beach area became and remains an Italian enclave. Often groups from the same village would live together in the same tenement. Earning poor wages because they were part of the unskilled labor force, they moved into rundown residential areas vacated by earlier immigrants whose children and grandchildren had moved up the social ladder and were out of the slum. Because of their numbers, they were able to create an Italian community replete with Italian stores, newspapers, theaters, social clubs, parishes, and schools. However, because of their village, family, and communal orientations, they failed to establish group-wide institutions.[61]

A variant of the extended-family system of southern Italian society was adapted to Italian life in America. Relatives were the principal focus of social life, and non-Italians were usually regarded as outsiders. True interethnic friendships rarely developed. Moreover, individual achievement (an American tradition) was not heavily encouraged. What mattered most were family honor, group stability, and social cohesion and cooperation. Each member of the family was expected to contribute to the economic well-being of the family unit.

In the old country, absentee landowners had usually exploited Italian tenant farmers, and priests and educators had silently supported this less than equitable system. Peasant children were rarely welcome in the schools. Landowner resistance to the political unification of Italy, which finally came about in 1870, further increased the hardships of tenant farmers and small landholders. Consequently, Italian immigrants generally distrusted priests and educated people.[62] In America, as in Italy, there was little involvement with the church, especially among males, and schooling was regarded as of only limited practical use. Children were permitted to attend school, for the most part, only as long as the law demanded; then they were sent to work to increase the family income. A few children were exceptions, but most second-generation Italian-Americans attending college did so in conflict with their families.

The studies of the immigrant would suggest that the move to America resulted in little change in the pattern of adult life. The social structure which the immigrants brought with them from Italy served them in the new country as well. Those who moved to the cities, for example, settled in Italian neighborhoods, where relatives often lived side by side, and in the midst of people from the same Italian town. Under these conditions, the family circle was maintained much as it had existed in Southern Italy.

The outside world continued to be a source of deprivation and exploitation. . . . Situated on the lowest rung of the occupational hierarchy, they were exploited by their employers and by the "padrone," the agent who acted as middleman between the immigrants and the labor market. Moreover, the churches in the immigrant neighborhoods were staffed largely by Irish priests, who practiced a strange and harsh form of Catholicism, and had little sympathy for the Madonna and the local saints that the Italians respected. The caretaking agencies and the political machines were run by Yankees and other ethnic groups. As a result of the surrounding strangeness, the immigrants tried to retain the self-sufficiency of the family circle as much as they could. They founded a number of community organizations that supported this circle, and kept away from the outside world whenever possible.[63]

Marginality

First-generation Italian-Americans, reinforced by so many of their compatriots, retained much of their language and customs. The second generation became more Americanized, producing a strain between the two generations. Those Italians who did not settle or remain long in the "Little Italies" assimilated much more quickly. Some changed their names and religion to accelerate the process.

In his study *Street Corner Society,* William Foote Whyte commented upon the problems of marginality experienced by Italian-American boys:

Some ask, "Why can't those people stop being Italians and become Americans like the rest of us?" The answer is that they are blocked in two ways: by their own organized society and by the outside world. Cornerville people want to be good

An Italian mother and her three children at Ellis Island seek
lost baggage. In the early years of operation at Ellis Island,
unscrupulous workers often stole from the immigrants'
meager belongings while they were processed upstairs.

American citizens. I have never heard such moving expressions of love for this
country as I have heard in Cornerville. Nevertheless, an organized way of life cannot be changed overnight. As the study of the corner gang shows, people became
dependent upon certain routines of action. If they broke away abruptly from these
routines, they would feel themselves disloyal and would be left helpless, without
support. And, if a man wants to forget that he is an Italian, the society around him
does not let him forget it. He is marked as an inferior person—like all other Italians.
To bolster his own self-respect he must tell himself and tell others that the Italians
are a great people, that their culture is second to none, and that their great men
are unsurpassed.[64]

Social Mobility

Upward mobility occurred more slowly for the Italians than for other groups coming at about the same time, such as the Greeks, Armenians, and Jews. Many factors, already discussed, contributed to this situation—a retreatist life style, disregard for education, negative stereotyping, and overt hostility protracted by the

continuing flow of new Italian immigrants. Sheltered within their ethnic communities in many large U.S. cities, the Italians adapted to an industrial society. They joined the working class and encouraged their children to do likewise as soon as they were able.

Second-generation adults, although drawn to *la via nuova*—the new way—through the schools, movies, and other cultural influences, still adhered to an extended-family-centered social structure. Most of them were employed in unskilled or semiskilled occupations. In 1976, Andrew Greeley reported that Italian Catholics ranked third behind Jews and Irish Catholics in terms of family income, but his data, as we shall discuss in Chapter 14, are somewhat misleading.[65]

Third-generation Italian-Americans are experiencing greater upward mobility than

BOX 6.4

> *"We heard a different language. . . . We didn't know what they were saying, maybe they were talking about us."*

"We came here on a large ship in 1910. We had a rough time coming here with storms and all, and my big sister was deadly sick. She never lifted her head up from her berth. It was a very long trip, about thirteen days, and the waters were rough. And when we got to Ellis Island, we were so happy to get out of that ship.

"When we got there my daddy was waiting for us and we got some nice gifts from the attendants in Ellis Island. Who got a doll, who got a jumping jack. But the funniest part was when they were selling bananas in the room, and my brother thought they were peppers and he wanted a pepper and discovered they were bananas.

"When my father took us down to the street, we heard a different language. We looked at each other. We went to my mother. We didn't know what they were saying, maybe they were talking about us. My father said, 'Don't worry. That's the language they speak here and you'll learn it yourself very fast.'

"Then my dad took us on a train to Old Forge, Pennsylvania, where he had rented rooms for us and we lived there six months. They were mostly all Polish people and German, and my mother didn't feel at home with no Italians around. My mother wanted to move to Paterson, New Jersey, because there were more Italian people there, but here she didn't understand anybody. And that's what we did. There were all Italians on the street where we lived. My dad was a musician but the other Italian immigrants worked on the trolley tracks, digging trolley tracks or to make streets.

"I got in right away with all the kids. They were all very friendly with me. As soon as recess used to come, they used to be in a playground. They would all come around me and they would talk to me in English, which helped me pick it up right away."

Italian immigrant who came to the United States in 1910 at age 8 their parents or grandparents. They are going to college and entering the professions and white collar fields. However, even though married sons and daughters move to the suburbs, the close-knit family ties remain. Frequently, the move includes two generations, not just the young.[66]

Nathan Glazer and Daniel P. Moynihan suggest that suburban Catholicism is stronger than that of the old neighborhood because the separate ethnic identities are merged into a common identity, that of American Catholics. No longer is there as much Italian antagonism to an Irish-run church. Instead, the suburban Catholic church serves more as an expression of middle-class status and acceptability than as an expression of a particular ethnic identity.[67]

THE GREEKS

Most of the Greeks who came to this country in the early twentieth century did not expect to stay long. They came as sojourners, planning to make money and then return to Greece. For many, the dowry system was an important "push" factor. Fathers and brothers found they could earn more money in the United States than in their homeland, and so these Greek men journeyed here to earn the money to provide substantial dowries for the prospective brides in their families. The fact that 95 percent of all Greek immigrants were male encouraged them to return home to their women.

Occupational Distribution

Many Greeks worked as laborers on railroad construction gangs or in factories. Those who did were often under the control of a padrone who, like the Italian *padroni,* acted as a labor agent and paternal figure. Abuses were common in such a system. Other Greek immigrants operated their own small businesses of many types, although Greeks came to be identified particularly with candy stores and restaurants.

The association of Greeks with candy and food was proverbial. Chicago became the center of their sweets trade, and in 1904 a Greek newspaperman observed that "Practically every busy corner in Chicago is occupied by a Greek candy store." After World War II the Greeks still maintained 350 to 450 confectionary shops and eight to ten candy manufacturers in the Windy City. Most Americans still connect the Greeks with restaurants and for good reason. Almost every major American city boasts of its fine Greek eating establishments, a tradition that goes back more than half a century. After World War I, for example, estimates were that the Greeks owned 564 restaurants in San Francisco alone.[68]

For many Greeks the restaurant provided a more stable economic base and a higher social status. Restaurant owners enjoyed more esteem than peddlers or manual laborers. Because so many immigrants sought a career in the restaurant business (and still do), they were continuously interacting with the general public.

A 1901 government survey showed Greeks faring better than Poles; at present, most Greeks, except for the newest arrivals, are economically secure, and many are in the upper middle class.[69]

Social Patterns

Although they came from a mostly agricultural country, the Greeks settled primarily in the cities. Like so many other ethnic groups, they resided in ethnic enclaves or "Greek colonies" within the major cities. A *kinotis,* or community council, served as the governing body; it was responsible for establishing and staffing schools and churches, and for the general welfare of the community. The *kaffeneion,* or coffeehouse, played a very important role, as Theodore Saloutos reports:

It was to the coffeehouse that the immigrant hurried after his arrival from Greece or from a neighboring community. It was in the coffeehouse that he sought out acquaintances, addresses, leads to jobs, and solace during the lonely hours. . . .

The coffeehouse was a community social center to which the men returned after working hours and on Saturdays and Sundays. Here they sipped cups of thick, black Turkish coffee, lazily drew on narghiles, played cards, or engaged in animated political discussion. Here congregated gesticulating Greeks of all kinds: railroad workers, factory hands, shopkeepers, professional men, the unemployed, labor agitators, amateur philosophers, community gossips, cardsharks, and amused spectators.[70]

Because of the favorable working conditions, many Greek males chose to remain in America. Since they preferred endogamous marriage, these men either returned home to marry a Greek woman or else sent money home to pay for the passage of a wife or wife-to-be. Like other immigrant peoples of this period, family ties among the Greeks in America were very close. The father was the unchallenged head of the household. Children were raised to be strictly obedient and had specific chores assigned to them. They studied Greek in addition to their regular studies in American public schools, and were frequently admonished to work hard and take advantage of the opportunities their parents had not had. The Greeks placed a high value on education and encouraged their children to enter the professions.

The Greek church—the Eastern Orthodox Church—and the Greek press bolstered Greek-American solidarity. Additionally, many organizations encouraged cohesiveness. The most notable of these was the American Hellenic Educational Progressive Association (AHEPA), founded in 1922. Its purpose was both to preserve the Greek heritage and to help the immigrant understand the American way of life.

Greek-Americans have blended certain aspects of pluralism (fierce love of homeland, pride in their heritage, slowness to become citizens, endogamy, institutional agencies) with some aspects of assimilation (geographic and occupational dispersion, low visibility, relatively high socioeconomic status). Cultural pluralism has been an important element in their adaptation to American society.

Societal Reaction

Not all Greek immigrants adjusted to American society smoothly. Many young males, away from family discipline and village controls, got into trouble with the law. Sociologist Henry Pratt Fairchild held a prejudiced and stereotyped view of the Greeks and other foreigners in America. He was concerned about the large overrepresentation of Greek immigrants among law violators and was pessimistic about the possibility of their assimilating or even being a benefit to American society. His comments about the effects of concentration in Greek colonies contain elements of the culture-of-poverty thesis developed in the 1960s with respect to Puerto Ricans, Mexicans, and Blacks. Fairchild states that the negative values within the community are not likely to be overcome unless there is effective interaction with members of the better (that is, middle) class. He also favored deconcentration and dispersal of Greeks.

It seems likely that the presence of this race (Greeks) in the country will add to, rather than diminish, the growing indifference to law as such, which is one of the most threatening signs of the times. This lack of reverence for law, and every form of authority, seems to be characteristic of every race. But the Greeks appear to have it when they come. What the character of their children will be in this respect we can only conjecture. . . .It has been frequently remarked in the course of the preceding discussion, that the evil tendencies of Greek life in this country manifest themselves most fully when the immigrants are collected into compact, isolated, distinctively Greek colonies, and that when the Greek is separated from the group and thrown into relations with Americans of the better class, he develops and displays many admirable qualities.[71]

Today few negative comments about Greek-Americans are heard. When Greeks are singled out as an ethnic group at all, the reference is usually positive or neutral. They often serve as a model of a nationality group that has been accepted, has achieved economic security, and has become Americanized, yet has also retained a strong pride in their ethnicity.

THE PORTUGUESE

Though it is a relatively small country, Portugal has provided the United States with immigrants of varying economic and cultural backgrounds. Whether their manner of adaptation was assimilationist or nonassimilationist has depended upon the part of the United States to which they migrated.

Early Immigrants

The fondness of many Portuguese for the sea was reflected in their early contributions to the United States. In the sixteenth century Portuguese mariners explored the California coast. In the eighteenth and nineteenth centuries, immigrants, primarily from the Azores Islands, settled in New England and became an important part of the fishing industry. Mostly of Flemish stock, these Portuguese had been whalers and fishermen for many generations. Recruited by business agents to bring their expertise to America, they came and settled in such coastal port cities as New Bedford and Newport. Though the Portuguese were predominantly Catholic, the Jews among them erected one of the first synagogues in the United States in Newport in 1763. Other Portuguese, some from the mainland and of Moorish lineage, worked on farms and in dairies. They started as farm laborers, then rented and eventually bought the old New England farms that became available. As the Portuguese continued to come and American industry grew, the newcomers turned to factory work; the majority of New England's Portuguese were working in factories shortly after the turn of the century.

A few Portuguese went to California, lured by the gold rush. Others followed in typical chain migration fashion. Thousands of other Portuguese went to the Hawaiian Islands in the late nineteenth century. By 1920 about 84,000 Portuguese lived in New England; the rest lived in California and Hawaii. Since transportation for laborers and their families was guaranteed and since they had labor contracts from the plantation owners, they were willing to make the long journey. Those in Hawaii assimilated, while those in California, encountering little conflict, retained their ethnic identity and sense of community to a much greater degree. The reason for this difference appears to be that the Portuguese quickly became a sizable working force on the pineapple and sugar plantations—about 12 percent of the population. The dominant group, from northern Europe, identified themselves separately through a special census classification and stereotyped the Portuguese as inferior. The Portuguese reacted by continuing to work hard, moving into crafts and skilled trades that paid better, and intermarrying and surrendering the usual accouterments of ethnic visibility—language, customs, residential clustering, and sometimes even their names—to achieve a respected status.

There is a wide cultural differentiation between the Portuguese in the Island setting and those in California today. Four decades of separation have shown the influence that environment can have in remolding a people. Although there have been changes in the cultural patterns of the Portuguese in California, it is in Hawaii, where the Portuguese people have gone through the processes of competition, conflict, and accommodation, and assimilation and have broken down social distance, that the distinction from old-world family patterns [is most evident.][72]

As the experiences of other groups have already shown, the adaptation of strangers in a new land moves along a continuum that may or may not end in total assimilation. The Portuguese in Hawaii and California exemplify two successful patterns under differing structural conditions.

Later Immigrants

As with other immigrant groups, the greatest number of Portuguese were encouraged to migrate here by the Industrial Revolution. Beginning in the late nineteenth century and peaking in 1921, after which immigration quotas restricted their numbers, 200,000 came, many to work in the mills of Massachusetts and Rhode Island. Their adaptation, as rural peasants in an urban setting, parallels that of other ethnic groups. They clung to the old ways and restricted their social relations to their own kind.

In an analysis of two Portuguese communities in New England in the late 1920s, Donald Taft noted a high infant mortality rate and low level of educational achievement. This lack of interest in education may have been due to their oc-

These Portuguese–American fishermen, sailing out of New Bedford, Massachusetts in 1940, are cutting up blackfish blubber. New England seaports such as New Bedford, Newport, and Provincetown attracted many Portuguese in the eighteenth century, and today thriving Portuguese communities continue in those places, and some of the men still earn a living as fishermen.

cupational preference for farming and fishing as well as to their high rate of illiteracy.[73] In the following passage note the ethnocentric outlook, patronizing tone, and stereotyping.

There seems no doubt that for the majority of Portuguese, immigration to New England has meant an improved status. Granting that they are poverty-stricken here, that they live far below our standards of comfort and decency, that women often work outside the home and that children leave school as soon as the law allows, that homes are unattractive and wages low; nevertheless their lot is far better than in the homeland, except perhaps in its picturesqueness. America gives the Portuguese a small wage but a higher one, a poor house but a better one, a meager sixth grade education but more than they know enough to want, and it is universal and compulsory.

. . . The presence of these people undoubtedly handicaps the public health organizations, increases the births where they should be fewest, and the death rates of all ages but especially of little children. It also makes possible economic and political exploitation whether by unscrupulous natives or by their own leaders. Indeed the presence of the Portuguese goes far to account for the poor record of our two communities [Fall River and Portsmouth] in official statistics and for the not altogether enviable reputation which they may have among sociologists.[74]

Though they are scattered throughout the nation, Portuguese-Americans are concentrated in Massachusetts, Rhode Island, California, Hawaii, and Newark, New Jersey, where *Luso-American,* the only Portuguese national weekly newspaper, is still published. A steady flow of new immigrants from Portugal has replenished the Portuguese communities. In the 1960s the numbers of arrivals increased sharply because of political unrest and worsening economic conditions in Portugal. As the situation there has become more stable in recent years, the numbers departing for America have declined.

THE ARMENIANS

Armenian immigrants settled in Jamestown in 1619. In that year Armenian workers, together with some Germans and Poles, struck to secure the political rights being denied them as "inferiors." The Virginia House of Burgesses granted them their freedom in response to this early civil rights protest in America.[75]

Confusion Over Refugee Identity

A number of factors appear to have initiated Turkish persecution of the Armenians, who had come under the rule of the Ottoman Empire after 1375. As Christians in a Moslem country, the Armenians became a special target for the authoritarian, religiously intolerant rulers. Moreover, they were often better educated and more prosperous than the Turks, who therefore suspected them of wanting political power. Over the years Armenians migrated for religious, political, and economic reasons, but the Turkish government's genocidal campaign against them between 1894 and 1916 was the primary reason for their movement to America. In 1915–1916 alone; the Turks killed 1 million Armenians.[76]

Because they traveled with Turkish passports and the U.S. government identified immigrants by country of origin, Armenian and Syrian Christians were classified as Turks. It is therefore difficult to determine exactly how many Armenians came here in the late nineteenth century. However, government estimates placed the number of Armenian immigrants between 1895 and 1899 at 70,982. The Turkish government then cut off further emigration until 1915. Because of the war, only a few thousand came until the 1920s, when 26,000 Armenians arrived in America.[77] After that, although Armenians continued to emigrate, their actual numbers were further obscured because the U.S. government identified them by their points of departure: usually Egypt, France, Lebanon, Iraq, Iran, Turkey, or Syria. Despite their high degree of ethnic consciousness, church records, and special censuses, the number of Armenians remained only an estimate. That estimate presently ranges from 350,000 to 500,000 Armenian-Americans currently residing in the United States.

Societal Reaction

As indicated in the social distance scales of Emory Bogardus, American public opinion and stereotypes of the Turks were quite negative, partly as a result of the atrocities committed against the Armenians.[78] Still, when Armenians attempted to become United States citizens, the federal government tried to stop them. The issue was resolved in 1925 in the U. S. District Court with the case of Tatos O. Cartozian, an Armenian rug merchant in Portland, Oregon. The government argued that Armenians were of Asiatic descent and thus not eligible for citizenship under the 1790 Naturalization Act, which allowed only Whites to become citizens. By this time Asians were the only group ineligible for citizenship; persons of African descent were given the right to citizenship by the Fourteenth Amendment and changes in the naturalization laws. After hearing expert testimony to the effect that they were Indo-European in language and origin, the court ruled in favor of the Armenians.

Cultural Differences

Armenians have had a long, continuous history because of their resiliency in maintaining their cultural identity. Two contributing factors have been language and religion. Not only do Armenians have their own language, they also have their own alphabet, increasing ingroup solidarity. A second source of ethnic cohesion among the Armenian people, both in their homeland and in America, has been the Armenian Apostolic Church. As the first national Christian church in the world, dating from the 3rd century, it never sought converts among other nationalities and functioned as much more than a religious institution. As Gary Kulhanjian reports:

The Armenian Church was and still is a fortress for preserving the cultural identity of Armenians in the world. Religion, social organizations, ethnocentrism, family life, and endogamy had all been potent social forces by which Armenians or Americans of Armenian descent have been culturally identifiable.[79]

Armenian art, architecture, literature, philosophy, and music are heavily interwoven within the fabric of the Church.

Another important factor in Armenian cohesiveness has been family life. But, as Kulhanjian observes, the assimilation process appears to be weakening some traditional influences.

The patriarchal family life of Armenians has played a major part in the cultural identification of these people throughout the world. Family life has traditionally advocated endogamy of the young generation. The young people have rebelled against many traditional ways of doing things, including endogamy. Americans of Armenian descent have drifted away from marrying within their minority, although some do; however, a great many still retail their subcultural identity with the Church, although they have married Americans from various backgrounds. This young group of second- and third-generation Armenian-Americans has not been as ethnocentrically minded as their parents or grandparents, who are foreign-born Americans. Cultural differentiation has been predominant among the older foreign-born Armenian-Americans.[80]

Armenians Today

The 1980 census identified 213,000 Armenians, as determined by nativity or parentage, living in the United States. However, the Armenians claim an ethnic community here and in Canada numbering between 350,000 and 500,000. They are scattered throughout the country, with larger concentrations in New England, New York, New Jersey, Michigan, and California.

SOCIOLOGICAL ANALYSIS

With so many millions of immigrants from diverse backgrounds discussed in this chapter, our study of them has necessarily covered a wide range of material. By applying the three major sociological perspectives, however, we can find unifying themes of common experiences in dominant-minority interrelations.

The Functionalist View

From this viewpoint, the arrival of significant numbers of immigrants served the rapidly industrializing nation well. Immigrants provided a valuable labor pool to meet the needs of an expanding economy, enabling the United States to emerge as an industrial giant. Unemployment was not a problem, and the poor of Europe were able to build a better life for themselves in their adopted land. Despite nativist fears, the freedom and economic opportunities created fervent patriotic converts among the newcomers. Later political and war refugees, many of them talented and skilled people, increased this hard-working, freedom-loving population. The American social system evolved into a complex, interdependent, and prosperous society, in large measure through the efforts of its first- and second-generation European Americans.

Accompanying problems of overcrowded tenements, social disorganization, crime, harsh working conditions, labor strife, and ethnic antagonism can all be understood within the context of rapid social change. For the mostly poor immigrants unable to afford better housing, the tenements at least offered a place to begin life anew, while also providing a dense concentration of compatriots for a social support system. For many, the abrupt change of life—language, customs, urban living—brought problems of adjustment resulting in various pathologies of behavior. The abuses of the industrial age—child labor, poor wages, and working conditions, lack of security—did cause severe hardship for many workers, but these factors were overcome in time through legislative safeguards and labor union organization. Massive immigration, especially in the first two decades of this century, further strained society's absorption capabilities, prolonging the assimilation process and thereby fostering negative reactions from native-born Americans. Gradually the necessary adjustments occurred: labor regulations, housing codes, acculturation, upward mobility. With the corrective actions, harmonious interrelations ensued, restoring the social system to a stage of equilibrium.

The Conflict View

Use and abuse of power, not societal inability to cope with rapid change, marks the conflict approach. American industrialists exploited immigrant workers, maximizing profits by minimizing wages and maintaining poor working conditions. When workers protested or went out on strike, employers blacklisted them, hired other ethnics as strikebreakers, secured court injunctions, or used vigilantes, police, or state militia to break up the demonstrations. Employers held absolute economic power to curtail worker agitation, since their position was reinforced by the other social institutions aligned with the powerful against the powerless. The power theory suggested by Lieberson places such actions in a conceptual framework consistent with earlier experiences of the Irish. Bonacich's split labor market theory becomes applicable, for example, in the use of Hungarians and Italians as strikebreakers, generating interethnic conflict as employers sought to thwart the "troublemakers."

Upward mobility for these "white ethnics" occurred not from gradual societal adjustments, say conflict theorists, but from an organized worker movement in opposition to the power structure. First- and second-generation American workers fought hard through the labor union movement—often at great risk and with great sacrifice against strong pressures—to secure their share of the American Dream. The change resulted from conflict, from class consciousness, and an unrelenting social movement against the entrenched economic interests. With economic gains came stability and respectability, enabling these ethnic groups to gain acceptance and overcome prejudice and discrimination against them.

The Interactionist View

Imagine yourself a native-born American living in a northeastern or midwestern city at the turn of the century. You would find your city filled with from two-thirds to three-fourths foreign-born. These people were mostly dark skinned and dark haired or else physically distinctive because of their clothing. Everything about them—their religion, life-style, behavior—seemed so different, so "un-American." The people you associated with did not live clustered together in such crowded slums. And there were so many of these people! You constantly read about them getting arrested for breaking some law or another. The city had changed, and not for the better! You worried that the country itself would lose its "authentic" identity as it was overrun by these European "misfits" who had little appreciation for American values and democratic principles.

Such a mental picture isn't that difficult, is it? Industrialization, urbanization, social disorganization, economic exploitation, and a host of other factors may have created the social problems regarding immigrants then, but the native-born mostly saw only the symptoms manifest in the immigrant communities. Believing such conditions had not existed until "these people" came, Americans defined the problems as inherent in the "new" immigrants. Indeed, everything the typical American saw or heard only reinforced the perception that the current floodtide of immigrants threatened the entire social fabric. The cries for immigration restrictions, eventually enacted, and the acts of avoidance, discrimination, and occasional violence all reflected the negative stereotyping of those who appeared "different."

RETROSPECT

Without question, the period from 1880 to 1920 was the greatest immigration epoch in American history, as 23 million persons left everything behind for the promise of "Golden America." Social and economic forces at work on both continents combined to encourage this mass migration. Europe's inability to offer a decent standard of living and America's need for great quantities of industrial labor were the major push-pull factors. Recruited or attracted to America because of its rapid industrialization, European immigrants fulfilled an important need in the growth and development of the United States.

Yet the "new" immigrants were hardly welcomed with open arms. Ethnocentric preconceptions of how an "American" should look and behave prejudiced large segments of the society against them. Their physical and cultural differences identified them as strangers and heightened nativist fears of an undesirable element populating America. By 1900 one-third of the total population were first- or second-generation Americans, a fact that spurred demands to close the "floodgates" to stem the "immigrant tide." Finally, in 1921 the first restrictive legislation against Europeans was enacted. Not until the late 1960s would the discriminatory quota system based on national origin be terminated entirely.

Many of the theoretical considerations in majority-minority relations apply to the European immigrants. Their cultural and structural differences set the stage for stereotyping, all three levels of prejudice, and discrimination. Progressive stages of culture shock, community organization, development of subcultural areas, and marginality were often the norm. Dominant patterns of nativism, antagonism, social and spatial segregation, and legislative controls were common, as were the minority responses of avoidance, deviance, defiance, and acceptance.

The immigrants settled in ethnic clusters and established their own institutions, and they generally followed the broad patterns of earlier groups of immigrants. The various new peoples differed from one another in language, customs, and value orientations, although Americans frequently found those who were not Italians or Jews indistinguishable, and lumped them all together. Not all of them wanted to stay, and not all of those who did stay assimilated. The immigrants in their ethnic clusters exhibited the same sort of cultural pluralism as, in more isolated settings, the "old" immigrants had shown. But the times were different. Urbanization had brought about a greater degree of functional interdependence, a reliance on one another for exchange of goods and services. Thus, the newcomers were not as isolated as the earlier immigrants had often been. Their numbers were great, and the dominant society wanted them to assimilate, although it also feared they could not do so.

For many, the transition from an agrarian to an industrial society was difficult. Those who had either come from an urban background or had to adapt to being a subordinate minority group in Europe, such as the Greeks, Jews, and Armenians, were able to adjust to city life more easily. They took advantage of educational opportunities, climbed the socioeconomic ladder when they or their children could, and adjusted to American society. Others, being mostly illiterate peasants, took longer to get established. Not all the immigrants became citizens, nor were they all successful. Some did not learn English. Today, the poorer areas of the cities, which originally housed newcomers, contain a number of poor and aged immigrants, for whom the American Dream, in economic terms at least, has proved elusive.[81]

American industry employed the immigrants because it needed them. The work was hard, the hours long, and the pay low, but most believed that the opportunities were better in America than in their homelands. Exploitation of workers led to labor unrest and the growth of the union movement. Some immigrants were attracted to radical movements, others returned home, but most toiled, indoors or outdoors, to succeed in their adopted land for themselves and their children.

REVIEW QUESTIONS

1. How had structural conditions in America changed for the "new" immigrants?

2. What factors aroused dominant antagonism against the newcomers? In what ways was this hostility expressed?

3. Were there any similarities in the ways in which the various ethnic groups adapted to American society?

4. Apply the concepts of stereotyping and the vicious circle to the immigrant experience during this period.

5. How does the power differential relate to these immigrants' experiences and the labor union movement?

6. How do the three major sociological perspectives explain the experiences of southern, central, and eastern Europeans?

SUGGESTED READINGS

Davis, Jerome. *The Russian Immigrant,* reprint ed. New York: Arno Press and *The New York Times,* 1969.

    A classic work still considered pertinent to understanding the Russian-American acculturation experience.

Gambino, Richard. *Blood of My Blood.* Garden City, N. Y.: Doubleday, 1974.

    Comprehensive and readable, a moving account of the Italian-American experience over the years.

Gans, Herbert. *The Urban Villagers,* 2nd ed. New York: Free Press, 1983.

    An excellent community study of an Italian-American neighborhood, examining its cohesive social network.

Halich, Wasyl. *Ukrainians in the United States,* reprint ed. New York: Arno Press and *The New York Times,* 1970.

    Originally published in 1937, but still the definitive study of early Ukrainian immigrants.

Lengyel, Emil. *Americans From Hungary,* reprint ed. Westport, Conn.: Greenwood Press, 1974.

    First published in 1948, a fine study of the Hungarian-American subculture and immigrant adjustment to the United States.

Lopata, Helena Z. *Polish Americans: Status Competition in an Ethnic Community.* Englewood Cliffs, NJ: Prentice-Hall, 1976.

    A concise, well-written study of the Polish-American community, with a primary focus on its multigenerational changes.

Soloutos, Theodore. *The Greeks in the United States.* Cambridge, Mass.: Harvard University Press, 1964.

A thorough study of the Greek-Americans, their economic mainstreaming and their retention of ethnic solidarity.

PART THREE
RACIAL MINORITIES

CHAPTER 7

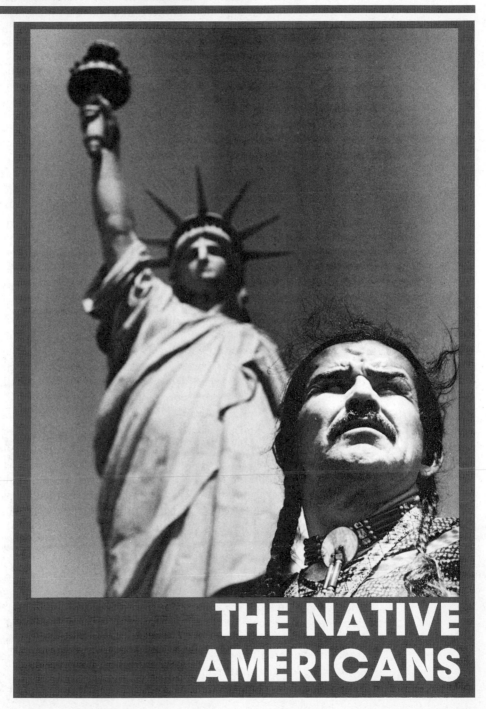

THE NATIVE AMERICANS

Different in race, material culture, beliefs, and behavior, the Europeans and the Indians at first were strangers to each other. The Europeans who first traded with and then conquered the natives showed little interest in or understanding of them. Brutalized and exploited, the American Indians experienced all the dominant group response patterns—legislative action, segregation, expulsion, xenophobia, and, for some tribes and groups, annihilation. In turn, they reacted with varying patterns of avoidance, defiance, and acceptance, steadfastly remaining a numerous and persistent subculture leading a marginal existence.

SOCIOHISTORICAL PERSPECTIVE

From the first European contact with the original population in the New World to the present day, the Native Americans have usually not been understood. Columbus called them Indians, since he thought he had reached the islands off the coast of Asia known as the Indies. Today some object to this word, preferring to use *Native American* or a tribal name such as Cherokee, Shoshone, or Blackfeet.

Early European explorers and settlers, reflecting ethnocentric views, condemned those aspects of Indian culture that they did not understand and related to other aspects only in terms of their own culture. Some considered the Indians to be savages, even though Indian societies had a high degree of social organization. Others idealized them as uncorrupted children of nature who spent most of their time engaging in pleasurable activities. In Europe, intellectual debate raged over how the presence of people so isolated from other human beings could be explained. Were they descended from the inhabitants of Atlantis, Carthage, ancient Greece, East Asia? Were they the Lost Tribes of Israel?[1] Were they no better than beasts, or were they intelligent, capable beings?

In colonial and frontier America, the stereotype of the Indians was often negative, especially when they were an obstacle to those Europeans who wanted to use the Indians' land. As a result of *self-justification,* the denigration of others to justify maltreating them, some Whites viewed Indians as cruel, treacherous, lying, dirty heathens. Although that very negative stereotype no longer prevails, even today Indians are portrayed in films, television, and comic strips as colorfully dressed but unemotional, humorless, and uncommunicative individuals. Supposedly, all they desired during the frontier period was scalps, firearms, and "firewater." Indians are often stereotyped as backward, lacking ambition, or continually drunk, or they are regarded as romantic anachronisms.

Some people overgeneralize about Indians, thinking of the many tribes as one people even though the various tribes have always been quite different from one another in language, social structure, values, and practices. Of the approximately three hundred different Indian languages spoken in 1492 in what is now the United States, only about fifty to a hundred still exist. At present there are 267 Indian reservations under federal jurisdiction, as well as scattered pieces of land at thirty-eight other locations maintained in federal trusteeship for Indians, Aleuts, and Eskimos. The Bureau of Indian Affairs recognizes 493 different tribal entities in the

United States.[2] Figure 7.1 shows the principal Indian tribes living in the United States today.

Native Americans share several distinguishing physical characteristics. Most Native Americans have thick, black, straight hair but very little facial or body hair. They tend to be dark-eyed with rather prominent cheekbones. Beyond these similarities they generally vary greatly in physical stature and features. The term *red-skin* is not at all accurate; their skin coloring ranges from yellowish to coppery brown.

The Indians' experiences in the American Colonies were unique in one respect: the Whites, not the Indians, were the newcomers, and the Whites were the minority for many years. The relationship between Indians and Whites was often characterized either by wariness and an uneasy truce or by violent hostilities. Even in colonial Massachusetts, where peaceful coexistence initially prevailed, the situation deteriorated.

As the two peoples interacted more fully, each group became more disenchanted with the other. The Indians could not understand the English settlers' use of beatings, hangings, and imprisonment as means of social control. The settlers could not understand the Indians' resistance to Christianity and to the Whites' more "civilized" way of life. These were but peripheral considerations, however: the major issue was whose way of life would prevail and whether the land would be further developed or allowed to remain in its natural state, replete with fish and wildlife.

The disenchantment grew as the settlers encroached more and more upon Indian lands. Eventually, hostilities broke out. Large-scale fighting, resulting in many killings, broke out in Virginia in 1622 and in Connecticut in 1637. Metacom, the leader of the Wampanoag, who was known as King Philip, united the Nipmuc and Narraganset behind him in 1675 and attacked fifty-two of the ninety New England settlements, completely destroying twelve of them. The Colonies seemed in danger of total defeat, but in 1676, Philip was killed and the Indian bands were wiped out one by one. Fighting between Indians and Whites continued sporadically and locally throughout the westward movement until the 1880s. Dominant-group attitudes toward the Indians, consisting of a mixture of racial and cultural prejudices, led to intergroup tensions and marked the beginning of a pattern that would be repeated with the Blacks, Asians, and Hispanics, although each group's experiences were different.

In the mid-nineteenth century, the government embarked upon a policy of containment as a means of controlling the Indians and encouraging westward expansion. The government used military force to displace the many tribes and resettle them on wasteland reservations, where they remained unless new settlement plans or the discovery of oil and valuable minerals resulted in further displacement. This program of forced segregation and dependency, compounded by attempts at forced "Americanization," reduced the Native Americans to the status of a subordinate colonized people—wards of the government—living at a subsistence level. Reflecting changing attitudes and interests in the late nineteenth and early twentieth centuries, Congress enacted various pieces of legislation ostensibly designed to help the Indians. These laws, to be discussed shortly, actually

FIGURE 7.1

Principal Indian Tribes in Continental United States, Showing Where They Live Today

Source: Based on data from "Indian Land Areas, General" (map), U.S. Department of the Interior, Bureau of Indian Affairs, U.S. Government Printing Office, 1971.

Tribal lands

Allotted reservations (few of these areas are now owned exclusively by Indians)

Federally terminated tribes

Former reservations in Oklahoma

* Iroquois (New York State) —largely state-supervised; federal consent required for alienation of land; some federal programs available

× Small Indian communities called "Rancherias" in California, and "Colonies" in Nevada

In 1834, most of what is now Oklahoma was designated Indian Territory by Congress. After this, many tribes were forced to move to this land. In 1907, Oklahoma became a state. The shaded areas are no longer reservations, but in them live over 100,000 Indians.

worked to the Indians' disadvantage and worsened their already low and dependent status.

Two short-lived Pan-Indian associations of the twentieth century, the Society of American Indians in the 1910–1920 decade and the National Congress of American Indians in the 1930s, failed to unify the tribes into an effective pressure group or to draw much outside support. New moves toward unity began in the 1960s, and new legislation and greater government sympathy helped the Indians' cause. The most significant factor in the Indians' new success, however, was the impact of the civil rights movement, for it created a greater social consciousness in the country and inspired the Indians to strive harder for self-determination. Though they had never been silent, they now became more vocal and organized, and they found non-Indians more receptive. They became more militant, as demonstrated by the occupation of Alcatraz Island in 1969, the takeover of the Bureau of Indian Affairs in Washington, D.C., in 1972, the long confrontation in 1973 at Wounded Knee, site of the 1890 massacre, and the march on Washington in 1978. A new generation of Red Power advocates took up the fight for Indian rights. Some attempted to achieve their goals through a national or Pan-Indian movement, whereas others preferred an emphasis on individual tribal culture and practices.

Throughout the five-hundred-year history of Indian-White relations, the Indians have frustrated Whites by their general refusal to believe that the Whites' religions and life styles are better. To understand the nature of these relations between dominant and majority groups is to understand the important role of ethnocentrism, stereotyping, cultural differences, and power differentials in intergroup relations.

EARLY ENCOUNTERS

To appreciate the significance of the first encounters, it is important to note that two human races were seeing each other's physical distinctions for the first time, but also that the vast differences in culture, knowledge, and life style made each a source of wonder to the other. Columbus's first impressions of the Arawak Indians in the Caribbean reflected ethnocentrism:

I knew they were a people who would better be freed and converted to our Holy Faith by love than by force . . . they are all generally of good height, of pleasing appearance and well built. . . . They must be good servants and intelligent . . . and I believe that they would easily become Christians, as it appeared to me that they had no sect.[3]

Though he admired the Indians, Columbus essentially saw them as "creatures." He looked upon them as potential servants, and he assumed that they had no religious convictions because he found no trappings of religion or written codes such as he was accustomed to seeing in Europe.

As Europeans became more curious about Indians, an idealistic concept of the Indian as the Noble Savage took hold. Michael de Montaigne, a sixteenth century French philosopher, after reading many travelers' journals and talking with explorers, wrote that the Indians were indeed Noble Savages, for they

---

[have] no kind of traffic, no knowledge of letters, no intelligence of numbers, no name of magistrate, nor of politics, no use of service, or riches, or of poverty; no contracts, no successions, no partitions, no occupation but idle, no apparel but natural, no manuring of lands, no use of wine. The very words that impart a lie, falsehood, treason, covetousness, envy, detraction, were not heard among them.[4]

While some Europeans were romanticizing Indians and a positive mystique about the Indians swept Elizabethan England and other parts of Europe, others viewed the Indians as bloodthirsty barbarians and cruelly exploited them. The early phases of Spanish military activity, particularly in Mexico, Peru, and the American Southwest, included Indian enslavement, plunder, rape, and slaughter. The Spanish put the peaceful Arawak Indians of the Caribbean islands into forced labor, using them in land clearing, building, mining, and plantation work. Since they had no weapons comparable to those of their conquerors, the subjugated peoples often responded by committing mass suicide and mass infanticide. The Indian population began to decline rapidly as a result of disease, warfare, and self-destruction.

The dichotomy of views of the Indian either as a Noble Savage or as a bloodthirsty barbarian was epitomized in the great debate between Bartolome de las Casas, a bishop serving in the New World, and Juan Ginés de Sepúlveda, a Renaissance scholar. The latter considered the Indians no better than "beasts" who should be enslaved. Las Casas presented a picture of the Indians as innocent children, both artistically and mechanically inclined, with intellectual capabilities for learning and a willingness to coexist with the Spanish intruders.[5] In 1550, King Charles V appointed the Council of the Indies, a panel of distinguished theologians and counselors, which met at Valladolid. The Council heard the arguments of the two antagonists, agreed in large measure with Las Casas, and thereby redirected Spanish policy toward the Indians.

As part of his long struggle to protect the Indians, Las Casas had returned to Spain in 1517 to plead their case directly to the king. In doing so, he revealed the extent of their decimation: "At my first arrival in Hispaniola (1497), it contained a million inhabitants and now there remain scarce the hundredth part of them." He felt that the Indians could survive only if another labor force replaced them. By convincing the Spanish authorities that Africans were sturdier and better adapted to agricultural operations, he opened the doors for the subsequent massive slave trade of Blacks to the Spanish possessions in the New World. It is cruelly ironic that the humane efforts of Las Casas on the Indians' behalf led to the brutalization and exploitation of black people and racial discrimination against them for over four hundred years.

The Indian populations in the United States and Latin America differ in their social, economic, and political status. Several factors, including habitability of terrain, migration patterns, degree of industrialization, and especially different attitudes in the various countries, have accounted for these differences. In the United States, the nineteenth century policy of removal, containment, and Indian dependency upon the federal government prevented most tribes from becoming full participants in American society. In Latin America, however, Spain adopted a more benevolent policy toward the Indians in 1550, following the recommendations of the Council of the Indies, and greater interaction, intermarriage, absorption, and gradual acculturation occurred among the Indians and the Spanish. Except for those living in the central Andes and other remote areas, the Indians became fuller participants in their society than their counterparts in the United States, and lived in relative cultural and racial harmony with the White, Black, *mulatto* (of mixed black and white ancestry), and *mestizo* (of mixed Indian and white ancestry) populations. Along with the other nonwhite groups, they were part of the large low-ranking social class, in sharp contrast to the small high ranking class. Despite racial harmony, they have had very little opportunity for upward mobility, and most Latin-American nonwhites live in economic stagnation. In contrast, most North American Indians have experienced both economic stagnation and a lack of racial harmony.

Indian populations in Latin America and North America were decimated by various sicknesses that had resulted from earlier contact with white explorers or traders. When the early settlers in New England found deserted Indian villages, they rejoiced; they considered this to be mute testimony of the judgment of Divine Providence upon these "heathens" as well as upon their own undertaking. The Lord had smitten the pagan to make way for the righteous! This accidental annihilation had often resulted from a serious contagion such as smallpox, tuberculosis, or cholera. The Indians also were often fatally susceptible to such diseases as measles, mumps, and chicken pox because they had not developed immunities to these European illnesses.

Cultural Strains

When the white settlers were few in number and depended upon Indian assistance, the Indians were hospitable and the Whites were receptive to them. The Indians along the Eastern Seaboard helped the colonists to get settled by teaching them what to plant and how to cultivate it as well as imparting to them the knowledge and skills they would need to survive in the wilderness. As the settlements became stabilized, the relations between the two races became more strained, as the following excerpt from Douglas Edward Leach's study of seventeenth-century New England reveals:

Ever since the coming of the white men there had been economic intercourse between Indians and English traders. At first it had seemed that the flourishing trade in furs, tools, cloth, and foodstuffs was as beneficial to the Indians as to the colonists, but as time went on and the English extended their activities the Indians grew more and more dissatisfied with the situation. It became apparent that they were gradually sinking into a position of complete economic subservience. Indian villages which had once enjoyed almost total sulf-sufficiency were now increasingly dependent upon products of English manufacture. Individual Indians became enmeshed in debt, which degraded them still further in the eyes of the English. The wiser leaders among the Indians saw that if the trend were not reversed, the time would soon come when the natives of New England would be completely stripped of their independence.

In the meantime, some of the Indians were exchanging their forest ways for the security and comfort of English habitations by engaging themselves as servants or laborers to the settlers, whose ambitious expansionism was fostering a continual shortage of labor. This meant that members of the two races were now being brought into frequent contact with each other on the streets of colonial villages, producing still more interracial friction. Furthermore, the migration of individual Indians to the English plantations was disturbing to the other Indians who chose to cling to their old independence, and who saw with dismay the weakening of tribal and family bonds. . . .

At the same time, the English colonists were being hardened in the conviction that the Indians were a graceless and savage people, dirty and slothful in their personal habits, treacherous in their relations with the superior race. To put it bluntly, they were fit only to be pushed aside and subordinated, so that the land could be occupied and made productive by those for whom it had been destined by God. If the Indians could be made to fit into a humble niche in the edifice of colonial religion, economy, and government, very well, but if not, sooner or later they would have to be driven away or crushed.[6]

Throughout the westward movement, if contact led to cooperation between the two cultures, the resulting interaction and cultural diffusion usually worked to the disadvantage of the Indians. They lost their self-sufficiency and became economically dependent on Whites. The Whites in turn demanded full compliance as the price of continued peaceful relations. Even if the Indians complied with the Whites' demands, however, many Whites continued to regard Indians as inferior, destined for a subservient role in white society.

Differing Values

Benjamin Franklin offered a classic example of different values in his account of a treaty signed between the Whites and the Iroquois in 1744.

After the principal Business was settled, the Commissioners from Virginia acquainted the Indians by a Speech, that there was at Williamsburg a College, with a Fund for Educating Indian youth; and that, if the Six Nations would send down half a dozen of their young Lads to that College, the Government would take care that they should be well provided for, and instructed in all the Learning of the White People. . . . [The Indians'] Speaker began . . . "We are convinc'd . . . that you mean to do us Good by your Proposal; and we thank you heartily. But you, who are wise, must know that different Nations have different Conceptions of things; and you will therefore not take it amiss, if our Ideas of this kind of Education happen not to be the same with yours. We have had some Experience of it;

Several of our young People were formerly brought up at the Colleges of the Northern Provinces; they were instructed in all your Sciences; but, when they came back to us, they were bad Runners, ignorant of every means of living in the Woods, unable to bear either Cold or Hunger, knew neither how to build a Cabin, take a Deer, or kill an Enemy, knew our Language imperfectly, were therefore neither fit for Hunters, Warriors, nor Counsellors; they were totally good for nothing. We are however not the less oblig'd by your kind Offer, tho' we decline accepting it; and, to show our grateful Sense of it, if the Gentlemen of Virginia will send us a Dozen of their Sons, we will take great Care of their Education, instruct them in all we know, and make *Men* of them."*

Almost one hundred years later, George Catlin offered insight into another manifestation of differing value orientations. Catlin, a nineteenth-century artist famous for his paintings of Indians and his sensitivity to their ways, observed in this passage how each of the two cultures viewed the other.

The civilized world look upon a group of Indians, in their classic dress, with their few and simple oddities, all of which have their moral or meaning, and laugh at them excessively, because they are not like ourselves—we ask, "why do the silly creatures wear such great bunches of quills on their heads?—Such loads and streaks of paint upon their bodies—and bear's grease? abominable!" and a thousand other equally silly questions, without ever stopping to think that Nature taught them to do so—and that they all have some definite importance or meaning which an Indian could explain to us at once, if he were asked and felt disposed to do so—that each quill in his head stood, in the eyes of his whole tribe, as the symbols of any enemy who had fallen by his hand—that every streak of red paint covered a wound which he had got in honourable combat—and that the bear's grease with which he carefully anoints his body every morning, from head to foot, cleanses and purifies the body, and protects his skin from the bite of mosquitoes, and at the same time preserves him from colds and coughs which are usually taken through the pores of the skin.

At the same time, an Indian looks at the civilized world, no doubt, with equal, if not much greater, astonishment, at our apparently, as well as really, ridiculous customs and fashions; but he laughs not, nor ridicules, nor questions,—for his natural good sense and good manners forbid him,—until he is reclining about the fireside of his wigwam companions, when he vents forth his just criticisms upon the learned world, who are a rich and just theme for Indian criticism and Indian gossip.

An Indian will not ask a white man the reason why he does not oil his skin with bear's grease, or why he does not paint his body—or why he wears a hat on his head, or why he has buttons on the back of his coat, where they can never be used—or why he wears whiskers, and a shirt collar up to his eyes—or why he sleeps with his head towards the fire instead of his feet—why he walks with his toes out instead of turning them in—or why it is that hundreds of white folks will flock and crowd round a table to see an Indian eat—but he will go home to his wigwam

*Excerpted with the permission of Farrar, Straus & Giroux, Inc. from *Benjamin Franklin,* Revised Edition, by Chester E. Jorgenson and Frank Luther Mott, eds., Copyright 1936,© 1962 by Hill and Wang (now a division of Farrar, Straus & Giroux, Inc.).

fireside, and "make the welkin ring" with jokes and fun upon the ignorance and folly of the knowing world.[7]

These two selections are excellent illustrations of how culture shapes an individual's view of reality. When people use their own group as a frame of reference in judging another group, the resulting ethnocentric judgments declare the outgroup to be strange and inferior.

White and Indian Governmental Relations

In 1754 the English Parliament adopted a new policy of treating the Indian tribes as independent nations and denied the Colonies all jurisdiction over them. Thereafter, if the colonists wanted to obtain additional Indian land or negotiate any trade pacts, they had to do so through the English government and not directly. Historians cite enforcement of this policy as an indirect cause of the American Revolution. In addition to the delay in gaining approval caused by drawing up petitions, making ocean crossings, and waiting for bureaucratic processing, the colonists fumed over heathens being accorded higher official status than they, loyal British subjects. Yet when the Colonies declared their independence from England, they adopted the same policy in 1778, and the tribes had quasi-national status.

One Indian nation, the Iroquois, had a pronounced influence upon some of the provisions of the U. S. Constitution. Iroquois is a name given to five Indian tribes located in New York State and the Ohio River Valley—the Cayuga, Mohawk, Oneida, Onondaga, and Seneca—who united in a league in 1570. They added a sixth tribe—the Tuscarora—in 1722, and also took other groups, including the Delaware, under their protection.[8] The League had not yet reached its full extent when it was curtailed by the white settlers; by 1851 it had virtually disappeared.

In its time, the League's democratic processes were so effective that romanticists called the Iroquois the "Greeks in America," and many aspects of their system served as a model for the colonists. One example is the means by which a Senate-House conference committee works out the differences between bills passed in each house in order to enable a compromise bill to become law.

INDIAN VALUES AND SOCIAL STRUCTURE

Although there were, and still are, a great many tribes whose cultures differ from one another, some marked similarities have existed among them. For one thing, the Indians have lived in a close and intimate relationship with nature, respecting and not abusing the land. They maximize the use of any animal prey—using its skin for clothing and shelter, its bones for various tools and implements, its sinews for thread, its meat for food, its bladder for a container, and so on.

Indian attitudes toward possession of the land itself ranged from single to joint to tribal ownership, depending upon the tribe. More frequently, the land belonged to the tribe, and as tribal members individuals or families could live on and possibly farm certain portions. Land no longer cultivated by one Indian could be cultivated by another. However, the nominal owner could not dispose of the property without considering the land use rights of the current user. More emphasis was thus placed upon the rights of the user than upon the rights and power of the nominal owner.[9] This practice is somewhat comparable, at least in terms of shared access, to a law in present-day Sweden that roughly translates to "every man's right." In that country a landowner cannot deny others access to the land, since all are entitled to enjoy its beauty. Thus campers or hikers do not encounter no-trespassing signs; since all respect the land, littering and other forms of abuse are quite rare.

Concerning personal interaction, Indians established primary relationships either through a clan system (descent from a common ancestor) or through a friendship system, much like other tribal societies.

Kin relationships were the basic building blocks of Indian society. These blocks were formed into social and political structures ranging from nuclear families to vast empires. The Indians, in their initial attempts to establish a basis of cooperation with the immigrant whites, attempted to incorporate the newcomers into the familiar kinship system. When proffered marriage alliances were turned down by the whites, the Indians sought to establish relationships based on the reciprocal responsibilities of brother to brother, nephew to uncle, and, finally, children to father. The white man refused the proferred relationships, misinterpreted Indian speech as weakness, and increasingly imposed his will on the disheartened remnants of once proud Indian nations.[10]

Indian children grow up under the encouragement and discipline of the extended family, not just the nuclear family. A generalized love of all children in the tribe, rather than just their own progeny, has been common among the Indians.[11] This factor may help explain the permissive and indulgent child-rearing practices many Europeans reported.[12] Whether the Indian tribe was a hunting, a fishing, or a farming society, social scientists have found that the children were raised in a cooperative, noncompetitive, and affectionate atmosphere. Considered from the outset as an individual, the child developed a sense of responsibility and interdependency at an early age. Unrestrained displays of affection or temper and the use of corporal punishment have rarely been part of traditional Indian child care practices. Instead, the means of social control are shame and ridicule, and the Indian matures into an individual keenly aware of any form of conduct that would lead other members of the tribe to have such reactions. Sometimes the price of emphasizing these forms of social control is heavy, for a great deal of psychological harm can be caused by shame and ridicule.

Closely related to the sensitivity to shame and ridicule is the Indian concept of personal honor, including the honor of one's word. Once pledged, whether to a

BOX 7.1

"The greatest object of their lives seems to be to acquire possessions—to be rich. They desire to possess the whole world."

"I had heard marvelous things of this people. In some things we despised them; in others we regarded them as *wakan* (mysterious), a race whose power bordered upon the supernatural. I learned that they had made a 'fire-boat.' I could not understand how they could unite two elements which cannot exist together. I thought the water would put out the fire, and the fire would consume the boat if it had the shadow of a chance. This was to me a preposterous thing! But when I was told that the Big Knives had created a 'fire-boat-walks-on-mountains' (a locomotive) it was too much to believe.

"I had seen guns and various other things brought to us by the French Canadians, so that I had already some notion of the supernatural gifts of the white man; but I had never before heard such tales as I listened to that morning. It was said that they had bridged the Missouri and Mississippi rivers, and that they made immense houses of stone and brick, piled on top of one another until they were as high as high hills. My brain was puzzled with these things for many a day.

"Certainly they are a heartless nation. They have made some of their people servants—yes, slaves! We have never believed in keeping slaves, but it seems these *Washichu* [white men] do! It is our belief that they painted their servants black a long time ago, to tell them from the rest, and now the slaves have children born to them of the same color!

"The greatest object of their lives seems to be to acquire possessions—to be rich. They desire to possess the whole world. For thirty years they were trying to entice us to sell them our land. Finally the outbreak gave them all, and we had already spread over the whole country.

"They are a wonderful people. They have divided the day into hours, like the moons of the year. In fact, they measure everything. Not one of them would let so much as a turnip go from his field unless he received full value for it. I understand that their great men make a feast and invite many, but when the feast is over the guests are required to pay for what they have eaten before leaving the house [restaurant].

"I am also informed, . . . but this I hardly believe, that their Great Chief (President) compels every man to pay him for the land he lives upon and all his personal goods—even for his own existence—every year! I am sure we could not live under such a law."

Sioux youth during the 1870s

white person or to another Indian, that word was never broken. Exceptions existed, for, Albert Britt reports, chiefs "lied only as a war measure, personal or tribal—later, in an attempt to please the white."[13] Some tribes had no word for *thief*, although an enemy's goods were always fair game. Sometimes, as among the Sioux, Crow, and Blackfeet, young men of one tribe would steal from another tribe as a form of sport or a joke, but normally they would not steal from one another.[14]

The Indian woman's role differed from the man's. Women's functions were to work and to raise children. However, the traditional view that women held a subservient position and labored long and hard while the men idled away their time is not completely accurate. Actually, there was a cooperative but not egalitarian arrangement between the sexes, with the men doing the heavy work and the women doing tasks that would not conflict with their child-rearing responsibilities. In hunting and fishing societies, the men would be away from the village for extended periods searching for food. In farming societies, the men cleared and cultivated the land, and the women tended the crops, collected edible foods, and gathered firewood as the men sought a fresh meat supply. Each member of the tribe, according to sexually defined roles, had responsibilities to fulfill for kin and tribe.

STEREOTYPING OF INDIANS

One popular misconception was that the Indian was a bloodthirsty savage. Some tribes, such as the Apache and Ute, were more warlike, but most sought to avoid conflict if they could. Rivalries did exist among various tribes, however, and the French, English, and Americans often exploited these rivalries for their own advantage. The Indians did believe strongly in retributive justice: a wrong had to be repaid, even if it took years, but not to a greater degree. Scalping, often depicted in films as a common Indian practice, in fact was not common. Even those tribes that did scalp frequently did so because of their belief in retributive justice. Some historians argue that the Indian first learned about scalping from white settlers.

Whatever its exact origins, there is no doubt that scalp-taking quickly spread over all of North America, except in the Eskimo areas; nor is there any doubt that its spread was due to the barbarity of White men rather than to the barbarity of Red men. White settlers early offered to pay bounties on dead Indians, and scalps were actual proof of the dead. Governor Kieft of New Netherland is usually credited with originating the idea of paying for Indian scalps, as they were more convenient to handle than whole heads, and they offered the same proof that an Indian had been killed. By liberal payment for scalps, the Dutch virtually cleared southern New York and New Jersey of Indians before the English supplanted them. By 1703 the colony of Massachusetts was paying the equivalent of about $60 for every Indian scalp. In the mid-eighteenth century, Pennsylvania fixed the bounty for a male Indian scalp at $134; a female's was worth only $50. Some White entrepreneurs simply hatcheted any old Indians that still survived in their towns.*

Another side of the Indian stereotype is the portrayal of the Indian as silent or aloof. This image probably grew out of normal Indian behavior in ambiguous situations, such as those faced by Indians transported to Europe for exhibition, transported to Washington, D.C., for treaty negotiations, or interacting with strangers.

*From *Man's Rise to Civilization as Shown by the Indians of North America from Primeval Times to the Coming of the Industrial State* by Peter Farb, p. 158. Copyright © 1968 by Peter Farb. Reprinted by permission of the publishers, E. P. Dutton.

Since they had developed from childhood a sensitivity to acting in any way that might bring about shame or ridicule, Indians often remained silent for fear of speaking or acting improperly. This practice is still common in courtship, in the greeting offered to children returning from boarding school, and in the face of harsh, angry words from a White. In each instance, the practice among most tribes is to allow some time, perhaps days or months, to elapse before the uncertainty is sufficiently reduced to permit conversation. Indian silence is a cautionary device to preserve respect and dignity on both sides.[15] The silence does not represent aloofness, and it is temporary, continuing only until the situation lends itself to speaking.

Hollywood has established the false Indian stereotype in the minds of many Americans. Ignoring their many ethnic identities, the movies have created a single fictional identity, often called "Sioux" or "Apache," and portrayed "the Indian" as either a noble redskin or a vicious savage, either of whom denies the "white man his proper Christian right to this continent."[16] As Will Rogers once said, "The problem ain't ignorance, but everyone knowing something that ain't true."

THE CHEROKEE: A TRAGIC CASE STUDY

Of all the broken treaties, confiscation of Indian lands, and disregard for minority rights and property, perhaps none is as poignant or as indicative of racist antagonism toward all Indians as the tragic experience of the Cherokee nation. Here was an Indian tribe that had succeeded in adapting to the white people's ways, but was nonetheless brutally victimized by the Whites.

When George Washington assumed the presidency in 1790, the federal government adopted the British policy of treating the Indian tribes as independent nations. This policy was continued until 1871, although if the Indians failed to accept the government's dictates, it frequently used military force against them. About 1790, the Cherokee, after some fourteen years of warfare with the Americans, decided to adopt American customs and culture. In other words, they embarked upon an active program of assimilation in an effort to live harmoniously with a different civilization.

Accomplishments

Over the next forty years, their success in achieving this goal was remarkable. They converted their economy to one based on agriculture and commerce, strengthened their self-governing political system, and prospered. They cultivated farmlands in the fertile soil of the tri-state region of Georgia, Tennessee, and North Carolina, and reaped bountiful harvests. The Cherokee patterned themselves after the Whites, setting up churches, schools, sawmills, grist mills, and blacksmith shops. They acquired spinning wheels, looms, plows, and all the other implements of white society.

Most extraordinary of all was the achievement of one Cherokee of part white ancestry named Sequoyah, after whom the redwoods and giant sequoia trees are named. In 1821, after a twelve-year struggle, this crippled genius succeeded in inventing a phonetic syllabary notation system for the Cherokee language. This immense accomplishment was unprecedented in world history. An untrained man had been able to write a language by himself, and to do so in a way that could be easily learned. What quickly followed is also remarkable. Within three years almost all the Cherokee could read and write their own language. By 1828, the tribe had its own newspaper and had adopted a written constitution and code of laws.

By American standards, the Cherokee were the most "civilized" tribe in the country. Driven by the desire for self-improvement, they had educated themselves, converted to Christianity, and learned the Whites' ways of agriculture, business, and government. They had successfully acculturated. Just one problem remained: the Whites wanted their rich land for cotton growing.

Legal Maneuvers

After much debate in Congress, with many legislators from the North against it, the Indian Removal Bill passed in 1830 by a close vote. This act called for the expulsion of all Indians east of the Mississippi. Georgia removed the Creek nation, but the Cherokee and their supporters succeeded in having the matter considered by the United States Supreme Court. On February 28, 1832, Chief Justice John Marshall delivered the majority opinion in favor of the Cherokee on the basis of long-standing treaties. President Jackson's reported response was, "John Marshall has rendered his decision, now let him enforce it." Indeed, two of the three branches of government favored removal, and Jackson interpreted his overwhelming re-election in November as a mandate from the electorate.

With public opinion against the Cherokee, the voices of John Marshall, Daniel Webster, Henry Clay, Sam Houston, Davy Crockett, and others could not help the Cherokee cause. Georgia confiscated Cherokee land and redistributed it through land lotteries, with the state militia stationed in the region to preserve the peace should the Indians resist.

> The premeditated brutality of the militia's daily conducts suggested their commanders' hope of provoking a Cherokee reaction which might provide an excuse for their immediate physical expulsion. The carefully disciplined Cherokee instead patiently submitted even when the provocations extended to the burning of their homes, the confiscation of their property, the mistreatment of their women, the closing of their schools, and the sale of liquor in their churches.[17]

The Cherokee retreated into the forests and continued their desperate legal maneuvering to avoid removal. Although federal troops removed the Choctaw and Chickasaw in Mississippi and the Creek in Alabama, they did not move against the Cherokee, who had won worldwide sympathy and whose legal efforts to prevent removal were still successful. Instead, the federal government intensified its efforts to promote disunity among the Cherokee through bribery, jailings, persecution, and denial of the services and support guaranteed under treaties. Most of the Cherokee remained loyal to their president, John Ross, and rejected the proposed treaty of removal and its five million dollars compensation payment.

Government officials finally succeeded in getting the treaty signed on December 29, 1835, by convening an ad hoc council of Ross's Cherokee opponents. Fewer than five hundred of the seventeen thousand Cherokee appeared, but they signed the treaty, and the Senate ratified it on May 18, 1836. Ross and the Cherokee people fought this pseudo-legitimate treaty, and in January of 1838 Ross presented the Senate with a petition signed by 15,665 Cherokee repudiating the treaty. The Senate rejected the petition by a 37–10 vote. A new wave of public protest in the North, including an impassioned open letter to President Van Buren from Ralph Waldo Emerson, had no result. On April 10, 1838, the president ordered General Winfield Scott to remove the Cherokee immediately, using whatever military force was necessary.

Expulsion

What followed is one of the ugliest episodes in this country's history. The United States government, through its military forces, acted against an entire people who had willingly adapted to the changing world around them. Soldiers forced them at gunpoint from their homes, first to stockades and then westward, far from all that had been theirs.

Families at dinner were startled by the sudden gleam of bayonets in the doorway and rose up to be driven with blows and oaths along the weary miles to the stockade. Men were seized in their fields or going along the road, women were taken from their wheels and children from their play. In many cases, on turning for one last look as they crossed the ridge, they saw their homes in flames, fired by the lawless rabble that followed on the heels of the soldiers to loot and pillage. So keen were these outlaws on the scent that in some instances they were driving off the cattle and other stock of the Indians almost before the soldiers had fairly started their owners in the other direction. Systematic hunts were made by the same men for Indian graves, to rob them of the silver pendants and other valuables deposited with the dead. A Georgia volunteer, afterward a colonel in the Confederate service, said: "I fought through the Civil War and have seen men shot to pieces and slaughtered by thousands, but the Cherokee removal was the cruelest work I ever knew." [18]

The Cherokee suffered extensively during this mass expulsion. Beginning in October 1838, army troops marched the Cherokee westward, along what the Cherokee later called the Trail of Tears: ten to twenty Indians died each day from exposure and other miseries. By March 1839, less than nine thousand out of thirteen thousand survived to reach the Indian Territory, which is now Oklahoma. At the midpoint in this sad episode—December 3, 1838—President Van Buren's message to Congress announced:

It affords me sincere pleasure to apprise the Congress of the entire removal of the Cherokee Nation of Indians to their new homes west of the Mississippi. The measures authorized by Congress at its last session have had the happiest effects. . . . They have emigrated without any apparent reluctance.[19]

CHANGES IN GOVERNMENTAL POLICY

A shift in governmental policy in the mid-nineteenth century changed Indian lifestyles to such an extent that one can see its aftereffects today on any reservation. Instead of using annihilation and expulsion as means of dealing with the Indians, the government embarked on a policy of segregation and isolation. Between 1850 and 1880, it established most of the reservations, of which there are now almost three hundred.

In 1871 Congress tacked onto an appropriations bill a rider that ended federal recognition of the Indian tribes as independent, sovereign nations and made them wards of the government instead. Bureaucrats were now responsible for the welfare of the Indians, issued them food rations, and supervised every aspect of their lives. The results were devastating. Proud and independent people, who had been taught self-reliance at an early age, were now totally dependent on non-Indian government agents. Many of the tribes had been nomadic, and did not easily adjust to reservation life. Moreover, such problems as inadequate administration by the Indian agents and irregular delivery of food, supplies, and equipment only made matters worse.

The government was still not through restructuring the Indians' life styles, as leaders at the time believed that what they were doing was ''for the best.'' Americanization became the goal. This meant destroying tribal organizations, suppressing ''pagan'' religions and ceremonies, allowing only the English language in the schools, requiring ''white'' hair and clothing styles, and teaching only American culture and history.

Most of the attention of the Americanizers was concentrated on the Indian children, who were snatched from their families and shipped off to boarding schools far from their homes. The children usually were kept at boarding school for eight years, during which time they were not permitted to see their parents, relatives or friends. Anything Indian—dress, language, religious practices, even outlook on life (and how that was defined was up to the judgment of each administration of the government's directives)—was uncompromisingly prohibited. Ostensibly educated, articulate in the English language, wearing store-bought clothes, and with their hair short and their emotionalism toned down, the boarding-school graduates were sent out either to make their way in a white world that did not want them, or to return to a reservation to which they were now foreign. The Indians had simply failed to melt into the great American melting pot.[20]

One value that was promulgated was the rugged individualism of white society, rather then the cooperative, noncompetitive approach of the Indian. This was the

Shown above is a small part of the carnage from the massacre of 150 Sioux men, women, and children on December 29, 1890. The U.S. Cavalry cut down many in this peaceful, unarmed group from behind, leaving the wounded to die from exposure from cold and snow. The soldiers then returned to bury their frozen bodies in a mass grave.

purpose of the General Allotment Act of 1887. Its sponsor, Senator Dawes, genuinely believed that it would create in the Indian that spirit of self-interest that he considered the major force in white civilization.

What this legislation actually did was deprive the Indians of even more land. Its intent was to break the backbone of Indian culture by ending the communal ownership of reservation lands and giving each Indian a share. Many of the Indians had no technical knowledge of farming and neither the cash nor credit to obtain farm implements. Some Indian peoples believed it was sacrilegious to plow open the earth. Loopholes in the Dawes Act enabled unscrupulous Whites to plunder the Indian land, either through low-cost long-term leases or by convincing the Indian owners to write wills leaving their property to white "friends." This practice was widespread, and a suspicious increase in the number of Indian deaths followed; some of these deaths were actually proven to have been murders.[21] By 1914 the 138 million acres of Indian land had been reduced to 56 million acres, all of it eroded and of poor quality.[22]

After 1933, the Roosevelt administration shifted from a policy of forced assimilation to one of pluralism. Secretary of the Interior Harold L. Ickes and Bureau of Indian Affairs Commissioner John Collier, in particular, were deeply sympathetic to the Indian cause. One outcome was the Indian Reorganization Act of 1934, which ended the land allotment program, encouraged tribal self-government, extended financial credit to the tribes, gave preference to BIA (Bureau of Indian Affairs) employment to Indians, and permitted consolidation of Indian lands split up through inheritance. Further, the Indians were encouraged to revive their ancient arts and crafts, their languages, their religions and ceremonies, and their customs and traditions. In keeping with an administrative philosophy of treating the Indians with dignity, the act was permissive, not mandatory; each tribe could vote to accept or reject the new law. Most chose to accept it.

In the 1950s, new top administrative personnel in the Interior Department and the BIA who had a different philosophy caused a shift back to attempts at assimilation. Some critics of the 1934 legislation had thought it regressive. Now, these people, believing that the only way to end the chronic poverty, disease, overpopulation, and hopelessness among the Indians was to end the isolation of reservation life, tried some new approaches.

Relocation

Beginning in 1952, the Bureau of Indian Affairs attempted to at least partially resolve the problem of overpopulation on the reservations. The BIA provided financial and other assistance to individuals or families who wanted to secure jobs and living accommodations in urban areas. For many Indians the word *relocation* had terrible connotations. That was the euphemism that had been used for the prison camps in which 110,000 Japanese-Americans had been placed during World War II. Furthermore, Dillon S. Myer, the government administrator who had been in charge of those camps, was now in charge of the Indian relocation program.

Most of the Indians who utilized this program (about 40,000) went to work in low-status unskilled or semiskilled jobs and to live in the poorer sections of the cities. Some adjusted and became acculturated; others felt uprooted and were driven to alcoholism. More than one-fourth of the total number returned to the reservations. The program tapered off after 1960, mostly because of other efforts to improve Indian life.

Termination

A series of bills passed in 1953–1954 sought to end federal responsibility for the Indians by ending all federal services and federal-liaison tribal organizations, and dispensing assets among members of the tribe. Two of the more prosperous tribes, the Klamath of southern Oregon and the Menominee of Wisconsin, both of whom owned considerable tracts of valuable timberland, some Paiute and Ute in Utah, and several other tribes were the first to be affected by this legislation.

For the Klamath, a tribe of 668 families totaling some 2,000 individuals, termination even threatened to end their tribal identity. In the spring of 1968, when 77 percent voted to withdraw from the tribe and receive a cash payment for their share of the land holdings, many government and business officials feared that liquidating tribal assets when the lumber market was already depressed would threaten the Pacific Northwest economy. Instead of selling the lumber, Congress voted to purchase the land, creating the Winema National Forest. A federal trusteeship for adults declared incompetent to handle their own affairs and for minors kept the government involved in 48.9 percent of the tribe members' affairs. With their tribal identity coming to an end, many Klamath are now professing interest in the Pan-Indian movement.[23]

In the case of the Menominee, the new policy brought economic disaster.

Almost overnight, many millions of dollars of tribal assets disappeared in the rush to transform the Menominee reservation into a self-supporting county. The need to finance the usual hospital, police, and other services of a county and pay taxes imperiled the tribe's sawmill and forest holdings, alienated tribal lands, threatened many Indians with the loss of their homes and life savings, and saddled Wisconsin with a huge welfare problem which it could not underwrite and which had to be met by desperate appeals for help from the same federal government that had thought it had washed its hands of the Menominees.[24]

Washington's hasty blunder cost the Menominee their hospital, their sawmill, and some of their best land, which they had to sell because they could not afford the taxes on it. President Nixon officially repudiated the termination policy in 1970 and Congress reversed the termination of all the tribes affected in December 1973, re-creating these reservations, but nobody gave the Menominee back their hospital or their sawmill. The following year the Menominee took over the abandoned sixty-four-room Alexian Brothers monastery to serve as their hospital. It had been built on Menominee land at a time when any church group could take as much Indian reservation land as it needed to build religious structures. Local Whites, who had bought tribal land cheaply when the tribe had to sell, objected, although the Alexian Brothers did not. When bloodshed seemed imminent, the governor of Wisconsin called out the National Guard to maintain order. Fortunately, a peaceful accommodation was reached, and the Menominee retained permanent possession of the building.

Other Approaches

In 1966 Lyndon Johnson appointed the first Native American—Robert L. Bennett, an Oneida from Wisconsin—to be Commissioner of Indian Affairs. However, paternalistic federal bureaucrats continued to impose their will upon a still subjugated people, as President Richard Nixon indicated in his July 8, 1970, message to Congress repudiating termination.

The story of the Indian in America is something more than the record of the white man's frequent aggression, broken agreements, intermittent remorse and prolonged failure. It is a record also of endurance, of survival, of adaptation and creativity in the face of overwhelming obstacles. It is a record of enormous contributions to this country—to its art and culture, to its strength and spirit, to its sense of history and its sense of purpose.

It is long past time that the Indian policies of the Federal government began to recognize and build upon the capacities and insights of the Indian people. Both as a matter of justice and of enlightened social policy, we must begin to act on the basis of what the Indians themselves have long been telling us. The time has come to break decisively with the past and to create the conditions for a new era in which the Indian future is determined by Indian acts and Indian decisions.

. . . Of the Department of the Interior's programs directly serving Indians, for example, only 1.5 per cent are presently under Indian control. Only 2.4 per cent of HEW's Indian health programs are run by Indians. The result is a burgeoning Federal bureaucracy, programs which are far less effective than they ought to be, and an erosion of Indian initiative and morale.

. . . This, then, must be the goal of any new national policy toward the Indian people: to strengthen the Indian's sense of autonomy without threatening his sense of community. We must assure the Indian that he can assume control of his own life without being separated involuntarily from the tribal group. And we must make it clear that Indians can become independent of Federal control without being cut off from Federal concern and Federal support.

Since that 1970 message, Presidents Nixon, Carter, and Reagan have made concerted efforts, usually through Justice Department advocacy in the courts or lobbying for legislation, to secure Indian rights. Although successful in a few instances, they have not improved much the quality of Native American life, as the following sections reveal.

PRESENT-DAY NATIVE AMERICAN LIFE

Of all the minorities in America, according to government statistics on income, employment, and housing, the Native American is "the poorest of the poor." It is cruelly ironic that most of the Native Americans' problems are due not only to their subordinate position as a result of conquest, but also to their insistence on their right to be different, to continue living as Native Americans. In a society that has long demanded assimilation, this insistence has not been popular.

Population

The 1980 census showed a 71.8 percent increase in the Native American population since 1970, going up from 792,730 to over 1.4 million. This statistic may reflect better data gathering, but it also supports other studies showing a Native American fertility rate higher than that of all other groups, a 3 percent annual population increase.[25] As Figure 7.2 indicates, the age stratification of American Indian and Alaska Natives is greater in the younger years than for the total U.S. population. This greater ratio of child-bearing age groups suggests continued faster rates of population increase among Native Americans. They are far from the "vanishing American" others have claimed. Yet more than half live on reservations which cannot offer adequate economic support for those already living there.

Employment

Chronic unemployment is a serious problem, averaging 45 to 55 percent on most reservations and sometimes as high as 80 percent. As many as 75 percent of those

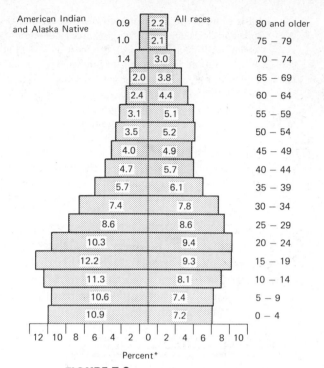

FIGURE 7.2

U.S. Population Structure, 1980

*Percentages may not add to 100 due to rounding.

Source: Indian Health Service, 1983.

who do work are on federal payrolls, providing education, health care, and social services to their fellow tribespeople. Others eke out an existence from fishing, raising a few head of sheep or cattle, or from a small garden if they are lucky enough to have water.

Federal budget cuts in both Indian programs and in general spending programs such as the Comprehensive Employment and Training Act (CETA) have cost jobs, although the government has increased by fifty million dollars annually its program contracts to Native Americans directly rather than through the Bureau of Indian Affairs (BIA). Since 1982, prompted by the Reagan administration, Congress has increasingly appropriated millions of dollars in seed money to attract light industry and business to reservations. Previous efforts of a similar nature have had only limited success. Owned by outsiders, the businesses experienced high employee turnover. Preferring to hire women, these businesses thus disrupted traditional family roles and further weakened the male Native Americans' self-image.[26] At this time, the median family income for Native Americans is only about 48 percent that of the national median.[27]

This impoverished Navaho mother and her daughter sit inside their hogan—a one–room, eight–sided log house with a sod roof. Lacking electricity and indoor plumbing, their home is situated on the nation's largest reservation, on harsh, barren land.

Life Expectancy

The demographic statistics (see Table 7.1) testify to the harshness and deprivation of reservation life, and the despair accompanying it.[28] The average life span of the Native American is about ten years less than the national average. The suicide rate among all Native Americans is twice the national average; that among young Native Americans is twice the national average; and that among boarding school students, five to seven times the national average. The infant mortality rate in 1970 was 30.9 per 1,000 live births for Indians, compared with 21.8 per 1,000 nationally.[29]

High chronic unemployment, together with a pervasive hopelessness and despair, contributes to the high suicide rate among adults. Another explanation for the suicide rates among the young people and adults is the problems engendered by marginality. Caught between two cultures, with assimilation unlikely and living as Native Americans difficult, the Native Americans are trapped in an unpleasant situation. According to Jack Bynum, inadequate acculturation and assimilation into

TABLE 7.1
Indians and Health: Age-Adjusted Death Rates
per 100,000 Population, 1979

	Indians and Alaska Natives	All Races
Motor-vehicle accidents	79.3	23.7
All other accidents	61.4	20.0
Alcoholism	57.3	7.4
Homicide	25.5	10.4
Pneumonia, influenza	23.1	11.4
Diabetes	22.8	10.0
Suicide	21.8	11.9
Tuberculosis	4.4	0.7

Source: Indian Health Service, Centers for Disease Control, 1983.

the ways and society of Whites has led to isolation, alienation, anomie, aggression, social disorganization of the minority subculture, and suicidal behavior.[30] Students at boarding schools are especially prone to suicide, as they experience extreme isolation and the denial of their culture and its values.

The most serious social problem among Native Americans on reservations, and a major factor in their high mortality rate, is alcohol consumption. Death from alcoholism is eight times the national average. The Indian Health Service reports that many accidents, suicides, and homicides are alcohol-related as well. Motor-vehicle accidents, the second greatest cause of death, is frequently alcohol-related and three times the national average (see Table 7.1).

Excessive drinking among the Navaho, for example, is one of the tribe's greatest problems. Theodore D. Graves reported that their alcohol intake is almost seven times greater than that for Anglos and more than three times greater than that for persons of Spanish descent.[31] Frances N. Ferguson cited a distinguished Navaho medicine man who estimated that 30 percent of the Navaho population drink to excess.[32] Strong peer pressures—refusal to buy a drink is an affront subject to ridicule—and lack of strong sanctions in Navaho society—a reluctance to interfere in another's behavior—appear to be contributing factors.[33]

Education

From 50 to 60 percent of all Indian children drop out of school before completing the twelfth grade, compared with a national average of 23 percent. Reasons for this include an unresponsive educational system, a poor curriculum, and inadequately trained educational personnel, but some improvements are being made in these areas.[34] The major difficulties occur in BIA boarding schools, currently attended by over 30,000 Indian children. Still other students attend off-reservation public schools but are housed in BIA dormitories. Some children are sent several hundred miles from home (Alaskan Indian children thousands of miles) and are often kept away from their families for the entire school year. Many become runaways, suicides, or dropouts. Off-reservation schools appear to be a carryover from the past BIA practice of removing children from the main socializing agency—the family. Observers have reported seeing children rounded up at the beginning of the school year to be sent away. If they hide in the hills, BIA officials threaten to stop the parents' welfare checks unless or until they produce their missing offspring for school.

In the fall of 1969, a Special Senate Subcommittee on Indian Education issued a scathing report on the BIA school system. This report, which was largely ignored, offered powerful arguments supporting Indian self-determination.

We are shocked at what we discovered. . . .

We have developed page after page of statistics. These cold figures mark a stain on our national conscience, a stain which has spread slowly for hundreds of years. They tell a story, to be sure. But they cannot tell the whole story. They cannot, for example, tell of the despair, the frustration, the hopelessness, the poignancy, of children who want to learn but are not taught; of adults who try to read but have no one to teach them; of families which want to stay together but are forced apart; or of 9-year-old children who want neighborhood schools but are sent thousands of miles away to remote and alien boarding schools.

We have seen what these conditions do to Indian children and Indian families. The sights are not pleasant.

We have concluded that our national policies for educating American Indians are a failure of major proportions. They have not offered Indian children—either in years past or today—an educational opportunity anywhere near equal to that offered the great bulk of American children. Past generations of lawmakers and administrators have failed the American Indian. Our own generation thus faces a challenge—we can continue the unacceptable policies and programs of the past or we can recognize our failures, renew our commitments, and reinvest our efforts with new energy.

. . . Creative, imaginative, and above all, relevant educational experiences can blot the stain on our national conscience. This is the challenge the subcommittee believes faces our own generation.[35]

In 1976 the American Indian Policy Review Commission issued a report on education criticizing the BIA for not acting to remedy any of the problems the subcommittee had pointed out.[36] Particularly singled out were the 19 boarding schools, which the Commission called "dumping grounds for students with serious social and emotional problems" that "do not rehabilitate" but "do more harm than good."[37]

The Commission reported that the official BIA policy of sending students to the school closest to home is in reality not practiced.[38] Alaskan Indian children have been sent to Fort Sill, Oklahoma. Others who are classified as "problems," such as the girl in Washington State who objected to a history test that called her ancestors "dirty savages," are also sent to distant boarding schools. In another report, the Commission also criticized the locations of the schools:

The sites of these schools were determined not merely by financial considerations of the Government, but by the conscious intention of forcing a separation between Indian parents and children and between Indian children and the idea of the reservation.[39]

Others have frequently commented on the teaching of American culture and history in reservation schools and on insensitivity and non-receptivity to Native American culture and history. One typical example is a composition given to Chippewa children at a reservation school in the Northwest: "Why we are all happy the Pilgrims landed."

While some improvements have occurred in recent years, only 6 percent of the Native American students entering high school presently graduate from college, compared to 12 percent of the Blacks and 23 percent of the Whites.[40]

Housing

One of the most visible signs of deprivation is reservation housing, called "open-air slums" by some. Mostly located down back roads unseen by reservation visitors, the various tribes live in small, overcrowded Western-style houses, in mobile homes, or in hogans—traditional, one-room, eight-sided log houses with sod roofs. About half the housing units lack bathrooms and a third completely lack indoor plumbing.[41] Most of those without a water supply must haul it from a mile or more away.[42] Indian dwellings often lack electricity also. In short, reservations present as bleak and desolate a picture of poverty as they did 100 years ago. Reservations were never meant to be successful or self-sufficient places; they were places to put people.

NATURAL RESOURCES

Trappers, settlers, oil drillers, and large companies have continually encroached upon Indian territory to obtain natural resources or fertile land. The situation is no different today. The need for water and energy has led government and industry to look covetously at reservation land once considered worthless. In July 1978, two thousand Native Americans participated in a 2,700-mile march to Washington, D.C. There they demonstrated against several proposed bills that would have allowed strip mining and siphoning of ground water from tribal land, and increased state police jurisdiction over the reservations.

The 53 million acres held by twenty-two Western tribes contain much of the nation's richest reserves of natural gas, oil, coal, and uranium, worth billions of dollars. In fact, one-third of the nation's low-sulfur coal and almost all the known uranium deposits are on tribal land. For some tribes, such as the oil-rich Osage in Oklahoma, the benefits are real.

Other impoverished tribes, such as the Navaho, gain very little, and their modest oil and natural-gas reserves may be exhausted in the next five to ten years.[43] The government's own watchdog, the General Accounting Office, has also criticized the BIA for frequently failing to protect Native American interests when encouraging and approving extraction of natural resources. The following examples are but a few of many present-day efforts to victimize the Native Americans for the sake of their land's riches.

Northern Cheyenne

Much of the 440,000-acre Cheyenne Reservation in Montana sits atop a 60-foot-deep deposit of high-quality coal. At BIA urging, the tribe approved a vaguely worded agreement that gave industry virtual carte blanche to use 243,808 acres—more than half the reservation. The company was free to strip mine and to build railroad lines, vast industrial complexes of power and conversion plants, and non-Indian towns for its workers. As the mammoth consequences became known to the Cheyenne and to environmentalists, organized, successful opposition arose to contain this development and protect the land.

Navaho

The Navaho, numbering over 160,000, live on the nation's largest Indian reservation; its 16 million acres in the four corners where Arizona, New Mexico, Colorado and Utah meet exceeds the size of West Virginia. This is a harsh, barren land where 2.5 billion tons of coal and 55 million pounds of uranium deposits remain in the ground because of slack demand and no railroad line to haul it away.[44]

Like most Western tribes, the Navaho have an agricultural economy. An 1868 treaty guaranteed them basic water rights, but the U.S. Bureau of Reclamation and the Army Corps of Engineers built a dam upstream, diverting their water to non-Indian users. Water levels dropped, fish died, and the Navaho farmland suffered. After years of protest, a massive federal irrigation project, begun in 1976, now brings water to part of the Navaho arid land in northwestern New Mexico.

Arapaho and Shoshone

The 4,800 members of the Arapahoe and Shoshone tribes live on the Wind River Reservation in central Wyoming. Its 2.3 million acres of flat, brown earth has little vegetation and is remote from any economic markets. Although the land has oil and natural gas, its 1980 sales of $169 million only brought tribal members $442.50 a person, which doesn't buy very much. Moreover, the Indians discovered tanker trucks driving away in the middle of the night with oil stolen from them. A federal investigation to determine the extent of the thefts revealed underpayment of $1.24 million in royalties by the three oil company purchasers.[45]

Paiute, Papago, Ak-Chin, and Pueblo

Nevada's Pyramid Lake, a spectacular thirty-mile expanse of water, belongs to the Paiute, whose water rights the government is supposed to protect. Instead, in 1906 it developed an irrigation project diverting 9.8 billion gallons of water each year before it reaches the lake. By the 1940s the water level had dropped 80 feet, killing the trout upon which the Paiute depended. In 1944 the U. S. Supreme Court decided the water rights case, awarding the tribe $8 million in damages. However, in settling the case on their behalf, the Justice Department did nothing about the fish crisis, the water level in the lake, or restrictions for future irrigation. Finally, the Justice Department, formally confessing its "breach of faith with the Indians," petitioned the Supreme Court to reopen the case to allow the Paiute to refill their lake.[46] In June 1983 the high court turned them down.

Water disputes are sharpest in the Southwest, where the water table is the lowest. Urban sprawl and agribusiness have prompted Whites to sink deep wells around reservations in Arizona siphoning off the water reserves of several tribes. To offset their loss, President Reagan in October 1983 approved a water system for the Papago, due for completion in 1992. The Ak-Chin in Arizona, whose 11,000 acres of cultivated land shrunk in the mid-1970s to less than 5,000 cultivatable acres because of dams and siphoned groundwater by non-Indian farmers, face the bleak prospect of a complete loss of water within five years, with no prospects of a water system being provided for them.[47] In New Mexico, farmers simply "appropriated a viable water system the Pueblo Indians had built 200 years before Cortes set sail," leaving that tribe without an adequate supply.[48]

The early 1970s witnessed increased Native American efforts to seek a redress of grievances and arouse the public conscience. Pictured above are some Native Americans staging a Protest march on Columbus Day at the Boston Common.

Water rights are the Western tribes' most valuable rights, providing a basis for achieving economic independence. Loss of water dooms them to an even worse existence. Most of the water fights end up in court, where they linger but seldom die. Over fifty lawsuits—from Arizona to Montana to California—await a decision.

RED POWER

As Alvin M. Josephy, Jr., a distinguished observer of Indian history and life, has noted, the Indians have never been silent about their needs and wishes.[49] Beginning with Seneca Chief Red Jacket's visit to Washington in 1792, Indians have repeatedly tried to tell the federal authorities what their people wanted and what was acceptable to them. Since they were seen as savages, the Indians found that government representatives usually ignored their views. When the forced removal programs and the bloodshed came to an end in the late nineteenth century, the government began trying to change the reservation Indians' way of life, to eliminate their poverty, and to encourage further integration. In the twentieth century, Indian militancy was quite rare until the 1960s. In the mid-1960s the Indians changed their approach, partly because the social climate was different. Many social forces were at work—the civil rights movement, the Vietnam protest, the idealism of the Great Society, and a growing social awareness in society itself. Perhaps taking their cue from other movements, a new generation of Native American leaders asserted themselves.

Pan-Indianism

This recent social movement, which attempts to establish an American Indian ethnic identity instead of just a tribal identity, has its roots in the past. The growing Iroquois Confederation of the seventeenth century, the mobility and social interaction among the Plains Indians in the nineteenth century, and the spread of the Ghost Dance religion were all early examples of Pan-Indianism. As Indian youths found comfort in one another's presence, first in boarding schools and later in urban areas, they found a commonality in their identity as Indians.

From this emerging group consciousness evolved several organizations dedicated to preserving Indian identity and gaining greater political clout. The Society of American Indians (SAI) and the National Congress of American Indians (NCAI) were the first twentieth-century attempts to organize. More recently, the National Indian Youth Council (NIYC) and the American Indian Movement (AIM) have attracted many young people who object to discrimination and white domination. The NIYC staged fish-ins to protest treaty violations of Indian rights in Washington State. In the ensuing legal battle, the Supreme Court ultimately ruled in favor of the Indians.

The Pan-Indian movement has not been completely accepted, however, even among young people. Many Native Americans are anxious to preserve their tribal identities and prefer to work for the cultural enrichment and social betterment of their own tribe rather than to engage in a national movement. As part of this tribal emphasis, these individuals also learn and teach their people silversmithing, pottery and blanket making, and other crafts that are part of their heritage. In an effort to increase tribal pride and economic welfare, they also establish cultural centers to exhibit and sell their artistic works and wares.

Alcatraz

On November 20, 1969, a group of seventy-eight Indians under the name "Indians of all Tribes" occupied Alcatraz Island, a former federal prison. This move, the first militant Indian action in the twentieth century, was both symbolic and an effort to establish a cultural center. The sarcasm in this excerpt from their proclamation attacks the paternalism, neglect, and deprivation fostered upon American Indians past and present.

We will give to the inhabitants of this island a portion of that land for their own, to hold in perpetuity—for as long as the sun shall rise and the rivers go down to the sea. We will further guide the inhabitants in the proper way of living. We will offer them our religion, our education, our life-ways, in order to help them achieve our level of civilization and thus raise them and all their white brothers up from their savage and unhappy state. We offer this treaty in good faith and wish to be fair and honorable in our dealings with all white men. We feel that this so-called Alcatraz Island is more than suitable for an Indian Reservation, as determined by the white man's own standards. By this we mean that this place resembles most Indian reservations in that:

1. It is isolated from modern facilities, and without adequate means of transportation.
2. It has no fresh running water.
3. It has inadequate sanitation facilities.
4. There are no oil or mineral rights.
5. There is no industry and so unemployment is very great.
6. There are no health care facilities.
7. The soil is rocky and nonproductive; and the land does not support game.
8. There are no education facilities.
9. The population has always exceeded the land base.
10. The population has always been held as prisoners and kept dependent upon others.

Further, it would be fitting and symbolic that ships from all over the world, entering the Golden Gate, would first see Indian land, and thus be reminded of the true history of this nation. This tiny island would be a symbol of the great lands once ruled by free and noble Indians.[50]

This militant action did not succeed. The group's cohesiveness collapsed when the twelve-year-old daughter of its leader, Michael Oakes, a Mohawk, accidentally fell down an elevator shaft on the island and died. Oakes, the unifying and motivating force, left Alcatraz with his daughter's body. Federal authorities then stepped in and removed the Indians. Oakes himself was later shot to death in California, supposedly mistaken for a trespasser. Today Alcatraz Island is a tourist attraction as a former prison, and its conversion to a gambling casino has been discussed.

Wounded Knee

On February 27, 1973, about two hundred members of the American Indian Movement seized control of the village of Wounded Knee, South Dakota, taking 11 hostages. The location was symbolic, since Wounded Knee had been the site of the last Indian resistance in 1890, when one hundred and fifty Sioux, including men, women, and children, were massacred by the U.S. Cavalry. Many were killed from behind, and the wounded were left to die in a blizzard the following night.[51]

A seventy-one-day siege following the seizure was a staged media event aimed at directing national attention to the plight of the Native Americans. Some Native American leaders criticized the action as rash, but most Native Americans appeared to be in sympathy with it. The holdout ended May 8, 1973, with two Indians killed, injuries on both sides, including a U.S. marshal paralyzed, and $240,000 in damages to property.[52]

Several months later the leaders—Dennis Banks, a Chippewa, and Russell Means, a Sioux—were brought to trial on charges directly related to the siege at Wounded Knee. The presiding judge dismissed all charges, severely criticizing the FBI and the Justice Department for misconduct in withholding or doctoring documents, illegal wiretaps, and spending money on liquor and women for a Native American progovernment witness.

Among other things, the militants had demanded that the government deal with the Sioux on the basis of an 1868 treaty that guaranteed them dominion over the vast Northern Plains between the Missouri River and the Rocky Mountains, land which the U.S. government confiscated in 1876. That Indian land claim has been described by Sioux representatives as the "largest, most historically and socially significant and, in terms of time taken in the courts, the oldest Indian land claim on record."

THE COURTS

Pending before various courts since 1920, the Sioux claim was upheld in July 1979 by the U.S. Court of Claims, reaffirmed by the U.S. Supreme Court in July 1980 despite a challenge by the Justice Department. The $105 million in compensation for illegal seizure of the Black Hills was to be distributed to 60,000 Sioux living on eight reservations in South Dakota, Montana, and Nebraska. Indian activist Russell Means urged Sioux chiefs to reject the U.S. offer and demand the land instead, claiming the Black Hills land was "our graveyard, our church, the center of our universe and the birthplace of our people . . . everything we hold sacred and dear, and this is the reason it is not for sale."[53] The Oglala Sioux in July 1980 then filed suit for return of the western half of South Dakota and for $1 billion in damages for "hunger, malnutrition, disease, and death" caused by loss of the land, also asking for tribal hunting rights on the land, a ban on removal of natural resources, and a ban on federal interference with Sioux use of the land for "subsistence and religious purposes."[54] In June 1981 the U.S. Court of Appeals rejected the suit, saying it had no jurisdiction on the matter, since Congress had created the Indian Claims Commission, since disbanded, as the sole remedy for Black Hills claims.[55]

The cash settlement for the Black Hills partially rested on a 1950 precedent, when the U.S. Court of Claims awarded $31.2 million to the Colorada Ute for lands illegally taken from them. This amounted to about $10,000 for each tribal adult and child. A precedent also existed for return of land. The Taos Pueblo of New Mexico had regarded the lands at and near Blue Lake as sacred since the fourteenth century. Demanding the land back from the Forest Service instead of a cash settlement, the Taos did regain 48,000 acres in 1970 through Congressional action at President Nixon's urging.

In spring 1977 the Passamaquoddy and Penobscot laid claim to about 5 million acres, or nearly one-third of Maine. The Carter administration threw its support behind the Indians and in 1978 reached an out-of-court settlement: $25 million cash, $1.7 million a year for fifteen years, and 300,000 acres at $5 an acre. The basis for these claims was that the Indian land had been bargained away in violation of the Nonintercourse Act of 1790, which reserved to Congress the power to negotiate with Indian tribes. Indians are pushing other claims throughout many other Eastern states as far south as South Carolina. In the Pacific Northwest federal courts have been upholding Indian fishing rights to the steelhead and salmon, based upon treaties over one hundred years old.

BUREAU OF INDIAN AFFAIRS (BIA)

The BIA, a government agency, can trace its origin to 1824. It has many critics, among Native Americans as well as among federal officials, sociologists, and anthropologists. Some view it as a bureaucracy staffed by some able, dedicated people who are restricted and frustrated by an inefficient organization and others see it staffed by self-serving, unsympathetic people who simply do not belong there.

There are undoubtedly weak, poor, and inefficient men within the Bureau. Some enter the system, especially at the area level, by patronage: some should never have been employed by the Bureau; some are poor because of inadequate training and orientation after they were employed; and some were good originally but, after many frustrations and defeats, gave up. . . One of the scores of "weaknesses," with which it appears unable to cope, is the continued presence within the Bureau of key personnel who long since should have been removed from it. . . . Many members of Indian communities are driven to desperation, some even to suicide, as a result of ineptitude, indifference or lethargy on the part of a poor superintendent or area official. Yet the record of the 1960's contains documentation of Commissioner Nash turning down Indian appeals to relieve them of intolerable agency personnel by telling them he would not remove a man while he was under fire, and of Commissioner Bennett answering tribal complaints of frustration and negativism with the retort that he was not interested in discussing "criticism of the BIA."[56]

Native American hostility toward the BIA goes beyond complaints about unsympathetic, incompetent, or even patronizing personnel; it is directed against its very structure. Although different government agencies touch all Americans in some ways, few non-Indians realize how totally the BIA dominates Native Americans' lives, as President Nixon's address and the Senate Subcommittee Report indicated. Every tribal decision throughout the United States is subject to BIA veto. A BIA official's mere supposition that certain individuals cannot properly handle their money or their personal affairs is sufficient to require formal BIA approval of any transactions those persons make. The BIA makes all decisions about school locations, staffing, and student residence. Additionally, all other aspects of Native American life—such as housing and economic development—are also the domain of the BIA. Only by comprehending the total pervasiveness of this bureaucracy can one begin to fathom the dependence, despair, and frustration the system engenders.

The problems inherent in all bureaucracies exist in the Bureau of Indian Affairs as well, and therein lies the problem of a complex organization running people's lives. Robert K. Merton has pointed out that working in a bureaucracy has a tendency to affect one's personality.[57] The very structure of a formal organization, with its hierarchy of authority, limitations on individual responsibility, specified work procedures, and emphasis upon objective criteria, encourages conformity to ongoing practices. To ensure job security and the approval of superiors, employees tend to follow guidelines rigidly. The means of achieving goals, rather than the goals themselves, become the point of emphasis. When criticisms mount, organization members become defensive and engage in obfuscation to ward off the outside pressures.

Yet Native Americans have mixed feelings about the BIA. They dislike many of its practices, but it is all they have, and so many oppose dismantling it. Vine Deloria, Jr., points out that dismantling the BIA would only lead to further deterioration of Native American conditions and loss of their remaining lands.[58] The disastrous termination policy showed what can happen when the government withdraws its support. Restoration of tribal sovereignty, or self-determination without termination as recommended by President Nixon, is the approach most favored today.

Still, little has changed since President Nixon's historic message to Congress in 1970, as Congress has failed to enact the necessary legislation. At that time there was a slight shakeup at the BIA, ostensibly to increase Indian self-determination. However, little really changed, as the American Indian Policy Review Commission, made up of 10 executives from private industry, indicated in its report to Congress in 1976. It concluded that every area of personnel management in the BIA was "inadequate" and recommended a massive restructuring to bring decision-making closer to tribal level.[59]

URBAN NATIVE AMERICANS

Over 627,000 Native Americans live in urban areas, but less is known about their ethnic identity than is the case for other urban dwellers. Yet 48,000 live in Los Angeles, the largest concentration of any city but only 0.6 percent of the total city population. Other cities with sizable numbers, often exceeding 10,000, include Boston, Chicago, Cleveland, Dallas, Denver, Detroit, St. Louis, Minneapolis, New York, Omaha, Phoenix, San Diego, San Francisco, and Seattle. Usually lacking job skills and adequate education, Native Americans generally experience the same poverty they left behind, but without the familiar environment and tribal support system. Because they blend in with the rest of the urban poor, society generalizes about their problems without identifying their ethnicity.

One interesting Eastern public image of the urban Native American is that of the Iroquois ironworkers, who regularly work high atop the structural steel frames of skyscrapers being built in the urban centers. While this group has a colorful image, most urban Native Americans are less visible to the non-Native American society. Consequently they have not received as much attention from sociologists as have those on reservations.[60] Urban living, however, helped to spawn the Pan-Indian movement. Contact with members of other tribes raised a group consciousness of being Indian, which led to an attempt to improve the lot of all by united action.

Though they are more scattered in residence than are the Blacks or Chicanos, approximately three-fourths of the urban Native Americans live in poverty in the poorer sections of the cities (see Figure 7.3) Their migration to urban areas has intensified in the last 15 years; almost half of the nation's Native Americans, especially those from 20 to 40 years old, have left the overpopulated reservations to seek better economic opportunities.[61]

Although urban Native Americans are not gathered in ethnic enclaves, all their other behavior patterns are similar to those of European immigrants. Situated in a social arena where they are the minority, they experience the culture shock of urban living away from the solidarity of the tribe. This shock sometimes leads to personal disorientation, and they seldom get relief or assistance from the dominant society.

A recent incident in Los Angeles highlights the problem of adjustment. A newly-arrived Navaho, who spoke no English, became quite ill, and on the street approached a woman wearing a white uniform, in the belief that she was a nurse. The woman, a beautician, thought she was being attacked and had the Indian arrested. Unable to communicate with the man, the police placed him in a hospital where he was classified as an insane Mexican-American.[62]

The newcomers often seek out other Native Americans, usually of the same tribe, and frequent the same bars. Drunkenness is as serious a problem in the cities as on the reservations. The Native Americans suffer from lack of preparedness, disorientation, and lack of job skills, and as a result seek solace in drink from

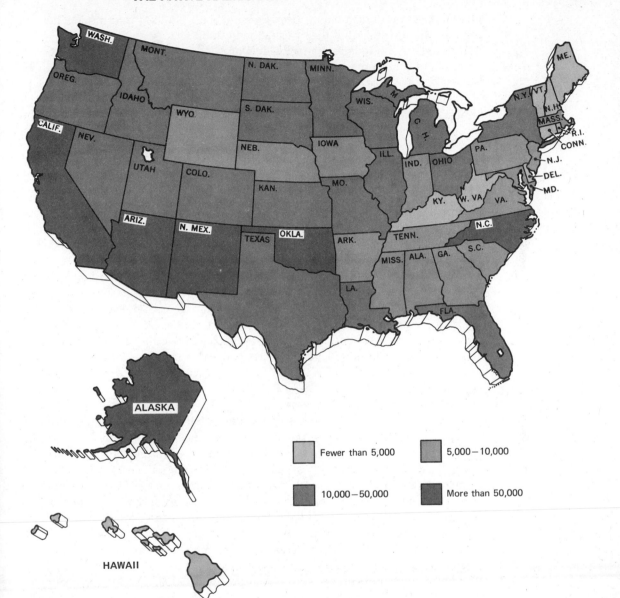

FIGURE 7.3
Where Native Americans Live

the harshness of the "cement prairies." In an in-depth study of Navaho migrants in Denver, Theodore D. Graves found drunkenness to be common as a result of structural and psychological variables. The Navaho had great difficulty adjusting to city life because their parents had not been role models for urban employment and because their cultural attitudes were dysfunctional for the work environment.[63] Custom and tradition, peer pressure, and drinking role models help to explain why they take out their frustration in drink.

Although urban Indians interact with Whites, these relationships tend to be superficial and functional rather than intimate. Bruce A. Chadwick and Joseph H. Strauss, for example, found a fairly low level of assimilation among urban Indians in Seattle, especially in terms of political participation and conflict with the dominant power structure. They found no relation between length of time lived in the city and degree of structural assimilation. For almost all, assimilation was quite low.[64]

Indians who succeed in adapting to urban living, usually over a two- to three-year period, settle into semiskilled or skilled jobs. Once they have gained some economic security, they frequently move out of the city to racially mixed suburban areas. While this shows some degree of acculturation and convergent social adaptation, other evidence suggests this trend is a limited one. Many middle-class urban-adapted Indians form their own ethnic institutions, including churches, powwow clubs, social centers, and athletic leagues.[65]

From the Pueblo, the first penthouse dwellers in the United States, to the city-dwelling Native American of today, urban living does not appear to have encouraged more rapid movement into the mainstream of American society. Today's urban Native Americans are relatively invisible, but that does not necessarily mean they have assimilated. There may have been some degree of acculturation, but most urban Native Americans attempt to preserve their ethnic identity and do not interact socially with non-Native Americans to any noticeable degree.

CULTURAL IMPACT

Perhaps no other ethnic group has had as great an impact upon American culture as have the Native Americans, primarily because they were already here and the Whites, who had to adapt to a new land, found it advantageous to learn from them. Cities, towns, counties, states, rivers, lakes, mountains, and other geographic entities by the thousands bear Indian names today. Over five hundred words in our language are Indian, including *wigwam, succotash, tobacco, papoose, chipmunk, squash, skunk, toboggan, oppossum, tomahawk, moose, mackinaw, hickory, pecan, raccoon, cougar, woodchuck, and hominy.*[66]

The Native Americans' knowledge of herbs and the more than eighty plants they domesticated brought Whites a wide variety of new tastes. Native Americans introduced the Europeans to corn, white and sweet potatoes, kidney beans, tomatoes, peanuts, peppers, pumpkins, avocados, pineapples, maple sugar, chicle, and cacao, as well as tobacco and long-fiber cotton. The Native Americans' knowledge of medicinal plants is also part of their legacy.

At least fifty-nine drugs, including coca (for cocaine and novocaine), curare (a muscle relaxant), cinochona bark (the source of quinine), cascara sagrada (a laxative), datura (a pain-reliever), and ephedra (a nasal remedy), were bequeathed to modern medicine by the Indians.[67]

The Indians also made various other objects many Americans still use today. Some of these are canoes, kayaks, snowshoes, toboggans, moccasins, hammocks, pipes, parkas, ponchos, dog sleds, and rubber syringes. Indian influence upon jewelry, clothing, art, architecture, literature, and Scouting is substantial. "Iron Eyes" Cody, an Indian actor, appeared in a television campaign against littering, and symbolized the likeness between traditional Indian reverence for the land and the positions that conservationists support today. The Iroquois influence upon House-Senate conferences as detailed in the Constitution has already been mentioned. Additionally, a new appreciation and adaptation of Indian child-rearing practices, group-directed activities, cooperatives, and ministrations to a patient's mental state are occurring.[68]

SOCIOLOGICAL ANALYSIS

Both Hollywood and the BIA use general Indian stereotypes in their treatment of Indians, even though extensive differences have always existed among tribes. In this chapter we have looked at their similarities and differences, noting the changes in attitude and public policy toward them over the years. Our three theoretical frameworks offer us not only a coherent approach to understanding the Indian experience, but provide insights into their problems.

The Functionalist View

Whites may never have fully understood the Indian social system, but anthropologists have found their tribal societies functioned with a high degree of social organization. Kin relationships, from the nuclear family to a vast clan system, formed the basis of interaction. Clearly defined, interdependent work roles for young and old, male and female, in cooperative tasks of living gave them a rather stable society. Living off the land, their pantheist belief system made them practicing conservationists, maintaining a harmonious relationship with their natural environment. They were self-sufficient people with institutionalized practices of gift-giving and property control—such as willful destruction of one's property in a competitive display of wealth among some Pacific Coast Indians—which helped sustain a fairly equitable society, without great extremes of poverty or riches.

Even early contacts with white explorers, trappers, and settlers were usually harmonious, both sides benefiting from what each had to offer the other. Dysfunctions occurred as Indians slipped into economic subservience, their way of life further threatened by encroachment on their land by steadily increasing numbers of white settlers. Whites saw the Indians as a hindrance to their making the land productive, forcibly removing the Indians as a nonvaluable part of their expanding society. Forced segregation on nonproductive reservations completely destroyed Indian society as a self-sufficient entity while reinforcing their culture. This systemic disorganization has been entrenched for over one hundred years, restricting life opportunities and continuing the poor education, income, housing, health, alcoholism, and other pathologies that are costly to the society and the people who endure them.

Functionalists stress that the most effective method of resolving these problems is to reorganize our social institutions to put the Native American social system back into balance. However, the plight of the Indians is functional to the few reservation Indians employed by government agencies to provide services and to BIA employees whose jobs rest on continued paternalistic control, as well as to Whites living near reservations who dominate that region's economy. All of these individuals, Indian and White alike, would find adjustments in the system dysfunctional to themselves and so do not advocate such changes.

The Conflict View

Lieberson's power theory provides an obvious model for studying Indian–White relations. As discussed in Chapter 4, here is a case of the white newcomers, superior in technology compared to the indigenous population, engaging in early conflict. The native population suffered numerical decline from warfare, disease, and disruption of sustenance activities, and their social institutions were undermined. Westward expansion, the nation's "manifest destiny," occurred by pushing aside the people whose land it was, without regard for their rights or wishes. Formal government agreements and treaties became meaningless to those in power if further land confiscation or exploitation offered profits.

What about today? Who benefits from Indian deprivation now? The battle over the precious commodity of water in the Southwest offers one answer. Water is about the only entity these tribes possess that might be developed in order for them to achieve economic independence, but it has been literally stolen out from under them by mining companies, farmers, and land developers. Prolonged court battles enable powerful business interests to maintain their dams, wells, and aqueducts at the expense of the Indians. You have read of abuses with other natural resources as well. Why doesn't Congress do something? Legislators respond to public pressure. Those not living near Indians are not motivated or sufficiently concerned to insist upon corrective action being taken. Those living near the Indians have a vested interest in maintaining the status quo, and they are the constituency with the power to influence their district's or state's national legislative representatives.

Yet Native Americans have achieved some positive results. They did so through an emerging group consciousness, whether tribal or Pan-Indian. Protest marches and demonstrations, militant acts of defiance—the Alcatraz, Wounded Knee, and BIA occupations—and class-action lawsuits have all brought public attention to their situation and some remedy. Conflict theory suggests organized social movements by the exploited can bring about social change. Native Americans are increasingly discovering that redress of their grievances will not occur without concerted public pressure.

The Interactionist View

Consider again the words of Columbus, Franklin, and Catlin earlier in this chapter. Ethnocentric views of Indian culture prompted a definition of the native population as inferiors, savages, even nonhumans! Once you create such social distance between groups by dehumanizing them, it is easy to justify any action taken against them. Compounding the negative labeling process was the racial differentiation. European-Americans even viewed the acculturated Indians working as servants or laborers in colonial villages, or the entire Cherokee people, as members of an inferior race fit to be subordinated and relegated to a noninterfering, humble role in society.

For their part, the Indians at first found white customs, fashions, and behavior amusing and astonishing. Later they perceived the Whites as threats to their existence, and as liars and treacherous people. The ensuing hostilities reaffirmed each group's negative view of the other, the conflict ending with total subjugation of the Indians.

Government national policy today mistakenly interprets the needs of all tribes and treats all tribes alike: the biggest and smallest, the agrarian and fishing, the ones with economic land bases and the ones without. Many Americans view the Indians as perpetuating their own problems, by remaining on reservations, depending upon government support, and refusing to blend in with white society. Growing up on a reservation, Indians find security in tribal life, viewing the outside world as alienating and without promise. Now the strangers in their own land, they believe it is their right to preserve their culture and to receive government assistance because of past abuses and broken treaties. With so many different interpretations of the current situation, the problems of the reservation appear difficult to resolve.

RETROSPECT

The white strangers who came among the Indians eventually outnumbered them, overpowered them, and changed their way of life. Once a proud and independent people, they were reduced to a state of poverty, despair, and dependency. The land they had known so well and roamed so freely was no longer theirs. Forced to live within an alien society that dominated all aspects of their lives, the Indians became strangers in their native land. Misunderstood and categorized as savages, they observed the taken-for-granted world of the whites more keenly than most whites did theirs.

Physical and cultural differences quickly became the basis for outgroup hostility as the groups competed for land and resources. Like other groups, the Indians faced the familiar patterns of stereotyping, prejudice, discrimination, and conflict because of their alleged inferiority and actual lack of power. Isolation on the reservations not only prevented the assimilation that most Indians did not desire anyway, but it also created for them a world of dependency and deprivation. Subsequent efforts at forced assimilation—boarding schools, relocation, termination—failed because of Indian resiliency and the BIA's lack of thoroughness in personal preparation, assistance, and follow-through.

The Native Americans are still misunderstood and exploited. One, two, or three hundred years ago, those who did not live near the Indians idealized them, and those who were closest often abused and humiliated them. It is no different today. Many people are oblivious to the Native Americans' problems and consider them quaint relics of the past, and others find them either undesirable or else in the way. Some still want their land and will use almost any means to secure it. Native Americans still encounter discrimination in stores, bars, and housing, particularly in cities and near the reservations. They are frequently beaten or killed, and their property rights are infringed upon.

Since the 1960s, some Native Americans have become more aggressive. Many young, better-educated Indians are forgetting tribal differences and finding a common bond—Pan-Indianism—uniting in the struggle to protect what they have and to restore what they have lost. Others prefer a more individualist approach within the tribe. Some gains have been made and more non-Native Americans are becoming aware of the facts, but at present the Native Americans are still one of the poorest American minorities.

REVIEW QUESTIONS

1. Why do some social scientists call the Native Americans the first victims of racism? Is racism an integral part of their experiences? Why?

2. Cite examples of ethnocentrism and stereotyping regarding Native Americans.

3. Why is the power differential so crucial in understanding the Native Americans' past and present problems?

4. Why have most government efforts to "help" the Native Americans failed?

5. In what ways can it be said that little has changed in the exploitation of the Native Americans?

SUGGESTED READINGS

Bahr, Howard M., Bruce A. Chadwick, and Robert C. Day, eds. *Native Americans Today: Sociological Perspectives.* New York: Harper & Row, 1972.

An excellent anthology covering studies and analyses of modern social problems among various Native American peoples on and off the reservation.

Brown, Dee. *Bury My Heart at Wounded Knee.* New York: Bantam, 1972.

A Native American viewpoint of past Indian–White interrelations, offering a valuable corrective to traditional historical coverage.

Deloria, Vine, Jr. ***Custer Died For Your Sins.*** New York: Macmillan, 1969.

    A humorous yet devastating indictment of white treatment of Native Americans by a leading Indian activist and founder of the National Congress of American Indians.

Farb, Peter. ***Man's Rise to Civilization.*** New York: E. P. Dutton, 1968.

    A fine, comprehensive study of North American Indians, from Pre-Columbian years to the industrial age, written in a very readable style.

Josephy, Alvin M., Jr. ***Red Power.*** New York: Avon, 1973.

    A good collection of speeches, declarations, and writings documenting the evolution of a social movement on behalf of Native Americans.

Wax, Murray L. ***Indian Americans: Unity and Diversity.*** Englewood Cliffs, NJ: Prentice-Hall, 1971.

    A succinct overview of Native Americans, from their past to the present, with emphasis on Pan-Indianism and tribal variation.

CHAPTER 8

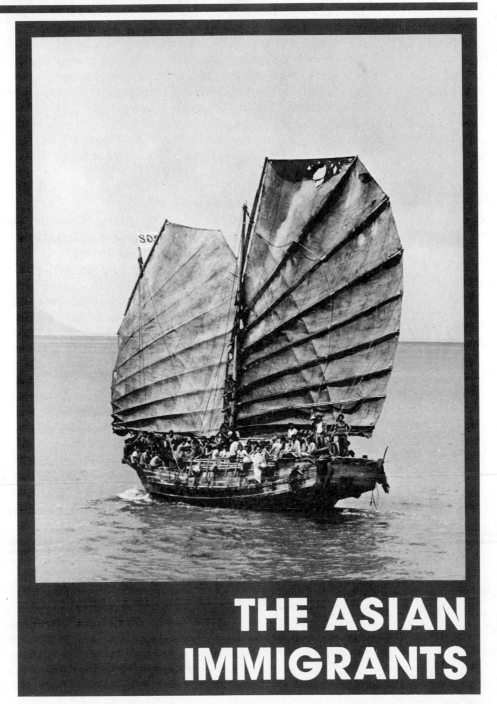

THE ASIAN IMMIGRANTS

Asian immigrants experienced the same dominant-group reaction as many other immigrant groups. Readily perceived as strangers because of their physical and cultural differences, they were broadly categorized as a single entity—Orientals—despite their diversity of nationality, history, language, customs, religion, politics, personality, and subgroup variances. The Asian groups also differed in rural-urban spread, occupations, ghettoization, life styles, and experiences with prejudice. Because so many of them encountered racial discrimination and suffered from a generalized negative image, many Asian-Americans today object to the designation "Oriental," looking upon it as an ethnic slur. In recent years the burgeoning Asian immigrant population has transformed the face of urban America, generating both a bustling mixture of Far Eastern cultures and occasionally some bad feelings between the newcomers and the more established residents.

SOCIOHISTORICAL PERSPECTIVE

Asians had some contact with the land and peoples of the Western Hemisphere before the beginning of recorded emigration in the mid-nineteenth century. Pottery and other archaeological finds suggest Japanese contact with Ecuador and Peru in 3000 B.C., and Chinese settlements in Mexico can be dated from the latter part of the Ming Dynasty (1368–1664). China played a role in early United States history, as New England merchants sought a monopoly on the lucrative China trade, an issue that became important in the struggle for American independence. Chinese sailors served on United States ships in the early 1800s, and a short-lived Chinese colony was established at Nootka Sound in 1792.[1] The first United States Consul outside the Western Hemisphere was Samuel Shaw, assigned to Canton in 1794.

The Chinese first came to the United States during the gold rush (1849); Japanese, Koreans, and Pilipinos came to the West Coast at least a generation later to seek their fortune. Some came to stay, but many came as sojourners, intending to return home after a limited work engagement. This view of America as a temporary overseas job opportunity, together with the white racism they faced and, in the case of the Chinese, a tradition of separate associations wherever they went, led the early Asian immigrants to form subsocieties. Throughout the first third of the twentieth century, when many Asians sought permanent residence in the United States, structural discrimination sharply limited their work and life opportunities.

The Chinese encountered racist hostility almost as soon as they arrived in California, despite the overwhelming need for manual labor in the mid-nineteenth century. They were often expelled from the mining camps, forbidden to enter schools, denied the right to testify in court, barred from obtaining citizenship, and even occasionally murdered. After the Civil War, anti-Chinese tensions increased, culminating in the Chinese Exclusion Act of 1882. The Japanese, Koreans, and Pilipinos who came to the West Coast later encountered racism and discrimination similar to that which the Chinese had faced. Many of them went to work as farm laborers in rural areas or as unskilled workers in urban areas.

A major social problem affecting most Asian immigrants through the 1940s was the shortage of women. Not only was this imbalance in the sex ratio significant in their personal, social, and community life; it also was the basis for racist complaints about prostitution or miscegenation. For the Chinese, the sojourner orientation, the custom that wives should remain in the household of the husband's parents, and subsequent immigration restrictions mostly account for this disproportionate sex ratio. By the turn of the century, the shortage of women had led to the rise of brothels in Chinatowns, and the Chinese were condemned for resorting to prostitutes. The Pilipinos were also mostly male and thus affected by the shortage of women. Whether the Asians patronized prostitutes or sought the company of white women, racists expressed moral indignation, and negative racial stereotypes resulted. Legislators in fourteen states passed laws against miscegenation to keep Asians from marrying Whites.

By 1920, the Japanese sex ratio was largely balanced. Following the Second World War, a greater number of females migrated to the United States, and the sex ratio for other Asian immigrant groups improved. Refugees and war brides from the Japanese, Korean, and Vietnamese wars account for part of the change, as do the brides of servicemen stationed overseas during the intervening years. The Immigration Act of 1965, in its relative-preference provisions, ensures both sexes equal opportunity to enter the United States.

After World War II, immigrants from these countries and from other parts of Southeast Asia were entering a much more industrialized American society. Many also came from lands that had been somewhat affected by Western influence. Some were political refugees, better educated and more skilled than earlier Asian immigrants. Many of these immigrants continued to prefer living in California, while others moved to the East Coast or elsewhere. Entering various occupations, these postwar immigrants were spared the violent hostility of previous times, although they still encountered resentment and discrimination.

THE CHINESE

Americans on both sides of the continent knew something about the Chinese long before they first came to the United States. The United States had established trade relations with China as early as 1785, and a great many Protestant missionaries had been sent there after 1807. Newspaper reports and magazine articles, inspired by the Anglo-Chinese War (1839–1842) and subsequent rebellions and incidents, gave lurid descriptions of filth, disease, cruel tortures, and executions. The American people gradually developed an unfavorable image of the Chinese. In 1842, seven years before the gold rush, the *Encyclopedia Britannica* gave an unflattering portrait of the Chinese people:

> A Chinaman is cold, cunning and distrustful; always ready to take advantage of those he has to deal with; extremely covetous and deceitful; quarrelsome, vindictive, but timid and dastardly. A Chinaman in office is a strange compound of insolence and meanness. All ranks and conditions have a total disregard for truth.[2]

Structural Conditions

Most of the Chinese who came to the United States in the nineteenth century were farmers, artisans, craftsmen, political exiles, and refugees. The discovery of gold in California proved to be an opportunity not only for easterners and Europeans but also for the Chinese from Kwangtung, who could get out easily, and who sought to recoup their losses from flood, famine, and the Tai Ping Revolution (1850–1864). A combination of push-pull factors thus brought the Chinese to the United States. Chinese males set out alone, often leaving wives and children within the village and the kinship circle of the extended family. The first wave of migrants came as sojourners, intending to earn some money and then return home.

The Chinese were visible because of their race, and their appearance and behavior aroused both curosity and suspicion. The sounds and characters of their language seemed most peculiar to the non-Chinese, as did their religions. Their "strange" clothes and hair worn in queues also seemed out of place in the crude pioneer surroundings. Since they had little or no command of English, kept mostly to themselves, and viewed California as a temporary workplace, the Chinese remained an enigma to most Americans.

When the Chinese began arriving in greater numbers in the late 1850s, the surface gold deposits were becoming exhausted. The white miners left these low-yield diggings to the Chinese, who in the 1860s moved on to become railroad construction workers, ranch hands, farm laborers, domestic servants, unskilled workers in the factories that had started to spring up, and anything else at which they could find work. Back in 1852, their industriousness had prompted Governor John MacDougall to praise them before the California legislature as the "most desirable of our adopted citizens" and to call for a land grant system to encourage more to come. However, the Chinese were not permitted to become U.S. citizens, and their reception in the years that followed could hardly be called a welcome.

By 1860, California's population had a large and varied ethnic segment. About 38 percent were foreign-born, and many others were Spanish-speaking natives or children of European immigrants.[3] The Chinese constituted about 9 percent of the state's population in 1860, but because they were mostly adult males, they represented close to 25 percent of the labor force at that time.[4] As the general population increased, the percentage of the total and working population that they represented decreased.

Hired as laborers who worked in gangs, the Chinese at this time helped to build the western portion of the transcontinental railroad for the Central Pacific. As many as nine thousand Chinese a year toiled through the High Sierra country, digging tunnels and laying tracks, and the task was completed sooner than expected. Leland Stanford, then president of the Central Pacific Railroad, described the Chinese as "quiet, peaceable, industrious, economical." While Chinese laborers received the same wages as non-Chinese, they fed and housed themselves, unlike the white workers, thereby costing the railroad company only two-thirds as much as Whites.[5]. The Chinese did not, however, pose an economic threat to the non-Chinese workers, who found their jobs upgraded.

Hiring Chinese resulted not in displacement of non-Chinese but in their upgrading. To the unskilled white railroad laborer of 1865, the coming of the Chinese meant his own advancement into that elite one-fifth of the labor force composed of straw-bosses, foremen, teamsters, skilled craftsmen. And one final reason was perhaps more cogent than all the others. No man with any choice would have chosen to be a common laborer on the Central Pacific during the crossing of the High Sierra.[6]

At the same time the railroad was being built, West Coast manufacturing was increasing. Wartime demands on eastern industries and the high cost of transporting eastern goods encouraged this growth.[7] A shortage of available women and children prompted the textile industry to hire many Chinese.[8] The end of the Civil War brought veterans seeking jobs and Eastern manufacturing concerns seeking West Coast markets, helped by efficient, low-cost shipment of goods over the transcontinental railroad. Fired when their work was completed, Chinese railroad laborers sought other jobs, but the economic conditions worsened, culminating in the Panic of 1873. Labor supply exceeded demand, and racist arguments of la-

THE ARGUMENT OF NATIONALITY.

EXCITED MOB—"*We don't want any cheap-labor foreigners intruding upon us native-born citizens.*"

Using stereotyped images to denote nationalities, this 1878 editorial cartoon perceptively identifies the anger of working—class ethnic Americans against Chinese laborers. This antagonism resulting from economic competition illustrates the split labor market theory.

borers, union organizers, and demagogues mounted against Chinese "competition."

Some of the ethnophaulisms directed against the Chinese during this period of labor agitation dealt with their being "dirty" and "disease-ridden." These epithets had originated decades earlier. In the 1840s Americans first became aware of the relationship between germs and dirt and disease. Negative stereotypes about the supposed Chinese preference for eating vermin, and crowded, unsanitary Chinatowns caused the Chinese to be associated with leprosy, cholera, and bubonic plague. By the 1870s the labor issue had become predominant, but as the labor unions joined together against the Chinese, they labeled them a menace to both the economy and the health of the society. The *real* issue by 1877 was race, disguised as labor conflict.

Societal Reactions

Racist attacks against the Chinese continued throughout the second half of the nineteenth century. Some compared their "racial inferiority" with that of the Blacks, and others attacked the "vices" of the Oriental race. In the 1850s one anti-slavery Southerner had attempted to draw parallels among several groups that were supposedly inferior.

No inferior race of men can exist in these United States without becoming subordinate to the will of the Anglo-Americans. . . . It is so with the Negroes in the South; it is so with the Irish in the North; it is so with the Indians in New England; and it will be so with the Chinese in California. . . . I should not wonder, at all, if the copper of the Pacific yet becomes as great a subject of discord and dissension as the ebony of the Atlantic.[9]

Cries for restrictions on Chinese immigration increased as racial antagonism rather than economic competition became the issue. In 1865, The *New York Times* viewed with alarm the effect of the increase in Asian immigration on American civilization, religion, morals, and political institutions:

Now we are utterly opposed to the permission of any extensive emigration of Chinamen or other Asiatics to any part of the United States. There are other points of national well-being to be considered beside the sudden development of material wealth. The security of its free institutions is more important than the enlargement of its population. The maintenance of an elevated national character is of higher value than mere growth in physical power.

. . . We have four millions of degraded negroes in the South . . . and if there were to be a flood-tide of Chinese population—a population befouled with all the social vices, with no knowledge or appreciation of free institutions or constitutional liberty, with heathenish souls and heathenish propensities, whose character, and habits, and modes of thought are firmly fixed by the consolidating influence of ages upon ages—we should be prepared to bid farewell to republicanism and democracy.[10]

In 1867 California Democrats used an anti-Chinese platform to such advantage that they swept the state elections, including the gubernatorial chair. Democrats elsewhere saw a bonanza in this subject, since many Republicans were identified with the railroads and with companies that recruited and employed the Chinese, and because the Democrats—identified with the defeated Confederacy and slavocracy—could not use Negro-baiting effectively after 1865. Republicans secured the Burlingame Treaty of 1868 between China and the United States, providing for free immigration and emigration to both countries "for the purpose of curiosity, or trade, or as permanent residents." Still, public hostility against the Chinese continued.

To some, the Chinese also posed the first real immigrant threat to the idealized concept of the melting pot. Individuals who held this belief argued that German and Irish Catholics at least were physically similar to the Protestant northern and western Europeans. The *New York Times* spoke of the undesirability of the Chinese:

Although they are patient and reliable laborers, they have characteristics deeply imbedded which make them undesirable as part of our permanent population. Their religion is wholly unlike ours, and they poison and stab. The circumstance would need be very favorable which would allow of their introduction into our families as servants, and as to mixing with them on terms of equality, that would be out of the question. No improvement of race could possibly result from such a mixture.[11]

As the prejudices of the 1850s developed into the sinophobia of the 1870s and 1880s, the negative stereotype of the "yellow menace" broadened. Senator James G. Blaine of Maine, a party leader and presidential hopeful, attacked even the Chinese family structure, since the Chinese, as sojourners, had temporarily left their families in China.

The Asiatic cannot go on with our population and make a homogeneous element. This idea . . . comparing European immigration with an immigration that had no regard to family, that does not recognize the relation of husband and wife, that does not observe the tie of parent and child, that does not have in the slightest degree the enabling and civilizing influence of the hearthstone and the fireside.[12]

Legislative Action

Several hundred thousand Chinese came to the United States between 1820 and 1882. As Chinese sojourners both came to America and returned to China in steady numbers, steamship companies found passenger trips a very profitable operation and so encouraged Chinese immigration. In 1881, 11,890 Chinese disembarked, and in 1882 the number jumped to 39,579.[13] Economic woes and labor agitation against the Chinese led to increasing pressures for restrictions. President Arthur vetoed the first restriction bill, which would have barred all Chinese immigration for twenty years. A few months later he signed a revised bill, barring Chinese laborers for a ten-year period, but permitting Chinese businessmen, clergy, students, and travelers to enter. The Chinese Exclusion Act of 1882 marked a significant change in national policy toward immigrants. For the first time the federal government had enacted a human embargo on a particular race of laborers. There were still sufficient exceptions to allow 8,031 legal Chinese immigrants in 1883, but legislative action in 1884 tightened the restrictions further, and the number of immigrants in 1885 dropped to 22.[14]

The exclusion law had a pronounced effect upon public opinion. Now that a ban on immigration of Chinese laborers was official policy, people's negative attitudes toward the Chinese became more and more evident in the media and in

Acts of violence against the Chinese occurred often in the late nineteenth century. This engraving by N. B. Wilkins depicts the anti–Chinese riot in Denver on October 31, 1880.

people's actions. Violence and killings, which had occurred prior to the legislation, continued. In 1871, twenty-one Chinese had been massacred in Los Angeles, and there had been anti-Chinese riots in Denver in 1880. Hostile actions became much more widespread after 1882. For example, at Rock Springs, Wyoming, in September 1885, a mob attacked and murdered twenty-eight Chinese, wounded many others, and drove hundreds from their homes. What appeared to be a carefully organized plan against the Chinese was put into effect by labor unions and politicians in the western United States. In Tacoma, Seattle, Oregon City, and many smaller towns, angry mobs expelled hundreds of Chinese residents, with considerable loss and destruction of property.

Congress renewed the exclusion act for another ten years in 1892, and extended it indefinitely in 1902. Other Anglo-Saxon countries on the Pacific rim also restricted Chinese immigration. Australia passed legislation in 1901, but Canada did not take such action until 1923. Americans frequently criticized Canada, especially British Columbia, because Chinese entered the United States from that province. The reverse migration also occurred after 1858, when the United States served as a point of entry into Canada for many Chinese.

Organized labor's creation and instigation of the anti-Chinese issue is illustrated in an 1893 AFL (American Federation of Labor) convention resolution, which held that the Chinese brought to America "nothing but filth, vice, and disease." It also maintained they had corrupted "a part of our people on the Pacific Coast to such a degree that could it be published in detail the American people would in their just and righteous anger sweep them from the face of the earth." [15]

Segregation

How did the Chinese react to all this abuse, vilification, and discriminatory legislation? Some reluctantly returned to China. Some sought redress in the courts, winning all cases involving state immigration restrictions but few involving assault or property damage complaints, as from 1854 to 1870, California courts did not allow Chinese to testify against Whites. Expelled from various trades and occupations, as well as from many residential areas, the Chinese had little choice but to congregate in Chinatowns and rely on the benevolent and protective associations for assistance. A large number congregated in San Francisco, but others moved to the larger eastern and midwestern cities, forming ethnic enclaves there. These Chinatowns were in low-rent ghetto areas, usually situated near major means of transportation, which at least allowed the Chinese to be readily accessible to friends and relatives. For example, in New York City and San Francisco they are in close proximity to the docks, while in Boston, Pittsburgh, and St. Louis they are near the railroad station.

The Chinese sought redress of grievances through the courts, petitioning for equal rights. They won for their children the right to attend public schools; then they fought to desegregate the schools. Housing codes kept them in the ghetto, and they found themselves segregated both socially and spatially. Securing jobs through the associations or from Chinese merchants, most entered occupations either not in competition with Whites (such as art and curio shops or Chinese restaurants) or serving only their own people. They settled disputes among themselves, partly because this was their custom and partly because they distrusted the white people's court. The traditional associations and the family clan offered them the familiarity and protection they needed. Chinese temples, newspapers, schools, and Old World festivals all were efforts to preserve their cultural and traditional practices.

Examining the early growth of the Chinatowns, and analyzing the present status of New York's Chinatown, D. Y. Yuan suggested that there was a four-stage process of development.[16] The first stage was marked by involuntary choice in response to societal prejudice and discrimination. Defensive insulation came next, as a mutual protection against racial hostility. As a group consciousness emerged, voluntary segregation became the third stage, sharing culture and problems of adjustment. The final stage is gradual assimilation, a process markedly slowed down by voluntary segregation and social isolation.

Albert Palmer drew from first-hand experience as a white boy growing up near San Francisco's Chinatown in the late nineteenth century in his social analysis of the stereotyped dominant view of these "foreign settlements":

Those who know only the picturesque Chinatown of today can hardly realize what the Chinatown of the eighties and nineties was like. It was dirty, overcrowded, rat-infested, and often diseased. It was poorly built with narrow alleys and underground cellars and secret passages, more like a warren of burrowing animals than a human city. It seemed uncanny because inhabited by a strange yellow race who wore "pigtails," talked an outlandish lingo in high falsetto voices, were reputed to eat sharks' fins and even rats, and to make medicine out of toads and spiders, and who sprinkled garments for ironing by sucking their mouths full of water and then squirting it out over the clothes. And Chinatown was accounted vicious because it was the haunt of gambling, opium smoking, lotteries, tong wars and prostitution, where helpless little slave-girls were bought and sold. . . .

Now, fear is a great disturber, and it largely created the old Chinatown. It did this partly, in fact, by herding Chinese into narrow, squalid quarters and surrounding them by hatred and suspicion; and partly in imagination, by creating the weird and distorted picture of their outlandish character. . . . Chinatown was never quite so bad as the prejudice and fear imagined it![17]

In an analysis of organizational life within San Francisco's Chinatown between 1850 and 1910, Stanford M. Lyman found that the traditional associations quickly came in conflict with one another.[18] As the clans (lineage bond), *hui kuan* (ethnic or regional bond), and secret societies (outlaw or protest bond) fought to secure the allegiance of immigrants and to dominate the community, the Chinese faced strife from both inside and outside their community.

The organizational developments and internecine fights that took place in Chinatown from 1850 to 1910 indicate that forming an overseas Chinese community was not an easy task. Principles of clan solidarity, barriers of language and dialect, allegiance to rebellious secret societies, and their own competitive interest in making enough money to permit retirement in China divided the loyalties of the Chinese immigrants. Yet during the same period the depredations of anti-Chinese mobs, the difficulties and indignities imposed by restrictive immigration legislation, the occupational discrimination created by state and local laws prohibiting or limiting the employment of Chinese, and the active opposition of the American labor movement to the Chinese workingman all seemed to call for a community united in the face of its enemies. What emerged out of this condition of pressures from without the ghetto and divisions within was a pattern alternating between order and violence. By 1910 this pattern had assumed a complex but recognizable sociological form: that of the community whose members are bound to one another not only because of external hostility but also because of deadly internal factionalism.[19]

The Chinese continued to encounter discrimination and hostility in the Caucasian world:

During most of this period, the lives of average Chinese in the United States were difficult and irregular. No matter how well educated they were, in their living quarters they were confined to a crowded Chinatown. . . . College training in engineering or other technical subjects did not guarantee decent positions to Chinese. If one should go out, dressed casually for a walk, or go to a club, or even to a church, he was liable to be picked up by the immigration officers on suspicion of illegal residence. For many years officials made a practice of picking up persons in the street or in public places on the suspicion that they were aliens illegally in this country. Such arrests were reported to be very common, especially in the late 1920s. . . . It was up to the Chinese to prove he was not an illegal alien or even an illegal citizen. But proof is sometimes difficult and takes time. Eventually he would solve his difficulty, but only after suffering much trouble and anxiety.[20]

Not all Chinese migrated to the crowded Chinatowns of the cities. A few hundred, many of whom became merchants, settled in the Mississippi Delta. Chinese grocers sold mostly to Blacks, extending them credit and providing other essential services (such as assisting illiterate rural Blacks with government forms and making telephone calls). Some Chinese married black women; others brought their families over from China. In this transition from sojourner to immigrant, the Chinese men with families tried to evade their "black" status and avoid discrimination against their children, who were attending white public schools. In the 1920s, however, as a result of segregationist actions, Chinese children were expelled from the white schools, and the action was upheld by the courts "to preserve the purity and integrity of the white race, and prevent amalgamation." Separate schools for Chinese were established, as the Mississippi Chinese developed parallel institutions when they were excluded from the white prototypes. By 1950, however, their status had improved, and white churches and schools were opened to them. Recently, the second-generation Mississippi Chinese have been migrating to other parts of the United States.

Social Factors

Perhaps the most tragic element in Chinese life in the United States was the scarcity of Chinese women. In the nineteenth century, single Chinese women did not usually venture forth alone seeking economic opportunity, and Chinese tradition demanded that the wife remain with her husband's parents, even if he worked far from home. About half the Chinese sojourners were married.[21] The imbalance in the male-female ratio was very significant: 1,858:1 in 1860; 1,284:1 in 1870; 2,106:1 in 1880; 2,678:1 in 1890; and 1,887:1 in 1900. The 1890 ratio converts to 102,620 Chinese males and 3,868 females. By 1920 the sex ratio, while still very much out of balance, had lessened to 695:1. By 1960 the disparity was still high but going down, with a total of 100,654 females and 135,430 males.[22] This overabundance of Chinese males and scarcity of Chinese females led to organized prostitution in Chinatowns. Numerous brothels dotted the Chinatowns, some of them run or protected by the secret societies and staffed with girls kidnapped from their villages, sold by impoverished parents, or lured abroad by the deceit of a proxy marriage.[23]

With the vast Pacific Ocean separating him from domestic joys and companionship, the Chinese sojourner relied on the tong-controlled brothels for sex, attending the gambling and opium dens for recreation and respite from the day's toil, and paid homage and allegiance to his clansmen, *Landsmänner,* and fraternal brothers to secure mutual aid, protection, and a job.[24]

Intermarriage was also generally impossible for the Chinese, since 14 states had passed laws forbidding miscegenation. Furthermore, in 1884, a federal court ruled that only wives of those males exempt from the Chinese Exclusion Act of 1882, namely merchants and businessmen, could emigrate to the United States. For nearly all the Chinese laborers in America, establishing a family was impossible. By 1890, forty years after the Chinese had first arrived, only 2.7 percent of the total Chinese population was American-born. The figure climbed to 30 percent by 1920. Legislation in 1943 allowed Chinese women to enter the country, enabling the American-born Chinese population to pass the halfway point in 1950. By 1960, the American-born Chinese were approximately two-thirds of the total.[25]

Recent Patterns

Congress ended the ban on immigration from China in 1943, and began a quota system. But first there was a dispute that reflected the lingering anti-Chinese feeling in America. Speaking against repeal, Congressman White of Idaho condemned the Chinese as a race unable to accept American standards:

The Chinese are inveterate opium-smokers most of the day. They brought that hideous opium habit to this country. . . . There is no melting pot in America that can change their habits or change their mentality. . . . If there are any people who have refused to accept our standard and our education, it is the Chinese.[26]

Actually, the 1943 legislation only permitted 105 Chinese to enter per year, and that quota included anyone in the world of Chinese descent, not just those from China. Special and separate legislative acts covering refugees, displaced persons, and brides allowed more Chinese to enter. However, not until the Immigration Act of 1965 would the Chinese be able to enter under regular immigration regulations.

Since 1965 the Chinese-American population has been rapidly increasing, almost doubling since 1970 to 806,000 in the 1980 census. As a result, the Chinatowns in San Francisco, Los Angeles, and New York have themselves almost doubled, spilling over their traditional boundaries into adjacent neighborhoods. The arrival of so many "FOB" (fresh off the boat) immigrants and refugees has raised commercial rents, squeezing out old-line shops. With the Chinatowns unable to absorb all the newcomers, Chinese are flourishing in nearby areas as well—in the Corona, Flushing, and Jackson Heights sections of Queens, New York and in the Richmond and Sunset districts outside San Francisco.[27] Chinese is now the third most common language in the United States, ranking behind English and Spanish.[28]

The San Francisco and New York Chinatowns, paradoxically, are both tourist attractions and slum communities. They are filled with overcrowded, dilapidated buildings, and troubled by the problems of youth gangs and high tuberculosis rates, but they retain historical, picturesque, and commercial importance. Less evident to tourists are the Chinese garment shops or sweatshops, notorious for their long hours and meager compensation. Also hidden above and behind the street-level storefront facades is the population density, ten to twelve times the city average, and a tuberculosis rate twice that of Whites.[29]

Chinese-Americans present a bipolar occupational distribution. Thirty percent are in professional and technical positions as against fifteen percent of the white labor force; but the Chinese are heavily overrepresented as low-skilled service workers, with 24 percent, as compared to 7 percent of the white labor force. Such employment characteristics partly reflect educational and immigration patterns. Also notable is a higher median family income for Chinese-Americans than for other Americans. However, since over 60 percent of Chinese families have more than one wage earner compared to the 51 percent of the total population, that fact may account for the difference more than higher paying positions.[30]

A Chinatown concern in recent years has been the increasing rebelliousness, criminality, and radicalism of many Chinese youth. The formation of delinquent gangs, particularly in New York and San Francisco, has resulted in a growing number of gang wars and killings. The growing problem of youthful militancy and delinquency appears to reflect the marginal status of those in the younger generation, who experience frustration and adjustment problems in America. Recent arrivals from Hong Kong are unfamiliar with the language and culture, they are either unemployed or in the lowliest of jobs, and they live in overcrowded, slum-like quarters with no recreational facilities. Gang behavior serves as an alternative and a means of filling status and identity needs.[31]

THE JAPANESE

When Commodore Perry sailed into Tokyo Bay in 1853, his arrival marked the beginning of a new era for Japan. For more than two hundred years the Japanese had lived in government-enforced isolation. The emperors had prohibited travel and foreign visitors, though castaways were treated hospitably and allowed to leave. No one was permitted to build large boats, and any Japanese attempt to emigrate was punishable by death.

The situation began to change in 1860, when the Japanese government sent its first official emissaries to Washington.

With their first major debarkation in the New World, the Japanese appeared to Americans to lack emotional expression. [A San Francisco reporter observed:] "This stoicism, however, is a distinguishing feature with the Japanese. It is part of their creed never to appear astonished at anything, and it must be a rare sight indeed which betrays in them any expression of wonder."

In the 85 years which passed between the arrival of Japan's first embassy and the end of World War II, this "distinguishing feature" of the Japanese became the cardinal element of the anti-Japanese stereotype. Characterized by journalists, politicians, novelists, and film-makers as a dangerous enemy, the Japanese were also pictured as mysterious and inscrutable.[32]

Beginning in 1868, the Japanese began emigrating, first as laborers and eventually as permanent settlers. Their numbers on the U.S. mainland were small at first. United States Census records show only 55 in this country in 1870, and 2,039 in 1890. After that they came in much greater numbers, reaching 24,326 in 1900, 72,157 in 1910, and 111,010 in 1920.

Economic Competition

Because many families in Japan still followed the practice of primogeniture (the eldest son inheriting the entire estate), many second and third sons came to the United States to seek their fortunes. They settled in the western states, where anti-Chinese sentiment was still strong, most of them becoming farmers or farm laborers. Their growing numbers, their concentration in small areas, and their racial visibility in a racist region led to conflict with organized labor, vegetable growers, and shippers in California.

Early Japanese immigrants entered various manufacturing and service occupations. Hostility from union members, who resented Asians' willingness to work for lower wages and under poor conditions, produced the inevitable clashes. Members of the shoemaker's union attacked Japanese cobblers in 1890, and members of the union for cooks and waiters attacked Japanese restaurateurs in

1892. Finding work difficult to get, most Japanese gravitated to the outlying areas and entered agricultural work, first as laborers and eventually as tenant farmers of small landholders; some Japanese became contract gardeners on the estates of Caucasians.

The Japanese, whose industriousness and knowledge of cultivation placed them in serious competition with the native farmers, encountered further discriminatory actions. In 1913 the California legislature passed the first alien land-holding law, prohibiting any person ineligible for citizenship from owning land and permitting such persons to lease land for only three years. Under the United States Naturalization Act of 1790, then still in effect, citizenship was available to "any alien, being a *free white* person [italics mine]." In 1868, the government modified this law to extend citizenship to persons of African descent (the recently freed slaves), but the Japanese were still excluded. In a remarkable and unsuccessful case (Ozawa v. U.S., 1921) the Japanese claimed to be Caucasoid.

Since their children, having been born in this country, were automatically United States citizens, the Japanese held land in their children's names, either directly or through land-holding companies in which they collectively owned the stock. After World War I, new agitation arose against the Japanese. In 1920, the California legislature passed a law prohibiting aliens from being guardians of a minor's property or from leasing any land at all. The United States Supreme Court upheld this law in 1923, and New Mexico, Arizona, Louisiana, Montana, Idaho, and Oregon passed similar laws. Because their opportunities were still best in agriculture, many Japanese continued in tenant or truck farming. Morton Grodzins suggests that their immense success (they raised 42 percent of California's truck crops by 1941) helps to explain why Caucasian vegetable growers and shippers pressed for their evacuation during the war.[33]

National Policy

Most non-Californians had no strong feelings about Japanese immigrants, but they were quite aware of Japan's growing military power after the Japanese defeated Russia in 1905. The catalyst that finally triggered a change in national policy toward the Japanese was a local incident. In 1906 the San Francisco Board of Education passed a resolution transferring ninety-three Japanese children, who were scattered throughout the city's twenty-three schools, into a segregated Oriental school in Chinatown. This action made national headlines and had international ramifications. Under pressure from the Japanese government, President Theodore Roosevelt instructed the attorney general to initiate lawsuits challenging the constitutionality of this action.

As a compromise, the school board rescinded its resolution, the government dropped its legal action, and Roosevelt issued an executive order, which remained in effect until 1948, barring the entry of Japanese from a bordering country or U.S. territory. Thus, Japanese who stayed even briefly in Hawaii, Canada, or Mexico could no longer enter the mainland United States. In addition, President Roosevelt secured the so-called Gentlemen's Agreement of 1908, whereby

Japan agreed to restrict, but not eliminate altogether, the issuance of passports. The big loophole in the Gentlemen's Agreement was permission for wives to enter. Many Japanese married by proxy and then sent for their "picture brides." Several thousand Japanese a year came until World War I, and almost six thousand a year after the war. As men brought their wives here and children were born, the Japanese birth rate became exaggerated. Questions about Japanese immigration began to shift from their economic competition to their "assimilability" because of their race, life style, and alleged birth rate. The anti-Japanese stereotype, long a part of dominant-group attitudes, played a key role.

The anti-Japanese stereotype was so widespread that it affected the judgements of sociologists about the possibilities of Japanese assimilation. Thus, in 1913 Robert E. Park was sufficiently depressed by anti-Japanese legislation and popular prejudice to predict: "The Japanese . . . is condemned to remain among us an abstraction, a symbol, and a symbol not merely of his own race, but of the Orient and of that vague, ill-defined menace we sometimes refer to as the 'yellow-peril.' " Although Park later reversed his doleful prediction, his observations on Japanese emphasized their uncommunicative features, stolid faces, and apparently blank character.[34]

The Immigration Law of 1924, which severely restricted the number of southern, central, and eastern Europeans who could enter, specifically barred the Japanese, since it denied entry to all aliens ineligible for citizenship. The bill passed by large majorities (323 to 71 in the House and 62 to 6 in the Senate), indicating widespread support for limiting immigration to the supposedly "assimilable" peoples. The Japanese government vehemently denounced this legislation, taking it as a personal affront, a violation of the terms of the Gentlemen's Agreement, and an insult to a nation only recently courted by the United States. Nevertheless, the legislation remained in effect until 1952.

Expulsion and Imprisonment

By 1940 there were about 127,000 Japanese in America, 94,000 of them in California. About 63 percent were American-born, and only 15 percent were of voting age. Japan's attack on Pearl Harbor in 1941 and the subsequent war led to what is now referred to as "our worst wartime mistake."[35] Approximately 110,000 Japanese, many of them second- and third-generation Americans, were removed from their homes and placed in what were euphemistically called relocation centers in Arkansas, Arizona, California, Colorado, Idaho, Utah, and Wyoming.[36]

The evacuees loaded their possessions onto trucks. . . . Neighbors and teachers were on hand to see their friends off. Members of other minority groups wept. One old Mexican woman wept, saying, "Me next. Me next."

 . . . People were starting off to 7 o'clock jobs, watering their gardens, sweeping their pavements. Passers-by invariably stopped to stare in amazement, perhaps in horror, that this could happen in the United States. People soon became accus-

Part of the 1942 mass evacuation, these Japanese–Americans—most of them born in the United States—board a special train in Seattle under Army guard. Forced to liquidate their possessions at a substantial financial loss, they will go to a "relocation center" in California.

tomed to the idea, however, and many profited from the evacuation. Japanese mortgages were foreclosed and their properties attached. They were forced to sell property such as cars and refrigerators at bargain prices.[37]

This mass expulsion of the Japanese from the West Coast was unnecessary for national security, although that was given as the primary justification. The traditional anti-Asian sentiment on the West Coast, fear of the "perfidious" character of the Japanese, and opposition to Japanese producing a sizable share of the area's agricultural products may all have been factors. There was no mass evacuation of the 150,000 Japanese in Hawaii, which was much more strategic and vulnerable to attack because of its location. The differences in the Japanese experience in Hawaii and on the mainland can perhaps best be understood by looking at the differences in structural discrimination. In Hawaii the Japanese were more fully involved in economic and political endeavors, partly because they lived in an environment of greater racial harmony. On the West Coast, the Japanese were more isolated from most of American society, and certain labor and agricultural groups saw them as an economic threat. Also, anti-Oriental attitudes and actions had prevailed in that area for almost a hundred years.

Besides the trauma that resulted from being uprooted and incarcerated, the Japanese had to make many cultural adjustments to their new surroundings. Instead of their preferred deep hot baths, they had only showers and common washrooms. Central dining halls prevented families from eating together intimately as a family unit. Outside and sometimes distant toilet facilities, not partitioned in the early months, were a hardship for the old and for the parents of small children. Almost six thousand babies were born while these centers were in existence, and proper hospital facilities were not always available. There were only partial partitions between rooms occupied by different families in the same barracks, and this did not allow for very much privacy. Ted Nakashima, a second-generation Japanese-American, offered a frightening portrait of what the early months of life in the Tule Lake camp were like:

The resettlement center is actually a penitentiary—armed guards in towers with spotlights and deadly tommy guns, fifteen feet of barbed wire fences, everyone confined to quarters at nine, lights out at ten o'clock. The guards are ordered to shoot anyone who approaches within twenty feet of the fences. No one is allowed to take the two-block-long hike to the latrines after nine, under any circumstances. The apartments, as the army calls them, are two-block-long stables, with windows on one side. Floors are . . . two-by-fours laid directly on the mud, which is everywhere. The stalls are about eighteen by twenty-one feet; some contain families of six or seven persons. Partitions are seven feet high, leaving a four-foot opening above. . . .

The food and sanitation problems are the worst. We have had absolutely no fresh meat, vegetables or butter since we came here. Mealtime queues extend for blocks; standing in a rainswept line, feet in the mud, waiting for the scant portions of canned wieners and boiled potatoes, hash for breakfast or canned wieners and beans for dinner. Coffee or tea dosed with saltpeter and stale bread are the adults' staples. Dirty, unwiped dishes, greasy silver, a starchy diet, no butter, no milk, bawling kids, mud, wet mud that stinks when it dries, no vegetables—a sad thing for the people who raised them in such abundance. . . .

Today one of the surface sewage-disposal pipes broke and the sewage flowed down the streets. Kids play in the water. Shower baths without hot water. Stinking mud and slops everywhere.

Can this be the same America we left a few weeks ago? . . . What really hurts most is the constant reference to us evacuees as "Japs." "Japs" are the guys we are fighting. We're on this side and we want to help.

Why won't America let us?[38]

Although the harsh physical conditions and sanitation problems were improved somewhat, the Japanese-Americans remained prisoners because of their background. They tried to make life inside the barbed wire fences a little brighter by fixing up their quarters and planting small gardens. However, these "residents" of the "relocation centers" still lived, for the most part, in concentration camps. About 35,000 young Japanese-Americans had left these centers by the end of 1943, going voluntarily to the East and Midwest for further schooling or a job. For those obliged to remain in the camps, life was monotonous and unproductive. The evacuation brought financial ruin to many Japanese families; they lost property, savings, income, and jobs for which they were never adequately compensated.

By weakening Japanese subcommunities and institutions, the evacuation program encouraged acculturation. The traditional authority of the first-generation Japanese-Americans (*Issei*) lessened, family structure and husband-wife roles underwent changes and became more equal because of camp life, and those sec-

At a "relocation center" in California, these Japanese–American "residents" stand in line to get supplies for their families. The hastily constructed barracks buildings in the background are their shared living quarters.

ond-generation Japanese (*Nisei*) who resettled found new opportunities. The Japanese relocated in Chicago, New Jersey, and a few other places, but later many families returned to the West. Many became more a part of American society in the postwar period because they had been forced to do so.

Finally, in 1976, President Ford signed an executive order officially closing the camps, but such mass evacuations could conceivably recur, because of the judicial precedent set by the United States Supreme Court in upholding the action. When the Supreme Court in 1944 upheld the Japanese evacuation by a 6–3 vote, the dissenting justices gave sharp minority opinions. Justice Francis Murphy called approving the evacuation "the legalization of racism." Justice Robert H. Jackson, who would later prosecute the Nazi war criminals at Nuremberg, wrote:

Once a judicial opinion rationalizes such an order to show it conforms to the Constitution, or rather rationalizes the Constitution to show that the Constitution sanctions such an order, the Court for all time has validated the principle of racial discrimination in criminal procedure, and of transplanting American citizens. The principle then lies about like a loaded weapon ready for the hand of any authority that can bring forward a plausible claim of an urgent need. Every repetition imbeds that principle more deeply in our law and thinking and expands it to new purposes.[39]

Prophetically, thirty-five years later the seizure of American hostages at the U. S. Embassy in Iran prompted calls from some politicians for the roundup of Iranian students then attending U.S. colleges and their detention in the very same concentration camps.

Recent Patterns

As internees and during the years following this mass incarceration, Japanese-Americans sought vindication and a redress of grievances. They have fought to obtain frozen bank deposits, receive compensation for land, and restore lost retirement benefits to Civil Service workers. Calling the mass evacuation a "disappointing" and "embarrassing occurrence," President Carter created a special commission of inquiry. After hearings in Washington, Los Angeles, San Francisco, Seattle, Anchorage, the Aleutian Islands, the Pribilof Islands, and Chicago, the panel formally acknowledged the government's mistake and recommended financial compensation to each internee. Although the payment was only a token amount, Japanese-Americans hailed the decision as a symbolic vindication of their civil rights as American citizens.

Because homeland influences are important in understanding immigrant orientations, changes in Japan since World War II are worth mentioning. American occupation of the country and foreign aid led to significant and rapid social change in Japan. The westernization and industrialization affected Japanese values and life styles; it also altered American attitudes toward and relations with that country. The 25,000 war brides who accompanied returning GIs encountered suspicion and hostility, but such attitudes can no longer be so clearly seen. Some may not be accepted by the Japanese-American ethnic community, but Japanese wives of Caucasians are usually looked upon as exotic.[40]

Traditionally, Japanese parents have encouraged their children to get a good education and, since the 1940s, Japanese-American males and females have been well above the national norms of those completing high school and college. Japanese emphasis upon conformity, aspiration, competitiveness, discipline, and self-control help to explain their high educational attainments.[41] Encouraged by their parents, the upwardly mobile Nisei (second generation), Sansei (third generation), and Yonsei (fourth generation) have increasingly entered the professional fields, especially engineering, pharmacy, electronics, and other technical fields. As a group, Japanese-American incomes are among the highest of all ethnic groups, yet one-third are also among the low-income groups, most of them elderly people.

The social organization and social controls within Japanese culture have long been strong enough to overcome any problems of marginality, as evidenced by their low rates of crime, delinquency, mental illness, and suicide. In 1969 Harry H.L. Kitano, a Japanese-American sociologist who had been interred during World War II, observed:

The ability of the Japanese family and community to provide ample growth opportunities, to present legitimate alternatives, to provide conditions of relative tolerance and treatments, to provide effective socialization and control, as well as the relative congruence between Japanese culture and middle-class American culture, has aided the group in adapting to acculturative changes with a minimum marginal population. Relatively few Japanese seek social friendships in the social cliques and organizations outside their own ethnic group. And those who do seek outside contacts appear to have many of the necessary requisites for such activity—high education, good training, and adequate income.[42]

In the 1970s the rates of delinquency, mental illness, and suicide edged upwards somewhat. Among the reasons given for this increase are urbanization and less effective social control over the Sansei and Yonsei, who feel more alienated from both white America and their parents' version of Japanese America. Today's Japanese-American youth, do experience marginality.[43] Another indicator of both structural assimilation and lessened ethnic cohesiveness has been outgroup dating and intermarriage, now reaching 50 percent.[44]

The Japanese-American population has not been increasing as fast as other Asian groups, dropping from the largest such group in 1970 to the third largest in 1980 with a total population of 701,000. Most live in Hawaii or California, with the newcomers also preferring to settle in those states. About half of all new arrivals are skilled and professional workers, who find many similarities between American society and their homeland. Most are Buddhists, a religion growing in membership in the United States because of the continuing entry of Japanese and other Asian believers in this faith. Japanese enjoy a much more favorable image in the United States today, but they are still a visible minority remaining stereotyped as a group.

One special group of Japanese in the United States is known as the *Kai-sha*—business people and employees of large corporations on two- or three-year assignments with their company's United States branch office. Their presence is more noticeable in the New York metropolitan region than ever before. Many suburban

TABLE 8.1
Asian-American and Pacific Islander Population

Nationality	1970 and 1980		
	1970	1980	Change
Chinese	435,000	806,000	+85.3%
Pilipino	343,000	775,000	+125.9%
Japanese	591,000	701,000	+18.6%
Korean	70,000	355,000	+407.1%
Vietnamese	n/a	262,000	*
Samoan	n/a	42,000	*
Guamanian	n/a	32,000	*

*Virtually all have entered the U.S. since 1970.

Source: U.S. Bureau of the Census

towns near New York City, particularly those across the Hudson River in Bergen County, New Jersey, have experienced a large influx of Japanese *Kai-sha* and their families. Long-time white residents, unaccustomed to Asian neighbors, have seen their neighborhoods racially integrated by a group they had not expected.[45]

THE PILIPINOS

Americans have traditionally called this ethnic group Filipinos. However, since there is no "F" sound in Tagalog, the second most widely spoken language in the Philippines, the shift to *Pilipino* is part of a very recent symbolic assertion of ethnic consciousness.[46] When racial or ethnic groups enter a stage of emerging self-consciousness and militancy, they often seek to transform their name to one representing greater racial or ethnic pride. Other examples are *Oriental to Asian, Negro to Black, Mexican to Chicano,* and *Indian to Native American.*

Early Immigrants

After the Gentlemen's Agreement of 1908 curtailed Japanese emigration, the Hawaiian Sugar Planters' Association recruited laborers from the Philippines to work the plantations. The modest number of Pilipinos in the continental United States (there were only 5,603 here in 1920, according to census records) began to increase in 1923. Why? California growers, faced with the loss of Mexican labor because of quota restrictions in the pending Immigration Act of 1924, turned to the Pilipinos as an alternative labor source. By 1930 their numbers had increased to over 45,000, with more than two-thirds of them living in California.

The Pilipinos came to this country with a unique status. After 1898 the Philippines had become an American possession and the inhabitants were considered nationals, although not United States citizens. Consequently, they were not designated as aliens and there was no quota restriction on their entry until 1935. Their Spanish heritage confused their status, however, since the federal government held that they were not Caucasians. The United States Supreme Court upheld this official position in a 1934 ruling on a case challenging the 1790 naturalization law limiting citizenship to foreign-born Whites.

"White persons" within the meaning of the statute are members of the Caucasian race, as Caucasian is defined in the understanding of the mass of men. The term excludes the Chinese, the Japanese, the Hindus, the American Indians and the Filipinos.[47]

Occupational Distribution

Many Pilipinos worked in agriculture at first, particularly in California and Washington. However, the promise of educational opportunities and the lure of the big city attracted many young Pilipino males to urban areas, where they sought jobs. Discrimination and their lack of education and job skills resulted in their getting only low-paying domestic and personal service work in hotels, restaurants, businesses, and residences. They were employed as bellboys, waiters, cooks, bus boys, janitors, drivers, house boys, elevator operators, and hospital attendants. By 1940 their employment in these areas peaked, with nine out of ten Pilipinos so employed.[48] Feeling that they were being exploited by their employers, they often joined unions, or formed their own unions when denied membership in existing unions, and went on strike, which only intensified management resentment. Ironically, the union hierarchy also disliked them and later joined in efforts to bar them from the United States.

As the Depression of the 1930s worsened and jobs became scarcer, increased objections were made to the presence of the Pilipinos. Race riots erupted in Exeter, California, on October 24, 1929, and in Watsonville, California, on January 19, 1930, when one Pilipino was killed. In both instances several hundred white men beat Pilipinos, shattered windows in cars and buildings, and wrecked property. Other clashes occurred in San Jose and San Francisco. Then on January 28, 1930, someone bombed the Filipino Federation of America Center in Stockton—called "the Manila of California" because of its large Pilipino population.

The Scarcity of Pilipino Women

Of every 100 Pilipinos coming to California between 1920 and 1929, 93 were male; almost 80 percent were single and between 16 and 30 years of age. Since there were few Pilipino women available, these males sought the company of women of other races. This situation enraged many Caucasian men, as the following racist statement illustrates.

The Filipinos have . . . demanded the right to run dance halls under the alias of clubs, with white girls as entertainers. And the excuse they have openly and brazenly given for their demand is that the Filipinos "prefer" white women to those of their own race and that besides there are not enough Filipino women in the country to satisfy their lust. . . . If that statement is not enough to make the blood of any white man, of any other decent man boil, then there is no such thing as justified indignation at any advocacy of immorality.[49]

This prejudicial, demogagic statement reflects the sort of sexually oriented charges often directed against racial groups. Association with Caucasian women through intermarriage, dance halls, and affairs led to increased tensions in Pilipino-Caucasian relations. The Pilipinos' reputation as great lovers emerged as a stereotype, causing a San Francisco judge to comment:

Some of these boys, with perfect candor, have told me bluntly and boastfully that they practice the art of love with more perfection than white boys, and occasionally one of the girls has supplied me with information to the same effect. In fact, some of the disclosures in this regard are perfectly startling in nature.[50]

Pilipino responses were quick to follow. Sylvester Saturday, editor of the Filipino Poets League in Washington, D.C., stated:

We Filipinos are tickled at being called "great lovers." Surely, we are proud of this heritage. We love our women so much that we work ourselves to death to gain and keep their affections.[51]

Another Pilipino from Chicago chided:

And as for the Filipinos being "great lovers," there is nothing surprising about that. We Filipinos, however poor, are taught from the cradle up to respect and love our women. That's why our divorce rate is nil compared with the state of which Judge Lazarus is a proud son. If to love and respect our womenfolks [sic] is savagery, then make the most of it, Judge. We plead guilty.[52]

White America was not amused. Several western states passed laws prohibiting marriages between Pilipinos and Caucasians. The Tyding-McDuffie Act in 1935 granted deferred independence to the Philippines and imposed an immediate rigid quota of 50 immigrants a year. Repatriation efforts in 1935–1937 succeeded in returning only 2,190 to the Philippines.[53]

Because of the lack of Pilipino women and legal restrictions on intermarriage, many Pilipino males remained single. These early immigrants became lonely old men with no family ties, living in poverty after years of hard work, although a small number did intermarry among Mexicans, Indians, mulattos, Asians, and Caucasians.[54]

Unlike the Chinese, who had a tradition of being sojourners and who formed benevolent and protective associations, the Pilipinos did not establish the institutions usually found in immigrant communities. Their lack of families and the seasonal, transitory nature of their employment were primary reasons for this. As a result of housing discrimination, they lived in hotels and rooming houses in less desirable sections of town. The pool hall and taxi-dance hall became their recreational outlets.[55]

Postwar Immigrants

Many Pilipinos circumvented the immigration quota by enlisting in the U.S. Armed Forces, particularly the navy and army, as completion of active military service entitles an alien to become a U.S. citizen. These Pilipino males emigrated with their families. It is mostly the children of these immigrants who lead the movement for increased Pilipino ethnic pride and identity.[56]

With the Philippines an ally during World War II, the social climate on the mainland became more liberal for Pilipinos. In January 1942, legislation was passed enabling Pilipino residents to become naturalized American citizens. They could buy land in California, and many did, often from Japanese-Americans who were being removed from such areas as Los Angeles. Many Pilipinos bought farms in the San Fernando Valley and the San Joaquin Valley as well as in the Torrance-Gardena area.[57]

Since the Immigration Act of 1965, Pilipino immigration has been quite high. Hawaii now has the largest concentration of Pilipinos living outside the Philippine Islands. On the mainland Pilipinos tend to settle on either the West or East Coast, a great many being professional workers in medicine, law, and education. Many are underemployed because they have difficulty securing jobs comparable to their education, skills, and experience.[58]

The Pilipino population in the United States more than doubled in size between 1970 and 1980, going from 343,000 to 775,000. Old-timers and female-headed families are particularly likely to live in poverty, especially in rural areas and in Hawaii. Like the Japanese, new arrivals tend to have better educational and occupational skills than most of their ethnic cohorts born in the United States. As a result, Pilipinos as a group have changed from the lowest Asian group in median family income and educational level in 1970 to ranking at or above the national norms by 1980.

THE KOREANS

Korea, because of its strategic location, has been a pawn in the expansionist efforts of several nations. Voyagers visited Korea frequently from the late seventeenth century onward. By the middle of the nineteenth century, English, French, and Russian whaling ships sailed Korean waters, and many Catholic missionaries had come to Korea. The United States, however, became the first Western nation to sign a treaty with Korea in 1882, when it formalized a relationship of friendship and trade. Other nations quickly followed suit, and all attempted to remove the Chinese influence from Korea. In 1910 Japan gained control of Korea as a result of a conflict with China.

Although various treaties and declarations by the different nations guaranteed Korea's independence, Japanese encroachment, both political and economic, continued. Japan's victory over Russia in 1905 solidified Japanese domination of Korea, and Japan retained colonial control until the end of World War II. Korea still did not gain national independence, however, for the Allied military strategy in 1945 was that Soviet troops would accept the Japanese surrender north of the thirty-eighth parallel and United States troops would do the same south of it. This temporary line, created out of military expediency, became a permanent delineation that still exists.

Early Immigrants

The Hawaii Sugar Planters' Association, needing laborers to replace the Chinese excluded by the 1882 legislation, recruited 7,226 Koreans, 637 of them women, between 1903 and 1905.[59] This was the first large group of Koreans to migrate to the United States. The Koreans, mostly peasants, sought economic relief from the famines plaguing their country at the turn of the century. In Hawaii they worked long hours for meager wages under harsh conditions.[60] Of this original group, about 1,000 returned to Korea, 2,000 males and 12 women went on to the mainland United States, and the rest remained in Hawaii.[61] The males were almost all between the ages of 20 and 40.[62]

Between 1907 and 1924 several thousand more Korean immigrants, mostly "picture brides," political activists fighting Japanese oppression, and students, migrated to the United States. As a result of the age disparity between the picture brides and the older males, many second-generation Korean-Americans spent a good portion of their formative years with non-English-speaking, widowed mothers who had had limited formal schooling.[63]

Recent Immigrants

Not until the Korean War and passage of the Refugee Relief Act in 1953 did Koreans migrate in substantial numbers. As refugees or as war brides, Koreans came to the United States in growing numbers beginning in 1958. The continued presence of U.S. troops in South Korea, and the cultural influence that resulted, was a constant inducement to the Koreans to intermarry or think about living in America. Also, the liberalized immigration law of 1965 opened the doors to Asian immigrants and allowed relatives to join family members already in the United States. This chain migration pattern resulted in an impressive fivefold population increase in ten years, from 70,000 in 1970 to 355,000 in 1980. The proportion obtaining U.S. citizenship is higher than that of immigrants from China, India, Japan, and Mexico.

Most Korean immigrants are Christians, and in a recent study of the role of Korean churches in the ethnic community of Chicago, where over 50,000 Koreans live, researchers found patterns reminiscent of earlier European immigrants.[64] Church affiliation was 57 percent compared to 12 percent in Korea. This heightened interest in church membership and frequent attendance at worship services is common among new immigrant groups seeking a communal bond in their ethnic identity. Not surprisingly, the study found religious involvement was the primary motive, but over 95 percent listed "loneliness and seeing friends and relatives" as the secondary reasons for involvement in church activities. Since the greater the participation the greater their identification with their homeland and culture, the Korean-American church, like other ethnic predecessors, serves as a focal point for enhancing ethnic identity.

Social Mobility

The majority of adult Korean immigrants since 1968, excluding housewives, held professional, technical, or managerial jobs in their home country. It appears that many who do not enter these fields in the United States start small businesses. On Olympic Boulevard in Los Angeles, on Clark Street in Chicago, and in lower Manhattan, these small Korean businesses are especially conspicuous.[65] In the Los

Box 8.1

> *"My mother and sister-in-law . . . scrubbed, ironed, and mended shirts*
> *for a nickel apiece. . . . Their knuckles became . . . raw from using the*
> *harsh yellow . . . soap."*

[The following comments, through the courtesy of Harold and Sonia Su-noo, are a composite of interviews with three Korean women who were among the first 12 women to come to the mainland.]

"We left Korea because we were too poor. We had nothing to eat. . . . There was absolutely no way we could survive.

"At first we were unaware that we had been 'sold' as laborers. . . . We thought Hawaii was America in those days. . . . We cut sugar canes, the thing you put in coffee. . . .

"I'll never forget the foreman. No, he wasn't Korean—he was French. The reason I'll never forget him is that he was the most ignorant of all ignoramuses, but he knew all the cuss words in the world. . . . [I] could tell by the sound of his words. He said we worked like 'lazy.' He wanted us to work faster. . . . He would gallop around on horseback and crack and snap his whip. . . . He was so mean and so ignorant!

". . . If all of us worked hard and pooled together our total earnings, it came to about fifty dollars a month, barely enough to feed and clothe the five of us. We cooked on the porch, using coal oil and when we cooked in the fields, I gathered the wood. We had to carry water in vessels from water faucets scattered here and there in the camp area. . . .

"My mother and sister-in-law took in laundry. They scrubbed, ironed, and mended shirts for a nickel apiece. It was pitiful! Their knuckles became swollen and raw from using the harsh yellow laundry soap . . . but it was still better than in Korea. There was no way to earn money there."

[On the mainland the Koreans encountered even worse problems than in Hawaii because of the more highly charged racial tension and the severe weather conditions, as the following account indicates.]

"We had five children at that time—our youngest was three and a half. I was paid fifteen cents an hour for weeding. Our baby was too young to go to school, so I had to take him along with me to the fields—it was so early when we started that he'd be fast asleep when we left so I couldn't feed him breakfast. Returning home, he'd be asleep again because he was so tired. Poor child, he was practically starved. He too suffered so much. . . . [In February] the ground . . . was frozen crisp and it was so cold that the baby's tender ears got frozen and blood oozed from him. . . . For all this suffering, I was paid fifteen cents an hour. . . ."

Three Korean immigrants, ranging in age from 19 to 25, who came to Hawaii between 1903 and 1905

Angeles area, which has the largest Korean-American population (about 80,000) perhaps one-fourth of the Korean families operate their own businesses.[66] Many other Koreans are employees of these firms, which penetrate the black and Hispanic markets.[67] Because the Koreans, themselves a minority group, occupy an intermediate position in trade and commerce between producer and consumer, elite and masses, the role they play is that of a middleman minority.[68]

Overall, Koreans are more highly educated than most other nonwhite groups. Their income, in proportion to their number of college graduates, lags behind that of native-born Americans, although their earnings are similar to those of other Asian-American groups.[69] Koreans have not fared so well in social as in economic status. If recent studies are any indication. Korean-Americans have never scored high in any measures of social distance, an important indicator of structural assimilation. In studies conducted in 1956 and 1966, Emory S. Bogardus found Koreans at or near the bottom in preference ranking, below other Asian peoples.[70] In a small replication study at Western Illinois University in 1976, Won Moo Hurh also found a near-bottom social distance ranking for Koreans.[71]

THE VIETNAMESE

In April 1975 the Vietnam War ended, and 127,000 Vietnamese and 4,000 Cambodian refugees entered the United States. As they waited in relocation centers at military bases for sponsors, public opinion polls showed the majority of Americans, especially the working class, were convinced the refugees would take jobs away from Americans. Labor and state officials raised serious objections to "flooding" the labor market and welfare rolls with so many aliens at a time when the economy was in a recession. Yet all the refugees were resettled within seven months in all fifty states, with potential sponsors—usually church groups—exceeding the number of refugees.

Box 8.2

"Our boat was thirty feet long and about seven feet wide and totally, we had about 103 people. It was so crowded, almost like a fish can, you know?"

"Our boat was kind of lucky, 'cause 70 percent of boats get captured by Vietnamese Coast Guard. That day there was no moon. It was totally dark. . . . Luckily we make it. . . . After one day and one night we get out of the control of the Vietnamese. Now we know we're free! . . . "Our boat was thirty feet long and about seven feet wide and, totally, we had about 103 people. It was so crowded, almost like a fish can, you know? Can you imagine? . . . "There was only enough water for one cup for each person in one day. So we rarely drank the water for, if we don't have water, we're going to die in the sea. The first day everyone got seasick. Nobody got used to it, the kind of high waves and ocean. So everyone got seasick and vomited. . . . But by the second day and the third day, we felt much better.

"We kept going straight into the international sea zone and we met a lot of ships. We tried to get signal for help, we tried to burn our clothes to get their attention. We wrote the big S.O.S. letter in our clothes and tried to hang it above the boat. No matter how we tried, they just passed us by. I think they might feel pity for us, have the good compassion, but I think they're afraid their government going to blame them because the law is, if you pick up any refugee in the ocean, your country got to have responsibility for those people. So finally we so disappointed because we got no help from anybody and our boat is now the only boat and we have only 3 h.p. motor.

"We have too many people and the wave is extremely high, about five feet. It is so dangerous. You can see the boat only maybe like one feet distant from the sea level. But we got no choice. We decide to keep going straight to Malaysia. The fifth day, the sixth day, we saw nothing. The only thing we saw is water, sun, and at night the stars. It's just like upside-down moon. And the sea. If you look down into the ocean, you get scared, because the water—color— is so dark. It's like dark blue. If you look down into the water, you had the feeling like it invite you, say "Go down with me." Especially at night, the water— it's black, like evil waiting for you. Say, "Oh, 103 people, I was waiting for you. Come down with us." We kept going, but we don't know where we're going to be, if we have enough food and water to make it. . . . We don't even know if we're going the right way. . . . we just estimate by looking at the sun and the stars.

. . . "The sixth day we saw the bird and a couple of floating things, so we are hoping we are almost come to the shore. We had some hope and we kept traveling one more day, the seventh day. That day is the day—our water—we have only one more day left. And the gasoline is almost gone. And we saw some fire, very little fire, very far away. And we went to that fire. One hour, two hours. And finally we saw that fire offshore drilling platform of Esso Company. Everybody's screaming and so happy because we know at least we have something we can turn to. . . . We know we cannot go any further. Most of the women and children in my boat are exhausted, and some of the children unconscious. Some of the children had been so thirsty, they just drank the water from the sea. And the water from the sea is terrible. The more you drank, the more you got thirsty. And the children, starving, got a bad reaction from the seawater. We all got skin disease and exhausted. . . . They took us in their boat to the refugee camp in Malaysia.

Vietnamese refugee who came to the United States in 1980 at age seventeen.

Like the Cuban exiles, many of the Vietnamese were middle class, migrating for political rather than economic reasons. Many were well educated, with marketable skills, and nearly half spoke English.[72] They were a cosmopolitan people, mostly from the Saigon region, and many had previously lived elsewhere, particularly in North Vietnam. A 1978 study of 350 refugees scattered in nine localities in Alabama, Florida, or California found 76 percent of household heads were male,

In 1979–80, tens of thousands of Vietnamese refugees such as these, fled their country in overcrowded boats on the open sea. These "boat people" took a heavy gamble against capture as well as against death from brutal pirates or drowning in a storm. Unlike these fortunate ones, the majority never made it. The United States accepted 14,000 Indochinese refugees a month for fifteen months during this time.

the average age was thirty-seven, with 68 percent employed in a full-time job.[73]

In 1979 tens of thousands of Vietnamese "boat people," many of them actually Chinese living in Vietnam, sought refuge in other countries, setting sail in flimsy, overcrowded boats. Many drowned or were killed by pirates, but several hundred thousand reached refugee camps in other countries. President Carter authorized 14,000 refugees a month for fifteen months, bringing in over 200,000 additional Indochinese refugees. Most of these newcomers—from Laos, Cambodia, and Thailand as well as Vietnam—spoke little English and had few occupational skills, making their adjustment and attainment of economic self-sufficiency more difficult.

Cultural Differentiation

Unlike Americans, who commonly believe in one's ability to establish one's own destiny, many Vietnamese believe life is essentially predetermined, with individual control over what occurs partial at best.[74] Two of the more important aspects of existence that the Vietnamese believe determine one's destiny are *phuc duc* and astrology. These are core elements within the family infrastructure of filial piety and ancestor worship, and they provide important insights into the Vietnamese ability to adapt to a new society with a minimal amount of emotional anxiety.

The concept of *phuc duc* refers to the amount of good fortune that comes from meritorious or self-sacrificing actions. This accumulation of rewards, primarily secured by the women for their family, also affects the lives of succeeding generations into the fifth generation. Phuc duc is quantifiable in that improper conduct diminishes the amount one has, while the nature of one's actions and one's degree of personal sacrifice determines the amount of phuc duc one acquires.

> To a great extent *phuc duc* acts as the social conscience of the nation, a collective superego. The children are conscientiously instructed in the ways of living that result in phuc duc. It is, in great part, related to the Confucian concept of Li, although it is actually Buddhist-Confucian in origin and unique to Vietnam. It has its place in future reincarnations but primarily it relates to the family and to future generations of the family. Thus the responsibility that it represents is impressively exacting: the future destiny of one's loved ones and those yet unborn depends upon one's conduct.[75]

So strong is the Vietnamese belief in horoscopes that parents accept no responsibility for a child's personality, believing that the configuration of the celestial bodies at the moment of conception has fixed the character of that individual. At the time of birth a Vietnamese astrologer specifically predicts the personality and events to come for the newborn infant. This often becomes a self-fulfilling prophecy, as the predictions influence actual behavior (parental child-rearing practices as well as the child's own actions, including mate selection as an adult). Thus the prophecy is confirmed by its result.

The important thing here is that the Vietnamese way of life includes belief in a deterministic life force over which one has minimal control. This concept has greatly influenced the accommodation of the Vietnamese to the United States.

> For many this is the second or third time that they have been refugees. It is not something that one ever gets used to, but there is a philosophic acceptance of fate. And this the Vietnamese can accept. It is assigned to bad phuc duc, to the heavens, to the land on which one's ancestors are buried, or whatever. The cause, however, is externalized and inasmuch as this is universally concurred in by one's peers, these adverse events are integrated into one's psychic apparatus with a minimum of emotional dislocation.[76]

Han T. Doan points out that Vietnamese believe human nature is basically good but corruptible.[77] Diligence is thus necessary in all activity: one must exercise caution, self-control, meditation, honor, modesty, and moderation. Vietnamese are strongly tradition-bound, revering their ancestors, homeland, and family traditions. They tend to live in harmony with nature rather than to dominate it. Instead of favoring individualism, Vietnamese culture is oriented toward group goal achievement, primarily within the extended family.

The doctrine of the "Golden Mean" of Confucius and that of the "Middle Path" of Buddha have been ingrained in the Vietnamese thinking and have dominated Vietnamese thoughts. These doctrines account for the harmony maintained in social relationships among Vietnamese and between Vietnamese and other peoples. In their relations with others, Vietnamese, in order to maintain the "just middle," try to avoid injuring others and hurting their susceptibility; they compromise. They are also delicate and tactful, gentle, polite, and flexible: what belongs to others is pretty and what belongs to them is ugly. Also, it is desirable for Vietnamese to show respect to their superiors and kindness to their inferiors. The desire to please others can be found in old folk sayings that "since one does not have to buy nice words, one should choose those pleasant to others' ears." To make others happy, one sometimes has to bend low and to live up to their expectation.[78]

According to Confucian thinking, a hierarchical system is the natural order of things. It is necessary, therefore, that individuals know their position in the system, and behave as befits that position.[79]

Acculturation

Although very few entire families succeeded in leaving Vietnam, enough members of Vietnamese extended families did arrive to enable continuance of traditional family structures. Although this arrangement would seem to ease their adjustment, early studies revealed immersion in the automated, specialized American culture caused tension between the vivid, persistent extended-family image and emotional reality.[80] Vietnamericans established separate households, often at a considerable distance from other relatives, making contacts, visits, and shared responsibility for older adult family members more difficult.

Refugee adaptation to American life appears to vary. One study found a higher education level and degree of Americanization prior to immigration eased the acculturation process.[81] A contradictory finding in another study was that higher education meant poorer adjustment because of underemployment.[82] Both studies agreed, however, that those Vietnamese with the most traditional point of view faced the greatest culture shock and adaptation.

An ongoing study by behavioral scientists at the University of Washington in Seattle, begun in 1976, uses the Cornell Medical Index to document the physical and mental health status of Vietnamese refugees.[83] Among their findings are that adaptation problems continue into the third and fourth year after arrival. Physical complaints are often the result of psychological stresses and are psychosomatic. Women are more likely than men to suffer from depression, anxiety, and tension. A greater frequency of feelings of inadequacy, anger, tension, and sensitivity occurs among the refugees than the general population. Principal causes of mental stress are loneliness, lack of community life, breakup of the family, uncertainty about the future, homesickness, grief over losses in fleeing one's homeland, and frustration in coping with American life. As found in earlier studies of Cuban and

Hungarian refugees, hostile and aggressive attitudes toward the host society or fellow refugees often proves to be an effective adaptive style. This emotional arousal helps Vietnamese overcome the passivity of their cultural values, discussed earlier in this section, and to seek out and find better ways to survive and surmount their problems.

The 1980 census reported 262,000 Vietnamericans living in the United States, the largest concentrations in California, Texas, Pennsylvania, Florida, and Washington. Recognizable ethnic communities, distinct from other Asian groups, can be found in New Orleans where over 4,000 live in a modern subdivision, and in Denver and Los Angeles.

SAMOANS

Samoans come either as immigrants from independent Western Samoa or as U.S. nationals from American Samoa. Their immigration to the United States began primarily in the 1950s, their current population numbering about 40,000, with most of them concentrated in southern California.

Like many other Asian groups, Samoan culture stresses the extended family and kinship system. For them, the family is the source of "security, safety, sustenance, and support."[84] One's contribution to the family is important, since wealth and property belong to the family, not to the individual.[85] Because their family structure emphasizes cooperation, sharing, and equivalence, Samoans possess a pride of self-sufficency, finding it difficult to ask for outside help. Lacking advanced education or work skills, they occupy lower-status positions, with some living in poverty. Yet the needy poor, unemployed, or elderly usually suffer in silence, since unreciprocated assistance, in their eyes, brings shame and loss of prestige to the family.[86]

Although the cooperative atmosphere of the Samoan family offers important psychological and economic advantages, it also creates acculturation problems. Unaccustomed to the competitive spirit in public schools, some young people find the pressures and frustrations of school too much, and they drop out.[87] Teenage dating, high-school activities, and outside agency events cause Samoan young people to spend more time outside the home, endangering family cohesion. Many urban Samoan families combat this aspect of Americanization by making their church (usually Congregational or Methodist) the center of their social activities and by stressing extended family interaction.[88]

Weddings and funerals are church-related events usually creating much financial strain on Samoan-American families, as they directly display family status and esteem. An extensive wedding feast, with gifts exchanged between the families of the bride and groom, costs from twelve to seventeen thousand dollars. A family death results in an elaborate ceremony and extensive feast, also with gifts and valuables given to all participants and those in attendance. These expenses run from sixteen to eighteen thousand dollars, and as high as twenty-five to thirty thousand dollars if the deceased was an important person in the ethnic community.[89]

Box 8.3

> *"I had the feeling I would never come back here. . . . I felt that I was losing the things that I really love. . . . It's a very lonely and scary feeling."*

"I came to the U.S. for the adventure. I had heard much about this country and seen many American films. My parents are Chinese and migrated to Thailand about twenty years before I was born. My father is a very successful businessman, having his own lumber business and a few hotels. So I really came here only to satisfy my own curiosity, but I stayed here for my undergraduate and graduate course work and I haven't returned yet.

"It's almost as if I sensed this before I left. I was going to America because I wanted to see that country, but before my parents took me to the airport, I cried. At the airport a lot of people came to say farewell to me and I just waved to them. I had the feeling I would never come back here. Especially when I got into the airplane, I felt that I was losing the things that I really love, and I wanted to get off. It's a very lonely and scary feeling. . . .

"Things seemed strange to me at first. Oriental people all have dark hair. Here I saw many people with different features, with blond hair, brown hair, and so on. At that time they looked funny to me. I had seen some American soldiers in Thailand, but they were a small minority. Now everyone around me was so very different. Another thing was being driven [so fast] on the highways. . . . We have few good highways in Thailand and this was a new experience.

"I can't describe to you how lonely and depressed I was in this country. I at first wished I had never come. The family I stayed with in New Hampshire was friendly and tried to teach me about America, but the language and cultural barriers were overwhelming in those first six or eight months. I was withdrawn because I was afraid of the people and didn't know how to do. Most people were impatient with me and so avoided me. I was sad and didn't like this country, but I felt obliged to my parents to stay for the year even though I was very homesick.

"At the end of the school year I went back home. I discovered I had changed. I was more independent and stubborn, and I enjoyed doing some things that Thai people thought were silly, like getting a suntan. Also, I really wanted to be somebody and make my parents proud, and I thought the best way was to get an education in the U.S. So I came back here and earned my bachelor's degree. This summer I'll finish my master's degree and then I'll go back home to my parents and give them my diplomas. They really belong to my parents because they gave me material and emotional support. I'll come back here . . . and maybe someday be a college professor."

Thai immigrant who came to the United States in 1971 at age 19.

A 1983 study of Samoans living in the Los Angeles and San Diego regions found 73 percent of the respondents with annual family incomes exceeding $10,000 desirous of maintaining these traditional costly events.[90] Possessing a strong sense of ethnic identity, the Samoans also indicated a fervent desire to keep it alive through membership in traditional Samoan churches rather than by joining available ones (86 percent), through endogamy (90 percent), and maintenance of Fa'a Samoa, the "Samoan way of life" (92 percent of those over twenty-five, 69 percent of those under twenty-five). As a fairly small group not experiencing much discrimination, whose cultural traditions are not very functional in urban America, the probability is high for their eventual assimilation into American society.

OTHER ASIAN-AMERICANS AND PACIFIC ISLANDERS

Other Asian immigrants have come to the United States from Bangladesh, Burma, Cambodia, Indonesia, Laos, Malaysia, Pakistan, and Thailand. There are also Pacific Islanders from Guam, Fiji, Tonga, and other parts of Micronesia. Their population sizes range from the 30,000 or more Guamanians, Laotians, and Thai, to the few thousand Fijians and Tonganese. Sometimes they form viable subcommunities like the 2,300 Tai Dam from Laos in Iowa or the Hmong from Laos in Seattle. In other places they blend with other Asian groups in urban neighborhoods. Their acculturation and life-style varies by their location, social contacts, occupation, and background, but most appear to possess some skills and education, suggesting eventual integration into the societal mainstream.

SOCIOLOGICAL ANALYSIS

Some of our discussion of Asian immigrants has covered events in previous generations, while other parts of this chapter have focused on the contemporary scene. If we apply the sociological perspective to these individual group chronologies, we find the time span is irrelevant in understanding the continuing patterns of intergroup relations.

The Functionalist View

Chinese in the nineteenth century filled important societal needs—working on railroads, farms, ranches, and in stores and factories. Their work effectively contributed to the building of a transportation system, the manufacture of needed goods, and the provision of valuable services. Although racial antagonism had existed earlier, nationwide economic hard times in the 1870s worsened the situation. Economic dysfunctions set off intensified labor antagonism, culminating in a system adjustment of immigration restrictions. The withdrawal of Chinese into their Chinatowns, despite occasional internal strife, helped promote ethnic solidarity and offer a social network for interaction in a hostile white society. Later these Chinatowns would function as absorption centers for tens of thousands of new arrivals, once the immigration restrictions were lifted.

Japanese, Korean, and Pilipino farm laborers, both in Hawaii and on the mainland, helped agriculture expand and prosper. An urbanizing West Coast needed many domestic and personal service workers, jobs filled mostly by Pilipinos who liked city life and its educational opportunities. Major societal dysfunctions—the trauma of a war begun with a surprise attack and a severe, long-lasting depression—triggered negative actions against the Japanese and Pilipinos respectively. Eventually a restoration of system balance enabled these minority groups to overcome past discrimination and become more fully assimilated. Problems remaining with Pilipino immigrants stem from their unemployment or underemployment and rapid increase in population, compounded by the recent recession and changing occupational structure of society.

Korean, Vietnamese, and other Indochinese refugees allowed Americans to act on one of their commonly held values—humanitarianism—by opening our doors to people from war-ravaged lands. Just as the host society provides freedom and opportunity to these Asian peoples, so too does the society gain from their labors and contributions to the American culture.

The Conflict View

From this perspective, when employers—railroads, farmers, urban businesses, Hawaiian plantation owners—needed inexpensive alien labor, they recruited it and reaped the profits. When times turned bad, those with power used it to protect their interests. So it was that the series of electoral victories by the anti-Chinese Workingmen's Party in California caused the Republican and Democratic political parties to coopt the anti-Chinese cause to defuse this new political movement. Similarly, the California growers advocated Japanese removal in 1942 to eliminate their competition. Labor organizations campaigned against the Chinese in the 1870s and against the Pilipinos and other groups in the 1930s to prevent their taking increasingly scarce jobs.

Originally based on the labor antagonism against the Chinese, the split labor market theory applies to several of the Asian groups. Coming from low-income countries, the wages Asian workers accepted, while reasonable by their standards, undermined the wage scale of the native workers. For instance, when the Chinese entered the shoemaking trade extensively in the 1870s, weekly wages dropped from $25 to $9. Complaints about unfair competition of Japanese farmers included their "willingness" to work for less than Whites, or to accept payment in crops or land instead of wages. More recently, white shrimpers burned Vietnamese-owned boats in Galveston Bay, Blacks in Harlem urged boycotts of Korean stores, Hispanics in Denver housing projects attacked Indochinese refugees, and Black–Pilipino animosity on the East Coast occasionally manifested itself among medical service workers competing for certain hospital jobs.

Economic exploitation or competition generates other forms of ethnic antagonism. The Chinatown sweatshops exploit immigrant labor and undermine the unionized garment workers, who are further affected adversely by imports from places like Taiwan and Hong Kong. Auto workers and steel workers experience layoffs and job insecurity because of Japanese products. As black, white, and Hispanic workers treat Asians as the enemy, conflict theorists point out that the real culprits are those benefiting—the sweatshop employers, the corporations that avoided capital modernization expenditures to maximize profits, and the America-based multinational corporations which establish factories in low-income countries, marketing their products in the United States and elsewhere for higher profits.

The Interactionist View

Americans have used the word *inscrutable* almost exclusively to describe the Asians, especially the Chinese and Japanese. This concept that Asians defied understanding rested on their marked non-Western differences in physical appearance, language, belief systems, customs, stoicism, and observable behavior. If you will recall our discussion in Chapter 1 about the perceived similarity factor and acceptance of strangers, the extreme social distance between native-born Americans and Asian immigrants becomes understandable. As the groups farthest from the dominant group's increasingly distant interaction patterns, Asians thus offered easy targets for negative stereotyping, prejudice, scapegoating, and discrimination. Cultural differences became intertwined with physical differences in the minds of many Americans, allowing racism to predominate in value judgments and avoidance—dominance responses.

Asian immigrants in the late nineteenth and early twentieth centuries gave the West Coast its immigrant experience in similar fashion to the European migration in the eastern United States. Spanish-Americans and Native Americans were already indigenous to the West, and so it was the Asians who created the new subcommunities, worked for low wages, and received the scorn and resentment of others. The Asian newcomers were replicating patterns of European immigrants in the eastern United States, but the Westerners intepreted these as threats to economic security and the American way of life. This social interpretation of reality set in motion the interaction problems which followed. As attitudes translated into actions, setting off reactions and reinforcing attitudes on both sides, the vicious circle intensified and perpetuated the ingroup's perception of the outgroup.

Recent Asian immigrants offer a bipolar model. Those who are preliterate and wedded to a tradition of the land, face a bewildering leap into an urban society. Schutz's observation, discussed in Chapter 1, that every taken-for-granted situation for the native presents a crisis for the stranger is overwhelmingly true for many Indochinese. Their adjustment and integration into society may be long and difficult. Others come with education and skills enabling them to define American society as not requiring a difficult adjustment. Since many Asian immigrants quietly work hard to succeed, some Americans have labeled them a "model minority," setting the tone for a more positive nativist reaction to their presence.

RETROSPECT

As a result of a combination of racial and non-Western cultural differences, a great many Asian immigrants from 1850 to 1940 remained outside the American mainstream all their lives. Lack of acceptance and social interaction in the dominant society, and frequent hostile actions directed against them, made the Asians acutely aware of the differences in the people and culture around them. Each succeeding wave of Asian immigrants, from whatever country, encountered some degree of hostility because of racial and cultural visibility. To some Americans, the Asians posed a serious challenge to the cherished notion of a melting pot because of their race, their non-Christian faith (though some were Christians), their language and alphabet, and their customs and practices. That many chose to settle on the West Coast near their port of entry, much as European immigrants had in the East, only accentuated their presence and led Whites to overemphasize their actual numbers. Many also believed that these immigrants posed an economic threat to American workers, and this further encouraged racist reactions.

Many white Americans came to accept negative stereotypes, first about the Chinese and later about the Japanese and Pilipinos. Normal ethnocentric judgments about a culturally distinct people, coupled with racial visibility that served as a distinct link to the stereotype, caused a generalized societal antagonism toward the Asians. The vast differences in culture and physical appearance, augmented by imagined racist fears of threats to economic security or to white womanhood from "lascivious Orientals," led to frequent hostility.

The Japanese were mostly concentrated in rural areas on the West Coast until 1940. On the mainland, racist antagonisms and fears culminated in 1942 with the removal of Japanese-Americans from their homes and jobs. Although a few Japanese-Americans were rounded up in Hawaii, there was no mass evacuation, because the Japanese lived in a less racist environment, with fuller political and economic participation. Pilipinos also encountered overt racial discrimination prior to 1940. Since the changes in the immigration law in 1965, over 250,000 Pilipinos have migrated to the United States. Although many are underemployed, they and the Chinese and Japanese encounter less hostility today than did their predecessors.

Koreans, Vietnamese, Cambodians, and Thais are among the more recent Asian immigrants. Some are war refugees, but all are from non-Western cultures and are racially distinct from white and black Americans. They enter an America far less racially hostile toward Asians than it was in the past. Many are either dependents of U.S. servicemen or individuals with marketable job skills. Most come from a region of the world where patience, stoicism, quiet industriousness, and the cohesiveness of the extended family are long-standing traditions. These traditional values aid the newcomers' transition to a new life.

Asia is presently the major supplier outside this hemisphere of immigrants to the United States. Approximately 40 percent of all immigrants now come from Asia. Obviously, that part of the world is having a profound effect upon the composition of our population. In the years ahead America will become even more a land of racial and cultural diversity.

REVIEW QUESTIONS

1. Discuss the interrelationship between labor conflict and racism with regard to the Chinese, Japanese, and Pilipinos.

2. How did the Chinese of the late nineteenth century respond to hostility and discrimination?

3. How can we explain the different treatment of Japanese-Americans in Hawaii and on the mainland during World War II?

4. How do the concepts of the ethnic church and middleman minority apply to the Korean-Americans?

5. What are some cultural characteristics of Vietnamericans?

6. Discuss the legislation and court rulings directed against Asian Americans.

7. How do today's Asian immigrants differ from their predecessors? How and why does society respond to them differently?

8. How do the three major sociological perspectives approach the Asian experience in the United States?

SUGGESTED READINGS

Bulosan, Carlos. *America Is in the Heart.* Seattle, Wash.: University of Washington, 1973.

   A moving autobiography of what it was like to be a Pilipino in California in the 1920s.

Daniels, Roger. *The Politics of Prejudice.* New York: Atheneum, 1972.

   A fine analysis of the use of political power against Asians in general, Japanese in particular.

Ignacio, Lemuel F. *Asian Americans and Pacific Islanders.* San Jose, Calif.: Pilipino Development Associates, 1976.

   A sometimes fiery analysis of experiences and efforts to succeed and be accepted of the diverse peoples from Asia and the Pacific Islands.

Kim, Hyung-Chan (ed.). *The Korean Diaspora.* Santa Barbara, Calif.: Clio Press, 1977.

   An excellent collection of writings about Korean-Americans, their organizations, and enterprises.

Kitano, Harry H.L. *Japanese Americans: The Evolution of a Subculture.* 2nd ed. Englewood Cliffs, N.J.: Prentice-Hall, 1976.

   Succinct yet comprehensive overview of the Japanese experience in America over four generations.

Lyman, Stanford M. *Chinese Americans.* New York: Random House, 1974.

   An excellent sociohistorical analysis of Chinese-Americans, written in an effective, comprehensive manner.

Lyman, Stanford M. *The Asian in North America.* Santa Barbara, Calif.: Clio Press, 1977.

   A comprehensive overview of major Asian immigrant groups to North America, the similarities and dissimilarities of their experiences.

CHAPTER 9

OTHER NON-WESTERN IMMIGRANTS

Other peoples from the non-Western world have come to the United States as permanent immigrants, students, or sojourners. They came from that part of the world situated between the area of Western thought and history on the one side, and the area of Eastern thought and history of the Orient on the other. In other words, these are the peoples from Africa, the Middle East, and other Asian countries, such as India and Turkey.

Although some of these peoples migrated before 1965 and had encounters similar to those of other racial and ethnic groups of earlier times, most have come in the past twenty years. Their acceptance as strangers and their adjustment to American life has differed from those of pre-1920 immigrants because structural conditions in both the sending and host countries have changed. Because of the occupational preference ranking of the 1965 legislation, many of those who have come are professional, managerial, or technical workers. Some are underemployed, but others are accepted in their occupational roles. Either way, most are generally isolated from informal social contact with others outside their nationality group. Thus the theoretical framework used in examining the experiences of past immigrant groups is not completely applicable to this group of immigrants, as we shall see.

SOCIOHISTORICAL PERSPECTIVE

Aside from special legislation allowing political or war refugees to enter, the immigration regulations prior to 1965 effectively limited the number of immigrants from the non-Western world. Eliminating the restrictive national origins quota system opened the door to America to many different peoples who had previously been denied entry. Since few had migrated to the United States prior to 1890, the year upon which the 1924 immigration legislation based its quotas, very few non-Western immigrants had been able to gain approval to migrate to the United States.

Since the immigration laws were changed in 1965, a third major wave of immigration has been underway, once again creating dramatic changes in the nation's population composition. European immigration in 1980, for example, was 72,121, a 36.4 percent decrease from the 113,424 European newcomers in 1965. African immigration rose from 3,383 in 1965 to 13,981 in 1980, an increase of 313.3 percent. Asian immigration exploded to 1041.5 percent, from 20,683 in 1965 to 236,097 in 1980.[1]

The Push–Pull Factors

For many non-Western immigrants, overpopulation and poverty have so seriously affected the quality of life in their homelands that they have sought a better life elsewhere. Sometimes restrictive governmental actions or limited socioeconomic opportunities have pushed the people to look elsewhere. America, with its cultural diversity, economic opportunities, and higher living standards, makes its influence felt throughout the world and is a powerful lure to those who are dissatisfied with their situation. For others, the United States offers educational or professional or career opportunities. Rapid air travel, which reduces the psychological distance from one's native country, has been a further inducement.

Structural Conditions

The non-Western immigrants discussed in this chapter have followed the same patterns as other ethnic groups who have emigrated to the United States. They usually settle in urban areas in close proximity to their compatriots, with whom they develop close, primary social contacts. Because many are trained professionals or skilled technicians, however, their job situation is quite different from that of the unskilled poor, who made up the majority of the 1880–1920 immigrant groups. Nor do they usually settle in decaying sections of cities, since with their income they can find better places to live. Wherever they congregate to live and work, one can find the various support facilities: churches or temples, food stores and restaurants specializing in their native victuals, social clubs or organizations, and perhaps their own schools and newspapers. They soon send for other members of their family or write home telling of their good fortune, and this stimulates others to come to the United States. The chain migration pattern of earlier immigrants is once again in evidence.

A great many of the new immigrants do not fit the acculturation patterns that worked so well for other immigrant groups. For instance, Middle Eastern prosperity and the new international image of the Arabs have not only strengthened that group's ethnic solidarity in the United States, but have also encouraged some to plan to return to their native country eventually. A Saudi Arabian, for example, might return from the United States after acquiring an advanced education or experience that would be preparation for a better life back home. Saudi Arabia collects no taxes whatsoever and offers free education and medical care, and its standard of living is improving rapidly. Arab recruitment of those with American know-how and an Arab background might even generate a "reverse brain drain."[2] Still, although immigration from Saudi Arabia may be extremely low, a greater number of newcomers from other Arab countries are seeking permanent residence here, as indicated in Table 9.1.

Because of new circumstances and conditions in the United States and because of the special character of this immigration, the theoretical framework for dealing with this new breed of immigrants needs revision. The emphasis is still upon structural conditions and the differentials of power, culture, and class, but the model is different.

Since many of this group of non-Western immigrants have marketable skills, they can get professional and salaried jobs without first having to play a subservient role in the economy. They need not yield to pressures to conform to the American way of life in order to gain middle-class respectability. Their income is high enough to enable them to enjoy the life style they want, and they are thus

TABLE 9.1
Middle-Eastern Immigrants Admitted to the United States

Country	1971–1975	1976–1980	Change %
Egypt	11,967	13,528	+13.0
Iran	13,413	32,739	+144.1
Iraq	8,838	14,566	+64.8
Jordan	13,210	16,368	+23.9
Lebanon	10,303	23,543	+128.5
Libya	334	501	+50.0
Morocco	2,102	2,329	+10.8
Saudi Arabia	252	448	+77.8
Syria	5,395	7,944	+47.2
Yemen (Sanaa)	3,491	1,679	−51.9

Source: Adapted from U.S. Immigration and Naturalization Service Annual Report, *Statistical Yearbook 1980*, Table 13.

free to continue their own cultural behavior patterns. Some Americanization will undoubtedly occur, but these immigrants do not have to make substantial adaptations in order to "make it" in American society.

Another sizable segment of non-Westerners in the United States is the nonimmigrant students, workers, and business people. Although they usually remain for only two to five years, their growing numbers make their presence of significant concern in the field of race and ethnic relations. In 1982, for example, 181,000 Asian and 42,000 African students arrived in the United States to study, and over 20,000 Africans and 70,000 Asians came to this country for business purposes.[3]

In many respects, these temporary visitors, although visible to others in work, residential, shopping, and entertainment settings, are similar to Americans who work for a multinational corporation overseas. Even if assigned to another country for a considerable number of years, they seldom lose their sense of ethnic identity. They live within the culture and enjoy the available opportunities without any thought of abandoning their own cultural ties and becoming assimilated in the country in which they work. Many aliens working here have the same orientation, whether they work for one of their own country's multinational corporations or for some American employer. U.S. citizenship and assimilation are not part of their plans. Many of today's sojourners may be more sophisticated than their predecessors, but their resistance to assimilation is just as strong.

Societal Reaction

About 8,000 Africans, 5,000 Asian Indians, and 325,000 Middle Easterners migrated to the United States between 1880 and 1920. They encountered far more prejudice and discrimination that their compatriots experience in America today. Americans are now more tolerant of what may seem to them to be the strange appearance and customs of the non-Western immigrants. Tolerance, though, is not the same thing as acceptance. People do categorize others and make judgments based on visible impressions, which often lead to stereotyping. Racial distinguishing features and distinctive apparel, such as a dashiki, turban, or sari, set these newcomers apart. Although there is no more overt discrimination than that along racial lines or among racial purists, other visible differences offer additional grounds for preferential treatment and limited social interaction.

In recent surveys of social distance among various minority groups,[4] the racially distinct non-Western immigrants have all scored at the bottom. Many newcomers find themselves accepted in their professional, managerial, and technical occupational roles by members of the dominant society, but usually not included in personal social activities. Once the workday or workweek ends, they seldom receive social invitations from dominant-group members, thus interacting mostly with family and compatriots. Economic mainstreaming may have occurred for the non-Western immigrants, but they have yet to achieve social integration.

THE SYRIAN–LEBANESE

A number of factors have contributed to a confusion of ethnic identities and a lack of accurate official statistics covering the immigrants from this part of the world. In the late nineteenth and early twentieth centuries, the Arabian peninsula was part of the Ottoman Empire; its inhabitants were Turkish citizens until the end of World War I. Although there was a great deal of cultural diversity in this single geographic region, all the inhabitants spoke Arabic and, except the Egyptians, used the term *Syrian* to identify themselves. Still, the immigrants had Turkish passports, and so United States officials identified them as Turkish until 1899, when a separate category for Syrians was begun. While approximately 85 percent of the immigrants came from the area known as Lebanon, only in the 1930s did the term *Lebanese* gain acceptance. Some Lebanese resisted, preferring to continue calling themselves Syrians, while some authentic Syrians began calling themselves Lebanese.

Ethnic Identity

Neither political authority nor specific regional residence determined group affinity; rather, religion defined the goals and boundaries of the "Syrian" community, as here indicated:

> Theological differences of Jews, Christians and Moslems have become translated into social and structural realities with each community becoming socially separate from the others. What the people believe is not so important as the fact that people who believe similarly are considered to belong to some social order qualitatively different from that of the rest. Since religion deals with things of primary impor- .

tance, a different religious persuasion turns others into members of a somewhat distinct society or "nation."

. . . Since the religions of the Middle East were all structurally and socially separate from one another, the Jewish community and the immigrant Moslem and Christian community continued this pattern of separation in the United States.[5]

Migration and Settlement

Although religious differences kept the three groups separate, the push-pull factors that led them to emigrate to the United States affected them similarly. In the main a combination of harsh living conditions—hunger, poverty, disease—and Turkish oppression—particularly against the Christians—led many Syrians to leave. The pull of the United States was the result of reports by missionaries and steamship agents of economic opportunities and religious and political freedom. Emigration to the United States began in the 1870s, reaching substantial proportions between 1890 and 1914 as Turkish oppression increased. The peak years were 1913 and 1914, when over 9,000 migrated to avoid conscription into the Turkish army, then being prepared for combat in the First World War.

A seven-block area on Washington and Rector Streets in lower Manhattan be-

In the Syrian quarter of New York City in 1913, this immigrant vendor sells cool drinks to passers—by. One out of three Syrian males became peddlers, many achieving economic security rather quickly, often within the first generation.

came a thriving Syrian community in the late nineteenth century. Other Syrians settled in downtown Brooklyn and elsewhere throughout the entire country. Most Syrian immigrants came either from cities or from densely populated villages; they usually located in American cities of 100,000 or more, and had little difficulty adjusting to urban life.

Culture Conflicts

Syrians often replaced the Irish in old city neighborhoods. This is an example of the sociological concept of *invasion-succession,* in which one group experiencing vertical mobility gradually moves out of its old residences. It is then replaced by another group at the previous residents' original socioeconomic level. Sometimes there may be hostility between the old and new groups. In the case of the Syrians, religious tension resulted in a clash with the Irish, as this 1920 account about the Dublin District of Paterson, New Jersey, reveals:

When the Syrians came to live there, the rentals became higher. This caused hard feelings between the Irish and the Syrians, which developed into a feud between the two nationalities. The fight started in the saloon on Grand and Mill Streets, first with bitter arguments and harsh words, and then threatening fist fights. From the saloon, the fight came out to the streets. It was like two armies in opposition facing each other. . . . The police force was called in to put an end to this fight. All they could do was to throw water on them to disperse them. These fights continued for three days in the evening. Finally, a committee of Syrians went to talk to Dean McNulty of St. John's, explaining to him that they were Christians coming from the Holy Land, not Mohammedans or Turks, as the Irish used to call them. They were good Catholics and they wanted to live in peace with everybody. Then the good Dean, at Sunday masses, urged the Irish to stop fighting with the Syrians, who were like them, Catholics. He succeeded in stopping this fighting better than the police.[6]

To be called a Turk was a bitter insult to the Syrian Christians, who had suffered religious persecution by the Moslem Turks. Americans frequently thought the Syrians were Turks, but they also frequently used the word in a derogatory sense, as an ethnophaulism much like "Jap," "kike," or "wop." Although these enthnophaulisms are still in evidence to a lesser degree today, Syrians no longer encounter this form of prejudice.

Another problem the Syrian immigrants encountered before World War I was racial classification. In 1909 the U.S. District Court in St. Louis ruled them ineligible for naturalization on the basis of the 1790 legislation, declaring them to be nonwhite. Many Syrian Christians were blond and blue-eyed, but the racial barrier was determined by country of origin. The Circuit Court of Appeals reversed this decision. Shortly thereafter the matter was again raised, this time in the United States District Court in New York, which ruled that they could be naturalized.

Early Patterns

Syrian males usually came alone and then sent for their wives and children. Though poor, they were mostly literate and insisted that their children complete primary school. The wife was more emancipated and less dependent on her husband than her counterparts in other ethnic groups at that time. She and the children, after they completed grade school, all worked together for the family's economic welfare. The family structure proved to be an important factor in the Syrians' economic success.

Generally, Syrians preferred to work at trade and shopkeeping, as trading was a time-honored occupation in their native land. Many Syrians became peddlers and traveled throughout the country, bringing both essential and exotic goods to many Americans. In the late nineteenth and early twentieth centuries, the peddler filled an economic need and was a welcome visitor to the home and community. About one out of three Syrian men became peddlers; others tried various ventures in commerce, started restaurants, or, in a few cases, worked in factories.

Upward Mobility

The Syrians achieved economic security quickly, often in the first generation. This is especially significant since less than one-fourth of those who came were professional or skilled workers. What aided them in their adjustment, acceptance, and upward mobility was (1) wide dispersal, negating any significant opposition to their presence; (2) business expertise and selection of self-employment, which allowed them greater rewards; and (3) cultural values of thrift, industriousness, and investment that were comparable to the middle-class values of the host society.

> Even while they were still in the lower income brackets and in working class occupations, the "Syrians" displayed the social characteristics of the middle classes in American urban centers. Studies of these Arab immigrants in Chicago, Pittsburgh and the South reveal a common pattern: low crime rates, better than average health, higher I.Q.'s, and more regular school attendance among the children, few intermarriages and divorces.[7]

Coming from a country in which nearly every man owned the house he lived in, determined to be independent, and highly motivated to succeed, the Syrians accumulated money rapidly and invested it either in property or in business ventures. By 1911 there were Syrians in almost every branch of commerce, including banking and import-export houses, and the government reported that their median income was only slightly lower than the $665 annual income of the adult native-born male.

> Unlike other immigrant groups who had to wait two or three generations to exert their independence from ghetto life and to satisfy their desire for mobility, it was

the Syrian immigrants (first generation) who amassed the wealth that their sons used as a lever for bringing themselves into wider contacts with society.[8]

Rapid economic success and the lack of either unfavorable stereotypes or discrimination barriers once they were known as Syrians, not Turks, allowed the Syrian-Lebanese to assimilate into American society quite easily, so that they did not need to duplicate the host society's institutions. True, they had social organizations and their own newspapers, but their mobility, wide dispersal, differing reli-

---

Box 9.1

"Sometimes in class I might say something with a super-heavy accent, and perhaps even say it completely wrong, and they would laugh at me."

"I am of Circassian origin, having been born in Syria. My father worked in government with the interior ministry. When the government changed from a moderate socialist to a radical socialist government following the Arab-Israeli War in 1968, my father was arrested as a pro-Western sympathizer. He escaped from jail, and we all fled to Jordan, where we received asylum. We migrated to West Germany, but very few Circassians live there, and so we came to the U.S. where other Circassians who had fled from Russia now lived.

"Before we came here, the idea I had about America was that the people were the same, that everybody was an American except the Blacks because they were different in color. I thought everybody would be an American, but when we came here—especially as soon as I went to high school—I found everyone identified with their parents' origin. In other words, they would call themselves Italian-American, Dutch-American, and so on. It was a little confusing to me because I expected them to say they were Americans. Instead they said their nationality first and then said American.

"Most Circassians live in northern New Jersey or in California, and so we settled in New Jersey where my father already knew some people. I did have a lot of trouble with the language here. I spoke two languages—Circassian and Arabic—but starting as a sophomore in high school I had trouble relating to the people. You know how high school kids are. They're immature. Sometimes in class I might say something with a super-heavy accent, and perhaps even say it completely wrong, and they would laugh at me. I didn't have many friends in high school because I worked after school, and besides, we didn't intereact very much with the Americans because the Circassian community had its own activities and clubs. Our language and culture were different and the Americans weren't so friendly. Besides, once you know you have an accent, that does stop you from even trying to make friends. It's a barrier. You're still trying to learn a language and it's hard. With my brothers I spoke Arabic, with my parents who were so nationalistic we had to speak Circassian, and in school I had to learn English, and it was all very confusing."

Syrian immigrant who came to the United States in 1968 at age 15 gions, and emphasis on the extended family rather than on ethnic organizations resulted in their being assimilated rather easily.

By the mid-1950s the Syrian-Americans had completely abandoned their "nomadic" occupations. They had entered the mainstream of American economic and social life and were represented in virtually every industry and profession.[9] Because they were prosperous, their children were able to enter the sciences, the professions, politics, and the arts, and many have distinguished themselves in each of these fields.

More than 40,000 Lebanese have left their war-ravaged country for the United States since 1971, yet they are not an ethnically visible group. Either joining friends and relatives already assimilated and dispersed, or coming as middle-class refugees, they usually blend in easily with the rest of American society in their work and residence. Lebanese-Americans maintain a strong social network of communication and interaction in social events. Their extended families have tended to do things together, including vacationing and relocating to different geographical areas.[10] In recent years a countertrend of large-scale intermarriage has been occurring, which Milton Gordon asserts is the last stage of the assimilation process.[11] It remains to be seen whether a continued exodus from Lebanon creates an institutionalized ethnic subculture or whether the assimilation process evident among those Lebanese residing longer in the United States quickly absorbs the newcomers as well.

THE IRANIANS

Immigrants from Iran are relatively new to the United States. During the reign of Shah Mohammed Reza Pahlevi, about 50,000 Iranian students studied in the United States annually. They maintained a sense of community among themselves, forming associations and interacting with one another. Fear of political repression under the Shah kept many from returning to their homeland until after his fall from power in 1979. Other Iranians living in the United States then were skilled professionals working as sojourners, with no intention of remaining, or political refugees hoping to return home someday. At that time, except for the college students, Iranians did not maintain an ethnic community or network, keeping to themselves, partly in fear of the Shah's secret police agents (SAVAK) reporting something about them and bringing harm to relatives still in Iran. Minority emigrants from Iran—the Armenians, Bahais, Jews—showed greater cohesiveness, intending to become U.S. citizens, but they comprised a very small percentage of all Iranian immigrants.

In a study of Iranian professional, middle-class immigrants living and working in the New York metropolitan region, Abdoulmaboud Ansari found that most do not intend to remain in the United States.[12] They do not form a territorially compact community, nor do they develop close personal ties with their compatriots other than their families. Most Iranian immigrants are physically and socially distant from other Iranians in this country and do not come together except at Now-Rooz, the Persian New Year, celebrated on the first day of spring.

The Now-Rooz party (which takes place in many major American cities) is the only major national event for Iranians in America. As the only publicly visible ceremony, it creates an atmosphere of national identity and a sense of belonging. However, it seems that somehow the ceremony has lost the meaning originally attached to it. For example, one of the most important aspects of Now-Rooz is to review or to extend friendships. The Iranians who attend the festivities in America are apt to come together as strangers and leave without exchanging any addresses or gaining any new friendships. Most of the festivities are characterized by a lack of intimacy and excessive self-consciousness in maintaining of social distance.[13]

Ansari found that Iranians fell into four self-designated categories. About 15 percent were "Persian Yankees," those who had become Americanized and had no desire to return to Iran. Others were "involuntary immigrants"—the political refugees who did return after the Islamic Revolution succeeded—and the "cosmopolitans," the "committed" or "universal" citizens of the world at ease working as professionals anywhere, with no "real" home. The fourth, and largest, group were the *Belataklif*, or ambivalent immigrants. Unable to choose between the two countries, they had become alienated in both. In Iran, their social prestige was much higher, but they had become Americanized enough to feel like foreigners in their own land. In America they were emotional aliens, thus becoming "dually marginal men."[14]

Here in America, not only is his social recognition limited to areas such as hospitals and universities, but as an alien he is subject to a discriminatory treatment because of his particular identity; he is an alien professional. It is as a result of such lowering of status that this type of immigrant finds his professional success has not completely satisfied his social needs.

A large proportion of the members of this group seem to be considering the idea of leaving this country. Such tendency to reemigration is one of the main characteristics of this type of immigrant. While some of the advantages of the present environment may exert pressure upon him to remain in America, personal ties, status aspirations, and cultural attachment constantly evoke the hope of returning home. The image of home, of course, is an over idealized image. From a distance of time and space, life at home is romanticized, thus intensifying the tendency to re-emigration. At the same time, the idea of returning gives the immigrant a convenient self-assurance against the creeping thought of his abandonment of home. But since his state of mind is one of skepticism and uncertainty, accompanied by an earlier alienation from home, many are likely to remain, up to a certain point, an undecided immigrant. The more he remains as an undecided immigrant, the less likely will he be to return, because as time passes, he becomes more convinced that he cannot afford another readjustment.[15]

Anti-Iranian feelings ran high in the United States throughout 1980, as the hostage crisis at the U.S. Embassy in Iran remained unresolved. Verbal abuse, boycotts, and arson against Iranian-American businesses, and physical attacks against Iranian students at several college campuses occurred. American-Iranians, with no anti-American feelings themselves, became the scapegoats of American frustration, suffering indignities and discrimination.

Over 46,000 Iranians immigrated to the United States in the 1970s, but few are now permitted to leave. Those living in the United States are mostly middle class, intent on forging a new life in this country. Large clusters can be found on the West Coast, the New York metropolitan area, and the Washington, D.C. region. A greater sense of ethnic consciousness and community is more evident than before, with "Little Irans" developing.

THE IRAQIS

It is necessary to distinguish between the immigrants from Iraq who came here before and after the Second World War because the political, social, and economic changes in the Middle East made these groups of immigrants very different. Studying one Iraqi subcultural group of Chaldeans living in the Detroit metropolitan area, Mary Sengstock observed its pre- and postwar changes due to the evolution of Iraq into a modern nation-state and the heightened Arab consciousness caused by Arab-Israeli tensions.[16]

The early immigrants had formed a community of village-oriented entrepreneurs with their religious traditions as their primary identification. They maintained a *gemeinschaft* subsociety within American society. Family orientations were strong, and a great many Iraqis were self-employed, operating grocery stores and other small businesses. They were, for the most part, a self-enclosed ethnic community.

Not only have recent Iraqi immigrants to Detroit had different value orientations than their predecessors, reflecting their increased education and their more urbanized backgrounds; they have also affected the self-perceptions and behavior of the earlier immigrants. Although the Chaldeans are Christian, they feel the pull of Arab nationalist loyalties,[17] and this national consciousness is infectious. Most now think of themselves as Arabs or Iraqis, not as Chaldeans or Telkeffes, another Iraqi subcultural group. Recent immigrants are less likely to be self-employed and more likely to be involved in bureaucratic endeavors that bring them into contact with many persons of different backgrounds.

In short, recent Iraqi immigrants rely more on formal organizations and interact more with outsiders. They are likely to join non-Chaldean organizations and to develop social relationships, including close friendship ties and marriage, with people from other backgrounds. With new immigrants arriving all the time (this particular community exceeds 6,000), these patterns may well continue and be the norm.

THE PALESTINIANS

At least 20,000 Palestinians now live in the United States.[18] Their exact numbers are difficult to determine since, having no official homeland, their passports indicate other countries, often Jordan. Their political cause serves as a unifying factor in ethnic identity and political activism. Many lack advanced education or occupation skills, so they work in a variety of working-class trades. Often living in urban neighborhoods near other Arab peoples, the males congregate in coffeehouses in their free hours, much like earlier Greek immigrants.

The Ramallah Federation, named after a town of 25,000 inhabitants just north of Jerusalem, is a nationwide ethnic organization, with local and regional social clubs designed to help those of Palestinian heritage adjust to life in the United States. The organization provides financial assistance, guaranteed bank loans, and expertise to enable the newcomers to start mom-and-pop grocery, liquor, and variety stores. The newcomers repay the loans, adding a small percentage to help others who follow them. One estimate places Palestinian ownership of San Francisco's small convenience stores at more than 25 percent. With these stores, the Ramallahans are earning money to prepare their children for more sophisticated businesses, building their future with help from the past.[19]

ARAB-AMERICAN ACCULTURATION PATTERNS

Arab is a broad term covering people of diverse nationalities, religions, and socioeconomic backgrounds. While they may share a sense of peoplehood, many differences separate them from one another. Two studies offer a basis for understanding this growing but diverse American minority group. Edward Hall's identification of traditional Arab values tells us of the "cultural baggage" some Arab immigrants bring to their adopted country. Vincent Parrillo shows us the emerging pattern of Arab immigrant settlement and interaction, a pattern unlike that of earlier immigrants.

Traditional Value Orientations

Edward Hall identified differences in the value orientations of most Arabs and Americans. Although the Arab nation-states are changing and other variables (such as specific nationality, socioeconomic status, or residence) may also shape Arabs' values, knowledge of these traditional values may help in understanding the perspective of some first-generation Arab-Americans. Hall indicates four principal areas of difference: rights to body space; privacy; facing; and olfaction.[20] To the Arab, all individuals have rights in their moving about, no one more than another. For example, pushing and shoving in public places is not considered rude or intrusive. What the Arab does consider rude or aggressive is an American's cavalier regard for moving space, such as some drivers' callousness toward pedestrians. All have rights in their movement. Physical privacy is rare in the Arab world; there is no Arabic word for the concept. Arabs enjoy lots of space within their homes, avoiding partitions so as not to be alone. Personal privacy is being alone with one's thoughts, not talking to others. Using the "silent treatment" on an Arab to show anger will not work, for the Arab will simply feel that the silent party wants to be in thought and not in conversation. Arabs consider it impolite to converse in one's peripheral view. Thus, speaking while walking side by side is not acceptable; the Arab will probably edge ahead, turn, and stop to see and to be involved in face-to-face contact. Perhaps most intriguing to Westerners is the prominent place of olfaction in traditional Arab life.

Not only is it one of the distance-setting mechanisms, but it is a vital part of a complex system of behavior. Arabs consistently breathe on people when they talk. However, this habit is more than a matter of different manners. To the Arab good smells are pleasing and a way of being involved with each other. To smell one's friend is not only nice but desirable, for to deny him your breath is to act ashamed. Americans, on the other hand, trained as they are not to breathe in people's faces, automatically communicate shame in trying to be polite. . . . Smell is even considered in the choice of a mate. When couples are being matched for marriage, the man's go-between will sometimes ask to smell the girl, who may be turned down if she doesn't "smell nice." Arabs recognize that smell and disposition may be linked.

In a word, the olfactory boundary performs two roles in Arab life. It enfolds those who want to relate and separates those who don't. The Arab finds it essential to stay inside the olfactory zone as a means of keeping tab on changes in emotion. What is more, he may feel crowded as soon as he smells something unpleasant.[21]

Residential Patterning

In an extensive field study of 5,973 Arab immigrants living in the Paterson, New Jersey metropolitan area, Vincent N. Parrillo and his investigators found them to be a religiously diverse group: 34.2 percent Moslem, 30.2 percent Orthodox Christian, 25.4 percent Melkite Catholic, and 10.2 percent Protestant.[22] Lebanese refugees, mostly middle class, tended to live in nearby suburbs, while Circassians, Jordanians, Palestinians, and Syrians lived on the northern and southern peripheries of the city, spilling over into adjacent exurbs. This settlement patterning of Arab immigrants on the edge of cities instead of in historic inner areas or zones in transition has been found in other American cities also.[23]

In the Paterson area, a few families lived fairly close to one another, but one had to journey several blocks to find the next grouping. Nevertheless, a shared sense of community and frequent interactional patterns existed. Ethnic solidarity was maintained through a cosmopolitan network of communication and life-cycle rituals, homeland concerns, political activism, or limited social situations (work, school, nearby families). Instead of a territorial ethnic community like past immigrants, Arab immigrants maintain an interactional community.

Racial composition of the neighborhood did not appear to be a factor in choice of residence or desire to relocate. No interracial tensions or conflicts were reported, as Arab-Americans shared a common assumption that those who lived where they did—White or Black—were respectable people. Coming from a part of the world steeped in religious rather than racial prejudices, Arab-Americans appear to be unconcerned about racial differences in this more secular society.

THE TURKS

The Immigration and Naturalization Service reports a total of about 400,000 Turkish immigrants have come to the United States since 1820. Ordinarily, that number would place Turkey in the top twenty suppliers of emigrants. However, if you recall our discussion on the Syrian–Lebanese, subjugated peoples of different languages and cultures left the Ottoman Empire with only Turkish passports prior to World War I. Over 300,000 people, three-fourths of the total "Turkish" immigration, entered the United States during this period (see Appendix). Though immigration officials identified them as Turkish by their passports, they really were Armenians, Syrians, Lebanese, or other nationalities. Slightly over 60,000 Turks have immigrated since 1921.

Factors Against Immigration

Several factors explain this low level of emigration from Turkey itself in comparison with other poor, undeveloped nations during the great migration period. Perhaps foremost, Moslem Turks had waged a relentless campaign against the Christians within their empire and would hardly be favorably inclined toward settling in an almost exclusively Christian country. Second, the Turks had traditionally always migrated in large groups. Consequently, there was little outside the country to attract families or individuals. In 1923 Turkey barred any emigrant from ever returning, even as a visitor. This law remained in force until 1950. With laws against emigration, few Turks decided to seek a better life elsewhere. Since 1965, however, a small but steady trickle of Turkish immigrants have migrated to the United States.

Societal Attitudes

Although relatively few Turks emigrated to the United States, feelings toward the Turks in this country were mostly negative, primarily because of the Ottoman Empire's political and religious repression.

Such sentiment towards Turkey as existed in America was largely anti-Turkish. We had of course inherited the ordinary western European prejudice against the Turks as champions of Islam. In addition, many groups in America had espoused the cause of one or another of those Ottoman subject peoples who in the nineteenth century were fighting to gain their independence from the Empire. Immigrants from that Empire had helped foster pro-Greek or pro-Macedonian or pro-Bulgarian sentiments in this country. What had principally aroused American interest in Turkey, however, and what had especially directed that interest towards the non-Turks were certainly the long-standing presence and activities of American missionaries in the Ottoman world. It was chiefly the Armenians' aspirations and woes to which those missionaries gave currency.[24]

The Ottoman Empire was often brutal in its attempts to suppress the Armenian and Syrian-Lebanese Christians. Annihilation of enemies was frequent, and Turkish massacres of thousands of Armenians in the 1890s and again in 1915 stirred the wrath of many Americans. To this day many Americans of Armenian descent mark the anniversary of these Turkish pogroms. American hostility toward the Turks was common during those times, and this helps explain further the initial hostility the Syrian-Lebanese encountered in this country when they were confused with Turks. In his survey of social distance in 1926, Emory S. Bogardus found that Turks ranked twenty-seventh out of thirty, above only Chinese, Koreans, and Indians from India. In 1946, 1956, and 1966, Turks shifted a position or two, finishing twenty-sixth in 1966, above Koreans, Mexicans, Blacks and East Indians.[25] In the same surveys Armenians ranked from five to eleven positions higher than Turks.

Immigrant Patterns

When the Balkan War of 1912 began, many young unmarried males came to the United States to avoid military service. When war-ravaged Europe was at peace again in 1918, over 30,000 of them returned to Turkey. The few thousand who remained settled primarily in New York, Massachusetts, Michigan, Illinois, and Indiana.

Most of the Turkish immigrants who came before World War II were illiterate and secured jobs as unskilled laborers. They settled mostly in New York City and Detroit, and they kept to themselves. Some gradually became acculturated, while others remained socially segregated within American society.

The more recent Turkish immigrants have been much better educated than their predecessors. They are often professionals or experienced business people, and they usually adjust fairly easily. The poor tend to migrate to places like West Germany, where they can more easily afford to go and find work as laborers. Those coming to the United States have averaged about 1,300 annually since 1971. Their relatively low numbers and occupational skills suggest they will probably assimilate fairly quickly, within the first or second generation.

THE ASIAN INDIANS

Emigration from India to the United States took place in two distinct phases. In the early twentieth century several thousand poorly educated Indian agricultural laborers migrated to the West Coast and settled in rural regions in Washington and California. They experienced much discrimination because of the then prevailing anti-Asian attitudes. Since 1965, a second group of immigrants—better educated, more urbanized and affluent—has come to the United States.

Early Immigrants

Between 1820 and 1900, fewer than eight hundred immigrants came to the United States from India. In the next two decades a small wave of almost 7,000 agricultural laborers from northern India journeyed to the West Coast of the United States, and still others chose Canada. Almost entirely male, this group—like so many other immigrant groups—intended to accumulate some savings and then return home. Between 1908 and 1920, a total of 1,656 did leave, and another 249 were deported as "undesirable" aliens.[26]

Societal Reaction

Even though the Japanese, Chinese, and Pilipinos far outnumbered the Asian Indians, the latter group also experienced discrimination and aggression because of their visibility and identification as Asians. Near a lumber camp in Bellingham, Washington, several hundred Whites raided the living quarters of Hindu workers on September 5, 1907, forcing about seven hundred of them to flee across the Canadian border. Two months later, in Everett, Washington, several hundred Whites drove the Hindu workers out of town. Racial prejudice manifested itself in Port Angeles, where real estate brokers published in the local newspaper the terms of their covenant not to sell to "Hindoos or Negroes." They justified their action on the grounds that wherever these groups settle, they "have depreciated [the] value of adjacent property and injured the reputation of the neighborhood, and are generally considered as undesirable."[27]

The San Francisco-based Asiatic Exclusion League quickly included the Asian Indians among their targets and warned the public that they were a "menace." League officials declared that the East Indians were untrustworthy, immodest, unsanitary, insolent, and lustful.[28] These pressures against the Asian Indians were effective from 1908 to 1910, when immigration officials rejected 1,130 immigrants at their ports of entry. Pressure from the Western Pacific Railroad in 1910 enabled 1,462 to enter between 1911 and 1920, but another 1,762 were denied entry, mostly on the grounds that they would become public charges.[29] The popular magazine *Collier's,* influenced by the Asiatic Exclusion League's exaggerated claim that there were 10,000 Asian Indians living in California, printed an article warning its readers about the "Hindu invasion."[30]

In this atmosphere of marked hostility toward Asians, the few thousand East Indians gradually established themselves primarily in California and relied chiefly on agriculture as a means of livelihood. Typically the Indians sought work in groups with a leader serving as their agent in negotiating with employers. Owing in part to the desire of many farmers to break the Japanese monopoly on the labor supply in those areas, they had little difficulty finding employment in the Sacramento and San Joaquin valleys. Also, Indians moved into the Imperial Valley, another rapidly growing agricultural area.[31]

In 1923 the U.S. Supreme Court reversed previous lower court decisions and ruled that Asian Indians were nonwhites and thus ineligible for citizenship under the terms of the 1790 naturalization act. The government than canceled the naturalization certificates that had previously been granted to sixty or seventy Asian Indians. This decision also prevented the Asian Indians from owning or leasing land in their own names because of state legislation against alien land-holding.

The Asian Indians thus became itinerant farm laborers. Few of them had any family life because of the itinerant nature of their work and the lack of women they could marry.

Minority Response

About 3,000 Asian Indians returned home between 1920 and 1940. A few hundred more were deported. The population dwindled from 5,441 in 1920 to 3,138 in 1930 and to 2,405 in 1940.[32] A few of those who remained married Mexican women. Most, however, lived in communal groups apart from the rest of society. Some congregated in Stockton, California—site of a large Pilipino community—and built a temple there for worship.

Physical appearance was an important factor setting these immigrants apart. In the early twentieth century, the long hair and full beards prescribed by the Sikh religion were not fashionable. Moreover, all the men wore turbans and were sometimes castigated as "ragheads." Those Indian women who had come before the Depression, as well as those who have come since the more liberal Immigration Act of 1965, were quite distinct in their wearing of the *sari,* a lightweight outer garment with one end wrapped about the waist and the other draped over the shoulder or covering the head. Most of the cultural differences—appearance, food taboos, social interaction—were an integral part of either the caste system or the religions of India. Therefore, the Asian Indians not only seemed strange to the Americans, but also had difficulty assimilating because they were reluctant to abandon their customs and practices.

Gary R. Hess reports that by the mid-1950s the Asian Indian community in Sutter County in north central California numbered about 900, and had grown stronger and more unified.[33] This had come about because the men preferred to marry Asian Indian women and because the caste system in India had a negligible influence in the United States, except perhaps in terms of status. Because of the small amount of intermarriage and the retention of important aspects of their culture, the rural Asian Indians, Hess concludes, remain only slightly acculturated even though they have adopted certain material comforts, dress, and other features of American life.

Recent Immigrants

Statistics reveal the dramatic change in the number of immigrants from India. Only 15,513 entered the United States over the sixty-five-year period from 1901 to 1965. In the next five years that total was easily surpassed, as 24,587 immigrated between 1966 and 1970; from 1971 to 1975, the number more than doubled to 66,650 immigrants; from 1976 to 1980, 97,484 Asian Indians. With a 20,000 maximum annual immigrant restriction, the numbers for 1981 to 1985 will be somewhere around 100,000.[34]

Since 1965, the immigration laws have allowed in an increased number of Asian immigrants, but this alone does not explain the increase in migration. Conditions

Blending the old and the new, this Indian woman wearing a sari prepares an old family recipe in her American home. Many Asian Indians possess the education and job skills to enter the economic mainstream while retaining their cultural traditions.

in India are an important factor. India is the world's second most populous country after mainland China, with 15 percent of the world's population on 2.5 percent of the world's land mass. This means that the population density is seven times greater than that of the United States.

The problem of overpopulation is quite serious. India's population has grown from 439 million in 1960, to 550 million in 1971, to over 700 million in 1983. The rapid growth is not due to any spurt in the birth rate, but rather to a decline in the mortality rate. Even so, 3 million of the 23 million babies born in India each year die before they reach their first year, and another million die before they complete childhood. Of the remaining 19 million, nearly 9 million will become adults with physical and mental impairments and reduced productivity because of serious undernourishment and poor health. Another 7 million will suffer milder malnutrition and less striking physical and mental impairment.[35] The population is nevertheless increasing by about 1.2 million people each month.

With over two-thirds of the population engaged in agriculture, a literacy rate of only 30 percent, and problems of severe poverty, hunger, and inadequate resources, India does not have very much to offer in terms of economic security. However, many of the recent immigrants have been professional workers—physicians, surgeons, dentists, teachers, and skilled workers—providing the United States with the very people India needs most to retain if the quality of life there is to improve.

Racial ambiguity marks the Asian-Indian acceptance pattern. Their skin color ranges from light brown to almost black, though most of the immigrants in the United States are of a light hue. Americans perceive them as racially different, but have difficulty categorizing them. Defined as "White" sometimes, "Asian" other times, and "Brown" or "Black" still other times, Asian Indians tend to classify themselves "White" and identify with the majority group.[36]

Over 400,000 Asian Indians now live in the United States. With their education and occupational skills, they can achieve economic security, but there are cultural strains. For example, they are uneasy with America's sexual mores. Parents have considerable difficulty convincing their children that the Indian custom of not dating before marriage has merit. As a result of societal pressures, many either wear American clothes or rarely venture out alone. Immigrants may also be lonely at holiday times and may feel guilty when their compatriots in India accuse them of having sold their skills to an already rich country.[37]

THE AFRICANS

Although many white Americans simply use Negroid racial features as the basis of group classification, there is much cultural diversity among Blacks in America. Generalizing about them is just as inaccurate as generalizing about Whites. Regional and social class differences create distinctions among American Blacks, and cultural differences make West Indian black immigrants unlike native-born Blacks. Black immigrants from Africa are culturally distinct not only from the two former groups but also from one another when they have different countries of origin. Also, although many native-born American Blacks call themselves Afro-Americans, in reality a wide cultural gulf separates them from the African immigrants.[38] This fact is often demonstrated at the student level when two separate groups form on college campuses. It has not been uncommon to see, for example, both a black student union and an African students' association at the same college.

Value Orientations

Professor Muruku Waiguchu, himself an immigrant from Kenya, has contrasted some of the value orientations of Black American and African college students in the United States.[39] He has found that African students tend to show some degree of contempt for and arrogance toward black students, commonly using such terms as "Negro" or "nigger" to refer to them. Africans are frequently more achievement oriented, competitive, and opportunistic than Black American students, partly because they have help from white supporters and no "history of denials and exclusion" from white America. The African student is also less racially conscious in the American sense and therefore is more likely to participate in interracial primary relationships (parties, dating, marriage) than black American college students. Waiguchu argues that the two black groups do not share a greater trust and understanding because both have been victimized by white social conditioning:

Unlike any other people, much of our history, and therefore our cultural continuity, has been written by our detractors and oppressors. The inevitable consequence has been that we look at one another through the eyes given and provided to us through the education process and other forms of communication owned and operated by white people. . . . We do not articulate our interests collectively because we oftentimes do not understand one another and waste valuable time labelling one another with the stereotypes we have collected from the white man.[40]

Whether Whites are the ultimate cause of Black American–African misunderstanding is debatable. It is true, though, that differing cultural orientations and ethnocentrism play important roles. Just as dominant and minority white groups have often mistrusted each other, so might different black groups display an outgroup negativism despite racial similarity.

As Table 9.2 indicates, African immigration has been significantly increasing in the past few decades. Chain migration, Americanization of foreign students enrolled in U.S. colleges, economic opportunities, and homeland events are the major push–pull factors at work.

African immigrants frequently face a double handicap in adjusting to American society. First, they encounter racial prejudice and discrimination in various social settings and on the job. For many, this is a new experience since they were not a racial minority at home nor did they experience any of these problems there. Second, because of their own cultural distinctions, they do not identify with American Blacks. Successful American Blacks who are interested in helping the less fortunate usually concentrate on the American black poor, not on newcomers from Africa, obliging the African immigrants to seek out one another for mutual comfort and security.

TABLE 9.2
African Immigration to the United States[a]

1901–1910	7,368
1911–1920	8,443
1921–1930	6,286
1931–1940	1,750
1941–1950	7,367
1951–1960	14,092
1961–1970	28,954
1971–1980	80,779

[a] Includes Egypt, Libya, and Morocco.

Source: U.S. Immigration and Naturalization Service, Annual Report, U.S. Government Printing Office, Washington, D.C., 1980; Table 2.

Since many African states have only recently been freed from colonial rule, their political boundaries are sometimes not as significant as tribal allegiances. Warring factions in some countries split along tribal lines, spilling over to similar divisions among first generation Afro-Americans. One example in the late 1970s was Biafra's unsuccessful attempt to secede from Nigeria, with the ensuing mass starvation and slaughter in that unfortunate land. Boundary disputes, invasions, and surreptitious aid to rebels can also affect attitudes among Africans in the United States toward one another. Angola's invasion of Katanga Province in Zaire, fighting between Ethiopia and Somalia, Kenya's logistical assistance to Israeli commandos rescuing hijacked Jewish passengers at Entebbe Airport in Uganda are a few recent examples of homeland events dividing Afro-American opinion. Grouping the immigrants from the African continent into one category is as much a mistake as generalizing about the southern, central, and eastern Europeans was two generations ago.

As a result of occupational preference classifications in current immigration law, many African immigrants are educated, and possess occupational skills placing them at a middle-class socioeconomic level. If their upsurge in immigration continues, their increased visibility and economic position may make them a more viable ethnic group than heretofore. Like Arab immigrants, they do not cluster in recognizable territories, forming interactional networks or "dispersed villages" instead.[41]

TABLE 9.3
African Immigration to the United States
By Country of Origin, 1971–1980

Country	1971–1975	1976–1980	% Change
Algeria	464	659	+42.0
Angola	155	1,282	+727.1
Cape Verde	963	4,568	+374.4
Ethiopia	953	2,928	+202.2
Ghana	1,639	3,556	+117.0
Kenya	1,758	2,747	+56.3
Liberia	799	1,601	+100.4
Mozambique	155	531	+242.6
Nigeria	3,250	5,517	+69.8
Senegal	169	393	+312.5
Sierra Leone	275	990	+260.0
Republic of South Africa	2,510	8,949	+256.5
Tanzania	1,265	1,724	+36.3
Uganda	1,774	1,596	−10.0
Zambia	279	1,052	+277.1
Zimbabwe	321	990	+208.4

Source: Adapted from U.S. Immigration and Naturalization Service Annual Report, *Statistical Yearbook 1980* (Washington, D.C.: U.S. Government Printing Office, 1984), Table 13.

SOCIOLOGICAL ANALYSIS

The immigrants from the countries discussed in this chapter have mostly arrived since 1965. Because they have lived in the United States less than one generation, their experiences lack the perspective of time for full analysis. Further, as we said at the beginning of the chapter, since most are educated with marketable occupational skills, they do not completely fit the theoretical framework of past immigrants. How well do they fit into the three theoretical perspectives? As you will see, each does provide a focus helpful to further understanding.

The Functionalist View

Has the social system been able to adapt smoothly in absorbing the newcomers, so many of them racially and religiously different? Functionalists would point to the immigration laws ensuring either sufficient earning power in occupational preference, or a support system in relative preference. These better-educated, better-skilled individuals quickly adjust, contribute to the economy, and appear to integrate society with a minimum of problems. Most rank low on the social distance scale at this time, but they do become functionally integrated fairly easily. Their economic power allows them to live in middle-class neighborhoods, accessible through fair housing laws. Some may even integrate areas, their comparable values and life-style making their native-born neighbors more receptive to them as a racially or culturally distinct people.

Lesser skilled non-Westerners have helped fill a population void in urban and exurban neighborhoods. Although some minor problems may occur, these newcomers bring stability to neighborhoods, preventing their decline, and helping maintain a racial balance. Urban density provides easy contact with one another, enabling ethnic solidarity to develop and sustain itself. Living in close proximity to their work, these newcomers find jobs other Americans are unwilling to take, yet fulfill societal needs. As they struggle to make it in America, they find better opportunities than they had known in their home countries, while society benefits from their work, purchasing power, and cultural contributions.

The Conflict View

Early non-Western immigrants provide grist for the analytical mill of conflict theorists. Industrialists often used Syrian–Lebanese as strikebreakers in the Northeast, particularly during the intense labor unrest in the early twentieth century. Just as they offered factory owners a cheaper alternative, so did Asian-Indians on the West Coast enable farmers, lumber companies, and railroads to benefit from their low-cost labor. Other workers resented their presence, fearing their growing numbers would jeopardize their own positions. Once again, the split labor market theory would seem applicable. Economic competition between two wage level groups generated ethnic antagonism and violence.

More recent arrivals suggest a different analysis. Tensions arise among American Blacks and Hispanics at the bottom of the socioeconomic ladder who see foreign-born Africans and Middle Easterners leapfrogging over them. Resentment builds against these newcomers whose hiring appears to deny upward mobility for native-born minority groups. Foreigners are benefiting at the expense of "Americans." Conflicts between American Blacks and African immigrants sometimes occur because of African achievement orientations and rising expectations of American Blacks. Additionally, the movement of Third World immigrants into white, middle-class apartment complexes and suburban neighborhoods changes the prior racial or cultural homogeneity, which sometimes stirs hostilities among the old-timers against the newcomers.

Though conflict may be less intense regarding these groups, an undercurrent of tensions and resentment can exist, as evidenced by occasional eruptions of public protest over the building of a Sikh temple in a suburban community or providing bilingual education for a group of Turkish-American children in an urban school (two actual incidents).[42]

The Interactionist View

Since visual clues are a major means of our categorizing strangers, those with different clothing or physical characteristics get classified as dissimilar types. Is it really surprising to learn the racially different (Africans, Asians) and the religiously different (Buddhists, Moslems) score so low on the social distance scale? If this perception of others as very different is coupled with a sense of overwhelming numbers of newcomers, fears of a "Hindoo invasion" or whatever the case may be, can easily lead to acts of exclusion, expulsion, and violence. Consider the case of the Irish in Paterson who attacked the Syrians moving into their neighborhood, thinking them to be Turks or "Mohammedans." Only when a respected religious leader redefined the situation for the Irish, did the fighting stop. Misinterpretations about an ethnic group have often caused problems, and the peoples in this chapter are no exception.

Because recent immigrants can often mainstream economically, their co-workers or neighbors assume they have integrated socially as well. Interaction may occur in work-related relationships, but socially the middle-class newcomers tend to become "unknown ethnics," at least in primary relationships. Socially isolated except on rare occasions, the non-Westerners by necessity interact with compatriots, remaining a generalized entity in the minds of Americans. This social segregation appears to result more from an attraction toward similarly perceived others than overt avoidance. Whatever the reason, non-Westerners are mostly social outcasts in American leisure activities. We may say, "Variety is the spice of life," but we don't apply that to racial and ethnic personal relationships.

RETROSPECT

Relatively few members of the racial and ethnic groups mentioned in this chapter came to the United States before 1940. The experiences of those who did were generally similar to those of other non-Western peoples here, and depended on the then prevailing American policies and regional attitudes.

For the most part, the immigrant experience of people from this part of the world is current. Although they are still identifiable because of physical and cultural differences, they usually have little difficulty with Americans because of their occupational status, their urban locale, and the relaxation of American norms about newcomers. Nevertheless, as strangers they are keenly aware of the society in which they find themselves, and Americans generally tend to avoid interacting with them in meaningful primary relationships. The non-Westerners are somewhat unusual in that many are able to secure a respectable social status in terms of education, occupation, income, and residence, but because of their cultural differences and their resistence to assimilation, they have little social participation with native-born Americans. This is often a two-way arrangement.

As larger numbers of immigrants from the non-Western world come to the United States, they are making their presence felt more and more. One aspect of this impact is in religion. Waves of immigrant peoples have changed the United States from an almost exclusively Protestant country to one of three major faiths. Now this Judeo-Christian population composition, if present trends continue, may be modified further as the numbers of Moslems, Hindus, Buddhists, and adherents of other Eastern religions swell.

As the United States becomes culturally diverse in the areas of religion, physical appearance, and value orientations, more Americans are becoming conscious of the differences in the people around them. Some argue that Americans today are more tolerant because of a resurgence of ethnicity and a more liberal government attitude toward cultural pluralism. Others contend that the past nativistic reaction to Asians in the West and to southern and eastern Europeans in the East is being replicated today against the non-Western immigrants. There may not be riots and violent confrontations, but there are more subtle and sophisticated acts of discrimination, in keeping with the changing times.

How accurate this analysis is has not yet been determined. What is known is that recent non-Western immigrants are better educated and better trained; they often speak English before they arrive; and thus they enter American society at a higher socioeconomic level than earlier immigrants did. Their ethnic community is more interactional than territorial for the most part, although some groups are more clustered and visible than others. They seem to adjust fairly easily to American life, although ingroup socializing is quite common, as with past immigrant groups. Perhaps we are still a generation away from being able to measure the full impact of their role within American society.

REVIEW QUESTIONS

1. Explain why the differences in economic power between non-Western immigrants and earlier immigrants make assimilation less necessary now than before.

2. How have structural conditions at home reshaped ethnic identity and attitudes among Arab immigrants to the United States?

3. What parallels are there between the East Indian and Asian immigrant experiences, both past and present?

4. How are the cultural orientations of African immigrants dissimiliar to those of black Americans?

5. What insights do the three sociological perspectives offer about non-Western immigrants?

SUGGESTED READINGS

Ansari, Abdoulmaboud. *The Iranians in the United States.* New York: Associated Faculty Press, 1985.

A fine and authoritative sociological study of Iranian emigrés and immigrants, their values and acculturation patterns.

Elkholy, Abdo A. "The Arab American Family," in Charles H. Mindel and Robert W. Habenstein, eds., *Ethnic Families in America* 2nd ed. New York: Elsevier, 1981.

A brief, well-written portrait of family structure, customs, and behavior patterns of Arab-American families.

Kayal, Philip M., and Joseph M. Kayal. *The Syrian-Lebanese in America.* New York: Twayne, 1975.

An excellent sociohistorical account of both early and recent Syrian–Lebanese immigrants, their encounters and accomplishments.

CHAPTER 10

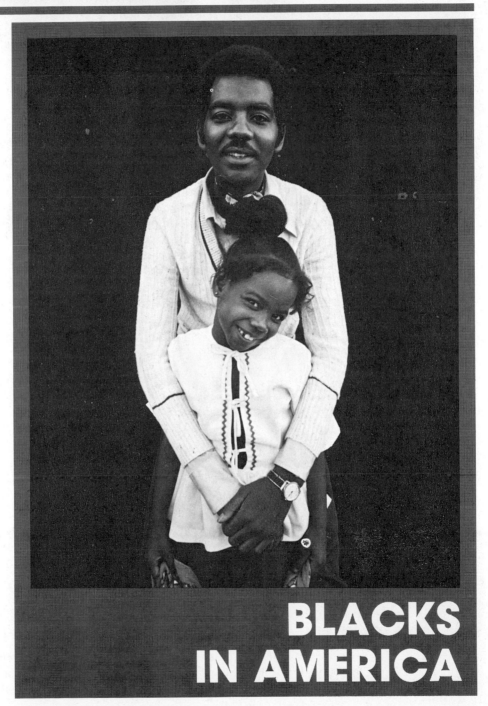

BLACKS
IN AMERICA

Most Africans who arrived in America from 1619 until the end of the slave trade in 1808 were unwilling immigrants, but twentieth-century black voluntary emigration to the United States has been substantial. Between 1899 and 1922, 115,000 African Blacks and over 25,000 West Indian Blacks were admitted. The restrictive immigration law of 1924 reduced the number of new immigrants from these groups; Africans, for example, were limited to only 122 annually.[1] In recent years black Africa has been averaging over 8,000 immigrants a year, while over 60,000 West Indians have been emigrating to the United States each year.

Differences in culture have prevented any unifying racial bond from forming between black immigrants and native-born Blacks. The newcomers are strangers in a new land, the native-born Blacks—like the Indians—are strangers in their own land, and both groups are strangers to each other. The new arrivals have come from an area where their race was the majority, or where a tripartite color system prevailed, or where color was not a primary factor in group life, into a society where color is an important determinant. They find that white Americans identify Africans with a partially assimilated and socially restricted native black population that itself does not accept or relate well to them.

The role of Blacks in American society, together with the recurring racial problems of prejudice and discrimination, has often been discussed, particularly in the past two decades. This chapter attempts to place Black–White relations in perspective by showing the similarities in, and differences from, the patterns of dominant-minority interaction of other racial and ethnic groups. Other major themes are the long-lasting impact of cultural conditioning and the changes wrought by the civil rights movement.

SOCIOHISTORICAL PERSPECTIVE

During the age of exploration, black crew members served under Columbus and sixteenth century Spanish explorers such as Balboa, Cortez, Pizzarro, and de Soto. The first known group of African immigrants were twenty voluntary immigrants who landed in Jamestown in August 1619, a year before the Pilgrims landed at Plymouth Rock. They came as indentured servants, as did many Whites, worked off their debt, and became masters of their own destiny. They were the fortunate few, for the labor demands of the Southern colonies soon resulted in the enslavement of millions of other Africans and their forced migration to the United States. Slavery replaced indentured servitude in the South. Blacks were forcibly taken from their African homelands and sold into a lifetime of slavery in a land they did not choose and in which they had no opportunity to advance themselves because they were not free.

The Years of Slavery

To ease the transition, other ethnic groups re-created in miniature the society they left behind, but the Africans were not allowed to do so. Other groups could use education to give themselves and their children a better future, but Southern state laws made the education of black slaves a criminal offense. Other groups may have encountered various degrees of hostility and discrimination, but through hard work and perseverance many were able to overcome nativist fears and prejudices. For the Blacks, however, two hundred years of master–slave relations did much more than just prevent their assimilation; they shaped values and attitudes about the two races that are still visible today.

As the industrial North and the slaveholding, agrarian South evolved into different societies, they developed different norms. Since norms are shared expectations of what does and does not constitute proper behavior, intergroup relations in these two regions might be expected to vary greatly. They did, but not in the way many Americans assume. To be sure, the institution of slavery created an inferior status for Blacks and led to much prejudice and discrimination. Yet there were free Blacks in the South too (nearly half a million by 1860)—those who had been set free by their owners, those who had purchased their freedom, or those who were descendants of free mothers. They lived in such urban areas as New Orleans, Mobile, and Charleston; in the tidewater regions of Virginia and Maryland; or in the Piedmont mountains of North Carolina and Virginia. Those who lived in the Southern cities worked in a wide variety of skilled and unskilled occupations; some were architects, teachers, store and hotel managers, clerks, and milliners. In the North, although there was some variance, the Blacks faced considerable discrimination in education, housing, employment, and voting rights. Since in the North no operative caste system delineated norms and interaction patterns, many Whites reacted more strongly to Blacks in their midst. As a result, Northern Blacks had considerable difficulty achieving economic security.

Racism and its Legacy

Although ancient civilizations considered themselves superior to others, they did so on the basis of culture, not race. Most historians agree that racism did not emerge until the sixteenth and seventeenth centuries.[2] This was the period of European exploration and imperialism, during which Europeans were brought into contact with many physically different, less technologically advanced peoples. Their physical characteristics, values, and ways of life were different, and so the Europeans naively concluded that there must be some relationship between how the people looked and how they behaved. This was another instance in which prejudices and stereotyping resulted from ethnocentric rationalization.

Myths about black racial inferiority emerged as a rationalization of slavery. Although slavery had existed under earlier systems, the ancient civilizations did not link skin color and social status. Statues and paintings from ancient Egypt, for example, depict slaves and rulers alike as both white and black.[3] Speculation about the causes of the rise of racism includes the rise of seagoing power among European nations and increased contact with red, brown, black, and yellow peoples; the influence of Christianity, linking slavery and skin color with the Curse of Ham; and European technological and military superiority over native peoples throughout the world. In the nineteenth century, evolutionary theory was also used to support racist thinking, as some argued that the white race was more highly evolved than the others.

W.E.B. DuBois interpreted this rise of racism as follows:

Labor was degraded, humanity was despised, the theory of "race" arose. There came a new doctrine of universal labor: mankind were of two sorts—the superior and the inferior; the inferior toiled for the superior; and the superior were the real men, the inferior half men or less. . . . Luxury and plenty for the few and poverty for the many was looked upon as inevitable in the course of nature. In addition to this, it went without saying that the white people of Europe had a right to live upon the labor and property of the colored peoples of the world.

In order to establish the righteousness of this point of view, science and religion, government and industry, were wheeling into line. The word "Negro" was used for the first time in the world's history to tie color to race and blackness to slavery and degradation. The white race was pictured as "pure" and superior: the black race as dirty, stupid, and inevitably inferior; the yellow race as sharing, in deception and cowardice, much of this color inferiority; while mixture of the races was considered the prime cause of degradation and failure in civilization. Everything great, everything fine, everything really successful in human culture, was white.

In order to prove this, even black people in India and Africa were labeled as "white" if they showed any trace of progress; and, on the other hand, any progress by colored people was attributed to some intermixture, ancient or modern, of white blood or some influence of white civilization.[4]

Although an extremely small percentage of white Southerners actually owned slaves, they were the most influential, and other Southern Whites were strong supporters of the system. The total separation of American slaves from the rest of society, unlike the partial separation of slaves in Latin American countries (where they had greater family stability and gradated freedom conditions), had important social consequences. As the dominant element of the Southern economy, plantation slavery affected the cultural life style and the shape of societal institutions. Illiteracy, nonexistent social and economic organizations, itinerant preachers, only local white law enforcement and protection, lack of medical and learning facilities, isolation, and dependency were the lot of the Blacks.

As a result of the racial ideology, stereotyping, and social isolation that survived the end of slavery, Blacks in the United States—despite their adaptability, willingness, and competence—were more excluded from participation in the free community than were the ex-slaves of Latin America. Once established, the impact of a master-slave social system and the concomitant theory of racial inferiority conditioned values, attitudes, and development of capacities that were to last well beyond the Civil War. Treated as if they were biologically inferior, the Blacks became socially inferior, first as a result of slavery and then as a result of discrimination in jobs, housing, and education.

Overcoming two hundred years of social conditioning is not easy. A generation after the close of the Civil War, many Blacks were making economic progress in the South, but the Whites still held deep-seated beliefs of racial superiority. Previous discussions of the vicious circle and the long-lasting effects of stereotypes help explain the continuance of institutionalized racism long after the end of slavery.[5]

In 1876, when Reconstruction ended and the status of Blacks became a Southern question rather than a national matter, Blacks were given a formalized inferior status. Segregation, disfranchisement, "black codes," job discrimination, and occupational eviction took place. Not until the 1960s did many deliberate segregationist practices end in the South.

Although there are now many laws to protect people against discrimination, racist beliefs continue to exist; they can be seen in the reasons people give for moving out of racially changing neighborhoods or for their attitudes toward cities, crime, and welfare. While fear of crime, violence, and other evils of the inner city is justified, some individuals attribute such problems to race. Deviance, it must be remembered, occurs among all groups who are poor, powerless, and victims of discrimination.[6]

The problem with racism is twofold: its legacy and its subtlety. *Legacy* here refers not only to its institutionalization within society, but also to its transmission from one generation to the next. Slavery may end, segregation may end, but some people still believe Blacks are inferior. This is part of the subtlety of racism, because people usually draw such conclusions from their observable world. They are not aware that this "objective" reality has been socially constructed over generations. The alleged inferiority is a myth, except as a social product. One sees primarily the effects of prolonged racist attitudes and actions. Even one's own attitudes, actions, and reactions may unwittingly contribute to the existence of racism.[7]

THE QUESTION OF RACIAL SUPERIORITY

Belief in white supremacy has existed for a long time in the United States. There have been, and still are, people who believe that Blacks are biologically inferior to Whites. This was the justification for segregation and for the Jim Crow laws, and this is the reason for many of the social problems of today. It is not only uneducated people who feel this way; some scientists and scholars also believe there are innate differences among the races. For example, in 1928 the noted American sociologist Pitirim Sorokin observed:

That there are mental differences among races seems to be definitely established. . . . No partisan of a belief in the uniformity of all races can disregard the differences in the historical role and in the cultural achievements of the different races. . . . The difference in the cultural contributions and in the historical roles played by different races is excellently corroborated by, and is in perfect agreement with, the experimental studies of race mentality and psychology. . . . So far as I know, all studies of the comparative intelligence of the contemporary Negro and white races . . . have unanimously shown that the I.Q. of the blacks, or even the Indians, is lower than that of the white or yellow. . . .

The only conclusion which it seems possible to make from the above and similar studies is that the mentality of various races . . . is different.[8]

Scientific attempts to prove racial superiority and inferiority have traditionally followed three primary approaches: anatomical, historical (or comparative achievement), and psychological.[9]

The Anatomical Approach

It has been mentioned elsewhere in this text that in many parts of the world, the group lowest on the socioeconomic ladder is often viewed as lowest on the evolutionary ladder as well. Some scientists have tried to use physical characteristics to show that Whites are further evolved than Blacks. The Blacks, they argue, most resemble the ape; they have a receding forehead, prognathous jaw, and broad, flat nose. What these proponents conveniently ignore is that the hair, texture, body hair, and lip form of Whites are closer to apes than are those of Blacks. Also, underneath their fur most simians have white skin. Using physical characteristics to rank the races in any evolutionary order is simply impossible, because no race is consistently more simian than another.

Whites generally have larger brains than Blacks, and some have contended that this proves they have superior intellectual capabilities.[10] However, physical size or cranial capacity is not in itself an indicator of mental capacity. Not only is there a wide range of size among all groups, but some peoples not particularly noted for

Fowler's *Phrenological Signs of Character* was based on the then popular notion that one's character could be read from the "bumps" on one's head. This illustration from the 1857 edition shows how this notion could support the prejudicial belief in the biological inferiority of Blacks, as well as stereotyped attributes for all Blacks regardless of individual differences.

their intellectual achievements (preliterate Eskimos and Neanderthals) have possessed larger-sized brains. Physical characterizations of skin pigmentation, hair texture, and brain size do not correlate with a comparative evolution of the human races.

The Comparative Achievement Approach

In other attempts to prove racial superiority, the achievements of different races have been compared. Some argue that since not all races have made "important" contributions to the world's culture and produced gifted artists, inventors, philosophers, geniuses, explorers, and conquerors, or built great civilizations and vast empires, they are not all equal. After all, they argue, a race that has produced all the engineering feats of today in architecture, computers, electronics, medicine, and space-age technology surely surpasses a primitive, illiterate, underdeveloped race of people, such as the Australian aborigines or Amazon jungle natives or African villagers.

Stanford M. Lyman attacks any attempt to measure the "contributions" of any ethnic group, since this involves a retrospective analysis of what has and has not been widely adopted or popularly acclaimed.

> The uselessness of contributions as a sociological concept is clear because its designative capacity is always post hoc. It forces a bifurcation of a natural class—the activities of a minority group—at an unnatural joint: those that are contributions and those that are not. When a minority is evaluated according to its contributions, its activities are classified in accordance with a concept that cannot be derived from their actual context. A people's activities should be regarded as contributions only when it can be shown that they were intended as such. Sociology should be faithful to the actual nature of its subject matter—people in active and creative existence.[11]

Another problem with this line of reasoning is that one should not confuse performance with potential. To do so is to misunderstand the dynamics of civilization as well as to lack perspective and to be ignorant of the history of culture. How, for example, do we measure achievement? Most of us would measure it by our standards, that is, using an ethnocentric approach. We may boast of our scientific knowledge and accomplishments, failing to realize that other people may not admire these things or consider them criteria for excellence. As Berry and Tischler point out:

> We would not come out so well in proving our superiority if our opponents insisted on using as criteria, not science and machines, but ability at sand painting, physical endurance, complexity of grammar, multiplicity of taboos, respect for the aged, ability in hunting, closeness to nature, fear of the deity, reverence for the soil, freedom from authority, disregard for material goods, the absence of neuroses, or

peace of mind. The fact is that no racial or ethnic group excels in all things, but each has its own interests and values, goals toward which it strives, and channels into which its efforts are directed.[12]

Even if someone were to argue that some peoples are superior because of the flowering of their civilization, time would show that attainment also to be relative. Some civilizations have exceeded others, only to be surpassed in later years by those very ones thought to be inferior. The history of some world civilizations— those of the Sumerians, Egyptians, Greeks, Romans, and English—is testimony to this fact. From the 9th century, when marauding tribes were still roving through parts of Europe, through the fifteenth century, various African kingdoms were building such sophisticated and affluent cities as Timbuktu, the intellectual capital of Western Sudan, with its stone palaces, many-windowed homes, city university, and busy marketplace; or Benin, Nigeria, with wide streets and civic splendor and a huge, magnificent palace; or the numerous tall stone towns on the East African coast. Early explorers noted some of these achievements, but ethnocentric mis-conceptions and the debilitating effects of enslavement distorted, dulled, and de-stroyed this knowledge of the Africans and their varied social systems. In the fol-lowing passage, Basil Davidson presents an undistorted picture of African civilizations:

Some of these systems produced societies whose standard of living—in terms of food, personal safety and freedom—equaled that of contemporary societies in Eu-rope. In some instances they were even more advanced: African societies practiced a simple but effective social welfare in their concern for widows and orphaned chil-dren.

This is the Africa . . . that Europeans began to see for themselves in the latter half of the fifteenth century. Instead of a primeval wilderness, these visitors found prosperous, self-contained cities linked to each other by a busy, carefully ordered trade. Their inhabitants—merchants, artisans, laborers, clerks—lived comfortable lives. . . .

Though far behind Europe in their technical knowledge, Africans developed tropical farming techniques that have scarcely been bettered to this day. They were good miners and metalworkers. . . . They were astute businessmen. . . . They operated political systems of considerable flexibility and sophistication. They were superb sculptors. . . .

But the record of achievement is not confined to big political systems alone. In the shadow of their pomp and glory rests the modest but impressive achievement of village-level Africa. In community attitudes that join man to man in a brother-hood of equals, in moral rules that guided social behavior, in beliefs that exalted the spiritual aspects of life above the material, the African village achieved a kind of social harmony that often functioned without any need for centralized authority. This, in fact, was where Africa best displayed its real genius—in its capacity for so-cial organization.[13]

In the United States and Africa, the subjugation of the African people and the creation of a social structure in which they were assigned a dependent, inferior status effectively hindered their further achievements. Civilizations flourish and wane for a variety of social, economic, political, and military reasons, not because of the "superiority" of a race or ethnic group.

Like all civilizations, the African civilization ebbed, partly as a result of imperialism, colonialism, and slavery. The subjugation of Blacks in the United States, first through slavery and then through continued discrimination and denial, effectively limited their advancement and thereby kept them from having as substantial an impact upon American society as they might have had until the mid-1950s. Individual black poets, authors, inventors, craftspeople, engineers, actors, and others flourished under slavery and in the following period, but black people as a whole had little or no education, poor-paying jobs and poor housing, and little upward mobility. Life for them was survival; there was not much opportunity for anything else.

Another counterargument to this historical approach to racial superiority is cultural diffusion. Each civilization is the beneficiary of the inventions and discoveries of others, and white civilizations are no exception; they have evolved further from the contributions of nonwhite civilizations. Whatever the United States has accomplished in world leadership and in achievement as a nation, it owes much to various other peoples for many of the elements within its culture.[14]

The Psychological Approach

The intelligence test, first developed by Alfred Binet in 1905, became a popular means of comparing the intelligence of different racial and ethnic groups, although that was not Binet's intention. Supposedly, this objective, scientific instrument would measure innate intelligence and not be influenced by any beneficial or detrimental effects of environment. Any question or claim of one group's intellectual superiority could now be determined. Early studies showed that northern and western Europeans, and often the Chinese and Japanese, scored consistently and decidedly higher than southern and eastern Europeans, Blacks, Mexicans, and American Indians.[15] Conveniently ignoring the results for Asians, nativists and segregationists seized upon these studies as arguments for immigration restrictions against "inferiors," for the Americanization of Indians, and to justify Jim Crow laws in the South.

Gradually, as nativist antipathy against the "new" immigrants abated, the argument shifted primarily to intelligence differences between Blacks and Whites. The disparity in the test results, actually reflecting a cultural bias within the tests, now became a basis for claiming white intellectual superiority.

In 1958 Audrey Shuey's book *The Testing of Negro Intelligence* appeared and caused a furor. Shuey surveyed some 240 studies of 60 different intelligence tests that had been given over a 44-year span to hundreds of thousands of servicemen from World Wars I and II and thousands of schoolchildren of all ages through college, from all regions of the country. She concluded:

The remarkable consistency in test results, whether they pertain to school or preschool children, to high school or college students, drafts of World War I or World

War II, to the gifted or mentally deficient, to the delinquent or criminal; the fact that the colored-white differences are present not only in the rural South and urban South, but in the border and northern areas; the fact that relatively small average differences are found between the I.Q.'s of northern-born and southern-born Negro children in northern cities; the evidence that the tested differences appear to be greater for abstract than for practical or concrete problems; the evidence that the differences obtained are not due primarily to a lack of language skills, the colored averaging no better on non-verbal tests than on verbal tests; the fact that differences are reported in all studies in which the cultural environment of the whites appeared to be no more complex, rich, or stimulating than the environment of the Negroes; the fact that in many comparisons (including those in which the colored appeared to best advantage) the Negro subjects have been either more representative of their racial group or more highly selected than are the comparable white subjects; all point to the presence of some native differences between Negroes and whites as determined by intelligence tests.[16]

For any scientist, interpretation of findings is as critical as the findings themselves and the methods employed to obtain them. Shuey was accurate in observing the consistent lower scoring of Blacks on intelligence tests. However, many disagreed with her conclusion that this was due to intellectual inferiority of the race. This conclusion of innate or generic differences was a quantum leap from her findings, which did not prove any such thing.

More recently, the IQ controversy has centered around two California professors: Arthur R. Jensen, an educational psychologist at the University of California (Berkeley), and William B. Shockley, a Nobel Prize-winning physicist at Stanford University. Jensen argued that the 10- to 20-point IQ differential between Blacks and Whites involves only certain mental functions. He pointed out that Blacks and Whites test equally well in such brain functions as rote learning and memory, but that Blacks test poorer in problem-solving, in seeing relationships, and in abstract reasoning. Since this material does not depend on specific cultural information, he maintained, the only conclusion is that the Blacks' lower scores are due to their genetic heritage.[17] Shockley also declared in the mid-1960s that the conceptual intelligence of Blacks, as measured by many different IQ tests, is significantly lower than that of Whites, and that some of this variance is genetically caused and therefore cannot be corrected.

Refuting this position, Thomas Sowell argued that white ethnic groups, such as the Poles, Jews, and Italians, scored in the 80s during the tests of the 1920s, but gained 20 to 25 points by the 1970s after experiencing upward mobility.[18] Those groups of European ancestry who have not experienced upward mobility, as well as the Mexican-Americans and the Puerto Ricans, continue to score in the 80s on IQ tests. Most significantly, at various times and places other low-IQ groups have also done poorly on the abstract portions of mental tests. Studies of immigrant groups in 1917, of white children in isolated mountain communities, of working-class children in England, and of early Chinese immigrants all show marked deficiencies on the abstract sections. Concerning the Chinese-Americans, recent studies show them to be strongest on the abstract portions of the mental tests, suggesting that upward mobility helps to improve powers of abstract reasoning. Other patterns—children's IQ scores declining as they become adults, and females consistently scoring higher than males—are also common among low-IQ groups, not just Blacks. Again, these results change once the group achieves a higher socioeconomic status.

In the late 1960s a number of tests were developed that were deliberately culturally biased in favor of Blacks, to protest culture-loaded tests and demonstrate how they can produce invalid scores. Among these were the BITCH test ("Black Intelligence Test to Counter Honkeyism") and the "Dove Counterbalance Intelligence Test," which became a part of the Air Force's race relations course for its personnel. It is important to note that some Blacks scored low on even these tests because their socioeconomic status, age, or residence made the questions unfamiliar to them (See Box 10.1.).

BOX 10.1

Black Intelligence Test of Cultural Homogeneity
by Robert L. Williams, Ph.D.

The purpose of tongue-in-cheek "tests" like these was to demonstrate both the subcultural language or understandings of a group and the unfairness of culture-loaded IQ tests on low-income people. Many of you will probably do badly on these questions, regardless of your ability, if the questions are alien to your cultural background, and that's the point of demonstrating cultural bias in tests. Note the acronym formed by the first letters of the test title.

1. **Alley Apple is a a) brick, b) piece of fruit, c) dog, d) horse.**
2. **CPT means a standard a) time, b) tune, c) tale, d) twist.**
3. **Deuce-and-a-quarter is a) money, b) a car, c) a house, d) dice.**
4. **The eagle flies means a) the blahs, b) a movie, c) payday, d) deficit.**
5. **Gospel Bird is a a) pheasant, b) chicken, c) goose, d) duck.**
6. **"I know you, shame" means a) You don't hear very well. b) You are a racist. c) You don't mean what you're saying. d) You are guilty.**
7. **Main Squeeze means a) to prepare for battle, b) a favorite toy, c) a best girlfriend, d) to hold up someone.**
8. **Nose Opened means a) flirting, b) teed off, c) deeply in love, d) very angry.**
9. **Playing the dozens means a) playing the numbers, b) playing baseball, c) insulting a person's parents, d) playing with women.**
10. **Shucking means a) talking, b) thinking, c) train of thought, d) wasting time.**
11. **Stone fox means a) bitchy, b) pretty, c) sly, d) uncanny.**
12. **T.C.B. means a) that's cool baby, b) taking care of business, c) they couldn't breathe, d) took careful behavior.**

Answers: 1-a,2-a,3-b,4-c,5-b,6-d,7-c,8-c,9-c,10-d,11-b,12-b.

Another problem with IQ tests is that they measure only some forms of intelligence—analytical, conceptual, and verbal. We are only beginning to understand how and why the brain functions as it does. Until we know more, any assumption of intellectual superiority or inferiority based on IQ scores is conjecture. Moreover, the only proven value IQ scores have is in predicting how well students will do in a traditional school setting. They do not predict performance in nontraditional approaches to education or in any job situation. Does a professor with a 135 IQ teach better than one with 120? Not necessarily, and that is another reason why IQ scores should not be a factor in questions of social interaction.

LANGUAGE AS PREJUDICE

Words are symbols connoting meanings to the world about us. That the very words used to describe the two races—white and black—usually convey positive and negative meanings, respectively, is unfortunate. For example, *white* often symbolizes cleanliness, purity, or heroes (clothes, armor, hats, horses), and *black* often stands for dirty, evil, or villains. A snow-covered landscape is beautiful, but a sky laden with black smoke is not. Black clouds are seen as threatening, but white clouds are not.

The power of words is such that the pervasiveness of such meanings for these two words can easily influence minds and attitudes. Ossie Davis had such concerns in mind when he said:

A superficial examination of Roget's *Thesaurus of the English Language* reveals the following facts: the word "whiteness" has 134 synonyms, 44 of which are favorable and pleasing to contemplate. For example: "purity," "cleanness," "immaculateness," "bright," "shiny," "ivory," "fair," "blonde," "stainless," "clean," "clear," "chaste," "unblemished," "unsullied," "innocent," "honorable," "upright," "just," "straightforward," "genuine," "trustworthy," and only 10 synonyms of which I feel to have been negative and then only in the mildest sense, such as "gloss-over," "whitewash," "gray," "wan," "pale," "ashen," etc.

The word "blackness" has 120 synonyms, 60 of which are distinctly unfavorable, and none of them even mildly positive. Among the offending 60 were such words as "blot," "blotch," "smut," "smudge," "sullied," "begrime," "soot," "becloud," "obscure," "dingy," "murky," "low-toned," "threatening," "frowning," "foreboding," "forbidding," "deadly," "unclean," "dirty," "unwashed." "foul," etc. In addition, and this is what really hurts, 20 of these words—and I exclude the villainous 60 above—are related directly to race, such as "Negro," "Negress," "nigger," "darkey," "blackamoor," etc.

If you consider the fact that thinking itself is subvocal speech (in other words, one must use words in order to think at all), you will appreciate the enormous trap of racial prejudgment that works on any child who is born into the English language.[19]

When *black* has so many negative connotations—blackening the reputation, being black-hearted, blacklisting or blackballing someone, being a blackguard, using black magic, running a black market, and so on—it is easy to see how language by itself can precondition a white person's mind against black people and can lead a black person's mind into possible self-hatred.

INSTITUTIONALIZED RACISM

During the Reconstruction period and almost to the end of the ninteenth century, Southern Blacks generally had greater access to stores, restaurants, public transportation, bars, and theaters than in the first half of the twentieth century. A typical pattern was for Whites to live on one street in large homes, while behind them on the parallel street were the lesser dwellings of Blacks, many of whom worked as domestics. Although there was a clear status distinction, in most places, no severe social distance occurred between the two races. Blacks lived in close proximity to Whites, and frequently interacted with them in secondary relationships through their occupational roles as domestic or service workers. In education, marriage, political participation, and major economic enterprises, however, Blacks did not share a commonality with Whites.

Immigration and Jim Crow

The change in Black White relations in the late ninteenth and early twentieth centuries is an example of *cultural drift,* a gradual and pervasive change in a people's values. Economic problems, scandals, and frustrations on the part of Southern Whites appear to be some of the factors that reshaped Southern attitudes. In a region in which they had long been considered inferior, many Blacks were achieving socioeconomic respectability and becoming economic competitors. Resentment of black upward mobility, flowing from the historical undercurrent of racist attitudes, was increased by economic troubles (declining cotton prices and unemployment). Since they were racially distinct, the Blacks were a convenient scapegoat for the frustrations and hostility of Southern Whites.

Less liberal attitudes in the North were also a factor increasing the number of racist acts of discrimination in housing, labor, associations, unions, schools, and churches in both North and South.[20] What caused this change in the North? It is not just coincidence that this change in racial attitudes occurred just when great numbers of southern and eastern European immigrants were settling in Northern urban areas. The arrival of so many dark-eyed, dark-haired, dark-complexioned newcomers set in motion a nativist reaction culminating with restrictive immigration laws. Northerners became more sensitive to the influx of foreigners and "anarchists" as well as to Southern Blacks coming to the North to seek work. There were racial overtones to the North's ethnocentric reaction to the "new" immigrants, and the South's reaction to the Blacks received greater sympathy from Northern nativists. The North ceased to pressure the South regarding Blacks, and allowed the Jim Crow laws to emerge without a challenge.

In the 1870s and 1880s, the Californians succeeded in making the Chinese question a national issue, and cleverly related it to that of the Blacks whenever

BOX 10.2

"In the South we had Whites live here, Colored live there and everybody would speak to you whether they knowed you or not. . . . People are not as friendly up here."

"I had heard so much talk about New York. People would say things were so good in New York until I felt that if I would get to New York, I would find money on the streets and wouldn't have no more worries. All my problems would be solved. When I got to New York, things were much different than that. Jobs were very hard to find, and the people were very different than in West Virginia.

"Finally I did get a job through the State Employment Office, working as a cook in the Brooklyn Navy Yard in a private canteen. I stayed there a year and then the war closed up—was over. Then I got another job in a seafood house on 34th Street and 3rd Avenue and I stayed there a year. Then a friend of mine and I went into our own business selling raw fish. Opened a store in Brooklyn selling raw fish. And, of course, it didn't pan out that way. The problem with that business was that we didn't have enough capital to carry us over the rough spots. And then my wife started having babies and so I had to give up that job and seek another, which I did, and finally I got a job right away at another seafood house.

"In the South we had Whites live here, Colored live there and everybody would speak to you whether they knowed you or not. But when I got to the North, I'd be out on the street, maybe walking around, before I got the jobs, looking around, trying to find my way around, and I would be saying, 'Good morning,' and 'Good evening,' whichever way the situation was, and people would look at me as if I was some dope or something. People would say, 'What's wrong with him?' People are not as friendly up here.

"And I also found out when we bought a house here, that the Whites started right away moving out. They started selling their houses, putting up signs for sale. That didn't bother me any. Only thing was that I was just saying to myself that I thought New York was so great. Why should this be happening? And in the South, where I was living, it didn't happen that way. Blacks and Whites lived side-by-side there, and we didn't have no problems with that. That kind of upset me that in New York, after hearing so much about it, this did go on."

Black migrant from West Virginia who came North in 1944 at age 26

necessary. Political deals were made, and later, Southern representatives voted overwhelmingly in favor of the Chinese Exclusion Act of 1882 and the 1921 immigration bill restricting southern and eastern Europeans, most of whom were settling in the North.

In 1896 the Supreme Court ruling on *Plessy v. Ferguson* upheld the principle of "separate but equal" railroad accommodations and education for Blacks and Whites. Only a few Southern states had had mandatory segregation laws covering

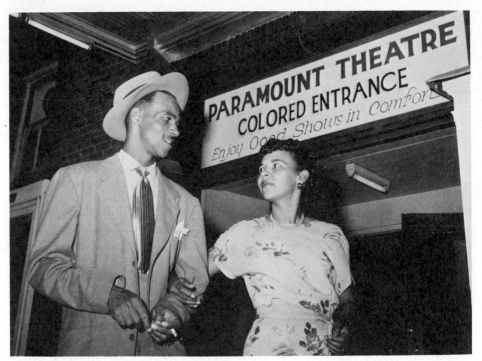

For the first six decades of the twentieth century, Jim Crow laws maintained a racially segregated society in the South. All aspects of public interaction, including the entrance and seating accommodations of this movie theater, distinguished use and accessibility by race. Such pervasive norms socialized many people into accepting a world of structural discrimination as "normal."

train passengers before the turn of the century. Between 1901 and 1910 most Southern states passed many different **Jim Crow laws.** What followed was the "snowball effect" of such legislation. Segregation became the norm in all areas of life—bars, barber shops, drinking fountains, toilet facilities, ticket windows, waiting rooms, hotels, restaurants, parks, playgrounds, theaters, and auditoriums. Through literacy tests, poll taxes, and other measures, the Southern states also succeeded in disfranchising black voters.

Effects of Jim Crow

The segregation laws, mostly of twentieth-century vintage, reflected racist attitudes that were still current throughout the South decades after slavery had ended. When the 1954 Supreme Court ruling overturned school segregation laws, seventeen states had mandatory segregation: Alabama, Arkansas, Delaware, Florida, Georgia, Kentucky, Louisiana, Maryland, Mississippi, Missouri, North Carolina, Oklahoma, South Carolina, Tennessee, Texas, Virginia, and West Virginia. Four other states—Arizona, Kansas, New Mexico, and Wyoming—permitted segregation as a local option.

The South

It is impossible to exaggerate the impact upon a society of legalizing such discriminatory norms. These laws existed for two generations. During that time both white and black children grew up in a society in which the two races were distinguished from one another and treated differently simply because of that racial difference. Since the white world of reality was one in which differential treatment was the norm, the inferior status of Blacks was taken for granted. For most Whites growing up in such an environment and in turn transmitting values and attitudes to their children, this was objective reality.

Structural discrimination in the South was pervasive. Despite challenges by the NAACP and by other groups and individuals, most Blacks and Whites appeared to accept the situation. To Whites, the inferior status of Blacks in Southern society appeared to justify continued differential treatment. It was, as Gunnar Myrdal concluded in his study of American race relations, a perfect example of the vicious circle in which "discrimination breeds discrimination."[21] As Blacks' education and job opportunities were restricted, the end result of that action was to reinforce the attitude supporting the action. Thus, suffering the consequences of deprivation and limited opportunity only aggravated the Blacks' situation. They were an easily recognizable group that did not hold better-paying jobs or become educated; they lived in squalor amidst poverty, disease, crime, and violence; they were not "good enough" to use the same facilities as Whites. This gave Whites more reason for their aversion to Blacks and increased their prejudicial attitudes and discriminatory actions. Myrdal calls this intensification a cumulative causation, in which there is an almost perpetual sequence of reciprocal stimuli and responses.[22]

The North

But what about the North, where few segregationist laws existed? Although there had been some migration to the North earlier, prior to 1914 almost all Blacks resided in the South; but then large numbers of Blacks began to migrate to the Northern urban areas. Clearly, the Jim Crow laws and poor economic conditions were the major "push" factors for moving north, while better wages, education, and political freedom were the primary "pull" factors.

By 1915, the North needed labor. The war was under way in Europe and Northern industry was reaping the benefits from it. The large supply of foreign immigrant labor was rapidly dwindling. In the fourteen years after 1900, over twelve million immigrants found their way to the United States. More than one million immigrants reached the United States in 1914 alone. The next year this figure was cut to about one third, in 1916 to about one fourth, and, by 1918, only 110,618 new arrivals landed on the shores of the United States, while 94,585 left. Other sources of labor were needed and Southern Negroes appeared as an available and willing substitute. . . .

The larger pay and increased economic opportunities in the North were heady inducements to migrants. But it was not only for economic reasons that the desire to come North existed in so many. . . . The desire of adults to see their children able to obtain an education caused many to move North. . . . According to a *New York Times* editorial (January 21, 1918), higher wages:

would have been far less attractive if the colored man had not felt, and felt for a long time and bitterly, that in the North and West he would not, as in his southern home, be reminded of his black skin every time he met a policeman, entered a street car, railway station or train, and in a hundred other less conspicuous ways in the course of a day.[23]

So the existence of Jim Crow in the South was an important cause of the migration to the North. By 1925 there were over 1.5 million Blacks living in the North, three-fourths of them concentrated in the following metropolitan regions:[24]

New York	251,300
Philadelphia	248,300
Chicago	131,600
St. Louis	102,600
Columbus–Cincinnati	89,600
Pittsburgh	88,300
Kansas City	65,400
Cleveland–Youngstown	58,800
Detroit–Toledo	55,900
Indianapolis	47,500

As their counterparts on the West Coast had done in response to Asian immigrants, the labor unions in the North organized against the Blacks. Seeing them either as an undesirable element or as economic competition, many workers quickly became antagonistic toward them. It was one more instance of people being liberals from a distance but reactionaries at close range. Although there was greater freedom in the North, the animosity led to majority patterns of avoidance and discrimination.

Race riots, basically an urban phenomenon reflecting the growing animosity in the North, swept through a number of cities during World War I. In 1917 in East St. Louis, Illinois, thirty-nine Blacks and eight Whites were killed, and hundreds seriously injured, in one of the worst riots. In 1919 the situation became even worse, with returning war veterans seeking jobs and more Blacks moving north.

That year there were race riots large and small in twenty-six American cities including thirty-eight killed in a Chicago riot of August; from twenty-five to fifty killed in Phillips County, Arkansas; and six killed in Washington. For a day, the city of Washington, in July, 1919, was actually in the hands of a black mob fighting against the aggression of the whites with hand grenades.[25]

The riots intensified the hostile racial feelings even more. The South had *de jure* segregation, but Jim Crow—as a cause of black migration and a model for Northern attitudes and actions—played an important role in the development of *de facto* segregation in the North. With race the determinant for various life opportunities in both the North and the South, succeeding generations of Blacks encountered the same obstacles to upward mobility. So the effects of Jim Crow upon

BOX 10.3

> *"I had heard there was no segregation in the North. . . . And I found all of this was, more or less, a fairy tale."*

"I came to the North not because of a lack, not being able to cope with economic situations in the South, because I was doing all right economically. I came, more or less, for a change of environment and for a higher income for the work I was doing.

"I was educated in the South and by the time I left I was not sharecropping any longer, I was teaching and so my standard of living was different from back when I was a child growing up. I had heard many rumors about the North when I was a child. I had heard there was no segregation in the North. You were at liberty to ride buses, use all facilities, no discrimination in jobs. And I found all of this was, more or less, a fairy tale in a lot of respects. As an adult, I had a more accurate picture of what the North was all about since I had relatives living in Detroit, Washington, and New Jersey.

"I worked at different jobs—office worker, in a nursery school, a dietician—before going to grad school and becoming a public school teacher as I was in the South.

"The biggest adjustment to me going from a rural to an urban setting was getting accustomed to rushing, rushing, rushing city life. To me the people were always running instead of walking. There was always the hustle-bustle to catch the buses and catch subways and this kind of thing. And this was the hardest thing for me to get accustomed to, and the rate at which people worked. The people in the North move much, much faster than people in the South.

"I lived in an apartment with my sister four months, got married and moved to another apartment with my husband. We lived there a year and then moved to the suburbs where we bought our house. Now things here have deteriorated to the extent we have higher unemployment in the North than we do in the South. The overcrowding situation and your housing situation is badly in need of improvement too."

Black migrant from South Carolina who came North in 1954 at age 22

black assimilation into the mainstream of American society went beyond the South and lasted longer than just the first half of the twentieth century.

The Ku Klux Klan

Once an organization primarily designed to intimidate Blacks, the Ku Klux Klan reorganized in the twentieth century with a broader range of target groups. As a social organization, the Klan has experienced several phases of popularity and decline, and several different sets of goals and objectives. Ex-Confederates had organized the original Klan during the Reconstruction period to frighten and discourage Blacks and carpetbaggers. In 1915 William J. Simmons resurrected the

In the early 1920s, the Ku Klux Klan attracted a large following, seizing upon nativist fears about the large numbers of recently arrived immigrants. Parades, such as this one in 1924 in Binghamton, New York, were commonplace at that time in many states, offering visible proof of the widespread support for an Anglo-Saxon Protestant version of Americanism.

movement, formalized its rituals and organization, and dedicated it to white supremacy, Protestant Christianity, and Americanism.

Protest or reactionary groups generally do not become popular unless there is a shared awareness of the problems or concerns to which the group addresses itself within a segment of the society. The Klan was no exception, both in the 1870s and again in the 1920s, when a combination of factors—the agricultural depression, Prohibition, immigration, and isolationism—brought it to a period of rapid expansion. By 1923 the Klan claimed 3 million enrolled members and operated in virtually every state in the union, with public ceremonies and parades.

At first the Klan concentrated on maintaining white supremacy by intimidating white employers as well as black workers and potential voters. While this remained an important theme, as the Klan spread northward, its racist orientation broadened into a more general nationalism and nativism. Fears and condemnation of Jews and foreigners, especially Catholics, led the Klan into a campaign of promoting an Anglo-Saxon version of Americanism with evangelical zeal. In almost puritanical fashion the hooded Klansmen used mass raids, tarring and featherings, floggings, and other strong-arm tactics aimed at either moral regulation or a stabilization of the old order. In reality they accomplished neither, since their actions only fomented additional strife and cruelty.

After a series of internal struggles, exposés of corruption, and mounting anti-Klan opposition, the Klan empire came apart. Although it retained some influence in rural regions of New York, Pennsylvania, Indiana, Texas, and North and South

Carolina, its heyday ended in the mid-1920s. It is still very active, however, particularly during times of racial troubles. Ironically, in the 1970s the Klan sought to recruit Catholics—one of its major targets in the past—from the South Boston area who were against school busing.

The Ku Klux Klan, then, evolved into a multi-xenophobic organization in which southern and eastern European Catholics and Jews, as well as Blacks, were seen as a threat to the American character. The Klan's enormous popularity in the early 1920s is a reflection of the times, since these minority peoples were felt to present an economic threat. As prosperity increased and immigration decreased, thereby reducing the tensions, support for the Klan also ebbed. Its success, like the success of the Native American Party and the Know-Nothing Party of the nineteenth century, indicates that many people were receptive to its philosophy and goals.

THE WINDS OF CHANGE

In the past, Blacks had made many concerted efforts to improve their lot. The Colored National Farmers' Alliance claimed 1,250,000 members in 1891, but had faded from the scene by 1910. In the twentieth century several black leaders arose to rally their people: Booker T. Washington, W. E. B. DuBois, Marcus Garvey, and A. Philip Randolph. In the 1920s, 1930s, and 1940s, the NAACP and other groups filed court cases that had limited success but laid the basis for the 1954 desegregation ruling. None of these attempts, however, resulted in as massive a restructuring of Black–White relations as the events of the midcentury.

Desegregation: The First Phase

Having experienced life outside their cultural milieu, many Blacks who fought in World War II returned home with new perspectives and aspirations. The GI Bill of Rights, Veterans Authority, and Federal Housing Authority offered increased opportunity for education, jobs, and housing. Expectations increased, and the growing popularity of television sets brought into more and more homes insights into life styles that previously could only be vaguely imagined.

Several court cases challenging the school segregation laws in Delaware, Kansas, South Carolina, and Virginia reached the U.S. Supreme Court in 1954. Consolidating the several suits, the Justices ruled unanimously on May 17, 1954, that the "separate but equal" doctrine was unconstitutional. Social science data, through amicus curiae briefs, played an important role in the decision.[26] The following year the Court established means of implementing its decree by giving the federal district courts jurisdiction over any problems relating to enforcement of the ruling. The Court insisted that the states move toward compliance with "all deliberate speed," but this guideline was vague enough to allow them to circumvent the ruling at first.

Although the National Association for the Advancement of Colored People (NAACP) quickly began a multipronged challenge to school districts in the seventeen states in which school segregation existed, their efforts met with mixed

A large crowd of spectators gathers in front of Little Rock Central High School in September 1957, as armed National Guardsmen keep watch to prevent black students from attending. President Eisenhower countered this defiance of the Supreme Court ruling by federalizing the state-controlled National Guard that the governor had called out, and sending in regular army troops as well to ensure the school's integration.

success. Many Whites, seeing their values, beliefs, and practices threatened by outsiders, resisted desegregation. State legislatures passed bills to stave off integration, Whites used economic and social pressures to intimidate any Blacks who attempted to integrate local schools, and the school districts themselves procrastinated in dealing with the problem. For three years the battle of wills resulted in continuation of the status quo despite the Supreme Court ruling.

On another front, an event occurred in Montgomery, Alabama, in 1955 that foreshadowed other minority actions in the 1960s. Mrs. Rosa Parks, a tired black seamstress on her way home from work, refused to give up her bus seat in the section reserved for Whites and was arrested. Through the organizing efforts of Martin Luther King, Jr., in the black community, a successful bus boycott occurred. Four months later the NAACP argued the case in the Federal District Court, which ruled against segregated seating on municipal buses. The U.S. Supreme Court upheld the decision.

The confrontation in the fall of 1957 at Little Rock Central High School in Arkansas was a watershed in desegregation. Here the state's defiance of the Supreme Court could not be ignored, since the governor called out the National Guard to forcibly block a concerted effort to integrate the high school. President Eisenhower, who had personally been against the 1954 ruling, acted decisively by federalizing the National Guard and sending regular army troops to assure compliance.

With all legal avenues of appeal exhausted and the federal government insisting that all citizens, including black children, be accorded equal rights, Southern resistance ebbed. Desegregation in the public schools, though sometimes merely tokenism, became the norm throughout the Southern states. That is not to say that everything was harmonious. Some Whites established private academies to avoid sending their children to integrated schools, and some Southern leaders publicly committed themselves to upholding Southern tradition at all costs. Still, Jim Crow had been dealt a severe blow, and opponents readied themselves for the next assault.

Desegregation: The Second Phase

In the 1960s the civil rights movement gained momentum, attracted many more followers, and moved against all other Jim Crow legislation. Sit-in demonstrations began in Greensboro, North Carolina, on February 1, 1960, when four freshmen from the all-black Agricultural and Technical College sat at the all-white lunch counter at the local Woolworth's store and refused to leave. During the spring of 1960, there were sit-ins throughout the South. From the sit-ins evolved a fourth social organization—the Student Nonviolent Coordinating Committee (SNCC, pronounced *snick*)—to compete with the NAACP, the Congress on Racial Equality (CORE), and the Southern Christian Leadership Conference (SCLC), which Dr. King had formed after the bus boycott.

The success of the sit-ins convinced many people that direct action was a quicker and more effective means of achieving total desegregation. James Farmer of CORE organized Freedom Rides from Washington, D.C., to selected Southern locations in 1961 to challenge the segregated facilities in bus terminals. These were followed by freedom marches, voter registration drives, and continued attacks upon Jim Crow legislation.

All the movements were symptomatic of the times. Kennedy's election as President in 1960 and his speaking of "a new generation of leadership" had inaugurated a period of high hopes and ideals. It was a time of commitment and change, of Vista and the Peace Corps, of promise and reachable goals. As the civil rights movement grew, "We Shall Overcome" became the rallying theme song, and Bob Dylan's "Blowin' in the Wind" captured the spirit of the times.

Civil rights activity met with fierce resistance. Dr. King urged nonviolence, but younger black activists grew impatient with such an approach.

Nonviolence was for him [King] a philosophical issue rather than the tactical or strategic question it posed for many younger activists in SNCC and CORE. The aim was "to awaken a sense of moral shame in the opponent." Such a philosophy presumed that the opponent had moral shame to awaken, and that moral shame, if awakened, would suffice. During the 1960's many civil rights activists came to

Rev. Martin Luther King, Jr.—flanked by other civil rights activists, including Rev. Ralph Abernathy, A. Philip Randolph, and Medgar Evans—makes a freedom march to Birmingham, Alabama, in 1962. Such public actions often produced jeers, taunts, insults, and physical attack, as challenges to generations of racial discrimination drew strong resistance from dominant Whites.

doubt the first and deny the second. The reasons for this did not lie primarily in white Southern terrorism as manifested in the killing of NAACP leader Medgar Evers, of three civil rights workers in Neshoba, Mississippi, of four little girls in a dynamited church in Birmingham, and many others. To a large extent, white Southern violence was anticipated and expected. What was not expected was the absence of strong protective action by the federal government.

Activists in SNCC and CORE met with greater and more violent Southern resistance as direct action continued during the sixties. Freedom Riders were beaten by mobs in Montgomery; demonstrators were hosed, clubbed, and cattle-prodded in Birmingham and Selma. Throughout the South, civil rights workers, Black and White, were victimized by local officials as well as by night-riders and angry crowds. It was not surprising, then, that student activists in the South became increasingly disillusioned with nonviolent tactics of resistance.[27]

Two events in 1963—the March on Washington and the integration of the University of Alabama—gave two civil rights activists—King and Kennedy—the opportunity to express the mood of the times. On August 28, 1963, tens of thousands of marchers of all races from all over the country and many walks of life gathered before the Lincoln Memorial. King addressed them (in part) as follows:

There are those who are asking the devotees of civil rights, "When will you be satisfied?" We can never be satisfied as long as the Negro is the victim of the unspeakable horrors of police brutality. We can never be satisfied as long as our bodies, heavy with the fatigue of travel, cannot gain lodging in the motels of the highways and the hotels of the cities. We cannot be satisfied as long as the Negro's basic mobility is from a smaller ghetto to a larger one. We can never be satisfied as long as a Negro in Mississippi cannot vote and a Negro in New York believes he has nothing for which to vote. No, no, we are not satisifed, and we will not be satisfied until justice rolls down like waters and righteousness like a mighty stream. . . .

I say to you today, my friends, that in spite of the difficulties and frustrations of the moment I still have a dream. It is a dream deeply rooted in the American dream.

I have a dream that one day this nation will rise up and live out the true meaning of its creed: "We hold these truths to be self-evident; that all men are created equal." . . . I have a dream that my four little children will one day live in a nation where they will not be judged by the color of their skin but by the content of their character.

On April 4, 1968, an assassin's bullet prevented Martin Luther King from seeing his dream move closer to reality. President Kennedy died on November 22, 1963, before the passage of the civil rights legislation he proposed after sending troops to enforce the integration of the University of Alabama in that same year. In explaining his actions, Kennedy had told the American public in a television address:

This nation was founded by men of many nations and backgrounds. It was founded on the principle that all men are created equal, and that the rights of every man are diminished when the rights of one man are threatened. . . .

It ought to be possible, therefore, for American students of any color to attend any public institution they select without having to be backed up by troops. It ought to be possible for American consumers of any color to receive equal service in places of public accommodation, such as hotels and restaurants, and theaters and retail stores without being forced to resort to demonstrations in the street.

And it ought to be possible for American citizens of any color to register and to vote in a free election without interference or fear of reprisal.

It ought to be possible, in short, for every American to enjoy the privileges of being American without regard to his race or his color.

In short, every American ought to have the right to be treated as he would wish to be treated, as one would wish his children to be treated. But this is not the case. . . .

One hundred years of delay have passed since President Lincoln freed the slaves, yet their heirs, their grandsons, are not fully free. They are not yet freed from the bonds of injustice; they are not yet freed from social and economic oppression.

And this nation, for all its hopes and all its boasts, will not be fully free until all its citizens are free.

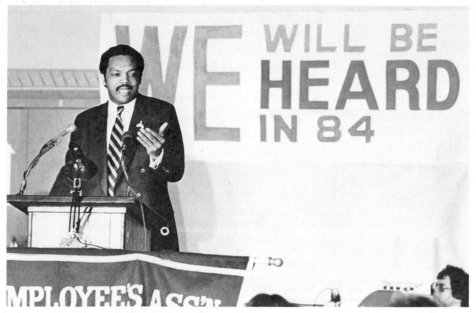

Rev. Jesse Jackson conducted a highly successful voter registration drive and primary presidential campaign in 1984. His fine showing in many states, North and South, served as a symbol to many of the growing political power of black voters. In the past twenty years the number of elected black officials has increased from 170 to over 5,700.

The Civil Rights Act of 1964 was the most far-reaching legislation against racial discrimination ever passed. It provided for equal standards for all voters in federal elections. It prohibited racial discrimination and refusal of service on racial grounds in all places of public accommodation, including eating and lodging establishments and places of entertainment, recreation, or service. It gave the attorney general broader powers to intervene in private suits regarding violation of civil rights. It banned racial discrimination by employers or unions or by any recipient of federal funds, and it directed federal agencies to monitor this and to withhold funds from any recalcitrant state or local agency. Unfortunately, black workers still meet resistance from many unions when they apply for membership.

Congress passed additional legislation in 1965 to simplify judicial enforcement of the voting laws and to extend them to state and local elections. In 1968 further civil rights legislation barred discrimination in housing and gave the American Indians greater rights in their dealings with courts and government agencies at all levels. Congress also set stiff federal penalties for those convicted of intimidating or injuring anyone who was exercising any of the civil rights provided by congressional action.

The effect of the legislation upon attitudes is difficult to measure, but it did give Blacks equal life opportunities. Black elected officials increased dramatically, from about 170 in 1964 to more than 5,700 in 1984, half of these in eleven Southern states. In the mid-1980s Blacks serve as mayors in 224 cities—among them such urban centers as Los Angeles, Chicago, Philadelphia, Detroit, Washington, Atlanta, Oakland, New Orleans, Newark, Birmingham, and Richmond.[28] Jesse Jackson's 1984 presidential bid succeeded in increasing black voter registration by several million, further strengthening their ballot power. In other areas to be discussed shortly, Blacks also improved their rate of participation. Perhaps "stateways" will change "folkways," as legislation opens doors to Blacks, thereby providing long-term opportunities for the social conditioning of people's attitudes toward racial harmony.[29]

Urban Unrest

As the civil rights movement gained momentum, it spread northward as well. Protests against discrimination in employment and housing and against *de facto* segregation in the schools began in the early 1960s in New York and Philadelphia and quickly spread.

None of the problems of the blacks in the North—slum schools, unemployment or residential segregation—were new, but an intensified awareness of them had grown. Part of this new awareness reflected the economic cramp that developed during the latter part of the fifties, particularly in the burgeoning ghettoes of northern and western cities. Ideological cramp was being felt outside the South, too. The promise of a new equality for all blacks, the struggle of southern blacks to realize this promise, and the complacency of white America as the white South turned the new equality into token equality spread disillusionment into black neighborhoods all over the nation. Ironically, the plaintive and oft-repeated plea of white southerners that the problem of race relations was not just a Southern problem finally began to be heard—but only because it was now sounded by black voices.[30]

In the North, ideological support for the black cause waned as the distance from the conflict diminished with increasing percentages of Blacks in Northern cities (Table 10.1). Changes were demanded nearer home, in particular open housing and busing. By 1964 Charles Silberman observed:

And so the North is finally beginning to face the reality of race. In the process, it is discovering animosities and prejudices that had been hidden in the recesses of the soul. For a brief period following the demonstrations in Birmingham in the spring of 1963—a very brief period—it appeared that the American conscience had been touched; a wave of sympathy for the Negro and of revulsion over white brutality seemed to course through the nation. But then the counteraction set in, revealing a degree of anti-Negro prejudice and hatred that surprised even the most sophisticated observers.[31]

As Blacks experienced some gains and some frustrations, a pattern of increased alienation, cynicism, hostility, and eventual violence ensued. When a social movement achieves some goals, its expectations are increased and so are its

TABLE 10.1
What Blacks and Whites Think of Each Other

Blacks on Whites

On the whole, do you think most white people want to see Blacks get a better break or want to keep Blacks down—or don't you think they care either way?

	1983 %	1969 %
Get better break	33	20
Keep Blacks down	23	43
Don't care	27	26
Don't know	17	11

Whites on Blacks:

	1963 %	1971 %	1978 %
Less ambitious	66	52	49
Want a handout	41	39	36
Less intelligent	39	37	25
Care less for family	31	26	18
Inferior to Whites	31	22	15

Source: Newsweek Polls, reported in *Newsweek,* August 29, 1983, p. 15, and February 26, 1979, 48–53.

frustrations, leading to greater militancy.[32] Militant leaders like Malcolm X, Eldridge Cleaver, Huey Newton, and Bobby Seale emerged to speak of the grievances of Northern Blacks. New organizations such as the Black Panthers and older ones such as the Black Muslims attracted many followers as they set out to meet the needs of Northern Blacks in the ghettoes.

In the summer of 1964, Blacks rioted in the tenement sections of Harlem, Philadelphia, and Rochester, attacking both police and property. The following summer, the violence and destruction were more massive; outbursts occurred first in the Watts section of Los Angeles and then in Chicago, Springfield, Massachusetts, and Philadelphia. Ghetto violence continued; in the summer of 1966 there were eighteen different riots, and in the summer of 1967, thirty-one cities experienced riots, of which those in Newark (twenty-six killed) and Detroit (forty-two killed) were the worst.

The increase in the number and intensity of riots in 1967 prompted an in-depth study of seventy-five of the disorders, including those in Newark and Detroit, by the National Advisory Commission on Civil Disorders. It found that, although specific grievances varied somewhat from city to city, there were consistent patterns in who the rioters were, how the riots originated, and what the rioters wanted. The most intense causal factors were police practices, unemployment and underemployment, and inadequate housing.

Disorder did not erupt as a result of a single "triggering" or "precipitation" incident. Instead, it was generated out of an increasingly disturbed social atmosphere, in which typically a series of tension-heightening incidents over a period of weeks or months became linked in the minds of many in the Negro community with a reservoir of underlying grievances. At some point in the mounting tension, a further incident—in itself often routine or trivial—became the breaking point and the tension spilled over into violence. . . .

The typical rioter was a teenager or young adult, a lifelong resident of the city in which he rioted, a high school dropout; he was nevertheless, somewhat better educated than his nonrioting Negro neighbor, and was usually underemployed or employed in a menial job. He was proud of his race, extremely hostile to both whites and middle-class Negroes and, although informed about politics, highly distrustful of the political system. . . .

What the rioters appeared to be seeking was fuller participation in the social order and the material benefits enjoyed by the majority of American citizens. Rather than rejecting the American system, they were anxious to obtain for themselves a place in it.[33]

The deaths, injuries, burnings, and extensive property damage in all the cities—Watts, Newark, and Detroit being the worst hit—produced government action at municipal, state, and federal levels to correct the conditions that encouraged violence. But the riots also caused a white backlash. The exodus of the white middle class from the cities, which had begun in the 1950s, now had added impetus. The migration increased, with some stores and businesses also moving to the suburbs. There are a number of complex reasons for the urban-suburban migration, but in the late 1960s urban violence was clearly a major factor for many people.

In 1966 Stokely Carmichael, the head of SNCC, advanced the slogan "Black Power," which became subject to many interpretations since it was never clearly defined. For many, it was not a wild cry of radicals, but rather a declaration that civil rights goals could be achieved only through concerted black efforts. It symbolized the attainment of what Kurt Lewin called a "sense of peoplehood" and Franklin Giddings identified as a "consciousness of kind." The word "Black" rather than "Negro" quickly became the accepted way of referring to this racial group.

Two factors contributed to the cooling of black urban violence. First, a new social movement protesting the war in Vietnam, to which many black youths were being sent, became a focus for public concern. Second, many black leaders were either assassinated (King, Medgar Evers, Malcom X) or imprisoned (Carmichael, Newton, Seale), or went into exile (Cleaver). Many Blacks redirected their energies toward community self-help programs, as other leaders were co-opted in leadership roles within the system and many Blacks began to strive for the Black Power goal Carmichael had enunciated. In May 1980 though, black economic frustrations and resentment against the growing Cuban community—sparked by an all-white jury's acquittal of four white police officers accused of bludgeoning to death a black man—set off three days of the worst outbreak of racial violence in thirteen years. When it ended, nine Blacks and six Whites were dead, with damages exceeding $200 million. Although an isolated incident, Miami served as a

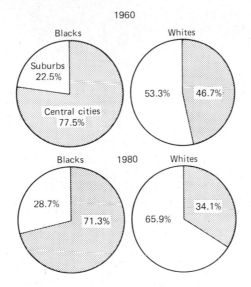

1960

Blacks

Suburbs
22.5%

Central cities
77.5%

Whites

53.3%   46.7%

Blacks   1980   Whites

28.7%   71.3%

34.1%

65.9%

FIGURE 10.1

Metropolitan Population Living Inside and
Outside Central Cities, Black and Whites:
1960 and 1980

chilling reminder of mounting frustrations in the nation's ghettos.

Figure 10.1 illustrates that, while a 6 percent shift of Blacks from central cities
to suburbs occurred between 1960 and 1980, Whites doubled that percentage
change in the same period. As many cities declined in population, this has meant
a larger concentration of Blacks in those cities.

SOCIAL INDICATORS OF BLACK PROGRESS

As Figure 10.2 shows, a larger percentage of Blacks are younger than Whites.
This demographic fact suggests both a more rapid future population growth for
Blacks and the importance of the socioeconomic environment in which young
people grow up. The more enriched their childhood socialization, the greater their
adult life opportunities.

Where are we today? How far have we gone toward true equality for Blacks
as well as Whites? Sociologists utilize quantifiable measurements or social indicators to identify specifically a group's achievements in comparison with others, as
well as its mobility within the stratification system. Three of the most common
variables—education, income, and occupation—offer an objective portrait of what
gains have been made, of how much the gap between the two races has been
narrowed.

Education

Most impressive have been the considerable gains in level of education. Even though
the national average for years of completed schooling has been rising, Blacks have
made such dramatic gains that they have narrowed the gap in median years of
schooling completed from a three-year differential in 1960 to a half-year differ-

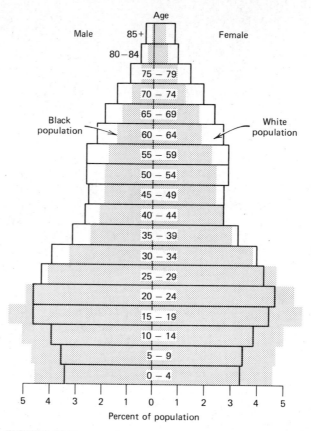

FIGURE 10.2

Age-Sex Composition of Black and White Populations: 1980

ential in 1981 (Table 10.2). Part of this success has been the "play it cool, stay in school" campaigns, which have effectively reduced the dropout rate (Table 10.3). Although still disproportionately high among Blacks, the dropout rate among black students dropped from 22.2 percent in 1960 to 15.5 percent in 1982. White students, including Hispanics, increased slightly in the same period, from 10.8 percent to 11.2 percent.

If we look more closely at those completing four years of high school or more, we find a slightly different picture. As Table 10.4 illustrates, the percentages for both Blacks and Whites have been steadily increasing, certainly a positive sign. However, despite the fact that Blacks went from 12.9 percent completing four or more years of high school in 1960 to 32.5 percent in 1982, a gap remains. Figure 10.3 shows the heart of the problem. Of those entering high school, 83 percent of the Whites and 72 percent of the Blacks graduated. Only 29 percent of the Blacks entered college compared to 38 percent of the Whites. Completing college were 12 percent of the Blacks, almost half the 23 percent white college graduates.

TABLE 10.2
Median Years of Schooling Completed
Selected Years, 1950–1982

	1950	1960	1970	1982
Black Males	6.4	7.7	9.6	12.2
White Males	9.3	10.7	12.2	12.7
Black Females	7.1	8.6	10.2	12.1
White Females	10.0	11.2	12.2	12.5

Source: U.S. Bureau of the Census, *Current Population Reports,* series P-20, No. 295, and *Statistical Abstract of the United States,* 1984 Table 223, p. 144.

TABLE 10.3
High School Dropouts By Race and Age
By Percent, 1968 to 1982

Race and Age	1968	1975	1982
White	11.9	10.5	11.2
16–17 years	7.2	8.4	7.6
18–21 years	15.5	14.7	15.2
22–24 years	20.1	12.6	13.7
Black	21.6	18.5	15.5
16–17 years	12.2	10.2	6.0
18–21 years	28.6	27.0	23.0
22–24 years	40.5	27.8	20.5

Includes other age groups not shown separately.

Source: Statistical Abstract of the United States, 1984, Table 254, p. 160.

TABLE 10.4
Years of School Completed, 1960 to 1982
By Age, Race, and Percent

Years of School Completed	Black			White		
	1960	1970	1982	1960	1970	1982
Under 5 years	23.8	15.1	7.3	6.7	4.2	2.4
5–7 years	24.2	16.7	10.6	12.8	8.3	5.0
8 years	12.9	11.2	6.8	18.1	13.6	7.2
High School 1–3 years	19.0	23.3	20.4	19.3	16.5	12.6
4 years	12.9	23.4	32.5	25.8	35.2	38.8
College 1–3 years	4.1	6.9	13.6	9.3	10.7	15.5
4 years or more	3.1	4.5	8.8	8.1	11.6	18.5
Median years completed	8.0	9.9	12.2	10.9	12.2	12.6

Source: U.S. Bureau of the Census, *Statistical Abstract of the United States,* 1984, Table 223, p. 144.

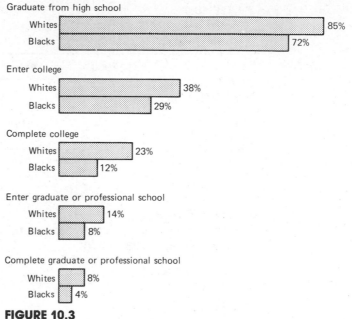

FIGURE 10.3

Black and White Educational Attainment Levels

Source: Ford Foundation study reported in *Chronicle of Higher Education,* February 3, 1982.

Given current trends, we may expect this situation to improve each succeeding year, continuing a positive picture for this social indicator.

Another barometer of improvement is comparative test scores. The College Board, which runs the national Scholastic Aptitude Test (SAT), found a narrowing of the traditional black–white gap in scores in the 1981 and 1982 tests. A more expansive study of scores on the verbal skills section of the National Assessment of Education Progress, SAT, and Graduate Record Exam over a seven-year period revealed a consistent reduction in the black–white average difference on all three tests.[34]

Income

Historically, black family income has always been significantly lower than white family income. From the civil rights legislation and War on Poverty programs of the mid-1960s to the late 1970s, the income percentage gap began to close. The 1980–1982 recession, resulting in high unemployment, together with federal domestic spending cutbacks, caused a substantial erosion. As indicated in Table 10.5, 1982 was a bleak year for black families, their median income dropping to 55.3 percent of white family median income, a figure not seen since the early 1960s.

Also worsening was the poverty rate. The War on Poverty programs of the 1960s

TABLE 10.5
Median Family Income, 1950 to 1982

Year	White	Black	Black Income as a Percent of White Income	Actual Income Gap
1950	$ 3,445	$ 1,869	54.3	$ 1,576
1955	$ 4,605	$ 2,549	55.4	$ 2,056
1960	$ 5,835	$ 3,233	55.4	$ 2,602
1965	$ 7,251	$ 3,994	55.1	$ 3,257
1970	$10,236	$ 6,516	63.7	$ 3,720
1975	$14,268	$ 9,321	65.3	$ 4,947
1980	$21,904	$13,843	63.2	$ 8,061
1981	$23,517	$14,598	62.1	$ 8,919
1982	$24,593	$13,598	55.3	$10,995

Source: U.S. Bureau of the Census.

had reduced black poverty from 55.1 percent in 1959 to 32.2 percent by 1969. For the next twelve years it hovered within a percentage point of the 1969 figure, but in 1982 the poverty rate rose to 35.6 percent for Blacks (Figure 10.4). A significant factor has been the "feminization of poverty," with the rise in female-headed families.[35] Since many women lack education and job skills, their poor earning potential is limited further by unavailable or unaffordable child-care centers, making female-headed families the fastest growing segment of the population living in poverty. One out of three female-headed families lives in poverty, up from a total of 1.8 million households in 1969 to 3 million in 1980.[36] In 1981, 41.7 percent

FIGURE 10.4

Black and White Families Below Poverty Level Selected years, 1959–1982, by percent of all black families were female-headed, compared to 11.9 percent female-headed white families.[37] Nearly half of all black youngsters now live in a single parent home.

For Black America both progress and regression have been occurring simultaneously. A larger segment than ever before has been able to secure better-paying positions and greater economic stability. At the same time, we have witnessed the growth of a multigenerational, poor underclass, mired in urban ghettoes and habitually unemployed or underemployed.

Occupation

For many Americans, occupation is a primary measure of status. Accordingly, comparisons of occupational distribution over a period of time demonstrate whether or not a group is achieving upward mobility. Because the occupational structure has also been changing—decline of farm and blue-collar jobs, increase of high technology jobs—we must consider changes not only within the group itself but also in comparison to other groups. Table 10.6 provides this view, showing parity for Blacks and Whites in clerical workers and larger growth for Blacks among white-collar, professional, and technical workers. A greater proportion of Blacks continue as operatives, service workers, and nonfarm laborers, most of which are low-pay, low-skill positions.

Occupational upgrading occurred among some Blacks. For example, a few occupational increases from 1970 to 1980 included: black female lawyers from 446 to 4,272; black female psychologists from 501 to 4,551; black male psychologists from 461 to 2,414.[38] Although the number of black men in professional positions grew at a slightly faster pace than that of white males during the 1970s, their pro-

TABLE 10.6
Occupational Distribution of U.S. Labor Force in 1970 and 1982, by Percent for Race

Classification	1970		1982	
	Black	White	Black	White
Professional, Technical Workers	6.2	14.8	11.8	17.4
Managers and Administrators	3.4	11.4	4.8	12.3
Salesworkers	8.8	6.7	2.8	7.1
Clerical Workers	12.3	18.0	18.9	18.5
Craft and Kindred Workers	10.6	13.5	9.0	12.8
Operatives	22.1	17.0	18.6	12.2
Nonfarm Laborers	12.5	4.1	7.4	4.2
Service Workers	19.9	10.7	25.0	12.6
Farm Workers	4.3	4.0	1.6	2.9

Source: U.S. Bureau of Labor Statistics and *Statistical Abstract of the United States, 1984,* Table 693, p. 417.

portional representation was only half that of white males. What we see, then, is slow progress in upward mobility and a slight improvement in occupation distribution but a remaining imbalance still to be corrected. For example, Blacks comprise 12 percent of the population but only 3 percent of those in sales, 4 percent of those in professional medicine and dentistry, and 8 percent of those in other professional and technical fields.[39]

RACE OR CLASS?

As growing class divisions within the black community became more apparent, a swirling controversy emerged among black social scientists as to the continuing cause of black difficulties. In his 1978 book, *The Declining Significance of Race,* sociologist William J. Wilson touched off the debate by arguing that the life chances of Blacks—their economic opportunities—are now determined far more by their social class than their race.[40] If educated, Blacks can compete equally with Whites, enjoying unprecedented opportunities for better-paying jobs. At the same time, Wilson said, the increasing job qualifications in this high-technology age may well keep the black underclass permanently trapped in economic subordination. Although race is not insignificant, Wilson stressed that social class, not racial discrimination, denies upward mobility to the black poor. Affirmative Action helps middle-class Blacks, not the poor. Until we recognize the dependency nature of welfare, the need to provide skills and education to the urban poor, we cannot effectively attack the problem of inequality.

Economist Thomas Sowell echoed this view, pointing out in *Ethnic America* the parallels between Blacks and other ethnic groups in social class and upward mobility as key factors in their acceptance and socioeconomic mainstreaming.[41] Carl Gershman, a white civil-rights activist and former research director of the A. Philip Randolph Institute, also called the current problem class-caused, suggesting black leaders remained preoccupied with racial bias as the sole cause of ghetto poverty, ignoring the reality of a bipolarization of American Blacks.[42]

Many other black social scientists do not agree with Wilson, Sowell, and Gershman. Sociologist Charles V. Willie in *Caste and Class Controversy* maintained that economics is but one facet of the larger society and should therefore not be considered in isolation. White racism permeates all social institutions, controlling entry to all desirable positions in education, employment, earnings, housing, and social status. By surrendering their blackness, Blacks may gain middle-class status, said Willie, but they become psychologically chained in a white world that permits only token entry while retaining actual power, control, and wealth.[43]

Psychologist Kenneth B. Clark called Wilson's position "wishful and premature optimism."[44] Death, retirement, and entry into judicial, political, or corporate careers has removed most effective civil-rights leaders, preventing action for remedying continuing and worsening racial problems. Those in corporate, government, or university life are less in genuine decision-making positions than in created positions of racial tokenism, with limited influence and a cautious attitude against jeopardizing their "personal gains and affable acceptance of their white colleagues." Institutionalized racism remains, said Clark, as seen in the failure of Whites to resolve the problem of the urban ghettos and in the use of such racial code words as "busing," "quotas," "reverse discrimination," "meritocracy," and "maintaining standards," which imply that efforts to correct racial injustice weaken the fiber of society.

The heated debate continues, with many others joining the fray. Wilson continues to argue it is wrong to emphasize a uniform racial experience for all Blacks, that the majority of Blacks have made great strides but a self-perpetuating underclass is becoming more entrenched. His opponents, including the Association of Black Sociologists, charge that Wilson misinterprets the situation because racial injustice still dominates the social system.

SOCIOLOGICAL ANALYSIS

Blacks have been victims of slavery, restrictive laws, or racial discrimination for most of the years they have lived in the United States. Many changes have occurred in the past twenty-five years, but problems remain. Some argue the unique experiences of black people in America require separate analysis, that their situation cannot be compared to other ethnic groups. Others maintain that, despite certain significant dissimilarities, sufficient parallels exist to invite comparative analysis in patterns of dominant–minority relations. Use of the three major perspectives incorporates both views.

The Functionalist View

Inequality exists in all societies, since people value more highly certain occupational roles and social positions over others. A value consensus develops about their functional importance in meeting the needs, goals, and priorities of society. Status, esteem, and differential rewards depend upon this orientation and the availability of qualified personnel. As one example, slavery offered the South a practical and effective means of developing an agricultural economy based on cotton; slaves provided a cheap labor force to work long hours, requiring only physical endurance—no training, skills, talent, or intelligence. The system worked, leaving slave owners free for "genteel" artistic, intellectual, and leisure pursuits while reaffirming in their minds the "inferiority" of their toiling "darkies."

This value consensus survived the social disorganization of the postbellum South. A generation later, the Jim Crow laws once again formalized a system of inequality through all social institutions. A new tradition of restricted opportunities and participation became entrenched, based on old values but feeding upon itself for justification of the existing order. In the North, Blacks filled a labor need, but remained unassimilated. This lack of societal cohesion and a continued presence of Blacks generated prejudice, avoidance, and reciprocal antagonism. In both North and South in the twentieth century, these system dysfunctions—the waste of human resources and lost productivity—produced social problems of poor education, low income and unemployment, crime and delinquency, poor housing, high disease and mortality rates, and other pathologies.

System corrections, in the form of federal judicial and legislative action, helped restore more of a balance to society, reorganizing our social institutions and eliminating barriers to full social, political, and economic opportunities. Other dysfunctions—the Vietnam War, rampant inflation in the 1970s, structural blue-collar unemployment, the 1980–1982 recession—curtailed some Black gains. Further adjustments are necessary to overcome the remaining problems.

The Conflict View

Slavery is an obvious past example of economic exploitation of Blacks, but more recent practices may be less obvious. Job discrimination, labor union discrimination—particularly in the building trades—and prejudices in educational institutions leading to low achievement and high dropout rates have together forced many Blacks into low-paying, low-status, economically vulnerable jobs. For many years confinement of Blacks to marginal positions preserved the better-paying job opportunities exclusively for Whites. Maintenance of a low-cost surplus labor pool, not in competition for jobs sought by Whites, benefited employers and the dominant society, providing domestic and sanitation workers, seasonal employees, as well as job opportunities for Whites in social work, law-enforcement, and welfare agencies.

Both de jure segregation and de facto segregation illustrate the success of those with power in protecting their self-interests by maintaining the status quo. Control of all social institutions kept Blacks confined to certain occupations and residential locations, away from participation in the political process and out of the societal mainstream. Although a black and mulatto elite did arise, and some positive white actions occurred, such as President Roosevelt's 1941 executive order banning racial discrimination in defense industries, Blacks mostly remained an oppressed minority.

Blauner's internal colonialism model is appropriate here: the outside control of black segregated communities as employers, teachers, social workers, police, and politicians represent the establishment, making the administrative, economic, and political decisions governing the ghetto. Unlike European groups, Blauner maintained, the Blacks did not gain control and ownership within a generation of their own buildings and commercial enterprises, remaining instead a subjugated and dependent colonized population.[45]

The civil rights movement of the 1960s, a culmination of earlier actions and court decisions, fits Marxian analysis of social change. Blacks developed a group cohesiveness, overcoming a false consciousness that equality was an unattainable goal, and formed an effective social movement. Sweeping changes through civil rights legislation, punctuated by urban violence from 1964 to 1968, brought improved life opportunities to Blacks and other minorities.

The Interactionist View

Just as our attraction to strangers is based upon perceived similarities, our anti-pathy to strangers can be based upon learned prejudices. In the United States, skin color has often triggered negative responses about busing, crime, housing, jobs, and poverty. Where do such attitudes originate? Earlier we discussed multi-generational stereotyping and social isolation of Blacks as the legacy of racism. If beliefs about a people, culturally transmitted and reinforced by external condi-tions, center on their differences or alleged inferiority, then avoidance, exploita-tion, or subjugation can become common responses.

Opposition to integration efforts usually comes from fear of these "unlike" strangers. Though expressed reasons may include preserving neighborhoods or neighborhood schools, the real reason is often concern Blacks will "contaminate" the school or area. Beliefs that the crime rate, school discipline, property values, and neighborhood stability will be adversely affected by their presence often prompts Whites to resist the proposed integration. Similarly, beliefs that Blacks are less re-liable, less honest, and less intelligent has frequently influenced hiring and accep-tance decisions in the past, and still sometimes today. What matters is not so much the unfairness or inaccuracy of such sweeping generalizations, but that people act upon them. Too many have spun a gossamer web of false reality and believed it.

Black racism works much the same way, seeing all Whites as the enemy, all Blacks as right, and suspicious of any friendly white action or criticism of any Black. Since both sides define a situation in a particular way, that interpretation usually results in reinforcing consequences. Upward mobility—in education, occupation, and income—does much to alter people's interpretations, as polls reported in this chapter indicate.

RETROSPECT

Through two hundred years of slavery and one hundred additional years of another form of subjugation, Blacks have found society unresponsive to their needs and wants. Negatively categorized by skin color, they have seen clearly that there are two worlds in this country: the white and the nonwhite. Many Blacks remain trapped in poverty and isolated in urban ghettos; others, who have achieved up-ward mobility, often find, at least in meaningful primary relationships, that they are still not accepted in white society.

There are many similarities between the black experience in the United States and the experiences of other minority peoples. Like the Asians and Indians, Blacks have frequently been judged on the basis of their skin color, not their individual capabilities. They have experienced, as have many immigrant groups, countless instances of stereotyping, scapegoating, prejudice, discrimination, social and spa-tial segregation, deprivation, and violence. When they have become too visible in a given area or have moved into economic competition with Whites, the domi-nant group has seen them as a threat and reacted accordingly. All of this is a fa-miliar pattern in dominant-minority relations.

More than two hundred years of slavery exacted a heavy toll upon the black people of America, and exploitation and discrimination did not end with the abolition of slavery. As a result of generations of social conditioning, many Whites continued to have a master-slave mentality long after the Civil War. Two generations later, when Blacks had made some progress, the Jim Crow laws eliminated those gains and reestablished unequal treatment and life opportunities, thereby increasing prejudice.

A change in values and attitudes became evident with the historic Supreme Court decision of 1954. Although school integration was slow, it did come about, and both Blacks and Whites were encouraged to seek even more changes. The growth of the civil rights movement—an idea whose time had come at last—peaked in the mid-1960s, when a broad range of laws were passed to offer black people a more equitable life experience.

A quarter of a century has elapsed since the 1954 decision. A great number of changes have taken place in the land, and there have been observable improvements in all aspects of life for many Blacks. Still, many problems remain. A disproportionate number of nonwhite poor continue to be concentrated in the cities, frequently trapped in a cycle of perpetual poverty. Despite all the legislation and court decisions, most Blacks still engage in primary relationships only with other Blacks. Social distance between Blacks and Whites in informal and private gatherings is still great. *De facto* segregation is still a problem, with the majority of Whites living in suburbs and the majority of Blacks living in urban areas.

Greater interaction occurs between the two races in places of public accommodation, and this may eventually reshape white attitudes. That, together with improved educational opportunities, may lead to greater structural assimilation for Blacks. One element crucial to black progress is the condition of the economy. Its ability to absorb Blacks into those positions in the labor force that permit upward socioeconomic mobility will, in large measure, determine the future status of Blacks in American society.

REVIEW QUESTIONS

1. In what ways is the black experience in the United States unique?

2. What similarities exist among the experiences of the Blacks, American Indians, and Asians in the United States?

3. What similarities are there between the responses of Blacks and of European immigrants to prejudice and discrimination?

4. What factors have delayed Blacks in gaining economic and political power as European and Asian immigrant groups did?

5. What is the present status of Blacks in America according to the leading social indicators?

6. What insights into the black experience do the three major sociological perspectives provide?

SUGGESTED READINGS

Billingsley, Andrew. ***Black Families in White America.*** Englewood Cliffs, N.J.: Prentice-Hall, 1968.

A now classic rebuttal to the Moynihan Report, detailing the wide range of black family structure and socioeconomic hierarchy.

Freeman, Richard B. ***Black Elite.*** New York: McGraw-Hill, 1976.

An analytical portrait of the success of this new group through education and the emergence of black professionals.

Lyman, Stanford M. ***The Black American in Sociological Thought: A Failure of Perspective.*** New York: Putnam, 1972.

Evaluative critique of other analyses of Black–White relations, suggesting guidelines for sociological study of America's largest minority.

Pinkney, Alphonso. ***Black Americans,*** 2nd ed. Englewood Cliffs, N.J.: Prentice-Hall, 1975.

A good overview of both the history and contemporary situation of American Blacks, emphasizing the role of power and social class.

Willie, Charles V. ***A New Look at Black Families,*** 2nd ed. New York: General Hall, 1981.

Excellent study of Black-American families, debunking myths yet identifying their problems engendered by poverty and racism.

Wilson, William J. ***The Declining Significance of Race.*** Chicago: University of Chicago Press, 1978.

A controversial argument that the current bipolar status of Blacks makes social class more important than race in their gaining status and power.

PART FOUR

OTHER MINORITIES

CHAPTER 11

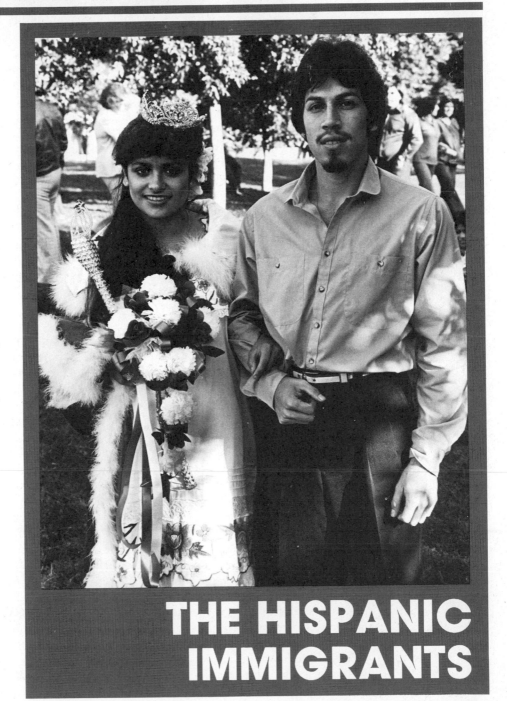

THE HISPANIC IMMIGRANTS

Perhaps no group attracts more public attention these days than do the Hispanic people. Their large numbers, their residential clustering, the bilingual programs and signs provided for them, and their poverty and its concurrent social problems make them a recognizable ethnic group. Although there are many differences in their cultural background, social-class status, and length of residence in the United States, they have one thing in common: the Spanish language. Because of this one factor, people often lump them all together despite the many differences among them.

SOCIOHISTORICAL PERSPECTIVE

Spanish influence has long been felt in the United States. Long before the English settled in their colonies in the New World, Spanish explorers, missionaries, and adventurers roamed through much of the Western Hemisphere, including Florida and the southwestern United States. In 1518 the Spanish established St. Augustine, Florida, and in the same year (1609) as the first permanent English settlement (Jamestown) was established, the Spanish founded Santa Fe, in what is now New Mexico. Spanish cultural influence was extensive throughout the New World in the areas of language, religion, customs, values, and town planning (for example, locating church and institutional buildings next to a central plaza).

Structural Conditions

The Hispanic-American experience varies greatly, depending upon the particular ethnic group, area of the country, and time period. In the American Southwest, agricultural needs and the presence of Mexican-Americans are crucial factors in dominant-minority relations. In the East, industrial employment, urban problems, and the presence of Cubans or Puerto Ricans provide the focal points of attitudes and actions. Figure 11.1 shows the percentage of Hispanics living in the 50 states in 1980.

Most low-skilled groups, including such Hispanic peoples as the Puerto Ricans and Mexicans, have at first obtained jobs that have low status, low pay, and little mobility. Unlike past groups, however, recent Hispanic immigrants have entered an industrial society in which the economy is no longer growing rapidly. Many Hispanic immigrants come from less industrialized nations and have few of the skills they would need in order to adjust easily to working in America. Technological progress has eliminated many of the jobs earlier immigrants could obtain to achieve some degree of economic security (such as unskilled factory work). The suburbanization of industry has meant that in older cities, where poor immigrants have traditionally lived and worked out of economic necessity, there are no longer enough manufacturing jobs for the newcomers. Unions once helped European immigrants to obtain job security, better wages, and improved working conditions, but today's unions often exclude or restrict the "new" minorities.

Because so many Hispanics are low-skilled workers, they are susceptible to downturns in the economy. For example, in the first quarter of 1983—the worst period for unemployment since World War II—the Hispanic unemployment rate

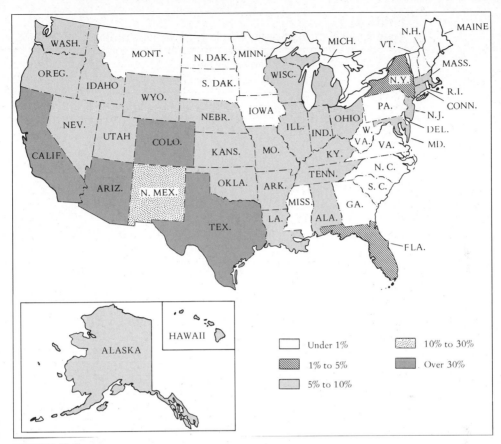

FIGURE 11.1

Percentage of Hispanics in the United States, 1980

was 16.7 percent. This was greater than the 11.2 white rate but below the 20.6 black rate. Puerto Ricans were highest at 19.9 percent unemployed, followed by Mexicans at 17.7 percent, and Cubans at 15.5 percent. Like the Blacks, Hispanics were overrepresented among the unemployed although their poverty rate is not as severe (see Tables 11.1 and 11.2). While they were only 5.4 percent of the total labor force (5.9 million), they constituted 9 percent of the total number unemployed (989,000) at that time.[1] Since that low period, their labor participation rate has improved somewhat.

Overpopulation throughout Latin American is a highly significant factor in the continued migration of large numbers of Hispanics to the United States (Table 11.3). High birth rates, improved sanitation, the reduction of child mortality, and negative attitudes toward birth control have led to population booms in countries whose resources and habitable land cannot support this many people. The Economic Commission for Latin America reports that the total population of Latin America grew from over 129 million in 1940 to over 284 million by 1970. Cur-

TABLE 11.1
Poverty Rate of Hispanic, Black, and White Families: 1973–1981

Year	Percent of Families Below Poverty Level			Ratio of Hispanic to White Poverty Rate
	Hispanic	Black	White	
1973	19.8	28.1	6.6	3.0
1974	21.2	26.9	6.8	3.1
1975	25.1	27.1	7.7	3.3
1976	23.1	27.9	7.1	3.3
1977	21.4	28.2	7.0	3.1
1978	20.4	27.5	6.9	3.0
1979	20.3	27.8	6.9	2.9
1980	23.2	28.9	8.0	2.9
1981	24.0	30.8	8.8	2.7

Source: Bureau of the Census, "Money Income and Poverty Status: 1981," Table 15.

TABLE 11.2
Median Income of Hispanic, Black, and White Families: 1972–1981 (in constant 1981 dollars)

Year	Median Family Income			Hispanic Family Income as Percent of White Income
	Hispanic	Black	White	
1972	17,790	14,922	25,107	71
1973	17,836	14,877	25,777	69
1974	17,594	14,765	24,728	71
1975	16,140	14,835	24,110	67
1976	16,390	14,766	24,823	66
1977	17,141	14,352	25,124	68
1978	17,518	15,166	25,606	68
1979	18,255	14,590	25,689	71
1980	16,242	13,989	24,176	67
1981	16,401	13,266	23,517	70

Source: Bureau of the Census, "Money Income and Poverty Status of Families and Persons in the United States: 1981 (Advance Data from the March 1982 Current Population Survey)," *Current Population Reports,* Series P-60, No. 134, July 1982, Table 3.

rent projections are that the population will reach about 500 million by 1990 and be over 650 million by the year 2000.[2] Suffering from poor living conditions, inadequate schools, limited job opportunities, and other aspects of poverty, many Latinos journey to the United States, legally or illegally, for a better life.[3] The United States has a 2,000-mile border with Mexico and open migration for Puerto Ricans, and many other Hispanic nationalities use these routes to enter illegally. The

TABLE 11.3
Legal Hispanic Immigration to the United States
By Decades, 1951–1980

	1951–1960	1961–1970	1971–1980
Mexico	299,811	453,937	640,294
Caribbean	123,091	470,213	741,126
Central America	44,751	101,330	134,640
South America	91,628	257,954	295,741

Source: U.S. Immigration and Naturalization Service.

U.S. government estimated that there were 6 to 8 million illegal aliens in the United States in 1984, almost all of them Hispanics. This large number of illegal aliens has an adverse effect upon the labor market, living conditions for poor people, and social service costs.

Cultural Differentiation

The cultures of the peoples from the various Caribbean and Central and South American countries differ. Value orientations within a particular country also vary, depending on such factors as degree of urbanization, amount of outside contact, and social class. With these qualifications in mind, we shall examine some general cultural traditions, shared to a greater or lesser degree by most Hispanics, that differ from traditional American values. Before we do so, we should also note that in areas of considerable acculturation, such as New Mexico, some of these cultural traits are muted, and Hispanics have adopted many Anglo (the Hispanics' term for American) behavior patterns.

The Cosmic Race

One cultural concept that is associated with Hispanics—especially Mexicans—is that of *La Raza Cosmica,* the cosmic race. The Mexican intellectual José Vasconcelos coined the term to refer to the amalgamation of the white, black, and Indian races, which he believed was occurring in Latin America.[4] Though in his old age he dismissed the idea as a juvenile fantasy, the concept evolved into a group categorization similar to what Kurt Lewin calls a recognition of an "interdependence of fate." In essence, *La Raza Cosmica* suggests that all the Spanish-speaking peoples in the Western Hemisphere share a cultural bond and that God has planned for them a great destiny that has yet to be realized. Recent studies of Mexican-Americans have found that this cultural belief is still significant, either directly or in terms of the behavioral values associated with it.[5] Reflecting centuries of European dominance, the concept is also one of fatalism; it implies that one should submit to the things of the present and not plan for the future. The song "Que sera, sera" (what will be, will be) illustrates this. Younger Hispanics appear to subscribe less to such fatalism than do their elders.

Machismo

Overstated in the Anglo stereotype, *machismo* is a basic value covering various qualities of masculinity. To Hispanic males, such attributes as inner strength in the face of adversity, personal daring, bravado, leadership, and sexual prowess are all measures of one's manhood.[6] The role of the man is to be a good provider for his family, to protect its honor at all times, and to be strong, reliable, and independent. He should avoid indebtedness or charity and any kind of relationship, formal or informal, that would weaken his autonomy. The culture and family system are male-dominated. The woman's role is within the family, and she is to be guarded against any onslaught upon her honor.

The result of these values can be not only a double standard of sexual morality but also difficulty adjusting to American culture. Women have more independence in the United States than in most Hispanic countries. Instead of males being the sole providers, females can also find employment here, sometimes earning more money than the men of the family. The labor-force participation of Spanish women appears to be related to educational level. The U.S. government has reported that the more highly educated Cuban and Central and South American women have labor-force participation rates similar to those of all white women in the United States, whereas Mexican and Puerto Rican women have especially low rates.[7]

Dignidad

This cultural value is the basis of social interaction; it assumes that the dignity of all humans entitles them to a measure of respect. It is primarily "a quality attributed to all, regardless of status, race, color or creed."[8] Regardless of status, each person acknowledges others' *dignidad* in a taken-for-granted reciprocal behavior pattern. Therefore, Hispanics—particularly Puerto Ricans—expect to be treated in terms of *dignidad*. Because it is an implicit measure of respect, one cannot demand it from others. Instead, one concludes that others are rude and cold if they do not acknowledge one's *dignidad*. More broadly, the concept includes a strong positive self-image.

Racial Attitudes

In most Latin American countries skin color is less important as an indicator of social status than is social class. There seems to be a correlation between darker skin color and low social standing, but the sharp racial line between Whites and Blacks found in the United States is deemphasized in Latin America. A great deal of color integration takes place in social interaction, intermarriage, and shared cultural value orientations. There is also a much wider range of color gradations, which helps to blunt any color prejudice. Still, in some places, such as Puerto Rico, color prejudice has increased, perhaps as a result of social and economic changes from industrialization.[9]

Color is often an unexpected basis of discrimination for Latinos coming to the

United States. Being stereotyped, judged, and treated on the basis on one's skin color is essentially unknown to these brown-skinned peoples. Therefore, encountering prejudice and discrimination based on their skin color is a traumatic experience for them. Before long they realize the extent of this regrettable aspect of American society. Some adapt to it, others forsake it and return home, but practically all resent it.

Other Cultural Attributes

Latinos generally have a more casual attitude toward time, and a negative attitude toward hurrying about. Another cultural difference that could easily lead to misunderstanding is their attitude about making eye contact with others. To them, not looking directly into the eyes of an authority figure such as a teacher or police officer is an act of respect, but Americans may interpret it as shyness, avoidance, or guilt. Like some Europeans, they regard physical proximity in conversation as a sign of friendliness, but Anglos are accustomed to a greater distance between conversationalists. One can envision an Anglo made uncomfortable by the ''unusual'' nearness of an Hispanic person and backing away, the latter re-establishing the physical closeness, the Anglo again backing away, and the Hispanic concluding that the Anglo is a cold or aloof individual. Each has viewed the situation from a different cultural perspective and thus interpreted the incident quite differently.[10]

Current Patterns

Hispanics are America's fastest growing minority, numbering over 14.6 million in the 1980 census, a 61 percent increase over their 9.1 million population in 1970. Although they only now comprise slightly more than 6 percent of the total U.S. population, demographers predict they should be the largest minority group by the year 2020, possibly amounting to 15 percent of the total.[11] This projection is based upon their high birth rate (almost twice that of other Americans), their low average age (half are under 21), and the fact that 40 percent of all legal immigrants come from Spanish-speaking lands (see Figure 11.3). Finally, there is the problem of the illegal immigrants. The U.S. Immigration and Naturalization Service estimates that at any one time there are probably 8 million or more illegal immigrants in this country, about 60 percent of them from Mexico and the others from other Latin American and Caribbean countries.

For the first time, the 1980 census asked respondents if they spoke a language other than English at home. Fully 11 percent reported that they did, about half of them speaking Spanish, making it the second most common language in the United States. Geographically, there are many Hispanic-Americans outside the large concentrations in California, Florida, and New York City. The Census Bureau reports that more Hispanics live in Illinois than in New Mexico and more live in New Jersey than in Arizona.[12] A large Mexican-American population in Chicago gives that

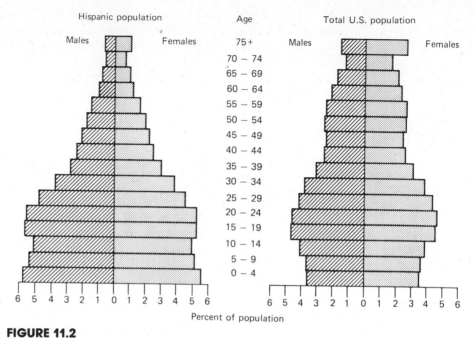

FIGURE 11.2

Age-Sex Composition of the Hispanic and Total U.S. Population: 1980

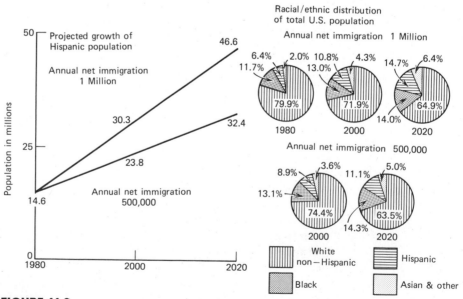

FIGURE 11.3

Population 1980 and as Projected for 2000 and 2020: Hispanics, Total U.S. Population, and Four Main Racial/Ethnic Groups city over 300,000 Latinos. Detroit has a mixture of almost 20 Spanish-speaking nationalities.

The degree of harmony in dominant-minority relations and of Hispanic assimilation varies by region and with the people and their culture. One pattern is relatively consistent, however, and that is the strong cultural vitality of various Hispanic-American groups. Mexican-Americans, for example, have long insisted on retaining their ethnic identity. Their large numbers in this country, their proximity to Mexico, and the fact that their predecessors in the Southwest were living in lands that had long been Spanish-controlled are undoubtedly all factors that reinforce cultural pluralism. Similarly, several influences encourage other Hispanic groups to retain their cultural identities. Primary among these are current migration patterns of newcomers from Spanish-speaking countries, psychological ties to the homeland because of rapid transportation and communications, actual proximity, endogamy, and high birth rates. Since there is less societal pressure for assimilation than there once was, and since Americans are more receptive to ethnicity, the Hispanics may become the first major immigrant group to be a lasting exception to the melting pot.[13]

THE MEXICAN-AMERICANS

About 83 percent of the 8.7 million Mexican-Americans in the United States live in the Southwest. Los Angeles, whose very name indicates its Spanish origin, has more than a million Mexican-American residents, making it second only to Mexico City in Mexican population. A great deal of diversity exists among this ethnic group in terms of degree of assimilation and socioeconomic status. For example, there is a very small group of old-family Spanish-Americans in northern New Mexico and southern Colorado who follow the old traditions and speak very little English.

Throughout New Mexico, which, unlike Texas and California, has not had constant contact with Mexico through border crossings, the employment pattern is brighter. In fact, Hispanic–Americans there are heavily represented in civil service occupations at the local, state, and federal levels. In a sense, they are like many recent non-Western immigrants in that they retain a cultural heritage (such as their diet, child-rearing philosophy, stress on the family, and extended family contacts), but hold economically secure occupational positions.

Second-generation Mexican–Americans living in Los Angeles are far more likely to be assimilated than their counterparts in Corpus Christi.[14] However, most present-day Mexican–Americans, whether they live in an urban or a rural area, are extremely poor, struggling to survive from day to day in a land that does not always look kindly upon them.

When the United States secured the southwestern region after the Mexican–American War of 1846–1848 and then added a small boundary section through the Gadsden Purchase of 1853, there were a relatively small number of Mexicans living in these areas. Most of these, quickly outnumbered by Anglos, lost their lands through legal maneuvering and became a subordinated population.

Recruiting Mexicans

In the second half of the nineteenth century a great need for agricultural labor developed and Mexicans from south of the border helped to fill it. Railroad lines were being built; cotton, fruit, and vegetable farms were expanding. The Chinese Exclusion Act of 1882 curtailed one source of laborers, and later the Immigration Acts of 1921 and 1924 curtailed another. But the demand for labor, especially for agricultural workers, increased, and the Mexicans left their poverty-stricken country for the economic opportunities available here.

It is important to understand the cultural milieu in their native land in order to understand the Mexicans' situation in the United States for over a hundred years. Most Mexicans were poor, illiterate peasants, virtually serfs, who eked out an existence laboring for the *hacendados,* the large landholding aristocracy of Mexico. Exploited by the hacienda owners and the Mexican government for years, and ignorant of the language and laws of this country, the Mexicans worked in the United States under servile conditions for meager wages. The degree of poverty in their native country is reflected in the fact that even though they worked for very low wages, they were still earning a great deal more than they could at home.

Although there were restrictions on immigration, it was easy for Mexicans to cross the largely unpatrolled border and enter the country illegally, and many did so. They were known as "wetbacks" because they had waded or swum across the Rio Grande. Some Mexican aliens also entered the United States legally as contract laborers. Under the *bracero* program, Mexican aliens were temporarily brought into the United States, then returned to Mexico after the harvest. This system provided the needed workers without the accompanying expenses of educating their children, giving them welfare during nonworking periods, and providing other social services. The program lasted from 1942 until 1964, when farm mechanization, labor shortages in Mexico, and the protests of native Hispanics in the United States ended it.

Expulsion

Although Mexican labor was a boon to the Southwestern economy, during a downturn in the national economy Mexicans usually were not welcome. One such time was the 1930s, when a great many Americans were jobless. Some Mexicans returned home voluntarily; others were pressured to do so by local residents. A great many more were rounded up and deported.

During the depression the U.S. Government and public agencies, in what was called a "repatriation program," deported literally hundreds of thousands of Mexicans and Mexican Americans to cut down on welfare costs. Roundups extended through southern California, to most cities of the Southwest, and as far north as Chicago and Detroit.

In Los Angeles, official trucks would grind into the barrios—the Mexican American neighborhoods—and the occupants would be herded into them. There was little or no determination of national origin. Citizenship or noncitizenship was not considered. Families were divided; the bringing of possessions was not permitted. . . .

"They pushed most of my family into one van," one of the victims, Jorge Acevedo, remembers bitterly. "We drove all day. The driver wouldn't stop for bathroom nor food nor water. Everyone knew by now we had been deported. Nobody knew why, but there was a lot of hatred and anger. . . . We had always known that we were hated. Now we had proof." [15]

During the recession of the mid-1950s, the U.S. Immigration and Naturalization Service launched "Operation Wetback" to find and return all illegal Mexican aliens. Concentrating on California and Texas, but ranging as far as Spokane, Chicago, Kansas City, and St. Louis, between 1954 and 1959 government officials found and expelled 3.8 million Mexicans, only 63,515 of whom had a formal hearing.[16] Not all were illegal aliens. Many American citizens, if they "looked Mexican," were stopped and questioned. If they could not immediately prove their legal status, they were often arrested and "sent home" without anyone even checking into their status.[17]

Violence

One infamous incident in which prejudices against the Mexicans erupted into violence is the Zoot Suit Riot of 1943. It was named thus because many Mexican-American youths at that time followed the then current fad of wearing long, loose-fitting jackets with wide shoulders; high-waisted, baggy trousers with tight cuffs; and flat-topped hats with broad brims. The gamblers in the original show and the film version of *Guys and Dolls* dressed in this fashion.

On June 3, 1943, two events occurred that triggered the riot. Some Mexican boys, returning from a police-sponsored club meeting, were assaulted by a group of non-Mexican hoodlums from the neighborhood in Los Angeles. That same evening, 11 sailors on leave were attacked, and one sailor badly hurt. The sailors said that their assailants were Mexican youths who outnumbered them 3 to 1. When the police, responding late, found no one to arrest in the area, about 200 sailors decided to settle the matter themselves the following evening. Cruising through the Mexican section in a caravan of twenty taxicabs, they savagely beat every Mexican they found. The police did nothing to stop this, and the press gave these events wide publicity.

The stage was now set for the really serious rioting of June seventh and eighth. Having featured the preliminary rioting as an offensive launched by sailors, soldiers, and marines, the press now whipped public opinion into a frenzy by dire warnings that Mexican zoot-suiters planned a mass retaliation. To insure a riot, the precise street corners were marked at which retaliatory action was expected and the time of the anticipated action was carefully specified. In effect these stories announced a riot and invited public participation. . . .

On Monday evening, June seventh, thousands of *Angelenos,* in response to twelve hours' advance notice in the press, turned out for a mass lynching. Marching through the streets of downtown Los Angeles, a mob of several thousand soldiers, sailors, and civilians, proceeded to beat up every zoot-suiter they could find. Pushing its way into the important motion picture theaters, the mob ordered the management to turn on the house lights and then ranged up and down the aisles dragging Mexicans out of their seats. Street cars were halted while Mexicans, and some Filipinos and Negroes, were jerked out of their seats, pushed into the streets, and beaten with sadistic frenzy. . . .

Here is one of the numerous eyewitness accounts written by Al Waxman, editor of *The Eastside Journal:*

Four boys came out of a pool hall. They were wearing the zoot-suits that have become the symbols of a fighting flag. Police ordered them into arrest cars. One refused. He asked: "Why am I being arrested?" The police officer answered with three swift blows of the night-stick across the boy's head and he went down. As he sprawled, he was kicked in the face. Police had difficulty loading his body into the vehicle because he was one-legged and wore a wooden limb. . . .

At the next corner a Mexican mother cried out, "Don't take my boy, he did nothing. He's only fifteen years old. Don't take him." She was struck across the jaw with a night-stick and almost dropped the two and a half year old baby that was clinging in her arms. . . .

A Negro defense worker, wearing a defense-plant identification badge on his work clothes, was taken from a street car and one of his eyes was gouged out with a knife. Huge half-page photographs, showing Mexican boys, stripped of their clothes, cowering on the pavements, often bleeding profusely, surrounded by jeering mobs of men and women, appeared in all of the Los Angeles newspapers. . . .

When it finally stopped, the Eagle Rock *Advertiser* mournfully editorialized: "It is too bad the servicemen were called off before they were able to complete the job. . . . Most of the citizens of the city have been delighted with what has been going on."[18]

This bloody incident, like the Know-Nothing riots, the anti-Chinese race riots, lynchings, and other past acts of violence, was the result of increasing societal tensions and prejudices against a minority, which erupted into aggression far in excess of the triggering incident. Whatever Mexicans thought about Anglo society before this wartime incident, they would long remember this race riot waged against them with official sanction from the police, the newspapers, and city hall.

Urban Life

For the past thirty-five years, most Mexican-Americans have lived in cities. In some places, like Los Angeles and New Mexico, they are better integrated into the mainstream of society. There they have higher intermarriage rates, nuclear instead of extended family residence patterns, and less patriarchal male roles. They are entering more diverse occupations, and many are attaining middle-class status and moving from the barrio to the suburbs and outskirts of the city. In other areas of the Southwest, particularly in smaller cities and towns, Mexican-Americans reside in large ethnic enclaves, virtually isolated from participation in Anglo society. Even those middle-class individuals whose families have resided in this country for generations choose to live among their own people and interact only with them.

Many Mexican-Americans live in substandard housing under crowded conditions. In the five Southwestern states their housing is more crowded than that of nonwhites—in Texas, twice as many Mexicans as Blacks live in overcrowded housing. Segregated in the less desirable sections of town, with their children attending schools that warrant the same criticisms as inner-city schools in the major cities, they experience many forms of discrimination.

In general, the sudden disappearance of ordinary urban facilities when a visitor enters exclusively Mexican poverty areas is striking. Streets are unpaved; there are no curbs and sidewalks or street lights; traffic hazards go unremedied, and the general air of decay and neglect is unmistakable. (In many cities in the Southwest, "improvements" considered normal and essential in other neighborhoods are financed by per capita assessments of local property owners. These special assessments are often impossible to obtain in poor neighborhoods.) Abandoned automobiles, uncollected refuse, hulks of burned out buildings and the famous cactus fences symbolize the civic status of these neighborhoods. In addition, it is typical of Mexican-American neighborhoods in the Southwest that they are carelessly zoned. Thus cheap shops, small factories, small tumble-down houses and even tiny urban farms sprawl together in unregulated confusion.[19]

Recent challenges to overt forms of discrimination have succeeded, but covert methods still persist. One landmark case protecting the civil liberties of Mexican-Americans was the 1953 U.S. Supreme Court decision concerning Peter Hernandez. This decision, which preceded the better-known *Brown* v. *Board of Education* segregation case, held that a community's laws cannot be written or applied against a particular class of people if this results in their being treated differently. The ruling, which had a far-reaching impact on discriminatory actions by public officials, was based on a case in which a nonrepresentative jury (Mexican-Americans never served on juries in that region) convicted a Mexican-American.

Stereotyping

Negative stereotypes of Mexican-Americans persist in American society. Such categorizations as their being lazy, unclean, treacherous, sneaks, or thieves frequently appear in the mass media. Even advertisements had used these derogatory stereotypes until adverse reaction forced advertisers to discontinue this practice. Consider from recent years the "Frito-Bandito" of potato chip fame; a Camel cigarette ad showing a sleepy Mexican village; an Arrid commercial showing a Mexican spraying his underarm while a voice says, "If it works for him, it will work for you"; a Liggett & Myers ad saying "Paco" never "feenishes" anything, not even a revolution.[20]

Sometimes scholarly works inadvertently contribute to the stereotype. Some people used Florence Kluckhohn's study of a remote village in New Mexico as the basis for generalizations about the values of all Mexicans.[21] Thus such cultural attributes as present-time orientation, emphasis on intangible gratification rather than material rewards, and emphasis on enjoyment rather than working hard became synonymous with being Mexican.[22] In reality, the values of most urban Mexican-Americans are quite similar to those of other Americans: they want upward mobility, a better life for their children, and community interaction.[23]

Like Blacks and Puerto Ricans, the Mexican-Americans also suffer from the culture-of-poverty beliefs of the dominant society.[24] All too often they are blamed for their low socioeconomic standing because of their supposed cultural values. However, it is much more likely that their lack of education and job skills, and sustained dominant–minority interactions, rather than the minority's cultural variations, cause them problems in achieving economic security.

Chicano Power

The term *Chicano* was originally a derogatory name applied to the "lower" class Mexican-Indian people, rather than to the Mexican-Spanish. Most Mexican-American youths and some older people have now adopted the term as a symbol of pride and peoplehood. Chicanos look to the past to reaffirm their ethnic identity, but they also look to the future , aiming at becoming more organized, collectively independent within the system, and stronger in socioeconomic status.

Ethnic murals, such as this one in Los Angeles, usually contain recognizable people, events, symbols, and hopes of the community within which they are located. Besides aesthetically enhancing the urban neighborhood, they serve as a stimulus for cultural identity and pride.

Leaders have emerged—Cesar Chavez and his United Farm Workers Union, Rodolfo Gonzales and his La Raza Unida movement, Reies Lopes Tijerina and his Alianza group seeking to recover land lost or stolen over the years, David Sanchez and his Brown Berets. The awakening Chicanos are making their presence known in a society that has previously either exploited or ignored them. Today they are seeking to restore their people's pride and dignity, but they have had only limited success. The very diversity of the Mexican-American population makes it difficult to develop a unified, cohesive social or political action program that will appeal to the various classes within the community and to the diverse regional groupings within the nation, particularly in the Southwest.

Current Patterns

Today's Mexican newcomers are mostly males from central Mexico; they are younger and less skilled and educated than other immigrants.[25] The median age of all Mexican-Americans residing in the United States is 19.6 years. Families tend to be large, reflecting the high fertility rate, and there are also high rates of separation without divorce.[26] Mexicans are disproportionately represented among those arrested and convicted, particularly in youth crimes. In large urban areas, vicious gangs frequently get into trouble because of narcotics offenses and other actions.[27]

In the predominantly Protestant Southwest, Mexicans' identification with Catholicism further increased their social isolation. The Catholic Church in the Southwest has constantly faced a shortage of funds to do more than perform its basic ministerial functions. With few Mexican-Americans in the priesthood or church hierarchy, as well as a primary church emphasis on meeting religious needs, the Church has not provided the leadership to address the social problems of the Mexican-Americans. Unlike other immigrant groups for whom the church or synagogue helped facilitate readjustment, the Chicanos lack church assistance in overcoming poor education, poverty, discrimination, and limited economic opportunities. Mexicans, like Italian immigrants and Puerto Ricans, have a general allegiance to the Church, but primarily only women and children are active participants in attending Mass.[28]

Perhaps the most significant factor contributing to many of the socioeconomic problems of the Mexican-Americans, and one of long duration, is the number of illegal aliens in the country. Mexico has about 73 million people and one of the world's highest birth rates. More than half of its labor force is unemployed or underemployed. Getting across the lightly patrolled border is easy; only one illegal entrant in five gets caught, and those who are returned to Mexico try again, often on the same day. An estimated 50–60 percent of all illegal aliens are Mexicans.[29] Current estimates of the total number of illegal aliens are 3.5 to 6 million.[30] That the number is increasing each year is suggested by figures on deportable aliens apprehended by the Immigration and Naturalization Service. From January through April 1983, there were 377,000 apprehensions at the Mexican border, a 46 percent increase over the same period in 1982.[31] In 1966 a total of 133,000 were deported, but figures increased to 420,000 in 1971, to over a million each year in 1977 through 1979, and 970,000 in 1982.[32] Some employers encouraged illegal aliens to come because these aliens accepted lower wages, and it was not illegal to employ them. The actual impact of illegal aliens on job displacement and the economy is a matter of debate, but many people cite them as the cause of crime, welfare, and economic troubles.[33] In Chapter 14, we shall discuss the issue of illegal aliens more fully.

THE PUERTO RICANS

Puerto Ricans frequently refer to their island as the "true melting pot," unlike the mainland, which has only claimed to be so. Originally inhabited by the Arawak and Caribe Indian tribes, Puerto Rico came under Spanish domination in 1493 and remained so for 400 years. When the Indian population was decimated, black slaves were imported. Miscegenation was quite common, resulting in a society that de-emphasized race. The high degree of color integration discussed earlier is reflected in words such as *moreno, mulatto, pardo,* and *trigueño,* indicating a broader range of color gradations. Structural assimilation in the island's multiracial society extends to housing, social institutions, government policy, and cultural identity.[34] A high degree of intermarriage often means people classified as one racial category have close kin relationships with other racial categories, either by blood line or adoption.

The racial scene in Puerto Rico has also been characterized by what I would call a high degree of two-way integration, while in the U.S. one-way integration has been and is the norm. That is, Blacks are usually sent to White schools, not vice-versa. Blacks integrate into White America, not Whites into Black America. . . . In this country it rarely happens that a Black couple adopts a White child. The number of White babies available for adoption and the limited income of many Blacks tend to discourage this action. In most agencies the action is not permitted and the reverse is encouraged. In Puerto Rico, it is a fairly common occurrence to rear other people's children as one's own. These "hijos de crianza" come in all colors. Thus, a "White" couple may rear the darker, orphaned children of a neighbor and vice-versa.[35]

Early Relations

In 1898, when the United States first annexed Puerto Rico after the Spanish-American War, there was an attempt at forced Americanization. The United States discouraged anything associated with the Spanish tradition and imposed the use of the English language. Presidents appointed governors, usually from the mainland, to rule the territory. The inhabitants were granted U.S. citizenship in 1917, but otherwise the island was virtually ignored and remained an undeveloped land with many poor people. Citizenship brought open migration because it eliminated passports, visas, and quotas, but it did not give the people the right to vote for President or to have a voting representative in Congress. By 1930 approximately

53,000 Puerto Ricans were living on the mainland. During the Depression and the war years, immigration virtually halted until the mass migration of the post-World War II era.

In the 1940s several improvements occurred. Luis Muñoz Marin's Popular Democratic Party *(Partido Popular Democratico)* emerged as a powerful force. President Franklin Roosevelt, as part of his Good Neighbor Policy, set about finding a new status for the island. Puerto Rico became a commonwealth, with the people writing their own constitution and electing their own representatives. Marin was elected governor, and was re-elected each time until 1964. In addition, the island was given complete freedom in its internal affairs, including maintaining its Spanish heritage and not being required to use English.

To help the island develop economically, the U.S. government launched "Operation Bootstrap" in 1945. Industries were given substantial tax advantages if they made capital investments in Puerto Rico. The tax breaks and abundant supply of low-cost labor resulted in 300 new factories being built by 1953, increasing to 660 by 1960 and creating over 48,000 new jobs. As a result, Puerto Rico became the most advanced and industrialized land in the Caribbean and in most of Central and South America, with the highest per capita income.

The Push-Pull Factors

Despite the creation of thousands of factory jobs through Operation Bootstrap, the collapse of the sugar industry kept the unemployment rate around 13 percent, triggering the beginning of *La Migración.* In the 1950s one of the most dramatic voluntary exoduses in world history occurred, as one of every six Puerto Ricans migrated to the mainland. Many of the 480,000 who came in the 1950s were rural people, settling in metropolitan urban centers where jobs could be found. Encouraged by inexpensive plane fares and freedom of entry as U.S. citizens, they were driven from the island's stagnant agrarian economy by the promise of jobs. The greatest total period of Puerto Rican migration was 1946–1964, when a total of 614,940 moved to the mainland. Only the Irish migration of the midnineteenth century offers a close comparison, but that was forced in part by the Potato Famine.

Thereafter a significant drop in Puerto Rican migration occurred. Many factors contributed to this. The "pull" factor lost its potency as cities such as New York lost hundreds of thousands of manufacturing jobs, no longer offering a promising job market. An island population of less than 2.4 million at that time and a declining fertility rate made sustaining a high exodus rate impossible. Further, the earlier exodus relieved pressure on the home job market; increases in U.S. government welfare support, combined with remittances from family members on the mainland encouraged many to stay on the island.[36] By the 1970s, migration dropped to 41,000 (see Table 11.4).

Hidden in these migration figures, however, is the large movement of people back and forth from the island. For example, while 109,842 came to the United States between 1965–1974, 92,603 returned to Puerto Rico, a net gain of only 17,239.[37] Analysis of figures for the 1970s shows a net outflow of people 35 years

TABLE 11.4
Hispanic Immigration into the U.S., by Ethnic Group: 1950–1980

Ethnic Group	1950–59		1960–69		1970–79	
	Number of Migrants	Percent of Total	Number of Migrants	Percent of Total	Number of Migrants	Percent of Total
Mexican	293,000	30.7	431,000	33.2	567,000	40.8
Cuban	71,000	7.4	249,000	19.2	278,000	20.0
Puerto Rican	480,000	50.2	222,000	17.1	41,000	3.0
Other Hispanic	112,000	11.7	397,000	30.6	503,000	36.2

Sources: Mexican, Cuban, Other Hispanic: Immigration and Naturalization Service annual reports 1950–1979, Table 9: Puerto Rican: Estimated from Puerto Rican census and vital statistics.

and older, as well as children aged 5 to 19, but a net influx of people aged 20 to 29 and children under age five.[38] It appears the prospect of better economic opportunities lures young adults and their children to the U.S. who then later choose to return to the island. This revolving door migration results partly from a sojourner orientation for some, buttressed by concern over deteriorating educational opportunities, housing conditions, health services, and personal safety in many urban areas.

Reasons for the return migration appear to be retirement; schooling of children (young parents who wish to educate their offspring in an environment less violent, less hostile, and less drug ridden than that in areas where they live in large cities in the four States); homesickness (strong longing for the more family-friend oriented society in which no discrimination against Puerto Ricans exists, in which there is less apparent discrimination against darkness of skin, and in which the sociological and moral fabric of the community is not perceived to be as deteriorated as in the areas of the large cities in the four States where Puerto Ricans live [New York, New Jersey, Connecticut, and Illinois]); and rising expectations about prospects in Puerto Rico.[39]

A new wave of migration began in 1982 when 33,000, three times the usual annual number, came to the mainland. These were mostly middle-class, skilled workers seeking escape from the Commonwealth's high tax rates and job opportunities. The trend continued into 1983 and, at the time of this writing, shows no sign of subsiding.[40]

The Family

In Puerto Rico, as in all Latin American countries, the individual's identity, importance, and security depend on family membership. There is a deep sense of family obligation that extends to dating and courtship; family approval is necessary because of the emphasis upon a marriage joining two families, not just two individuals. An indication of family importance is the use of both the father's and mother's surnames, but in reverse order to the American practice. José Garcia Rivera, whose father's last name is Garcia and his mother's Rivera, should be called Mr. Garcia, not Mr. Rivera. The sociologist Joseph Fitzpatrick reveals that American confusion about use of these names is a constant source of embarrassment to Spanish-speaking people.[41] José's wife retains her family name and calls herself Maria Gonzalez de Garcia. On formal occasions she may use both sets of family names, such as Maria Gonzalez Medina de Garcia Rivera, while her husband would write his name José Garcia Diaz y Rivera Colon.[42]

Fitzpatrick identifies a fourfold typology among Puerto Rican families: (1) the extended family residing either in the same household or in separate households with frequent visits and strong bonds; (2) the nuclear family, increasingly common among the middle class; (3) the nuclear family plus other children of different names from previous union(s) of husband or wife, a not uncommon pattern among Puerto Ricans; (4) the female-headed household, with children of one or more men, but with no permanent male in the home.[43] The last type is frequently found among welfare families and is thus the target of much criticism.

Religion

The Catholic church has traditionally played an important role with immigrant groups, in succession assisting the French, Irish, Germans, Italians, Slavs, Poles, Syrian-Lebanese, and others.[44] This pattern has not been repeated with the Puerto Ricans in terms of representation in the church hierarchy, church leadership in the ethnic community, or immigrant involvement in the church.

> The Puerto Ricans have not created, as others did, national parishes of their own. Thus the capacities of the Church are weak in just those areas in which the needs of the migrants are great—in creating a surrounding, supporting community to replace the extended families, broken by city life, and to supply a social setting for those who feel lost and lonely in the great city. . . .
>
> Most of the Puerto Ricans in the city are Catholic, but their participation in Catholic life is small.[45]

Several factors have contributed to this break in the usual pattern. Because the island was a colony for so long, first Spanish and then American priests predominated within the church hierarchy on the island. Few Puerto Ricans became priests, and what few there were did not come to the mainland with the immigrants. The distant and alien nature of the church in Puerto Rico resulted in the Puerto Ricans having an internalized sense of Catholic identity without formally attending Mass and receiving the sacraments. Baptisms, weddings, and funerals all became important as social occasions, and the ceremony itself was of secondary importance. Throughout all of Latin America, Catholicism means personal relationships with the saints and a community manifestation of faith, not the individual actions and commitments expected in the United States. Another aspect of religious life in Puerto Rico, Brazil, and other parts of Latin America is the widespread belief in spiritualism and superstition. These practices undoubtedly are remnants of old folk rites, but they are still observed by various cults as well as by many Catholics.[46]

On the mainland a few other factors weakened any possibility that the Puerto Ricans would develop a strong ethnic church. Joseph Fitzpatrick indicates that the movement of other third-generation immigrants out of the city left behind clusters of old national churches with few parishioners.[47] Because of these existing church buildings and parochial schools, Cardinal Spellman decided in 1939 that New York City parishes would be integrated to accommodate the newcomers. Instead of having their own churches, the Puerto Ricans had the services of one or more Spanish-speaking priests, with special Masses and services performed in a basement chapel, school hall, or some other area of the parish. Although this practice was cost effective for the Catholic church, it prevented the parish from becoming the basis for a strong, stable community, since the group could not identify with it.

For many lower-class people of all racial and ethnic backgrounds, religion serves as an emotional escape from the harsh realities of everyday life. Pentecostalism is the fastest-growing religious movement among Puerto Ricans; it is the largest Protestant body both on the island and on the mainland. Storefront churches, with small and intimate congregations of about 60 to 100, offer their members a sense of community they cannot find elsewhere. Second-generation participation falls off sharply; Pentecostalism appears to be a first-generation phenomenon and therefore of limited duration.[48]

Church estimates reveal that only 6 percent of the Puerto Rican population on the mainland are involved with any Protestant denomination, including Pentecostalism, and only 20 percent with the Catholic church.[49] It is doubtful, then, that religious identification will be an important factor in either assimilation or cultural pluralism, as it was for earlier immigrant groups.

Puerto Rican Communities

The New York metropolitan area emerged as the Puerto Rican center, at one time containing three-fourths of all Puerto Ricans living on the mainland. According to the 1980 census, a dispersion became evident: only 43 percent of the 2 million Puerto Ricans now live in the New York metropolitan area, and 49 percent remain in New York State compared to 64 percent in 1970.[50] New Jersey accounts for another 12 percent, and Illinois 6 percent.[51] From 20 percent in 1970, now fully one-third of the "Ricans"—a name some prefer to differentiate themselves from those living in Puerto Rico—are scattered in other states.

For many years the continuous shuttle migration kept an organized community life from fully developing. Hometown clubs—voluntary organizations based upon one's place of birth—offered social opportunities in providing a place for celebration of weddings, birthdays, First Communions, and Confirmations. Because they drew members from scattered New York neighborhoods, they did not serve as a community center, nor did any other social institution. Only the annual Puerto

BOX 11.1

> *"We felt we had all the rights in the world to enjoy all the privileges others had. We were honest, hard-working, respectable citizens too. So we took legal action. . . ."*

"My husband and I bought our own house in Brooklyn after the Second World War, and a few years later we bought other property on Long Island, where we moved to raise our family. In 1956 we were employed by the U.S. Military Academy, West Point, and purchased a lovely home in a so-called exclusive area not too far away. This was a quaint neighborhood where custom-built homes ranged from $40,000 up to $100,000.

"Shortly after we moved in, we went down to Florida on vacation. When we came back, the house was empty. We slept on the floor and the following day our attorney by telephone searched every place high and low until he found our possessions in a warehouse in Nyack. Some of our neighbors had learned we were originally from Puerto Rico, were unhappy to have us as neighbors, and had plotted this against us.

"The harassment continued for a long time. They threw their garbage every night on our lawn. They even sent the police to intimidate us and even tried to buy us out. We told them they couldn't afford the luxury of buying us out. We felt we had all the rights in the world to enjoy all the privileges others had. We were honest, hard-working, respectable citizens too. So we took legal action and demanded for damages. The judge was fair and ruled for us."

Puerto Rican couple who came to the mainland in 1946 during their twenties

Rican Day Parade, begun in 1958, served as a focal point of group identity. By 1977, however, Clara Rodriguez was able to discern increased ethnic neighborhood organization:

> Note, for example, the growth of what are today Puerto Rican "cuchifrito" stands, social clubs, and after-hour clubs. These and other institutions did not exist years ago or existed in a very different form. Today they are identifying symbols of a Puerto Rican neighborhood. This same phenomena of change is also reflected in the speech of many second generation Puerto Ricans who no longer speak continuous Spanish, but whose English is decidedly "Rican."[52]

As with most ethnic communities, a great many civic and social organizations evolved. Some, born out of the War on Poverty and dependent on federal funding, have declined, but others remain strong. Most notable is *Aspira*, founded in 1961. Through guidance, encouragement, and financial assistance, *Aspira* seeks to develop cultural pride and self-confidence in youth, and to encourage them to further their education and enter the professions, technical fields, and the arts. Begun in New York City, its grass-roots program has achieved national fame, and it has expanded to other cities as well. A more direct community action group is the Puerto Rican Community Development Project, which attempts to promote a sense

For more than a quarter of a century, the annual Puerto Rican Day Parade has served as a rallying event for group solidarity. This popular activity serves as an effective means of instilling ethnic pride in the young generation, helping negate any marginality they may experience growing up as minority group members.

of identity among Puerto Ricans and to develop community strength. Another organization begun in New York is the Puerto Rican Family Institute, which provides professional social services to Puerto Rican families. Parent action groups, athletic leagues, cultural organizations, and social clubs also exist, providing services and fulfilling community needs.[53]

Activist organizations such as the Young Lords, the Puerto Rican Student Union, and *El Comite,* and collective community efforts on issues relating to education, antipoverty programs, public welfare, and housing have helped to develop a group consciousness. The problem is that militant actions, ranging from aggressive challenges to the status quo, to the radical FALN bombings dramatizing their demand for Puerto Rican independence, create tension and conflict within the Puerto Rican community and negative responses outside the community. For people who are trying to adjust and improve their life situations, the increased militancy may complicate things rather than improve them.

Socioeconomic Characteristics

Many Puerto Ricans have replaced the European immigrants on the urban slums and low-status jobs. They often do the work no one else will do because they can find no other work. Unlike their European predecessors, however, they cannot assume that hard manual labor will enable them to improve their lot. The United

States is a more technologically advanced society today, and many of the unskilled jobs of the past are no longer available. Many of the blue-collar and white-collar jobs presently available require skills that the Puerto Ricans do not have.

Living in the cities' worst neighborhoods, Puerto Ricans have the same problems other poor minority peoples have had. There are high levels of tuberculosis, venereal disease, drug addiction, juvenile delinquency, illegitimate births, and chronic unemployment among the Puerto Rican population just as there have been among almost all other ethnic groups in low-income situations. The severity of these social problems is directly related to the low economic status of the Puerto Ricans on the mainland. Rodriguez argues that U.S. technological development in Puerto Rico creates a surplus unskilled labor force that migrates to the mainland. As long as this surplus population remains and there continues to be open migration because of the political ties, Puerto Ricans "will continue to come and join the lower ranks of the working or non-working class."[54]

In October 1976, the U.S. Commission on Civil Rights reported that "the incidence of poverty and unemployment for Puerto Ricans is more severe than that of virtually any other ethnic group in the U.S."[55] (See Table 11.2.) It added that "the economic situation of Puerto Ricans in the continental United States has deteriorated during the last decade." With a disproportionate number of Puerto Ricans in the low-income group, their median income in 1959 was 71 percent of the national norm, but it had shrunk to 50 percent by 1979.

By 1982, only 51 percent of adult Puerto Ricans on the mainland were in the labor force, compared to 62 percent of Cubans and Mexican-Americans. This was partly due to the low 37 percent of Puerto Rican women working compared to about 50 percent for Cuban and Mexican-American women.[56] Puerto Rican men were most likely to work in nontransport operatives jobs (21 percent), with large proportions employed as service workers and craft workers. Nearly 25 percent of Puerto Rican women work in operatives jobs—dressmakers, assemblers, packers, graders, and the like.[57]

As might be expected, Puerto Ricans have the highest unemployment rate among Hispanics. Their unemployment rate has generally remained about twice that of Whites and about the same as Blacks for a number of years. It is difficult to determine whether Puerto Ricans are having difficulty achieving upward mobility, or if an immigration of poor islanders and return migration of those achieving some economic security is clouding the true picture.

THE CUBANS

Although the United States granted Cuba its independence after the 1898 war with Spain, it continued to exercise control over the island. The United States had Cuba relinquish a naval base at Guantánamo, which it still maintains, and through the Platt Amendment it reserved the right to intervene in Cuba if necessary to protect American interests. The Cubans resented these infringements upon their newly granted sovereignty. Later, in the 1930s, Franklin Roosevelt's Good Neighbor Policy helped to ease relations between the two countries.

Since the government listed Cuban immigrants among those from the West

Indies until 1950, exact numbers prior to that time are impossible to determine. Almost 500,000 people came to the United States from the West Indies between 1820 and 1950. Cubans had little impact upon the American scene during that period, although a Cuban community in northern New Jersey that dated back to 1850 did attract many refugees in the 1960s.

Cuban Migration

Since 1959, over 765,000 Cubans—more than came from the entire West Indies over a period of 130 years—have entered the United States. Touched off by Castro's rise to power, Cuban immigration surged in the first years of the revolution, then ebbed and flowed with shifts in both U.S. and Cuban government policies. Low points were Castro's cutoff of emigration after the 1962 missile crisis and in 1973.

In the 1960s and early 1970s, the first waves of postrevolutionary refugees had been "displaced bourgeoise"—well-educated, middle- and upper-class professionals and businesspeople alienated by the new regime.[58] Sympathetically received by the nation as resisters and refugees from the first communist regime in the Western Hemisphere, Cubans began to concentrate in several major cities, notably Miami and New York. Initial concern in those regions about overburdening the educational, welfare, and social service systems quickly dissipated as the Cubans made rapid economic progress and became a part of the community. By 1976, Cuban median income was $2,000 below the national norm, but higher than that of other Hispanic groups and Blacks, as well as in comparison to previous percentages of the national income of other newly arrived groups.

The largest single influx of Cubans occurred in late 1980, when the Mariel boatlift brought 125,000 Cubans to the United States in just a few months. Most were urban working-class and lower-class people, with at least several thousand hardened, vicious criminals among them. One consequence of this boatlift was it took place after completion of the 1980 census, thereby undermining its relevancy regarding the Cuban population. To the census total of 803,000, we must add the 1980 boatlift total of 125,000, making a total of 928,000. About 83 percent of all Cubans in the United States are first-generation Americans.[59]

Cuban Communities

In some instances Cubans found themselves treated disparagingly because non-Hispanic residents did not differentiate them from other, poorer Spanish-speaking groups such as the Puerto Ricans and Dominicans. Although they had looked upon such other Caribbean peoples with disdain in the past, the Cubans found that it was in their own best interests to work cooperatively with other Hispanic groups. In a pattern reminiscent of the Sephardic and Ashkenazic Jews, who first resisted and then were very helpful to the central and eastern European Jewish immigrants, the Cubans sometimes established closer relations with other Hispanic groups, particularly in New York. These cooperative efforts, where found, have helped to bring greater stability and visible progress to Hispanic neighborhoods.

Cubans often settled in blighted urban areas, but their motivation, education, and entrepreneurial skills enabled them to bring color, vitality, stability, and improvement to previously declining neighborhoods. Long-time residents of areas heavily populated by Cubans often credit them with restoring and increasing the beauty and vigor of the community.

Miami offers an excellent example. Its climate and closeness to Cuba made it the ideal choice of many exiles, thereby increasing the fears of residents about so large an ethnic group in their midst. Yet, by 1966 an observer could comment:

Though some ill-feeling still persists in Miami, by and large the city has come to count its new Cuban community as its own good fortune. . . . There is even something of a real-estate boom in Miami—one of the few cities in the U.S. where housing markets are strong—and an estimated 30 percent of the new FHA commitments there are to Cubans. Enterprising Cubans have been credited with bringing a new commercial vigor to much of the downtown area, especially the former commercial center of Flagler Street, which had been rapidly running down. Many of the former Havana cigar manufacturers and their employees have set up nearly a dozen companies in Miami, helping the city to displace Tampa as the hand-rolled-cigar capital of the U.S. At least one cigarette company, Dorsal & Mendes, is thriving; there are also sizable and prosperous Cuban-owned garment companies, shoe manufacturers, import houses, shopping centers, restaurants and night clubs. To the northwest of Miami, Cuban entrepreneurs have set up sugar plantations and mills.[60]

This picture of a Cuban section of Miami typifies urban scenes of Hispanics throughout the country. Like millions of European immigrants in earlier years, the Hispanic newcomers create and interact in their own ethnic communities, recognizable to outsiders by the foreign language commercial signs.

The Cuban impact upon Miami, now dubbed "Little Havana," has been significant. Over half the country's Cuban-Americans live in the Miami area, where Cubans comprise 70 percent of all Hispanics. The Cuban influence has transformed Miami from a resort town to a year-round commercial center with linkages throughout Latin America and made it into a leading bilingual cultural center.

The New York City metropolitan region has the second largest concentration of Cubans. Over 80,000 Cubans live there, often near groups from other parts of Latin America. Because Cubans have had a high status throughout the Caribbean for a long time, their presence in Hispanic-American neighborhoods has brought a new dimension in intracommunity relations, expectations, and cohesion:

> In the Caribbean, the Dominicans, Puerto Ricans and Jamaicans are all highly regarded as entrepreneurs. However, even they acknowledge, sometimes ruefully, that it is the Cubans who are to the tropics what the Parisians are to France and the Genoans to Italy: People who possess that special admixture of diligence and brashness, making the shrewd and prudently risky decisions that are the difference between high success and just making a living.[61]

As the Cubans began to organize within their new communities, their efforts also helped other Hispanics in the neighborhood. In the Washington Heights section of New York, for example, the Hispanic-American Alliance exerts political pressure to improve local schools and increase police protection, while the Cuban-backed Capital National Bank and Latin American Chamber of Commerce work to encourage successful small business enterprises. Across the Hudson River in New Jersey communities like Union City, West New York, and Elizabeth, as well as in other parts of the United States, Cuban influence has been positive.

Cultural Values

In addition to a commonality of values shared with other Latinos discussed earlier in this chapter, Cubans also share certain subcultural values that differ from those of the dominant American culture.[62] Among these are attitudes toward work, personal qualities, and the role of individuals in society.

American values stress hard work as a means of achieving material well-being, while the Cuban orientation is that material success should be pursued for personal freedom, not physical comfort. Work is not considered to be an end in itself, that one should live in order to work, as Cubans believe Anglos do. Instead, one should work to enjoy life. Intellectual pursuits are highly valued, idleness is frowned upon.

Unlike the American Puritan value of thrift and frugality, Cubans are fervent believers in generosity. Common group traits include a sharing of one's good fortune, a warm open-house policy, and an extensive social outreach to others. Cubans believe one of the worst sins is to be a *tacaño,* a cheapskate who does not readily show affection and friendship through kindnesses and hospitality.

BOX 11.2

> *"When we needed an escape from Cuba, we only had America. America was the only country that opened the door."*

"I have to tell you that the Spanish-speaking people are always talking about brotherhood and the brotherhood of the Latin American countries. They say our brother country Mexico and our brother country Venezuela, and every time they mention a Latin American country, they say the brother country. Well, in reality, it is wrong. When we needed an escape from Cuba, we only had America. America was the only country that opened the door. America is the only place where you can go for freedom and where you can live as a human being.

"I love Cuba very much but I can tell you that we never had the freedom that we have here. I can sincerely say that the opportunities in this country—America—are so great and so many, that no matter how bad they say we are as far as economics right now—they're talking about recession and everything—no matter how bad they say, it will never be as bad as it was and it is, actually, in Cuba.

"America took us in and we are grateful to America and to the Americans. And remember, when we came over, we were looking for freedom and liberty. Now we have freedom, we have liberty, and we have the chance to make money. Many Cubans are doing very well, better than me. I make enough to support my family and to live decently. I am very happy and grateful.

"Believe me, I am not only speaking for myself, but for a large group of Cubans who feel the same way I feel. We are happy here. We miss Cuba. Sometimes we get tearful when we think about the old friends and the old neighborhoods, but we are lucky. We are lucky because we still can say what we want to say, and we can move around wherever we want, and be what we want to be."

Cuban refugee who came to the United States in 1960 at age 18

Individualism is a value best shown through national and personal pride, which Anglos often misperceive as haughtiness. Yet Cubans believe individualism is not so much self-assertiveness as much as it is attitudes and actions oriented toward a group, sometimes a large number of people. Hostility needs to be directed through *choteo* and *relajo,* the continuous practice of humor, jokes, and wit, and accepted by others in good part. This is because one should avoid being a *pesado*—someone dislikeable, disagreeable, unwitty—which is the worst of all cultural sins.

Socioeconomic Characteristics

The population pyramid for Cubans (Figure 11.4) shows the significant difference of this Hispanic group compared to others. The bulges at ages 40–59 and 15–24 reflect the young and middle-aged Cubans who arrived in the 1960s and early

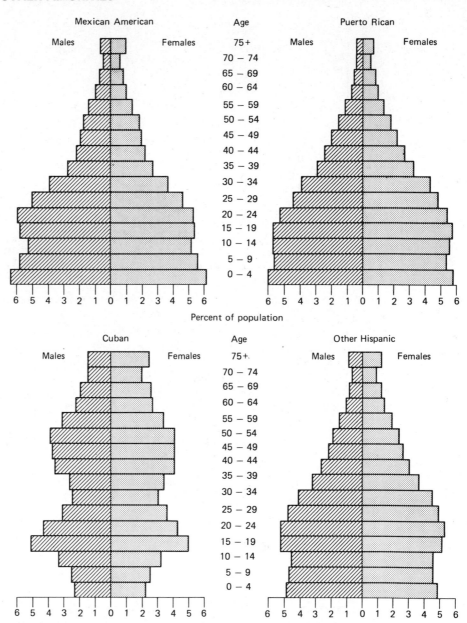

FIGURE 11.4

Age-Sex Composition of the Four Hispanic Groups: 1980

Based on data from *1980 Census of Population, General Population Characteristics,* Bureau of the Census.

TABLE 11.5
Occupations of Hispanic and All Workers, by Sex: 1981
(Numbers in Percent of Total Workers, by Sex)

Occupation	All Workers		Total Hispanics		Mexican American		Puerto Rican		Cuban	
	Men	Women	Men	Women	Men	Women	Men	Women	Men	Women
Professional and technical	15.9	17.0	7.7	8.8	5.7	8.0	8.5	11.6	12.9	9.9
Managers, Administrators	14.6	7.4	7.8	4.7	6.3	4.3	6.9	6.1	14.5	5.5
Sales	6.1	6.8	3.1	5.1	2.6	5.2	2.6	3.0	6.2	4.9
Clerical	6.3	34.7	6.4	31.9	5.0	32.4	13.1	36.4	9.4	31.9
Craft and kindred workers	20.7	1.9	20.1	2.4	20.9	2.5	15.4	2.5	20.7	2.2
Operatives, except transport	11.1	9.7	18.9	22.0	20.2	21.6	20.6	25.8	12.5	29.7
Transport equipment operatives	5.5	0.7	6.6	0.4	6.8	0.5	6.2	0.5	6.6	—
Nonfarm laborers	7.1	1.3	10.9	1.6	12.7	2.2	8.5	0.5	7.4	1.1
Service workers	8.9	19.4	13.3	21.4	12.2	21.1	17.6	13.1	9.4	14.8
Farm workers	3.9	1.1	5.2	1.6	7.5	2.5	0.3	0.5	0.4	—

Source: Dennis M. Roth, "Hispanics in the U.S. Labor Force," in Cary Davis, Carl Haub and JoAnne Willette, "U.S. Hispanics: Changing the Face of America," *Population Bulletin,* 38 (June 1983), 34, Population Reference Bureau.

1970s and their children. The narrow base shows their very low current fertility. Not included in this graphic depiction are the 125,000 Marielitos, mostly young males who arrived after the April 1, 1980 census.

Cubans are the most metropolitan of Hispanics, with virtually 100 percent living in metropolitan areas, particularly in Florida, New Jersey, New York, and California.[63] Cubans have a lower fertility rate, lower unemployment rate, higher median family income, greater education, and greater middle-class population composition than other Hispanic groups. Although 20 percent of the Marielitos are unemployable because they are unskilled, elderly, or physically or mentally handicapped, other Cubans secure well-paying jobs. As Table 11.5 shows, 27 percent are in professional, technical, or managerial positions, a figure comparing favorably with the national figure of 30 percent. They have an equal proportion of craft and kindred workers, the skilled workers category.

OTHER HISPANICS

The government's "Other Hispanics" category includes immigrants from sixteen different nations. The largest contingents come from the Dominican Republic, Colombia, Argentina, and Ecuador, joined, in recent years, by growing numbers of escapees from the political turmoil in El Salvador and Nicaragua. In the thirty-year period indicated in Table 11.4, the Other Hispanics have registered the largest gain, from 112,000 or 12 percent in the 1950s to 503,000 or 36 percent in the 1970s. The population doubles in these sixteen countries every thirty-five years, suggesting an ever-growing immigration for this group in future years.

Also included in this category in the census data are the Hispanos, people whose ancestors have lived for many generations in the United States. They properly belong in the Mexican-American category but distinguish themselves from the newer and poorer arrivals. Spaniards also fall under this classification.

During the 1970s, a total of 148,016 people emigrated to the United States from the Dominican Republic. In recent years they have been approaching the 20,000 maximum immigrants allowed annually from a single country. Most of the Dominicans are dark-skinned people, fleeing the poverty of their land. Because of lack of skills, they have a high unemployment rate. Many live in poor urban neighborhoods, suffering the deprivation and family disruption so common among those with low education and job skill levels. Racial discrimination further compounds their problems, and some find work as migrant farm laborers, away from urban troubles.

Spanish

Approximately 265,000 immigrants have come to the United States from Spain since 1820. In recent years an average of more than five thousand immigrants have arrived each year. Many of them settle in urban areas, seek employment in a variety of skilled and semiskilled occupations, and keep primarily to themselves. Although they speak the same language and usually have the same religion as other Hispanic groups, they do not, as a rule, interact with them in meaningful primary relationships.

One subcultural group from the Spanish mainland are the Basques, who began coming to the United States in the late nineteenth century. Though never large in number—there are only about 10,000 to 15,000 here today, including the second and third generations—they have played an important role in the West. Primarily settling in the bordering regions of Oregon, Idaho, Wyoming, Colorado, Nevada, and California, they came as sheepherders and dominated the sheep industry, including the support services of transportation and marketing, by the end of the nineteenth century. The old Western plot of conflict between cattle ranchers and sheepherders is based on fact, and these conflicts often involved the Basques. An intense hostility sometimes developed between the two groups, resulting in the Basques being stereotyped as "dirty" foreigners who were destroying the open range. But the Basques were a tenacious people who valued achievement in the face of adversity. Their quiet but ironlike determination held them in good stead, and they eventually overcame outgroup hostility. Although many Basques came to this country to stay, a good number also came as sojourners and returned to their native land.[64]

Colombians

Colombia is the South American country supplying the most immigrants, a total of 77,556 in the 1970s. Population pressures, better economic opportunities, and chain migration networking have increased the annual immigration totals recently, now averaging over 11,000 yearly. In addition, many illegal aliens come from Colombia, leading one observer to suggest over 300,000 Colombians now live in the United States.[65]

Colombians are mostly a light tan-skinned people, making them less susceptible to racial discrimination than some Caribbean Hispanics. They are a mixture of educated professionals and low-skilled peasants seeking a better life. Living mostly in urban neighborhoods near other Hispanics, they too form their own social clubs and institutions, attempting to preserve their culture through ethnic folk dance groups and holiday celebrations.

OTHER CARIBBEAN PEOPLES

English- and French-speaking Caribbean people have also emigrated to the United States in substantial numbers. While they come from the same region, their languages and cultures set them apart from each other and from the Hispanic peoples as well. Most of them are dark-skinned; encountering racial discrimination in housing, jobs, and other social interactions is a common, though new, experience for them.

Guadeloupe, Martinque, and French Guiana send very few immigrants. English-speaking immigrants from The Bahamas, Bermuda, British Virgin Islands, Dominica, and other small islands also send a few hundred or less each year. Barbados, Trinidad, and Tobago average several thousand immigrants yearly, and they may become larger suppliers soon as the chain migration process intensifies. The two major suppliers are Haiti and Jamaica, whose immigrants we shall now briefly discuss.

Haitians

In the 1970s, 58,705 legal immigrants from Haiti entered the United States. In the 1980s, slightly more than 6,000 are entering annually. What drew public attention, however, was the 15,000 Haitian boat people in 1980, and another 8,000 arriving on the South Florida shore in small, rickety boats in 1981. Not officially recognizing the Duvalier regime as politically oppressive, the U.S. government defined the refugees as ineligible for asylum because they were fleeing for economic, not political, reasons. Placed in one of seventeen detention camps, most Haitians

BOX 11.3

> *"I think the melting pot idea . . . is not a workable idea."*

"The Colombians here are the poor people. They are the ones who had no chance for an education in Colombia. They are the ones who—because they had no education—their pay was very meager. And so over here they have a better life than they would in Colombia. So over here they really—if you can call it the American Dream—has been fulfilled in them.

"Emotionally they're very attached to their country. See, this is the thing that is very hard for people to understand. They want them to become American and to forget everything. You can't! The ties—the blood ties—are too strong! You just can't become—as I said, I cannot even become an American. I can't! Even if I wanted to. You would have to make me all over again. And I love this country and I choose to stay in this country.

"Now with these people—take some of them. They have come because of necessity—sheer necessity. We criticize them because they don't love America, but I don't think that is the fact. Also, if you notice the kind of people that come here. For instance, I had students who were the children of my father's workers on the coffee plantation. Now in my country they were tilling the soil. You know, the children of the owner go to school. The children of the worker go to till the soil. They had no chance of an education. They had huts up in the mountains where they had no running water, no electricity. Now they come here and they have all the conveniences. If they live poorly, Americans criticize them but they don't realize where they were living before. If they're not clean and spotless and they don't keep the shades the right way—but these people have been doing this for a hundred years! The people who just came in never even had a shade to talk about. They never had a venetian blind. They never even had a window to talk about!" (Laughs.)

"I think we have to be careful because we often make the mistake of imposing our way to the people. Now you could say, we're not going to them, they're coming here. But if you accept them in the country, I think you also have to accept a big risk. I think the melting pot idea is not the prevalent idea. It is not a workable idea. Each one has a culture. Each people has a culture and if you want them in America, if you allow them to stay here, you have to work something by which each one is able to live. I don't mean to say that we have independent little countries, but that they are comfortable. Because you cannot remove—those are strong things that you cannot remove from a person."

Colombian immigrant who came to the United States in 1952 at age 16

lingered for almost a year until a federal court ruling declared the policy illegal. Now the Coast Guard actively turns back Haitian refugees at sea, preventing further boatloads. The 1980 census found 90,000 people identifying themselves as Haitian-Americans, though government officials estimate an equal number of Haitians are also here illegally.

From 50,000 to 60,000 Haitians live in Dade County, Florida. A 1983 study by the Behavorial Science Institute at Coral Gables concluded that the 22,800 Haitians living in the Edison-Little River community, which includes Little Haiti, "face substantial problems."[66] Half were unemployed, half could not speak English, and two-thirds had a household income of less than $150 a week, paying $175 monthly for crowded, deteriorating housing infested with rats and roaches. Their strong desire to be self-sufficient made them reluctant to turn to public agency assistance, despite an unemployment rate four times the national average.

Another large concentration of Haitians lives in New York City, perhaps over 100,000. Besides problems of employment and racial discrimination, Haitians face the stigma of association with AIDS, since about 5 percent of AIDS victims have been Haitian. About one-third of all migrant farm laborers on the East Coast are Haitians.[67] Others work usually in low-paying jobs in service industries, mainly because of the language barrier and lack of skills. Some are also middle-class professionals, particularly the earlier arrivals and some of the legal immigrants.

Most Haitians are French-speaking Catholics with a fierce pride in themselves and their heritage. One study showed their insistence upon retaining a Haitian identity was to avoid entry into the racial structure as black Americans. They received better treatment from white Americans that way, they discovered, than by claiming a black identity.[68] As a result, second-generation Haitian-Americans have been slow to make an identity transition as well.

Jamaicans

Jamaicans are rapidly becoming a sizable minority. A total of 103,752 emigrated to the United States in the 1970s (Table 11.6) and, given their yearly totals thus far in the 1980s, they should surpass that total in this decade. Most appear to be settling on the East Coast in urban environments.

Jamaica itself is a plural society, with three layered sections: a small white section at the top, at the bottom a black section comprising about four-fifths of the population, and a brown section in between.[69] Within this "hierarchally arrayed mosaic of total communities," each provides its members with the entire range of life experience.[70] Most of the immigrants coming to the United States, reflecting their nation's population composition, are Blacks. On the island they practice a folk culture containing numerous elements reminiscent of African societies and Caribbean slavery.[71] Their first language is English, although their rapid speech patterning and clipped accent cause some difficulty for a first-time listener.

Economic opportunity is the primary motivation for immigration. Tourism and the limited economy cannot support the growing population base. Adapting quite easily to American society, first-generation Jamaican-Americans find their initial encounters with racism bitter and difficult experiences. Some become disillusioned and return home, but most remain to pursue their goals. Second-generation Jamaican-Americans appear to be integrating into society as black Americans. It remains to be seen whether the present Jamaican communities become more structured, encouraging cultural pluralism through the continuing arrival of newcomers, or if a short-term integration process continues.

TABLE 11.6
Western Hemisphere Immigrants
Leading Countries, 1971–1980

1. Mexico	640,294
2. Cuba	276,788
3. Dominican Republic	148,016
4. Canada	114,845
5. Jamaica	103,752
6. Colombia	77,556
7. Trinidad & Tobago	61,776
8. Haiti	58,705
9. Ecuador	50,161
10. El Salvador	34,347
11. Peru	29,098
12. Guatemala	25,574

Source: U.S. Immigration and Naturalization Service.

SOCIOLOGICAL ANALYSIS

Like other immigrant groups before them, the new arrivals from the Caribbean and Latin America are beginning to change the face of America, making their distinctive contributions to the neighborhoods in which they live. But with their growing numbers they are also encountering the hostility historically accorded almost all newly arriving ethnic groups. Application of sociological perspectives can thus place their current experiences in a comparative context.

The Functionalist View

Rapid population growth has been a mixed blessing for Hispanic-Americans. They have been able to develop supportive ethnic subcommunities, providing social institutions and an interactive network which ease readjustment to a new country. Cuban settlement in deteriorated urban neighborhoods has both revitalized those areas and brought, out of necessity, interethnic assistance to other Hispanic groups. Because 85 percent of all Hispanics live in nine states (California, Arizona, Colorado, New Mexico, Texas, Illinois, New York, New Jersey, Florida), they are quickly realizing their potential political power, enabling them to make their presence felt for improvement of their life situation. Concern exists that their numbers and common language may be dysfunctional, delaying assimilation and creating a "Hispanic Quebec" within the United States.

Most of the newcomers lack sufficient education and job skills to escape a below- or near-poverty existence (See Figure 11.5). Yet the existence of a dual economy—industries on the periphery such as garment factories, restaurants, and hotels dependent on low-skill workers, even illegals or minors—provides barrio residents with job opportunities.[72] Illegals or low-skill legal immigrants even promote domestic employment, keeping alive some manual labor that might other-

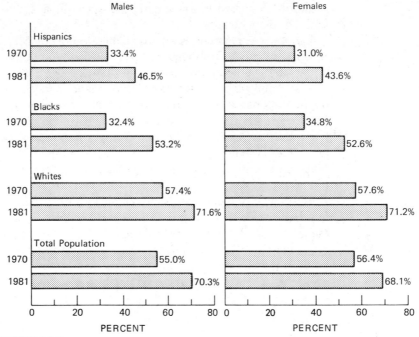

Males   Females

Hispanics

1970   33.4%   31.0%
1981   46.5%   43.6%

Blacks

1970   32.4%   34.8%
1981   53.2%   52.6%

Whites

1970   57.4%   57.6%
1981   71.6%   71.2%

Total Population

1970   55.0%   56.4%
1981   70.3%   68.1%

0   20   40   60   80 0   20   40   60   80
PERCENT   PERCENT

FIGURE 11.5

Hispanics, Blacks, Whites, and Total Population Aged 25 and Over Who Completed
Four Years of High School or More: 1970 and 1981

wise be automated. Although they take poor-paying jobs other U.S. workers do
not want, they have a dysfunctional impact in that they tend to hold wages down.
Further, by condoning the existence of an underclass, legal or illegal, we undermine fundamental concepts of personal rights, equality of opportunity, and tolerance of cultural diversity.

Rapid social change is the keystone to functional analysis of existing problems.
The influx of large numbers in a short period of time and the changing occupational structure of American society have prevented the social system from absorbing so many low-skill workers right away. Adjustments must be made to ease
Hispanic integration into society, and time is necessary for the acculturation and
assimilation process to work.

The Conflict View

Internal colonialism analysts maintain the continued residential segregation of
Mexican-Americans in ghetto areas of cities in five southwestern states is unlike
the European immigrant pattern, where the level of segregation declined with length
of residence in the United States. Instead of a gradual acculturation or structural
assimilation process, they see the persistence of subordination, with Mexican-
Americans confined to certain areas of rental properties controlled by absentee

landlords, restricted to low-paying job opportunities, inferior schools, and many forms of discrimination.

Economic exploitation is another dimension of conflict analysis. Mexicans, Puerto Ricans, and other Caribbean peoples work as migrant farm laborers in many parts under abysmal conditions for meager pay despite repeated exposes. City sweat-shops—employing thousands of illegal aliens, refugees, and low-skilled legal immigrants—operate in clandestine settings, prospering from the toil of low-wage employees. The rise of an ethnic bourgeoise—the *padrino* in urban or farm settings, the token elite among the Chicano population, or the small middle class with other Hispanic groups—only helps control the rest, say conflict theorists, and does not foretell an economic upgrading and assimilation of the remaining group members.

Resolution of the inferior status of millions of Hispanic-Americans, according to this view, will occur through protest movements, organized resistance to exploitation, and the flexing of political muscle. Spanish-speaking people need to realize more fully their commonalities, take a lesson from the Irish and use their ballot power to create the necessary changes to benefit themselves. If they effectively wield their political clout, they will begin to overcome the power differential existing in the social and economic spheres as well.

The Interactionist View

Anglo–Hispanic relations are often strained by inaccurate perceptions. Dominant group members tend to think of one Spanish-speaking public, when a variety exist, each preferring different foods, music, recreation, and possessing different cultural attributes. Too many Anglos interpret Hispanic ethnic subcommunities, parallel social institutions, and limited command of English as detrimental to the cohesiveness of American society, failing to realize that 83 percent are first-generation Americans repeating a resettlement pattern of earlier European immigrants. Extensive poverty among most Hispanics, including about 20 percent of the Marielitos, often generates the classic "blaming the victim" approach or culture-of-poverty thinking. Instead of confronting the problem of poor education, lack of job skills and job opportunities, some find fault with the group itself, reacting with avoidance, indifference, or paternalistic actions.

In our previous discussion about eye contact, physical proximity, the notions of hurrying, and revelance of time, we identified a few areas of potential cultural misunderstanding. Add to this Anglo impatience with language problems, black concern about economic competition, taxpayer resistance to increased welfare demands, labor union fears of wages undermined by cheap labor, and nativist alarm at the failure of the melting pot to "melt" the Hispanics, and you have further reasons for dominant-group members to stereotype the Latinos as an increasing social problem. Since perceptions influence interaction patterns and social policy, the potential for tensions and conflict is strong. The antibilingual ordinance passed by Florida's Dade County voters in 1980 is but one illustration of people defining a situation and acting upon that definition.

For Hispanics, clinging to one's culture and ethnic identity is a matter of pride and personal commitment to a rich heritage. Some find it their only solace against discrimination in a hostile land, but even those who achieve economic mobility retain a strong ethnic identification. Washed afresh with new waves of Hispanic immigrants, the ethnic communities retain an ethnic vitality, prompting even successful Hispanics to hold onto their ethnic traditions. Interactionists thus point to the resiliency of an ethnic self-definition, somewhat at odds with assimilationist views.

RETROSPECT

In many ways the Hispanic immigrants have been repeating the patterns of earlier racial and ethnic groups. Coming in large numbers from impoverished lands, many have entered the lowest strata of society, clustered together in substandard housing units, and faced the problems of adjustment, deprivation, frustration, and pathology (sickness and crime). Marked as strangers by their language, customs, and physical appearance, they have difficulty being accepted and gaining economic security. Ironically, the Hispanic poor face the same problems and are condemned for them in the same way as earlier groups. They are also condemned for failing to overcome these problems immediately, even though other groups often took three generations to do so. Dominant-minority response patterns are thus quite similar to those of earlier immigrant peoples.

What is particularly significant for the Hispanic immigrants in comparison to other groups is the changed structural conditions. The restrictive immigration laws in the 1920s drastically curtailed the great influx of southern, eastern, and central Europeans. This meant that those immigrants already here did not receive continuous cultural reinforcement from new arrivals. Not only is there a sizable flow of new Hispanic arrivals, but rapid and inexpensive communications and transportation encourage return trips to the not-so-far-away homeland. In addition, the earlier European immigrants encountered sometimes heavy-handed attempts at Americanization, whereas the Hispanics come at a time when pluralism and ethnic resurgence is common among dominant-group members.

Another crucial change in structural conditions has taken place in technology and the job market. When the European poor came to America, they could find many unskilled and semiskilled jobs. There were many evils and abuses in industry, but an immigrant could secure a little piece of the American Dream through hard physical labor. The Hispanic immigrant today enters a contracting labor market, not an expanding one, and so jobs are harder to find. Technology has eliminated a great many low-skill jobs and reduced the total number of blue collar jobs, and the demand now is for skilled blue collar and white collar workers. The poor of the Western Hemisphere are not qualified for these positions; they find they cannot improve their lot through hard physical labor because this labor is no longer there to be found.

During the mass European migration, the fledgling labor unions struggled to improve, and eventually did improve, the economic situation of the immigrant workers. As the economy contracts, the government uses welfare as the answer to the economic problems of today's nonworking poor. In fact, throughout the

1950s and 1960s the government encouraged individuals to apply for welfare by liberalizing eligibility requirements. With structural unemployment leaving no alternative, the system maneuvers many Hispanics into dependence on welfare.

Highly visible because of their numbers, language, culture, and poverty, many Hispanic-Americans find themselves the objects of resentment, hostility, and overt discrimination from the dominant society. The familiar pattern of blaming the victim results in negative stereotyping, social segregation, and all shades of prejudice and discrimination against the Hispanic poor.

Not all Hispanic-Americans are poor, of course. For those who are not, attaining economic security means a very different life experience. Other positive factors offer some promise of easing the transition to American life: bilingual education, increased public awareness, a greater tolerance for cultural pluralism, civic and governmental programs. Serious problems still remain for a disproportionate number of Hispanic-Americans, however, and it is too soon to tell whether the new legislation designed to control illegal aliens will have any impact on the Hispanic poor.

Even if greater upward mobility occurs, this will not necessarily lead to assimilation. Many variables within both the dominant and minority societies are encouraging cultural and structural pluralism. The present-day public focus is more upon eliminating the problems of poverty among culturally distinct groups than upon eliminating the cultural distinctions. Just how successful these efforts will be has yet to be determined.

REVIEW QUESTIONS

1. What are some of the cultural value orientations shared to some degree by most Hispanics?

2. What changes in American structural conditions make upward mobility difficult for many of the newcomers?

3. How diverse a group are Mexican-Americans? What factors continue poverty status among so many of them?

4. What factors distinguish the Puerto Rican experience from that of other Hispanic groups?

5. How do Cubans differ in cultural values and economic mobility?

6. Who are some of the other Hispanic and Caribbean peoples migrating in significant numbers, and why are they doing so?

SUGGESTED READINGS

Acuna, Rodolf. *Occupied America,* 2nd ed. New York: Harper & Row, 1980.
　　A comprehensive analysis of current Chicano problems and struggles, rooted in nineteenth-century military conquest.

Ashabranner, Brent. *The New Americans.* New York: Dodd, Mead, 1983.
   Fine, sweeping study of the various Hispanic groups in the United States, with analytical data on each.

Cortés, Carlos E. (ed.) *Latinos in the United States.* New York: Arno Press, 1980.
   A rich anthology of useful overviews and studies of all Latinos in Florida, Chicago, and New York City, including Dominicans and Haitians.

Fitzpatrick, Joseph P. *Puerto Rican Americans,* 2nd ed. Englewood Clffs, N.J.: Prentice-Hall, 1976.
   A still pertinent, classic portrait of Puerto Ricans on the mainland, their values, traditions, and problems.

Lewis, Oscar. *La Vida: A Puerto Rican Family in the Culture of Poverty—San Juan and New York.* New York: Random House, 1965.
   Controversial yet classic case study of Puerto Rican families, arguing the existence of a self-perpetuating poverty subculture.

Moore, Joan W. *Mexican Americans,* 2nd ed. Englewood Cliffs, N.J.: Prentice-Hall, 1976.
   Good overview of the socioeconomic characteristics of Mexican Americans and contributing factors toward their deprivation.

CHAPTER 12

RELIGIOUS
MINORITIES

Any study of race and ethnicity must include religion as well. For some immigrant groups—German and Russian Jews or Irish and Italian Catholics, for instance—religion and ethnicity have been heavily intertwined, providing the focus for understanding both their group solidarity and initial societal hostility toward them. Sometimes the religious group itself is an ethnic group—the Amish, for example. Another aspect of intergroup relations is the unfortunate reality that religion can also generate ingroup–outgroup stereotyping, misunderstandings, and conflict, just as racial and ethnic groups sometimes do.

Religion, like race and ethnicity, often evokes an emotional response in people, sometimes more so. Many individuals find it difficult to be neutral about religion. For some, it is impossible to accept the idea that religious beliefs other than their own are equally legitimate. Since religion often serves as the basis for accepting or rejecting mates, friends, neighbors, schools, and employees, it often has a polarizing effect. Religious differences not only differentiate persons, but can be divisive as well, by emphasizing separateness or superiority, thereby defining others as inferior (heretics, infidels, heathens, nonbelievers). Because religion does stir strong emotional feelings, our previous considerations of how people respond to defined strangers become even more pertinent when discussing religious minorities.

We are a more secular society today, religious differences no longer fanning the flames of intense bigotry and acts of mob violence. Though we may not be torn apart like Northern Ireland or Lebanon, to assume religious harmony prevails throughout the land would be a mistake. Religious conflicts still occur, incorrect stereotypes still find acceptance, and religious prejudice still exists. Because of their beliefs, some religious minorities—such as the Amish and Rastafarians—encounter conflicts with the dominant society. Issues such as abortion, birth control, and school prayer continue to bring people of varying religious beliefs into conflict with one another as well. In this chapter we shall examine both past and present patterns of religious tolerance and conflict in the United States, specifically discussing some groups who have either experienced problems similar to racial or ethnic groups discussed in previous chapters, or who continue as viable religious subcultures in this pluralistic society.

SOCIOHISTORICAL PERSPECTIVE

Since the time of the Pilgrims, this nation has been the haven for many religious groups fleeing persecution and seeking religious freedom. Some instances of religious intolerance did occur during colonial times though, such as the expulsion of Anne Hutchinson and Roger Williams and their followers from Massachusetts, and denial of political office holding to Catholics in Maryland. As the isolated settlements, many of a single religious persuasion, evolved into interactive colonies, Anglo-Saxon Protestantism dominated. Nevertheless, the Founding Fathers built into the Constitution two fundamental principles: separation of church and state, and freedom of religion. Those two hallmarks bestowed a unique legacy on American culture which continues to the present day. Unlike most nations where one or a few faiths dominate, the United States has an immense diversity of faiths. Over 1,500 religious groups exist, 200 of which are conventional Christian and Jewish denominations, 24 of which have a membership exceeding one million.[1]

What is notable about so many immigrant groups is the significance religion has played in their lives. The church, synagogue, or temple so often became the major social institution of their ethnic communities, functioning both as a spiritual bond reinforcing group identity and as the social, educational, even political base of their activities. Strikingly, Harvard University—founded in 1630—illustrates an early effort to educate clergy to minister to the spiritual needs of the people. Visits to various New England towns reveal a church prominently situated by the village green, in the center of the community, the place in which town meetings brought participatory democracy to reality. Similarly, in the remnants of white ethnic neighborhoods in northeastern cities, in midwestern farming communities, in the southwestern states, and in specific places like St. Augustine, Florida or New Orleans, the still-standing religious edifices and recorded ethnic community histories and studies offer abundant testimony to the role religion played among first- and second-generation Americans.

The clergy have always provided important leadership among racial and ethnic groups. In addition to spiritual guidance, they often have provided the rallying force to enhance community cohesiveness, economic, and social welfare, while advocating to the host society improved circumstances for their people. Priests, rabbis, and ministers frequently have been in the forefront of concerted efforts to ease immigrant transition to American life and their entry into the economic mainstream. Black ministers, such as Martin Luther King and Jesse Jackson, have consistently been in the vanguard for civil rights and equality. Driving the point home, religious leaders throughout American history have played an important role, not only in shaping the values and moral behavior of their congregations, but in influencing public policy, encouraging charitable activities, and implementing the spirit of the Constitution.

Unfortunately, not all religious leaders have been magnanimous in promoting equality nor have all religions experienced tolerance in the American experience. Some—Catholics, Jews, and Mormons—have been victims of discrimination, persecution, and even violence. Others—Amish, Christian Scientists, Jehovah's Witnesses, Rastafarians—have come into conflict with society over their religious beliefs. Even though the ideal culture stresses freedom of religion, in practice religious bigotry and intolerance have caused suffering and hardship to some religious minorities in the United States.

AMERICAN CATHOLICS

Catholicism did not gain easy acceptance in the United States. By the midseventeenth century, all the colonies had passed laws designed to thwart Catholic immigration, most of them denying Catholics citizenship, voting, and office-holding rights.[2] Until 1830, the nation remained almost exclusively a Protestant domain. For the next thirty years, immigration had a profound political and social impact on the nation. Over a half-million immigrants in the 1830s, 1.7 million in the 1840s, and 2.6 million in the 1850s—the great bulk of them Roman Catholics, mostly Irish and German peasants—entered the country. A feeling of alarm spread among American Protestants who believed Catholics would subvert the nation.

Societal Hostility

Samuel F.B. Morse, inventor of the telegraph and son of a militant minister, railed against an alleged Papist conspiracy to overwhelm the nation with Catholic immigrants and take control. He exhorted Americans not to be "deceived by Jesuit-controlled immigrants." Instead, they should "fly to protect the vulnerable places of your Constitution and Laws. Place your guards; you will need them, and quickly too.—And first, shut your gates."[3]

Lurid, best-selling exposés of the Catholic Church appeared. Rebecca Reed fabricated a story about her life in a convent in Charlestown, Massachusetts, resulting in the burning of that Ursuline Convent in 1834. Two years later, the most infamous of these inflammatory works appeared: *Awful Disclosures of the Hotel Dieu Nunnery of Montreal* by Maria Monk. The author claimed to be an escaped nun, kept prisoner in the Montreal convent against her will, and forced to have sexual relations with priests. Resisting nuns were killed, as were any babies born; all bodies were thrown into a lime pit. Even though Maria Monk was later discredited as a prostitute and fraud when investigations uncovered no evidence to support her charges, many believed her story. The monograph was frequently reprinted, selling hundreds of thousands of copies, spawning a sequel and many imitators.

Throughout the 1850s nativist hostility against Catholics intensified, with the Know-Nothing movement spearheading most of the agitation. Not unexpectedly, violence erupted. Mobs rioted, burning Catholic churches, schools, convents, and homes. One particularly effective diatribe against Catholics was Josiah Strong's *Our Country* (1855), accusing Catholic immigrants of immorality, crime, corruption, and socialism. Reprinted in numerous editions, it incited the public for decades. Reverend Justin H. Fulton was also effective, his anti-Catholic books, *Rome in America* (1887) and *Washington in the Lap of Rome* (1888), claiming a Catholic threat to America's liberty through the school system and control of the government. Another Maria Monk type, Margaret Lisle Shepherd, published her autobiography, *My Life in a Convent* (1887), claiming to be an escaped nun who fled priests' carnal lust. Her story, though false, was widely believed and added to the anti-Catholic chorus.

In 1887, a short-lived but highly successful anti-Catholic organization, the American Protective Association (APA), emerged out of Iowa to a national force of about 500,000 members.[4] Dedicated to keeping Catholics out of office, employing only Protestants, and being noncooperative with Catholics in any strikes, the APA struck a responsive chord with many working-class Americans believing Catholic immigrants were coming to take their jobs, particularly after the panic of 1893 and the ensuing unemployment. Enjoying some success in the East and none in the South, the APA was most successful throughout the Midwest. Although its endorsed candidates gained control of city governments in Detroit, Kansas City, and Milwaukee, resulting in the firing of all Catholic officials in those cities, the APA sowed the seeds of its own destruction. Internecine fighting, charges of corruption and embezzlement of funds, and a violent reputation combined to bring a rapid decline to the APA so that it had no power after 1896.[5]

Anti-Catholicism did not end, however. In 1911, General Nelson Miles, former Army Chief of Staff and Congressional Medal of Honor recipient, organized the Guardians of Liberty in upstate New York in 1911. Dedicated to keeping Catholics out of office because they would supposedly take their orders from Rome, this group never did have any real political clout. An anti-Catholic publication, *The Menace,* developed over 1.5 million readers, mostly rural. The Catholic Church lost its lawsuit to revoke *The Menace*'s mailing privileges on the grounds of obscenity because of its graphic depictions of the alleged immorality of the Catholic Church.[6] A total of sixty-one anti-Catholic periodicals appeared prior to World War I.[7]

The post-World War I period saw the resurrection of the Ku Klux Klan, dedicated to the theme of Catholicism and Judaism as alien to Americanism. As discussed more fully in Chapter 6, the KKK grew to a membership of 2 to 3 million members, and was partly responsible for passage of the restrictive immigration laws of 1921 and 1924. Thereafter, it declined in numbers and influence, its final hurrah a slanderous campaign in 1928 against Democratic presidential candidate, Al Smith, the Catholic governor of New York.

Values and Practices

Several factors help explain nativist hostility against American Catholics in past years. We must first remember religion played a far greater role in people's lives in previous centuries, making religious differences of greater concern. Generations of Catholic–Protestant conflict in Europe had formed a legacy of latent antagonism among European Americans. American Protestantism had evolved along with the American culture, stressing individualism and self-reliance, whether in making one's fortune or gaining salvation through the teachings of the Bible. Several of the parallel social institutions of Catholics provided ammunition for Protestant attack and anxiety.

Religion

Because Catholics followed church dogma, or prescribed doctrine, operating their local churches as part of a vast bureaucracy with a hierarchy of authority reaching back to the Pope in Rome as the head of the Church, many Protestants feared this structure would undermine the American way of life. They envisioned millions of Catholic immigrants marching to the orders of a foreign potentate (the Pope), as unthinking, indoctrinated, docile followers; if such people gained political office, some Protestants feared control of the country from Rome. The physical presence of priests and nuns, the building of churches, convents, and parochial schools— all virtually nonexistent in the United States before—served to confirm the worst Protestant fears.

Other Catholic practices puzzled and disturbed many Protestant Americans. They considered vows of celibacy among priests and nuns as unnatural, leading many to believe the lurid fabrications that were printed about the sexual practices amongst the religious orders and the priesthood. Mandatory attendance at the weekly repetition of the same Mass ceremony then spoken in Latin seemed to them both un-American and repressive of individual thought. Use of a private confessional booth to tell one's sins to a priest, unlike the usual Protestant practice of silent confession during worship services, seemed bizarre to some. While Catholics themselves understood and accepted the context of their own beliefs and practices, to Protestants these outgroup differences were not only strange but threatening.

Education

Perhaps more than anything else, Catholic education generated the most conflict between Catholics and Protestants. In public schools, daily reading from the King James Bible was one of several factors prompting Catholics to establish parochial schools in order to provide religious training and moral guidance for their children. Efforts in the 1840s to obtain public funding for parochial schools, or substitution of the Catholic version of the Bible for Catholic students in public schools, generated fierce controversy in Boston, New York, Philadelphia, and Cincinnati.[8] The issue of public funding for parochial schools flared up again in the 1870s, but the opposition of President Grant and the Republican party negated any organized nativist opposition. Efforts in the 1880s in Massachusetts and several midwestern states (Ohio, Illinois, Wisconsin) to regulate parochial schools generated intense controversy.[9] Throughout this period Protestant periodicals argued that the public school system would end the "ignorance and superstition" of Catholic children, and so campaigned not only against public funding of parochial schools but for their elimination.[10]

The Present Scene

Today Roman Catholics in the United States number over 51.2 million, the largest single religious denomination in the country. Overt discrimination against them has ended, and except for recent Hispanic-Catholic immigrants, they are assimilated into the economic and political mainstream. They can be found in all occupations and in many leadership roles. John F. Kennedy became the first Catholic president in 1960, and in the 98th Congress, Catholics totaled 142, ranking first among denominations and continuing a twenty-year upward trend in electing national legislators.

Greater dialogue occurs between Protestant and Catholic religious leaders, an outgrowth of the ecumenical movement initiated by Pope John XXIII two decades ago. An acute shortage of priests has obliged the laity to become more active: reading Scripture, leading music, and distributing Communion at services, and taking leadership positions in nearly every phase of the church's life: religious instruction, family life bureaus, financial, and administrative positions. With both men and women handling these church tasks, Catholics have in some ways become more like several Protestant denominations and thus less "different" to outsiders. Catholic social views tend to agree with those of conservative Protestants in regard to a variety of subjects, including pornography, abortion, birth control, and school prayer.

Problem areas still remain. Public funding for parochial schools, though endorsed by President Reagan, remains a controversial subject and has been consistently rejected by Congress. In May 1983, American Catholic bishops released a pastoral letter condemning most uses of nuclear arms as immoral, thereby plunging the Church into the arms race controversy. Similarly, Church positions on abortion and birth control create controversies both among Catholics themselves and within American society. These difficult moral issues offer no easy solution, pitting people with strong but opposing convictions against one another, with the Catholic Church right in the middle.

JEWISH-AMERICANS

Jewish people are a unique minority, since they are not a specific nationality, racial, ethnic, or even religious grouping. Although religion has been an important bond among Jews, it is not a cohesive force in that three separate branches of Judaism exist—Orthodox, Conservative, and Reform; many agnostics and atheists also identify themselves as Jews. Varying in physical appearance, native languages, and cultural attributes, Jewishness is that elusive quality Franklin Giddings called "consciousness of kind." Jews are people who think of themselves as such, with outgroup members treating them accordingly.

Immigration Prior to 1880

The first group of Jewish immigrants—four men, six women, and thirteen younger people—arrived in New Amsterdam in 1654 as refugees from the Portuguese takeover of Dutch-ruled Brazil. Benefiting from tolerant Dutch rule, Jews experienced open acceptance in this settlement. Later many Jewish refugees of Spanish and Portuguese origin, fleeing the Spanish Inquisition, came to the United States by way of Holland, the West Indies, or South America. By the end of the eighteenth century, about 2,000 to 3,000 Sephardic Jews were living in America.[11]

Most of our earlier comments about nativist hostility against Catholics apply equally well to Jewish immigrants. All of the English colonies discouraged Jewish immigration, also passing statutes against their voting or holding office. When Jews were permitted to vote in New York in 1736, a group of residents claimed the election was fraudulent on that basis.[12] When the Know-Nothing movement reached its heights in the 1850s, the Know-Nothings criticized and discriminated against "this peculiar race of people."[13] During the Civil War, former Know-Nothing member, Ulysses S. Grant, acting on unwarranted charges that Jews were profiteering through smuggling and cotton speculation, issued General Order Number 11, expelling all civilian Jews from his military jurisdiction.[14] On January 4, 1863, Lincoln revoked this order.

By the midnineteenth century, the second wave of Jewish migration had begun. These Ashkenazic Jews came mostly from the German provinces; they were more prosperous and better educated than earlier German-Jewish immigrants. This was the first mass Jewish immigration—groups of entire families from a single locality or community. From an 1840 Jewish population of 15,000, Jewish-Americans increased to 50,000 in 1850, 150,000 in 1860, and 250,000 in 1880. By that time, Jewish-American communities were almost exclusively German communities.

Newcomers and Tension

The third wave was the most significant—in numbers, cultural influence, work contributions, and dominant-group reaction. From 250,000 in 1880, the Jewish population rose to almost 3 million before generally restrictive immigration laws were enacted in the 1920s. The initial impetus for this massive migration was the pogroms that followed the assassination of Czar Alexander II (1881). Though no Jews were involved in the regicide, the Czarist government used them as a scapegoat to divert people's attention from long-festering social, political, and economic grievances. This marked the beginning of a long series of pogroms, with many attacks, loss of lives, and extensive property damage in Jewish communities throughout the Russian Empire's Pale of Settlement. In addition to the need to escape government-incited violence, there were powerful economic incentives for emigration. Some people came to escape from destitution. Others fled from economic instability that resulted from government efforts to industrialize Russia.

Considerable cultural tensions developed among Jews from the different areas of Europe. Some Sephardic Jews, the first to be transplanted to America, considered themselves superior to German Jewish newcomers (Ashkenazic), who later looked with disdain on newcomers from eastern Europe. Although a few Jewish immigrants from central and eastern Europe had arrived as early as the eighteenth century, for some Jewish ethnics the distinctions based on place of origin and time of arrival in America persisted well into the mid-1940s, as this report indicates:

The earlier arrivals scarred the later ones as crude, superstitious, and economically indigent, and the latter despised the former as snobs and religious renegades. As recently as 1925, one student of immigrant groups asserted that "intermarriage between a Sephardic Jew and a Russian Jew, for instance, is as rare, if not rarer, than intermarriage between Jew and Gentile." Even within each of these divisions of Jews there was at first aversion to marriage with some of the subdivisions. Bavarian Jews hesitated to marry with those German Jews who came from the area near the Polish border, derisively labelled "Pollacks." The Russian Jew looked down on the Polish and Galician Jews and refused to marry them or permit his children to do so. Although these intra-Jewish barriers to marriage have largely disappeared in recent times, first generation Jewish parents may still go through the motions of embarrassment when their children marry the sons and daughters of a ridiculed sub-group.[15]

Thus ethnic prejudices as well as cultural and class differences led to strain between the "old" Jewish population and the "new" Jewish arrivals. Some German Jews, who had by this time supplanted the Sephardic Jews as an ethnic elite, were embarrassed by their lowly coreligionists with their strange appearance, Yiddish language, and orthodox religious practices. At first, many rejected the new arrivals, partly out of fear that growing anti-Semitic feeling in American society would place all Jews—old and new—into one negative category. Soon, however, the established community developed organizations that helped the newcomers adjust to their surroundings. Additionally, they made strenuous efforts to settle the newcomers in widely dispersed farm communities, away from the congested urban centers.[16]

Anti-Semitism

Anti-Jewish stereotyping spread in the arts and the media as it had for other immigrant groups, such as the Irish and Asians. On stage the Jew was sometimes depicted as either a scoundrel or a comic character. Newspapers and magazines at times ran cartoons and editorials that were clearly anti-Semitic in nature. One example was *Life* magazine, published in New York City, where the Jewish population rose from 4 percent in 1880 to 25 percent in 1910. The magazine called the city "Jew York" and attacked the ostensible Jewish clannishness, pushiness, and domination of the theater. In the early twentieth century about half of the actors, songwriters, publishers, and entrepreneurs in New York City were Jewish; this included those who worked in the flourishing Yiddish language theater serving the immigrant community. *Life*'s editors launched a ten-year attack on the "Jewish Theatrical Trust," accusing it of poisoning American values, of lowering the moral tone by running lascivious plays for profit. The accusations were false or distorted. The Yiddish theater may have catered to a specific ethnic group and thus have been "different," but the plays were not lewd or lascivious.

Two notorious incidents emphasize the heights anti-Semitic feelings reached in the late nineteenth and early twentieth centuries. In the first instance, Joseph Seligman, an eminent banker and frequent guest of President Grant at the White House, was denied accommodations in 1877 at a fashionable resort hotel in Saratoga Springs, New York. Although he and his family had stayed there several times before, the hotel's new policy of "not accepting Israelites" made headlines across the country. This incident brought latent anti-Jewish attitudes into the open, and many other establishments quickly followed suit.

The second incident concerned Leo Frank, the manager of an Atlanta pencil factory, who was hastily convicted, on very flimsy evidence, of murdering a young factory girl. Many felt that he was convicted because he was a Jew. His case in 1913 led directly to the formation of the B'nai B'rith's Anti-Defamation League.

This anti-Semitic cartoon, appearing in the March 29, 1900 issue of *Life,* was part of the magazine's ten-year campaign against the ''Jewish Theatrical Trust.'' The publication inaccurately accused Jewish theatrical producers and actors of attempting to corrupt American morals by staging lewd and lascivious plays.

With prominent Georgia newspapers and clergymen calling for a new trial and many Jews financing his appeal, anti-Semitic feelings intensified in the state. When the governor commuted Frank's execution to life imprisonment, an act praised by the Georgia press, some of the dead girl's friends and neighbors abducted Frank from the state prison, transported him 175 miles to the girl's home town, and lynched him.

It was more than a local episode. The nationwide press coverage of the incident included comments about racial nationalism and antagonism toward the ''Parasite Race.'' Anti-Semitism of varying intensity has continued to the present day. It ebbed in the 1920s and flourished again during the Depression. The Silver Shirts, led by William Pelley, and the Christian Front, headed by Father Charles Coughlin, were two of the most active movements against the Jews in the late 1930s. Anti-Semitic behavior has declined since World War II, in part because of revulsion against Nazi genocide and in part because pluralism has become more generally accepted. Incidents still occur at rare intervals, mostly acts of vandalism or desecration. Some analysts suggest that the roots of anti-Semitism can be found in the teachings of Christianity (now renounced in the Catholic Church by Vatican II), which had blamed the Jews for the death of Christ.[17] Latent anti-Semitism may manifest itself for many reasons, such as status or economic rivalries.

BOX 12.1

> *"And you know what the judge answered me? 'You go back to your
> . . . . country where you came, if you don't like the laws of this country!'"*

"One night someone broke my store window and took out some leather hats and shirts (1950). They caught three boys and they called me up at home in the middle of the night and said we have to go right away to the store to fix the window and then go to the police station. So, naturally, it was a big shock for us and we went to the store.

"Then we went to the police station. We came there and the captain said, 'You have to press charges.' So we said, 'We don't want to press charges. If they're young boys, if it's the first or second time, give them a warning and let them go.' Then came a sergeant and he said that these boys already have been in many troubles, and they wouldn't let me not press charges. So I did.

"I had to go next day to court. There were the hats there and the shirts and so on. I went maybe four-five times and nothing happened. Once, one boy was missing. Next time the other boys were missing and so on. I went maybe six times more and I explained to the judge, 'Mister Judge, please, I gave all my answers what you need.' And I said to the Assistant District Attorney, 'Please, will you tell the judge that I am an only storekeeper. I am only one in the store and I have to close up always the store and so on.' And he told the story, what I said to the judge.

"And you know what the judge answered me? 'You go back to your government, to your country where you came, if you don't like the laws of this country!'

"So I started to cry, because in front of these thieves, in front of the old people in the room, he said it to me. This I call really prejudice, very bad prejudice."

Czechoslovakian Jewish immigrant who came to the United States in 1948 at age 31 (He was the sole survivor of his family of the Holocaust.)

Upward Mobility

Like other "new" immigrants, many of the East European Jews who came here were very poor. Most thus settled in great numbers in the large cities that were ports of entry (Boston, New York, and Philadelphia). A great many went to work in the garment industry, while others became street peddlers until they saved enough capital to open their own stores. Since two-thirds of the Jewish male immigrants were skilled workers, compared with an average of 20 percent of the males from other immigrant groups, their absorption into the American economy was eased somewhat.[18] Many social scientists cite this immigrant group as one that climbed the socioeconomic ladder more quickly and more widely than most other groups,[19] although prejudices have limited their ascent to middle-management positions.

BOX 12.2

> *"People still believed the streets were paved with gold. All what you needed was a shovel."*

"I heard a lot about the streets in America being paved with gold but I knew one thing, because I came in contact with GI's and I saw they came from different backgrounds in different parts of the country, and I knew one thing—that I was going to have to work in the United States. People didn't actually still say the streets were paved with gold, but this was still the belief in Europe because, you know, the dollar was the Almighty. In Europe you could buy five-six times with the dollar what you could buy in the United States. So this was why people still believed the streets were paved with gold. All what you needed was a shovel. But I knew. I was prepared. I never was disappointed in coming here to the United States.

"What is to me the American Dream? To some people maybe it's a bigger car or a bigger house. This is their dream. Take more vacations. Sure, we need vacations, but I think our way of life should be to practice just what we preach, just what we have in our Constitution. I mean, not to discriminate against people of all kinds, because this country—if it really is a melting pot—for this one reason, because it is so great this country, because from so many countries, the idea can be put together."

Polish Jewish immigrant who came to the United States in 1948 at age 35

Several cultural factors have contributed to the success of some first- and many second-generation Jewish-Americans. First, because of discrimination in Europe, they had been relegated to such self-sustaining occupations as merchant, scholar, and self-employed artisan. Thus they brought with them skills and knowledge useful in an industrial society, together with values that encouraged deferred gratification, seriousness of purpose, patience, and perseverance—precisely those virtues stressed by the Protestant Ethic of middle-class America. Second, during the period of great immigration, 1880 to 1920, most Jews came here along with members of their families; in many other ethnic groups males usually came first and then either returned to the old country or else sent for their families.[20] Jews had traditionally placed a heavy emphasis on family responsibility, and having the entire family unit together from the outset gave them greater emotional stability and an advantage in cooperative efforts to start a new life. Sometimes the immigrant experience produced emotional and psychological strain within families, however. Third, and perhaps most important, was the Jewish people's traditional emphasis on learning—especially for boys. Even if the children were illiterate in the language of their country of origin, and this was less often true than with many other immigrant groups, they had learned Hebrew and, as a result, the discipline of study. By the time he was thirteen, a Jewish boy, if raised in a religious family, was prepared to read from the Torah for his bar mitzvah. Today, a large number of Jewish girls also participate in this ceremony (called bat mitzvah, for girls). Within the

Jewish culture this positive orientation toward learning carried over to American public education and secular studies. While parents toiled in low-status factory jobs, they were encouraging their children to further their education and then enter the professions. The high percentage of Jewish youth attending public and private colleges in the first few decades of the twentieth century is all the more remarkable because of their limited residency in the United States and because most Americans placed less emphasis upon a college education in those times.[21]

Gordon reports that by the 1940s the occupational distribution of Jews was comparable to that of members of high-status Protestant denominations.[22] Yet Jews have been virtually unrepresented in some industries, such as steel, oil, banking, and insurance. Not all experienced upward mobility. Thousands of Jewish poor, especially the aged, exist on a level far from the stereotyped portrait of the successful Jews.

Social Interaction

Social ostracism often accompanied the economic successes of the Jewish people. Higher economic status did not necessarily mean a comparable increase in social prestige. Even when Jews gained positions with higher levels of income, they still found themselves excluded from social and recreational clubs and were forced to establish parallel social and recreational organizations for themselves. They also encountered restrictions in housing; admissions quotas for colleges, universities, and professional schools; and other obstacles designed to keep them at a social, economic, and educational distance from white Protestants.

Although many Jewish middle-class families moved to the suburbs after World War II, in keeping with a trend in the larger society, many social scientists reported continuing social segregation in the 1950s and 1960s. Social distance is sometimes measured by the degree of primary relationships between Jews and Gentiles. In his Detroit study, Gerhard Lenski found that the frequency of close associations between the two groups declined after adolescence, particularly at the time of choosing a mate.[23] In his study of Elmira, John P. Dean found that approximately 75 percent of his Jewish sample socialized occasionally with their closest non-Jewish friends, but few were regular participants in a mixed social clique.[24] Herbert J. Gans reported that the Jewish suburban housewives of Park Forest, outside of Chicago, participate in the daytime social activities of the entire neighborhood, but that in the evening and on weekends their social relationships are confined to other Jews.[25] Albert Gordon suggested that this pattern of relative isolation in suburban evening or weekend social gatherings is fairly common and not necessarily a voluntary choice.[26] Milton Gordon, echoing the concept of the triple melting pot,[27] suggested that Catholics, Protestants, and Jews each tend to interact in meaningful primary relationships with members of their own religio-ethnic group.[28]

The situation appears to be changing somewhat. About 40 percent of the 5.9 million American Jews (table 12.1) marry outside their faith, up from 31.7 percent in the 1960s and 5.9 percent in the 1950s.[29] Obviously, increased intermarriages

This family, gathered together for the Passover Seder, repeat a traditional ceremony that is part of their heritage dating back thousands of years. Such primary group interaction strengthens one's sense of religious identity and shared cultural bonds.

imply improved primary group relationships between Christians and Jews. Once the cause for concern about the survival of Judaism in the United States, these intermarriages, Jewish leaders believe, have the potential of expanding their community. Studies show seven out of ten children in mixed marriages are raised as Jews.[30] Reform rabbis recently eased the path for such children into Judaism, modifying ancient tradition to declare the child of a Jewish father and gentile mother is also a Jew, a bold departure from past centuries. Moreover, non-Jews marrying Jews are increasingly converting to Judaism.[31]

Jewish Identity

Among the large numbers of Jewish immigrants in the late nineteenth and early twentieth centuries, the synagogue played a significant role in their community structure. At the same time it had to compete with a variety of cultural, ideological, and self-help organizations supported by many Jews. Classes offered by organizations such as the Educational Alliance, on New York's Lower East Side, provided opportunities for acculturation. Together, the synagogues and organizations served as cohesive bonds, laying the foundation for community organization, social activities, and a feeling of belongingness.[32]

More recently, the state of Israel and its continuing conflicts with its Arab neighbors have cemented Jewish identity among diverse Jewish-Americans. A survey

TABLE 12.1
Jews in the U.S.

How Many

	Number	Share of Population
1950	5,000,000	3.5%
1982	5,921,000	2.5%

Where They Live
States with largest Jewish population—

	1982 Estimate	Share of State Total
New York	1,872,150	10.6%
California	775,995	3.2%
Florida	478,180	4.7%
New Jersey	435,165	5.9%
Pennsylvania	415,125	3.5%
Illinois	266,985	2.3%
Massachusetts	248,545	4.3%
Maryland	195,915	4.6%
Ohio	138,795	1.3%
Connecticut	102,075	3.3%

Source: American Jewish Committee, 1983; *Statistical Abstract of the United States, 1984,* Table 79, p. 57.

found 37 percent of U.S. Jews have visited Israel, yet only about half the nation's Jews belong to a synagogue.[33] Even though the number of Jewish children is declining because of a drop in the birth rate, attendance at all-day Jewish schools has climbed from 60,000 in 1962 to 110,000 in 1983.[34] A recent rise in anti-Semitism—linked to Middle East tensions and renewed Ku Klux Klan activity—concerns Jewish leaders, but they are optimistic about the growing consciousness of American Jews who are moving closer to their religious heritage.[35]

Recent Immigrants

More than 500,000 Jews from around the world have emigrated to the United States in the past twelve years. About 350,000 Israelis and over 80,000 Soviet Jews comprise the two largest groups of recent immigrants. Most are well-educated and highly skilled, seeking professional and economic opportunities as well as personal and religious freedom. Nowadays one out of every ten to twelve Jews in the United States has been here less than ten years.[36]

THE MORMONS

The Church of Jesus Christ of Latter-Day Saints offers a fascinating portrait of a religious group evolving from a despised and persecuted people to a highly successful and respected church. As we shall discuss, they are unique as an ethnic group since their principal migration was to leave the United States, their resettlement in the Rocky Mountains in the 1840s giving them an enduring sense of territoriality and shared tradition.[37]

The Early Years

By his own account, at age 18 Joseph Smith received the first of several visitations from the angel Moroni who guided him to a hidden stack of golden plates, each eight inches square.[38] Aided by two stones called the Urim and Thummin, Joseph Smith translated the hieroglyphics into the *Book of Mormon,* a massive and controversial work. Mormons believe it to be the true word of God, providing the foundation of their faith. Two years later in 1830, Joseph Smith—now 25 years old—founded the Mormon faith in the western New York State region in which he then lived. Within a year the church had over 1,000 members.

As the church continued to grow rapidly under the charismatic leadership of Joseph Smith, it attracted enemies. Fleeing harassment in New York and then Ohio, the Mormons resettled in Missouri, incurring further hostility because of their antislavery views, growing political power, and cooperative communities seen as threatening by their more individualistically oriented neighbors on the sparsely settled frontier.[39] Expelled by the Governor in 1838, the Mormons moved to Illinois where they would face their worst clashes. By now their encouragement of plural marriage, together with their growing numbers and strength, inflamed societal hostility into frequent acts of violence. When Joseph Smith and his brother Hyrum were murdered in 1844 by a mob storming the jail in which they had been incarcerated, further violence ensued. Raids, pitched battles, burned homes and temples, rape of Mormon women, even artillery pieces used by both sides brought Mormon existence to a crisis stage.

Facing extermination or forced assimilation, most of the Mormons—under the leadership of Brigham Young—migrated westward until they reached the Great Salt Lake Valley in 1847. Intergroup conflict had strengthened their group identity and cohesiveness, and now the Mormons experienced steady and rapid growth in the isolated Salt Lake region.[40] Part of this growth was due to the arrival throughout the nineteenth century of tens of thousands of converts from England and Scandinavia. The discovery of gold in California ended Mormon isolation, however, since they were located along the best route to the California gold fields.

Mormon scholars Bruce Campbell and Eugene Campbell suggest that Mormon theocratic political power apparently threatened federal control of the Utah territory and thus control of the route to California, generating several decades of government attempts to alter Mormon economic, political, and social institutions.[41] One instance was President Buchanan's sending troops to Utah in 1857 to force

Hostility against the Mormons was quite severe from 1830 to 1847, prompting frequent acts of violence and murder. On October 30, 1838, two hundred militiamen—urged by Governor Lilburn Boggs of Missouri to exterminate or drive the Mormons from the state "for the public good"—attacked the Mormons at member Jacob Haun's flour mill. They left fifteen wounded and seventeen dead, including a nine-year-old boy deliberately shot through the head because one trooper feared that "nits will make lice."

the replacement of Brigham Young as territorial governor with a non-Mormon. An actual short war followed in which over 100 people were killed, with the Mormons prevailing and Young remaining as governor.

Government efforts next shifted to an attack on polygyny, the Mormon practice of men having more than one wife. Though permitted by church doctrine, polygyny occurred only among 10 to 15 percent of the eligible males, two-thirds of whom had one additional wife.[42] Lurid newspaper stories about alleged Mormon depravity inflamed public opinion and created a stereotype of Mormon males as evil, seductive, promiscuous, sexually virile libertines. Non-Mormon opportunists produced such products as Brigham Young Tablets and Mormon Bishop Pills supposedly able to increase sexual desire or ability.[43] In 1862 Lincoln signed the Morill Act, forbidding bigamy in U.S. territories. Continually harassed by federal agents after the Civil War, the Mormons challenged the law as an infringement on their religious freedom. In 1878 the U.S. Supreme Court ruled in *Reynolds* v. *United States* that the law was constitutional.

Unable to gain access to church records to prove the multiple marriages, the government passed a new law in 1882 against anyone living in "lewd cohabitation," effectively sending hundreds of Mormon polygamists to jail. In 1887 the Edmunds-Tucker Act dissolved the Mormon Church as a legal entity and provided for the confiscation of church property. When this law was upheld by the Supreme Court in 1890 as constitutional also, church president Wilford Wood-

An incredibly successful missionary program in Europe brought tens of thousands of converts in the nineteenth century to Utah, helping the Mormon Church to grow and prosper. This scene from Frank Leslie's *Illustrated Newspaper* (November 23, 1878) shows new arrivals at the immigrant processing center at Castle Garden, New York City, bound for Salt Lake City.

ruff's Manifesto ended the open practice of plural marriage. President Benjamin Harrison then granted a pardon to all imprisoned polygamists. In 1896 Utah was permitted to become a state, beginning a new era of relations between Gentiles and Mormons.

Values and Practices

Following the behavioral code set by Joseph Smith, whom they believe is a prophet of God, Mormons do not smoke nor drink any form of alcoholic beverages, coffee, tea, or carbonated beverages. Emphasis is upon group rather than individual activities so that group identification is promoted. Especially encouraged are any of the performing arts, team sports, or organized recreational activities. Other aspects of the Mormon faith, as described below, are deeply embedded in their social institutions.

Family

Mormons place heavy emphasis on the family, both as the primary agent for socializing people into the Mormon belief system and as the basic social organization in the eternal Kingdom of God.[44] Anything undermining family growth or stability is discouraged; for example, premarital or extramarital sex, indecent language, immodest behavior, abortion, birth control, intermarriage, divorce. Among active, observing Mormons these problems occur far less often than amongst those who are less religiously involved. Drugs and premarital sex are a problem among Mormon teenagers and young adults, though to a lesser degree than the national average, particularly among active Mormons.[45]

Unlike typical American families where each person pursues individual interests and activities, Mormon families do many things together. Monday is set aside as home family night and entire families attend other social and sporting events with the emphasis upon the intermingling of different age groups. The extended family-kinship network manifests itself in annual summer reunions and in the search for dead ancestors to secure for them a proxy baptism or sealing ceremony in a Mormon temple to allow them into God's presence in the Celestial World. Through the Mormon Genealogical Society more than ten billion names have been preserved on microfilm—from vital statistics, census materials, church records, and other official records. This extensive collection is increased every year, available free of charge to Mormons and non-Mormons alike for ancestor research investigation.

Education

Following Joseph Smith's revelation in 1833 about intelligence as the glory of God, Mormons place great stress on education. Mormons founded both the University of Utah (the oldest university west of the Mississippi) and Brigham Young University (the nation's largest church-related university with 25,000 students enrolled). Utah leads the nation in literacy, and in the percentage of enrolled college students and college graduates.[46]

Religion

A vigorous and systematic missionary program brings in about 80,000 converts annually.[47] About 25,000 young missionaries, aged 19 to 22, are in the field at any given time, fulfilling a cherished two-year assignment. Their world membership now exceeds 6 million, and their 3.5 million American membership makes them the seventh largest religious body in the United States.[48] Another significant factor in the spectacular growth of the Mormon church is their practice of tithing, giving 10 percent of their gross income to the church. Income from tithing supports the missionary program and the operational costs of Brigham Young University where tuition costs are only about $1,000 annually.

Economics

Mormons take care of their own poor, without public welfare assistance. Each stake (a district comparable to a Catholic diocese) operates a farm, ranch, orchard, cannery, or factory producing goods through donated labor. Through a national exchange program to 150 bishops' storehouses resembling small supermarkets, the Mormon poor receive their needed foodstuffs. Other items—clothing, toiletries, household items—are also available there, provided through monthly cash donations of other Mormons, about $15 per family.

The Mormon Church is possibly the richest church in the world, with daily revenues of about $3 million.[49] In addition to its income from tithing it includes a wide variety of investments:

> The Mormon Church owns some of the choicest hotels and motels in the West. It owns department stores, insurance companies, radio and television stations, and a newspaper. It has vast real estate holdings, both in the United States and abroad. It owns skyscrapers in such diverse places as Salt Lake City and New York City.
>
> LDS also has a major interest in the United States beet sugar industry. It owns 700,000 acres of Florida ranchland, which means that the church is probably the largest landowner in the state. Additionally, LDS has 100,000 acres of ranchland in Canada and a large sugar plantation in Hawaii. It owns dozens of mills, factories, and stores and hundreds of farms. The church also has large holdings in a number of well-known corporations. And the list of assets could be extended.[50]

Current Problem Areas

Although the Mormons had incurred the wrath of many whites for their opposition to slavery in the 1840s, by the 1960s they were under attack for "racist" church doctrine. While Blacks could become church members, they could not join the priesthood. In June 1978, church president Spencer W. Kimball announced a divine revelation that Blacks could be given the priesthood. Only two other revelations—Brigham Young's guidance to Utah and Wilford Woodruff's ending plural marriage—had been reported since Joseph Smith's death. Wide acceptance followed, usually with great relief, and the Church adapted rather easily.

Charges of sexism have also been brought against the church. Church leaders believe the women's liberation movement and the Equal Rights Amendment (ERA) divert women from their primary role, thereby undermining family stability.[51] Higher education for women has always been encouraged, and women are not prohibited from working; they are not permitted, however, to be part of the church hierarchy. All church leaders are male and some Mormon women have been excommunicated for publicly protesting this practice. Most Mormon women appear satisfied with their role, but some are obviously dissatisfied.

Some observers believe Mormon society has been turning inward since the 1960s, reversing an earlier pattern of both outreach and receptivity to external influence.[52] The more permissive attitudes toward abortion, divorce, gay rights, sexual permissiveness, and women's liberation all point, in the Mormons' view, to a disintegration of moral values, prompting a growing cultural insularity, a sharper boundary between Mormons and the rest of society. Only time will determine how much separatism in values, attitudes, and behavior between the dominant society and this religious group actually occurs.

THE AMISH

The Amish, direct descendants of the Swiss Anabaptists believing only in adult baptism as practiced by the early Christians, are also a branch of the Mennonites. Their founder, a Mennonite bishop named Jakob Ammann, began a sectarian movement when a schism arose in 1693 over enforcement of the *Meidung.* Still practiced among the Amish today, the *Meidung,* or shunning, is a powerful social control mechanism that enables them to maintain their way of life.

When a bishop, acting on the near-unanimous vote of the congregation, imposes the *Meidung* on an errant member, others, including family members, cannot look upon, talk, or associate with that person without also being placed under the ban. Informal sanctions such as ridicule and group disapproval, followed by formal admonition by clergy if necessary, precede such an action. Seldom imposed but also not rare, the Meidung can be revoked if the transgressor admits the error and personally asks the congregation for forgiveness.[53]

Though some may have come earlier, the first documented arrival of the Amish in America is 1727, when a few families left Switzerland and settled in Pennsylvania.[54] Migration continued from this region and from Germany from 1727 to 1780, with large numbers of Alsatian and Bavarian Amish migrating from 1815 to 1840, establishing communities in Ontario, Illinois, and Ohio.[55] With an intensive agricultural orientation, the Amish found the unlimited availability of land in the New World so attractive an inducement that they completely transplanted to America. Their subculture became extinct in Europe, the Amish remaining there being absorbed into the dominant society.

Values, Symbols, and Practices

Forming gemeinschaft communities—intimate, homogeneous, and characterized by strong religious tradition—the Amish have remained remarkably constant in a radically changing dominant society. Their communities are highly integrated, as their social institutions—family, school, church, and economic endeavors—are complementary and consistent in values and expectations; young and old live similar lives. The entire group shares the same life-style and restrictions, accepting them as the will of God.

Pride is a major sin, so wearing jewelry or other efforts at promoting physical attraction are forbidden; boasting is rare, and seeking a leadership role is frowned upon. No Amish seeks political office of any kind, many not even registering to vote. Here we must make a distinction between the more conservative Old Order Amish living mostly in Pennsylvania, and the somewhat less conservative communities in midwestern states. The latter tend to vote Republican and adamantly oppose farm subsidies, believing they would undermine their self-help social system.

Clothing is an important symbol of group identity, maintaining separatism from outgroups and continuity within the community. In an unchanged 250-year tradition, the men wear low-crown, wide-brim hats; coats without collars, lapels, or pockets; trousers with suspenders but without cuffs or creases. Belts and gloves, even in cold weather, are not permitted. Women wear solid color, one-piece dresses, with long skirts and aprons, keeping their heads covered at all times, whether indoors or outdoors. Clothing thus expresses a common understanding and mutual affection among those sharing similar traditions and expectations.[56] Other aspects

Their Sunday worship service ended, these Amish folk socialize for a while before returning home. This picture offers a good illustration of their traditional clothing, the facial hair of the men, and the special braids of the women, all of which help maintain group identity and multi-generational continuity.

of appearance—beards but not mustaches for all married men, a special braided hairstyle for females—reinforce further this orientation.

Language serves as another symbolic attribute of the *unser Satt Leit* (our sort of people). Pennsylvania Dutch (the word *Dutch* derives from *Deutsch* meaning German) is a German dialect resembling Palatine German folk speech and is common to all Amish, regardless of where they live.[57] English is their second language, usually introduced to a child upon entering school and learned without difficulty. High German is used exclusively for the preaching service and formal ceremonies; the family teaches High German to their children so all can understand it when used in sermons and hymns.[58]

Amish farmers use a team of horses instead of tractors and gain an additional benefit from the natural supply of fertilizer. Amish homes may be lacking in modern conveniences, but they are clean, solid, kept in good repair, and like the farms, well run.

Floors are without rugs or carpets, though linoleum is often used. There are no curtains, mirrors, photographs, or paintings in an Amish household. Even wallpaper is taboo. Electrical appliances are also forbidden, although in some districts gasoline-powered washing machines are permitted. Telephones are prohibited, as are electric lights. For illumination, oil lamps are used.

Amish homes contain no furnaces, no running water, and, in some outlying districts, no indoor toilets. Television sets, radios, and electric refrigerators are out of the question. There are no doorbells. Neither houses nor barns have lightning rods.[59]

Some Amish congregations have accepted parts of modern life. The Beachy Amish, founded by Amish bishop Moses M. Beachy in 1927, permit ownership of automobiles and certain other modern conveniences, and the "New Amish" allow telephones, electricity, and tractors.[60]

The Amish consider adolescence the most dangerous period of an individual's life. Because of physical and emotional changes, peer group influence exceeding family control, adolescents strain for independence, to be children no longer. As a result, the Amish community has somewhat institutionalized adolescent rebellion, allowing teenagers to make mistakes, test the cultural boundaries, and date. However, exposure to high-school worldliness is forbidden, the teens receiving vocational training instead. Since baptism does not occur until the late teens or early twenties, adults are more tolerant of discreet adolescent other-worldly activities, which may include going to the movies, having a photograph taken, owning a radio, occasionally wearing non-Amish clothes.[61] A small degree of youth problems—drunkenness, disrespect, joyriding, even buying a car—occasionally confront the Old Order Amish, but most return to Amish ways upon baptism and the assumption of adult responsibilities. As much as 22 percent of Amish youth may leave and join a more liberal Mennonite group[62] However, only 6 percent of the baptized Amish, ever leave.[63]

If an individual wishes to remain part of the community, the Amish insist upon an endogamous marriage. The Amish do not practice birth control and so have a high birth rate; they have grown from 59,304 in 1970 to 91,900 in 1980. Social class has no meaning to the Amish and all share a strong sense of social obligation to one another. This includes helping others when disaster or tragedy strikes, and home care rather than institutionalization for the aged.

Conflicts With Society

The Amish oppose social security or any form of insurance, believing the Christian brotherhood is responsible for its own people. Because they would not accept social security payments, they refused to pay the mandatory self-employment social security tax. In the years of conflict with the government over this issue, the government confiscated some Amish farms and horses to collect the owed taxes. Finally, Amish leaders went to Washington, astounding the legislators by their request to be exempted from government benefits. Consequently a law was passed, exempting them from both payments and benefits.

Compulsory school attendance until age 16 provided another arena of conflict for the Amish with society. Because the Amish refused to send their children to high school, they were harassed and arrested by state officials. A Wisconsin case ultimately reached the U.S. Supreme Court, resulting in a unanimous ruling in favor of the Amish. For them eighth-grade education is sufficient, with farm vocational training occurring thereafter.

An Indiana sect permits car ownership but forbids having photographs taken, believing them to be graven images. When that state required photographs on driver licenses in 1976, the Amish requested an exemption. When the state refused, the Amish were once again drawn into conflict with authority over their religious principles.

Tourism is an annoyance for the Amish, especially in Lancaster County, Pennsylvania. Ignoring Amish religious beliefs against having their pictures taken, camera-wielding tourists routinely do so. In 1983, some Amish were having a church service in a home as is their custom, with their buggies parked outside. Some tourists pulled up in cars, went up on the porch, looked through the windows at them, and took their pictures.[64] Guided bus tours clog the narrow roads, block their vehicles, and park in front of their schools and farms. Motels, commercial "museums," and handicraft and souvenir outlets cover the region, none run by or approved of by the Amish.[65]

Despite the problems, the Amish persist and survive. Non-Amish neighbors and leaders praise their integrity, work ethic, and neighborliness. Their birth rate, in-group solidarity, and resistance to outside influences suggest they will continue as a persistent subculture for many more years.

THE RASTAFARIANS

Rastafarians provide a contemporary example of a misunderstood religious minority group, that frequently experiences prejudice and harassment. They fulfill the characteristics of a minority group: unequal treatment, easily identifiable, self-conscious identity, real or assumed common ancestry, and endogamy.[66] The factors that direct attention to them are their skin color, distinctive hairstyling, and use of *ganja* (marijuana) for much the same purpose as the Navaho and Huichol Indians use peyote.

The Early Years

Marcus Garvey, Jamaican-born founder of the Back to Africa movement, was influential in Jamaica before leaving the island for the United States in 1916. Upon his departure, he is supposed to have said, "Look to Africa, [where] a black king shall be crowned, for the day of deliverance is near."[67] When Ras Tafari was crowned as Emperor Haile Selassie in 1930, he added the titles "King of Kings" and "Lion of the Tribe of Judah," placing himself in the legendary line of King Solomon. The coronation of the young Ethiopian emperor reminded Garvey's followers of his words and seemed to fulfill the Biblical prophecy of Revelation 5:2–5:

And I saw a mighty angel, who announced in a loud voice, "Who is worthy to break the seals and open the scroll?" But there was no one in heaven or on earth or in the world below who could open the scroll or look inside it. Then one of the elders said to me, "Don't cry. Look! The Lion from Judah's tribe, the great descendant of David, has won the victory, and he can break the seven seals and open the scroll.

Finding other collaborating scriptural passages (Revelation 19:16, Psalm 68:4, and Daniel 7:9 describing the king's hair "like pure wool"), the Rastas believed themselves to be the black Israelites of the Diaspora. Four ministers—Leonard Howell, Joseph Hibbert, Archibald Dunkley, and Robert Hinds—spread the message, attracting many followers. To Black Jamaicans experiencing economic frustration at the time of a worldwide depression, as well as white colonial rule, the movement offered hope and the promise of a better day coming.

Three major themes dominated the early phase of the Rastafarian movement: the wickedness of Whites, the superiority of Blacks, and the eventual revenge of Blacks against Whites by means of enslavement.[68] Living at the bottom of the ladder in a highly stratified society, Jamaican Blacks thus protested against white racism and economic exploitation through the Rastafarian movement. Since then, most Rastafarians have taken a more conciliatory stance toward Whites, no longer condemning them en masse.[69]

Believing the colonial social institutions enchained them, the Rastas flouted the laws denying the jurisdiction of the rulers. Even working for taxpayers or social institutions implied recognition of the existing social structure, so the Rastas refused to do so. Instead, they eked out an existence off the land, living as squatters in temporary shacks. Since the Rastas were poor, these attitudes provided them with coping mechanisms while they awaited the end of their exile from Africa.

From Outcasts to Social Acceptance

The Rastas' rebelliousness, though passive, brought quick condemnation in the early years of the movement. Newspapers called them unpatriotic, despicable, and ganja-smoking criminals. Some schools refused to admit their children, while the government disrupted their meetings, arrested cult members, raiding and burning their homes.[70] Dominant group persecution only served to further unify the Rastafarians. Finally, the Rastas invited the University of the West Indies to conduct an impartial investigation of their movement. The UWI report did rehabilitate their public image, and a new period of reciprocal cooperation began between the Rastas and the dominant society. A high point was reached on April 21, 1966, when Haile Selassie visited Jamaica and some Rastas were invited to the residence of the Governor General for the first time to meet with the Emperor in private. Each year on that date Rastafarians in Jamaica and the United States celebrate the event.

In the past twenty years Rastas have become assimilated into the sociocultural milieu of the island society. Their expressive art forms have been featured in public exhibitions and at the annual National Festival; their imprint on Jamaican music, from ska to reggae, has been significant. Its appeal has widened to include many different groups amongst the American public as well as Jamaicans. As a socially recognized group, Rastafarians in Jamaica now attract members from the middle and upper classes as well.

Values, Symbols, and Practices

Although some Rastafarians do not wear long hair, most do so as a symbol of unity, power, freedom, defiance to outgroups, and in accordance with Biblical custom.[71] Because they reject almost all chemically processed goods, Rastafarians do not use soap, shampoo, or combs. They are far from unsanitary, however, washing their hair and body in water and herbs very frequently. The hair grows long, left undisturbed to curl of its own volition into dreadlocks.

Food is another symbol of religious identification. Rastafarians rarely eat meat, abhorring pork, and preferring small fish and vegetables instead. They will not drink liquor, milk, or coffee, preferring instead herbal tea. No manufactured foods, salt, or processed shortening is used; natural foods and oil from dried coconut are the staples in *I-tal* food and cooking, the name signifying the Rastafarian diet.

Smoking *ganja* (marijuana) gave the Rastas *communitas,* a sense of cohesive unity.[72] By producing an altered state of consciousness, they could gain temporary escape from their lives of hardship. Gradually, smoking *ganja* became identified with seeking communion with the supernatural, experiencing the self as God.[73]

The Rastafarians' language also symbolizes their philosophy and reality perceptions. A form of creole English, Rastafarian speech is almost devoid of subject–object opposition; "you" and "me" are almost never used, an "I and I" primary combination being used instead, even to outgroup members. Shedding the cognitive shell and asserting a new self-concept and world view that they believed to be their natural, African state, Rastafarians use "I and I" to identify soulfully with others at a higher level than I–Thou or I–It relationships. An actual example from *The Rastafarian Voice,* is, "Government claims it is interested in I and I planting the land. Yet when I and I plant food to feed I fellow African, I and I are harassed and driven off the land."[74]

Rastafarian-Americans

Rastafarianism survives because of its adaptive capabilities. An existential interpretation of their doctrines has enabled the Rastas to adjust to industrialism and to American society without sacrificing their naturistic ethic. As increased numbers of Jamaicans migrated to the United States (103,752 in the 1970s), many Rastafarians were among them.

Mostly poor, unskilled workers, the Rastafarians tend to live in low-rent urban neighborhoods. Their cultural orientations isolate them from both white and black Americans, the social distance forging a small, cohesive subculture. Rastafarians frequently encounter problems with the police, their appearance and regular use of marijuana making them inviting targets. Their ingroup solidarity, adaptability, and social distance from the dominant society make the Rastafarians likely to remain a persistent subculture, much like the Gypsies.

The long dreadlocks of this Rastafarian man clearly set him apart from outgroup members. While his unique hairstyle carries on his customs and serves as a mutually recognizable bond within his group, it also places him low on the similarity-attraction scale to others, heightening his visibility and vulnerability for harassment or other forms of conflict.

THE SHAKERS

Even though the United Society of Believers in Christ's Second Appearing—or Shakers, as they are most commonly known—may now be disappearing, leaving behind no religious legacy, they have left their mark in other ways. With a 200-year history, they have been both the largest and longest-lasting communistic movement in the United States. At the peak of their membership in the mid-nineteenth century, they numbered at least 17,000 and possibly as high as 64,000.[75]

The Early Years

Ann Lee, an illiterate Englishwoman from a poor family, was the founder of the United Society. Born in Manchester in 1736, at age 22 she joined a radical religious sect whose worship services included both silent meditation and sudden bursts of shouting, singing, and agitated shakings of the body. Because leaders Jane and James Wardley were former Quakers, the group became known as "Shaking Quakers" or "Shakers." After four children died in early infancy, the last birth a most difficult one seriously endangering her life, Ann Lee became convinced sexual desire and carnal pleasure violated God's will. Sex was the root of all evil—the reason Adam and Eve were driven from the Garden of Eden and the cause of problems in her own time.

Convincing her colleagues about the sins of the flesh through her charismatic powers, she began preaching against the established church for allowing marriage and sexual practice. Arrested for disturbing the peace and kept in solitary confinement for two weeks, her colleagues—already anticipating the imminent second coming of Christ—now saw Ann Lee as a female messiah, since they believed in the male–female duality of God and all spiritual beings. Mother Ann Lee, as she was now called, was the female counterpart of a spirit earlier appearing in the person of Jesus.

A divine revelation led Ann Lee and eight followers to migrate to the New World in May 1774. By August 1774 they were in Niskayuna, an area just outside Albany, where they built a settlement. Within a few years they began attracting many converts, but at the same time gained many enemies. Suspected in those revolutionary times of being British sympathizers, and unpopular for their religious views, female leadership, and claims to the female reincarnation of Christ, the Shakers experienced brutal abuse. They were imprisoned, fined, attacked by mobs, beaten, and clubbed. Ann Lee was stoned and badly mauled on several occasions, her brother once suffering a severe skull fracture from a rock.

From 1781 to 1783, Ann Lee and her disciples traveled throughout the Northeast, gaining many converts and establishing a base for several new Shaker communities. Within a year though, Mother Ann was dead at age 48. Effective leadership and missionary activities enabled the Believers to expand over the next seventy-five years, with nineteen communities developing in eight states.[76] Some of these communities also encountered mob violence and persecution, as well as the frontier perils of Indian attack, inadequate medical facilities, and battles against the elements. Nevertheless, they grew and prospered despite their isolation from one another, most communities situated hundreds of miles apart from each other.

Values and Practices

With celibacy as a basic tenet of their faith, Shakers employed extensive sex segregation in their daily activities. Men and women had separate work areas, dined in silence at separate tables seating four to eight in a communal dining room, and avoided all physical contact with one another, including shaking hands. They had separate doorways in many of their buildings, wide hallways to prevent brushing by one another, and were not permitted to pass by one another on the stairs. Children—either those of converts or adopted from orphanages—attended sex-segregated schools and grew up untouched by members of the opposite sex. Since they also thought the millennium was near, Shakers had no concern about the need to propagate.

Believing idleness, even in conversation, was a temptation for the devil to corrupt them, Shakers glorified work and spent most of their waking moments engaged in some form of manual labor. Their deep commitment to work resulted in top-quality products, whether in their buildings, distinctive furniture, or farm produce, earning them a reputation for selling choice quality goods. Their strict moral code and ordered existence, while unique to their life-style, followed a pattern of deliberately planned and coordinated activities found in typical utopian communes.[77]

The Shakers also believed in the ideal of common property practiced by the early Christians (Acts 4:32). Their common ownership of all property made everyone equal regardless of age, race, or gender, enabling them to fulfill the Christian virtues of humility and charity; no one was servant or master. In the eighteenth and nineteenth centuries, such pioneering of women's rights and racial equality (Blacks and slaves were fully admitted as free and equal members) was a bold concept for the times.

Why would total sexual denial and extensive work schedules appeal to thousands of converts? We must first remember that in the eighteenth and nineteenth centuries divorce was rare and socially unacceptable; with sexual gratification considered a male prerogative, women seldom viewed marriage in sexual terms.[78] Unhappy couples had an alternative to their present state by joining the Shakers. Widows—having no means of support since both life insurance and jobs for women were rare—could gain both emotional and economic security in the Shaker community. Others—unable to function in a competitive society due to personality, limited ability, or life orientation—could find a peaceful haven with the Shakers.

Whatever the reason, Shaker life appealed to people from all walks of life—professionals, skilled and unskilled workers, merchants, artisans, and craftspeople; most were Protestant, some Jewish, generally from working-class backgrounds. Blacks and foreign-born also joined. Out of their combined efforts came a number of significant inventions: the circular saw, screw propeller, clothespin, cut nail, brimstone match, flat broom, revolving oven, threshing machine, and various machines for printing labels, cutting leather, and making broom handles.[79] Their simple, straight, functional styling has also made an indelible mark on American furniture.

Shaker observance of the Sabbath was a joyous event, culminating in an emotional release through frenzied and animated dancing. Again, the sexes never touched each other. One frequent version of dance was formation of two circles, one within the other, males forming one circle and females another. They would chant, sing, clap hands, grouping, and regrouping in various patterns. Some dances were actually marches in rhythm, accompanied by varying body movements such

The frenzied and animated exuberance of Shaker dancing serves as an enjoyable group activity and emotional outlet from the hard work and personal restraint practiced all week. This photograph depicts one version of the circle dance, with numerous participants and "wallflowers." Note the gender-segregated seating.

as swinging arms. A more ecstatic dance included jerking one's head back and forth or side to side with limbs and trunk twitching in every direction.[80] Undoubtedly such participation was an effective outlet from the total restraint practiced all week long.

Decline and Virtual Disappearance

Several factors contributed to the decline of the United Society. Industrialization ushered in the factory system, undermining the Shaker economy whose handicraft system could not compete with less expensive, mass-produced products. Values about sex changed, Americans developing more positive attitudes about sexual pleasure. Improvements in transportation (railroad, automobile) and communication (telegraph, telephone), together with national population growth and land development, reduced Shaker isolation and separatism. The emergence of governmental social welfare programs for the elderly, widowed, orphaned, or sick eliminated economic security as a motive for joining. As American society changed, the Shakers found it increasingly difficult to gain new converts and keep their younger members. As their membership aged, their dance rituals lost their vigor, replaced by more conservative songs and instrumental music, ending the exuberance of the sect.[81] By the turn of the century most of the Shaker communities were in a state of precipitous decline and by 1925, most had vanished.

Most of the Shaker buildings still stand, serving as museums or being used as facilities for schools, state institutions, religious orders, or private residences. One Shaker community still exists at Sabbathday Lake, Maine. Less than a dozen, mostly elderly members live there, benefiting from revenues generated through tourism. Although gaining a trickle of converts, even in the past few years, the community may not remain viable for much longer.

RELIGION AND AMERICAN SOCIETY

Religion is a very important aspect of American culture. Public opinion polls have consistently found 94 to 96 percent of Americans saying they believe in God, and nearly 75 percent believing in a life after death. Such responses are from two to three times greater than in other Western nations. Some 130 million Americans belong to a church or synagogue, about 60 percent of the population.[82] After a steady decline through the mid-1970s, the proportion of Americans attending weekly worship services and finding religion an increasing influence on their lives has been rising (see Figure 12.1). While 41 percent weekly worship service attendance may appear low, it is by far the highest of all developed countries; for example, only 15 percent of the British attend church weekly. Undoubtedly, some Americans use religion for social rather than religious purposes, finding in their church a source of community and reaffirmation of American values of humanitarianism, work, individualism, and anticommunism.

As we mentioned earlier, much religious diversity exists in the United States. The influx of Asian immigrants, for instance, has increased the number of followers of Eastern religions such as Buddhism or Hinduism to over one million. Another ten million practice disciplines derived from Hinduism, including Yoga and Transcendental Meditation.

Even Catholicism and Protestantism have great diversity within their churches; they are not the monolithic entities some assume them to be. The ethnic diversity of the Catholic Church—French, German, Hispanic, Irish, Italian, Polish, to name

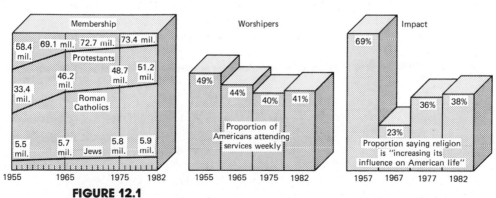

FIGURE 12.1
Vital Signs
Source: U.S. News & World Report, April 4, 1983.

but a few—results in varying forms of religious behavior among these subgroups.[83] The Irish, as the Italians and Poles have long recognized, dominate American Catholicism; at present Irish-Americans represent 17 percent of the Catholic population yet comprise 57 percent of the U.S. bishops. Protestants range from the more liberal Congregationalists and Episcopalians with their formal religious ceremonies, to the more conservative American Lutherans and American Baptists with their less elaborate worship services. The Amish and Mormons are but two of the many different Protestant faiths, as are such fundamentalists as the Missouri Synod Lutherans and Southern Baptists with their strict interpretations of the Bible.[84]

Civil Religion

Sociologist Robert Bellah has suggested the United States has a "civil religion," a shared belief system incorporating all religious elements into a sanctification and celebration of the American way of life.[85] Our Pledge of Allegiance identifies us as a nation "under God." All our coins and paper money declare, "In God We Trust," the back of our one-dollar bills also containing the now obscure symbols of the Trinity (triangle) and the omniscience of God (the eye within the triangle). Congress begins each session with a prayer; presidents regularly schedule prayer breakfasts with government leaders and they mention God in almost all their state of the union and inaugural addresses. Religion is an important element in oaths of office, courtroom procedures, and most formal public occasions. Scouting emphasizes "God and Country" in the Scout Oath and in an award by that name. The list is virtually endless.

Current Controversies

The U.S. Supreme Court has often been involved in controversial decisions interpreting the First Amendment's stipulation about separation of church and state. In its efforts to maintain government neutrality in maximizing religious freedom, the Court has sometimes outraged religious advocates of particular moral issues. Its most controversial decisions have been those banning prayer in public schools and approving abortion. Other decisions—upholding Amish exemption from compulsory education laws, permitting certain forms of federal assistance to parochial schools (lunches, books), and allowing local governments to set up Nativity displays—encourage certain religious activities while striving to maintain First Amendment principles.

School prayer and abortion continue as controversial issues. Proposed constitutional amendments have not gained sufficient support for passage, though religious groups persist in their efforts. Catholics, Mormons, Lutherans, Baptists, and other conservative sects and denominations have combined their efforts to overturn the abortion ruling through lobbying and support of sympathetic legislators. School prayer does not generate the same degree of emotion, but it too unites people of different faiths to effect a change. Opposing them are both strict constitutionalists and people of more liberal religious persuasions.

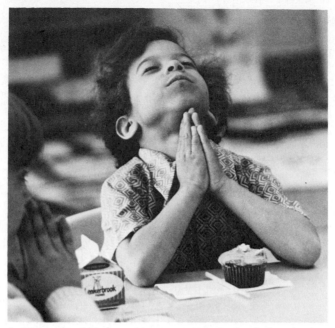

Is this scene of kindergarten youngsters praying before having milk and cupcakes a violation of the U.S. Constitution? The question has stirred strong emotional feelings on both sides, those arguing for separation of church and state in the public schools, and those insisting on religious rights and the school's responsibility to instill moral strength in children.

Creationists, those supporting a literal interpretation of the Bible, have been crusading over the past ten years for a "balanced treatment" about the origins of life. Objecting both to textbooks and curriculum on the subject of evolution, Christian fundamentalists insisted the book of Genesis be included as well. Arkansas, Louisiana, and Mississippi passed legislation requiring such an approach, and eighteen other states were considering similar laws when a Federal District Court in early 1982 struck down the Arkansas law as a violation of the First Amendment. Creationists scored a victory anyway, as textbook publishers reduced or eliminated coverage of evolution, fossils, and geology to keep their sales markets. As with other moral issues, creationism generates strong emotions and the lobbying efforts continue.

SOCIOLOGICAL PERSPECTIVES

Our three theoretical frameworks each provide a means of understanding the significance of religion in intergroup relations and within the activities of convergent and persistent subcultures as well. Though different in emphasis, these perspectives offer unifying themes to religious pluralism in the United States.

The Functionalist View

In *The Elementary Forms of Religious Life* (1912), Emile Durkheim identified religion as an integrative bond for society, a theme elaborated upon by modern functionalists. Religion, they maintain, serves as a social "cement," uniting people with shared values and beliefs, bringing them together to celebrate harvests and life-cycle events. Religion gives meaning and purpose to one's life, offering individuals emotional and psychological support in both good and bad times. Religious teachings also help maintain social control, reinforcing important values and norms and providing moral standards.

Each of the groups discussed in this chapter—Catholics, Jews, Mormons, Amish, Rastafarians, Shakers—found their religious bond a means of strengthening their resolve and identity in a pluralistic and sometimes harsh society. Catholic and Jewish immigrants usually lived in ethnic neighborhoods with their church or synagogue as the focal point of their community activities, easing their transition to the American life-style. Experiencing acts of hostility, Mormons, Rastafarians, and Shakers—often Catholics and Jews also—drew closer to other ingroup members and sustained hope through their faith. Because of their strong religious convictions, the Amish and Shakers remained constant in their ways despite a changing world all around them. Mormons and Rastafarians, in particular, function in the secular world but maintain their sense of identity and purpose through adherence to specific religious tenets.

As separatist minorities, the Amish and Shakers developed economic and social interaction patterns intensifying their values and beliefs. All aspects of their daily lives have functioned together in harmony, eliminating stress and conflict between religion and daily living. Amish institutionalization of adolescent rebelliousness and Shaker dancing exuberance both operate as safety releases for otherwise strict communes. The socialization efforts by Amish, Catholics, Jews, and Mormons of children and youth, though varying greatly in approach and intensity, serve to transmit and sustain over generations a continuing social system organized around specific religious beliefs and practices. Language, symbols, and rituals further instill a shared religious identity and social bond.

The Conflict View

Karl Marx and later conflict theorists thought religion a social control mechanism to protect the interests of those in power. The dominant religion of a society represents the ruling economic and political class, and it legitimizes the existing social structure, blunting people's frustration, anger, and pain with the promise of an afterlife reward. Religion can be a divisive factor, breeding dissension and violence, though conflict theorists suggest the real reasons behind such altercations are economic and political in nature. What appears to be religious bigotry or fanaticism is usually, say the conflict theorists, a struggle for power and control disguised as a religious matter. Even the participants may be unaware of the reality of the situation, caught up as they are in the religious justification given for the conflict.

Note how nativist alarm over midnineteenth-century Catholic immigrants centered on their perceived growing political strength; fears of papal rule of America were very real then. Loss of political control still haunted Protestant Americans thirty years later. The American Protective Association even dedicated itself to keeping Catholics out of office! Problems arose for Rastafarians in Jamaica because they challenged the political status quo, while the Mormons in Illinois and Missouri made enemies because of their political strength in those states. Shakers, thought to be Tory sympathizers, incurred the wrath of their neighbors during the revolutionary period. The Amish, on the other hand, sought no political leadership nor economic competition and so encountered little hostility for those reasons.

Economic competition did create religious antagonism against Catholic and Jews. The rebelliousness of striking Irish laborers against mine and factory owners sparked anti-Catholic reactions, as did the recessions in the 1870s and 1890s, causing workers to fear Catholics taking away their jobs. Rapid upward mobility among Jewish-Americans ignited fears of their dominance, resulting in unflattering Shylock stereotyping and exclusion from organizations and establishments of affluent Christians. Such actions support conflict theory argumentation that the roots of religious confrontation, whether peaceful or violent, actually lie in political and economic resource distributions.

The Interactionist View

Appearance is one key element in perceptions of those religiously different. Away from their worship services, most Americans offer few clues about their religious preference, but some do, however. When an outsider sees a physically distinct believer—a Hasidic Jew, a Hare Krishna follower, an Amish person, or a Rastafarian, for instance—those dissimilarities announce a social distance and tend to lessen chances of close interaction patterns. Those physical clues may even foster negative responses. Conversely, this outward appearance becomes a source of comfort and reinforced religious identity to a fellow believer. Wearing of religious symbols—perhaps ashes on one's forehead on Ash Wednesday or a Star of David on a necklace—may also induce positive or negative reactions.

Self-identity emerges out of the orderliness of day-by-day accomplishments of individuals interacting face to face, interpreting and reinterpreting their ways of doing things. These shared definitions become more solidified and the group members a more cohesive unit under insulated conditions. Amish and Shakers living in their separate communities, and the Mormons in the Utah Territory, succeeded in developing their own social systems whose totality encompassed all aspects of daily life, thereby reinforcing the precepts of their religious beliefs. Rastafarians, in rejecting the dominant economic system and language syntax, created their own symbolic world so differentiated from the dominant society that their everyday interrelationships with one another reinforced their group solidarity. Even Catholics and Jews, as well as the Mormons of modern times, benefit from such cooperative interpretation with one another, since studies show each tends to interact in primary group relations outside religious settings with same faith members.[86] For members of all faiths, the religious bond serves both to unite and insulate, preserved and maintained through daily interactions with like-minded individuals.

Societal labeling of dissimilar religious minorities often results in negative attitudes and actions, with an avoidance response thereby promoting subcultural insularity. If Catholics are attacked as "docile and superstitious," Jews as "mercenary," Mormons as "chauvinistic," Amish as "backward," Rastafarians as "potheads," and Shakers as "weird," group members are more likely to turn inward for the sense of personal worth denied them in the outside world.

RETROSPECT

Founded on the principle of religious freedom, the United States became a place of refuge for people of many faiths. Yet religious tolerance has not always prevailed; some groups have been harassed, experiencing both verbal and physical abuse as they sought the right to follow their beliefs.

Throughout much of the nation's history, Catholics have been vilified and abused. Anti-Catholic actions include colonial statutes against political participation, vicious pamphlets and books, hostile political party platforms, Know-Nothing and Ku Klux Klan demonstrations and violence, American Protective Association activities. Proposed aid to parochial schools remains controversial, as do Catholic positions on abortion, birth control, and nuclear arms. Catholics today are the largest single religious denomination in the country.

Jewish-Americans encountered many of the same problems as Catholics, often from the same nativist groups. Overt anti-Semitic stereotyping and actions continued well into the twentieth century. Jewish upward mobility occurred more quickly than for most other immigrants because more came as skilled workers with families intact, and their religious emphasis on learning encouraged secular education and entry into better-paying jobs. A high intermarriage rate, once a cause for concern, now appears a means of religious expansion.

The Latter-Day Saints offer an example of a persecuted minority, expelled from several states, growing into a large, successful, and respectable church. Their emphasis on family and education earns them high praise, as do their economic investments and assistance to their poor. While criticisms about plural marriages and racism have ended through changes in church doctrine, charges of sexism still remain, though most Mormon women appear satisfied in their role.

Both the Amish and Shakers are long-lasting examples of a persistent subculture. While the Amish remain a vibrant and growing community, the Shakers appear to be disappearing after a 200-year existence. Rastafarians are becoming more numerous as Jamaican immigration increases, and they too are a separatist minority opposed to assimilation.

Today religion remains an important aspect of American culture, as indicated by public opinion polls and rising church attendance. A civil religion exists, as do controversies over abortion, school prayer, and teaching evolution theory.

Functionalists stress the integrative aspects of religion, while conflict theorists analyze the underpinnings of economic and political power struggles as the basis for religious conflict. Interactionists examine how social interpretations foster ingroup solidarity and outgroup acceptance or hostility.

SUGGESTED READINGS

Anderson, Charles H. *White Protestant Americans: From National Origins to Religious Group.* Englewood Cliffs, N.J.: Prentice-Hall, 1970.
   A readable, comprehensive account of cultural dominance of Anglo-Americans and their role in interethnic relations.

Baltzell, E. Digby. *The Protestant Establishment.* New York: Vintage Books, 1966.
   A classic study of the history, power, and life-styles of the white, Anglo-Saxon elite in the United States.

Barrett, Leonard. *The Rastafarians: Sounds of Cultural Dissonance.* Boston: Beacon Press, 1977.
   A highly readable study of Rastafarian history, ideology, and impact on society.

Curran, Thomas J. *Xenophobia and Immigration, 1820–1930.* New York: Twayne Publishers, 1975.
   A detailed historical account of nativist efforts and political actions against Catholics and Jews.

Herberg, Will. *Protestant-Catholic-Jew,* rev. ed. Garden City, N.Y.: Anchor Books, 1960).
   A somewhat controversial argument that a religious triple melting pot now forms group affiliation and identity.

Higham, John. *Strangers in the Land.* (New York: Atheneum, 1973).
   An excellent historical narrative of the patterns of American nativism from 1860 to 1925.

Hostetler, John A. *Amish Society,* 3rd ed. (Baltimore, Md.: Johns Hopkins Press, 1980).
   A classic and outstanding study of Amish society, with a thorough insider's view of their values and practices.

Kephart, William M. *Extraordinary Groups: The Sociology of Unconventional Life-Styles,* 2nd ed. (New York: St. Martin's Press, 1982).
   A fine sociological examination of the Amish, Mormons, and Shakers, as well as several other groups.

Sklare, Marshall. *America's Jews.* New York: Random House, 1971.
   Broad, comprehensive account of Jewish-Americans, a definitive study by a leading authority on the subject.

CHAPTER 13

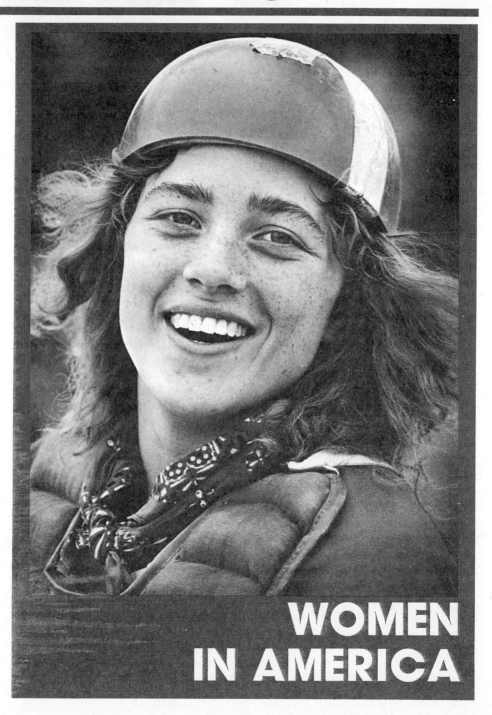

**WOMEN
IN AMERICA**

Sexism—institutionalized prejudice and discrimination based on sex—has only recently become a public concern. In fact, the words **sexism** or *sexist* did not even appear in American dictionaries until the mid-1960s. Previously, women had been subordinate to men in virtually all societies throughout history, recorded comments reflecting this cultural bias.[1] Aristotle, for example, thought men active by nature and women passive, making women intellectually and morally inferior to men.[2] In 1879 Gustave LeBon, a founder of social psychology, made the following observation:

> In the most intelligent races, as among the Parisians, there are a large number of women whose brains are closer in size to those of gorillas than to the most developed male brains. This inferiority is so obvious that no one can contest it for a moment; only its degree is worth discussion. All psychologists who have studied the intelligence of women, as well as poets and novelists, recognize today that they represent the most inferior forms of human evolution and that they are closer to children and savages than to an adult, civilized man. They excel in fickleness, inconstancy, absence of thought and logic, and incapacity to reason. Without doubt there exist some distinguished women, very superior to an average man, but they are as exceptional as the birth of any monstrosity, as, for example, of a gorilla with two heads; consequently, we may neglect them entirely.[3]

More recently, Freudian psychologists have advanced notions of gender differences affecting behavior. Freud believed that the fact that males have a penis made them more aggressive, while "penis envy" made females feel shame and a sense of inferiority. Erik Erikson suggested male genitalia influenced boys to be questing, aggressive, and outward thrusting, and female genitalia directed girls to be concerned about boundaries, limits, and "interiors." Today such notions have been refuted by cross-cultural studies demonstrating variances in sex role norms and behavior as developed through the socialization process and societal expectations of men and women.

Not everyone had been blind to the effects of male domination. In an appendix to his classic and influential analysis of Black–White relations, *An American Dilemma* (1944), Gunnar Myrdal noted a parallel to the position of women and Blacks in American society.[4] In fact, he observed, the legal position of women and children defined as being under the control of the male head of the household had provided the basis for the legal position of black servants in the seventeenth century. Sociologist Helen Hacker in 1951 identified major areas of sexual discrimination in American society, describing women as marginal in a masculine society.[5] Not until the 1960s, however, did the feminist movement make any headway, partially launched by Betty Friedan's consciousness-raising book, *The Feminine Mystique* (1963).

As public awareness of women as an oppressed group increased, the parallels of their status to that of racial and ethnic groups became more obvious. For example, the minority group characteristics we discussed in Chapter 1 apply to women, too.[6] Women are born into their gender identity and are easily identifiable by physical and cultural characteristics. In addition, women now recognize their commonality with one another as victims of sexism, an ideology, like that of racism, used to justify their unequal treatment.

A fifth characteristic, the practice of endogamy may seem inappropriate, yet in marriage the domination–subordination lines also manifest themselves. Traditional marriage ceremonies provide for the male to cherish his wife while she promises to obey her husband. When the ceremony ends, they are pronounced not "husband and wife," but "man and wife," grafting her identity and maiden name onto her relationship to her husband. Property laws, credit regulations, social security benefits, divorce laws, even telephone listings have long reinforced this less than equal status, although recent changes have occurred in some of these areas.

SOCIOHISTORICAL PERSPECTIVE

Early colonists in the new world, recreating in miniature the social systems of their homelands, continued male dominance patterns. In settlements and the advancing frontier, women were valuable "commodities," both for their skills and labor in the battle for survival and as sexual property in a region with a shortage of women. Although some instances of female independence in land ownership, inheritance, and voting rights did occur in those early years, for the most part women remained subordinate to men, with few individual rights except as appendages to

BOX 13.1

"Remember all men would be tyrants if they could."

"I long to hear that you have declared an independency—and by the way in the new Code of Laws which I suppose it will be necessary for you to make I desire you would Remember the Ladies, and be more generous and favourable to them than your ancestors. Do not put such unlimited power into the hands of the Husbands. Remember all men would be tyrants if they could. If particular care and attention is not paid to the Ladies we are determined to foment a Rebellion, and will not hold ourselves bound by any Laws in which we have no voice, or Representation.

"That your Sex are Naturally Tyrannical is a Truth so thoroughly established as to admit of no dispute, but such of you as wish to be happy willingly give up the harsh title of Master for the more tender and endearing one of Friend. Why then, not put it out of the power of the vicious and the Lawless to use us with cruelty and indignity with impunity. Men of Sense in all Ages abhor those customs which treat us only as the vassals of your Sex. Regard us then as Beings placed by Providence under your protection and in imitation of the Supreme Being make use of that power only for our happiness."

Letter from Abigail Adams to John Adams, March 31, 1776

their husbands. The U.S. Constitution did not give voting rights to women, nor did the courts until many decades later interpret its other provisions regarding full and equal participation as applicable to women either.[7]

As the nation grew and prospered, as the Industrial Revolution changed the very nature of American society, a dichotomy emerged regarding the role of women. Poor women, mostly from immigrant families, went to work in the factories at low-skilled jobs for lower wages than men.[8] Middle- and upper-class women, usually native-born, from families of prosperous merchants and industrialists, were elevated to a pedestal, as towers of moral strength, refinement, and soothing comfort to their world-weary males. Prevailing values in the nineteenth and early twentieth centuries held that the nature of women was to please and the nature of men was to achieve.[9]

Legal restrictions denied women any right to self-determination. They could not vote, own property in their own name, testify in court, make a legal contract, spend their own wages without their husband's permission, or even retain guardianship over their own children if their husband died or deserted them. Since men were supposedly active and women passive, only men were thought to enjoy sex; any woman who also enjoyed it was considered deviant and degenerate. A double standard in sexual conduct thus emerged. In a similar vein, female public speaking was a strong taboo, since a passive, refined lady would not behave so crudely.

Did everyone think and act this way in the nineteenth century? Certainly not, but these were the prevailing norms. Still, the abolitionist movement attracted female activists to fight against the continuance or expansion of slavery. The New York State legislature in 1848 acted to protect the property rights of married women, and in 1869 Wyoming Territory gave women the right to vote, continuing that practice after becoming a state in 1890, the first state to do so.

Suffragettes march in Washington, D.C. to urge passage of legislation giving women the right to vote. These first feminists incurred the wrath of many men as well as the disdain of numerous women for challenging existing norms. When their goal was achieved, the women's movement lay dormant until reactivated in the 1960s.

This editorial cartoon appearing in the *Louisville Times* on
November 24, 1913, successfully amused its readers.
Underneath the humor, however, lay the commonly shared
belief by many that both masculinity and femininity would
suffer if the defined sex roles were altered.

Efforts to give all women the right to vote met with fierce resistance. As the
suffragettes held rallies, protest marches, and demonstrations, they were ridiculed,
insulted, and abused—slapped, tripped, pelted with overripe fruits and vegetables
and burning cigar stubs. Chaining themselves to the posts, fences, and grillwork
of public buildings, these early feminists were arrested and jailed. In 1913, in
Washington, D.C., federal troops were brought in to quell the unrest. In 1916 six
months of picketing at the White House ended with mass arrests and imprisonment when the women refused to pay what they labeled "unjust" fines. Hostility
against such challenges to the male establishment is indicated by this account of
how the prison guards maltreated the demonstrators:

I saw Miss Lincoln, a slight young girl, thrown to the floor. Mrs. Nolan, a delicate old lady of seventy-three, was mastered by two men. . . . Whittaker [the prison superintendent] in the center of the room directed the whole attack, inciting the guards to every brutality. Two men brought in Dorothy Day, twisting her arms above her head. Suddenly they lifted her and brought her body down twice over the back of an iron bench . . . The bed broke Mrs. Nolan's fall, but Mrs. Cosu hit the wall. They had been there a few minutes when Mrs. Lewis, all doubled over like a sack of flour, was thrown in. Her head struck the iron bed and she fell to the floor senseless. As for Lucy Burns, they handcuffed her wrists and fastened the handcuffs over her head to the cell door.[10]

Finally, in 1919 Congress passed the Nineteenth Amendment, giving women the right to vote. Ratified a year later, it became the law of the land. Yet other feminist reforms did not follow. Women did not use their newly gained political power much, and a very few won elective office in proportion to their numbers. About 90 percent of the suffragettes ceased further activist measures, as the feminist movement faded, until it was resurrected some forty years later. Antisuffrage groups remained active though, successfully campaigning against forbidding women to serve on juries, holding elected office, or getting jobs competitive with males.

Following passage of the Nineteenth Amendment, labor force participation by women increased to about 25 percent, though job discrimination continued. Females rarely held decision-making positions and were the first fired during the Great Depression.[11] Society still frowned on the career woman, tolerating only women working for needed supplemental income. The approved female role was still as the good wife and mother, her prime responsibility being to the home.[12]

World War II changed all that—temporarily. Now women were needed in all work areas, contributing to the war effort while the men fought the enemy. The percentages of women working increased to 36 percent, with training programs and child-care centers often available to them. Both a postwar recession and GIs returning to their former jobs resulted in 2 million women fired within fifteen months after the war ended. As child-care centers were dismantled, public propaganda led to women leaving their jobs and returning to their home responsibilities full time. Nevertheless, the proportion of women working gradually increased, exceeding 50 percent by the 1980s.

The 1960s was a decade of social activism inspired by many factors, including the Camelot promise of the Kennedy administration, with Kennedy being the nation's first president born in the twentieth century. Kennedy appointed a Presidential Commission on the Status of Women, which documented extensive sexual discrimination in the country. When Congress failed to act on the commission's recommendations, a number of feminist advocates formed the National Organization for Women (NOW) in 1966, and a new phase of the feminist movement began. Resisted at first by most other women's groups, the New Left, even civil rights groups, the feminist movement eventually gained acceptance, succeeding in its efforts to end many forms of sex discrimination.

THE REALITY OF SEXUAL DIFFERENCES

Men and women differ biologically, but do they differ in other ways too? Are women naturally more tender, loving, nurturing, passive? Are men more aggressive, intelligent, dominant? When Freud argued that biology was destiny, he was simply restating a prevailing belief that had existed for centuries. Abundant evidence almost everywhere demonstrated a lower status for women, suggesting their inferiority rested on biological differences. Yet how much of these "natural" differences actually results from sociocultural factors and how much is truly innate? We still do not know, because untangling the impact of cultural molding from inherent capabilities has been virtually impossible so far. Still, we do have some clues from research investigations.

Biological Explanations

Aside from physical and reproductive differences, males and females are biologically distinct in other ways. Females tend to have a lower infant mortality rate, a higher tolerance for pain, and greater longevity. Their size and weight tends to give males greater physical strength. Scientists studying newborn infants, however, have not detected any significant differences in personality traits between the sexes.

Greater aggressiveness in boys appears between the ages of two and three, a pattern some scientists at least partially attribute to hormonal differences. Males have higher levels of certain hormones, such as testosterone, while females have higher concentrations, of other hormones such as the estrogens. Animal studies have indicated early hormonal differences produce different neural patterns in males and females. Additionally, other studies of humans and animals show a direct link between higher levels of testosterone and increased aggression. A possible biological advantage in establishing male dominance may thus result from aggressive tendencies, combined with greater size and strength.

Another possible biological difference may lie in intellectual capabilities. Females tend to have an edge in verbal ability while males tend to be somewhat better in spatial conceptualization. As we shall discuss shortly, socialization factors may shape these differences, but some scientists suggest a physiological explanation. The left hemisphere of the brain generally controls verbal abilities and the right hemisphere generally controls spatial abilities. Females appear to develop this specialization of brain hemispheres at an earlier age, leading to an advantage for them in developing verbal skills, while the delay aids males in developing their spatial skills.[13] Even so, such differences do not establish sexual superiority any more than individuals excelling in one skill are better than people excelling in other skills. The fact that all of us possess different talents and skills makes us complementary to one another, not superior/inferior.

Socialization and Sex Roles

While gender identity is an ascribed status, one given at birth, society shapes that identity through socialization. In this process of learning traits and activities as desirable and correct, individuals internalize approved sex role behavior as a real part of themselves. These cultural dictates of appropriate male–female conduct sometimes vary from one society to another, as anthropologist Margaret Mead found, for example, among three tribes in New Guinea.[14] The Arapesh culture produced both men and women with decidedly feminine traits, while the Mundugamor produced both sexes with pronounced masculine traits. However, among the Tchambuli the usual sex role behavior of western society was completely reversed. Mead's findings emphasized the influential role of culture and socialization in developing sexual differentiation.

In much of the world male dominance has both existed and been reinforced by the writings of male philosophers and religious leaders. Sexist ideology is promoted in the sacred books of the world's three major religions, evoking supernatural justification for male supremacy. Islam's Koran states, "Men are superior to women on account of qualities in which God has given them pre-eminence." In the New Testament, Saint Paul proclaims, "Let the woman learn in silence with all subjection. But I suffer not a woman to teach, nor to usurp authority over the man, but to be in silence . . . she shall be saved in childbearing, if they continue in faith and charity and holiness with sobriety." Finally, the morning prayer of the Orthodox Jews includes the line, "Blessed art Thou, oh Lord our God, King of the Universe, that I was not born a woman."

Childhood Socialization

Influenced by such value pronouncements, but even more so by their own upbringing, parents convey their expectations to children in thousands of ways. Studies show mothers and fathers touch, handle, speak to, play with, and discipline children differently, depending on the child's sex. Children learn to play differently, girls more often in exclusive dyadic relationships and boys more likely in larger groups.[15] Boys usually grow up experiencing more expansive territory on their bikes or hikes, requiring numerous adaptive decisions, while girls generally experience a more structured, narrower world, limiting their opportunities to develop self-reliance. Children also learn from parental and other adult role models, assuming attitudes and evaluations of their gender.

The impact of parents, family, friends, school, and the media in shaping differences in gender behavior extends to personalities as well. Because of childhood experiences, boys tend to become more inquisitive, self-assured, and convinced they can control things while girls tend to become more passive, timid, and fearful of new situations. Though individuals vary in personality and temperament, this pattern emerges through the socialization process to match self-evaluations with the unequal rewards of the system, thereby completing the vicious circle of justification.[16]

Based upon an eleven-year longitudinal study of culturally influenced sex differences among boys and girls, psychologist Jeanne Bloch has identified seven areas where the two sexes vary:

1. *Aggression.* Boys tend to be more aggressive in various activities.

2. *Activity.* Boys tend to have more outdoor activities, to be more curious and explore unfamiliar worlds.

3. *Impulsiveness.* Boys tend to resist temptations less, partly indicated by their higher accident rate.

4. *Anxiety.* Girls tend to be more fearful and anxious, their greater compliance and obedience manifesting their anxiety.

5. *Importance of Social Relations.* Girls tend to have greater concern for the welfare of the group, to compromise more, and understand better the feelings of others.

6. *Quality of Self-Concept.* Males tend to view themselves as more powerful and in control, seeing themselves as able to make things happen.

7. *Achievement-related Activities.* Males tend to set higher goals and be more confident, blaming failure on external factors, while females blame themselves.[17]

Socialization is a lifelong process, and throughout one's childhood, adolescence, and adulthood a continuous array of experiences reinforces early influences. Toys, games, textbooks, teachers' attitudes and actions, and peer influence have all helped maintain sexual stereotypes. Most influential is the role of the media, particularly television commercials and programming. If we are to believe television, only males live life with gusto, buy cars, and have group fun, while women use the right shampoo to avoid the "frizzies," wear a seductive perfume, or get their floors to really shine. From Smurfette playing a less important role as the only female on the popular cartoon show, to Mary Tyler Moore as the only female in the TV newsroom and the only one to call the boss Mr. Grant, women are constantly portrayed as subservient or supportive fluff, or sex objects in shows and advertising.[18] A content analysis of the lyrics of rock 'n roll songs also reveals sexual stereotyping.

Advertising

The impact of advertising in reinforcing traditional sex roles and sterotypes is very pervasive. Lucy Komisar argues that

Advertising is an insidious propaganda machine for a male supremacist society. . . . [It] legitimizes the idealized, stereotyped roles of woman as temptress, wife, mother, and sex object, and portrays women as less intelligent and more dependent than men. . . . It makes women feel unfeminine if they are not pretty enough and guilty if they do not spend most of their time in desperate attempts to imitate gourmet cooks and eighteenth century scullery maids. . . . It creates false, unreal images of women that reflect males' fantasies rather than flesh and blood human beings.[19]

Research on television advertising reveals: (1) males mostly do commercial voiceovers; (2) women tend to perform typical family activities, usually in the home, benefiting men, but men carry out a wide variety of activities; (3) women are younger than men; (4) fewer girls and women appear than boys and men.[20] Moreover, as Erving Goffman observed, subtle forms of sexism are common in print advertising as well:

(1) Overwhelmingly, a woman is taller than a man only when the man is her social inferior; (2) a woman's hands are seen just barely touching, holding or caressing—never grasping, manipulating or shaping; (3) when a photograph of men and women illustrates an instruction of some sort the man is always instructing the woman—even if the men and women are actually children (that is, a male child will be instructing a female child); (4) when an advertisement requires someone to sit or lie on a bed or a floor that someone is almost always a child or a woman, hardly ever a man; (5) when the head or eye of a man is averted it is only in relation to a social, political, or intellectual superior, but when the eye or head of a woman is averted it is always in relation to whatever man is pictured with her; (6) women are repeatedly shown mentally drifting from the scene while in close physical touch with a male, their faces lost and dreamy, "as though his aliveness to the surroundings and his readiness to cope were enough for both of them"; (7) concomitantly, women, much more than men, are pictured at the kind of psychological loss or remove from a social situation that leaves one unoriented for action (e.g., something terrible has happened and a woman is shown with her hands over her mouth and her eyes helpless with horror).[21]

Today's world is hardly static regarding sexual inequality, as women continue to make gains in all areas. Yet we remain in a transitional stage, and socialization inequities continue. One team of researchers pointed out that the computing culture puts out obstacles for little girls, even though computers will be the principal tools in 25 percent of all jobs in a few years.[22] The video arcade is a den of teenage male culture, they say, where the main role of girls is to admire the performance of their boyfriends, not to play themselves. Arcade games and home computer software transplant street corner society to a TV monitor with games of destruction, sports, and tests of spatial skills—games designed by males for males— hardly the kind of world girls find enticing.

IMMIGRANT AND MINORITY WOMEN

Before we look at women in contemporary America in the next section, we first need to consider the impact of socialization and subcultural communities upon the role of many women in American society. Almost all immigrants, past and present, have come from traditional societies with clearly defined sex role models of behavior and responsibility. Those internalized self-concepts and expectations were not only part of everyday life in their homeland, but also continuing norms within their ethnic communities after immigration. In those culturally insulated neighbor-hoods with their parallel social institutions, women seldom worked outside the home, performing instead their traditional responsibilities for their families within the home.

Vestiges of White Ethnic Orientations

In many northeastern U.S. cities numerous elderly immigrant poor live on mea-ger, fixed incomes, struggling to survive in decaying neighborhoods no longer cohesive or homogeneous. Most of these oldtimers are female, with a limited command of English, since their traditional role in an ethnic community did not necessitate English fluency, and most arrived in the United States long before the advent of the feminist movement. Lacking job skills and much formal education, unfamiliar with the workings of a bureaucratic society or reluctant to seek public assistance, they cling to the remnants of their familiar world. For them, being a woman, advanced in years, and unprepared for independence, life presents daily challenges.

Often overlooked in any discussion of most aspects of ethnicity are second-generation adult Americans. Yet their primary socialization revolved around Old World value orientations and traditional sex role models, shaping their percep-tions of the world somewhat differently than that of children of native-born par-ents. Studies of working-class Americans, many of whom are second-generation Americans of central, southern, and eastern European heritage, reveal some of these continuing values and attitudes. In a typical working-class family, the woman does not work outside the home, devoting her energies entirely to the family, while the male serves as breadwinner and supreme authority of the household.

The women's movement has brought problems to these families. Lillian Rub-in's field research shows many working-class women are frustrated and lonely, not experiencing in their lives the heralded liberation television portrays.[23] Males, providing their wives with all the attributes of a good life—home, car, necessities, and luxuries—are puzzled by their wives' unhappiness. Because their value ori-entations are sex-segregated, working-class husbands and wives may experience great difficulty communicating with each other.

One avenue of role expansion for workingmen's wives has been increased par-ticipation in the civic arena of service, politics, and social action. Sociologist Irene Dabrowski reports their widespread neighborhood involvement stems from urban problems disrupting "Little Italies," "Polish Towns," and "South Sides," thereby "weakening family ties, eroding economic self-sufficiency, and even threatening the very existence of these largely white ethnic communities."[24] In a case study of Carondelet, an ethnic working-class neighborhood on the south side of St. Louis, Dabrowski found neighborhood women in three-fourths of all community orga-nizations and half of all leadership positions, achieving moderate success in pre-serving the vitality and stability of their community.[25]

Today's Minority Women

Machismo, the pervasive value orientation of the male as provider and dominant force in the family, impacts heavily on the daily lives of Hispanic women. Most Hispanics are Catholic, and the position of the Church against ordained women priests and limited, supportive roles only for nuns, reinforces sex role differentiation. Problems arise among low-income Hispanic-Americans when only the female is able to find work, or earns more than her spouse, creating family strain as internalized male self-image and role behavior—as culturally prescribed—are threatened by economic reality. Hispanic women who work or go to school must still completely fulfill their traditional home responsibilities, placing extensive demands upon them to maintain both spheres of work adequately.

The status and roles of Asian-American women vary with their place of birth and that of their husbands, as well as their educational levels. Generally, those foreign-born maintain very traditional family and sex roles. The higher the education and the more Americanized the women are, the higher their status. Although more Asian women are combining career and family roles, Lucy Jen Huang reports that the Chinese wife tends to assume the role of "co-pilot and helper to her husband rather than be totally equalitarian in the relationship."[26] Akemi Kikumura and Henry H. L. Kitano suggest the personal dissatisfaction among Japanese-American women in their expected female roles may be a primary reason for their more rapid acculturation and greater outgroup marriage rate.[27]

The dichotomy among Blacks, discussed in Chapter 10, relates directly to the status and role of the black female in American society. College-educated black females are more likely to benefit from the women's liberation movement in employment, income, and equalitarian marriages, although their higher ratio to black male college graduates indicates a disadvantage in finding a spouse of the same race.[28] In contrast, low-income black women do not identify with the women's movement, since many of its demands seem irrelevant to their needs. Sociologist Robert Staples observes:

They have always been in the labor force, whether they wanted to or not. Black women have not been depicted as sex objects as much as they have been used as sex objects. Motherhood and marriage were two institutions that were denied to them in the past. Because they had to work, many were deprived of the time to enjoy their children. Marriage was a luxury many could not afford or the conditions of their lives would not provide. To the many black women who are heading households, a husband would be a welcome figure.[29]

What emerges from a consideration of women in various racial and ethnic groups are two basic themes: cultural attributes and intensified subordinate status. Not only do immigrant groups recreate in miniature their old familiar worlds to obtain a secure place in an alien country, but their evolving ethnic self-consciousness and community organization foster maintenance of accompanying male dominance patterns as well. These traditional gender roles have either reflected sexism within the entire society or else resisted recent advances in sexual equality. Moreover, as both a woman and a minority group member, an individual is at a double disadvantage, simultaneously encountering prejudice and discrimination on two fronts— her sex and her race or ethnicity.

Special concerns of minority women include: involuntary sterilization, monolingual education and services, high infant- and maternal-mortality rates, housing, psychological and employment testing, reduced enforcement of affirmative action, deportation of Hispanic mothers of American-born children, special-admission quality education programs, unemployment, welfare programs, and the family.[30] One black delegate to the National Women's Convention in Houston in November 1977 summed up the double disadvantages of minority women:

> Minority women share with all women the experience of sexism as a barrier to their full rights of citizenship. . . . But the institutionalized bias based on race, language, culture and/or ethnic origin in governance of territories or localities has led to the additional oppression and exclusion of minority women and to the conditions of poverty from which they disproportionally suffer.[31]

WOMEN IN CONTEMPORARY AMERICA

The justification for considering women as a minority group and speaking of the existence of sexism becomes readily understandable through examination of leading social indicators. As we did for Blacks and Hispanics in earlier chapters, we shall now direct our attention to the comparative status of women in terms of education, employment, and income. Additionally, we shall look at sexual harassment, law, and politics to illustrate why the U.S. Commission on Civil Rights in 1976 concluded, "Discrimination against women exists in every facet of American society."[32]

Education

For many generations, education was sex-segregated. Males and females often attended different schools or were physically and academically separated in "coeducational" schools. For example, the still-standing Henry Street grammar school in New York's Lower East Side—a well-known white ethnic area for over a century—contains either the word "Boys" or "Girls" engraved over one of its two opposite-end entrances. Women were once taught only the social graces and given moral education. Teaching academic subjects to females was then considered a waste of time, one Harvard Professor in 1911 even proclaiming such an attempt would "weaken the intellect of the teacher."[33]

Even after females overcame these prejudices and took academic subjects alongside males, the educational system maintained sexism in both obvious and subtle ways. Teachers and counselors, with traditional sex-role expectations, fostered sex-linked aspirations and career choices. Children's books and textbooks

BOX 13.2

Barbarous Rituals

Woman Is:

- kicking strongly in your mother's womb, upon which she is told, "It must be a boy, if it's so active!"

- being confined to the Doll Corner in nursery school when you are really fascinated by Tinker Toys.

- being labeled a tomboy when all you wanted to do was climb that tree to look out and see a distance.

- seeing grownups chuckle when you say you want to be an engineer or doctor when you grow up—and learning to say you want to be a mommy or nurse, instead.

- dreading summertime because more of your body with its imperfections will be seen—and judged.

- liking math or history and getting hints that boys are turned off by smart girls.

- discovering that what seems like everything worthwhile doing in life "isn't feminine," and learning to just delight in being feminine and "nice"—and feeling somehow guilty.

- swinging down the street feeling good and smiling at people and being hassled like a piece of meat in return.

- brooding about "how far" you should go with the guy you really like. Will he no longer respect you? Will you get—oh God—a "reputation"? Or, if not, are you a square? Being pissed off because you can't just do what you feel like doing.

- finding that the career you've chosen exacts more than just study or hard work—an emotional price of being made to feel "less a woman."

- being bugged by men in the office who assume that you're a virginal prude if you don't flirt, and that you're an easy mark if you are halfway relaxed and pleasant.

- wanting to go back to school, to read, to join something, do something. Why isn't home enough for you? What's wrong with you?

- feeling a need to say "thank you" when your guy actually fixes himself a meal now that you're dying with the 'flu.

- being widowed, or divorced, and trying to get a "good" job—at your age.

- getting older, getting lonelier, getting ready to die—and knowing it wouldn't have had to be this way after all.

from Robin Morgan, *Going Too Far: The Personal Chronicle of a Feminist* (New York: Vintage Books, 1978), pp. 107–113.

TABLE 13.1

Years of School Completed, by Sex, Race, and Spanish Origin, 1981

Race and Sex	Population (1,000)	Percent of Population Completing							Median School Years Completed
		Elementary School			High School		College		
		0–4 Years	5–7 Years	8 Years	1–3 Years	4 Years	1–3 Years	4 Years or More	
White	116,647	2.6	5.1	7.9	12.8	38.5	15.3	17.8	12.6
Male	55,213	2.7	5.3	7.7	12.3	34.1	15.7	22.2	12.6
Female	61,435	2.5	5.0	8.1	13.3	42.4	14.9	13.8	12.5
Black	13,259	7.9	11.1	6.8	21.4	31.6	13.1	8.2	12.1
Male	5,848	9.3	10.2	7.1	20.1	31.1	13.9	8.2	12.1
Female	7,411	6.8	11.8	6.5	22.4	32.1	12.4	8.2	12.1
Spanish Origin	6,308	15.6	16.7	8.8	14.4	26.3	10.5	7.7	10.7
Male	2,993	15.2	16.5	9.0	13.9	24.5	11.3	9.7	11.0
Female	3,316	16.1	16.8	8.7	14.9	27.9	9.8	5.9	10.5
Total, All Races	132,899	3.3	5.8	7.7	13.6	37.6	15.1	17.1	12.5

Source: U.S. Bureau of the Census.

reinforced sex stereotypes, with male characters heavily outnumbering females, active and adventuresome in contrast to the more passive females. Stereotypical activities—boys creating or earning money and girls shopping, cooking, and sewing—existed in all texts, even in mathematics. Throughout all of them the exclusive use of male pronouns further biased children's education. Most of these stereotypical depictions have been eliminated through court challenges and pressures on publishers, though problems still remain.[34]

As Table 13.1 shows, the median school years completed is very close between males and females when controlled for race. These are deceptive statistics, however. In fact, a greater percentage of females graduate from high school than males, due to the higher male dropout rate, usually caused by a need to assume a share of the family's financial responsibilities. Over 42 percent of the white females have graduated from high school, compared to 34 percent of the white males. Among Blacks and Hispanics, the percentages and differences are much less, though females remain higher. Among all three groups fewer women enter college, and those who do are less likely to earn a degree than males entering college. Even fewer women go on to graduate or professional school.

Another indication of gender differentiation in education lies in field study. If men and women were truly equal in their socialization and life opportunities, we would expect to find a fairly even distribution of both sexes in all areas. Instead, as Table 13.2 illustrates, women are underrepresented in such male-dominated fields as business and management, computer and information services, engineering, and the physical sciences. Women remain overrepresented in traditional

TABLE 13.2
Female-earned Bachelor's Degrees
by Field of Study, 1980

Biological Sciences	42.2
Business and Management	33.6
Communications	52.1
Computer and Information Sciences	30.4
Education	73.2
Engineering	9.3
Fine and Applied Arts	63.1
Foreign Languages	75.7
Health Professions	82.8
Home Economics	95.1
Law	42.9
Math	42.1
Physical Sciences	23.6
Psychology	63.3
Social Sciences	43.6
Theology	25.8

Source: U.S. National Center for Education Statistics.

female career areas: education, nursing, home economics, and letters. Advanced degrees conferred in medicine, dentistry, law, and engineering in 1980 show a strong imbalance in sex ratio, ranging from more than 2 to 1 in law to 11 to 1 in engineering (see Table 13.3).

TABLE 13.3
Degrees Conferred in Selected Professions

Type of Degree	1960	1970	1980
Medicine (M.D.)			
Men	6,645	7,615	11,416
Women	387	699	3,486
Dentistry (D.D.S., D.M.D.)			
Men	3,221	3,684	4,558
Women	26	34	700
Law (LL.B, J.D.)			
Men	9,010	14,115	24,893
Women	230	801	10,754
Engineering			
Men	45,453	63,227	80,001
Women	171	526	7,642

Source: U.S. National Center for Education Statistics.

Employment

Sex segregation has long been a reality in the work force, creating a female oc-cupational ghetto. We still have a traditional set of low-pay, low-status jobs over-whelmingly filled by women and another set of higher-pay, higher-status occu-pations that are predominantly male (see Table 13.4). "Pink collar" jobs include sales clerks, bank tellers, bookkeepers, cashiers, key punch operators, secretaries, telephone operators, health technicians, and librarians.

When we examine the percentage distributions of workers by sex in the major occupational categories (Figure 13.1), we find men dominate the higher-paid managerial positions while women disproportionately occupy the much lower-paying clerical positions. This pattern repeats itself in blue-collar occupational fields: men dominate in the unionized, high-paying jobs and women far outnumber men in the generally nonunionized, low-paying service and household work fields. Blue-collar supervisory positions for females are unusual, males being nine times more likely to hold such positions.[35] A similar pattern occurs in white-collar occupations, where most of the 27.5 percent females in managerial and administrative posi-tions tend to be in lower management with little power or upward mobility poten-tial.[36]

Although women appear almost proportionately represented among profes-sional and technical workers, the distribution within this category is very uneven. Women are heavily concentrated in the lower-pay, lower-prestige occupations, ones requiring fewer qualifications and labeled traditionally female: librarians, nurses,

TABLE 13.4
Employed Persons, Selected Occupations
By Sex and Percent: 1981

Female		Male	
Registered Nurses	96.8	Engineers	95.6
Elementary school teachers	83.6	Lawyers and judges	85.9
Bank tellers	93.5	Dentists	95.4
Billing clerks	88.2	Physicians	86.3
Bookkeepers	91.1	Religious workers	88.1
Cashiers	86.2	Science technicians	81.2
File clerks	83.8	Stock and bond sales agents	83.0
Key punch operators	93.5	Wholesale trade sales reps	88.1
Receptionists	97.3	Manufacturing sales reps	80.0
Secretaries	99.1	Mail carriers, post office	84.3
Stenographers	85.1	Carpenters	98.1
Telephone operators	92.9	Automobile mechanics	99.4
Typists	96.3	Electricians	98.4
Waiters	89.3	Blue-collar supervisors	88.7
Health and nursing aides	89.2	Machinists and jobsetters	96.0
Private household workers	96.5	Radio and TV mechanics	96.3

Source: Statistical Abstract of the United States, 1982–83, Table 651.

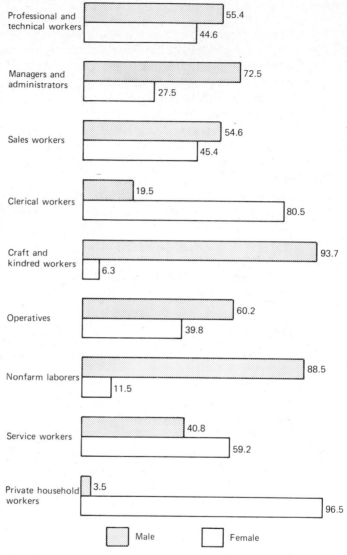

FIGURE 13.1

Occupations of Employed Persons, by Sex and Percent, 1981

dieticians, therapists, noncollege teachers, and social workers. Men heavily domi- nate the high-status professional positions: medicine, dentistry, law, engineering. While the situation is improving (see Figure 13.2), a woman remains eleven times more likely to become a nurse but only one-eighth as likely to become a physi- cian. She is only one-fourth as likely to become a computer specialist but five times more likely to become a librarian than men.

FIGURE 13.2

Female Professional and Technical Workers, by Percent, 1981

Source: U.S. Bureau of Labor Statistics.

More than 52 percent of all women are now working, up from less than 40 percent in 1965. The greatest increase in working women has been among married mothers with preschool and school-age children. By 1982, nearly two-thirds of women with children aged 6 to 17 were working, up from 49.2 percent in 1970. Nearly half of all mothers with children under 6 were working, up from 30.3 percent in 1970 and 18.6 percent in 1960.[37] By 1982, 32 million children under 18—or 55 percent of all American children—had working mothers. Even though more women are in the labor market, gaining entry and increased proportions in previously all or mostly male occupational domains, they remain underrepresented in many fields.

While more women enter the labor force, men continue a decades-old trend of leaving it. Since 1951, adult males in the labor force have declined from 87.3 percent to 77 percent.[38] Those 65 and older had a labor force participation rate of 19.9 percent in 1981 compared to 44.6 percent in 1955.[39] The drop-off participation of males accelerates after age 45, apparently encouraged by early retirement plans, better pensions, and disability benefits. In 1982, the U.S. labor force totaled 110 million, 56 percent male and 44 percent female. Projections for the

Walter Mondale's selection of New York Congresswoman Geraldine Ferraro, the daughter of Italian immigrants, as the Democratic Vice-Presidential candidate was a major step forward for women in politics, as well as for Italian Americans. Neither group had previously been represented by a major party candidate for national office. Regardless of the election outcome, another barrier in female political participation had come tumbling down.

year 2000 are a labor force of 134 million, 52 percent male and 48 percent female.[40] Because their proportionate representation in the labor force continues to grow, women are increasingly found in all occupational endeavors.

Income

As you would expect, a sex-segregated occupational structure results in differential income levels. Comparing the median income of full-time workers in 1981, women earned $12,457, or 60 percent of male earnings of $20,692.[41] What makes this pay gap more significant is that 60 percent figure has been virtually unchanged for twenty-five years! Despite all the heralded claims about female gains in education and job opportunities, women have not been gaining in their earnings relative to men.

TABLE 13.5
Median Earnings by Occupation of Longest Job Held and Sex: 1980

Major Full-Time Occupational Groups	Women	Men	Ratio: Women to Men
Professional and Technical Workers	$15,285	$23,026	.66
Managers and Administrators	$12,936	$23,558	.55
Sales Workers	$ 9,748	$19,910	.49
Clerical Workers	$10,997	$18,247	.60
Craft Workers	$11,701	$18,671	.63
Operatives	$ 9,440	$15,702	.60
Laborers, except farm	$ 9,747	$12,157	.76
Service Workers	$ 7,982	$13,097	.61
Total	$11,197	$18,612	.60

Source: Bureau of the Census, *Current Population Reports,* Series P-60, No. 132.

In discussing employment, we said women were often in lower positions within occupational categories. When we examine the female to male median earnings ratio within these categories, by longest job held, the differential still remains (see Table 13.5). The disparity in income between men and women occurs on all levels of the occupational scale. A portion of this difference may be due to variations in qualifications, seniority, and number of hours worked, but even when these variables are controlled for, the disparity still exists. Catherine MacKinnon has observed:

> Controlling for differences in education, skills, and experience (factors which themselves could be created by discrimination), studies have found a remaining difference between men's and women's salaries of between 20 and 43 percent, a difference which can be explained only as discrimination.[42]

Even when we control for race, the income differences remain. The median income of males, regardless of race, is higher than the median income of females, regardless of race. In 1982, for example, white males had median earnings of $15,964, and black males $10,510. The median income of black females was $7,802, followed by white females with $7,640.[43] Sexual discrimination in the workplace appears a more potent force than racial discrimination.

When we consider the growing number of households headed by women (see Figure 13.3), this pattern takes on alarming significance. About 15 percent of all white families and almost half of all black families are headed by women, whose greater probability of limited earning power negatively impacts on the family's economic health. Female-headed families are the fastest growing segment of the population living in poverty, prompting many to call this trend the "feminization of poverty."[44] One out of three female-headed families now lives in poverty, having increased from 1.8 million families in 1969 to over 3 million in 1980.[45]

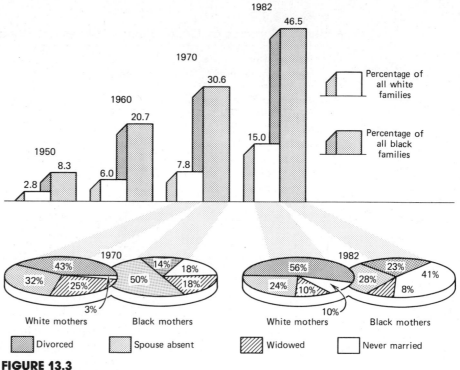

FIGURE 13.3

Households Headed by Women

Source: Bureau of the Census.

Sexual Harassment

For years sexual harassment continued because it was kept secret and considered to be an individual, personal problem. Supposedly, a male, attracted to a particular female, made sexual advances and received a positive, negative, or "maybe" response. Until 1976, women kept mostly silent, thinking the experience an individual encounter and not realizing it was part of a larger pattern connected to their subordination and vulnerability in the occupational structure.

Redbook magazine's 1976 survey of 9,000 women defined the extent of the problem, as 90 percent reported having experienced sexual harassment at work. The woman's movement brought heightened awareness of the group basis of this problem. Then the federal government's Merit System Protection Board, in a 1978–1980 study, reported a $189 million cost in hiring, training, absenteeism, and job-turnover expenses caused by harassment. When private industry costs are included, the figure probably runs into billions. The government survey also estimated that 1 percent, or about 9,000 female federal employees, had been victims of attempted rape by supervisors or co-workers.

In 1979, attorney and university professor Catherine A. MacKinnon wrote the first book on this subject, *Sexual Harassment of Working Women: A Case of Sex*

Discrimination. She identified sexual harassment as either a single occurrence at work or a series of incidents, ranging along a continuum of varying intensity, including:

> verbal sexual suggestions or jokes, constant leering or ogling, brushing against your body "accidentally," a friendly pat, squeeze or pinch or arm against you, catching you alone for a quick kiss, the indecent proposition backed by the threat of losing your job, or forced sexual relations.[46]

Some men's assumption that their superior position at work also involves sexual privileges is rooted in centuries of male domination:

> Sexual harassment by a boss or supervisor harkens back, in a way, to the medieval practice of *droit du seigneur,* which gave the feudal lord the right to sleep the first night with the bride of any of his vassals. Athough feudalism ended many centuries ago, some people still feel that to be a boss is to be at least semi-divinely ordained —to have certain inalienable rights. . . . The idea of using a paycheck as a license for sex seems ludicrous, if not sick, but it happens all the time. Men who would never think or at least never follow through on, the idea of pinching a woman's breast in a bus or on the street, feel free to subject their secretary to this humiliation as if it were a job-given right.[47]

Prospects for reduction of this type of harassment seem promising. Official guidelines formulated by the Equal Employment Opportunities Commission set standards protecting employees from certain forms of sexual harassment, defined as follows:

> Unwelcome sexual advances, requests for sexual favors, and other verbal or physical conduct of a sexual nature . . . when submission is made a condition of employment, or rejection of the advance is used as the basis for future employment decision, or interfering with the individual's performance or creating an intimidating, hostile, or offensive working environment.

While this sounds formidable, it does not encompass many obnoxious and questionable behaviors found in everyday examples. California's Fair Employment and Housing Department has established more down-to-earth guidelines: unsolicited written, verbal, or physical contacts; suggestive or obscene notes; continual leering; obscene gestures; display of obscene objects or pictures; blocking movements by physical touching; and forced involvement in obscene joking. Since these forms of sexual harassment are not specifically mentioned in the EEOC guidelines, they can escape definition and punishment. A General Motors representative, however, has suggested a good "rough measure" of sexual harassment: "Would you be embarrassed to have your remarks displayed in the newspaper or actions described to your family?"[48]

Sexism and the Law

Stereotyping females as passive and in need of protection became institutionalized in law. Many labor laws, originally intended to prevent the exploitation of women, became a means of restricting their job opportunities and income potential. A vast array of state laws, assuming certain female inabilities, ran counter to reality. As sociologist Rosalind J. Dworkin wryly commented:

A mother can carry her 40-pound child, move furniture in her home, and finish her housekeeping chores late at night. But the same woman, working outside the home, legally could not carry more than 30 pounds of weight or work overtime in some states. . . . [T]hese protective laws . . . degrade women to a childlike status by assuming they are unable, or not wise enough, to protect themselves, individually or collectively, from exploitation.[49]

Though many of these laws are changing, compliance does not necessarily follow. Many women do not know their legal rights, or find the difficulties involved in securing them outweigh the rewards. Moreover, the courts are hardly free of sexism themselves. In 1983 New Jersey became the first state to complete a self-review of sexism in the state court system. Among other findings, it discovered:

1. Women received lower personal injury settlements, especially if they were housewives, because juries failed to recognize the value of their work;

2. Judges failed to enforce the new law against wife beating and domestic violence;

3. Judges set child-support payments in divorce cases too low, with no strong enforceable sanctions against nonpayment by fathers.

Female attorneys also complained that 86 percent of their colleagues and 66 percent of the judges had made demeaning jokes or hostile remarks about their sex.[50] As New Jersey acts to eliminate such practices, some of the other forty-nine states are beginning to conduct similar self-reviews, as pressure for change mounts from the growing number of female lawyers nationwide.

Because changing hundreds of state laws is a long, difficult process, Congress approved the Equal Rights Amendment (ERA) in 1972, intending it to extend full and legal rights to women. The proposed Amendment's wording was brief: "Equality of rights under the law shall not be denied or abridged by the United States or by any state on account of sex." Required to be ratified by three-fourths of the states, a total of thirty-eight, it only gained approval by thirty-five. The failure of the ERA was caused by the opposition of numerous groups, including many women, labor leaders or activists, as well as conservatives, religious groups, and insurance companies.

Is the ERA dead? Many feminists have not given up, vowing to replace state and federal legislators opposed to the measure. Others argue the Amendment is unnecessary, that full property and credit rights for women, and more equal divorce and child custody rights for men, for example, are simply evolving through

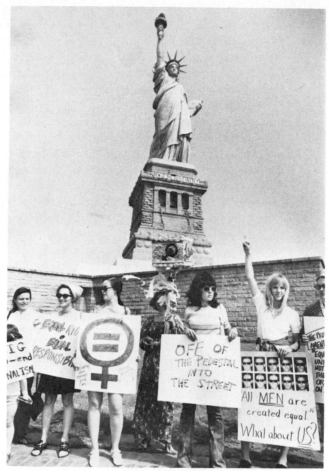

Members of the Women's Liberation movement display their banners in front of a sea wall at the Statue of Liberty. On this day, August 10, 1970, the House of Representatives passed the Equal Rights Amendment. However, only 35 of the required 38 states ratified the amendment.

changing societal norms. The issue remains highly controversial, sometimes surrounded by emotion-charged fears and myths, but with well-intentioned people on both sides of the argument. If an ERA does pass, one thing is certain: it is still years away.

Women and Politics

Earlier we noted that, once they secured voting rights, women did not use their political power to improve their lives or win their proportional share of elected office. Only a handful of women have been elected governor, the late Ella Grasso of Connecticut being the first in 1974. Only 2 of 100 U.S. senators are female, and 19 of 435 Congressional representatives. Women comprise 14 percent of township or municipal councils, 9 percent of all mayors, and 12 percent of all state legislators.[51] With women constituting slightly over 51 percent of the population, with more female than male registered and active voters, they nevertheless remain vastly underrepresented in elected, decision-making positions.

What accounts for this lack of female political involvement? The question has intrigued both sociologists and political scientists, with emerging explanations many and varied. Most political careers evolve out of training, experience, and leadership in law or business careers, areas in which women have participated only slightly. Both men and women also prefer male leaders, placing more confidence in them. Furthermore, males control the political parties, often resisting placement of women in organizational power positions or as viable candidates for "serious" offices.[52] Politics has been a male bastion for so many generations that male politicians tend to view the female politican as a stranger, one whose feminine values and way of life appear incompatible with the world of politics. Evidence of this attitude was seen in the lively debate in the summer of 1984, with presidential candidate Walter Mondale's consideration of a female running mate.

A woman seeking a political career experiences marginality, unable to retain her past "feminine" ways if she is to be an active political participant, yet unwilling to reject them either. Both choices present threats to her self-esteem, and the simpler choice is avoiding disorientation and personal isolation by not running for office.[53] Women also do not form a voting bloc, since they are not residentially segregated and tend to vote along socioeconomic lines.

SOCIOLOGICAL PERSPECTIVES

Every society has had a gender-based division of labor, but this has not always meant sexual inequality. Why, then, has the male role been considered superior in many soceites? Functionalists, conflict theorists, and interactionists differ in explaining both the reasons for male dominance and in what steps should be taken.

The Functionalist View

In preindustrial societies, from which most immigrants to America have come, assigned work tasks by gender effectively created a smoothly functioning society. Such was also the case in early nineteenth-century America, as distinct sex roles facilitated social stability, women and men understanding their place and function in the society. Sociologists Talcott Parsons and Robert Bales maintained the efficient functioning of a society, indeed its very survival, depends upon satisfying both instrumental and expressive needs.[54] Males have traditionally performed the instrumental tasks —goal-oriented activities necessary for family survival, such as earning a living or finding food. Females have handled the expressive tasks—providing harmony, love, emotional support, and stability within the family. Today, many are questioning why these necessary tasks should be gender-linked and not shared or reversed, if desired.

As mentioned earlier under biological explanations, the tendencies of males to be larger, stronger, and more aggressive may explain their emergence as dominant in the social order.[55] As male dominance continued over the generations, a sexist ideology evolved to justify the existing order as "natural," gender role and status becoming institutionalized through socialization and practice. As long as a society remains relatively unchanged, sex role differentiation did not emerge as a concern to most people nor generate a female group consciousness and desire for change.

Social changes caused by the industrial revolution threw the gender-based social structure out of balance. Machines reduced the male advantage of greater strength for work tasks, while reductions in the infant mortality rate and family size, together with labor-saving home applicances, freed women from spending most of their adult lives and waking hours raising small children. Values, attitudes, and expectations about women's proper role did not change as rapidly as social and economic conditions. This cultural lag caused strain among individuals, families, and in society itself.

Among twentieth century immigrants, both past and present, family and traditions have been two vital means of preserving identity and stability in a new country. Those with traditional sex-role value orientations experience problems adapting to a more egalitarian society. Working Hispanic women present a conflict to the machismo concept of the male as the sole provider. Social activities and dating practices among teenage girls challenge traditional homeland norms about adolescent male–female interaction. Higher education for women runs counter to traditional notions about its value for females who should just marry and bear children.

Achieving sexual equality, functionalists stress, requires a restoration of a balance between expectations and actual conditions. To some, changes have been too extensive and system harmony requires a return to the past, with clearly defined sex roles restoring a stable family life and an efficient division of labor. Most functionalists, however, call for redefined sex roles and adjustments in the family system and other social institutions to eliminate sexual discrimination. Changes in societal conditions and expectations require system adjustments if the dysfunctions are to be overcome.

The Conflict View

Male dominance and subordination of women, sexual inequality and discrimination, are simply illustrations for conflict theorists of the universal human problems of exploitation and oppression. Substituting the words "men" and "women" for names of dominant and minority groups, or "gender" for "class," enables us to incorporate women as a group in Marxian concepts of false consciousness, exploitation, awakened awareness, and organized challenges to the social order. In fact, Friedrich Engels had observed that the first class oppression in history was of "the female sex by the male."[56]

When the economic contributions of the two sexes were fairly even, as in hunting and gathering societies, sexual equality existed to a high degree. Women in

those societies gathered a good share of edible foods, but the men were not always successful in their hunting expeditions, thus making the gender-based activities of both important. Agrarian and pastoral societies drew upon greater male
strength for needed labors in plowing, irrigation, building, crafts, and military defense. Sexual inequality then became more marked as disparities in economic
contributions, a pattern continuing into early industrial societies, with women working
only in low-paying positions.[57]

In industrial societies, female dependence on male breadwinners kept women
in an inferior position, an unchallenged situation until increasing numbers of women
entered the labor force. The demands of recent years for sexual equality correlates with women's growing economic contributions. In other words, conflict theorists maintain women's economic position determines the degree of equality in
relations between men and women in society.[58] As they achieved greater economic independence, women developed a heightened awareness of a shared bond
of exploitation, and the feminist movement gained momentum and many successes in eliminating sexist discrimination.

A society's cultural characteristics, the product of generations of thought and
reinforced patterns of behavior, live on through the social institutions perpetuating
the sexist ideology that women are childlike, passive, and inferior. For centuries
the social structure of most societies placed males in controlling positions of political, economic, and social power. The subordinate role of women in society and
in the family clearly benefited men, giving them little incentive to change the sex-
role patterns. A prevailing male value system placed men in a superior status by
putting women in an inferior one, defining the female role as supportive to the
more highly valued male activities. In classic Marxian theory, only the social action
of the subordinate group in challenging this arrangement can effect a change.

Who benefits from sexual inequality? Males do, in terms of higher status, better
jobs, higher pay, greater life satisfaction, and more leisure time at home as their
wives fulfill domestic and child-care chores. Business and industry reap higher profits,
possibly 23 percent of all corporate profits, by employing women at lower rates
than men.[59] This oppression of women exacts some costs for both sexes as well:
denial of full human development and full use of one's talents; loss to the society
of much human creativity and leadership; and individual suffering in economic
deprivation, emotional and psychological strain.

The Interactionist View

Through social interaction, as well as the internalization of others' expectations,
the self emerges. From birth through adulthood, children go through a socialization process shaping their sense of identity based upon cultural value orientations
about sex roles. All the socialization agents—family, school, peers, church, media—promote sex role identity and norms in various ways, including example and
reinforcement. Social definitions of appropriate behavior, emotions, and goals for
boys or girls become internalized as desirable attributes for acceptance and praise.
Because these social definitions begin so early, are so pervasive, and are accepted

by those so defined, they appear to be "natural," explaining how "Nature" or God intended us to be.

In this socially constructed reality of shared expectations about gender capabilities and proper behavior, people interact with one another on the basis of their cultural conditioning. Men do not, however, consciously and deliberately subjugate women, who passively submit to their masters. For the most part, both sexes long interacted with one another in a taken-for-granted manner as to their "place" in the social structure. William I. Thomas's famous statement (1911) indicates both the consequences of social definitions, including sexism, as well as the "male reality" of his time: "If men define a situation as real, it is real in its consequences."

Technological changes have altered our social structure and life expectations. As a result, traditional sex roles no longer find acceptance among many women. Yet a consensus does not exist about what it means to be male and female, a fact that creates an ambiguous situation. Sex roles may be blurring, but strongly held concepts of masculinity and femininity remain popular and influential. We live in a transitional period, when we are redefining sex roles while many aspects of traditional sex-role attitudes and practices continue. How long and difficult will this transitional period be? No one knows, though evidence from surveys on sex-role attitudes shows increased acceptance of women in nontraditional sex roles among both men and women.[60] As new patterns of male–female interaction become institutionalized in various social arenas, we may expect to find greater acceptance of sexual equality.

Because the socialization process is so critical, interactionists stress the need to change its content and approach. Thus, parents can be made more aware of existing sexual biases in behavioral expectations of their children, encouraging them to develop fully all aspects of their personalities. Through education and the media, a more enlightened approach, eliminating sexual stereotypes, and providing varied role models of either gender, could do much to promote change and sexual equality. The media and academic world could also do much to resocialize women to overcome their past conditioning and to resocialize all adults to a more egalitarian value system. This perspective holds that ideas tend to have a life of their own and, by concentrating on how we interpret the world, we can create a new social reality.

RETROSPECT

Sexism has only recently been recognized as a problem, although it has existed for centuries. Minority group characteristics—ascribed status, physical and cultural visibility, unequal treatment, and shared group awareness—apply to women, as they do to various racial and ethnic groups. The practice of endogamy does not apply, but in marriage the dominant–subordinate roles are often quite obvious.

Throughout much of American history, male dominance patterns prevailed. Women lacked voting, contract, and property rights, and were even denied the right to enjoy sex without being thought deviant. After a long struggle, women gained the right to vote nationally in 1919, but did not harness any political power to effect change or elect many women to office. During World War II many women worked, but peacetime brought an emphasis on the home as a "woman's proper place." In the 1960s, the feminist movement began anew, fostering social awareness and still unfolding social change.

Despite some biological differences between the sexes in size, strength, and longevity, socialization is what shapes gender identity and sex-role behavior. Entrenched value orientations result in a conditioning process producing differential behavior patterns and life goals. The resultant sexual inequality is evident throughout society, and doubly so among minority women. In education, employment, income, legal status, and political power, women's status has improved but still remains far removed from parity with men.

Functionalists see gender-based division of labor as an efficient means to a smoothly functioning society in the past, but that technology has since thrown the social system out of balance, requiring some form of adjustment. Conflict theorists stress the oppression of women as economically based and beneficial to male status and power. Interactionists focus on the social interpretation of reality through socialization and interaction patterns, suggesting changing the content of the socialization process will eliminate sexual inequality.

REVIEW QUESTIONS

1. How can we consider women as a minority group?

2. What are some examples of past male discrimination against women?

3. Discuss the biological and sociological explanations of sex-role behavior.

4. What are some examples of problems of sexism among first- and second-generation Americans?

5. What examples of sexual discrimination can we find in education, work, income, and law?

6. How do the three major sociological perspectives explain sexism?

SUGGESTED READINGS

Freeman, Jo (ed.). *Women: A Feminist Perspective,* 2nd ed. Palo Alto, Calif.: Mayfield, 1979).

A fine collection of feminist writings about women and their encounters with male-dominated society.

Friedan, Betty. *The Feminine Mystique.* New York: Norton, 1963.

A classic and still pertinent work criticizing myths about female passivity and fulfillment only as wife and mother.

Giele, Janet Zollinger. *Women and the Future: Changing Sex Roles in Modern America.* New York: Free Press, 1978.

A very fine coverage of sex-role images and changes in major social institutions, with discussion of future possibilities.

Kanter, Rosabeth Moss. *Men and Women of the Corporation.* New York: Basic Books, 1977.

A well-written account of subtle and overt forms of sexual discrimination and gender career choices in corporations.

MacKinnon, Catharine A. *Sexual Harassment of Working Women: A Case of Sex Discrimination.* New Haven, Conn.: Yale University Press, 1979.

An excellent legal and sociological analysis of actual instances of sexual harassment in the work place.

Mead, Margaret. *Sex and Temperament in Three Primitive Societies.* New York: Morrow, 1963.

A classic demonstration of the different effects of socialization on male–female attitudes and behavior in three New Guinea tribes.

Morgan, Robin (ed.). *Sisterhood Is Powerful.* New York: Random House, 1970.

Still the most comprehensive collection of writings from the women's liberation movement covering virtually all aspects of life.

PART FIVE

PRESENT AND FUTURE STATUS OF MINORITY GROUPS

CHAPTER 14

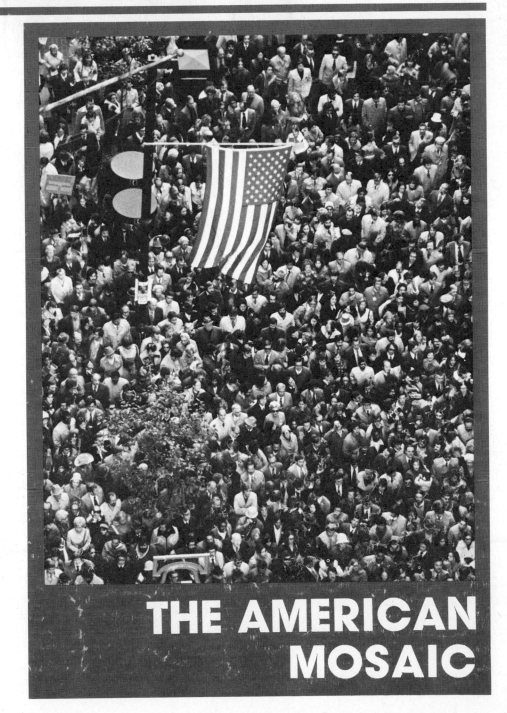

THE AMERICAN
MOSAIC

As a nation of immigrants, the United States has had many different groups of strangers arrive and interact with its people. The strangers have perceived a different world than the native population took for granted, and their reactions have ranged from wonder to bewilderment to dismay, from fulfilled expectations to culture shock. Because their language, appearance, and cultural background often made them conspicuous, the newcomers were categorically identified and judged as a group, rather than individually. Native-born Americans sometimes welcomed these strangers, sometimes were impatient, and sometimes were intolerant; they helped or exploited or ignored the newcomers.

Throughout the nation's history, then, varied patterns of majority-minority relations have existed. Ethnocentric values have prompted the natural development of ingroup loyalty and outgroup hostility among both indigenous and migrant groups. Competition for scarce resources, colonialism, and political dominance by the Anglo-Saxon core groups also provided a basis for conflict. However, the resulting prejudicial attitudes and discriminatory actions varied greatly in intensity. Additionally, both attitudes and social and economic conditions in this country have changed over the years, and this has affected the newcomers' experience.

Not all groups have come for the same reasons, nor have they come from the same backgrounds. Because of variations in social class, education, and occupational skills, not all immigrants have begun at the bottom of the socioeconomic ladder. Some have come as sojourners, intending to stay only long enough to earn enough money for a better life back in their homeland. Some have come with the desire to be American citizens in every sense of the word; others have insisted upon retaining their own culture.

American attitudes toward the newcomers have also varied. Dominant attitudes, as well as sociological analyses, have tended to focus on either assimilation or pluralism as the preferred minority adaptation. Which process the public considers more acceptable will greatly influence dominant-minority relations. For example, if assimilation is held to be the "proper" goal, then evidence of pluralism will probably be a target for negative reaction. In recent years many people, but not all, have been more receptive to pluralism, and government policies and actions have reflected this orientation. Also, there has been a resurgence of ethnicity among the so-called white ethnics and other minority groups. Manifestations of the social processes of pluralism suggest that while minority groups may still encounter problems of adjustment and acceptance, these are not compounded by overt pressures for Americanization to the same extent as in the past.

How important is ethnicity today? Are immigration and assimilation concerns justified? What is the future of ethnicity in the United States? In this chapter we shall attempt to answer those questions, as we examine theories of ethnic consciousness and behavior, ethnic stratification in today's society, and the issues of bilingual education, legal, and illegal immigration.

ETHNIC CONSCIOUSNESS

Sociologists have long been interested in the attitudinal and behavioral patterns that emerge when people migrate into a society with a different culture. For example, what factors encourage or discourage ethnic self-awareness or maintenance of one's culture? If succeeding generations supposedly identify less with their country of origin, how do we explain the resurgence of ethnicity among white ethnics in recent years? Are there ethnic differentials in social mobility, social change, and behavior patterns even among third-generation Americans? Sociologists have frequently raised these questions, and a number of sociological theories have been offered in an effort to synthesize the diversity of ethnic experience.

Country of Origin as a Factor

Mary Sengstock believes that focusing on the relationship between the migrant and the country of origin will lead to a better understanding of the degree of assimilation.[1] She contends that the assumption that a migrant group is affected primarily by factors in the receiving country is wrong. This may have been more true of those groups that came here prior to the First World War, when transportation and communication were limited. Furthermore, immigration restrictions in the 1920s sharply curtailed the number of new immigrants and the assimilation process was less impeded when newcomers were not arriving to reinforce the language and customs of the old country. In today's world, however, an immigrant group can maintain contact with the country of origin not only through air-mail letters but, more importantly, through long-distance telephone calls, rapid transportation, and the continued arrival of newcomers. The Mexican and Puerto Rican communities benefit from geographical proximity, and the mother country can exert more influence over its emigrants than in years past. Where there is greater social contact, cultural transmission is also greater.

The degree of stability or social change in the homeland will have a profound effect on the migrant community's sociocultural patterns and life style.

Where the country of origin has experienced a relatively stable or gradually changing culture, the effect on the immigrant community will most likely be to encourage retention of the ethnic culture. This is much the same case as has occurred with Puerto Ricans and Mexican-Americans.

Some societies, however, have experienced drastic changes in recent years. When groups of immigrants from such areas experience constant immigration and other types of contact with the mother country, one might expect such contact to produce profound effects on the immigrant community as well.[2]

Sengstock uses a study of Chaldean immigrants from Iraq who settled in Detroit both before and after the Second World War to illustrate her position. Iraq is now an independent nation-state, not a colonial land of different tribes all under the control of another nation. It is struggling to replace centuries-old tribal rivalries with the unity of nationalism. The changes have reached the Detroit community through visitors and immigrants.

> Recent immigrants are less likely to exhibit the traditional family orientation of their predecessors. They are more likely to exhibit the bureaucratic, urban, secular characteristics of the modern nation-state Iraq now is. They are also more likely to identify themselves as Iraqis or Arabs than were the early immigrants. . . . It seems likely that the "modern" pattern will eventually be the established pattern in the Detroit community, since the older immigrants remain the sole repository for the village tradition, and most of them are well advanced in age.[3]

As the Chaldeans illustrate, it appears that recent immigrants who have more education and more experience with urban settings and bureaucracies will be more likely to interact with others. Thus willingness to extend one's social contacts to members of other groups could, suggests Sengstock, produce a more "assimilable" group.

The social structure of an immigrant group's country of origin, then, may help to explain both nationalistic sentiment and social interaction with others in the adopted country.

The Three-generation Hypothesis

Historian Marcus Hansen conceptualized a normal pattern of ethnic revival in what he called the "Law of the Return of the Third Generation."[4] The third generation, more secure in its socioeconomic status and American identity, becomes interested in the ethnic heritage that the second generation neglected in its efforts to overcome discrimination and marginality. Simply stated, "What the child wishes to forget, the grandchild wishes to remember." Hansen, who based his conclusions mainly upon Midwestern Swedish-Americans, reaffirmed his position several years later:

> Whenever any immigrant group reaches the third-generation stage in its development a spontaneous and almost irresistible impulse arises which forces the thoughts of many people of different professions, different positions in life and different points of view to interest themselves in that one factor which they have in common: heritage—the heritage of blood.[5]

What Hansen has suggested here is a pattern in the fall and rise of ethnic identity in succeeding generations of Americans. His hypothesis generated extensive discussion in the academic community, resulting in studies and commentaries that both supported and criticized his views.

Supporters and Detractors

Some early studies, using religion as a major criterion of ethnicity, found evidence of continuing or revitalized ethnic consciousness. Ruby Jo Reeves Kennedy's findings of religious endogamy despite intermarriage across national origin lines led her to conclude that assimilation in the United States followed one of three religious routes: a "triple melting pot" pattern.[6] In other words, consciousness of national origin declined, but consciousness of religion remained. Critics of the triple-melting-pot thesis pointed to places where religious intermarriage does occur, particularly those locations where the Jewish or Catholic population is a very small segment of the community.[7]

Will Herberg blended the Kennedy and Hansen hypotheses into a construct that stressed religion rather than national origin as the basis for a third-generation ethnic revival.[8] Many critics have argued that national-origin endogamy can be just as strong as religious endogamy in many areas. Low national-origin intermarriage rates among Catholics,[9] ethnically balanced political tickets,[10] and the flourishing of many ethnic associations[11] all point to ethnic consciousness regarding national origin.

Conflicting Findings

In a study of Irish and Italian Catholics in Providence, Rhode Island, John Goering had mixed results.[12] He found that ethnic consciousness was steadily declining in succeeding generations in some respects, but emerging in a negative sense in other respects as a backlash to the black civil rights movement and the hippie phenomenon. He concluded that this ethnic revival was "less as a source of cultural or religious refreshment than as the basis for organizing the skepticism associated with discontent and racial confrontation."[13] Another interesting observation by Goering was that the ideology of the first- and second-generation Irish- and Italian-Americans living in the ethnic ghetto is more "American" and tolerant of American society than that of the third generation living outside the ghetto:

Ethnicity is not clearly perceived in the ghetto. The boundaries of the ghetto became the boundaries of the real world. The awareness of ethnicity, and its divisiveness, comes with the "children of the uprooted." All forms of ethnic consciousness are not associated with the ethnic ghetto.[14]

These comments are similar to "Hansen's law" in that they assume that the second generation perceives its ethnicity as a disadvantage in being accepted in American society. However, Goering perceives growing ethnic awareness not as a progression but as a regression to the "seclusiveness of ethnicity in resentment against unattained promises."[15]

Neil Sandburg's study, cited in the section on Polish-Americans, found that subjects in the Los Angeles area tended to be less ethnic over several generations.[16] In a similar study of Italian-Americans in two suburbs of Providence, Rhode Island, John P. Roche also found increased assimilation over several generations and lower levels of attitudinal ethnicity.[17] Other writers have suggested that events in one's homeland or the situation of one's fellow ethnics in other parts of the world may heighten ethnic awareness.[18]

Perhaps one of the most comprehensive rebuttals of the three-generation hypothesis was that of Harold Abramson, who argued that the many dimensions of ethnic diversity preclude any macrosocial theory about ethnic consciousness.[19] In addition to differences in time period, which may have influenced the experience, adjustment, and intergenerational conflict or consensus of ethnic groups, there is also a diversity within the groups themselves. Possibly only the better educated among each ethnic group, being in wider contact with the outside world and more ambivalent about their identity, experience an ethnic resurgence, while the majority have quietly progressed in some steady fashion. The enormous variability of the American social structure also affects what will happen to the grandchildren of all ethnic groups.

Here I am talking about the diversity of region, of social stratification, of urban and rural settlement. In other words, the immigrants of Old and New and continuing migrations, the blacks of the North and of the South, the native American Indians, all experience *their* encounters with America under vastly different conditions. The French-Canadians in depressed mill towns of New England, the Hungarians and Czechs in company coal towns of Pennsylvania, and the Chicanos in migrant labor fields of California, do not experience the social mobility or social change of the Irish in Boston politics, the Jews in the garment industry of New York, or the Japanese in the professions of Hawaii. Not only are there traditional cultural factors to explain these phenomena, but there are structural reasons of settlement, region, and the local composition of the ethnic mosaic as well.[20]

Additionally, the responses of different traditional cultures to the forces of society vary. For example, the Irish and Italians have different levels of attachment to Catholicism. Persisting diversity makes it difficult to describe the American experience in any generalized manner.

The White Ethnic Revival

In the late 1960s and 1970s some observers noted an increased ethnic consciousness among urban Catholic groups, whom they categorized as "white ethnics." Some, like Goering,[21] saw this as a backlash to the efforts of Blacks, hippies, and liberals. Others, such as Andrew Greeley, saw it as an affirmation of Hansen's law.[22] Greeley suggested that the final stage of assimilation included the new generation's interest in its heritage. It had nothing to do with the militant black and Indian social movements, since that was an earlier stage in the assimilation process. Greeley attributed the white ethnic revival to the last phase, when Hansen's law becomes operative. The third generation has a strong interest in the cultural and artistic background of their ethnic tradition. They take trips to the old country out of curiosity and occasional "amused compassion." Greeley saw this increased ethnic awareness as a deliberate, self-conscious effort among young ethnics.[23]

Michael Novak interpreted the ethnic revival not as a part of the assimilation process but as evidence of "unmeltable ethnics," or pluralism.[24] He noted that many working-class ethnics resented the limitations the Protestant Establishment imposed upon their realization of the American Dream.

> Ordinary workers . . . resent the liberties, privileges, wealth, and securities of the professional elites based in the universities. They also resent the actual, daily contacts of their own culture with black culture. No amount of good will, theory, or ideology blinds them to the actual experience of that contact: it is very often characterized by economic penalties for both whites and blacks, by rising violence and conflict, by insolence and insult, by mutual stereotype and prejudice.[25]

According to Novak, it is the Anglo-Saxon Protestant, not the working-class ethnic, who harbors strong anti-Black sentiment. The white ethnics have discovered their solidarity not for use against Blacks; but as a necessary and effective weapon against the established power, which ignores their problems, such as inflation, unemployment, and declining neighborhoods. All of this is to the good, Novak claims, for this ethnic pride allows these groups to feel more a part of America.

> In any case, millions of Americans, who for a long time tried desperately even unconsciously to become "Americanized," are delighted to discover that they no longer have to pay that price; are grateful that they were born among the people destiny placed them in, are pleased to discover the possibilities and the limits inherent in being who they are; and are openly happy about what heretofore they had disguised in silence. There is a creativity and new release, there is liberation, and there is hope.
> America is becoming America.[26]

The resiliency of ethnic consciousness makes it endure, observes Perry Weed.[27] Many people have erroneously assumed that acculturation eliminates ethnic identity, but it persists, sometimes intensifies, and has meaning into and beyond the third generation. The majority of ethnic Americans, now that pluralism is tolerated, are recognizing that they have not lost their foreign identity or ethnic consciousness. Many factors have contributed to preserving ethnicity:

> A high level of nationality consciousness has always been maintained by the churches, local newspapers and political organizations wherever there are large concentrations of ethnic groups. Both immigrant neighborhoods and residential movement demonstrate that ethnics prefer to live among those who share their cultural heritage and immigrant experience.[28]

A Dissenting View

Not everyone agrees that there is a resurgence of ethnicity. Some see the apparent resurgence either as a temporary adjustment, similar to others in the past, or as a much more limited phenomenon. One notable sociologist who has taken this position is Herbert Gans. As one who has long taken exception to the three-generation hypothesis, Gans has seen a steadily diminishing ethnic consciousness and progressive social and cultural assimilation among American Jews[29] and in an Italian-American community in Boston.[30] Gans believes that the so-called ethnic revival is a misnomer, much like the so-called religious revival of the mid-1950s, when many churches and synagogues were constructed in the new suburbs.[31] Since, by and large, American ethnicity today is a working-class ethnicity, ethnic politics is actually an interethnic grouping of members of the same social class to achieve desired goals.

One reason is the decline of Irish and WASP control of American politics, and the political mobility of Italian-Americans, Polish-Americans, and others into important local and national positions. This political mobility has been developing for a long time and has more to do with the fact that many members of these ethnic groups have achieved middle class status, and thus economic power and political power, than with a new ethnic consciousness. . . .

Second, and far more important, the urban and suburban white working class has also achieved more political power in the last few years, and since many of the members of that class are Catholic ethnics, their new influence has been falsely ascribed to a newly emerging ethnic pride. What has actually happened is that for the first time in a long time, the white working class has become politically visible, but their demands have been labeled as ethnic rather than working class.[32]

Gans sees the so-called ethnic revival as being popularized by a new group of Catholic intellectuals, such as Greeley and Novak. As members of a small academic community that has sometimes had to face covert discrimination from the academic establishment, they may well be expressing their own ethnic consciousness rather than that of all or even many members of their ethnic group. Perhaps, concludes Gans, Hansen's law really applies only to academics and intellectuals, among whom most of the scholarly and theoretical discussions occur, not to the majority of ethnic peoples.

An Alternative View

Recently some sociologists have argued that ethnicity should be regarded not as an ascribed attribute with only the two discrete categories of assimilation and pluralism, but as a continuous variable.[33] In a review of the recent literature, William L. Yancey, Eugene P. Ericksen, and Richard N. Juliani conclude that ethnic behavior is conditioned by occupation, residence, and institutional affiliation—the structural situations in which groups have found themselves. The "old" immigrants, migrating before the Industrial Revolution, had a more dispersed residential pattern than did the "new" immigrants, who were "bunched together" because of concentrated large-scale urban employment and the need for low-cost housing near the place of employment. Similarly, when immigrants arrived, they were drawn to the areas of economic expansion, and the migration chains—the subsequent arrival of relatives and friends—continued the concentrated settlement pattern.

The Germans and Irish, who were earlier immigrants, concentrated in the older cities such as Philadelphia and St. Louis. By contrast, the new immigrants from Poland, Italy and Russia concentrated in Buffalo, Cleveland, Detroit and Milwaukee, as well as in some of the older cities with expanding opportunities. Different migration patterns occurred for immigrants with and without skills. . . . Rewards for skilled occupations were greater, and the skilled immigrant went to the cities where there were opportunities to practice his trade. Less highly skilled workers went to the cities with expanding opportunities. Thus, the Italian concentration in construction and the Polish in steel were related to the expansion of these industries as these groups arrived. The Jewish concentration in the garment industry may have been a function of their previous experience as tailors, but it is also dependent upon the emergence of the mass production of clothing in the late nineteenth century.[34]

Like Gans, these authors conclude that group consciousness is generated and becomes crystallized within the work relationships, common residential areas, interests, and life styles of working-class conditions. Moreover, normal communication and participation in ethnic organizations on a cosmopolitan level can reinforce ethnic identity even among residentially dispersed groups.[35] This "situational ethnicity" may be characterized by such things as:

Church and synagogue attendance, marching in a St. Patrick's or Columbus Day parade, voting for a political candidate of a similar ethnicity, or supporting a political cause associated with the country of origin, such as the emigration of Russian Jews to Israel or the reunification of Ireland.[36]

Three observations are of interest to the student in this alternative view: (1) the importance of structural conditions, such as predetermined residential or occupational choices; (2) the existence of ethnic networks among geographically dispersed groups; and (3) ethnicity as the result of a process that continues to unfold, not a constant ascribed trait inherited from the past.

Stanford M. Lyman and William A. Douglass believe that social process offers a more dynamic conception of race and ethnicity, but they suggest that such processes are not necessarily unidirectional or evolutionary, leading to acculturation and assimilation.[37] Instead, there are several different possible strategies as contending ethnic groups attempt to adjust to one another.

A minority might attempt to: (1) become fully incorporated into the larger society; (2) participate actively in the public life of the larger society while retaining significant aspects of its own cultural identity; (3) emphasize ethnic identity in the creation of new social positions and patterned activities not formerly found within the society; (4) retain confederational ties with the larger society at the same time that it secures territorial and communal control for itself; (5) secede from the larger society and form a new state or enter into the plural structure of another state; (6) establish its own hegemony over the society in which it lives.[38]

Not all of these strategies have been used in the United States, but any or all of them may lead to problems and disruption in a pluralistic society. Each of these

These marchers relax before beginning their 1978 St. Patrick's Day Parade in New York City. For many groups now residentially dispersed and no longer self-conscious entities, such events of situational ethnicity crystallize group consciousness and reaffirm one's cultural heritage.

strategies, it should be added, is in dialectical relationship with patterns in the larger society; a minority's "choice" is heavily dependent upon these prevailing patterns. (See Box 14.1 for a summary of various explanations for ethnic consciousness.)

What about third- and fourth-generation Americans, of mixed or ambiguous European ancestry? Do they maintain an ethnic identification or are they too assimilated to pay attention to ethnic identity? Examining over 3500 responses from the NORC General Social Survey for 1977, 1978, and 1980, Richard D. Alba and Mitchell B. Chamlin found that later generations attending college still re-

BOX 14.1

Reasons for Ethnic Consciousness

Country of Origin

1. Psychological nearness through rapid communications and transportation
2. Geographical proximity
3. Degree of stability or social change in the homeland
4. Social contact with recent immigrants

Three-Generation Hypothesis

1. Second generation emphasizes American ways and neglects own heritage
2. Third generation rediscovers ethnic identity

Other Explanations

1. Religion replaces national origin as basis of identity
2. Ethnicity less perceived in ethnic community than in real world
3. Outside events may heighten ethnic awareness
4. Only better educated of a group become ethnically self-conscious
5. Variations in time, social structure, and within ethnic groups encourage different types of responses

White Ethnic Revival

1. Backlash to efforts of Blacks, hippies, and liberals
2. Affirmation of Hansen's law
3. Discovery of group consciousness as a reaction to social and economic problems
4. Resiliency of ethnic identity even through acculturation
5. Revival is a misnomer; it is really a temporary structural adjustment reflecting attainment of some political power by working-class ethnics
6. Really a situational ethnicity because of changed structural conditions

tained a strong ethnic identification, with a rising number of individuals identifying with a single group.[39] Despite social assimilation, ethnic identifications remain salient over the generations. What form of ethnic identity flows from this ethnic identification is not yet clear.

ETHNIC BEHAVIOR

Some sociologists, like Gordon and Gans, think that social class is more important than ethnicity. They believe that people of different ethnic backgrounds but the same social class tend to act similarly, more so than people of the same ethnic background but different social classes. Others believe that ethnic differences lead to differences in behavior. Numerous studies have been undertaken to test these hypotheses.

Reaction to Pain

In interviewing male patients in a veterans' hospital, Mark Zborowski found some notable differences in responses to pain among Irish, Italians, Jews, and "Old Americans" (white Protestants).[40] Although definitive patterns emerged, he noted that there were individual differences within each group as a result of social class, personality differences, generation (first-, second-, or third-generation American), or the nature of the disease. Zborowski observed that although these differences affected behavior, the attitudes toward pain were relatively consistent within each group.

Old Americans suffer pain privately, neither crying nor complaining because it does no good and they do not want pity. They consider the body a machine in the hands of a skilled professional; so they prefer being in a hospital, have confidence in their treatment, and are optimistic about the future. The Irish are also stoic about pain, and almost noncommunicative, making few complaints and forcing the doctor to probe further to learn the symptoms. For the Irish, pain is a test of manhood, and they look upon it as a unique personal challenge. The Old American, on the other hand, views pain as useless except as a warning signal of mechanical failure.

Zborowski found both Italians and Jews to be emotional about pain, to cry openly and unashamedly, and to believe that pain is something social, something that should be shared with family and friends. Jews are more skeptical of doctors than are the other three groups, and are interested in the precise diagnosis, something the Old American is reluctant to know. Jews are pessimistic about their health and afraid to take drugs lest they be habit-forming or mask the source of the pain. Italians are more present-oriented, and for them the pain is what is important. Its relief greatly affects their mood, and this buoyancy, along with their belief that dependency is normal in such a situation, makes them favorite patients among the nurses. Zborowski suggests that these attitudinal differences are the result of cultural variances in the socialization process, ranging from parental overprotectiveness to the stressing of self-reliance.

Zborowski's study helped us to understand culture determines one's pain responsivity. Other studies have demonstrated ethnic differences to shock and pain as well, corroborating Zborowski's specific findings.[41] Emphasizing the psychophysiological dimensions of patient response, one study found that Jews have a lower pain tolerance than Protestants, but increase their tolerance when told this.[42] Studies of the pain threshold among dental patients also revealed ethnicity as a significant variable.[43] Much research does confirm ethnic differences in pain reactivity exist among ethnic groups, and that these differences are likely based on the symbolic meaning of pain in different cultures. Nevertheless, we must again emphasize this sweeping statement may not necessarily hold true for an individual member of an ethnic group.

Homeland Influence

In a 1974 study, Andrew M. Greeley and William C. McCready attempted to measure the extent to which ethnic differences among Irish, Italians, and Anglo-Saxons are predictable from cultural patterns in the country of origin.[44] They tested forty-five hypotheses comparing personality variables, political participation, drinking behavior, and sexual attitudes. The hypotheses, established on the basis of the sociological literature about the three homelands, were proven correct twenty-two times—a statistically significant level. Six cases, primarily concerning the Irish, were statistically significant in the opposite direction.

Both Irish and Italians were more fatalistic than Anglo-Saxons. Italians and Anglo-Saxons were more similar in such personality variables as trust, anxiety, conformity, and being authoritarian and moralistic, while the Irish scored lower in these categories. Irish-Americans proved to be the most active politically (in voting, campaigning, and civic activities), Italian-Americans the least active, and Anglo-Saxons in between. The Irish also respected democratic processes much more than did the Anglo-Saxons, who in turn held them in higher regard than did the Italians. Italians were much more conservative in their drinking behavior and more sexually restrictive than either the Irish or the Anglo-Saxons, who tended to be more alike in these areas. The fact that there are similarities and differences among the three groups was just as important to the researchers as the distinctions themselves:

What have we demonstrated with our exploratory research? It is apparent that we can no longer believe that there are no important differences among native Americans, Irish Americans, and Italian Americans. We are not all alike. On the other hand, we cannot believe that ours is a mosaic society in which differences among the three groups are to be expected on almost every variable. The truth seems to be somewhere in between. We are both alike and different.

. . . If one assumes (and many commentators in American life seem to have made this assumption) that European heritages of the American ethnic groups are irrelevant to an understanding of the present attitudes and behaviors of such groups, one can find very little substantiation in the research reported here. The European heritage may not be *all* important, but it is important, probably more so than many of us would have thought.[45]

Michael Novak makes much the same point when he comments on the uniqueness of cultural influences upon particular ethnic groups. It would appear, according to these observers, that subcultural variables tend to shape differences in attitude and behavior in certain areas, although not uniformly throughout an entire group.

When a person thinks, more than one generation's passions and images think in him. Below the threshold of the rational or the fully conscious, our instincts and sensibilities lead backwards to the predilections of our forebears. More deeply than

Americans have been taught to recognize, their own particular pasts live on in their present judgments and actions.[46]

Drinking Patterns

The prevalence of norms among certain ethnic groups about alcohol consumption further illustrates the differences in learned behavior patterns. Orthodox Jews restrict drinking to special occasions among relatives and close friends, consider excessive drinking a bad reflection on their culture, being more the deviant behavior of non-Jews. Having learned norms of moderation in childhood, even adult Jews who have drifted away from orthodoxy continue their restraint in drinking.[47] Italian-American children grow up in households where wine drinking is an integral part of eating, and again, moderate consumption is the norm. Neither Italians nor Jews tend to drink to relieve stress, since they have not defined drinking as an acceptable means of relieving problems, but as a part of family life.[48] Irish-Americans, on the other hand, have traditionally associated drinking to create a good time at any social gathering. Traditional Irish values do not hold public drunkenness as disgraceful, as do Jews and Italians, unless it results in loss of income or property. Consequently, excessive drinking at Irish-American gatherings is not uncommon. A relatively high rate of alcoholism exists among Irish-American males, but is rare among Italians and Jews.[49]

Andrew J. Gordon found the varying cultural context among three Hispanic-American communities in a small New England city affected drinking behavior patterns.[50] Dominicans drink moderately and only the very best of liquors, their sobriety and tastes reflecting their sense of upward mobility from the poverty-stricken years in their homeland. Guatemalan men, working as sojourners, tend to drink heavily to pass away their loneliness for families back home. Puerto Ricans, particularly young adult males, often mix alcohol and drugs—usually cocaine or marijuana—to make a *bomba* (become utterly narcotized), as they seek escape from economic hardship. Other Puerto Ricans, either older or more economically secure, conform to a more typical middle-class style of moderate social drinking.

Other Factors

Obviously, the preceding sections cover only a few aspects of ethnic behavior. Others, such as dating and marriage patterns, male-female relationships, child-rearing practices, actions toward outsiders, education, religion, authority, occupations, eating, drinking, and socializing, are all at least partially dependent upon cultural orientations. If all important forms of social behavior are learned, and if culture shapes our learning experience, then it follows that certain forms of behavior will differ among groups according to cultural variance. To that degree most of us can accept certain generalizations about differences in ethnic behavior.

When we discuss ethnic behavior in any sense, however, we must consider several factors. Is the behavior we are attempting to analyze a reflection of culture, social class, the particular situation only, the prevailing attitudinal climate, or some combination of these or other factors? Does this behavior generally prevail among all members of the group, or is there variance within the group itself? If so, why? Would another ethnic group, behave in the same way under the same set of conditions? Is there a more universal explanation for behavioral differences? That is, are behavioral differences attributable to certain idiosyncrasies of one group, or would other groups who shared similar visibility, deprivation, discrimination, generational seniority in America, and rural, tribal, or village life orientations behave in the same fashion? Or is the answer to be found in certain subcultural values and attitudes that are transmitted from one generation to the next despite whatever acculturation or assimilation may have occurred?

These are provocative questions, and not all of them can be easily answered. The basic question is whether it is the degree of minority integration into the society or inherent minority characteristics that determines any ethnic variations in behavior. Some research suggests that there are both similarities and differences among various ethnic groups. More research must be done before we can know the reason for behavioral differences among ethnic groups with any degree of certainty.

ETHNIC STRATIFICATION

Some groups, like the Blacks, Hispanics, and American Indians, have received much attention; those findings are reported in the chapters in this book dealing with each specific group. For other ethnic groups, the data are limited, both in frequency of reporting and in recording generational change. Much of the information from the Census Bureau is limited to foreign-born, thereby restricting available information on second- and third-generation Americans, except in the regional studies done by social scientists. Also, the Department of Labor's measurement of occupational position and shift does not specifically measure ethnic movement except by race and for Hispanics. Moreover, many of the more recent Third World immigrants have yet to be included in the data that are reported.

When Volume 2 of the 1980 Census of the population is published in late 1984, that report will offer ethnic group characteristics, such as age, family composition, income, and poverty status. While these long-awaited data will provide valuable information about the relative standings and variances among ethnic groups, recent sociological research has offered us some excellent insights into white ethnic stratification.

Achievement and Mobility

In a composite study of almost 18,000 respondents, Andrew M. Greeley reported some surprising findings in his comparisons of non-Spanish-speaking white ethnics.[51] In terms of occupational stratification and occupational mobility, Jews, Episcopalians, and Presbyterians were the most successful of all religious groups. In terms of educational stratification, the same three groups rank first, second, and third, respectively but in terms of educational mobility the most successful are Jews, Catholics, and Presbyterians, in that order. For average income, Jews, Catholics, and Episcopalians are in the first three positions, and the standard deviation is far greater among Episcopalians and Presbyterians than for other groups, indicating a much wider range in income levels.

When Greeley refined the data to control for both religion and nationality, the rank order in terms of family income in 1974 was Jews, Irish Catholics, Italian Catholics, German Catholics, Polish Catholics, Episcopalians, Presbyterians, Slavic Catholics, British Protestants, French Catholics, Methodists, German Protestants, Lutherans, Scandinavian Protestants, "American" Protestants, Irish Protestants, Baptists. When only northern metropolitan regions are considered, the Catholic groups do even better. This ranking contrasts with the prevailing stereotype of wealthy WASPs and working-class Catholic ethnic groups. According to this study, the Jewish and Catholic ethnic groups have surpassed the older Protestant ethnic groups in terms of average family income.

One stratification expert, David Featherman, pointed to several misleading interpretations by Greeley.[52] Most importantly, he stresses that Greeley uses family income as a measure of economic achievement and ambition. There is a difference in occupational achievement between income from the full-time employment of the household head only and income from the simultaneous employment of several family members, even if some work only part-time. Larger immigrant families have more potential earners. Higher income from overtime employment taken out of economic necessity or from blue collar union power does not necessarily imply occupational achievement either. Moreover, says Featherman, the data actually show that "few substantive educational and occupational differences remain among white, non-Spanish groups once the disadvantages and advantages of social backgrounds are controlled."[53] Featherman disputes Greeley's interpretation that Catholics have "made it big" economically, instead seeing them from the same data as very close to the national average. Both men agree that many white ethnic groups and denominations have been generally integrated into the American economy.

Each racial and ethnic group is represented at all levels of income, and so one must also be careful in discussing the average incomes Greeley reports. Also, since that study did not include Asians, Indians, Hispanics, and Blacks, it does not give a complete picture of ethnic stratification. Increasing intermarriage by national origin, religion, and race, in declining order of frequency, further complicates the measurement of ethnic occupational distribution.

Stanley Lieberson and Donna K. Carter used the rates of inclusion in *Who's Who* between 1924 and 1974 as a measure of assimilation and achievement of Blacks and five white ethnic groups.[54] Since 1944 Jews have moved significantly ahead of the English, who are closely followed by the Scandinavians. Italians and Slavs have also significantly increased their representation, and all five groups are becoming similar. Blacks rank lowest, sharply different from the Whites, but have been moving upward since 1944.

Another major study by Richard D. Alba and Gwen Moore revealed greater ethnic heterogeneity among the American elite in major economic, political, and social institutions.[55] White Anglo-Saxon Protestants were overrepresented in most sectors of the elite, dramatically so in business and Congress, where they were

TABLE 14.1
Ethnic Representation in the Elite[a]

	Wasps	Other Protes-tants	Irish Catho-lics	Other Catho-lics	Jews	Minor-ities
Overall Elite	43.0%	19.5%	8.5%	8.7%	11.3%	3.9%
Business	57.3	22.1	5.3	6.1	6.9	0.0
Labor	23.9	15.2	37.0	13.0	4.3	2.2
Political Parties	44.0	18.0	14.0	4.0	8.0	4.0
Voluntary Organizations	32.7	13.5	1.9	7.7	17.3	19.2
Mass Media	37.1	11.3	4.8	9.7	25.8	0.0
Congress	53.4	19.0	6.9	8.6	3.4	3.4
Political Appointees	39.4	28.8	1.5	13.6	10.6	3.0
Civil Servants	35.8	22.6	9.4	9.4	15.1	3.8
National Population						
Men Born Before 1932	22.9	22.5	4.2	17.2	2.9	14.4
College-Educated Men						
Born Before 1932	31.0	19.8	6.0	15.5	8.9	5.2

[a]Americans who are not White or Protestant tend to be underrepresented in positions of decision-making authority. Although the situation is improving, the disparity still remains.

Source: From Richard D. Alba and Gwen Moore, "Ethnicity in the American Elite," *American Sociological Review,* Vol. 47, June 1982, p. 377. Reprinted by permission of the American Sociological Association and the authors.

also numerically dominant (see Table 14.1). Constituting only 22.9 percent of all men born before 1932 and 31 percent of the college educated, they comprise 43 percent of the elite group. Jewish representation among the elite places them second, at or above their population proportion in all elite sectors, particularly the mass media. Irish Catholics were also at or above their population proportion in most sectors, particularly as labor and political party leaders. Other underrepresented Catholics include groups of European ancestry and protected minority groups. Ethnicity remains an important factor for entry into the elite, though not an exclusionary one.

Immigrant Occupations

Table 14.2 shows, except for a fairly stable level for craftspeople, a gradual upward trend in the percentages of professional and technical workers among immigrants. However, the number of immigrants reporting no occupation stands at 60 percent, compared with 26 percent in 1901–1910. This is partly explained by the great numbers of males who came here either as sojourners or ahead of their families in the early twentieth century; fewer dependents came over then. Also, the immigration laws now favor relatives joining the immigrants already here. Then too, for many, it was simpler to report being farm laborers when the entire family participated in that endeavor.

TABLE 14.2
Occupational Distribution of Immigrants, 1900–1980

Period	Professional, Technical, etc.	Clerical, Sales, etc.	Craftsmen, Foremen, Operators, etc.	Laborers Exc. Farm	Misc.[a]	No Occupation
1971–1980	10.3	4.8	10.2	3.6	11.1	60.0
1961–1970	10.2	7.4	11.1	3.9	11.6	55.9
1951–1960	7.3	7.8	14.4	5.3	12.3	52.8
1941–1950	7.9	7.9	13.3	2.4	13.8	54.7
1931–1940	7.2	4.5	8.1	3.6	18.5	58.1
1921–1930	2.7	4.3	14.4	15.0	24.3	39.2
1911–1920	1.7	2.0	12.9	17.9	35.9	29.6
1901–1910	1.0	1.1	13.2	26.1	32.9	25.7

[a]Includes farmers, farm managers, managers, officials, proprietors, private household workers, service workers, farm laborers, and farm foremen.

Source: U.S. Department of Commerce, Bureau of the Census, "We Are the American Foreign Born," June 1973, p. 13; Statistical Abstract of the United States, 1982–83, Table 132.

TABLE 14.3
Leading Suppliers of Emigrants to the United States, 1820–1981

1.	Germany	6,998,056
2.	Italy	5,310,516
3.	United Kingdom	4,978,524
4.	Ireland	4,692,856
5.	Austria/Hungary[a]	4,318,845
6.	Canada	4,149,838
7.	U.S.S.R.	3,394,999
8.	Mexico	2,334,154
9.	Caribbean	1,904,427
10.	Sweden	1,274,289
11.	Norway	857,646
12.	France	756,979
13.	Greece	669,888
14.	China	593,432
15.	Poland	528,098

[a]Data for Austria/Hungary was not reported until 1861. Austria and Hungary have been reported separately since 1905. From 1938 to 1945, Austria is included in figures for Germany.

Source: U.S. Immigration and Naturalization Service, Annual Report, *Statistical Yearbook 1981*, Table 2.

TABLE 14.4
Major Sources of Newcomers to United States

1965		1981	
1. Canada	38,327	1. Vietnam	43,483
2. Mexico	37,969	2. Philippines	42,316
3. United Kingdom	27,358	3. Korea	32,320
4. Germany	24,045	4. China	27,651
5. Cuba	19,760	5. India	22,607
6. Colombia	10,885	6. Jamaica	18,970
7. Italy	10,821	7. Dominican Republic	17,245
8. Dominican Republic	9,504	8. United Kingdom	15,485
9. Poland	8,465	9. Cuba	15,054
10. Argentina	6,124	10. Laos	13,970
11. Ireland	5,463	11. Canada	13,609
12. Ecuador	4,392	12. Colombia	11,287
13. China and Taiwan	4,057	13. U.S.S.R.	10,543
14. France	4,039	14. Iran	10,410
15. Haiti	3,609	15. Portugal	8,408

Source: U.S. Immigration and Naturalization Service, Annual Report (Washington, D.C.: U.S. Government Printing Office, 1984), Table 13.

The extent to which other countries begin, continue, or cease to send large numbers of immigrants will partially determine the cultural impact of these immigrants upon American society. Moreover, as different parts of the world become primary sending areas, the interests of the newly naturalized citizens, and in turn American foreign policy, become increasingly involved in developments in those parts of the world. Table 14.3 shows the leading suppliers of immigrants since 1820, and Table 14.4 shows some recent changes in immigration patterns. The first table shows the past dominance of countries from Europe and the Western Hemisphere in the total numbers, while the second table shows the impact of the current immigration law, with significant shifts in country representation among the leaders. Many immigrants still come from European countries, but there has been a decided increase in the number of immigrants from Asia. As the chain migration process occurs among these immigrants, it is reasonable to assume that there will continue to be large numbers of them among the strangers coming to these shores.

CURRENT ETHNIC ISSUES

Two highly controversial issues punctuate race and ethnic relations in the United States: immigration and bilingual education. Although the latter is a fairly new issue, arguments against both are repetitions of those hotly debated issues in the late nineteenth and early twentieth centuries. Nativist fears of being overrun by too many "non-American types" and of their cultural pluralism undermining societal cohesion are quite similar to concerns raised by past generations.

Immigration Fears

Almost 6.4 million legal immigrants came to the United States in 1971–1980, exceeding the number from every other decade in the nation's history except 1901–1910, when 8.8 million arrived. The 1980s appear to be heading toward at least 5 million immigrants, if current trends continue. For some, such large numbers are cause for concern about the country's ability to absorb so many immigrants or that Americans will "lose control" of their country to foreigners. These reactions are very similar, though not as intense, as those in other peak immigration periods—the midnineteenth century and early twentieth century. Actually, the impact of 6.4 million arrivals upon a population exceeding 232 million will probably be much less than that of 8.8 million upon a population of 76 million in 1910. In addition, the proportion of foreign-born citizens in the total population is actually the lowest since 1850, when the federal government began keeping such statistics.

Besides numbers, another major alarm has been raised about the changing racial composition of the nation. Asia and Latin America now account for 82 percent of all immigration. Asians and Pacific Islanders increased 127.6 percent between 1970 and 1980, from 1.5 million to 3.5 million, while the Hispanic population grew by 61 percent, going from 9 million to 14.6 million.[56] One demographer has projected that, if current migration patterns and birth rates continue, this country's population in 100 years will be one-fourth Asian and one-third Hispanic.[57]

The current wave of Asians and Latinos results from the 1965 immigration law eliminating percentage quotas in effect since 1924, which had virtually excluded these peoples and established preferences for close relatives of those already here. Presidential historian Theodore White called the 1965 law "Probably the most thoughtless of the many acts of the Great Society," while Eugene McCarthy, former Minnesota senator and presidential candidate, lamented that America was becoming a "colony to the world" and suffered a "loss of control" over immigration.

Refugees have always been welcomed to the United States, but a backlash against the new "imported poverty class" has been occurring for the past several years. The 1980 boatlift of 125,000 Cuban refugees, and the arrival of over 350,000 Indochinese and 60,000 Haitians since 1975, have brought reactionary violence to Florida, the Gulf Coast, and California. Arson and rioting in Miami against Cubans, as well as harassment, arson, shootings, and violence in Texas, Louisiana, and Mississippi against Vietnamerican fishermen occurred in 1981 and 1982. In California where 350,000 Asian refugees now live, beatings, bomb threats, and vandalism have been reported. Most of the hostility stems from concerns over job competition, public welfare and education costs, and the numerical threat to "American" values and moral fiber.

Senator Alan Simpson of Wyoming cosponsored the Immigration Reform and Control Act in 1982, expressing concern about "Hispanic dominance" in immigration and the "inability" of Latinos to assimilate as rapidly as other groups. The bill passed in the Senate 80–19, but did not come to a vote in the House until June 1984, when it narrowly passed 216–211. A 1984 *Newsweek* poll showed many Americans echoing Sen. Simpson's concerns: 53 percent of those surveyed thought too many Latin American immigrants were entering the country while 49 percent said too many Asians were coming in.[58] A 1982 Roper survey showed two of three Americans in favor of decreasing the annual maximum allowance of immigrants.

Illegal Aliens

A major cause for concern among political and civic leaders is the growing number of illegal aliens in the United States, for which estimates range from 3.5 to 8 million. The Border Patrol apprehends over 80,000 illegal aliens each month, but estimates it catches only 1 in 3. Slipping across the 1,933-mile southern border is easy, many doing so in broad daylight after reaching a border town by bus.

The illegal alien population is overwhelmingly comprised of Mexicans, who are about four out of every five illegal immigrants. Other major sources of illegal aliens are Columbia, Dominican Republic, El Salvador, Guatemala, Haiti, and Jamaica. With the number of illegal aliens continuing in record numbers, a loud clamor exists for the United States to regain control of its borders. Suggested solutions in the Simpson-Mazzoli bill passed in 1984 include amnesty for those already here,

Their faces registering varying degrees of fear and disappointment, these apprehended illegal aliens await deportation. Perhaps twice as many escape detection as the 80,000 caught monthly, many of the latter simply trying again. With widespread poverty and unemployment in their homeland, the illegal aliens act out of desperation to escape their fate and the bureaucratic processing delays of legal immigration.

an identification card system for job applicants, and penalties for employers knowingly hiring undocumented workers.

The most frequent complaints are that illegal aliens depress the wage scale, displace low-skilled American workers who are often minority group members themselves, and thereby increase the cost of assistance and social service programs. Others dismiss the charges, claiming the illegals are taking jobs no one else wants and their consumerism actually helps the economy. Except for those illegally in the country for criminal purposes (drug trafficking, theft, robbery), crime is not a serious problem, since undocumented aliens must walk a narrow line to remain unknown to the authorities. To what extent the illegal aliens are thus victims of unreported crimes is unknown.

Compounding reaction against illegal aliens was a June 1982 ruling by the U.S. Supreme Court, which held that Texas must provide free education for children who have entered the country illegally. This 5–4 decision was based upon the Fourteenth Amendment, that says in part: ". . . nor shall any state . . . deny to any person within its jurisdiction the equal protection of the laws." Critics claim the Constitution's definition of "Person" does not include noncitizens arriving in a state against the law by their own determination, without accepting the jurisdiction of that sort.[59] In addition to requiring public funding for schooling children, state officials in Texas and California worry about the extension of such a ruling into unemployment and welfare benefits, health services, and free college education.

Bilingual Education

Offering *bilingual education*—teaching subjects in both English and the student's native language—can be a transition program (gradually phasing in English completely over several years) or a maintenance program (continual native-language teaching to sustain one's heritage). For many Americans who assumed that English-speaking schools provided the heat for the melting pot, the popularity of bilingual education—particularly maintenance programs—became a sore point. Some saw such efforts as counterproductive because they would reduce assimilation and cohesiveness in American society, while simultaneously isolating ethnic groups from one another. Advocates of bilingual programs emphasize they are developing *bilingualism*—fluency in both English and one's native tongue—and that many youngsters are illiterate in both when they begin school.

Public funding for bilingual education began in 1968 when Congress passed the Bilingual Education Act, designed for low-income families only. Two years later, the Department of Health, Education, and Welfare specified that school districts with any national origin group of more than 5 percent had a legal obligation to provide bilingual programs for low-income families. In 1974 two laws significantly expanded bilingual programs. The Bilingual Act eliminated the low-income requirement and urged children receive a variety of courses that provided appreciation of their cultural heritage. The Equal Opportunity Act included failure to take "appropriate action" to overcome language barriers that impeded equal par-

While adults debate the pro-con issues of bilingual education, these children poignantly demonstrate acceptance through shared understandings. Americans have always looked to the schools as Americanization agents, causing some to fear bilingual programs will foster ethnic tribalism instead of assimilation.

ticipation in school as an illegal form of denying equal educational opportunity. Presently, close to 700 bilingual programs exist in sixty-eight languages, including twenty Native-American languages, Arabic, Chinese, French, Greek, Punjabi, Samoan, Spanish, and Vietnamese.[60]

Difficulty with the English language while they were students is often cited by older naturalized American citizens as one of their most difficult times of adjustment and gaining acceptance. Bilingual proponents argue their program eases that adjustment and accelerates the learning process. Carmel Sandoval of the National Education Association, which strongly supports bilingual education, maintains the program not only "helps the kids who don't speak English—(but) it even reduces their astronomical dropout rates."[61]

Opponents find the programs too costly, frequently staffed by paraprofessionals who themselves are not very fluent in English, or simply subsidizing political activities of vocal minority groups. A primary fear is that the program encourages "ethnic tribalism," fostering separation instead of a cohesive society. Critics point to the increased divisiveness and cries of separatism from French Canadians in Quebec and Basques in Spain, arguing bilingual programs can sow such seeds of dissension here.

One example of the bilingual backlash occurred in Florida's Dade County in November 1980, when voters passed by a 3–2 margin an antibilingual ordinance.

Although the ordinance dealt with spending county funds only and therefore did not affect election ballots, emergency services (police, fire, hospital, hurricane alert programs), or even schools, the Cuban community expressed strong resentment. In the long run this vote will probably prove inconsequential because of a shift in the balance of power, with more Anglos moving out and more Cubans moving in. Still, the controversy over bilingual education is likely to continue for many years throughout the nation.

Some scholarship on bilingualism has found a positive association between the maintenance of the native language and academic performance.[62] These findings have led to suggestions that a thorough cognitive development in the native language contributes to a better cognitive development in the second language. However, Benjamin Hadis, after analyzing the academic performance of over 4,000 New York City high-school students in 1980–1981, concludes this relationship is a spurious one, since it no longer exists after controlling for length of residence in the United States.[63] However, Hadis found maintenance of the native language has a positive effect on students' school attendance, and indirectly on their academic performance, but only in socially and academically deprived contexts.

Briefly, an insistence on "building" on the basis of the native language and, thus, placing emphasis on the development of native language arts as a vehicle for an effective transition into the mainstream would only make sense when the student's cognitive development in the native language has reached a step which is above a minimum threshold. . . . On the other hand, the maintenance of the native language as a boost of self-esteem, coupled with a bi-cultural approach. makes more sense in socially and academically deprived contexts. In school contexts which are not haunted by poverty and which are more conducive to learning, factors other than those pertaining to boosting the pride in the students' culture of origin work just as well.[64]

Hadis's findings return us once again to a major point raised in Chapter 2 and illustrated throughout this book: the interrelationship between ethnicity and social class. Bilingual education appears less necessary among those economically secure, but an important factor among low-income ethnic Americans, giving them an enhanced self-image and achievement motivation.

THE FUTURE OF ETHNICITY

The ethnic experience in the United States has been vast and complex. This nation of immigrants has substantial diversity within its population, which has sometimes resulted in antagonism and conflict. Some have struggled to overcome their ethnicity, and others have struggled to preserve theirs, but all have fought to make a better life for themselves and their families in the new country.

Many differences of opinion exist among sociologists concerning what changes have occurred in the immigrants' value orientations and behavior patterns and whether there is or is not a current ethnic revival, and if so, why. Certainly there is more scholarship and theoretical discussion on the matter than ever before, and many Americans have shown that they are interested in learning more about their own roots. Is this interest the result of curiosity arising out of better education, increased leisure time, affluence, and rapid transportation opportunities, or is it a rediscovery of ethnicity? Is it a temporary phenomenon or part of an ongoing process? Is it based on security in American identity or on uneasiness in a depersonalized society? And what of the new immigrants who have been coming here? What effect will they have upon American society? Will governmental acceptance of pluralism and such controversial practices as bilingual education improve or weaken the fabric of American society?

Most important of all, what kind of society are we becoming? Of the many possibilities, two distinct ones are a pluralistic society that is truly integrated in all respects, or a pluralistic society with the degree of integration dependent upon race and ethnicity. Which of these possibilities is likely to occur, and when? Is there an evolutionary process at work, or is government action necessary? In so complex and dynamic a subject as race and ethnic relations, with so many influencing variables, discussing future directions is a challenge. Nevertheless, here are some observations relating to future possibilities:

1. Economic growth is a critical factor in curbing ethnic antagonism and absorbing more minority people into the mainstream of American life. In recent years illegal immigration had led to greater ethnic antagonism, particularly in the Southwest, when the economy has been unable to grow fast enough to absorb the illegal aliens. Moreover, a continuing pattern of illegal immigration also fans antagonism between the illegal and legal aliens with the same heritage who are competing for jobs, an issue over which the Chicano community is currently seriously split.

It would appear that a concentrated federal effort aimed at sustained economic growth, full employment, and urban revitalization would do much to reduce many of the tensions and problems of dominant-minority relations. When economic security for all U.S. residents replaces chronic unemployment, underemployment, dependency, hopelessness, frustration, and despair, then we will have eliminated one of the major causes of negative judgments and treatments of various racial and ethnic groups.

2. Many social scientists feel that more and more Americans are becoming aware of the pluralistic reality of American society and that often their own "hangups" cause them to be prejudiced. If this awareness becomes more widespread and can be translated into action, this may be the beginning of a truly integrated society.

3. It may be argued that heightened racial and ethnic self-awareness will ultimately lead to greater societal cohesion, not to divisiveness. The predominance of an Anglo-conformity assimilationist viewpoint worked to the disadvantage of those who were considered "different" or "unassimilable." An awareness of diversity and an insistence upon acceptance of one's own particular racial and ethnic identity will, hopefully, lead people to allow others that same prerogative. In time, greater tolerance for other groups might even lead to an appreciation of their differences.

4. Racism, which is relatively new in human history but as old as American history, is another critical factor in dominant-minority relations. America is no longer as racist a society as it once was, but it would be naive to think that this ideology has been overcome completely. Again, economic independence would seem to be a key means of overcoming much of the racial condemnation, as it has been to a large extent for the Chinese and Japanese. We could express the very same thoughts about sexism and sex discrimination as well, as both retreat in the face of heightened awareness and economic independence among American women.

5. Finally, young people seem to have an increasing tendency to relate to people as individuals rather than on the basis of race, religion, nationality, or even social class, although they remain interested in those factors. The degree to which that attitude spreads among others and is retained by the young people as they grow older will greatly determine what American society will become.

Economic growth, increased awareness of pluralism, and a greater tendency to relate to individuals as individuals may allow the strangers in our midst to be perceived more favorably than their predecessors were. When the predominant attitude toward strangers becomes one of acceptance rather than suspicion, and when the newcomers are perceived as equals and sources of cultural enrichment rather than as inferiors and threats to the status quo, then race and ethnic relations will be more positive. Whether this ideal can ever become reality is the challenge before us.

REVIEW QUESTIONS

1. What are some of the explanations for ethnic consciousness? Which seems most plausible? Why?

2. Is it correct to suggest ethnic differences in behavior, even in reaction to pain? How so?

3. What does ethnic stratification suggest about upward mobility in the United States?

4. What do current immigration patterns indicate to us? Is immigration a problem for native-born Americans?

5. What are the pros and cons of bilingual education?

6. What is the future of ethnicity in the United States?

SUGGESTED READINGS

Gordon, Milton. M. *Assimilation in American Life.* New York: Oxford University Press, 1964.

A highly influential and still pertinent book offering an analysis of the role of race and ethnicity in American life, and the different forms assimilation takes.

Miller, Randall M. (ed.). *The Kaleidoscopic Lens: How Hollywood Views Ethnic Groups.* Englewood, NJ: Jerome S. Ozer, 1980.

An interesting, illustrated examination of the origins, development, and significance of ethnic representations in American feature films, from silent films to 1980.

Mindel, Charles H. and Robert W. Habenstein (eds.). *Ethnic Families in America: Patterns and Variations,* 2nd ed. New York: Elsevier, 1981.

An excellent portrait of fifteen racial and ethnic groups, their family characteristics, and the impact of the women's movement on ethnic family life.

Newman, William M. *American Pluralism.* New York: Harper & Row, 1973.

An argument for a social pluralism theory and analysis of the consequences of discrimination and conflict.

Novak, Michael. *The Rise of the Unmeltable Ethnics.* New York: Macmillan, 1971.

A provocative and influential book examining assimilation problems of white ethnics and their reactions to efforts for today's identified minorities.

Sowell, Thomas. *Ethnic America: A History.* New York: Basic Books, 1981.

A fine comparative analysis of major racial and ethnic groups in the United States, with discussion of reasons for their varying success in American society.

GLOSSARY

Abstract Typification The generalization of people or things into broad categories.

Acceptance A minority response to prejudice and discrimination; based on powerlessness, fear for personal safety, or economic security, or fatalism.

Accommodation A tendency to accept the situation as it exists, without seeking to change it or make others conform; pluralism.

Acculturation The process by which a group changes its distinctive cultural traits to conform with those of the host society.

Achieved Status One's socially defined position in a society based on individual accomplishments or failings.

Action-Orientation Level of Prejudice A positive or negative predisposition to engage in discriminatory behavior toward members of a particular group.

Amalgamation The biological and cultural blending of two or more groups of people into a distinct new type; the melting-pot theory.

Americanization The effort to have ethnic groups quickly give up their cultural traits and adopt those of the dominant American group.

Anglo-conformity A behavioral adherence to the established white Anglo-Saxon Protestant prototype; what many ethnocentric Americans mean by assimilation.

Annihilation The extermination of a specific group of people.

Ascribed Status One's socially defined, unchangeable position in a society based on such arbitrary factors as age, sex, race, or family background.

Assimilation The process by which members of racial or ethnic minorities are able to function within a society without indicating any marked cultural, social, or personal differences from the people of the majority group.

Authoritarian Personality A set of distinct personality traits, including conformity, insecurity, and intol-erance, said to be common among many prejudiced people.

Avoidance A minority-group response to prejudice and discrimination by migrating or withdrawing to escape further problems; a majority-group attempt to minimize contact with specific minority groups through social or spatial segregation.

Bilingual Education Teaching subjects in both English and one's native language to develop fluency in both.

Categoric Knowing A stereotype of others based merely on information obtained visually and perhaps verbally.

Chain Migration A sequential flow of immigrants to a locality previously settled by friends, relatives, or other compatriots.

Cognitive Level of Prejudice The beliefs and perceptions about other racial or ethnic groups.

Conflict Theory A sociological perspective emphasizing conflict as an important influence and permanent feature of life.

Convergent Subculture A subgroup gradually becoming completely integrated into the dominant culture.

Cultural Assimilation Changing cultural patterns of behavior to those of the host society; acculturation.

Cultural Determinism A theory that a group's culture explains its position in society and its achievements or lack of them.

Cultural Differentiation Those differences between cultures making one group distinguishable from another.

Cultural diffusion The spread of ideas, inventions, and practices from one culture to another.

Cultural drift A gradual change in the values, attitudes, customs, and beliefs of the members of a society.

Cultural pluralism Two or more culturally distinct groups coexisting in relative harmony.

Cultural relativism The perception and judging of another culture or subculture from the perspective of the other culture rather than that of one's own culture.

Cultural transmission The passing on of a society's culture from one generation to another.

Culture The values, attitudes, customs, beliefs, and habits shared by members of a society.

Culture of Poverty A controversial viewpoint arguing the disorganization and pathology of lower-class culture is self-perpetuating through cultural transmission.

Culture Shock Feelings of disorientation, anxiety. and a sense of being threatened when unpreparedly brought into contact with another culture.

Cumulative causation Gunnar Myrdal's term for the vicious-circle process in which prejudice and discrimination each mutually "cause" the other, thereby continuing and intensifying the cycle.

De facto discrimination Unequal and differential treatment of a group or groups that is entrenched in social customs and institutions.

Defiance A peaceful or violent action to challenge openly what a group considers a discriminatory practice.

De jure discrimination Unequal and differential treatment of a group or groups that is established by law.

Deviance Characteristics or behavior violating social norms and thereby negatively valued by many people in that society.

Differentiation The social theory that societies tend to treat their members differently because of race, religion, age, sex, or other factors.

Discrimination Differential and unequal treatment of other groups of people, usually along racial, religious, or ethnic lines.

Displaced aggression Hostility directed against a powerless group rather than against the more powerful cause of the feelings of hostility.

Dominant Group Any culturally or physically distinctive social grouping possessing economic, political and social power, and discriminating against a subordinate minority group.

Dysfunction A disruption of the equilibrium in a social system or of the functioning of some unit within the system.

Economic determinism A theory that a society's economic base establishes its culture and general characteristics.

Emotional level of prejudice The feelings aroused in a group by another racial or ethnic group.

Endogamy The tendency for people to marry only within their own social group.

Ethclass A social group classification based on a combination of race, religion, social class, and regional residence.

Ethnic antagonism Various forms of intergroup hostility, including ideologies, beliefs, behavior, and institutionalized practices.

Ethnic behavior A concept that members of different ethnic groups behave differently in similar situations.

Ethnic consciousness A self-awareness of ethnic identity; the deliberate maintenance of one's culture in another cultural environment.

Ethnic group A group of people who share a common religion, nationality, culture, and/or language.

Ethnicity A cultural concept in which a large number of people who share learned or acquired traits and close social interaction regard themselves and are regarded by others as a single group on that basis.

Ethnocentrism A tendency to judge other cultures or subcultures by the standards of one's own culture.

Ethnography The study of the way of life of a people.

Ethnophaulism A derogatory word or expression used to describe or refer to a racial or ethnic group.

Exogamy The tendency for people to marry outside their own social group.

Exploitation The selfish utilization of the labor of others for profit at their expense.

Expulsion   The forced removal of a group of people from an area.

False Consciousness   Holding attitudes not accurately reflecting the objective facts of the situation.

Fatalism   A belief that events are determined by fate and thus beyond human control.

First-generation American   Someone born in another country who migrated to the United States.

Folkways   Norms that a society considers useful but not essential; their violation evokes only a mild negative response.

Frustration   A behavioral response when expectations remain unsatisfied; sometimes linked to scapegoating.

Functional Theory   A sociological perspective emphasizing societal order and stability, with harmonious interdependent parts.

Gemeinschaft   A small, tradition-dominated community characterized by intimate primary relationships and strong feelings of group loyalty.

Group   A collectivity of people closely interacting with one another on the basis of shared expectations about behavior.

Hansen's law   A theory that what the child of an immigrant wishes to forget, the grandchild wishes to remember; also called the three-generation hypothesis.

Hegemony   Leadership or predominant influence exercised by one group over others, whether on a racial, religious, cultural, or linguistic basis.

Historicity   Historical actuality or authenticity; past experiences.

Ideology   A generalized set of beliefs that explains and justifies the interests of those who hold them.

Ingroup   The group to which an individual belongs and feels loyalty.

Institution   Patterns of behavior organized to meet a basic need of a society, such as family, education, religion, economics, or politics.

Institutionalized discrimination   Differential and unequal treatment of a group or groups that deeply pervades social customs and institutions, and is usually subtle and informal.

Interactionist Theory   A sociological perspective emphasizing the shared interpretations and interaction patterns in everyday life.

Intergenerational mobility   The change in social status within a family from one generation to the next.

Internal Colonialism   A concept explaining the experiences of Blacks, Chicanos, and Native Americans in terms of economic exploitation and rigid stratification.

Invasion–Succession   The ecological process in which one group displaces another group in a residential area or business activity.

Jigsaw Method   A teaching technique to promote cooperation and better intergroup understanding.

Jim Crow laws   Southern state segregation laws, passed in the 1890s and early twentieth century, which covered use of all public facilities, including schools, restaurants, transportation, waiting rooms, rest rooms, drinking fountains, and parks.

Linguistic relativity   The recognition that different languages dissect and present reality differently.

Marginality   The situation of individuals who are the product of one culture but are attempting to live within another, and therefore are not fully a part of either one.

Marital Assimilation   A pattern of intermarriage of minority group members with dominant group members.

Melting-Pot Theory   An idealistic idea that many diverse peoples would blend both biologically and culturally, forming a distinct new breed—the American; amalgamation.

Middleman Minority   A minority group occupying an intermediate occupational position in trade or commerce between the top and bottom strata.

Minority Group   A culturally and physically distinctive group receiving unequal treatment, an ascribed status, a sense of shared identity, and practicing endogamy.

Mores Norms that society considers essential; their violation evokes a strong negative response.

Nativist One who advocates a policy of protecting the interests of native inhabitants against those of immigrants.

Negative Self-Image The result of social conditioning or differential treatment or both, causing people or groups to believe themselves inferior.

"New" immigrants A term used by the Dillingham Commission (1907–1911) to identify immigrants from southern, central, and eastern Europe.

Norms The internalized rules of conduct that embody the fundamental expectations of society.

Objectivity Disciplining oneself to examine and interpret reality with the least possible amount of personal bias and distortion.

Occupational Mobility Ability to change one's job position in terms of status and economic reward.

"Old" immigrants A term used by the Dillingham Commission (1907–1911) to identify immigrants from northern and western Europe.

Outgroup Any group to which an individual does not belong nor feels loyalty.

Paralinguistic Signals Use of sounds, but not words, which convey distinct meanings.

Parallel Social Institutions A subcultural replication of institutions of the larger society, such as churches, schools, organizations.

Paternalism A condescending treatment of adults, managing and regulating their affairs as a father would handle his children's affairs.

Persistent Subculture A subgroup adhering to its own way of life and resisting absorption into the dominant culture.

Personality An individual's typical patterns of thought, feeling, and action.

Pluralism A state in which minorities can maintain their distinctive subcultures and simultaneously interact with relative equality in the larger society.

Power differential The uneven distribution of power, whether economic, political, or social.

Power Theory A concept that the relative power of the indigenous and migrant groups determines the outcome of their interaction.

Prejudice A system of negative beliefs, feelings, and action-orientations regarding a certain group or groups of people.

Primary group A small number of people who interact with one another in close, personal, and meaningful relationships.

Push–pull factors The forces that encourage migration from one country to another.

Race A categorization in which a large number of people sharing visible physical characteristics regard themselves or are regarded by others as a single group on that basis.

Racial stratification Differences in socioeconomic status within a society that is structured according to race.

Racism An ideology that establishes a link between the biological conditions of a human organism and its sociocultural capabilities and behavior.

Random sample A scientific selection of people from a larger population in which everyone has an equal chance to be chosen.

Reciprocal typifications People's categorizations of one another based upon their shared experiences.

Reference group A group to which people may or may not belong, but to which they refer when evaluating themselves and their behavior.

Relative deprivation A lack of resources, or rewards, in one's standard of living in comparison with others in the society.

Reputational Method A technique for measuring social class by questioning people of others' social standing.

Reverse Discrimination An action to overcome discrimination against one group resulting in discrimination against another group.

Role Behavior determined by the status the individual occupies.

Scapegoating Placing blame on others for something that is not their fault.

Second-generation American   A child born in the United States of immigrant parents; can also refer to a child born elsewhere but raised from a young age in the United States by immigrant parents.

Secondary group   A collectivity of people who interact on an impersonal or limited emotional basis for some practical or specific purpose.

Selective Perception   A tendency to see or accept only that information agreeing with one's value orientations or consistent with one's attitudes about other groups.

Self-fulfilling prophecy   A prediction that so influences behavior that the consequence is a realization of the prediction.

Self-justification   A defense mechanism whereby people denigrate another person or group to justify maltreatment of them.

Sexism   Institutionalized prejudice and discrimination based on gender.

Situational ethnicity   Ethnic consciousness generated by residence, special events, work relationships, or working-class life style.

Social change   Any alteration, whether gradual or swift, in the patterns of social behavior or the social structure.

Social class   A categorization designating people's places in the stratification hierarchy on the basis of similarities in income, property, power, status, and life style.

Social conditioning   A socialization process through which people are molded to fit into the social system.

Social Construction of Reality   The process by which definitions of reality are socially created, objectified, internalized, and then taken for granted.

Social Discrimination   Exclusion of outgroup members from close relationships with ingroup members.

Social Distance   The degree of closeness or remoteness one desires in interaction with members of a particular group.

Social hierarchy   The stratified levels of status within a group or society.

Social interaction   The reciprocal process by which people act and react toward one another.

Social mobility   The change from one status to another in a stratified society.

Social norms   Generally shared rules or expectations of what is and is not proper behavior.

Social organization   Any grouping formed to provide a means of social interaction among individuals.

Social segregation   A situation in which participation in social, fraternal, service, and other types of activities is confined to members of the ingroup.

Social stratification   The hierarchy within a society based upon the unequal distribution of resources, power, or prestige.

Social structure   The organized patterns of behavior in a social system governing people's interrelationship with one another.

Socialization   The process of social interaction by which people acquire personality and learn the culture or subculture of their group.

Society   A group of individuals who share a common culture and territory.

Socioeconomic status (SES) A social prestige ranking as determined by numerous factors, including occupation, income, educational background, and place of residence.

Spatial segregation   The physical separation of a minority group from the rest of society, such as in housing or education.

Split Labor Market   A concept explaining ethnic antagonism on the basis of conflict between higher-paid and lower-paid labor.

Status   A socially defined position in society.

Stereotype   An oversimplified generalization attributing certain traits or characteristics to any person in a group without regard to individual differences.

Structural assimilation   The large-scale entrance of minority-group members into primary-group relationships with the host society in its social organizations and institutions.

Structural conditions Those large-scale factors affecting society, such as industrialization, economic vitality, and stratification.

Structural differentiation Status distinctions for different racial and ethnic groups entrenched within the social system.

Structural discrimination Differential treatment of groups of people that is entrenched in the institutions of a society.

Structural pluralism Coexistence of racial and ethnic groups in separate subsocieties also divided along social class and regional boundaries.

Subculture A group that shares in the overall culture of a society while retaining its own distinctive traditions and life style.

Subjectivity Observing the world from one's own viewpoint, as shaped by cultural input, personal opinion, emotions, and experiences.

Subordinate Less powerful than another group that possesses political, economic, or technological advantages.

Superordinate Possessing superior power, whether political, economic, or technological.

Symbol Anything that can be understood to signify something else, such as a word or gesture that symbolizes an attitude or feeling.

Symbolic interaction The use of symbols such as signs, gestures, and language through which people interact with one another.

Third-generation American Someone born in the United States whose grandparents migrated to the United States.

Three-generation hypothesis See Hansen's Law.

Thomas theorem An observation that if people define situations as real, then they are real in their consequences.

Triple-melting-pot theory The concept that intermarriage is occurring among various nationalities within the three major religious groupings.

Value judgment A personal or subjective opinion based on the values of the observer.

Value neutrality An ideal state, never fully possible, in which the observer eliminates all personal bias in order to be completely objective.

Value Stretch The concept that the poor adapt their values to cope with more realistic expectations.

Values Shared general concepts regarding what is good, right, useful, or desirable.

Vertical mobility A change to a higher or lower social or occupational status than previously held.

Vicious circle A self-perpetuating process in human behavior, as when a negative attitude influences a negative action, which results in a reaction that reaffirms or intensifies the negative attitude.

Victimological approach Blaming the victim for his or her situation, rather than looking for other causes for the problem.

Xenophobia An irrational fear of or contempt for strangers or foreigners.

NOTES

Chapter 1

1. Aristotle, *The Rhetoric*, Appleton, New York, 1932.

2. See, for example, Theodore Newcomb, "The Acquaintance Process: Looking Mainly Backward," *Journal of Personality and Social Psychology*, 36(1978), 1075–1083.

3. Donn Byrne, et al., "The Ubiquitous Relationship: Attitude Similarity and Attraction. A Cross-Cultural Study," *Human Relations*, 24 (1971), 201–207.

4. Emory S. Bogardus, "Comparing Racial Distances in Ethiopia, South Africa, and the United States," *Sociology and Social Research*, 52 (1968), 149–156.

5. Lyn H. Lofland, *A World of Strangers*, Basic Books, New York, 1973, p. 16.

6. Georg Simmel, "The Stranger," in *The Sociology of Georg Simmel*, ed. Kurt H. Wolff, Free Press, New York, 1950.

7. Alfred Schutz, "The Stranger," *American Sociological Review*, 69 (May 1944), 449–507.

8. William Graham Sumner, *Folkways*, Ginn, Boston, 1906, p. 13.

9. See Marc J. Schwartz, "Negative Ethnocentrism," *Journal of Conflict Resolution*, 5 (March 1961), 75–81.

10. Robin M. Williams, Jr., *Strangers Next Door*, Prentice-Hall, Englewood Cliffs, N.J., 1964, p. 23.

11. Robert A. Levine and Donald T. Campbell, *Ethnocentrism: Theories of Conflict, Ethnic Attitudes, and Group Behavior*, Wiley, New York, 1972, pp. 68, 202.

12. Kenneth E. Boulding, *Conflict and Defense: A General Theory*, Harper, New York, 1962, pp. 162–163; Lewis A. Coser, *Sociological Theory: A Book of Readings*, Macmillan, New York, 1957, pp. 87–110; P. C. Rosenblatt, "Origins and Effects of Group Ethnocentrism and Nationalism," *Journal of Conflict Resolution*, 8 (1964), 131–146; M. Sherif and C. W. Sherif, *Groups in Harmony and Tension*, Harper, New York, 1953, p. 196.

13. Brewton Berry, *Race and Ethnic Relations*, 3rd ed., Houghton Mifflin, Boston, 1965, p. 55.

14. Morton Klass and Hal Hellman, *The Kinds of Mankind*, Lippincott, New York, 1971, p. 61.

15. Immanuel Velikovsky, *Oedipus and Akhnaton*, Doubleday, New York, 1960, p. 96.

16. See Albert Szymanski, "Racial Discrimination and White Gain," *American Sociological Review*, 41 (1976), 403–414; Sidney M. Willhelm, "Can Marxism Explain America's Racism?" *Social Problems*, 28 (1980), 98–112.

17. Erving Goffman, *The Presentation of Self in Everyday Life*, Doubleday, Garden City, N.Y., 1959.

18. Peter L. Berger and Thomas Luckmann, *The Social Construction of Reality*, Doubleday, Garden City, N.Y., 1963.

19. Donald Young, *American Minority Peoples*, Harper, New York, 1932, p. viii.

20. Louis Wirth, "The Problem of Minority Groups," in *The Science of Man in the World Crisis*, ed. Ralph Linton, Columbia University Press, New York, 1945.

21. Richard Schermerhorn, *Comparative Ethnic Relations*, Random House, New York, 1970, p. 8.

22. Tamotsu Shibutani and Kian M. Kwan, *Ethnic Stratification*, Macmillan, New York, 1965.

23. Schermerhorn, *Comparative Ethnic Relations*, p. 12.

24. Charles Wagley and Marvin Harris, *Minorities in the New World*, Columbia University Press, New York, 1964.

25. See Ashley Montagu, *Man's Most Dangerous Myth: The Fallacy of Race*, 5th ed., Oxford University Press, New York, 1974.

26. Brewton Berry and Henry L. Tischler, *Race and Ethnic Relations*, 4th ed., Houghton Mifflin, Boston, 1978, pp. 30–32.

27. Milton Gordon, *Assimilation in American Life*, Oxford University Press, New York, 1964, p. 27;

Shibutani and Kwan, *Ethnic Stratification,* p. 47; Jerry D. Rose, *Peoples: The Ethnic Dimension in Human Relations,* Rand McNally, Chicago, 1976, pp. 8–12.

Chapter 2

1. Louis Schneider and Charles Bonjean (eds.), *The Idea of Culture in the Social Sciences,* Cambridge University Press, Cambridge, U.K., 1973.

2. The importance of symbols to social interaction has drawn much attention in sociology. See Benjamin L. Whorf, *Language, Thought and Reality,* Wiley, New York, 1956; Gertrude Jaeger and Philip Selznick, "A Normative Theory of Culture," *American Sociological Review,* 29 (October 1964), 653–659; Herbert Blumer, *Symbolic Interaction: Perspective and Method,* Prentice-Hall, Englewood Cliffs, N.J., 1969.

3. Harry C. Bredemeier and Richard M. Stephenson, *The Analysis of Social Systems,* Holt, Rinehart, and Winston, New York, 1962, p. 3.

4. Giraffe going by a second-story window. Hot dog on a hamburger roll. Aerial view of two Mexicans in a canoe.

5. This connection between Lippmann's comments, the Droodles, and human response to definitions of stimuli was originally made by Harry C. Bredemeier and Richard M. Stephenson, *The Analysis of Social Systems,* pp. 2–3.

6. Edward O. Wilson, *Sociobiology,* The Belknap Press of Harvard University Press, Cambridge, Mass., 1975, p. 550.

7. Desmond Morris, *Manwatching: A Field Guide to Human Behavior,* Abrams, New York, 1977.

8. William I. Thomas, "The Relation of Research to the Social Process," in *Essays on Research in the Social Sciences,* The Brookings Institution, Washington, D.C., 1931, p. 189.

9. See the discussion on pp. 91–92.

10. Gregory Razran, "Ethnic Dislike and Stereotypes: A Laboratory Study," *Journal of Abnormal and Social Psychology,* 45 (1950), 7–27.

11. Copyright ©1949 by Richard Rodgers and Oscar Hammerstein II. Copyright renewed. Williamson Music, Inc., owner of publication and allied rights for the Western Hemisphere and Japan. International copyright secured. All rights reserved. Used by permission.

12. John Gillis, *The Ways of Men,* Appleton-Century-Crofts, New York, 1948, p. 556.

13. For a case study of England from 1000 to 1899, see Margaret T. Hodgen, *Change and History,* Wenner-Gren Foundation for Anthropological Research, New York, 1952.

14. Stanley Lieberson, "A Societal Theory of Race and Ethnic Relations," *American Sociological Review,* 26 (December 1961), 902–910.

15. Mary C. Sengstock, "Social Change in the Country of Origin as a Factor in Immigrant Conceptions of Nationality," *Ethnicity,* 4 (March 1977), 54–69.

16. E. Franklin Frazier, *The Negro Family in Chicago,* University of Chicago Press, Chicago, 1932; see also *The Negro Family in the United States,* rev. ed., University of Chicago Press, Chicago, 1966.

17. Daniel P. Moynihan, *The Negro Family: The Case for National Action,* U.S. Department of Labor, Washington, D.C., 1965.

18. Ibid., p. 5.

19. Ibid., p. 6.

20. Ibid., pp. 30, 47.

21. Oscar Lewis, *La Vida,* Vintage, New York, 1966, pp. xlii–lii.

22. Ibid., p. xlv.

23. Edward C. Banfield, *The Unheavenly City: The Nature and Future of Our Urban Crisis,* Little, Brown, Boston, 1970, pp. 210–211.

24. Joe R. Feagin, "Poverty: We Still Believe that God Helps Those Who Help Themselves," *Psychology Today,* 6 (November 1972), 101–110, 129.

25. Michael Harrington, *The Other America: Poverty in the United States,* Penguin, Baltimore, Md., 1963, p. 21.

26. Charles A. Valentine, *Culture and Poverty,* University of Chicago Press, Chicago, 1968, p. 129.

27. Lola M. Irelan, Oliver C. Moles, and Robert M. O'Shea, "Ethnicity, Poverty, and Selected Attitudes: A Test of the 'Culture of Poverty' Hypothesis," *Social Forces*, 47 (1969), 405–413.

28. Eliot Liebow, *Tally's Corner: A Study of Negro Streetcorner Men*, Little, Brown, Boston, 1967, pp. 222–223. See also Ulf Hannerz, *Soulside: Inquiries into Ghetto Culture and Community*, Columbia University Press, New York, 1969.

29. See Alan S. Berger and William Simon, "Black Families and the Moynihan Report: A Research Evaluation," *Social Problems*, 22 (1974), 145–161; Barbara E. Coward, et. al., "The Culture of Poverty Debate: Some Additional Data," *Social Problems*, 21 (1974), 621–634.

30. James E. Blackwell, *The Black Community: Diversity and Unity*, Dodd, Mead, New York, 1975.

31. Charles V. Willie, *A New Look at Black Families* 2nd ed., General Hall, New York, 1981; R. Hill, *The Strengths of Black Families,* Emerson Hall Publishers, New York, 1972; Andrew Billingsley, *Black Families in White America*, Prentice-Hall, Englewood Cliffs, NJ, 1968.

32. Hyman Rodman, "The Lower Class Value Stretch," *Social Forces*, 42 (1963), 205–215.

33. L. Richard Della Fave, "The Culture of Poverty Revisited: A Strategy for Research," *Social Problems*, 21 (1974), 609–621.

34. Alan C. Kerckhoff, *Socialization and Social Class*, Prentice-Hall, Englewood Cliffs, N.J., 1972, pp. 126–128.

35. W. Lloyd Warner and Paul S. Lunt, *The Social Life of a Modern Community*, Yankee City Series, Vol. 1, Yale University Press, New Haven, Conn., 1941.

36. W. Lloyd Warner and Leo Srole, *The Social System of American Ethnic Groups,* Yankee City Series, Vol. 3, Yale University Press, New Haven, Conn., 1945.

37. John C. Leggett, "Working Class Consciousness in an Industrial Community," unpublished Ph.D. thesis, University of Michigan, 1962, reported in Bruno Bettelheim and Morris Janowitz, *Social Change and Prejudice*, Free Press, New York, 1964, p. 33.

38. Richard Centers, *The Psychology of Social Classes: A Study of Class Consciousness*, Princeton University Press, Princeton, N.J., 1949; Oscar Glantz, "Class Consciousness and Political Solidarity," *American Sociological Review*, 23 (August 1958), 375–382; Robert W. Hodge and Donald J. Treiman, "Class Identification in the U.S.," *American Journal of Sociology*, 73 (March 1968), 535–547; Werner S. Landecker, "Class Crystallization and Class Consciousness," *American Sociological Review*, 28 (April 1963), 219–229; Robert T. Morris and Raymond J. Murphy, "A Paradigm for the Study of Class Consciousness," *Sociology and Social Research,* 50 (April 1966), 298–313.

39. Colin Greer (ed.), *Divided Society*, Basic Books, New York, 1974, p. 34

40. Milton M. Gordon, *Assimilation in American Life,* Oxford University Press, New York, 1964.

41. William M. Newman, *American Pluralism*, Harper & Row, New York, 1973, p. 84.

42. Gordon, *Assimilation in American Life,* p. 47.

43. See August B. Hollingshead, "Trends in Social Stratification: A Case Study," *American Sociological Review*, 17 (December 1952), 685–686; Raymond Mack (ed.), *Race, Class and Power*, 2nd ed., Van Nostrand Reinhold, New York, 1963; John Leggett *Class, Race and Labor*, Oxford University Press, New York, 1968.

44. Robert E. Park, *Race and Culture,* Free Press, Glencoe, Ill., 1949, p. 150.

45. Seymour M. Lipset, "Changing Social Status and Prejudice: The Race Theories of a Pioneering American Sociologist," *Commentary*, 9 (May 1950), 479.

46. Stanford M. Lyman, *The Black American in Sociological Thought: A Failure of Perspective,* Putnam, New York, 1972, pp. 49–50.

47. Warner and Srole, *The Social System of American Ethnic Groups,* pp. 285–286.

48. See Fred B. Silberstein and Melvin Seeman, "Social Mobility and Prejudice," *American Journal of Sociology*, 60 (November 1959), 258–264; Joseph Greenblum and Leonard J. Pearlin, "Vertical Mobility and Prejudice: A Socio-Psychological Analysis," in

Class, Status and Power, ed. Richard Bendix and S. M. Lipset, Free Press, Glencoe, Ill., 1953, pp. 483–491.

49. Bettelheim and Janowitz, Social Change and Prejudice, pp. 29–34.

50. Donald L. Noel, "A Theory of the Origin of Ethnic Stratification," *Social Problems,* 16 (Fall 1968), 157–172.

51. Lewis A. Coser, "Conflict: Social Aspects," in *International Encyclopedia of the Social Sciences,* ed. David Sills, Macmillan, New York, 1968, pp. 234–235.

52. Ralf Dahrendorf, *Class and Class Conflict in Industrial Society,* Stanford University Press, Stanford, Calif., 1959, pp. 215–218.

53. Max Weber, "Class, Status, Party," 1922, in *From Max Weber,* trans. and ed. Hans Gerth and C. Wright Mills, Oxford University Press, New York, 1946, pp. 193–194.

54. See Hubert M. Blalock, Jr., *Toward a Theory of Minority-Group Relations,* Wiley, New York, 1967, pp. 199–203.

55. James M. O'Kane, "Ethnic Mobility and the Lower-Income Negro: A Socio-Historical Perspective," *Social Problems,* 16 (1969), 309–311; see also Leonard Reissman and Michael N. Halstead, "The Subject Is Class," *Sociology and Social Research,* 54 (1970), 301–304.

56. Ibid., pp. 303–311.

57. See Robert Blauner, "Internal Colonialism and Ghetto Revolt." *Social Problems,* 16 (1969), 397; Stuart L. Hills, "Negroes and Immigrants in America," *Sociological Focus,* 3 (Summer 1970), 85–96; Nathan Glazer, "Blacks and Ethnic Groups," *Social Problems,* 18 (1971), 444–461.

58. Newman, *American Pluralism,* p. 53.

59. Barbara Solomon, *Ancestors and Immigrants,* University of Chicago Press, Chicago, 1956, pp. 59–61.

60. John Higham, *Strangers in the Land,* Rutgers University Press, New Brunswick, N.J., 1955, p. 247.

61. George R. Stewart, *American Ways of Life,* Doubleday, Garden City, N.Y., 1954, pp. 23, 28.

62. Gordon, *Assimilation in American Life,* pp. 70–71.

63. Ibid., p. 81.

64. See Gerhard Lenski, *The Religious Factor,* Doubleday, Garden City, N.Y., 1961, pp. 326–330; Will Herberg, *Protestant-Catholic-Jew,* Doubleday, Garden City, N.Y., 1955; William M. Dobriner, *Class in Suburbia,* Prentice-Hall, Englewood Cliffs, N.J., 1963; Bennett M. Berger, *Working Class Suburbs,* 2nd ed., University of California Press, Berkeley, Calif., 1960.

65. Louis Wirth, "The Problem of Minority Groups," in *The Science of Man in the World Crisis,* ed. Ralph Linton, Columbia University Press, New York, 1945.

66. Solomon, *Ancestors and Immigrants,* pp. 59–81.

67. Newman, *American Pluralism,* p. 63.

68. J. Hector St. John de Crèvecoeur, *Letters from an American Farmer,* Albert and Charles Boni, New York, 1925, pp. 54–55. Reprinted from the original edition, London, 1782.

69. Frederick Jackson Turner, *The Frontier in American History,* Henry Holt, New York, 1920, p. 351.

70. Israel Zangwill, *The Melting-Pot: Drama in Four Acts,* Macmillan, New York, 1921, p. 33.

71. Actually, any student of western civilizations would point out that centuries of invasions, conquests, boundary changes, etc., had often resulted in cross-breeding and that truly distinct or pure ethnic types were virtually nonexistent long before the eighteenth century.

72. Gordon, *Assimilation in American Life,* pp. 109–110.

73. Ruby Jo Reeves Kennedy, "Single or Triple Melting Pot? Intermarriage Trends in New Haven, 1870–1940," *American Journal of Sociology,* 49 (January 1944), 331–339; see also her follow-up study in *American Journal of Sociology,* 58 (July 1952), 56–59.

74. See Will Herberg, *Protestant-Catholic-Jew,* Doubleday, Garden City, N.Y., 1955.

75. Henry Pratt Fairchild, *Immigration,* Macmillan, New York, 1925, p. 396 ff.

76. Herberg, *Protestant-Catholic-Jew,* pp. 33–34.

77. Newman, *American Pluralism,* p. 67.

78. Horace M. Kallen, "Democracy *Versus* the Melting Pot," *The Nation,* Feb. 18, 1915, pp. 190–194; Feb. 25, 1915, pp. 217–220.

79. Gordon, *Assimilation in American Life,* p. 135.

Chapter 3

1. See Hortense Powdermaker, *Probing Our Prejudices,* Harper, New York, 1941, p. 1.

2. Louis Wirth, "Race and Public Policy," *The Scientific Monthly,* 58 (1944), 303.

3. Ralph L. Rosnow, "Poultry and Prejudice," *Psychology Today,* (March 1972), p. 53.

4. Reported by Daniel Wilner, Rosabelle Price Walkley, and Stuart W. Cook, "Residential Proximity and Intergroup Relations in Public Housing Projects," *Journal of Social Issues,* 8, No. 1 (1952), 45. See also James W. Vander Zanden, *American Minority Relations,* 3rd ed., Ronald Press, New York, 1972, p. 21.

5. Bernard M. Kramer, "Dimensions of Prejudice," *Journal of Psychology,* 27 (April 1949), 389–451.

6. L. Perry Curtis, Jr., *Apes and Angels: The Irishman in Victorian Caricature,* Smithsonian Press, Washington, D.C., 1971.

7. Eliot Aronson, *The Social Animal,* and ed., Freeman, San Francisco, 1984, p. 174.

8. David Katz and Kenneth Braly, "Racial Stereotypes of One Hundred College Students," *Journal of Abnormal and Social Psychology,* 28 (October–December 1933), 280–290; G. M. Gilbert, "Stereotype Persistence and Change Among College Students," *Journal of Abnormal and Social Psychology,* 46 (1951), 245–254; Marvin Karlins, Thomas L. Coffman, and Gary Walters, "On the Fading of Social Stereotypes: Studies in Three Generations of College Students," *Journal of Personality and Social Psychology,* 13 (1969), 1–16.

9. Howard J. Ehrlich, *The Social Psychology of Prejudice,* Wiley, New York, 1973, p. 22.

10. Erdman Palmore, "Ethnophaulisms and Ethnocentrism," *American Journal of Sociology,* 67 (January 1962), 442–445.

11. See Jeffrey H. Goldstein, "Theoretical Notes on Humor," *Journal of Communication,* 26 (1976), 102–112.

12. Jeffrey H. Goldstein, *Social Psychology,* Academic Press, New York, 1980, p. 368.

13. U.S. Commission on Civil Rights, *Window Dressing on the Set: Women and Minorities in Television,* U.S. Government Printing Office, Washington, D.C., 1977; *Window Dressing on the Set: An Update,* 1979.

14. George Gerbner, quoted in "Life According to TV," *Newsweek,* December 6, 1982, pp. 136 ff.

15. Ibid.

16. Gaye Tuchman, Arlene K. Daniels, and James Benet, eds., *Hearth and Home: Images of Women in the Mass Media,* Oxford University Press, New York, 1978, pp. 76–77.

17. Sheryl Graves, "How to Encourage Positive Racial Attitudes," paper presented at the biennial meeting of the Society for Research in Child Development, 1975, Denver, Colo.

18. For an overview of research on this program see Stuart H. Surlin, "Five Years of 'All in the Family': A Summary of Empirical Research Generated by the Program," *Mass Comm Review,* 3 (1976).

19. Neil Vidmar and Milton Rokeach, "Archie Bunker's Bigotry," *Journal of Communication,* 24 (1974), 36–47.

20. Herbert Blumer, "Race Prejudice as a Sense of Group Position," *Pacific Sociological Review,* 1 (1958), 3–7.

21. William M. Newman, *American Pluralism,* Harper & Row, New York, 1973, p. 197.

22. See Marvin B. Scott and Stanford M. Lyman, "Accounts," *American Sociological Review,* 33 (February 1968), 40–62.

23. Philip Mason, *Patterns of Dominance,* Oxford University Press, New York, 1970, p. 7. Also, Philip Mason, *Race Relations,* Oxford University Press, New York, 1970, pp. 17–29.

24. T. W. Adorno, Else Frankel-Brunswik, Daniel J. Levinson, and R. Nevitt Sanford, *The Authoritarian Personality,* Harper & Row, New York, 1950.

25. H. H. Hyman and P. B. Sheatsley, "The Authoritarian Personality: A Methodological Critique," in *Studies in the Scope and Method of "The Authoritarian Personality,"* ed. R. Christie and M. Jahoda, Free Press, Glencoe, Ill., 1954.

26. Solomon E. Asch, *Social Psychology,* Prentice-Hall, Englewood Cliffs, N.J., 1952, p. 545.

27. E. A. Shils, "Authoritarianism: Right and Left," in *Studies in the Scope and Method of "The Authoritarian Personality."*

28. D. Stewart and T. Hoult, "A Social-Psychological Theory of "The Authoritarian Personality,'" *American Journal of Sociology,* 65 (1959), 274.

29. H. C. Kelman and Janet Barclay, "The F Scale as a Measure of Breadth of Perspective," *Journal of Abnormal and Social Psychology,* 67 (1963), 608–615.

30. For an excellent summary of authoritarian studies and literature, see John P. Kirscht and Ronald C. Dillehay, *Dimensions of Authoritarianism: A Review of Research and Theory,* University of Kentucky Press, Lexington, 1967.

31. George E. Simpson and J. Milton Yinger, *Racial and Cultural Minorities: An Analysis of Prejudice and Discrimination,* Harper & Row, New York, 1953, p. 91.

32. Ibid., pp. 62–79.

33. John Dollard, Leonard W. Doob, Neal E. Miller, O. H. Mowrer, and Robert P. Sears, *Frustration and Aggression,* Yale University Press, New Haven, Conn., 1939; A. F. Henry and J. F. Short, Jr., *Suicide and Homicide,* Free Press, New York, 1954; Neal Miller and Richard Bugelski, "Minor Studies in Aggression: The Influence of Frustration Imposed by the Ingroup on Attitudes Expressed Toward Out-groups," *Journal of Psychology,* 25 (1948), 437–442; Stuart Palmer,

The Psychology of Murder, T. Y. Crowell, New York, 1960; Brenden C. Rule and Elizabeth Percival, "The Effects of Frustration and Attack on Physical Aggression," *Journal of Experimental Research on Personality,* 5 (1971), 111–188.

34. Leviticus 16:5–22.

35. Gordon W. Allport, "The ABC's of Scapegoating," 5th rev. ed., Anti-Defamation League pamphlet, New York.

36. Carl I. Hovland and Robert R. Sears, "Minor Studies of Aggression: Correlation of Lynchings with Economic Indices," *Journal of Psychology,* 9 (Winter 1940), 301–310.

37. Miller and Bugelski, "Minor Studies of Aggression," pp. 437–442.

38. Donald Weatherley, "Anti-Semitism and the Expression of Fantasy Aggression," *Journal of Abnormal and Social Psychology,* 62 (1961), 454–457.

39. Talcott Parsons, "Certain Primary Sources and Patterns of Aggression in the Social Structure of the Western World," *Essays in Sociological Theory,* Free Press, New York, 1964, pp. 298–322.

40. For an excellent review of Parsonian theory in this area, see Stanford M. Lyman, *The Black American in Sociological Thought: A Failure of Perspective,* Putnam, New York, 1972, pp. 145–169.

41. See Leonard Berkowitz, "Whatever Happened to the Frustration-Aggression Hypothesis?" *American Behavioral Scientist,* 21 (1978), 691–708; L. Berkowitz. *Aggression: A Social Psychological Analysis,* McGraw-Hill, New York, 1962.

42. Seymour Feshback and Robert Singer, "The Effects of Personal and Shared Threats Upon Social Prejudice," *Journal of Abnormal and Social Psychology,* 54 (1957), 411–416.

43. John Dollard, "Hostility and Fear in Social Life," *Social Forces,* 17 (1938), 15–26.

44. Muzafer Sherif, O. J. Harvey, B. Jack White, William Hood, and Carolyn Sherif, *Intergroup Conflict and Cooperation: The Robbers Cave Experiment,* University of Oklahoma Institute of Intergroup Relations, Norman, Okla., 1961. See also M. Sherif,

"Experiments in Group Conflict," *Scientific American,* 195 (1956), 54–58.

45. Donald Young, *Research Memorandum on Minority Peoples in the Depression,* Social Science Research Council, New York, 1937, pp. 133–141.

46. Andrew Greeley and Paul Sheatsley, "The Acceptance of Desegregation Continues to Advance," *Scientific American,* 210 (1971), 13–19.

47. See Harry H. L. Kitano, "Passive Discrimination in the Normal Person," *Journal of Social Psychology,* 70 (1966), 23–31.

48. Thomas Pettigrew, "Regional Differences in Anti-Negro Prejudice," *Journal of Abnormal and Social Psychology,* 59 (1959), 28–36.

49. Jeanne Watson, "Some Social and Psychological Situations Related to Change in Attitude," *Human Relations,* 3 (1950), 15–56.

50. John Dollard, *Caste and Class in a Southern Town,* 3rd ed., Doubleday Anchor Books, Garden City, N.Y., 1957.

51. See Gordon W. Allport, *The Nature of Prejudice,* Addison-Wesley, Reading, Mass., 1954, p. 261 ff.; Robin M. Williams, Jr., *Strangers Next Door,* Prentice-Hall, Englewood Cliffs, N.J., 1964, p. 150 ff.; James W. Vander Zanden, *American Minority Relations,* 3rd ed., Ronald Press, New York, 1972, pp. 460–469.

52. Brewton Berry and Henry L. Tischler, *Race and Ethnic Relations,* 4th ed., Houghton Mifflin, Boston, 1978, p. 250.

53. Eliot Aronson and Neal Osherow, "Cooperation, Prosocial Behavior, and Academic Performance: Experiments in the Desegregated Classroom," *Applied Social Psychology Annual,* 1 (1980), 163–196.

54. Gertrude J. Selznick and Stephen Steinberg, *The Tenacity of Prejudice,* Harper & Row, New York, 1969.

55. For evidence of both findings, see Robin M. Williams, Jr., *The Reduction of Intergroup Tensions,* Social Science Research Council, Washington, D.C., 1947, p. 27 ff.; Gordon W. Allport, *The Nature of Prejudice,* p. 483 ff.

56. Charles H. Stember, *Education and Attitude Change,* Institute of Human Relations Press, New York, 1961.

57. Blumer, "Race Prejudice as a Sense of Group Position," pp. 3–7.

58. Allport, *The Nature of Prejudice.*

59. Williams, *Strangers Next Door,* pp. 124–125.

60. Robert K. Merton, "Discrimination and the American Creed," in *Discrimination and National Welfare,* ed. Robert M. MacIver, Harper, New York, 1949, pp. 99–126.

61. Hubert M. Blalock, Jr., *Toward a Theory of Minority Group Relationships,* Capricorn Books, New York, 1970, pp. 204–207. For insight into the origin of this argument, see Stanford M. Lyman, "Cherished Values and Civil Rights," *The Crisis,* 71 (December 1964), 645–654, 695.

62. William M. Newman, *American Pluralism,* Harper & Row, New York, 1973, p. 231.

63. John Rawls, *A Theory of Justice,* The Belknap Press of Harvard University, Cambridge, Mass., 1971.

64. Joseph Tussman and Jacobus ten-Broek, "The Equal Protection of the Laws," *California Law Review,* 37 (September 1949), 341–381.

65. Ibid., p. 380.

66. Ibid., p. 381.

Chapter 4

1. See Robin M. Williams, Jr., "The Reduction of Intergroup Tensions," *Social Science Research Council Bulletin,* 57 (1947), 61; William J. Wilson, *Power, Racism, and Privilege,* Free Press, New York, 1973, pp. 47–68.

2. President's Commission on Law Enforcement and Administration of Justice, *Task Force Report: The Courts,* U.S. Government Printing Office, Washington, D.C., 1967; Lee Silverstein, *Defense of the Poor in Criminal Cases in American State Courts,* I, American Bar Association, New York, 1965; Caleb Foote, "The Bail System and Equal Justice," *Federal Probation,* 23 (September 1959), 45–47; Rita M. James,

"Status and Competence of Jurors," *American Journal of Sociology,* 64 (May 1959), 565–566.

3. Clifford R. Shaw and Henry D. McKay, *Juvenile Delinquency and Urban Areas,* University of Chicago Press, Chicago, 1942.

4. John P. Clark and Eugene P. Wenninger, "Socioeconomic Class and Area as Correlates of Illegal Behavior Among Juveniles," *American Sociological Review,* 27 (December 1962), 826–843; Karl Schnessler, "Components of Variation in City Crime Rates," *Social Problems,* 9 (1962), 314–323.

5. Albert K. Cohen, *Delinquent Boys,* Free Press, Glencoe, Ill., 1955.

6. For a study of Chinese gangs, see Stanford M. Lyman, "Red Guard on Grant Avenue: The Rise of Youthful Rebellion in Chinatown," *The Asian in North America,* A-B-C Clio Press, Santa Barbara, Calif., 1977, pp. 177–200. The classic study on Italian gangs is William F. Whyte, *Street Corner Society,* University of Chicago Press, Chicago, 1943.

7. Jackson Toby, "Hoodlum or Business Man: An American Dilemma," in *The Jews,* ed. Marshall Sklare, Free Press, Glencoe, Ill., 1958, pp. 544–549.

8. See Charles S. Johnson, *Patterns of Segregation,* Harper & Row, New York, 1943, pp. 244–266; *Minority Responses: Comparative Views of Reactions to Subordination,* ed. Minako Kurokawa, Random House, New York, 1970, pp. 187–227.

9. Brewton Berry and Henry Tischler, *Race and Ethnic Relations,* 4th ed., Houghton Mifflin, Boston, 1979, p. 389.

10. Kurt Lewin, *Resolving Social Conflicts,* Harper & Row, New York, 1948, pp. 186–200.

11. Gordon W. Allport, *The Nature of Prejudice,* 1954, Addison-Wesley, Reading, Mass., pp. 152–153.

12. Gunnar Myrdal, *An American Dilemma,* McGraw-Hill, New York, 1964, pp. 25–28; originally published by Harper, 1944.

13. Gordon W. Allport, "The Role of Expectancy," in *Tensions that Cause Wars,* ed. H. Cantril, *University of Illinois Press,* Urbana, 1950, chap. 2.

14. Allport, *The Nature of Prejudice,* p. 160.

15. Robert K. Merton, *Social Theory and Social Structure,* Free Press, Glencoe, Ill., 1957, pp. 290–291.

16. Robert E. Park, "Human Migration and the Marginal Man," *American Journal of Sociology,* 33 (May 1928), 891; see also Everett V. Stonequist, *The Marginal Man,* Scribner, New York, 1937.

17. George E. Simpson and J. Milton Yinger, *Racial and Cultural Minorities: An Analysis of Prejudice and Discrimination,* 4th ed., Harper & Row, New York, 1972, p. 186.

18. Milton M. Goldberg, "A Qualification of the Marginal Man Theory," *American Sociological Review,* 6 (February 1941), 52–58.

19. Hubert M. Blalock, Jr., *Toward a Theory of Minority Group Relations,* Wiley, New York, 1967 pp. 79–84.

20. Edna Bonacich, "A Theory of Middleman Minorities," *American Sociological Review,* 38 (1973), 583–594.

21. Edna Bonacich and John Modell, *The Economic Basis of Ethnic Solidarity,* University of California Press, Berkeley, Calif., 1980, p. 30.

22. See Gideon Sjoberg, "The Preindustrial City," *American Journal of Sociology,* 60 (March 1955), 438–445; Claude S. Fischer, *The Urban Experience,* 2nd ed., Harcourt Brace Jovanovich, New York, 1984, p. 13; Lyn H: Lofland, *A World of Strangers,* Basic Books, New York, 1973, p. 50.

23. See Noel P. Gist and Sylvia F. Fava, *Urban Society,* 6th ed., Thomas Y. Crowell, New York, 1974, p. 204.

24. See Allport, *The Nature of Prejudice,* pp. 53–54.

25. Deuteronomy 2:32–35; 3:1, 3–4, 6–7.

26. Arnold J. Toynbee, *A Study of History,* Oxford University Press, London, 1934, p. 465.

27. G. P. Murdock, *Our Primitive Contemporaries,* Macmillan, New York, 1934, pp. 16–18.

28. See I. D. MacCrone, *Race Attitudes in South Africa,* Oxford University Press, London, 1937, pp. 89–136.

29. Donald Pierson, *Negroes in Brazil,* University of Chicago Press, Chicago, 1942, p. 6.

30. See Gunnar Myrdal, *An American Dilemma,* Harper & Row, New York, 1944, pp. 566, 1350.

31. Stanley Lieberson, "A Societal Theory of Race and Ethnic Relations," *American Sociological Review,* 26 (December 1961), 902–910.

32. William J. Wilson, *Power, Racism, and Privilege,* Free Press, New York, 1973, pp. 47–65.

33. Robert Blauner, "Internal Colonialism and Ghetto Revolt," *Social Problems,* 16 (Spring 1969), 393–406.

34. Ibid., p. 397.

35. Edna Bonacich, "A Theory of Ethnic Antagonism: The Split Labor Market," *American Sociological Review* 37 (1972), 547–559.

36. Ibid., p. 554.

37. Ibid., p. 550.

38. See Alexander Saxton, *The Indispensable Enemy: Labor and the Anti-Chinese Movement in California,* University of California Press, Berkeley, Calif., 1971.

39. Mike Hilton, "The Split Labor Market and Chinese Immigration, 1848–1882." presented at the 72nd annual meeting of the American Sociological Association, 1977.

40. Ibid., pp. 4–5.

Chapter 5

1. Nathan Glazer and Daniel P. Moynihan. *Beyond the Melting Pot,* 2nd ed., M.I.T. Press, Cambridge, Mass., 1970, p. 1.

2. Maldwyn Allen Jones, *American Immigration,* University of Chicago Press, Chicago, 1960, p. 40.

3. Quoted in *American Observer,* 50 (November 29, 1971), 4.

4. Quotations and commentary taken from John C. Miller, *Crisis in Freedom,* Little, Brown, Boston, 1951, pp. 41–42.

5. W. S. Shaw to Abigail Adams, Cambridge, Mass., May 20, 1798, *Adams Papers,* Vol. 8, No. 48, Massachusetts Historical Society.

6. R. Ernst, "The Living Conditions of the Immigrant," in *The Urbanization of America,* ed. A. M. Wakestein, Houghton Mifflin, Boston, 1949, p. 266.

7. Carleton Beals, *Brass Knuckle Crusade,* Hastings House, New York 1960, p. 5.

8. Ibid.

9. Ray Allen Billington, *The Protestant Crusade, 1800–1860,* Macmillan, New York, 1938, p. 388.

10. John Higham, *Strangers in the Land,* Atheneum, New York, 1973, p. 7.

11. Harriet Martineau, *Society in America,* 1837, quoted in *American Observer,* 50 (November 29, 1971), 4.

12. *The Journals and Miscellaneous Notebooks of Ralph Waldo Emerson,* eds. Ralph H. Orth and Alfred K. Ferguson, The Belknap Press of Harvard University Press, Cambridge, Mass., 1971, IX, 299–300.

13. William Bradford, *Of Plymouth Plantation,* ed. Harvey Wish, Capricorn Books, New York, 1962, p. 29.

14. Ibid., p. 33.

15. Ibid., pp. 16–17, 184.

16. Rowland Berthoff, *British Immigrants in Industrial America, 1790–1950,* Harvard University Press, Cambridge, Mass., 1953, pp. 30–56.

17. Ibid., pp. 125–131.

18. Ilja M. Dijour. "A Seminar on the Integration of Immigrants," 1960, p. 6, quoted in Wilbur S. Shepperson, *Emigration and Disenchantment: Portraits of Englishmen Repatriated from the United States,* University of Oklahoma Press, Norman, 1965, p. 182.

19. Wilbur S. Shepperson, *Emigration and Disenchantment: Portraits of Englishmen Repatriated from the United States,* University of Oklahoma Press, Norman, 1965, pp. 16–17, 184.

20. A Report of the Commissioner of Immigration upon the Causes Which Incite Immigration to the U.S.,

52nd Congress, 1st session (1891–1892), *House Executive Document 235*, Part I, pp. 260, 282.

21. Berthoff, *British Immigrants in Industrial America, 1790–1950*, pp. 103–104.

22. U.S. Immigration and Naturalization Service, *Annual Report: 1980*, Washington, D.C., 1981, Table 13, p. 88.

23. Ibid.

24. Hans Koningsberger, *Holland and the United States*, Netherlands Information Service, New York, 1968, p. 20.

25. Arthur Henry Hirsch, *The Huguenots of Colonial South Carolina*, Shoe String Press, Hamden, Conn., 1962, p. 95.

26. Miller, *Crisis in Freedom*, pp. 13, 42–43.

27. T. Lynn Smith and Vernon J. Parenton, "Acculturation Among the Louisiana French," *American Journal of Sociology*, 44 (November 1938), 357.

28. Ibid., p. 364.

29. Vernon J. Parenton, "Socio-Psychological Integration in a Rural French-Speaking Section of Louisiana," *The Southwestern Social Science Quarterly*, 30 (December 1949), 195.

30. Marcus L. Hansen and J. B. Prebner, *The Mingling of the Canadian and American Peoples*, Yale University Press, New Haven, Conn., 1940, pp. 123–168.

31. Albert B. Faust, *The German Element in the United States*, Arno Press, New York, 1969, I, 66–72.

32. Quoted in W. C. Smith, *Americans in the Making*, Appleton-Century, New York, 1939, p. 394.

33. Maurice R. Davie, *World Immigration*, Macmillan, New York, 1936, p. 36.

34. Brewton Berry and Henry I. Tischler, *Race and Ethnic Relations*, 4th ed., Houghton Mifflin, Boston, 1978. p. 186.

35. Beals, *Brass Knuckle Crusade*, p. 168.

36. Quoted in James M. Smith, *Freedom's Fetters*, Cornell University Press, Ithaca, N.Y., 1956, p. 25.

37. Charles F. Marden and Gladys Meyer, *Minorities in American Society*, 5th ed., Van Nostrand Reinhold, New York, 1978, p. 77.

38. Edward Everett, "Letters on Irish Emigration," in *Historical Aspects of the Immigration Problem, Select Documents*, ed. Edith Abbott, University of Chicago Press, Chicago, 1926, pp. 462–463.

39. Peter I. Rose, *They and We*, 2nd ed., Random House, New York, 1974, p. 39.

40. For information about middleman minorities, see Hubert M. Blalock, Jr., *Toward a Theory of Minority Group Relations*, Wiley, New York, 1967, pp. 79–84; Edna Bonacich, "A Theory of Middleman Minorities," *American Sociological Review*, 38 (October 1973), 583–594.

41. Oscar Handlin, *Boston's Immigrants*, rev. ed., Harvard University Press, Cambridge, Mass., 1959, p. 176.

42. Arnold Shrier, *Ireland and the American Emigration, 1850–1900* University of Minnesota Press, Minneapolis, 1958, p. 34.

43. Carl Wittke, *The Irish in America*, Russell and Russell, New York, 1970, pp. 191–192.

44. Robert Kelley, *The Cultural Pattern in American Politics: The First Century*, Knopf, New York, 1979, pp. 195, 237.

45. Joel T. Headley, *The Great Riots of New York, 1712–1873*, Bobbs-Merrill, Indianapolis, 1970; James McCague, *The Second Rebellion*, Dial Press, New York, 1968.

46. Joseph P. O'Grady, *How the Irish Became Americans*, Twayne, New York, 1973; Edgar Litt, *Beyond Pluralism: Ethnic Politics in America*, Scott, Foresman, Glencoe, Ill., 1970, chap. 8.

47. Richard Krickus, *Pursuing the American Dream: White Ethnics and the New Populism*, Indiana University Press, Bloomington, 1976, chap. 4; D. W. Brogan, *Politics in America*, Harper, New York, 1954).

48. Rose, *They and We*, p. 68.

49. Ole E. Rolvaag, *Giants in the Earth*, Copyright, 1927, by Harper & Brothers, p. 425.

50. Paul C. Nyholm, *The Americanization of the Danish Lutheran Churches in America,* Augsburg Publishing House, Minneapolis, Minn., 1963, pp. 249–291.

51. Merle Curti, *The Making of an American Community: A Case Study of Democracy in a Frontier County,* Stanford University Press, Stanford, Calif., 1959, pp. 84, 96, 101, 104, 112.

52. Kendric C. Babcock, *The Scandinavian Element in the United States,* 1914, reprint ed., Arno Press and The New York Times, New York, 1969, pp. 15–16.

53. James G. Leyburn,' *The Scotch-Irish: A Social History,* University of North Carolina Press, Chapel Hill, 1962, chap. 16.

54. Ibid.

55. J. Hector St. John de Crèvecoeur, *Letters From an American Farmer,* Albert and Charles Boni, New York, 1925, pp. 54–55. Reprinted from the original edition, London, 1782.

Chapter 6

1. "From Farm to Factory: Immigrant Adjustment to American Industry," *Spectrum,* 1 (May 1975), 1.

2. Milton M. Gordon, *Assimilation in American Life,* Oxford University Press, New York, 1964, p. 136.

3. Madison Grant, *The Passing of the Great Race,* 1916; reprint edition, Arno Press and the New York Times, 1970, p. 91.

4. Gordon, *Assimilation in American Life,* p. 97.

5. Ronald M. Pavalko, "Racism and the New Immigration: Toward a Reinterpretation of the Experiences of White Ethnics in American Society," paper presented at the 72nd annual meeting of the American Sociological Association, 1977.

6. Isaac A. Hourwich, *Immigrants and Labor,* B. W. Huebach, Inc., New York, 1922; quoted in Pavalko, "Racism and the New Immigration," p. 8.

7. Pavalko, p. 2.

8. Ibid., p. 24.

9. See the discussion on pp. 90–91; see also Gordon, *Assimilation in American Life,* pp. 137–138.

10. Ellwood P. Cubberly, *Changing Conceptions of Education,* Houghton Mifflin, Boston, 1909, pp. 15–16.

11. John Higham, *Strangers in the Land: Patterns of American Nativism,* 1860–1925, Rutgers University Press, New Brunswick, N.J., 1955, pp. 137–138.

12. *Public Opinion,* I (1886), 82–86.

13. *The Age of Steel,* quoted in *Public Opinion,* I (1886), 355.

14. Henry Pratt Fairchild, *The Melting Pot Mistake,* Little, Brown, Boston, 1926, quoted in *American Observer,* 50 (November 29, 1971),5.

15. Victor R. Greene, *The Slavic Community on Strike,* University of Notre Dame Press, South Bend, Ind., 1968, pp. 40–41.

16. Ibid., pp. 49–50.

17. See Charles B. Nam, "Nationality Groups and Social Stratification in America," *Social Forces,* 37, (1959), 328–333.

18. Henryk Sienkiewicz, *Portrait of America, Letters of Henryk Sienkiewicz,* ed. & trans. Charles Morley, Columbia University Press, New York, 1959, pp. 272–273.

19. Ibid., p. 279.

20. William I. Thomas and Florian Znaniecki, *The Polish Peasant in Europe and America,* 5 vols., B. G. Badger, Boston, 1918–1920.

21. "Immigrants and Religion: The Persistence of Ethnic Diversity," *Spectrum* 1 (September 1975), 2.

22. Helena Znaniecki Lopata, *Polish Americans: Status Competition in an Ethnic Community,* Prentice-Hall, Englewood Cliffs, N.J., 1976, p. 92.

23. Ibid.

24. Ibid., p. 145.

25. Beverly Duncan and Otis Dudley Duncan, "Minorities and the Process of Stratification," *American Sociological Review,* 33 (June 1968), 356–364; Stanley Lieberson, *Ethnic Patterns in American Cities,* Free Press, New York, 1963, p. 189.

26. Lopata, *Polish Americans,* p. 95.

27. Neil C. Sandberg, *Ethnic Identity and Assimilation: The Polish-American Community,* Praeger, New York, 1974.

28. See the discussion on pp. 40–41.

29. Lopata, *Polish Americans,* p. 148.

30. Emil Lengyel, *Americans from Hungary,* Lippincott, New York, 1948, p. 128.

32. New York *Tribune,* September 11–12, 1897, pp. 1, 3.

32. See Peter I. Rose, *They and We,* 2nd ed., Random House, New York, 1974, p. 135.

33. Ian Hancock, "Gypsies," in Stephen Thernstrom ed., *Harvard Encyclopedia of American Ethnic Groups,* Harvard University Press, Cambridge, Mass.: 1980, p. 441.

34. Werner Cohn, "Some Comparisons Between Gypsy (North American Rom) and American English Kinship Terms," *American Anthropologist,* 71 (June 1969), 477–478.

35. Glen W. Davidson, " 'Gypsies': People with a Hidden History." in *The Rediscovery of Ethnicity, ed.* Sallie TeSelle, Harper and Row, New York, 1973, p. 84.

36. Allan Pinkerton, *The Gypsies and the Detectives,* G. W. Carleton & Company, New York, 1879, pp. 68–69.

37. Rena C. Gropper, *Gypsies in the City,* Darwin, Princeton, N.J., 1975, pp. 60–66.

38. Gulbun Coker, "Romany Rye in Philadelphia: A Sequel," *Southwestern Journal of Anthropology,* 22 (1966), 85–100.

39. Jean-Paul Clebert, *The Gypsies,* Vista, London,: 1963, p. 96.

40. Jan Yoors, *The Gypsies,* Simon & Schuster, New York, 1967, p. 7.

41. Anne Sutherland, *Gypsies: The Hidden Americans,* Free Press, New York, 1975.

42. Gropper, *Gypsies in the City,* p. 162.

43. Carol Miller, "American Rom and the Ideology of Defilement," in Farnham Rehfisch, ed., *Gypsies,*

Tinkers, and Other Travelers, Academic Press, New York, 1975, p. 41.

44. Ronald Lee, *Goddam Gypsy: An Autobiographical Novel,* Tundra, Montreal, 1971, pp. 29–30.

45. Sutherland, *Gypsies: The Hidden Americans,* p. 264.

46. Gropper, *Gypsies in the City,* pp. 92–93.

47. Miller, "American Rom and the Ideology of Defilement," pp. 45–46.

48. Peter Maas, *King of the Gypsies,* Viking, New York, 1975, pp. 29–31.

49. Ibid., p. 29.

50. Sutherland, *Gypsies: The Hidden Americans,* p. 98.

51. Hancock, "Gypsies," p. 441.

52. Wasyl Halich, *Ukrainians in the United States,* University of Chicago Press, Chicago, 1937; reprint edition by Arno Press and *The New York Times,* 1970, pp. 28–29.

53. Jerome Davis, *The Russians and Ruthenians in America,* Doran, New York, 1922; reprint edition by Arno Press and *The New York Times,* 1970, p. 104.

54. Based on data from Mark Wischnitzer, *Visas to Freedom,* prepared by Hebrew Immigration Assistance Society, World Publishing Company, Cleveland, 1956; U.S. Immigration and Naturalization Service, *Annual Report: 1980,* Washington, D.C., Table 13, p. 63.

55. Jerome Davis, *The Russian Immigrant,* Macmillan, New York, 1922; reprint edition by Arno Press and *The New York Times,* 1970, p. 98.

56. Edward T. Devine, "Family and Social Work," in Jerome Davis, *The Russians and Ruthenians in America,* p. 32.

57. Davis, *The Russian Immigrant,* pp. 173–174.

58. John Higham, *Strangers in the Land: Patterns of American Nativism, 1860–1925,* Rutgers University Press, New Brunswick, N.J., 1955, pp. 230–231; See also Frederick R. Barkley, "Jailing Radicals in Detroit," *Nation,* 110 (1920), 136.

59. *The Letters of Sacco and Vanzetti,* ed. Marion D. Frankfurter and Gardner Jackson, Viking, New York, 1928, p. 377.

60. Higham reports, for example, that under the heading "Italians" in the 1902 *New York Tribune Index,* 55 of the 74 entries were clear accounts of crime and violence (*Strangers in the Land,* p. 363).

61. For an excellent insight into the Italian community of Chicago's West Side, see Gerald D. Suttles, *The Social Order of the Slum,* University of Chicago Press, Chicago, 1968.

62. See Rudolph Vecoli, *The Peoples of New Jersey,* Van Nostrand, Princeton, N.J., 1965, pp. 221–236.

63. Herbert J. Gans, *The Urban Villagers,* Free Press, New York, 1962, pp. 204–205.

64. William Foote Whyte, *Street Corner Society,* University of Chicago Press, Chicago, 1943, p. 274.

65. Andrew M. Greeley, *Ethnicity, Denomination, and Inequality,* Sage Research Papers in the Social Sciences, Vol. 4, Series no. 90–029 (Studies in Religion and Ethnicity), Sage Publications, Beverly Hills, Calif., 1976.

66. Nathan Glazer and Daniel P. Moynihan, *Beyond the Melting Pot,* 2nd ed., M.I.T. Press, Cambridge, Mass., 1970, p. 187.

67. Ibid., pp. 203–204.

68. Dinnerstein and Reimers, *Ethnic Americans,* p. 43.

69. In 1972 a Boston city survey, the Omnibus Survey, revealed that its sizable Greek immigrant population had a zero unemployment rate, no one on welfare, and a median income $4,000 above the Boston average.

70. Theodore Saloutos, *The Greeks in the United States,* Harvard University Press, Cambridge, Mass., 1964, pp. 78–79.

71. Henry Pratt Fairchild, *Greek Immigration,* Yale University Press, New Haven, Conn., 1911, pp. 239, 241–242.

72. Gerald A. Estep, "Portuguese Assimilation in Hawaii and California," *Sociology and Social Research,* 26 (September 1941), 64.

73. Donald R. Taft, *Two Portuguese Communities in New England,* reprint edition, Arno Press, New York, 1969, p. 79.

74. Ibid., p. 348.

75. See Louis Adamic, *A Nation of Nations,* Harper, New York, 1945, pp. 287–288.

76. Marjorie Housepian, *The Unremembered Genocide,* "A Commentary Report," American Jewish Committee, New York, 1965, p. 31.

77. Frank A. Stone, *Armenian Studies for Secondary Students,* Parousia Press, Storrs, Conn., 1975, p. 8.

78. Emory S. Bogardus, "Comparing Racial Distance in Ethiopia, South Africa, and the United States," *Sociology and Social Research,* 52 (1968), 149–156.

79. Gary A. Kulhanjian, *The Historical and Sociological Aspects of Armenian Immigration to the United States,* 1890 to 1930, R. and E. Research Associates, San Francisco, 1975, p. 25.

80. Ibid., p. 29

81. In Chapter 14 we shall examine white ethnic upward mobility.

Chapter 7

1. See Lee E. Huddleston, *Origins of the American Indians: European Concepts, 1492–1729,* University of Texas Press, Austin, 1967.

2. Bureau of Indian Affairs, "You Asked About . . . Facts About American Indians and Alaskan Natives," Washington, D.C., 1976.

3. John Boyd Thacher (ed.), *Christopher Columbus,* Vol. 1, AMS Press, Inc., New York, 1967, I, 533.

4. Michel de Montaigne, "Of Cannibals," Book I, Ch. 31, in *The Complete Works of Montaigne,* translated by Donald M. Frame, Stanford University Press, Stanford, Calif., 1957, pp. 150–159.

5. See Lewis Hanke, *The First Social Experiments in America: A Study in the Development of Spanish In-*

dian Policy in the Sixteenth Century, Peter Smith, Gloucester, Mass., 1964.

6. Douglas Edward Leach, *Flintlock and Tomahawk, New England in King Philip's War,* Norton, New York, 1958, pp. 20–22.

7. George Catlin, *Letters and Notes of the Manners, Customs and Conditions of the North American Indians* (London, 1841), Dover, New York, 1973, I, 102–103.

8. Peter Farb, *Man's Rise to Civilization as Shown by the Indians of North America from Primeval Times to the Coming of the Industrial State,* E. P. Dutton, New York, 1968, p. 128.

9. Wilcomb E. Washburn, *The Indian in America,* Harper & Row, New York, 1975, p. 32.

10. Ibid., pp. 39–40.

11. See D'Arcy McNickle, *They Came Here First: The Epic of the American Indian,* J. B. Lippincott, Philadelphia, 1949, p. 128.

12. Anthony F. C. Wallace, *The Death and Rebirth of the Seneca,* Knopf, New York, 1970, p. 28; John Axtell, "The Scholastic Philosophy of the Wilderness," *William and Mary Quarterly,* 29 (1972), 359.

13. Albert Britt, *Indian Chiefs,* Books for Libraries Press, Freeport, N.Y., 1969, p. 8.

14. *Ibid.,* p. 26.

15. See Keith H. Basso, " 'To Give Up on Words': Silence in Western Apache Culture." *Southwestern Journal of Anthropology,* 26 (1970), 213–230.

16. Alice Marriott and Carol K. Rachlin, *American Epic: The Story of the American Indian,* Mentor, New York, 1969, p. 114.

17. Dale Van Every, *Disinherited: The Lost Birthright of the American Indian,* Discus Avon Books, New York, 1966, p. 163.

18. James Mooney, *Myths of the Cherokee,* 19th Annual Report, Bureau of American Ethnology, Washington, D.C., 1900, p. 130.

19. James D. Richardson, *Messages and Papers of the President,* Washington, D.C., 1897, III, 497.

20. From *Man's Rise to Civilization as Shown by the Indians of North America from Primeval Times to the Coming of the Industrial State* by Peter Farb, p. 310. Copyright © 1968 by Peter Farb Reprinted by permission of the publishers of E. P. Dutton.

21. Ibid., p. 309.

22. Ibid.

23. See Theodore Stern, *The Klamath Tribe,* University of Washington Press, Seattle, 1966.

24. Alvin M. Josephy, Jr., *The Indian Heritage of America,* Knopf, New York, 1968, p. 354.

25. Sar A. Levitan, William B. Johnston, and Robert Taggart, *Minorities in the United States: Problems, Progress and Prospects,* Public Affairs Press, Washington, D.C., 1975, p. 86.

26. Ibid., p. 91.

27. Richard J. Margolis, "A Long List of Grievances," *The New York Times,* November 12, 1972; *The New York Times,* February 19, 1967, p. 33; Josephy, *The Indian Heritage of America,* p. 359; Bureau of Indian Affairs, "You Asked About . . ."

28. For an excellent depiction of the harshness of reservation life, see Murray Wax, *Indian-Americans: Unity and Diversity,* Prentice-Hall, Englewood Cliffs, N.J., 1971, pp. 65–87.

29. *The New York Times,* November 12, 1972.

30. Jack Bynum, "Suicide and the American Indian: An Analysis of Recent Trends," in *Native Americans Today: Sociological Perspectives,* eds. Howard M. Bahr, Bruce A. Chadwick, and Robert C. Day, Harper & Row, New York, 1972, p. 375.

31. Theodore D. Graves, "Acculturation, Access, and Alcohol in a Tri-Ethnic Community," *American Anthropologist,* 69 (April 1967), 306–321.

32. Frances Northend Ferguson, "Navaho Drinking: Some Tentative Hypotheses," *Human Organization,* 27 (Summer 1968), 159–167.

33. Graves, "Acculturation, Access, and Alcohol in a Tri-Ethnic Community."

34. See Alvin M. Josephy, Jr., *Red Power,* McGraw-

Hill, New York, 1971, p. 3; *The Indian Heritage of America,* p. 359.

35. 1969 Report of U.S. Senate Committee on Labor and Public Welfare, Special Subcommittee on Indian Education, quoted in Josephy, *Red Power,* pp. 156–157.

36. American Indian Policy Review Commission, "Report on Indian Education," Washington, D.C., 1976, p. 253.

37. Ibid., p. 245.

38. Ibid., p. 123.

39. American Indian Policy Review Commission, "Report on Urban and Rural Non-Reservation Indians," Washington, D.C., 1976, p. 25.

40. Ford Foundation study reported in *Chronicle of Higher Education,* February 1, 1982, p. 11.

41. Levitan, et. al., *Minorities in the United States,* p. 84.

42. Josephy, *The Indian Heritage of America,* p. 359.

43. Steve Huntley, et. al., "America's Indians: 'Beggars in Our Own Land'," *U.S. News & World Report,* May 23, 1983, p. 71.

44. Ibid., p. 72.

45. Ibid., pp. 70–71.

46. Aric Press, et. al., "The Indian Water Wars," *Newsweek,* June 13, 1983, pp. 80–81.

47. Ibid., p. 82.

48. Ibid., p. 80.

49. Josephy, *Red Power,* p. 4.

50. Quoted in Morris Freedman and Carolyn Banks (eds.), *American Mix,* Lippincott, Philadelphia, 1972, pp. 46–47.

51. See Dee Brown, *Bury My Heart at Wounded Knee,* Holt, New York, 1970.

52. "Wounded Knee: The Media Coup d'Etat," *Nation,* 216 (June 25, 1973). 807.

53. "Sioux Chiefs Urged to Reject U.S. Offer," *The New York Times,* September 2, 1979, p. 22.

54. "Tribe Files Suit for $11 Billion Over Black Hills," *The New York Times,* July 19, 1980, p. 5.

55. "Appeals Court Rejects Suit by Indians Over Black Hills," *The New York Times,* June 3, 1981, p. 18.

56. Alvin M. Josephy, Jr., "The American Indian and the Bureau of Indian Affairs," Special Report to the President, Feb. 11, 1969, Sec. V.

57. Robert K. Merton, *Social Theory and Social Structure,* Free Press, Glencoe, Ill., 1957, p. 197 ff.

58. Vine Deloria, Jr., *Custer Died for Your Sins,* Avon, New York, 1970, p. 145.

59. American Indian Policy Review Commission, "Report on Trust Responsibilities and Federal-Indian Relations, Including Treaty Review," Washington, D.C., 1976, pp. 3–6.

60. See Howard M. Bahr, "An End to Visibility," in *Native Americans Today,* pp. 404–407. One significant exception is Edmund Wilson, *Apologies to the Iroquois,* Farrar, Straus and Cudahy, New York, 1960. This book includes Joseph Mitchell's study, "The Mohawks in High Steel."

61. American Indian Policy Review Commission, "Report on Urban and Rural Non-Reservation Indians," p. 35.

62. John A. Price, "The Migration and Adaptation of American Indians to Los Angeles," *Human Organization,* 27 (Summer 1968). 168–175.

63. Theodore D. Graves, "The Personal Adjustment of Navaho Indian Migrants to Denver, Colorado," *American Anthropologist,* 72 (1970), 35–54.

64. Bruce A. Chadwick and Joseph H. Strauss, "The Assimilation of American Indians into Urban Society: The Seattle Case," *Human Organization,* 34 (Winter 1975), 359–369. See also Joan Ablon, "Relocated American Indians in the San Francisco Bay Area: Social Interaction and Indian Identity," *Human Organization,* 23 (Winter 1964), 296–304.

65. John A. Price, "North American Indian Families," in *Ethnic Families in America,* eds. Charles H. Mindel and Robert W. Haberstein, Elsevier, New York, 1976, p. 266.

66. Josephy, *The Indian Heritage of America,* p. 32.

67. Ibid.

68. Ibid., p. 34.

Chapter 8

1. Edwin P. Hoyt, *Asians in the West,* Nelson, New York, 1974, p. 123.

2. "China," *Encyclopedia Britannica,* 7th ed., 1842, Vol. 6.

3. Otis Gibson, *The Chinese in America,* Hitchcock and Walden, Cincinnati, 1877, pp. 51–52.

4. Ibid.

5. Alexander Saxton, *The Indispensable Enemy: Labor and the Anti-Chinese Movement in California,* University of California Press, Berkeley, 1971, p. 63.

6. Ibid.

7. Mike Hilton, "The Split Labor Market and Chinese Immigration, 1848–1882," presented to the 72nd annual meeting of the American Sociological Association, 1977, p. 7.

8. Ibid., p. 5.

9. Hinton Helper, *The Land of Gold: Reality Versus Fiction,* Baltimore, 1855, pp. 94–96, quoted in Saxton, *The Indispensable Enemy,* p. 19.

10. "The Growth of the U.S. Through Emigration—The Chinese," The *New York Times,* Sept. 3, 1865.

11. *The New York Times,* June 7, 1868.

12. Senator James G. Blaine, *Congressional Record* (February 14, 1879), p. 1301.

13. U.S. Immigration and Naturalization Service, *Annual Report,* U.S. Government Printing Office, Washington, D.C., 1926, pp. 170–181.

14. *Ibid.*

15. American Federation of Labor, Proceedings, 1893, p. 73.

16. D. Y. Yuan, "New York Chinatown," in *Minority Problems,* eds. Arnold M. Rose and Caroline B. Rose, Harper & Row, New York, 1965, pp. 277–284.

17. Albert W. Palmer, *Orientals in American Life,* Friendship Press, New York, 1934, pp. 1–2, 7.

18. Stanford M. Lyman, "Conflict and the Web of Group Affiliation in San Francisco's Chinatown, 1850–1910," *Pacific Historical Review,* 43 (November 1974), 473–499. This work is based upon Georg Simmel's two theoretical essays, "Conflict" and "The Web of Group Affiliation."

19. Ibid, 494–499.

20. S. W. Kung, *Chinese in American Life,* University of Washington Press, Seattle, 1962, p. 89.

21. Stanford M. Lyman, "Marriage and the Family Among Chinese Immigrants to America," *Phylon,* 29 (Winter 1968), 324.

22. Ibid., pp. 322–323.

23. Ibid., p. 327.

24. Ibid., p. 330.

25. Ibid., p. 328.

26. *Congressional Record,* Oct. 21, 1943, p. 8626.

27. "Our Big Cities Go Ethnic," *U.S. News & World Report,* March 21, 1983, p. 50.

28. U.S. Bureau of the Census, *1980 Census of the Population: National Origin and Language,* Vol. 2 U.S. Government Printing Office, Washington, D.C., 1984, Table 99.

29. U.S. Public Health Service, Centers for Disease Control.

30. U.S. Bureau of the Census.

31. Lucy Jen Huang, "The Chinese American Family," in *Ethnic Families in America,* eds. Charles H. Mindel and Robert W. Habenstein, Elsevier, New York, 1976, p. 144.

32. Stanford M. Lyman, "Generation & Character: The Case of the Japanese-Americans," in *East Across the Pacific: Historical and Sociological Studies of Japanese Immigration and Assimilation,* eds. Hilary Conroy and T. Scott Miyakawa. Reprinted by permission of American Bibliographical Center—Clio Press, Inc., Santa Barbara, Calif., © 1972, p. 279. Also in Lyman, S., *The Asian in North America,* Clio Press, Santa Barbara, Calif., 1977, pp. 151–176.

33. Morton Grodzins, *Americans Betrayed,* University of Chicago Press, Chicago, 1949.

34. Lyman, "Generation & Character: The Case of the Japanese-Americans," pp. 279–280. Reprinted by permission of ABC-Clio, Inc., Santa Barbara, Calif., © 1972.

35. Eugene V. Rostow, "Our Worst Wartime Mistake," *Harper's Magazine,* 191 (September 1945), 193–201.

36. See Michi Weglyn, *Years of Infamy: The Untold Story of America's Concentration Camps,* Morrow, New York, 1976.

37. Esther B. Rhoads, "My Experience with the Wartime Relocation of Japanese," in *East Across the Pacific: Historical and Sociological Studies of Japanese Immigration and Assimilation,* eds. Hilary Conroy and T. Scott Miyakawa, pp. 131–132. Reprinted by permission of ABC-Clio, Inc., Santa Barbara, Calif., © 1972.

38. Ted Nakashima, "Concentration Camp, U.S. Style," *The New Republic,* June 15, 1942, 822–823.

39. Justice Robert H. Jackson, dissenting opinion, *Korematsu v. United States of America,* Vol. 65, Supreme Court Reporter, 1944, pp. 206–208.

40. Harry H. L. Kitano, *Japanese Americans: The Evolution of a Subculture,* 2nd ed., Prentice-Hall, Englewood Cliffs, N.J., 1976, p. 132.

41. See Kitano, Japanese Americans, pp. 23–24, 107–108.

42. Ibid., p. 127. See also John Connor, *Tradition and Change in Three Generations of Japanese Americans,* Nelson-Hall, Chicago, 1977.

43. Harry H. L. Kitano, "Japanese-American Crime and Delinquency," *Journal of Social Psychology,* 66 (1967), 253–263.

44. Akemi Kikumura and Harry H. L. Kitano, "Interracial Marriage: A Picture of the Japanese Americans," *Journal of Social Issues,* 29 (1973), 1–9.

45. Vincent N. Parrillo, private interviews with community residents, 1976.

46. Lemuel F. Ignacio, *Asian Americans and Pacific Islanders,* Pilipino Development Associates, San Jose, Calif., 1976, pp. 3–4.

47. *Morrison et al. v. California* (1934), No. 487, Vol. 291, United States Supreme Court Reports, U.S. Government Printing Office, Washington, D.C., 1934, pp. 85–86.

48. Davis McEntire, *The Labor Force in California: A Study of Characteristics and Trends in Labor Force, Employment and Occupations in California,* 1900–1950, University of California Press, Berkeley, 1952, p. 62.

49. Carey McWilliams, *Brothers Under the Skin,* Little, Brown, Boston, 1951, p. 239.

50. Sylvain Lazarus, San Francisco Municipal Court, January 1936, quoted in Manuel Braken, *I Have Lived with the American People,* Caxton, Caldwell, Calif., 1948, pp. 136–138.

51. Letter from Sylvester Saturday, in *Time,* 27 (May 11, 1936), 4.

52. Letter from Ernest D. Ilustre, in *Time,* 27 (April 27, 1936), 3.

53. McWilliams, *Brothers Under the Skin,* p. 244.

54. Bernicio T. Catapusan, "Filipino Intermarriage Problems in the United States," *Sociology and Social Research,* 22 (1938), 265–272.

55. For an excellent sociological study of Pilipinos in dance halls, see Paul G. Cressey, *The Taxi-Dance Hall,* University of Chicago Press, Chicago, 1932, pp. 145–176.

56. Ignacio, *Asian Americans and Pacific Islanders,* p.7.

57. R. T. Feria, "War and the Status of the Filipino Immigrants," *Sociology and Social Research,* 31 (1946), 50.

58. Department of Health and Human Services, *A Study of Selected Socioeconomic Characteristics of Ethnic Minorities Based on the 1980 Census. Volume II: Asian Americans,* Washington, D.C., 1984, pp. 105, 134, 145.

59. Harold H. Sunoo and Sonia S. Sunoo, "The Heritage of the First Korean Women Immigrants in the United States: 1903–1924." *Korean Christian Journal,* 2 (Spring 1977), 144.

60. Ibid., p. 146.

61. Ibid., pp. 144, 165.

62. Bernice H. Kim, "The Koreans in Hawaii," *Social Science,* 9 (1934), 409.

63. Lee Houchins and Chang-su Houchins, "The Korean Experience in America, 1903–1924," *Pacific Historical Review,* 43 (November 1974), 560.

64. Hei Chu Kim, Won Moo Hurh, and Kwang Chung Kim, "Ethnic Roles of the Korean Church in the Chicago Area," paper presented at the annual meeting of the Korean Christian Scholars Association, 1979.

65. Kwang C. Kim, "Intra- and Inter-Ethnic Group Conflicts: The Case of Korean Small Business in the United States," presented to the 11th annual meeting of the Korean Christian Scholars, 1977, p. 3.

66. Edna Bonacich, Ivan Light, and Charles Choy Wong, "Small Business Among Koreans in Los Angeles," presented to the 71st annual meeting of the American Sociological Association, 1976, p. 10.

67. Kim, "Intra- and Inter-Ethnic Group Conflicts: The Case of Korean Small Business in the United States," p. 23.

66. See Edna Bonacich, "A Theory of Middleman Minorities." *American Sociological* Review, 38 (1973), 583–594.

69. *A Study of Selected Socioeconomic Characteristics of Ethnic Minorities Based on the 1980 Census. Vol. 2: Asian Americans,* pp. 105, 134, 142.

70. Emory S. Bogardus, "Comparing Racial Distance in Ethiopia, South Africa, and the United States," *Sociology and Social Research* 52 (1968). 149–156.

71. Won Moo Hurh, "Comparative Study of Korean Immigrants in the United States: A Typology." p. 68.

72. "Future of Refugees: The Furor and the Facts," *U.S. News and World Report,* May 19, 1975, 16.

73. Paul D. Starr and Alden E. Roberts, "Community Structure and Vietnamese Refugee Adaptation: The Significance of Context," *International Migration Review,* 16 (1982), 595–608.

74. The author acknowledges a substantial debt and gratitude to Walter H. Slote, Ph.D.; and Stephen Young, J. D., for sharing their expertise about the Vietnamese and Vietnamericans.

75. Walter H. Slote, "Adaption of Recent Vietnamese Immigres to the American Experience: A Psycho-Cultural Approach," paper presented at the 29th annual meeting of the Association for Asian Studies, March 1977, p. 9.

76. Ibid., p. 11.

77. Han T. Doan, "Vietnamericans: Bending Low or Breaking in the Acculturation Process?" presented to the 72nd annual meeting of the American Sociological Association, 1977, pp. 14–15.

78. Ibid., p. 12.

79. Ibid.

80. See Walter H. Slote, "Psychodynamic Structures in Vietnamese Personality," *Transcultural Research in Mental Health,* 2 (1972).

81. Doan, "Vietnamericans: Bending Low or Breaking in the Acculturation Process?", pp. 9–11, 15.

82. Starr and Roberts "Community Structure and Vietnamese Refugee Adaptation," pp. 595–608.

83. Bayard Webster, "Studies Report Refugees Plagued by Persistent Stress," *The New York Times,* September 11, 1979, p. C1.

84. La'auli Ale Filoiali'i and Lyle Knowles, "Attitudes of Southern California Samoans Toward Maintaining the Samoan Way of Life," *Sociology and Social Research,* 67 (1983), 301–311.

85. Ibid., p. 302.

86. Ibid.

87. Ibid., p. 305.

88. Ibid., pp. 305–306.

89. Ibid., p. 306.

90. Ibid., p. 309.

Chapter 9

1. U.S. Immigration and Naturalization Service Annual Report, *Statistical Yearbook 1980,* U.S. Government Printing Office, Washington, D.C., 1984, Table 2.

2. Abdo A. Elkholy, "The Arab American Family," in *Ethnic Families in America,* eds. Charles H. Mindel and Robert W. Habenstein, Elsevier, New York, 1976, pp. 166–167.

3. Bureau of the Census, *Statistical Abstract of the United States, 1984,* Table 261; p. 162.

4. Emory S. Bogardus, "Comparing Racial Distance in Ethiopia, South Africa, and the United States," *Sociology and Social Research,* 52 (1968). 149–156; Won Moo Hurh, "Comparative Study of Korean Immigrants in the United States," *Korean Christian Journal,* No. 2 (Spring 1977), 60 –99.

5. Philip M. Kayal and Joseph M. Kayal, *The Syrian-Lebanese in America,* Twayne, New York, 1975, pp. 50, 61.

6. Rev. Cyril Anid, *I Grew with Them,* Paulist Press, Jounieh, Lebanon, 1967. p. 18.

7. Morris Berger, "America's Syrian Community," *Commentary,* 25, No. 4 (1958), 316.

8. Ibid., p. 111.

9. Kayal and Kayal, *The Syrian-Lebanese in America,* p. 108.

10. Ibid., pp. 197–200.

11. Milton M. Gordon, *Assimilation in American Life,* Oxford University Press, New York, 1964.

12. Abdoulmaboud Ansari, "A Community In Process: The First Generation of the Iranian Professional Middle Class Immigrants in the United States," *International Review of Modern Sociology,* 7 (Spring 1977), 96.

13. Ibid., p. 99.

14. Abdoulmaboud Ansari, "The Dually Marginal Man: The Iranian Immigrant in the United States," unpublished doctoral dissertation, New School for Social Research, 1974, pp. 12–13.

15. Ibid., pp. 12–13.

16. Mary C. Sengstock, "Social Change in the Country of Origin as a Factor in Immigrant Conceptions of Nationality," *Ethnicity,* 4 (March 1977), 54–69.

17. Ibid., p. 61.

18. Philip Harsham, "Arabs in America: The Transplanted Ones," *Aramco World Magazine,* 26, No. 2 (1975), 6.

19. Ibid.

20. Edward T. Hall, *The Hidden Dimension,* Doubleday, Garden City, N.Y., 1966, pp. 144–153.

21. Ibid., p. 149.

22. Vincent N. Parrillo, "Arab American Immigrant Communities: Diversity and Parallel," paper presented at annual meeting of Eastern Sociological Society, Baltimore, Md., March 1983; Vincent N. Parrillo, "Arab American Residential Segregation: Differences in Patterns," paper presented at annual meeting of Eastern Sociological Society, Boston, March 1984.

23. See Carol Agocs, "Ethnic Settlement in a Metropolitan Area: A Typology of Communities," *Ethnicity,* 8 (1981), 127–148; B. Aswad, *Arabic Speaking Communities in American Cities,* Center for Migration Studies, New York, 1974.

24. Lewis V. Thomas and Richard N. Krye, *The United States and Turkey and Iran,* Harvard, Cambridge, Mass., 1952, pp. 139–140.

25. Bogardus, "Comparing Racial Distance in Ethiopia, South Africa, and the United States," p. 152.

26. Gurdial Singh, "East Indians in the United States," *Sociology and Social Research,* 30 (1946), 210–211.

27. Joan M. Jensen, "Apartheid: Pacific Coast Style," *Pacific Historical Review,* 38 (1969), 335–340

28. Gary R. Hess. "The Forgotten Asian Americans: The East Indian Community in the United States," *Pacific Historical Review,* 43 (1974), 580.

29. Singh, "East Indians in the United States," pp. 210–211.

30. "Hindu Invasion," *Collier's,* 45 (March 26, 1910), 15.

31. Hess, "The Forgotten Asian Americans: The East Indian Community in the United States," pp. 583–584.

32. Ibid, p. 590.

33. Ibid., pp. 593–594.

34. U.S. Immigration and Naturalization Service Annual Report, Table 2.

35. William Claiborne, "Mother India's Children—Born to Lose," *Washington Post News Service,* February 6, 1983.

36. Rosalind J. Dworkin, "Differential Processes in Acculturation: The Case of the Asiatic Indians," Educational Resources Information Center (ERIC) ED 178–430, 1980.

37. George Becker, "Asian Spice in the Melting Pot," *New York Sunday News Magazine,* November 28, 1976, pp. 7–21.

38. For a comparative analysis of native-born and foreign-born Blacks, see Ira De Augustine Reid, *The Negro Immigrant,* 1939, reprint ed., Arno Press and *The New York Times,* New York, 1969.

39. Muruku Waiguchu, "Relations Between African and Afro-American Students in the United States," paper presented at the 7th annual meeting of the African Heritage Studies Association, 1978.

40. Ibid., pp. 5, 16.

41. Lyn H. Lofland, *A World of Strangers,* Basic Books, New York, 1973.

42. *Ridgewood News,* September 11, 1983, p. 1; *Paterson News,* September 6, 1982. p. 5.

Chapter 10

1. Ira De Augustine Reid, *The Negro Immigrant, 1939,* reprint ed., Arno Press and *The New York Times,* New York, 1969, p. 32.

2. See James O. Buswell, III, *Slavery, Segregation and Scripture,* Eerdmans, Grand Rapids, Mich., 1964; George D. Kelsey, *Racism and the Christian Understanding of Man,* Scribner's, New York, 1965; W. E. B. DuBois, *The World and Africa,* International Publishers, New York, 1965; Keith Irvine, *The Rise of the Colored Races,* Norton, New York, 1970.

3. Irvine, *The Rise of the Colored Races,* p. 13.

4. DuBois, *The World and Africa,* pp. 19–20.

5. See the discussion on pp. 60–64.

6. See the discussion on pp. 87–88.

7. See the discussion on pp. 24–28.

8. Pitirim A. Sorokin, *Contemporary Sociological Theories,* Harper, New York, 1928, pp. 291–301.

9. The following three sections are partly drawn from Brewton Berry and Henry L. Tischler, *Race and Ethnic Relations,* 4th ed., Houghton Mifflin, Boston, 1978, pp. 48–52.

10. See Kenneth Pearson, "On Our Present Knowledge of the Relationship of Mind and Body," *Annals of Eugenics,* 1 (1925–1926), 382–406; Otto Klineberg, *Race Differences,* Harper & Row, New York, 1935, pp. 84, 86.

11. Stanford M. Lyman, *Chinese Americans,* Prentice-Hall, Englewood Cliffs, N.J., 1974.

12. Berry and Tischler, *Race and Ethnic Relations,* p. 51.

13. Basil Davidson, *African Kingdoms,* Time-Life, New York, 1966, pp. 21–22.

14. See the discussion on pp. 28–29.

15. See Thomas Sowell, "New Light on Black I.Q." *The New York Times Magazine,* March 27, 1977, p. 57.

16. Audrey Shuey, *The Testing of Negro Intelligence,* J. P. Bell, Lynchburg, Va., 1958, p. 318.

17. Arthur R. Jensen, "How Much Can We Boost I.Q. and Scholastic Achievement?" *Harvard Educational Review,* 39 (1969), 1–123. In December 1979, Jensen reexamined this issue, claiming that assumptions about biased tests are inaccurate, since mean differences remain despite attempts to raise black test scores; see Arthur R. Jensen, *Bias in Mental Testing,* Free Press, New York, 1980.

18. Sowell, "New Light on Black I.Q.," p. 57 ff.

19. Ossie Davis, "The English Language Is My Enemy," *IRCD Bulletin,* 5 (Summer 1969), 13.

20. See C. Vann Woodward, *The Strange Career of Jim Crow,* 2nd ed., Oxford University Press, New York, 1966.

21. Gunnar Myrdal, *An American Dilemma,* McGraw-Hill, New York, 1964.

22. Ibid., pp. 25–38.

23. Dewey H. Palmer, "Moving North: Migration of Negroes During World War I," *Phylon*, 27 (Spring 1967), 52–62.

24. *The New York Times*, March 9, 1925, p. 16.

25. W. E. B. DuBois, *Dusk of Dawn*, Harcourt, Brace, New York, 1940, p. 264.

26. The Supreme Court specifically cited Kenneth B. Clark's study on negative self-image among black school children. For detailed information on the social scientists' role in the decision, see Kenneth B. Clark, *Prejudice and Your Child*, 2nd ed., Beacon Press, Boston, 1963.

27. Jerome H. Skolnick, *The Politics of Protest: Violent Aspects of Protest and Confrontation*, National Commission on the Causes and Prevention of Violence, Washington, D.C., 1969, pp. 101–102.

28. "Blacks New Bid for Bigger Role in Politics," *U.S. News & World Report*, April 18, 1983, p. 69.

29. See Alphonso Pinkney, *Black Americans*, Prentice-Hall, Englewood Cliffs, N.J., 1969.

30. Lewis M. Killian, *The Impossible Revolution, Phase II*, Random House, New York, 1975, p. 70.

31. Charles Silberman, *Crises in Black and White*, Random House, New York, 1964, p. 8.

32. See Robin M. Williams, Jr., "Social Change and Social Conflict: Race Relations in the United States, 1944–1964," *Sociological Inquiry*, 35 (Winter 1965), 20–24. Also, Stanley Lieberson and Arnold R. Silverman, "The Precipitants and Underlying Conditions of Race Riots," *American Sociological Review*, 30 (1965), 887–898.

33. From the Report of the National Advisory Commission on Civil Disorders, U.S. Government Printing Office, Washington, D.C., 1968.

34. Findings reported by Lyle Jones at annual meetings of American Psychological Association, Anaheim, California, August 1983.

35. Diane Pierce, *The Feminization of Poverty: Women, Work, and Welfare*, University of Chicago Press, Chicago, 1978.

36. U.S. Bureau of the Census, "Characteristics of the Population Below the Poverty Level: 1981," *Current Population Reports*, Series P-60, No. 138, March 1983, Table 5, p. 18.

37. U.S. Bureau of the Census, *Statistical Abstract of the United States*, 1984 Table 61, p. 48.

38. John Herbers, "Women and Blacks Gained in Jobs, U.S. Says," *The New York Times*, April 24, 1983, pp. 1, 38.

39. *Statistical Abstract of the United States, 1984*, Table 696, p. 419.

40. William J. Wilson, *The Declining Significance of Race*, University of Chicago Press, Chicago, 1978.

41. Thomas Sowell, *Ethnic America*, Basic Books, New York, 1981.

42. Carl Gershman, "A Matter of Class," *The New York Times Magazine*, October 5, 1980, pp. 24 ff.

43. Charles V. Willie, *Caste and Class Controversy*, General Hall, New York, 1979.

44. Kenneth B. Clark, "The Role of Race," *The New York Times Magazine*, October 5, 1980, pp. 25 ff.

45. Robert Blauner, "Internal Colonialism and Ghetto Revolt," *Social Problems*, 16 (1969), 393–408.

Chapter 11

1. Bureau of Labor Statistics, U.S. Department of Labor, "Employment in Perspective: Minority Workers," First Quarter 1983, Report 694.

2. Reported in Ronald Hilton, *The Latin Americans: Their Heritage and Their Destiny*, Lippincott, New York, 1973, p. 16.

3. See Glen H. Beyer, *The Urban Explosion in Latin America*, Cornell University Press, Ithaca, N.Y., 1967; David Chaplin, *Population Policy and Growth in Latin America*, Heath, New York, 1971; Eric R. Wolf and Edward C. Hanson, *The Human Condition in Latin America*, Oxford University Press, New York, 1972.

4. Hilton, *The Latin Americans*, pp. 40–41.

5. Celia S. Heller, *Mexican-American Youth: Forgotten Youth at the Crossroads*, Random House, New York, 1966; William Madsen, *The Mexican-Americans of South Texas*, Holt, New York, 1964, pp. 15–17.

6. Joseph P. Fitzpatrick, *Puerto Rican Americans,* Prentice-Hall, Englewood Cliffs, N.J., 1971, p. 91.

7. McKay, "Americans of Spanish Origin in the Labor Force: An Update," pp. 4–5.

8. Clara Rodriguez, *The Ethnic Queue in the U.S.: The Case of the Puerto Ricans,* R & E Research Associates, San Francisco, 1974, p. 92.

9. Fitzpatrick, *Puerto Rican Americans,* p. 105.

10. For some excellent cross-cultural analyses of attitudes regarding distance between people, see Edward Hall, *The Hidden Dimension,* Doubleday, Garden City, N.Y., 1966; E. Hall, *Silent Language,* Doubleday, Garden City, N.Y., 1959.

11. Cary Davis, Carl Haub, and JoAnne Willette, "U.S. Hispanics: Changing the Face of America," *Population Bulletin,* Vol. 38, No. 3 Population Reference Bureau, Washington, D.C., 1983, 38–39.

12. U.S. Department of Commerce: Bureau of the Census, "Ancestry of the Population by State: 1980," Supplementary Report PC 80-S1-10, April 1983, p. 28–31.

13. Michael T. Malloy, "We Want No Melting Pot," *The National Observer,* August 7, 1976, pp. 1, 12.

14. Joan W. Moore, *Mexican Americans,* Prentice-Hall, Englewood Cliffs, N.J., 1970, p. 100.

15. Ed Ludwig and James Santibanex (eds.). *The Chicanos,* Penguin, Baltimore, 1971, pp. 2–3.

16. Moore, *Mexican Americans,* p. 43.

17. Ibid.

18. Carey McWilliams, *North from Mexico,* Greenwood Press, New York, 1968, pp. 247-250.

19. Moore, *Mexican Americans,* p. 72.

20. See Thomas M. Martinez, "Advertising and Racism: The Case of the Mexican-American," *El Grito,* Summer 1969.

21. Florence Kluckhohn and Fred L. Strodtbeck, *Variations in Value Orientations,* Row, Peterson, Evanston, Ill., 1961.

22. See Moore, *Mexican Americans,* pp. 129–130.

23. Leo Grebler, Joan Moore, and Ralph Guzman, *The Mexican American People,* Free Press, New York, 1970, pp. 423–439.

24. See the discussion on pp. 35–38.

25. Moore, *Mexican Americans,* pp. 44–45.

26. Ibid., pp. 57–59.

27. Ibid., p. 75.

28. Ibid., pp. 85–88.

29. Michael S. Teitelbaum, "Right Versus Right: Immigration and Refugee Policy in the United States," *Foreign Affairs,* 59 (1980), 23.

30. Jacob S. Siegel, et. al., "Preliminary Review of Existing Studies of the Number of Illegal Residents in the United States," Bureau of the Census, prepared for the staff of the Select Commission on Immigration and Refugee Policy, January 30, 1981.

31. Robert Pear, "Immigration Reform is Alive and Well," *The New York Times,* May 22, 1983.

32. Davis, Haub, and Willette, "U.S. Hispanics: Changing the Face of America," p. 27.

33. See James P. Sterba, "From Mexico to Hard Times in the Southwest U.S.," *The New York Times,* May 1, 1977, p. E3.

34. Rodriguez, *The Ethnic Queue in the U.S.: The Case of the Puerto Ricans,* pp. 83–85.

35. Ibid., p. 83.

36. Davis, Haub, and Willette, "U.S. Hispanics," pp. 23–24.

37. Centro de Estudios Puertorriqueños, *Labor Migration Under Capitalism: The Puerto Rican Experience,* Monthly Review Press, New York, 1979, pp. 108, 186–87.

38. Davis, Haub, and Willete, "U.S. Hispanics," pp. 24–25.

39. Rita M. Maldonado, "Why Puerto Ricans Migrated to the United States in 1947–73," *Monthly Labor Review,* U.S. Department of Labor, Bureau of Labor Statistics, September 1976, p. 14.

40. See Howard Bray, "The New Wave of Puerto Rican Immigrants," *The New York Times Magazine,* July 3, 1983, pp. 22 ff.

41. Fitzpatrick, *Puerto Rican Americans,* p. 78.

42. The example is from Fitzpatrick, pp. 78–79.

43. Ibid., pp. 83–84.

44. See Oscar Handlin, *The Uprooted,* Little, Brown, Boston, 1951, p. 135.

45. Nathan Glazer and Daniel P. Moynihan, *Beyond the Melting Pot,* 2nd ed., M.I.T., Cambridge, Mass., 1970, pp. 103–104.

46. For a more detailed discussion of the role of religion among Puerto Ricans, see Fitzpatrick, *Puerto Rican Americans,* pp. 115–129; also Rodriguez, *The Ethnic Queue in the U.S.: The Case of the Puerto Ricans,* pp. 95–99.

47. Fitzpatrick, *Puerto Rican Americans,* pp. 123–127.

48. Ibid., p. 129.

49. Ibid., p. 128.

50. "Lands of our Fathers," *Newsweek,* January 17, 1983, p. 23.

51. Davis, Haub, and Willette, "U.S. Hispanics: Changing the Face of America," p. 13.

52. Clara Rodriguez, "Assimilation in the Puerto Rican Communities of the U.S.: A New Focus," presented to the 72nd annual meeting of the American Sociological Association, 1977, p. 8.

53. Fitzpatrick, *Puerto Rican Americans,* pp. 66–70.

54. Ibid., p. 78.

55. Rodriguez, "Assimilation in the Puerto Rican Communities of the U.S.: A New Focus," p. 15.

56. U.S. Commission on Civil Rights, "Puerto Ricans in the Continental U.S.: An Uncertain Future," October 1976.

57. Bureau of Labor Statistics, U.S. Department of Labor, "Employment and Earnings, January 1983," Table 45.

58. Dennis M. Roth, "Hispanics in the U.S. Labor Force: A Brief Review," in Congressional Research Service, *The Hispanic Population of the United States: An Overview,* U.S. Government Printing Office, Washington, D.C., 1983, Tables 5 and 6.

59. Diaz-Briquets, Sergio and Lisandro Perez, "Cuba: The Demography of Revolution," *Population Bulletin,* 36(1)(April 1981).

60. Davis, Haub, and Willette, "U.S. Hispanics," p. 23.

61. Tom Alexander, "Those Amazing Cuban Emigres," *Fortune Magazine,* 74 (October 1966), 144–146.

62. Richard Severo, "Spanish Influx Felt in Washington Heights," *The New York Times,* August 12, 1976, p. 33. ©1976 by The New York Times Company. Reprinted by permission.

63. Rolando A. Alum and Felipe P. Manteiga, "Cuban and American Values: A Synoptic Comparison," *Mosaic,* 3 (1977), 11–12.

64. Davis, Haub, and Willette, "U.S. Hispanics", pp. 13–14.

65. A definitive study on the Basques in America is William A. Douglass and Jon Bilbao, *Amerikanuak: Basques in the New World,* University of Nevada Press, Reno, 1975.

66. Juan de Onis, "From Columbia with Skills and High Hopes," *The New York Times,* May 1, 1977, p. E3.

67. Reginald Stuart, "Haitians, Seeking Freedom and Jobs, Find Heartaches Instead in America," *The New York Times,* June 28, 1983, p. A18.

68. Carey W. English, "Sweatshops Are Back—And They're Thriving," *U.S. News & World Report,* January 16, 1984, p. 68.

69. Tekle M. Woldemikael, "Becoming Black American: A Case Study of Haitian Immigrants to the U.S.A.," paper presented at the annual meetings of the Eastern Sociological Society, Philadelphia, March 1982.

70. M. G. Smith, *The Plural Society in the British West Indies,* University of California Press, Berkeley, Calif., 1965, pp. 163–164.

71. Benjamin B. Ringer, *"We the People" and Others,* Tavistock, New York, 1983, p. 19.

72. Smith, *The Plural Society.*

73. Joan W. Moore, "American Minorities and 'New Nation' Perspectives," in F. James Davis (ed.), *Understanding Minority-Dominant Relations,* AMH Corporation, Arlington Heights, Ill., 1979, pp. 40–53.

Chapter 12

1. "Many Seek Faith Along Other Paths," *U.S. News & World Report,* April 4, 1983, pp. 42–43; Constant Jacquet (ed.), Yearbook of American and Canadian Churches 1983, Abingdon Press, Nashville, Tenn., 1983, pp. 225–231.

2. Thomas J. Curran, *Xenophobia and Immigration, 1820–1930,* Twayne Publishers, Boston, 1975, pp. 12–13.

3. Samuel F. B. Morse, *Imminent Dangers to the Free Institutions of the United States through Foreign Immigration and the Present State of the Naturalization Laws: A Series of Numbers Originally Published in the New York Journal of Commerce Revised and Corrected with Additions,* New York, 1835.

4. Curran, *Xenophobia and Immigration, 1820–1930,* pp. 99–108.

5. Ibid., p. 107.

6. Ibid., p. 130.

7. Ibid., p. 131.

8. Ibid., pp. 32–35.

9. John Higham, *Strangers in the Land,* Atheneum, New York, 1973, p. 59.

10. Curran, *Xenophobia and Immigration, 1820–1930,* p. 78.

11. Nathan Glazer, *American Judaism,* 2nd ed. University of Chicago Press, Chicago, 1972, p. 14.

12. Curran, *Xenophobia and Immigration, 1820–1930,* p. 13.

13. Ibid., p. 76.

14. Ibid., pp. 76–77.

15. Milton L. Barron, "The Incidence of Jewish Intermarriage in Europe and America," *American Sociological Review,* 1 (February 1946), 11.

16. See Joseph Brandes, *Immigrants to Freedom,*

University of Pennsylvania Press, Philadelphia, 1971; Fred Rosenbaum, *Free to Choose: The Making of a Jewish Community in the American West,* Berkeley, Calif. The Judah I. Magnes Memorial Museum, 1976.

17. See Jules Isaac, *The Teaching of Contempt: Christian Roots of Anti-Semitism,* Harcourt, Brace & World, New York, 1964; Malcolm Hay, *Europe and the Jews,* Beacon Press, Boston, 1960.

18. Leonard Dinnerstein and David M. Reimers, *Ethnic Americans,* Harper & Row, New York, 1975, p. 44.

19. See Bernard C. Rosen, "Evaluation of Occupations: A Reflection of Jewish and Italian Mobility Differences," *American Sociological Review,* 22 (1957), 546–553; Herbert J. Gans, "American Jewry: Present and Future," *Commentary,* May–June 1956, pp. 422, 430, 555, 563.

20. "Distribution of Immigrants," *Senate Documents,* 20 (61st Congress, 3rd Session), 47 ff.

21. Dinnerstein and Reimers, *Ethnic Americans,* p. 53: "By 1915 Jews comprised 85 percent of the student body at New York's free but renowned City College, one-fifth of those attending New York University and one-sixth of the students at Columbia."

22. Gordon, *Assimilation in American Life,* p. 185.

23. Gerhard Lenski, *The Religious Factor,* Doubleday, New York, 1961, pp. 33–34.

24. John P. Dean, "Patterns of Socialization and Association Between Jews and Non-Jews," *Jewish Social Studies,* 17 (July 1955), 252–254.

25. Herbert J. Gans, "The Origin and Growth of a Jewish Community in the Suburbs: A Study of the Jews of Park Forest," in *The Jews: Social Patterns of an American Group,* ed. Marshall Sklare, Free Press, Glencoe, Ill., 1958, p. 227.

26. Albert I. Gordon, *Jews in Suburbia,* Beacon Press, Boston, 1956.

27. See the discussion on p. 50.

28. Milton M. Gordon, *Assimilation in American Life,* pp. 173–224.

29. Alvin P. Sanoff, "Jews Find New Solace in the Old Traditions," *U.S. News & World Report,* April 4, 1983, p. 44; Fred Massarik, "Intermarriage: Facts for

Planning," *National Jewish Population Study,* Council of Jewish Federations and Welfare Funds, New York, 1974.

30. Sanoff, "Jews Find New Solace in the Old Traditions," p. 44.

31. Ibid.

32. See Hutchins Hapgood, *The Spirit of the Ghetto,* Belknap Press, Cambridge, Mass., 1967.

33. Sanoff, "Jews Find New Solace in the Old Traditions," p. 44.

34. Ibid., p. 43.

35. Ibid., pp. 43–45.

36. Drora Kass and Seymour Martin Lipset, "America's New Wave of Jewish Immigrants," *The New York Times Magazine,* December 7, 1980, p. 44.

37. Dean L. May, "Mormons," in Stephan Thernstrom (ed.), *Harvard Encyclopedia of American Ethnic Groups,* Harvard University Press, Cambridge, Mass., 1980, pp. 720–721.

38. Joseph Smith, *Pearl of Great Price,* The Church of Jesus Christ of Latter-Day Saints, Salt Lake City, Utah, 1974, pp. 50–51.

39. See Marvin S. Hill, "The Rise of the Mormon Kingdom of God," in Richard Poll (ed.), *Utah's History,* Brigham Young University Press, Provo, Utah, 1978.

40. Val Dan MacMurray and Perry H. Cunningham, "Mormons and Gentiles: A Study in Conflict and Persistence," in Donald F. Gefland and Russell D. Lee (eds.), *Ethnic Conflicts and Power: A Cross-National Perspective,* John Wiley & Sons, New York, 1973, pp. 205–218.

41. Bruce L. Campbell and Eugene E. Campbell, "The Mormon Family," in Charles H. Mindel and Robert W. Habenstein (eds.), *Ethnic Families in America,* 2nd ed., Elsevier, New York, 1981, p. 389.

42. Stanley Ivins, "Notes on Mormon Polygamy," *Western Humanities Review,* 10 (1956), 233.

43. Lester E. Bush, "Mormon Elder's Wafers: Images of Mormon Virility in Patent Medicine Ads," *Dialogue: A Journal of Mormon Thought,* 10 (1976), 89–93.

44. Campbell and Campbell, "The Mormon Family," p. 390.

45. John F. Galliher and Linda Basilick, "Utah's Liberal Drug Laws: Structural Foundations and Triggering Events," *Social Problems,* 26 (1979), 284–297; Harold T. Christensen, "Some Next Steps in Mormon Family Research," in Phillip R. Kunz (ed.), *The Mormon Family,* Brigham Young University Press, Provo, Utah, 1977, p. 413.

46. William J. Whalen, *The Latter-Day Saints in the Modern-Day World,* Day, New York, 1964, p. 17.

47. William M. Kephart, *Extraordinary Groups: The Sociology of Unconventional Life-Styles,* 2nd ed., St. Martin's Press, New York, 1982, p. 265.

48. U.S. Bureau of the Census, *Statistical Abstract of the United States, 1984,* Table No. 79, pp. 57–58.

49. Marilyn Warenski, *Patriarchs and Politics,* McGraw-Hill, New York, 1978, p. 82.

50. Kephart, *Extraordinary Groups,* p. 273.

51. May, "Mormons," p. 729.

52. Ibid., p. 731.

52. John A. Hostetler, *Amish Society,* 3rd ed., Johns Hopkins Press, Baltimore, 1980, pp. 62–65.

54. Ibid., p. 38.

55. Ibid., p. 40.

56. Ibid., p. 138.

57. Ibid., pp. 139–144.

58. Ibid.

59. Kephart, *Extraordinary Groups,* p. 58.

60. Hostetler, *Amish Society,* pp. 276–277.

61. Gertrude Enders Huntington, "The Amish Family," in Mindel and Habenstein, *Ethnic Families in America,* p. 314.

62. Hostetler, *Amish Society,* pp. 276–277.

63. Ibid., p. 293; Kephart, *Extraordinary Groups,* p. 89.

64. Leon Daniel, "Amish Try to Hold Reins on Their

Plain Way of Life," *United Press International,* August 12, 1983.

65. Kephart, *Extraordinary Groups,* pp. 86–87.

66. Charles Wagley and Marvin Harris, *Minorities in the New World,* Columbia University Press, New York, 1958, p. 10.

67. M. G. Smith, R. Augier and R. M. Nettleford, *The Rastafari Movement in Kingston, Jamaica,* Institute of Social and Economic Research, Kingston, Jamaica, 1960, p. 5.

68. George E. Simpson, "Political Cultism in West Kingston, Jamaica," *Social and Economic Studies,* 4 (1955), 133–149.

69. Barry Chevannes, "Dread: The Rastafarians of Jamaica—A Review," *Caribbean Quarterly,* 24 (1976), 61–69.

70. Neville G. Callam, "Invitation to Docility: Defusing the Rastafarian Challenge," *Caribbean Journal of Religion Studies,* 3 (1980), 39.

71. Leonard Barrett, *The Rastafarians: Sounds of Cultural Dissonance,* Beacon Press, Boston, 1977, p. 138.

72. See Victor Turner, *The Ritual Process,* Cornell University Press, Ithaca, N.Y., 1969, p. 128.

73. Callam, "Invitation to Docility," p. 33.

74. *The Rastafarian Voice,* July 1975, quoted in Barrett, *The Rastafarians,* p. 144.

75. Kephart, *Extraordinary Groups,* p. 208.

76. See Marguerite Fellows Melcher, *The Shaker Adventure,* Western Reserve Press, Cleveland, 1968; Edward Andrews, *The People Called Shakers,* Oxford University Press, New York, 1953.

77. Rosabeth Moss Kanter, *Commitment and Community: Communes and Utopias in Sociological Perspective,* Harvard University Press, Cambridge, Mass, 1973, p. 39.

78. Kephart, *Extraordinary Groups,* p. 205.

79. See Andrews, *The People Called Shakers;* Melcher, *The Shaker Adventure;* Henri Desroche, *The American Shakers: From Neo-Christianity to Preso-cialism,* University of Massachusetts Press, Amherst, Mass., 1971.

80. Desroche, *American Shakers,* pp. 118–119.

81. Ibid., pp. 116–117.

82. James P. Mann, "A Search for the Sacred," *U.S. News & World Report,* April 4, 1983, p. 36.

83. Harold J. Abramson, *Ethnic Diversity in Catholic America,* John Wiley & Sons, New York: 1973; Elmer Spreitzer and Eldon E. Snyder, "Patterns of Variation Within and Between Ethnoreligious Groupings," *Ethnicity,* 2 (1975), 124–133.

34. Charles Y. Glock and Rodney Stark, "Is There an American Protestantism?" *Trans-action,* 3 (November–December 1965), pp. 8–13,48–49.

85. Robert Bellah, "Civil Religion in America," *Daedalus,* 96 (1967), 1–21.

86. Lenski, *The Religious Factor;* Dean, "Patterns of Socialization and Association Between Jews and Non-Jews."

Chapter 13

1. Marvin Harris, "Why Men Dominate Women," *The New York Times Magazine,* November 13, 1977, p. 46.

2. See Vern L. Bullough, *The Subordinate Sex: A History of Attitudes Toward Women,* Penguin Books, New York, 1974.

3. Gustav LeBon, *Révue d'Anthropologie* (1879), pp. 60–61, quoted in Stephan Jay Gould, *The Mismeasure of Man,* W. W. Norton, New York, 1981, pp. 104–105.

4. Gunnar Myrdal, *An American Dilemma: The Negro Problem and Modern Democracy,* Harper, New York, 1944, pp. 1073–1078.

5. Helen M. Hacker, "Women as a Minority Group," *Social Forces,* 30 (1951), 60–69.

6. Charles Wagley and Marvin Harris, *Minorities in the New World,* Columbia University Press, New York, 1958, p. 10.

7. Mary P. Ryan, *Womanhood in America: From*

Colonial Times to the Present, 2nd ed., New Viewpoints, Franklin Watts, New York, 1979.

8. *See* Edith Abbott, *Women in Industry: A Study in American Economic History,* 1919 New York, quoted in Ryan, *Womanhood in America,* p. 54.

9. Ibid., p. 56.

10. Joyce Cowley, *Pioneers of Women's Liberation,* Merit, New York, 1969, p. 13.

11. William H. Chafe, *The American Woman: Her Changing Social, Economic, and Political Role,* Oxford University Press, New York, 1972.

12. Jo Freeman, *The Politics of Women's Liberation,* David McKay, New York, 1975, pp. 19–25.

13. Irene H. Frieze, et. al. *Women and Sex Roles,* W. W. Norton and Company, New York, 1978, pp. 91–93.

14. Margaret Mead, *Sex and Temperament,* William Morrow, New York, 1935,1950,1963.

15. Donna Eder and M.T. Hallinan, "The Meek Shall Not Inherit the Earth: Self-Evaluation and the Legitimacy of Stratification," *American Sociological Review,* 45 (1978), 247.

16. Richard Della Fave, "Sex Differences in Children's Friendships," *American Sociological Review,* 43 (1980), 955–970.

17. Featured in "The Pinks and the Blues," *Nova,* Public Broadcasting System, 1982.

18. *See* Gaye Tuchman, Arlene K. Daniels, and James Benet (eds.), *Hearth and Home: Images of Women in the Mass Media,* Oxford University Press, New York, 1978; see also discussion in Chapter 3.

19. Lucy Komisar, "The Image of Women in Advertising," in *Woman in Sexist Society: Studies in Power and Powerlessness,* (eds.) Vivian Gornick and Barbara K. Moran, Basic Books, New York, 1971, pp. 204, 211–212.

20. *See* Tuchman, Daniels, and Benet, *Hearth and Home: Images of Women in the Mass Media;* Matilda Butler and William Paisley, *Women and the Mass Media,* Human Sciences Press, New York, 1980, pp. 103–114.

21. Erving Goffman, *Gender Advertisements,* Harper/Colophon, New York, 1979, p. viii.

22. Sara Kiesler, Lee Sprovel, and Jacquelynne S. Eicles, "Second-Class Citizens?" *Psychology Today,* 17 (March 1983), 40–48.

23. Lillian B. Rubin, *Worlds of Pain: Life in the Working-Class Family,* Basic Books, New York, 1976.

24. Irene Dabrowski, "Working-Class Women and Civic Action: A Case Study of an Innovative Community Role," *Policy Studies Journal,* 2 (1983), 427–435.

25. Ibid.

26. Lucy Jen Huang, "The Chinese American Family," in Charles H. Mindel and Robert W. Habenstein (eds.) *Ethnic Families in America,* 2nd ed., Elsevier, New York, 1981, p. 124.

27. Akemi Kikumura and Harry H. L. Kitano, "The Japanese American Family," in Mindel and Habenstein (eds.) *Ethnic Familes in America,* pp. 54–56.

28. Robert Staples, *The World of Black Singles: Changing Patterns of Male/Female Relations,* Greenwood Press, Westport, Conn., 1981.

29. Robert Staples, "The Black American Family," in Mindel and Habenstein (eds.), *Ethnic Families in America,* pp. 236–237.

30. Janus Adams, "The Power Hook-up," *Essence,* 8 (1978), 80–81, 114–129.

31. Ibid., p. 125.

32. U.S. Commission on Civil Rights, *A Guide to Federal Laws and Regulations Prohibiting Sex Discrimination,* U.S. Government Printing Office, Washington, D.C., 1976, p. 1.

33. C. P. Gilman, *Women and Education* (1911), in N. Reeves, *Womankind: Beyond the Stereotypes,* Aldine-Atherton, Chicago, 1971, p. 301.

34. Carol A. Whitehurst, *Women in America: The Oppressed Majority,* Goodyear, Santa Monica, Calif., 1977.

35. Karen M. Mills and Thomas J. Palumbo, "A Statistical Portrait of Women in the United States: 1978," *Current Population Reports,* Series P-23, No. 100,

U.S. Government Printing Office, Washington, D.C., 1980.

36. Rosabeth Moss Kanter, *Men and Women of the Corporation,* Basic Books, New York, 1977.

37. "The Work Revolution," *Newsweek,* January 17, 1983, p. 31.

38. Constance Sorrentino, "International Comparisons of Labor Force Participation," *Monthly Labor Review* (February 1983), pp. 23–27.

39. Ibid.

40. Malcolm H. Morrison, "The Aging of the U.S. Population: Human Resource Implications," *Monthly Labor Review* (May 1983), p. 15.

41. U.S. Bureau of the Census, *Statistical Abstract of the United States, 1984,* Table 774, p. 469.

42. Catharine A. MacKinnon, *Sexual Harassment of Working Women: A Case of Sex Discrimination,* Yale University Press, New Haven, Conn. 1979.

43. Bureau of Labor Statistics, reported in *The New York Times,* November 20, 1983.

44. See Diane Pierce, *The Feminization of Poverty: Women, Work, and Welfare,* University of Chicago Press, Chicago, 1978.

45. "Characteristics of the Population Below the Poverty Level: 1981," *Current Population Reports,* Series P-60, No. 138, U.S. Government Printing Office, Washington, D.C., March 1983, p. 18.

46. P. D. Horn and J. C. Horn, *Sex in the Office: Power and Passion in the Workplace,* Addison-Wesley, Reading, Mass., 1982, p. 70.

47. Ibid., p. 64.

48. MacKinnon, *Sexual Harassment of Working Women,* p. 2.

49. Rosalind J. Dworkin, "A Woman's Report," *The Minority Report,* 2nd ed., Holt, Rinehart and Winston, New York, 1982, p. 384.

50. *The New York Times,* November 27, 1983, p. E7.

51. *Statistical Abstract of the United States, 1982–83,* Table 800, p. 489.

52. See Marianne Githens and Jewel L. Prestage, *A Portrait of Marginality: The Political Behavior of the American Women,* David McKay, New York, 1977.

53. Ibid.

54. Talcott Parsons and Robert Bales, *Family Socialization, and Interaction Process,* Free Press, Glencoe, Ill., 1955.

55. See Susan Brownmiller, *Against Our Will: Men, Women, and Rape,* Simon and Schuster, New York, 1975.

56. Friedrich Engels, *The Origin of the Family, Private Property, and the State,* International Publishers, New York, 1942.

57. See Alice Schlegel (ed.), *Sexual Stratification: A Cross-Cultural View,* Columbia University Press, New York, 1977.

58. Michael Gordon, *The American Family: Past, Present, and Future,* Random House, New York, 1978, p. 199.

59. Jan M. Newton, "The Political Economy of Women's Oppression," in Jean Ramage LePaluoto (ed.), *Women on the Move: A Feminist Perspective,* University of Oregon Press, Eugene, Ore., 1973, p. 121.

60. P. B. Walters, "Trends in U.S. Men's and Women's Sex Role Attitudes: 1972–78," *American Sociological Review,* 46 (1981), 453–460.

Chapter 14

1. Mary C. Sengstock, "Social Change in the Country of Origin as a Factor in Immigrant Conceptions of Nationality," *Ethnicity,* 4 (March 1977). 54–69.

2. Ibid., pp. 56–57.

3. Ibid., pp. 61, 64.

4. Marcus L. Hansen, "The Third Generation in America," *Commentary,* 14, No. 5 (November 1952), 492–500.

5. Marcus L. Hansen, "The Third Generation," in Oscar Handlin (ed.), *Children of the Uprooted,* Harper & Row, New York, 1966, pp. 255–271.

6. Ruby Jo Reeves Kennedy, "Single or Triple Melting Pot? Intermarriage in New Haven, 1870–1940,"

American Journal of Sociology, 49 (January 1944), 331–339; also, Ruby Jo Reeves Kennedy, "Single or Triple Melting Pot? Intermarriage Trends in New Haven, 1870–1950, *American Journal of Sociology,* 58 (July 1952), 56–59.

7. Marshall Sklare, *America's Jews,* Random House, New York, 1971, p. 185; John L. Thomas, "The Factor of Religion in the Selection of Marriage Mates," *American Sociological Review,* 16 (August 1951), 487–491.

8. Will Herberg, *Protestant-Catholic-Jew,* Doubleday, Garden City, N.Y., 1955.

9. Harold J. Abramson, *Ethnic Diversity in Catholic America,* Wiley, New York, 1973, pp. 51–68.

10. Mark R. Levy and Michael S. Kramer, *The Ethnic Factor,* Simon and Schuster, New York, 1973.

11. Jerry D. Rose, *Peoples: The Ethnic Dimension in Human Relations,* Rand McNally, Chicago, 1976, p. 21.

12. John M. Goering, "The Emergence of Ethnic Interests: A Case of Serendipity," *Social Forces,* 49 (March 1971), 379–384.

13. Ibid., p. 383.

14. Ibid., pp. 381–382.

15. Ibid., p. 382.

16. Neil C. Sandberg, *Ethnic Identity and Assimilation: The Polish-American Community,* Praeger, New York, 1974.

17. John P. Roche, "Suburban Ethnicity: Ethnic Attitudes and Behavior Among Italian Americans in Two Suburban Communities," *Social Science Quarterly* 63 (1982), 145–153.

18. See, for example, Richard O'Connor, *The German Americans,* Little, Brown, Boston, 1968; or Bernard Wasserstein, "Jewish Identification Among Students at Oxford," *Jewish Journal of Sociology,* 13 (December 1971), 131–151.

19. Harold J. Abramson, "The Religioethnic Factor and the American Experience: Another Look at the Three-Generation Hypothesis," *Ethnicity,* 2 (1975), 163–177.

20. Ibid., p. 173.

21. John M. Goering, "The Emergence of Ethnic Interests," pp. 379–384.

22. Andrew M. Greeley, *Why Can't They Be Like Us?,* Dutton, New York, 1971, pp. 148–152.

23. Ibid., p. 152.

24. Michael Novak, *The Rise of the Unmeltable Ethnics,* Macmillan, New York, 1971.

25. Ibid., p. 30.

26. Ibid., p. 291.

27. Perry L. Weed, *The White Ethnic Movement and Ethnic Politics,* Praeger, New York, 1973, p. 48.

28. Ibid.

29. Herbert Gans, "American Jewry: Present and Future," *Commentary,* 21 (May 1956), 422–430; and "The Future of American Jewry: Part II," *Commentary,* 21 (June 1956), 555–563.

30. Herbert Gans, *The Urban Villagers,* Free Press, New York, 1962.

31. Herbert Gans, p. xii of Foreword in Sandberg, *Ethnic Identity and Assimilation.*

32. Ibid., p. xi.

33. William L. Yancey, Eugene P. Ericksen, and Richard N. Juliani, "Emergent Ethnicity: A Review and Reformulation," *American Sociological Review,* 41 (June 1976), 391–403.

34. Ibid., p. 393.

35. See also Amitai Etzioni, "The Ghetto. A Reevaluation," *Social Forces,* 39 (1959), 255–262.

36. Yancey, et al., "Emergent Ethnicity," p. 399.

37. Stanford M. Lyman and William A. Douglass, "Ethnicity: Strategies of Collective and Individual Impression Management," *Social Research,* 40 (Summer 1973), 344–365.

38. Ibid., p. 345.

39. Richard D. Alba, "A Preliminary Examination of Ethnic Identification Among Whites," *American Sociological Review,* 48 (1983), 473–498.

40. Mark Zborowski, "Cultural Components in Response to Pain," *Journal of Social Issues,* 8 (1952),

16–30; *see also* M. Zborowski, *People in Pain,* Jossey-Bass, San Francisco, 1969.

41. R. A. Sternbach and B. Tursky, "Ethnic Differences Among Housewives in Psychophysical and Skin Potential Responses to Electric Shock," *Psychophysiology,* 1 (1965), 241–246; B. Tursky and R. A. Sternbach, "Further Physiological Correlates of Ethnic Differences in Response to Shock," *Psychophysiology* 4 (1967), 67–74.

42. W. E. Lambert, E. Libman, and E. G. Poser, "The Effect of Increased Salience of a Membership Group on Pain Tolerance," *British Journal of Social and Clinical Psychology,* 3 (1964), 130.

43. Barry J. Wepman, "Psychological Component of Pain Perception," *Dental Clinics of North America,* 22 (1978), 101–113; F. Graham Spear, "Cultural Factors in Clinical Pain Assessment," *International Dental Journal,* 27 (1977), 284–287.

44. Andrew M. Greeley and William C. McCready, "Does Ethnicity Matter?," *Ethnicity,* 1 (1974), 91–103.

45. Ibid., p. 102.

46. Novak, *The Rise of the Unmeltable Ethnics,* p. 32.

47. Barry Glassner and Bruce Berg, "How Jews Avoid Alcohol Problems," American Sociological Review, 45(1980), 647–664.

48. Georgio Lolli, et. al., *Alcohol in Italian Culture,* Free Press: Glencoe, Ill., 1958.

49. Richard Stivers, *A Hair of the Dog: Irish Drinking and the American Stereotype,* University of Pennsylvania Press: University Park, Penn., 1976.

50. Andrew J. Gordon, "The Cultural Context of Drinking and Indigenous Therapy for Alcohol Problems in Three Migrant Hispanic Cultures," *Journal of Studies on Alcohol, Suppl.* No. 9, 1981, pp. 217–240.

51. Andrew M. Greeley, *Ethnicity, Denomination, and Inequality,* Sage Research Papers in the Social Sciences, Vol. 4, series 90–029 (Studies in Religion and Ethnicity), Sage Publications, Beverly Hills, Calif., 1976.

52. David L. Featherman in a review of Greeley's book in *Sociological Analysis,* 38 (Summer 1977), 176–179.

53. Ibid., p. 178.

54. Stanley Lieberson and Donna K. Carter, "Making It in America: Differences between Eminent Blacks and White Ethnic Groups," *American Sociological Review,* 44 (June 1979), 347–366.

55. Richard D. Alba and Gwen Moore, "Ethnicity in the American Elite," *American Sociological Review,* 47 (1982), 373–383.

56. "Lands of Our Fathers," *Newsweek,* January 17, 1983, p. 70.

57. Barry Siegel, "Here We Come Again," *Los Angeles Times,* December 1982.

58. "A *Newsweek* Poll on Immigration," *Newsweek,* June 25, 1984, p. 21.

59. Marvin Stone, "Help for Illegals—How Much?," *U.S. News & World Report,* August 16, 1982, p. 74.

60. "Teaching in English-Plus," *Newsweek,* February 7, 1977, pp. 64–65.

61. Ibid., p. 65.

62. James Cummins, "Linguistic Interdependence and the Educational Development of Bilingual Children," *Bilingual Education Paper Series,* National Dissemination and Assessment Center at UCLA, Los Angeles, 1981; Joti Bhatnaser, "Linguistic Behavior and Adjustment of Immigrant Children in French and English Schools in Montreal, *International Journal of Applied Psychology,* 29 (1980), 141–158.

63. Benjamin F. Hadis, "The Role of Native Language Maintenance and the Learning Social Context in the Academic Performance of Immigrant Students," paper presented at the annual meetings of the Eastern Sociological Society, Boston, March 1984.

64. Ibid.

APPENDIX

Immigration by Country, for Decades 1820–1981[1]

Countries	1820	1821–1830	1831–1840	1841–1850	1851–1860	1861–1870	1871–1880
All Countries	8,385	143,439	599,125	1,713,251	2,598,214	2,314,824	2,812,191
Europe	7,690	98,797	495,681	1,597,442	2,452,577	2,065,141	2,271,925
Austria-Hungary[2,5]	—	—	—	—	—	7,800	72,969
Belgium	1	27	22	5,074	4,738	6,734	7,221
Denmark	20	169	1,063	539	3,749	17,094	31,771
France	371	8,497	45,575	77,262	76,358	35,986	72,206
Germany[2,5]	968	6,761	152,454	434,626	951,667	787,468	718,182
Great Britain:							
England	1,782	14,055	7,611	32,092	247,125	222,277	437,706
Scotland	268	2,912	2,667	3,712	38,331	38,769	87,564
Wales	—	170	185	1,261	6,319	4,313	6,631
Not specified[3]	360	7,942	65,347	229,979	132,199	341,537	16,142
Greece	—	20	49	16	31	72	210
Ireland	3,614	50,724	207,381	780,719	914,119	435,778	436,871
Italy	30	409	2,253	1,870	9,231	11,725	55,759
Netherlands	49	1,078	1,412	8,251	10,789	9,102	16,541
Norway	3	91	1,201	13,903	20,931	71,631	95,323
Sweden[4]						37,667	115,922
Poland[5]	5	16	369	105	1,164	2,027	12,970
Portugal	35	145	829	550	1,055	2,658	14,082
Romania[12]	—	—	—	—	—	—	11
Spain	139	2,477	2,125	2,209	9,298	6,697	5,266
Switzerland	31	3,226	4,821	4,644	25,011	23,286	28,293
U.S.S.R.[5,6]	14	75	277	551	457	2,512	39,284
Other Europe	—	3	40	79	5	8	1,001
Asia	6	30	55	141	41,538	64,759	124,160
China	1	2	8	35	41,397	64,301	123,201
India	1	8	39	36	43	69	163
Japan[7]	—	—	—	—	—	186	149
Turkey	1	20	7	59	83	131	404
Other Asia	3	—	1	11	15	72	243
America	387	11,564	33,424	62,469	74,720	166,607	404,044
Canada & New-foundland[8]	209	2,277	13,624	41,723	59,309	153,878	383,640
Mexico	1	4,817	6,599	3,271	3,078	2,191	5,162
West Indies	164	3,834	12,301	13,528	10,660	9,046	13,957
Central America	2	105	44	368	449	95	157
South America	11	531	856	3,579	1,224	1,397	1,128

See notes and source at end of table.

Immigration by Country, for Decades 1820–1981 (continued)

Countries	1881–1890	1891–1900	1901–1910	1911–1920	1921–1930	1931–1940	1941–1950
All Countries	5,246,613	3,687,564	8,795,386	5,735,811	4,107,209	528,431	1,035,039
Europe	4,735,484	3,555,352	8,056,040	4,321,887	2,463,194	347,552	621,124
Albania [11]	—	—	—	—	—	2,040	85
Austria	353,719	529,707	2,145,266	453,649	32,868	3,563	24,860
Hungary [2,5]				442,693	30,680	7,861	3,469
Belgium	20,177	18,167	41,635	33,746	15,846	4,817	12,189
Bulgaria [10]	—	160	39,280	22,533	2,945	938	375
Czechoslovakia [11]	—	—	—	3,426	102,194	14,393	8,347
Denmark	88,132	50,231	65,285	41,983	32,430	2,559	5,393
Estonia	—	—	—	—	—	506	212
Finland [11]	—	—	—	756	16,691	2,146	2,503
France	50,464	30,770	73,379	61,897	49,610	12,623	38,809
Germany [2,5]	1,452,970	505,152	341,498	143,945	412,202	114,058	226,578
Great Britain:							
England	644,680	216,726	388,017	249,944	157,420	21,756	112,252
Scotland	149,869	44,188	120,469	78,357	159,731	6,887	16,131
Wales	12,640	10,557	17,464	13,107	13,012	735	3,209
Not specified [3]	168	67	—	—	—	—	—
Greece	2,308	15,979	167,519	184,201	51,084	9,119	8,973
Ireland	655,482	388,416	339,065	146,181	220,591	13,167	26,967
Italy	307,309	651,893	2,045,877	1,109,524	455,315	68,028	57,661
Latvia [11]	—	—	—	—	—	1,192	361
Lithuania [11]	—	—	—	—	—	2,201	683
Luxembourg [15]	—	—	—	—	—	565	820
Netherlands	53,701	26,758	48,262	43,718	26,948	7,150	14,860
Norway [4]	176,586	95,015	190,505	66,395	68,531	4,740	10,100
Poland [5]	51,806	96,720	—	4,813	227,734	17,026	7,571
Portugal	16,978	27,508	69,149	89,732	29,994	3,329	7,423
Romania [12]	6,348	12,750	53,008	13,311	67,646	3,871	1,076
Spain	4,419	8,731	27,935	68,611	28,958	3,258	2,898
Sweden [4]	391,776	226,266	249,534	95,074	97,249	3,960	10,665
Switzerland	81,988	31,179	34,922	23,091	29,676	5,512	10,547
U.S.S.R. [5,6]	213,282	505,290	1,597,306	921,201	61,742	1,356	548
Yugoslavia [10]	—	—	—	1,888	49,064	5,835	1,576
Other Europe	682	122	665	8,111	22,983	2,361	3,983
Asia	69,942	74,862	323,543	247,236	112,059	16,081	32,360
China	61,711	14,799	20,605	21,278	29,907	4,928	16,709
India	269	68	4,713	2,082	1,886	496	1,761
Japan [7]	2,270	25,942	129,797	83,837	33,462	1,948	1,555
Turkey	3,782	30,425	157,369	134,066	33,824	1,065	798
Other Asia	1,910	3,628	11,059	5,973	12,980	7,644	11,537
America	426,967	38,972	361,888	1,143,671	1,516,716	160,037	354,804
Canada & New-foundland [8]	393,304	3,311	179,226	742,185	924,515	108,527	171,718
Mexico [9]	1,913	971	49,642	219,004	459,287	22,319	60,589
West Indies	29,042	33,066	107,548	123,424	74,899	15,502	49,725
Central America	404	549	8,192	17,159	15,769	5,861	21,665
South America	2,304	1,075	17,280	41,899	42,215	7,803	21,831
Other America [13]	—	—	—	—	31	25	29,276

See notes at end of table.

Immigration by Country, for Decades 1820–1981 (con't)

Countries	1951–1960	1961–1970	1971–1980	1981	Total: 1820–1981
All Countries	2,515,479	3,321,677	4,493,314	596,600	50,252,552
Europe	1,325,640	1,123,363	800,368	66,695	36,405,952
Albania[11]	59	98	329	11	2,622
Austria[2,5]	67,106	20,621	9,478	367 ⎫	
Hungary[2,5]	36,637	5,401	6,550	581 ⎬	4,318,845
Belgium	18,575	9,192	5,329	467	203,490
Bulgaria[10]	104	619	785	124	68,266
Czechoslovakia[11]	918	3,273	6,023	793	139,367
Denmark	10,984	9,201	2,609	506	365,548
Estonia[11]	185	163	91	22	1,179
Finland[11]	4,925	4,192	2,868	317	34,398
France	51,121	45,237	25,069	1,745	756,979
Germany[2,5]	477,765	190,796	43,986	6,552	6,998,056
Greece	47,608	85,969	92,369	4,361	669,888
Ireland	57,332	37,461	44,731	902	4,692,856
Italy	185,491	214,111	129,368	4,662	5,310,516
Latvia[11]	352	510	207	39	2,661
Lithuania[11]	242	562	248	44	3,980
Luxembourg[15]	684	556	307	18	2,950
Netherlands	52,277	30,606	10,492	999	362,993
Norway[4]	22,935	15,484	3,941	331	857,646
Poland[5]	9,985	53,539	37,234	5,014	528,098
Portugal	19,588	76,065	101,710	7,049	467,879
Romania[12]	1,039	2,531	12,393	1,974	175,958
Spain	7,894	44,659	39,141	1,711	266,426
Sweden[4]	21,697	17,116	6,531	832	1,274,289
Switzerland	17,675	18,453	8,255	601	351,191
U.S.S.R.[5,6]	584	2,336	38,961	9,223	3,394,999
United Kingdom:					
Total	204,468	214,518	155,572	14,997	4,978,524
England	156,171	174,452			
Scotland	32,854	29,849			
Wales	2,589	2,052			
Not specified[3]	3,884	3,675			
Yugoslavia[10]	8,225	20,381	30,540	2048	119,557
Other Europe	8,155	4,203	4,049	405	56,324
Asia[16]	150,106	427,771	1,507,178	264,343	3,537,170
China[17]	9,657	34,764	124,326	25,803	593,432
India	1,973	27,189	164,134	21,522	226,452
Japan[7]	46,250	39,988	49,775	3,896	419,055
Turkey	3,519	10,142	13,399	2,766	391,860
Other Asia	88,707	315,688	1,236,544	210,356	1,906,371
America	996,944	1,716,374	1,982,529	246,340	9,698,457
Canada and New-foundland[8]	377,952	413,310	249,560	11,191	4,149,383
Mexico[9]	299,811	453,937	640,294	101,268	2,334,154
Caribbean	123,091	470,213	741,126	73,301	1,904,427
Central America	44,751	101,330	134,640	24,509	376,049
South America	91,628	257,954	295,741	35,913	824,369
Other America[13]	59,711	19,630	789	158	109,620

See notes at end of table.

Immigration by Country, for Decades 1820–1981[1]

Countries	1820	1821–1830	1831–1840	1841–1850	1851–1860	1861–1870	1871–1880
Africa	1	16	54	55	210	312	358
Australia & New Zealand	—	—	—	—	—	36	9,886
Pacific Islands (U.S. Adm.)	—	—	—	—	—	—	1,028
Not Specified	301	33,032	69,911	53,144	29,169	17,969	790

Countries	1881–1890	1891–1900	1901–1910	1911–1920	1921–1930	1931–1940	1941–1950
Africa	857	350	7,368	8,443	6,286	1,750	7,367
Australia & New Zealand	7,017	2,740	11,975	12,348	8,299	2,231	13,805
Pacific Islands (U.S. Adm.)	5,557	1,225	1,049	1,079	427	780	5,437
Not Specified[14]	789	14,063	33,523	1,147	228	—	142

Countries	1951–1960	1961–1970	1971–1980	1981	Total 102 Years 1820–1981
Africa	14,092	28,954	80,779	15,029	172,281
Australia and New Zealand	11,506	19,562	23,788	1,947	125,140
Pacific Islands (U.S. Adm.)[16]	4,698	1,769	1,806	108	24,963
Not Specified[14]	12,493	3,884	15,866	2,138	291,589

[1] From 1820–1867, figures represent alien passengers arrived; from 1868–1891 and 1895–1897, immigrant aliens arrived; from 1892–1894 and 1898 to the present time, immigrant aliens admitted. Data for years prior to 1906 relates to country whence alien came; thereafter, to country of last permanent residence. Because of changes in boundaries and changes in lists of countries, data for certain countries is not comparable throughout.
Since July 1, 1868, the data is for fiscal years ending June 30. Prior to fiscal year 1869, the periods covered are as follows: from 1820–1831 and 1843–1849, the years ended on September 30—1843 covers 9 months; and from 1832–1842 and 1850–1867, the years ended on December 31—1832 and 1850 cover 15 months. For 1868, the period ended on June 30 and covers 6 months.

[2] Data for Austria-Hungary was not reported until 1861. Austria and Hungary have been recorded separately since 1905. From 1938–1945, Austria is included in Germany.

[3] Great Britain not specified. From 1901–1951, included in other Europe.

[4] From 1820–1868, the figures for Norway and Sweden are combined.

[5] Poland recorded as a separate country from 1820–1898 and since 1920. From 1899–1919, Poland is included with Austria-Hungary, Germany, and Russia.

[6] From 1931–1963, the U.S.S.R. is broken down into European U.S.S.R. and Asian U.S.S.R. Since 1964 total U.S.S.R. has been reported in Europe.

[7] No record of immigration from Japan until 1861.

[8] Prior to 1920, Canada and Newfoundland are recorded as British North America. From 1820–1898, the figures include all British North American possessions.

[9] No record of immigration from Mexico from 1886–1893.

[10] Bulgaria, Serbia, and Montenegro were first reported in 1899. Bulgaria has been reported separately since 1920; also in 1920, a separate enumeration was made for the Kingdom of Serbs, Croats, and Slovenes. Since 1922, the Serbs, Croat, and Slovene Kingdom has been recorded as Yugoslavia.

[11] Countries added to the list since the beginning of World War I are included with the countries to which they belonged. Figures available since 1920 for Czechoslovakia and Finland and, since 1924, for Albania, Estonia, Latvia, and Lithuania.

[12] No record of immigration from Romania until 1880.

[13] Included with countries not specified to 1925.

[14] The figure 33,523 in column headed 1901–1910 includes 32,897 persons returning in 1906 to their homes in the United States.

[15] Figures for Luxembourg are available since 1925.

[16] Beginning with the year 1952, Asia includes the Philippines. From 1934–1951, the Philippines are included in the Pacific Islands. Prior to 1934, the Philippines are recorded in separate tables as insular travel.

[17] Beginning with the year 1957, China includes Taiwan.

Source: U.S. Immigration and Naturalization Service, Annual Report, U.S. Government Printing Office, Washington, D.C., 1981, Table 2.

PHOTO CREDITS

Chapter 1

Opener: Charles Gatewood/The Image Works. Page 9: The Distorted Image, courtesy Anti-Defamation League of B'nai B'rith, John and Selma Appel Collection.

Chapter 2

Opener: Peter Southwick/Stock Boston, Page 33: Jacob A. Riis/Jacob A. Riis Collection, Museum of the City of New York. Page 37: Arthur Grace/Stock Boston. Page 44: UPI/The Bettmann Archive. Page 47: Jacob A. Riis/Jacob A. Riis Collection, Museum of the City of New York. Page 51: Courtesy Anti-Defamation League of B'nai B'rith, John and Selma Appel Collection.

Chapter 3

Opener: Jim Holland/Stock Boston. Page 61: Courtesy Anti-Defamation League of B'nai B'rith, John and Selma Appel Collection. Page 61: Jacob A. Riis/Jacob A. Riis Collection, Museum of the City of New York.

Chapter 4

Opener: Peter Southwick/Stock Boston. Page 89: AP/Wide World Photos. Page 97: "The Trail of Tears" by Robert Lindneux, Woolaroc Museum, Bartlesville, Oklahoma. Page 99: Culver Pictures.

Chapter 5

Opener: Culver Pictures. Page 114: Painting by Samuel B. Waugh, Museum of the City of New York. Page 115: Jacob A. Riis/Jacob A. Riis Collection, Museum of the City of New York. Page 124: Museum of the City of New York. Page 130: Brown Brothers. Page 134: Courtesy Anti-Defamation League of B'nai B'rith, John and Selma Appel Collection. Page 138: Culver Pictures.

Chapter 6

Opener: Lewis Wickes Hine/George Eastman House Collection. Page 149: Brown Brothers. Page 152: The Library of Congress. Page 154: Courtesy Anti-Defamation League of B'nai B'rith, John and Selma Appel Collection. Page 158: Culver Pictures. Page 172: Brown Brothers. Page 177: Culver Pictures. Page 179: Lewis Wickes Hine/George Eastman House Collection. Page 185: Old Dartmouth Historical Society/The Whaling Museum, New Bedford, Mass.

Chapter 7

Opener: Gianfranco Gorgoni/Contact Press Images. Page 213: National Archives. Page 217: Martha Stewart/Picture Cube. Page 244: Michal Heron/Woodfin Camp.

Chapter 8

Opener: Magnus Bartlett/Woodfin Camp. Page 243: Culver Pictures. Page 246: Brown Brothers. Page 255: UPI/The Bettmann Archive. Page 257: Brown Brothers. Page 268: Magnus Bartlett/Woodfin Camp.

Chapter 9

Opener: Peter Menzel/Stock Boston. Page 284: The Library of Congress. Page 297: Owen Franken/Stock Boston.

Chapter 10

Opener: Michael Weisbrot/Stock Boston. Page 310: Courtesy Anti-Defamation League of B'nai B'rith, John and Selma Appel Collection. Page 319: Bern Keating/Black Star. Page 323: UPI/The Bettmann Archive. Page 325: UPI/The Bettmann Archive. Page 327: Dan Budnik/Woodfin Camp. Page 329: Christina Thomson/Contact.

Chapter 11

Opener: Peter Menzel/Stock Boston. Page 371: Michal Heron/Woodfin Camp. Page 360: Peter Menzel/Stock Boston. Page 368: Jason Laure/Woodfin Camp.

Chapter 12

Opener: Ira Berger/Woodfin Camp. Page 396: Culver Pictures. Page 400: Andrew Brilliant/Picture Cube. Page 403: Culver Pictures. Page 404: Museum of the City of New York. Page 408: David S. Strickler/Picture Cube. Page 413: Alan Carey/The Image Works. Page 416: Brown Brothers. Page 419: David Strickler/Picture Cube.

Chapter 13

Opener: Michael Hayman/Stock Boston. Page 428: Brown Brothers. Page 429: The Library of Congress. Page 444: UPI/The Bettmann Archive. Page 449: UPI/The Bettmann Archive.

Chapter 14

Opener: Owen Franken/Stock Boston. Page 468: Jim Anderson/Woodfin Camp. Page 479: Olivier Rebbot/Woodfin Camp. Page 481: Owen Franken/Stock Boston.

INDEX